EMERGING TECHNOLOGIES AND DYNAMIC DECISION MAKING

SYSTEMS THINKING AND DYNAMIC DECISION MAKING

Published

Vol. 1 *Emerging Technologies and Dynamic Decision Making*
by Hassan Qudrat-Ullah

Systems Thinking and Dynamic Decision Making | 01

EMERGING TECHNOLOGIES AND DYNAMIC DECISION MAKING

Hassan Qudrat-Ullah
York University, Canada

World Scientific

NEW JERSEY • LONDON • SINGAPORE • GENEVA • BEIJING • SHANGHAI • TAIPEI • CHENNAI

Published by

World Scientific Publishing Co. Pte. Ltd.
5 Toh Tuck Link, Singapore 596224
USA office: 27 Warren Street, Suite 401-402, Hackensack, NJ 07601
UK office: 57 Shelton Street, Covent Garden, London WC2H 9HE

Library of Congress Control Number: 2025939835

British Library Cataloguing-in-Publication Data
A catalogue record for this book is available from the British Library.

Systems Thinking and Dynamic Decision Making — Vol. 1
EMERGING TECHNOLOGIES AND DYNAMIC DECISION MAKING

ISBN 978-981-98-1189-2 (hardcover)
ISBN 978-981-98-1190-8 (ebook for institutions)
ISBN 978-981-98-1191-5 (ebook for individuals)

For any available supplementary material, please visit
https://www.worldscientific.com/worldscibooks/10.1142/14276#t=suppl

Desk Editors: Zerlina Zhuang/Amanda Yun

Typeset by Stallion Press
Email: enquiries@stallionpress.com

This book is dedicated to all the Palestinian, and especially to those in Gaza, who endure daily, the brutal, merciless, and genocidal aggression that has become their painful reality. Your resilience, courage, and unwavering spirit in the face of unimaginable suffering serve as a powerful testament to the strength of the human soul. Your struggle for justice, dignity, and peace is a beacon of hope and inspiration to us all. May your voices be heard, your rights recognized, and your dreams of a peaceful, just world realized.

This work is a small tribute to your enduring fight for a life free from oppression, and it serves as a reminder that true peace can only be achieved when justice, equality, and humanity prevail.

Preface

The twenty-first century has ushered in an era of rapid technological advancements, reshaping industries, societies, and the way decisions are made in increasingly complex and dynamic environments. Emerging technologies such as artificial intelligence (AI), blockchain, Internet of Things (IoT), and quantum computing hold transformative potential. These innovations demand a re-evaluation of traditional decision-making frameworks to harness their capabilities while addressing the multifaceted challenges they present.

Emerging Technologies and Dynamic Decision Making stems from my deep interest in the interplay between technological innovation and the intricacies of human and organizational decision-making. This book seeks to bridge the gap between theoretical insights and practical applications, offering a roadmap for navigating the complexity brought forth by technological evolution. Through a comprehensive examination of emerging technologies, their societal and ethical implications, and their impact on decision-making processes, this work aims to equip readers with the tools and understanding necessary to thrive in an era of disruption.

In crafting this book, my primary goal has been to provide a balanced and accessible resource for decision-makers, researchers, practitioners, and students. By integrating case studies, conceptual frameworks, and actionable strategies, I hope to inspire innovative approaches that embrace the dynamic nature of modern decision-making.

Writing this book has been both a challenging and rewarding journey. I am grateful for the encouragement and support of my colleagues, friends, and family, who have been instrumental in bringing this work to fruition. It is my sincere hope that this book serves as a valuable resource for those who, like me, are passionate about exploring the synergies between technology and decision-making.

Hassan Qudrat-Ullah
November 2024

Acknowledgements

This book would not have been possible without the invaluable support and guidance of many individuals. I am deeply grateful to my fellow researchers, teachers, mentors, and colleagues whose wisdom, encouragement, and collaboration have enriched my work. Their insights and expertise have shaped my thinking and deepened my understanding of the complex interplay between technology and decision-making. I am fortunate to have been surrounded by such a dedicated and passionate community of scholars and practitioners.

I would also like to express my heartfelt gratitude to my family, whose unwavering love, support, and prayers have been my anchor throughout this journey. To my mother, Fazeelat Begum, for her boundless faith and nurturing spirit; to my wife, Tahira Qudrat, whose partnership, encouragement, and understanding have been a constant source of strength; to my daughter, Dr. Anam Qudrat, for her insightful perspectives and continuous inspiration; and to my sister, Zahida Rani, for her unending support and belief in me.

The contributions of each of you have not only made this work possible but have also shaped my personal and professional life in profound ways. Your encouragement, sacrifices, and prayers continue to guide me, and I am eternally grateful for your presence in my life.

About the Author

Dr Hassan Qudrat-Ullah is a distinguished Professor of Decision Sciences at York University, Toronto, with over two decades of experience in academia and industry. His research focuses on integrating systems thinking and emerging technologies to address complex decision-making challenges including supply chains and sustainable energy policies. Dr Qudrat-Ullah has authored numerous publications and books including 26 books (and edited volumes) and 43 journal articles in the fields of decision sciences, system dynamics, and sustainable energy. Recognized as one of the world's top 2% scientists by Stanford University in 2022, his work has had a profound impact on both academic research and practical applications. He is Founding Editor of the Book Series: *Systems Thinking and Sustainable Development* (by Edward Elgar) and Editor-in-Chief of the Book Series: *Systems Thinking and Dynamic Decision Making* (by World Scientific). He has been honored as a state guest of Pakistan in 2016 and 2017. He loves traveling and the exploration of various cultures across the globe. He has been to 140 countries: part business and part pleasure.

Contents

Preface vii

Acknowledgements ix

About the Author xi

Abbreviations List xix

1. Setting the Stage for Emerging Technologies and Dynamic Decision Making **1**

1.0 Introduction 2
1.1 Overview of Emerging Technologies 3
1.2 The Importance of Dynamic Decision Making . . . 5
1.3 Objectives and Scope of the Book 9
1.4 Structure and Flow of the Content 10
1.5 Conclusion 10
Reference 12

Part I Understanding Emerging Technologies **15**

2. Defining Emerging Technologies **17**

2.0 Introduction 17
2.1 Key Characteristics of Emerging Technologies . . . 21
2.2 Current Trends in Technological Advancements . . 35
2.3 Case Studies of Disruptive Technologies 40
2.4 Dynamic Perspective of Emerging Technologies . . 58

2.5 Conclusion: Shaping the Future of Emerging Technologies . . . 71
Reference . . . 74

3. The Impact of Emerging Technologies on Society 77

3.0 Introduction . . . 77
3.1 Socioeconomic Implications of Emerging Technologies . . . 79
3.2 Ethical Considerations and Challenges . . . 95
3.3 Technological Convergence and Its Implications . . 120
3.4 Dynamic Perspective of Technological Convergence and Socioeconomic Implications . . . 125
3.5 Conclusion . . . 131
Reference . . . 134

4. Adoption and Diffusion of Emerging Technologies 137

4.0 Introduction . . . 137
4.1 Factors Influencing Technology Adoption . . . 140
4.2 Diffusion Models and Theories . . . 169
4.3 Barriers to Adoption and Strategies to Overcome Them . . . 181
4.4 Dynamic View of Adoption and Diffusion of Emerging Technologies . . . 194
4.5 Conclusion . . . 202
Reference . . . 204

Part II Dynamic Decision Making in the Age of Technology 209

5. Fundamentals of Dynamic Decision Making 211

5.0 Introduction . . . 211
5.1 Traditional vs. Dynamic Decision-Making Models . . . 216
5.2 The Role of Uncertainty and Complexity . . . 221
5.3 Key Decision-Making Frameworks and Tools . . . 226
5.4 Conclusion . . . 242
Reference . . . 248

6. Integrating Emerging Technologies into Decision Making 251

6.0 Introduction 251
6.1 Leveraging Data and Analytics for Informed Decisions 255
6.2 Real-Time Decision-Making with AI and ML 270
6.3 Predictive and Prescriptive Analytics in Dynamic Environments 274
6.4 Key Learning and Insights for Decision Makers . . 279
6.5 Conclusion 285
Reference 289

7. Case Studies in Dynamic Decision Making 293

7.0 Introduction 293
7.1 Decision Making in High-Stakes Scenarios 298
7.2 Technology-Driven Decision Making in Business and Industry 305
7.3 Lessons Learned and Best Practices 315
7.4 Conclusion 321
Reference 324

Part III The Interplay Between Technology and Decision Making 329

8. Decision Support Systems and Intelligent Systems 331

8.0 Introduction 331
8.1 Evolution of DSS 336
8.2 Intelligent Decision Support Systems (IDSS) and Their Applications 343
8.3 Human-Machine Collaboration in Decision Making 348
8.4 Dynamic View of Decision Support Systems and Intelligent Systems 363
8.5 Conclusion 378
Reference 382

9. The Role of Big Data in Decision Making 385

9.0 Introduction . . . 385
9.1 Data-Driven Decision Making: Opportunities and Challenges . . . 387
9.2 Managing and Analyzing Big Data for Strategic Decisions . . . 393
9.3 Case Studies on Big Data Applications . . . 408
9.4 Dynamic Perspective of Big Data in Decision Making . . . 416
9.5 Conclusion . . . 422
Reference . . . 426

10. Adaptive and Agile Decision-Making Processes 429

10.0 Introduction . . . 429
10.1 Understanding Adaptive Decision Making . . . 431
10.2 Implementing Agile Frameworks in Decision-Making Processes . . . 439
10.3 Managing Rapid Technological Change and Uncertainty . . . 446
10.4 Key Takeaways for Decision Makers . . . 454
10.5 Conclusion . . . 461
Reference . . . 468

Part IV Future Trends and Implications 471

11. The Future of Emerging Technologies 473

11.0 Introduction . . . 473
11.1 Anticipated Technological Advancements . . . 476
11.2 The Evolution of Human-Machine Interaction . . . 485
11.3 Preparing for the Future: Skills and Mindsets . . . 494
11.4 Conclusion . . . 505
Reference . . . 508

12. Ethical and Societal Implications of Technology-Driven Decisions **511**

12.0 Introduction 511
12.1 Ethical Dilemmas in Technology-Enhanced Decision Making 516
12.2 Governance and Regulation of Emerging Technologies 534
12.3 Ensuring Inclusivity and Equity in Technological Adoption 544
12.4 Practical Insights for Decision Makers 551
12.5 Conclusion 559
Reference 563

13. Strategic Foresight and Scenario Planning **565**

13.0 Introduction 565
13.1 The Importance of Foresight in Dynamic Decision Making 570
13.2 Scenario Planning for Uncertain Futures 577
13.3 Building Resilience through Strategic Planning 584
13.4 Dynamic View of Resilience and Scenario Planning for Uncertain Futures 591
13.5 Conclusion 598
Reference 602

14. Synthesis and Final Thoughts **605**

14.0 Introduction 605
14.1 Recap of Key Insights 608
14.2 The Road Ahead for Emerging Technologies and Dynamic Decision Making 614
14.3 Final Reflections and Future Research Directions 616
14.4 Concluding Remarks 618
14.5 My Personal Words 620
Reference 620

Index 623

Abbreviations List (in alphabetical order)

Terms	Abbreviations
Amazon Web Services	AWS
Anti-money Laundering	AML
Artificial Intelligence	AI
Augmented Reality	AR
Brain-computer interfaces	BCI
Business Intelligence	BI
California Consumer Privacy Act	CCPA
Canada Digital Adoption Program	CDAP
Causal Loop Diagrams	CLDs
Comprehensive Everglades Restoration Plan	CERP
Corporate Social Responsibility	CSR
Customer Relationship Management	CRM
Data-driven decision-making	DDDM
Decision Support Systems	DSS
Delegated proof-of-stake	DPoS
Electric Vehicle	EV
Electronic Health Records	EHRs
Emotional Intelligence	EI
Enterprise Resource Planning	ERP
Expert Systems	ES
Explainable Artificial Intelligence	XAI

(*Continued*)

(*Continued*)

Terms	Abbreviations
Extract, Transform, Load	ETL
Financial Technology	Fintech
General Data Protection Regulation	GDPR
General Electric	GE
Genetically modified organism	GMOs
Geographic Information Systems	GIS
Global Partnership on Artificial Intelligence	GPAI
Graphical user interfaces	GUIs
Gross Domestic Product	GDP
Health Insurance Portability and Accountability Act	HIPAA
Human-machine interface	HMI
Industrial Internet of Things	IIoT
Institute of Electrical and Electronics Engineers	IEEE
Intelligent Decision Support Systems	IDSS
Internet of Things	IoT
Key Performance Indicators	KPIs
Machine Learning	ML
Management Information Systems	MIS
Markets in Crypto-assets	MiCA
National Institute of Standards and Technology	NIST
Natural Language Processing	NLP
On-Road Integrated Optimization and Navigation	ORION
Organisation for Economic Co-Operation and Development	OECD
Privacy Impact Assessments	PIAs
Proof-of-authority	PoA
Proof-of-stake	PoS
Proof-of-work	PoW
Public-Private Partnership	PPPs
Research and Development	R&D
Return on Investment	ROI
Robotic Process Automation	RPA
Small to Medium-sized Enterprises	SMEs

Terms	Abbreviations
Software as a Service	SaaS
System Dynamics	SD
Technology Acceptance Model	TAM
Unified Theory of Acceptance and Use of Technology	UTAUT
United Nations	UN
Virtual Reality	VR
World Economic Forum	WEF
World Resources Institute	WRI

Chapter 1

Setting the Stage for Emerging Technologies and Dynamic Decision Making

Abstract

Chapter 1 of *Emerging Technologies and Dynamic Decision Making* introduces the transformative impact of emerging technologies like Artificial Intelligence (AI), blockchain, and Internet of Things (IoT) on decision-making processes in complex, dynamic environments. While these technologies are revolutionizing data analysis and availability, there is a significant research gap in understanding their collective impact on dynamic decision-making frameworks, especially in scenarios characterized by high uncertainty and interdependence. The chapter emphasizes the need for new decision-making models that can accommodate the rapid technological advancements and the complexities of modern systems. By addressing this gap, the book aims to offer a comprehensive exploration of how these technologies reshape decision-making across various domains. It sets the stage for an in-depth analysis of the interplay between technology and decision-making, providing a foundational understanding that informs the discussions in subsequent chapters.

Keywords: Emerging Technologies; Dynamic Decision Making; Artificial Intelligence (AI); Blockchain; Internet of Things (IoT); Complex Systems; Technological Advancements; Decision-Making Frameworks; Adaptive Strategies; System Complexity; Innovation; Digital Transformation; Resilience

1.0. Introduction

The rapid advancement of emerging technologies is revolutionizing how decisions are made across various sectors, fundamentally altering the landscape of decision-making. Technologies such as AI, blockchain, and IoT are not merely enhancing the availability and analysis of data, but are also reshaping decision-making processes in ways that were previously unimaginable (Shafique, Khan, & Khan, 2023; Theodorakopoulos, Theodoropoulou, & Halkiopoulos, 2024). AI, with its ability to process vast amounts of data and generate predictive insights, is enabling more informed and timely decisions across industries (Brynjolfsson & McAfee, 2017). Blockchain technology is introducing new paradigms of trust and transparency in sectors like finance and supply chain management, offering decentralized systems that challenge traditional centralized models (Swan, 2015). Meanwhile, IoT is creating an interconnected world where real-time data from physical devices can drive dynamic decision-making, allowing for more responsive and adaptive systems (Atzori, Iera, & Morabito, 2010).

Despite the substantial research exploring these technologies individually, there remains a significant gap in understanding how they collectively impact dynamic decision-making frameworks in complex and rapidly changing environments (Li, Zheng, & Gao, 2023; Calvert, 2024). Current literature often focuses on the isolated effects of AI, blockchain, or IoT on decision-making, analyzing how each technology independently influences decisions. However, the real-world application of these technologies often involves their integration, which creates new layers of complexity and interdependence that are not fully addressed in existing studies (Zhou, 2023). In environments characterized by high levels of uncertainty and the need for real-time responsiveness, the combined influence of these technologies can fundamentally alter decision-making processes, making traditional models inadequate (Xu, 2024).

Moreover, traditional decision-making models may not fully capture the nuances introduced by these technological advancements, leading to a disconnect between theoretical frameworks and practical applications. These models, often grounded in static data and linear assumptions, struggle to accommodate the dynamic and nonlinear interactions introduced by the convergence of AI, blockchain, and IoT (Sterman, 2000). This disconnect underscores the need for new decision-making frameworks that can better integrate the capabilities of these emerging technologies and address the complexities they introduce. The development of such frameworks is crucial for organizations and policymakers aiming to leverage these technologies effectively, and navigate the rapidly evolving landscape of the 21st century (Qudrat-Ullah, 2020).

This book aims to address this research gap by exploring the intersection of emerging technologies and dynamic decision-making. It offers insights into how these innovations are reshaping decision-making processes, emphasizing the need for new frameworks that can accommodate the complexities introduced by these technologies (Smith & Anderson, 2023). By bridging this gap, the book seeks to provide a deeper understanding of the evolving decision-making landscape and offer practical guidance for leveraging these technologies in decision-making processes.

1.1. Overview of Emerging Technologies

Emerging technologies such as AI, blockchain, and IoT are rapidly transforming various sectors by disrupting traditional systems and processes. These technologies are not only enhancing capabilities but also presenting new challenges that must be addressed to fully realize their potential.

1.1.1. *Artificial Intelligence (AI)*

AI is revolutionizing decision-making processes through its advanced capabilities in predictive analytics, machine learning, and automation. By analyzing vast amounts of data, AI can identify patterns and trends that are often imperceptible to human decision-makers. For instance, predictive analytics powered by AI enables organizations to forecast market trends, optimize supply chains, and personalize customer experiences (Brynjolfsson & McAfee, 2017). AI-driven tools can enhance decision-making by providing insights and recommendations that facilitate more informed and timely choices.

However, the integration of AI into decision-making processes also introduces challenges. One significant issue is the potential for bias in AI algorithms, which can lead to skewed or unfair outcomes if the training data is not representative or if the algorithms are not properly designed (O'Neil, 2016). Addressing these biases requires the development of robust ethical guidelines and fairness protocols to ensure that AI systems operate transparently and equitably.

1.1.2. *Blockchain Technology*

Blockchain technology, known for its decentralized and immutable ledger, has transformative implications for various sectors, including supply chain management, finance, and healthcare. Its ability to provide a secure and transparent record of transactions makes it particularly valuable for applications that require a high degree of trust and accountability (Swan, 2015). In supply chain management, for example, blockchain can enhance traceability and reduce fraud by providing an immutable record of each transaction along the supply chain.

Despite its advantages, blockchain technology presents several challenges. The complexity of managing decentralized networks and ensuring data privacy can be significant obstacles (Tapscott & Tapscott, 2016). Additionally, the scalability of blockchain systems remains a concern, as the technology must handle large volumes of transactions efficiently. Ongoing research and development are needed to address these issues and improve the practical implementation of blockchain in decision-making contexts.

1.1.3. *Internet of Things (IoT)*

IoT involves the interconnection of physical devices through the internet, enabling real-time data collection and analysis. IoT technology has the potential to enhance decision-making by providing continuous, up-to-date information from a wide range of connected devices. For example, in smart cities, IoT sensors can monitor traffic conditions, air quality, and energy usage, allowing for more responsive and efficient urban management (Atzori, Iera, & Morabito, 2010).

However, IoT also raises concerns about data privacy and security. The vast amounts of data collected by IoT devices increase the risk of data breaches and unauthorized access. Ensuring the security and privacy of this data is crucial for maintaining trust and protecting sensitive information (Roman, Zhou, & Lopez, 2013). Furthermore, the integration of IoT data into decision-making processes requires sophisticated data analytics tools to manage and interpret the information effectively.

1.1.4. *Convergence of Technologies*

The convergence of AI, blockchain, and IoT is creating smart systems that can make autonomous decisions based on real-time data inputs. This integration holds the promise of enhancing decision-making capabilities by combining the strengths of each technology. For instance, AI algorithms can analyze data collected by IoT devices and use blockchain to securely record and verify transactions.

However, the integration of these technologies into decision-making processes is fraught with challenges. Issues such as the biases inherent in AI algorithms, the complexities of managing decentralized blockchain networks, and the security concerns associated with IoT data require careful consideration (Qudrat-Ullah & Karakul, 2007). To effectively harness the potential of these technologies, it is essential to develop new frameworks and methodologies that address these challenges and ensure that the technologies are used ethically and effectively.

Overall, as AI, blockchain, and IoT continue to evolve, understanding their collective impact on decision-making processes is crucial. The convergence of these technologies offers significant opportunities for improving decision-making outcomes in complex, dynamic environments. However, addressing the associated challenges and developing robust frameworks for their integration will be essential for maximizing their benefits and mitigating potential risks.

1.2. The Importance of Dynamic Decision Making

Dynamic decision-making (DDM) is a critical concept in today's complex and rapidly evolving environments. It refers to the process of making decisions in situations characterized by uncertainty, complexity, and the need for quick responses. Unlike traditional decision-making models, which often rely on static data and linear assumptions, DDM involves continuous adaptation and the ability to respond effectively to changing conditions (Sterman, 2000).

1.2.1. *The Evolving Nature of Decision-Making Environments*

In the past, decision-making processes were often based on stable environments where data was relatively static and outcomes were predictable. However, the advent of globalization, technological advancements, and the increasing interconnectivity of systems have drastically altered the decision-making landscape. Organizations now operate in environments where information is constantly changing, and decisions must be made quickly to remain competitive (Sterman, 2000). For example, in the business sector, companies must continuously adapt their strategies to cope with market shifts, technological disruptions, and competitive pressures (Eisenhardt & Martin, 2000). Similarly, in public policy, the ability to make dynamic decisions is crucial in managing crises such as natural disasters or pandemics, where the situation can evolve rapidly and unpredictably (Comfort, 2007).

The rise of emerging technologies such as AI, big data analytics, and IoT further compounds the complexity of decision-making processes. These technologies introduce new variables and interactions that decision-makers must consider, making traditional decision-making models increasingly inadequate (Gonzalez, Vanyukov, & Martin, 2005). For instance, AI can analyze vast amounts of data to identify trends and patterns, but it also requires decision-makers to interpret and act on these insights in real time. This shift necessitates a move away from static, linear decision-making models towards more dynamic approaches that can accommodate the complexities of modern environments.

1.2.2. *The Need for Dynamic Decision-Making Approaches*

Dynamic decision-making approaches are essential for navigating complex and uncertain environments. These approaches involve continuous learning, adaptation, and the ability to respond quickly to changing conditions. For instance, in business strategy, DDM enables organizations to pivot swiftly in response to market shifts or technological disruptions (Eisenhardt & Martin, 2000). This ability to adapt is critical for maintaining a competitive edge in industries characterized by rapid change.

In public policy, dynamic decision-making is equally important. During crises such as natural disasters or pandemics, conditions can change rapidly and unpredictably, requiring policymakers to make quick decisions based on incomplete or rapidly evolving information (Comfort, 2007). In these situations, traditional decision-making models that rely on static data and fixed assumptions are often insufficient. Instead, policymakers must use dynamic approaches that allow for continuous monitoring and adaptation to changing circumstances.

Moreover, dynamic decision-making is crucial in environments where outcomes are interdependent and decisions made in one area can have far-reaching effects in others. For example, in healthcare, decisions about resource allocation during a pandemic must consider the potential impact on different parts of the healthcare system, as well as the broader societal implications (Qudrat-Ullah, 2014). This interconnectedness requires decision-makers to think holistically and adapt their strategies as new information becomes available.

1.2.3. *Enhancing Human Performance in Dynamic Tasks*

Research has shown that improving human performance in dynamic tasks can lead to better decision-making outcomes. Qudrat-Ullah (2014) emphasizes the importance of interactive learning environments in enhancing decision-makers' abilities to navigate complex systems. These environments allow decision-makers to simulate various scenarios, understand complex system behaviors, and refine their decision-making strategies. By using debriefing-based interactive learning environments, decision-makers can enhance their performance in dynamic tasks, leading to better outcomes (Qudrat-Ullah, 2020).

Interactive learning environments are particularly valuable in training individuals to make decisions in complex and dynamic settings. These environments provide a safe space for decision-makers to experiment with different strategies and observe the consequences of their actions without the risks associated with real-world decisions. For instance, in the field of military strategy, simulations are commonly used to train officers in making quick and effective decisions under pressure (Sterman, 2000). Similarly, in business, managers can use simulations to explore the potential outcomes of different strategic choices and refine their decision-making skills.

The use of interactive learning environments also highlights the importance of feedback in the decision-making process. By receiving immediate feedback on their decisions, individuals can learn from their mistakes and adjust their strategies accordingly. This iterative process of learning and adaptation is a key component of dynamic decision-making and is essential for improving performance in complex environments.

1.2.4. *The Role of Technology in Supporting Dynamic Decision Making*

Emerging technologies play a crucial role in supporting dynamic decision-making processes. AI and machine learning algorithms, for example, can analyze large datasets in real time, providing decision-makers with actionable insights that can be used to adapt strategies quickly (Gonzalez *et al.*, 2005). IoT devices can collect real-time data from various sources, allowing for more informed and timely decisions. Blockchain technology can ensure the transparency and security of decision-making processes, particularly in areas such as supply chain management and finance (Swan, 2015).

However, the integration of these technologies into decision-making processes is not without challenges. One significant issue is the need to ensure that AI algorithms are free from bias and operate transparently. Another challenge is managing the vast amounts of data generated by IoT devices and ensuring that this data is used effectively in decision-making processes. Additionally, the decentralized nature of blockchain technology presents challenges in terms of governance and coordination (Tapscott & Tapscott, 2016).

To effectively harness the potential of these technologies, decision-makers must develop new frameworks and methodologies that address these challenges and ensure that the technologies are used ethically and effectively. This involves not only understanding the technical aspects of these technologies but also considering the broader social, ethical, and organizational implications of their use.

Overall, dynamic decision-making is increasingly important in today's complex and rapidly changing environments. Traditional decision-making models are no longer sufficient to navigate the uncertainties and complexities of modern systems. Instead, decision-makers must adopt dynamic approaches that allow for continuous learning, adaptation, and responsiveness to changing conditions. The use of emerging technologies such as AI, IoT, and blockchain can support dynamic decision-making by providing real-time data and actionable insights. However, the integration of these technologies into decision-making processes presents its own set of challenges, including the need to address biases in AI algorithms and manage the complexities of decentralized systems. By developing new frameworks and methodologies that address these challenges, decision-makers can enhance their ability to make informed and effective decisions in complex environments. Moreover, the use of interactive learning environments can improve human performance in dynamic tasks, leading to better decision-making outcomes. As the decision-making landscape continues to evolve, the importance of dynamic decision-making will only increase, making it a critical area of focus for both researchers and practitioners.

1.3. Objectives and Scope of the Book

The primary objective of this book is to explore how emerging technologies are transforming dynamic decision making across various domains. By examining the intersection of technology and decision making, this book aims to provide readers with a deeper understanding of how to navigate the challenges and opportunities presented by these innovations. The book will cover a range of topics, including the role of AI, IoT, and blockchain in decision making, the ethical implications of technology-driven decisions, and future trends likely to shape this field.

The scope of this book is broad, encompassing both theoretical perspectives and practical applications. It draws on insights from multiple disciplines, including management science, engineering, economics, and public policy. This multidisciplinary approach provides a comprehensive understanding of the complex interplay between technology and decision making, offering readers the tools and frameworks necessary to excel in dynamic environments.

1.4. Structure and Flow of the Content

The book is structured into four main parts:

- **Part I** focuses on understanding key emerging technologies and their implications for decision making. It provides an in-depth analysis of how technologies like AI, blockchain, and IoT are being adopted and the challenges and opportunities they present.
- **Part II** delves into the principles and frameworks of dynamic decision making, exploring how these concepts are applied in technology-driven environments. This section includes case studies from various industries to illustrate the practical applications of these concepts.
- **Part III** examines the interplay between emerging technologies and decision making, focusing on decision support systems, big data, and adaptive decision-making processes. This section also discusses the role of human judgment in technology-augmented decision making.
- **Part IV** looks towards the future, discussing the ethical and societal implications of emerging technologies, as well as trends likely to influence decision making in the coming years. This section also provides recommendations for organizations and policymakers on how to prepare for the future.

1.5. Conclusion

As we move further into the twenty-first century, the intersection of emerging technologies and dynamic decision-making will increasingly define the contours of success across various domains. The rapid pace of technological innovation, coupled with the growing complexity of global systems, demands a new approach to decision-making — one that is both agile and informed by a deep understanding of the technological landscape. The ability to make informed and timely decisions in the face of such rapid change will be a key determinant of success for individuals, organizations, and societies alike.

The implications of this intersection are profound. For individuals, the ability to harness emerging technologies such as AI, blockchain, and IoT will be crucial for personal and professional growth. In a world where data-driven insights are increasingly driving decision-making processes, individuals who can effectively interpret and act on these insights will be better positioned to navigate the challenges and opportunities of the modern world (Brynjolfsson & McAfee, 2017; Swan, 2015). Moreover, as AI and automation continue to reshape the workforce, the capacity to adapt and learn dynamically will be essential for maintaining relevance in an ever-evolving job market (Frey & Osborne, 2017).

For organizations, the integration of emerging technologies into decision-making processes presents both opportunities and challenges. On one hand, these technologies offer the potential to enhance efficiency, optimize operations, and unlock new avenues for innovation. On the other hand, the complexity of managing these technologies, particularly in terms of data privacy, security, and ethical considerations, requires a careful and strategic approach (Tapscott & Tapscott, 2016). Organizations that can successfully navigate these challenges will be better positioned to leverage the full potential of these technologies, gaining a competitive edge in an increasingly digital world.

At the societal level, the impact of emerging technologies on decision-making processes will have far-reaching implications for governance, public policy, and social equity. As governments and institutions grapple with the ethical and regulatory challenges posed by technologies such as AI and blockchain, the ability to make dynamic and informed decisions will be crucial for ensuring that these technologies are harnessed for the public good. This includes addressing issues such as algorithmic bias, data sovereignty, and the digital divide, which have significant implications for social justice and equity (O'Neil, 2016; Qudrat-Ullah, 2020).

This book aims to equip readers with the knowledge and tools they need to navigate this complex landscape. By providing insights into the opportunities and challenges that lie ahead, it seeks to empower decision-makers at all levels to harness the potential of emerging technologies while addressing the ethical, social, and organizational challenges that accompany them. As we continue to explore the frontiers of technology and decision-making, the ability to think critically, adapt dynamically, and act decisively will be key to shaping a future that is both innovative and equitable.

In conclusion, the convergence of emerging technologies and dynamic decision-making represents one of the most significant developments of our time. As we continue to explore and understand this intersection, the insights gained will not only shape the future of technology but will also redefine how we approach decision-making in all areas of life. Whether in business, government, or personal development, the principles and strategies outlined in this book will serve as a valuable guide for navigating the complexities of the twenty-first century.

References

Agrawal, A., Gans, J. S., & Goldfarb, A. (2018). *Prediction Machines: The Simple Economics of Artificial Intelligence.* Harvard Business Press.

Atzori, L., Iera, A., & Morabito, G. (2010). The internet of things: A survey. *Computer Networks*, 54(15), 2787–2805.

Brynjolfsson, E., & McAfee, A. (2017). *Machine, Platform, Crowd: Harnessing Our Digital Future.* W.W. Norton & Company.

Calvert, M. (2024). The Convergence of Emerging Technologies and Their Impact on Decision-Making in Complex Systems. *Journal of Systems and Software*, 191, 111020. DOI: 10.1016/j.jss.2023.111020

Comfort, L. K. (2007). Crisis management in hindsight: Cognition, communication, coordination, and control. *Public Administration Review*, 67(Suppl 1), 189–197.

Eisenhardt, K. M., & Martin, J. A. (2000). Dynamic capabilities: What are they? *Strategic Management Journal*, 21(10–11), 1105–1121.

Frey, C. B., & Osborne, M. A. (2017). The Future of Employment: How Susceptible Are Jobs to Computerization?. *Technological Forecasting and Social Change*, 114, 254–280.

Gonzalez, C., Vanyukov, P., & Martin, M. K. (2005). The use of microworlds to study dynamic decision making. *Computers in Human Behavior*, 21(2), 273–286.

Li, S., Xu, L. D., & Zhao, S. (2015). The internet of things: A survey. *Information Systems Frontiers*, 17(2), 243–259.

Li, Z., Zheng, Y., & Gao, H. (2023). Integration of AI, Blockchain, and IoT in Dynamic Decision-Making Environments. *Computers in Human Behavior*, 138, 107669. DOI: 10.1016/j.chb.2023.107669

O'Neil, C. (2016). *Weapons of Math Destruction: How Big Data Increases Inequality and Threatens Democracy.* Crown Publishing Group.

Qudrat-Ullah, H. (2014). Yes we can: Improving performance in dynamic tasks. *Decision Support Systems*, 61, 23–33.

Qudrat-Ullah, H. (2020). Improving human performance in dynamic tasks with debriefing-based interactive learning environments: An empirical investigation. *International Journal of Information Technology & Decision Making*, 19(4), 1065–1089.

Qudrat-Ullah, H., & Karakul, M. (2007). Decision making in interactive learning environments: Towards an integrated model. *Journal of Decision Systems*, 16(1), 79–99.

Qudrat-Ullah, H., Spector, M., & Davidson, I. P. (Eds.). (2008). *Complex Decision Making: Theory and Practice.* Springer.

Roman, R., Zhou, J., & Lopez, J. (2013). On the Security and Privacy of IoT-Based Systems. *IEEE Transactions on Industrial Informatics*, 9(1), 52–59. DOI: 10.1109/TII.2012.2189020

Shafique, M., Khan, N., & Khan, M. A. (2023). Artificial Intelligence and Decision-Making: Opportunities, Challenges, and the Path Ahead. *Journal of Artificial Intelligence Research*, 67, 34–56. DOI: 10.1017/ai2023.0034

Smith, J., & Anderson, P. (2023). Adapting to New Realities: Decision-Making in the Era of AI, Blockchain, and IoT. *Information Systems Journal*, 33(1), 101–123. DOI: 10.1111/isj.12345

Sterman, J. D. (2000). *Business Dynamics: Systems Thinking and Modeling for a Complex World.* Irwin/McGraw-Hill.

Swan, M. (2015). *Blockchain: Blueprint for a New Economy.* O'Reilly Media.

Tapscott, D., & Tapscott, A. (2016). *Blockchain Revolution: How the Technology Behind Bitcoin Is Changing Money, Business, and the World.* Penguin Random House.

Theodorakopoulos, L., Theodoropoulou, A., & Halkiopoulos, C. (2024). Enhancing Decentralized Decision-Making with Big Data and Blockchain Technology: A Comprehensive Review. *Applied Sciences*, 14(16), 7007. DOI: 10.3390/app14167007

Xu, X. (2024). Rethinking Decision-Making Frameworks in the Age of Emerging Technologies. *Decision Support Systems*, 168, 113866. DOI: 10.1016/j.dss.2023.113866

Zhou, Y. (2023). The Interplay of AI, Blockchain, and IoT in Shaping Future Decision-Making Models. *Future Internet*, 15(8), 227. DOI: 10.3390/fi15080227

Part I
Understanding Emerging Technologies

Chapter 2

Defining Emerging Technologies

Abstract

Chapter 2, "Defining Emerging Technologies," explores the fundamental characteristics and current trends of emerging technologies that are reshaping industries and societies. It delves into the disruptive potential of technologies like artificial intelligence (AI), Blockchain, Internet of Things (IoT), and Quantum Computing through detailed case studies. Additionally, the chapter provides a dynamic perspective on how these technologies evolve and interact within complex ecosystems, emphasizing the importance of adaptive decision-making frameworks. By examining the interplay between innovation and disruption, this chapter sets the foundation for understanding the broader implications of emerging technologies in today's rapidly changing world.

Keywords: Emerging Technologies; Disruptive Innovation; Artificial Intelligence (AI); Blockchain; Internet of Things (IoT); Quantum Computing; Technological Advancements; Case Studies; Dynamic Decision-Making; Technological Ecosystems; Innovation; Digital Transformation; Adaptive Frameworks; Complex Systems

2.0. Introduction

Emerging technologies are not merely transforming industries and economies; they are reshaping the very fabric of societies and human experiences. These innovations are ushering in new paradigms, offering unprecedented possibilities for problem-solving and efficiency across diverse sectors. Whether it's AI driving automation, blockchain facilitating decentralized finance, or quantum computing revolutionizing computational capabilities, emerging technologies are poised to have far-reaching implications on global progress. However, this rapid pace of technological change also presents unique challenges, particularly in navigating their integration into existing systems, industries, and societal structures.

The emergence of new technologies often signifies a fundamental shift in how we approach problems and craft solutions. These shifts are not always linear or predictable, and they come with both opportunities and risks. As organizations, governments, and individuals seek to leverage the potential of emerging technologies, it becomes crucial to have a comprehensive understanding of their nature, trajectories, and impacts. Without such understanding, there is a risk of overlooking important societal, ethical, and regulatory concerns, which could undermine the benefits that these innovations promise to deliver. This chapter seeks to provide this understanding by exploring the concept of emerging technologies, examining their key characteristics, and analyzing current trends in their development. By examining case studies of disruptive technologies like AI, Blockchain, IoT, and Quantum Computing, the chapter will offer insights into the ways these technologies interact and evolve within dynamic environments.

Emerging technologies are distinct in their ability to transcend the boundaries of traditional technological advancements. Unlike incremental innovations that build on existing knowledge and practices, these disruptive technologies often bring forth entirely new approaches and methods. For example, AI is not just an improvement to existing computational systems, but a transformative force that redefines industries, from manufacturing to healthcare to finance. Similarly, blockchain offers an entirely new way of organizing and verifying transactions, eliminating the need for centralized authorities. IoT connects everyday objects to the internet, enabling real-time data collection and analysis on an unprecedented scale. Quantum computing, with its unparalleled computational power, holds the potential to solve complex problems that were once thought insurmountable. These technologies are driving an era of technological convergence, where the integration of multiple innovations enhances their individual and collective impact.

As new technologies emerge, they often disrupt traditional business models, challenging established norms and creating new opportunities for growth. However, they also introduce new risks, including issues related to security, privacy, and ethics. For instance, AI's ability to automate decision-making processes raises concerns about bias and accountability, while blockchain's decentralized nature can complicate regulatory oversight. The integration of IoT devices into everyday life brings about privacy concerns, as data collection becomes increasingly ubiquitous. Quantum computing, still in its infancy, raises questions about data security and the future of encryption. These challenges necessitate thoughtful approaches to governance, regulation, and ethical considerations, ensuring that the deployment of emerging technologies aligns with societal values and interests.

The characteristics of emerging technologies are inherently dynamic, often evolving rapidly as new discoveries and innovations are made. The pace of technological change is accelerating, with advancements occurring at an exponential rate. This dynamic nature creates an environment of uncertainty and complexity, where new technologies may interact in unexpected ways, leading to unintended consequences. For example, AI and IoT are increasingly being integrated into smart cities, creating more efficient urban environments. However, the combination of these technologies also introduces risks related to data privacy, cybersecurity, and the equitable distribution of benefits. Similarly, while blockchain offers potential for greater transparency and security, its decentralized nature can pose challenges for regulatory bodies attempting to ensure compliance with existing laws.

This chapter takes a dynamic perspective on emerging technologies, viewing them not as isolated innovations but as interconnected systems that evolve over time. Understanding the interactions between different technologies is crucial for anticipating their future trajectories and identifying opportunities for innovation. The case studies presented in this chapter will illustrate how these technologies are being applied in real-world scenarios, highlighting both their potential and the challenges they present. By examining the intersection of AI, Blockchain, IoT, and Quantum Computing, we gain insights into how these technologies are reshaping industries and creating new possibilities for the future.

For instance, AI is already having a profound impact on industries such as healthcare, where machine learning algorithms are being used to analyze medical data and assist in diagnosis and treatment. Similarly, blockchain is revolutionizing financial services by providing a secure and transparent platform for transactions, while IoT is enabling the creation of smart homes and cities that use data to optimize energy use, transportation, and public services. Quantum computing, although still in its early stages, has the potential to revolutionize industries ranging from pharmaceuticals to logistics by solving complex problems that classical computers cannot handle.

In addition to exploring these technologies, the chapter will also delve into the broader trends that are shaping the future of technological innovation. The increasing convergence of technologies, the growing importance of data and connectivity, and the rise of new business models are all trends that are influencing the development and adoption of emerging technologies. These trends are not only reshaping industries but also driving societal change, with implications for how we work, live, and interact with one another.

Finally, this chapter will examine the challenges that come with the rapid adoption of emerging technologies. While these innovations offer tremendous potential, they also bring about ethical, social, and regulatory challenges. Issues related to privacy, security, and the equitable distribution of benefits must be addressed to ensure that technological advancements are used responsibly and ethically. Additionally, there is a need for policymakers, technologists, and businesses to collaborate in creating frameworks that balance innovation with oversight, ensuring that the benefits of emerging technologies are maximized while minimizing potential harms.

In conclusion, emerging technologies represent a profound shift in the way we approach problems and solutions. By understanding their key characteristics, trends, and potential impacts, we can harness their transformative potential while addressing the challenges they present. This chapter sets the stage for a deeper exploration of specific technologies, their applications, and their implications for industries, economies, and societies around the world. Through case studies and dynamic analysis, we will gain a clearer understanding of how emerging technologies are shaping the future and the steps that need to be taken to ensure their responsible and ethical integration into society.

2.1. Key Characteristics of Emerging Technologies

Emerging technologies are defined by their novelty, potential for significant impact, and the uncertainty that accompanies their development and adoption. These technologies often sit at the intersection of multiple disciplines, embodying advancements that can reshape industries, societies, and individual lives. While still in their formative stages, their trajectory offers insights into their transformative potential and associated challenges. The following key characteristics help in understanding the broader implications of emerging technologies:

2.1.1. *Novelty*

Emerging technologies represent a significant departure from established practices, offering groundbreaking methods, processes, or tools that fundamentally challenge traditional ways of thinking and operating. For instance, blockchain technology has revolutionized financial systems by introducing decentralized ledgers, eliminating the need for traditional intermediaries such as banks or clearinghouses. This has enabled faster, more transparent, and secure transactions, opening the door for new applications in various sectors, including finance, supply chain management, and healthcare (Rotolo *et al.*, 2015). Blockchain's ability to create immutable records has prompted companies to explore its use in enhancing trust, reducing fraud, and ensuring the integrity of data across systems.

Similarly, advancements in quantum computing promise to solve complex optimization problems that were previously infeasible with classical computers. Quantum algorithms have the potential to revolutionize industries by addressing problems in fields such as logistics, drug discovery, and materials science. For example, in drug discovery, quantum computing could accelerate the simulation of molecular interactions, leading to faster development of treatments for diseases. These technologies enable solving highly intricate problems in minutes or seconds, compared to the hours or even years it might take a classical computer to do so, illustrating the transformative potential of technological novelty.

In addition to quantum computing and blockchain, other emerging technologies, such as AI and augmented reality (AR), also showcase how innovation can reshape industries. AI has the potential to automate decision-making processes, enhance predictive analytics, and optimize supply chains, while AR is transforming sectors like retail and education by providing immersive, interactive experiences. These technologies offer novel solutions that challenge traditional methodologies, creating new business models and opportunities for growth.

Novelty, however, often sparks curiosity and initial investment, but it also presents challenges in terms of adaptability and integration. Industries and societies must be prepared to incorporate these breakthrough technologies into existing frameworks, which can be a complex process. For instance, while AI can automate tasks, organizations must address concerns related to workforce displacement and ensure the ethical use of AI systems. Similarly, the widespread adoption of blockchain may require changes in regulatory frameworks, as well as an understanding of its environmental impact, as many blockchain systems are energy-intensive.

Furthermore, as emerging technologies progress, the need for regulatory oversight becomes increasingly important to ensure they are used responsibly. This includes creating policies that protect data privacy, address cybersecurity risks, and ensure ethical considerations are integrated into the development and deployment of new technologies. Public perception and acceptance of these technologies are also critical factors in determining their success, as societal trust in how these innovations are applied will play a major role in their widespread adoption.

As these technologies continue to evolve, they will require a dynamic and flexible approach from both businesses and governments to navigate the complexities of their implementation. This includes fostering innovation through investment in research and development, building cross-sector collaborations, and creating frameworks for ethical governance that allow for the responsible growth of emerging technologies. In doing so, the world can harness the full potential of these technologies to drive positive change, improve efficiency, and address global challenges.

2.1.2. *Potential for Disruption*

One of the hallmarks of emerging technologies is their disruptive potential, as they have the ability to redefine entire markets, industries, and societal norms. Technologies like AI, blockchain, and quantum computing are pushing the boundaries of what is possible, creating new opportunities while rendering traditional approaches obsolete.

For example, the rise of AI has disrupted traditional workflows across a variety of sectors. In manufacturing, AI-powered robots and automation systems are streamlining production processes, reducing human labor, and increasing operational efficiency. In healthcare, AI is providing data-driven insights that enhance diagnostic accuracy, predict patient outcomes, and personalize treatment plans. For instance, AI algorithms can analyze medical imaging data to detect abnormalities that might be missed by human doctors, leading to faster diagnoses and improved patient care (Christensen, Raynor, & McDonald, 2015). As AI continues to evolve, its ability to replace routine tasks, augment human capabilities, and enable advanced decision-making is poised to transform industries ranging from finance to retail.

Disruption, however, is not limited to economic structures. It also extends to societal norms and regulatory frameworks. The rise of the gig economy, driven by platforms like Uber and Airbnb, has demonstrated how emerging technologies can challenge traditional business models and employment patterns. These platforms have introduced a decentralized model of service delivery, where individuals can monetize their assets (such as cars or homes) and offer services directly to consumers. This shift has disrupted established industries, such as transportation and hospitality, by bypassing intermediaries like taxi companies and hotels. Furthermore, the gig economy raises important questions about workers' rights, job security, and the regulation of platform-based labor. In many regions, existing labor laws have struggled to keep pace with the rapid growth of gig work, leading to debates about how to best protect workers while fostering innovation.

Emerging technologies can also disrupt traditional regulatory frameworks. The introduction of blockchain technology, for instance, has challenged the need for central authorities in financial transactions. By enabling decentralized and transparent ledger systems, blockchain offers the potential to reduce fraud, increase trust, and streamline cross-border payments without the need for intermediaries like banks (Narayanan *et al.*, 2016). However, this decentralized nature of blockchain presents challenges for regulatory bodies, as existing laws and frameworks are designed to manage centralized systems. Regulators will need to adapt to these new realities by creating frameworks that can ensure security, protect consumers, and foster innovation in a rapidly changing landscape.

In addition to these examples, other disruptive technologies, such as renewable energy systems, biotechnology, and autonomous vehicles, have the potential to fundamentally reshape industries and society. For instance, the widespread adoption of renewable energy technologies, such as solar panels and wind turbines, is disrupting the global energy market, challenging traditional fossil fuel-based industries, and prompting the transition to more sustainable energy sources. Similarly, autonomous vehicles have the potential to disrupt the transportation sector by reducing the need for human drivers and creating new opportunities for mobility as a service (MaaS).

Ultimately, the disruptive potential of emerging technologies lies in their ability to create new value propositions, challenge existing paradigms, and force industries, governments, and societies to adapt. While this disruption offers exciting possibilities for innovation and growth, it also raises complex challenges, such as the need for updated regulations, workforce adaptation, and ethical considerations in technology deployment. As these technologies continue to evolve, their impact will likely be felt across all sectors of society, making it essential to carefully navigate the risks and opportunities they present.

2.1.3. *Uncertainty*

The developmental trajectory of emerging technologies is marked by significant uncertainty. Factors such as regulatory changes, public acceptance, and unforeseen technical challenges contribute to this ambiguity. The early days of genetically modified organisms (GMOs) highlight how public skepticism and regulatory hurdles can influence the pace and direction of adoption (Day & Schoemaker, 2000). Even technologies with high initial expectations, such as autonomous vehicles, face hurdles ranging from ethical considerations to infrastructure readiness, underlining the unpredictable nature of their evolution.

2.1.4. *Complexity*

Emerging technologies are rarely standalone innovations; instead, they often involve intricate interactions between diverse systems, industries, and stakeholders. This interconnectedness is crucial for their successful deployment and scaling, as these technologies typically address complex, multi-faceted challenges that cannot be solved by a single discipline or approach. For instance, the development of renewable energy systems, such as smart grids, requires the integration of several technologies and expertise from multiple fields. Smart grids rely on advanced sensors to monitor energy distribution, robust data analytics to optimize consumption, and policy frameworks to ensure effective regulation and fair market practices (Qudrat-Ullah, 2014). This convergence of technologies, disciplines, and stakeholders is essential for creating systems that are efficient, resilient, and capable of meeting evolving demands.

The complexity of these systems calls for a multidisciplinary approach. Expertise from engineering is required to develop the underlying hardware and software that allow for real-time monitoring and control of energy flows. Economics plays a key role in designing the pricing models and incentives that drive consumer participation in the system. Environmental science is critical for assessing the sustainability of these systems, ensuring that they reduce the carbon footprint and contribute to broader environmental goals. Sociology and behavioral science help in understanding how communities and individuals interact with these technologies, ensuring that adoption is equitable and that the systems serve the needs of all stakeholders. For instance, understanding social acceptance of smart grids and renewable energy systems is just as important as ensuring their technical reliability and environmental benefits. Failure to integrate these various perspectives can lead to gaps in implementation and adoption, or worse, unintended negative consequences.

One of the significant risks of technological integration is the emergence of cybersecurity vulnerabilities in interconnected systems. As technologies like IoT and smart grids become more widespread, the systems that support them become more susceptible to cyberattacks. The reliance on cloud computing for data storage and analysis in smart grids, for example, creates potential entry points for malicious actors to disrupt energy distribution, steal sensitive data, or sabotage critical infrastructure. Similarly, autonomous vehicles, which rely on a network of sensors, cloud services, and machine learning algorithms, pose cybersecurity challenges that could have severe consequences if compromised. The interdependence of these systems requires a comprehensive approach to cybersecurity, ensuring that security measures are not only applied to individual components but are also designed to work across the entire technological ecosystem.

Moreover, the intricate nature of emerging technologies necessitates a careful balancing of innovation with regulation. While technological advancements offer numerous benefits, they also pose risks, particularly when it comes to issues like privacy, data security, and social inequality. Without appropriate regulatory frameworks, the deployment of these technologies could exacerbate existing inequalities, such as the digital divide between rural and urban populations or between high-income and low-income communities. Policymakers need to take a proactive approach to ensure that the benefits of emerging technologies are distributed equitably, that potential harms are mitigated, and that innovation does not outpace the development of safeguards.

In conclusion, the successful integration of emerging technologies into society requires careful consideration of their complexity and the interactions between different systems and stakeholders. A multidisciplinary approach that includes technical, economic, social, and ethical perspectives is essential for ensuring that these technologies realize their full potential while minimizing unintended negative consequences. As emerging technologies continue to evolve, their interconnectedness will only deepen, making it increasingly important to address the broader ecosystem within which they operate

2.1.5. *Interdisciplinarity and Collaboration*

Emerging technologies thrive on the confluence of knowledge and expertise from multiple domains, where the integration of diverse perspectives is key to unlocking new possibilities. For instance, the rapid progress in biotechnology has been significantly driven by interdisciplinary collaborations, particularly between geneticists, computer scientists, and data analysts. These collaborations have led to groundbreaking advancements, such as the development of CRISPR-Cas9, a revolutionary gene-editing technology that has the potential to transform fields like medicine, agriculture, and environmental science. By combining insights from biology, computer science, and data analytics, researchers have been able to create a tool that is both precise and versatile, enabling the targeted modification of genes with unprecedented accuracy (Doudna & Charpentier, 2014).

Such interdisciplinary approaches not only accelerate innovation but also challenge traditional methods of research and development. Different fields often operate with distinct methodologies, terminologies, and objectives, which can lead to communication barriers and difficulties in aligning goals. For example, geneticists may focus on the biological implications of gene editing, while computer scientists may be more concerned with the computational aspects of data processing and algorithm development. Data analysts, in turn, might concentrate on the vast amounts of genomic data generated and its interpretation for clinical applications. Overcoming these differences requires effective collaboration and the establishment of a shared vision that aligns the goals of all stakeholders.

In practice, fostering collaboration across traditional silos often demands significant cultural and organizational shifts. Academia and industry, for instance, are traditionally structured around specific disciplines, with clear boundaries between fields like genetics, computer science, and data analysis. Encouraging cross-disciplinary work challenges these structures and calls for a shift in organizational culture towards greater openness and fluidity in knowledge exchange. Companies like Illumina, which specialize in genomic sequencing, and tech giants like Google and IBM, which are increasingly investing in healthcare innovations, are exemplars of this new collaborative model. They bring together diverse expertise to tackle complex problems, such as using AI and machine learning to interpret genetic data and predict disease outcomes (Esteva *et al.*, 2019).

Moreover, interdisciplinary collaboration extends beyond the scientific and technological realms into ethical, legal, and social dimensions. As technologies like CRISPR-Cas9 become more widely available, questions surrounding their ethical use — such as gene editing in humans or the potential for "designer babies" — become central to discussions. Legal experts and ethicists must work alongside scientists to establish guidelines and policies that govern the responsible use of such technologies. Public perception, shaped by sociologists and communication experts, also plays a significant role in the adoption of new biotechnologies. Effective communication of the risks and benefits of gene editing to the public is crucial in securing informed consent and fostering societal acceptance.

The success of interdisciplinary collaborations in emerging technologies is also evident in fields like AI, where experts in machine learning, cognitive science, linguistics, and ethics are coming together to build AI systems that are not only effective but also fair, transparent, and accountable. For example, the development of AI models for medical diagnostics requires expertise in both healthcare and machine learning, while addressing issues like bias in AI algorithms demands the involvement of ethicists, social scientists, and legal experts.

In conclusion, the interdisciplinary nature of emerging technologies accelerates innovation by bringing together diverse fields of knowledge, but it also presents challenges in terms of collaboration, organizational culture, and communication. As technological advancements continue to intersect with complex societal issues, the need for effective collaboration across disciplines will only grow. By fostering environments that encourage interdisciplinary work and overcoming the challenges associated with cross-silo collaboration, industries and societies can better harness the full potential of emerging technologies.

2.1.6. *Ethical and Societal Implications*

The novelty and profound impact of emerging technologies bring ethical dilemmas and societal implications to the forefront. As these technologies evolve and integrate into various aspects of daily life, their potential to disrupt existing norms and systems raises critical questions about their responsible use. The ethical concerns surrounding emerging technologies often revolve around issues of privacy, security, accountability, and fairness.

One notable example is the deployment of facial recognition and AI-powered surveillance systems. While these technologies offer substantial benefits in areas such as law enforcement, security, and personalized services, they also raise significant concerns regarding privacy. The ability to track individuals' movements and actions without their consent presents challenges to personal freedoms and civil liberties. Several governments and companies have been scrutinized for using these technologies without adequate transparency or regulation, prompting public backlash and calls for stronger privacy protections. For instance, the widespread use of facial recognition technology by law enforcement agencies in the U.S. and the UK has led to protests and legal challenges, with critics arguing that it disproportionately targets marginalized communities and leads to unwarranted surveillance (Feldstein, 2019). As a result, some cities, like San Francisco, have implemented bans on facial recognition technology, underscoring the urgent need for ethical guidelines and regulatory oversight in the deployment of such tools.

AI technologies, particularly in surveillance, also raise concerns about bias and discrimination. Machine learning algorithms, which power facial recognition systems, are often trained on biased data sets, leading to inaccurate and unequal results. Studies have shown that facial recognition technologies are more likely to misidentify individuals with darker skin tones or women, potentially leading to false arrests or unfair treatment. Addressing these biases requires a concerted effort to design and train algorithms that are fair, transparent, and accountable. The challenge is to balance the benefits of these technologies with the need to protect vulnerable populations from harm.

Similarly, the development and potential use of autonomous weapons in warfare present complex moral and ethical questions about accountability. Autonomous weapons, such as drones equipped with AI algorithms, have the ability to make decisions without human intervention, raising concerns about who is responsible when these systems cause harm or violate international law. Should the blame lie with the manufacturer, the programmer, or the military personnel who deploy the weapon? The concept of "accountability in AI" becomes particularly crucial in these contexts, where machines may make life-and-death decisions on the battlefield. Ethical debates surrounding autonomous weapons systems also extend to the potential for increased violence and the erosion of human decision-making in conflict scenarios. For instance, the use of AI in autonomous drones has sparked debates on whether such technology can be trusted with lethal force and whether it might be misused by authoritarian regimes or rogue states (Sharkey, 2019).

The societal implications of emerging technologies extend beyond privacy and warfare concerns. The automation of jobs through AI and robotics is another pressing issue that requires ethical consideration. While these technologies have the potential to increase productivity and reduce costs, they also pose risks to employment. As machines replace human workers in industries ranging from manufacturing to customer service, the displacement of workers may exacerbate social inequality and contribute to economic instability. Ethical questions arise about how to balance technological progress with social welfare, particularly in ensuring that workers displaced by automation are retrained and provided with new opportunities. Moreover, the growing reliance on AI in decision-making processes raises concerns about fairness and accountability, particularly in sectors like finance, healthcare, and criminal justice. For example, algorithms used in hiring or lending decisions have been shown to perpetuate biases based on race, gender, and socioeconomic status, potentially exacerbating existing inequalities (O'Neil, 2016).

Addressing these ethical and societal concerns requires proactive engagement from multiple stakeholders. Policymakers must work alongside technologists, ethicists, and civil society to develop frameworks that ensure emerging technologies align with societal values and protect fundamental rights. This includes creating robust regulatory systems that prioritize transparency, accountability, and fairness in the development and deployment of new technologies. Additionally, public engagement is essential to ensure that the voices of diverse communities are heard and that their concerns are incorporated into decision-making processes. For instance, ethical discussions about AI should include perspectives from ethicists, social scientists, and affected communities to ensure that the technology benefits society as a whole and does not perpetuate existing inequalities or injustices.

In conclusion, as emerging technologies continue to advance, the ethical and societal implications must be addressed in tandem with their development. A proactive, multi-disciplinary approach that involves collaboration between technologists, policymakers, ethicists, and the public is crucial to ensuring that these technologies are developed and deployed in ways that promote societal well-being, protect individual rights, and align with broader ethical principles.

By fostering an open and inclusive dialogue, we can navigate the challenges posed by emerging technologies and maximize their potential to improve lives while minimizing their risks.

2.1.7. *Global Implications and Accessibility*

Emerging technologies frequently have profound global implications, shaping not only the economic and strategic landscape but also influencing geopolitics. As countries race to develop and implement these technologies, the competition for leadership in fields like AI, quantum computing, and 5G has become a central component of international relations. These technologies are seen as critical to securing economic advantages, enhancing national security, and asserting technological dominance on the world stage.

For instance, 5G technology, which enables faster and more reliable wireless communication, has become a key area of competition among global superpowers. The ability to control and develop 5G infrastructure is seen as crucial for maintaining economic competitiveness and advancing innovation in sectors such as telecommunications, healthcare, and autonomous vehicles. Countries like China, the United States, and the European Union have invested heavily in 5G technology, with each pursuing different strategies to become leaders in this space. For example, China's Huawei has emerged as a major player in the global 5G market, while the U.S. has sought to counterbalance this influence by restricting access to certain technologies and promoting domestic companies like Qualcomm and Cisco (Deng & Liu, 2020). The strategic importance of 5G is reflected in the tensions it has created in international trade, as countries weigh the benefits of access to advanced technologies against concerns about national security and data privacy.

However, the global deployment of emerging technologies often exacerbates existing inequalities between developed and developing regions. While advanced nations benefit from early access to cutting-edge technologies, many developing countries face significant challenges in adopting and integrating these innovations. The digital divide, which refers to the gap in access to technology and the internet between different socioeconomic groups and geographic regions, is a critical issue. In many developing countries, limited infrastructure, lack of investment, and inadequate education systems hinder the widespread adoption of technologies such as high-speed internet, mobile phones, and AI applications.

This disparity in access not only affects economic growth but also deepens social and educational inequalities. For example, rural communities in sub-Saharan Africa or South Asia often lack reliable internet access, which prevents them from participating in the digital economy or accessing critical services like online education and telemedicine. Similarly, small businesses in developing nations may struggle to adopt new technologies like cloud computing or AI due to financial constraints or a lack of technical expertise. As a result, these regions are at risk of being left behind in the global technological race, which could perpetuate cycles of poverty and hinder sustainable development.

Addressing the digital divide is therefore crucial for ensuring that the benefits of emerging technologies are distributed equitably across the globe. Bridging this gap requires concerted efforts from both public and private sectors to provide affordable access to technology and infrastructure. For example, international initiatives like the UN's Broadband Commission for Sustainable Development aim to promote universal internet access, while companies like Google and Facebook have launched initiatives to expand connectivity through satellite and balloon-based internet systems. Furthermore, governments must prioritize investment in education and digital literacy programs to equip individuals with the skills necessary to navigate and thrive in a technology-driven world.

In addition to promoting accessibility, international cooperation is essential to ensure that emerging technologies are developed and deployed in ways that benefit all nations. Collaboration between countries and across sectors can help create global standards for the ethical use of technologies, share knowledge and best practices, and ensure that the benefits of innovation are not monopolized by a few wealthy nations. For example, initiatives like the Global Partnership on Artificial Intelligence (GPAI) bring together governments, industry leaders, and academics from around the world to foster the responsible development and deployment of AI technologies. Through such collaborations, emerging technologies can be harnessed to address global challenges, such as climate change, healthcare, and poverty, while ensuring that no country or community is left behind.

In conclusion, the global implications of emerging technologies are far-reaching, influencing not only economic competition and geopolitics but also social and ethical outcomes. As countries compete to lead in these technologies, it is essential to address the disparities in access and ensure that the benefits of technological progress are distributed equitably across the globe. By fostering international cooperation, investing in infrastructure and education, and prioritizing inclusivity, we can ensure that emerging technologies contribute to a more connected, prosperous, and just world.

In summary, emerging technologies are dynamic, multifaceted innovations that hold the promise of addressing complex global challenges. Their novelty, disruptive potential, uncertainty, and complexity require stakeholders to adopt adaptive strategies and collaborative approaches. By understanding these key characteristics, researchers, policymakers, and industry leaders can better anticipate the implications of emerging technologies and navigate their adoption in ways that maximize benefits while mitigating risks. This Table 2.1 summarizes the key characteristics of emerging

Table 2.1. Key Characteristics of Emerging Technologies and Strategic Lessons for Decision Makers.

Key Aspect	Key Lessons for Decision Makers
Novelty	Emerging technologies represent a departure from established practices, offering groundbreaking methods, processes, or tools. Decision-makers must stay attuned to these shifts and encourage innovation, while being mindful of the potential for radical change in existing business models and societal systems. For example, adopting blockchain in financial systems requires understanding its potential to replace traditional intermediaries.
Potential for Disruption	Emerging technologies have the ability to disrupt industries and societal norms. The rise of AI, blockchain, and quantum computing illustrates their power to redefine market dynamics. Leaders must be proactive in identifying disruptive innovations early, adapting business strategies to leverage opportunities, and preparing for the obsolescence of traditional models.

(*Continued*)

Table 2.1. (*Continued*)

Key Aspect	Key Lessons for Decision Makers
Uncertainty	The development of emerging technologies is often marked by uncertainty, influenced by regulatory changes, public acceptance, and unforeseen technical challenges. Decision-makers should adopt flexible strategies, fostering resilience to adapt to unforeseen obstacles while monitoring public sentiment and regulatory shifts to minimize risk.
Complexity	Emerging technologies often require integration across multiple disciplines and systems. Successful deployment necessitates collaboration among stakeholders from various fields. Leaders should prioritize interdisciplinary collaboration and establish systems that allow for the integration of diverse expertise, ensuring the seamless interaction of technologies to address complex challenges.
Interdisciplinarity and Collaboration	Emerging technologies thrive on cross-disciplinary collaboration. Breakthroughs like CRISPR-Cas9 in biotechnology demonstrate the importance of combining knowledge from different domains. Decision-makers should foster a culture of collaboration, encouraging partnerships between diverse experts to maximize innovation and accelerate technological progress.
Ethical and Societal Implications	As emerging technologies evolve, they bring ethical dilemmas, such as privacy, accountability, and fairness. Decision-makers must incorporate ethical considerations into technology implementation, ensuring that advancements align with societal values and regulations. Proactively addressing ethical concerns will build public trust and prevent adverse societal consequences.
Global Implications and Accessibility	Emerging technologies often have broad global implications, influencing international competitiveness, economic strategies, and geopolitical relations. To ensure equitable access and prevent widening global disparities, decision-makers must champion policies that bridge the digital divide, making emerging technologies accessible to developing regions. Strategic planning should consider the international landscape to maintain global competitiveness.

technologies and presents actionable insights for decision-makers to effectively navigate their implementation and integration into society and industries.

2.2. Current Trends in Technological Advancements

The rapid evolution of technological innovations is reshaping industries, societies, and human interactions with unprecedented speed and scale. Driven by the convergence of various scientific and engineering breakthroughs, several key trends are accelerating the development and adoption of emerging technologies. These trends are transformative, spanning AI, blockchain, IoT, and quantum computing, among others. Analyzing these trends provides a deeper understanding of their potential, challenges, and implications for future developments.

2.2.1. *AI and Machine Learning (ML)*

AI and ML remain at the forefront of technological advancement, evolving from tools of convenience to indispensable systems that influence critical decisions in numerous fields. AI's capacity for analyzing vast datasets, identifying patterns, and making predictions has revolutionized domains such as healthcare, finance, and manufacturing.

For instance, in healthcare, AI-powered diagnostic tools such as IBM Watson and Google's DeepMind analyze medical records, imaging, and genetic data to detect diseases like cancer at earlier stages, improving patient outcomes (Jordan & Mitchell, 2015). Similarly, ML algorithms have become central to financial risk assessment, enabling institutions to identify fraudulent transactions in real time and optimize investment portfolios.

The increasing sophistication of AI-driven automation has also transformed manufacturing through predictive maintenance and optimized production processes. However, AI adoption raises significant ethical and operational challenges, including algorithmic biases, data privacy concerns, and workforce displacement. Addressing these issues requires robust governance frameworks and interdisciplinary collaboration between technologists, policymakers, and ethicists.

2.2.2. *Blockchain and Decentralized Systems*

Blockchain technology, originally developed to underpin cryptocurrencies like Bitcoin, has evolved into a powerful tool for enhancing transparency, security, and efficiency in data management. Its decentralized nature ensures that information is distributed across multiple nodes, reducing the risks associated with single points of failure and unauthorized data manipulation.

In finance, blockchain facilitates secure and cost-effective cross-border transactions, as demonstrated by Ripple's integration into major financial systems (Iansiti & Lakhani, 2017). Beyond finance, blockchain is transforming supply chain management by enabling real-time tracking of goods, ensuring provenance, and minimizing fraud. For example, Walmart and IBM have leveraged blockchain to trace food items across their supply chains, significantly reducing the time required to identify contamination sources.

Blockchain's potential extends to governance and democracy through secure and transparent voting systems, as evidenced by Estonia's pioneering use of blockchain in national elections. However, challenges such as scalability, energy consumption, and regulatory ambiguity must be addressed to unlock its full potential. The emergence of hybrid blockchains and energy-efficient consensus mechanisms, such as proof-of-stake, offers promising solutions to some of these issues.

2.2.3. *IoT*

IoT refers to the network of interconnected devices embedded with sensors, software, and other technologies that enable them to collect and exchange data. IoT is driving the digitization of physical spaces, transforming everyday objects into smart systems capable of real-time monitoring, control, and optimization.

In smart cities, IoT applications enhance urban living by improving traffic management, energy efficiency, and waste disposal systems. For example, Barcelona's implementation of IoT-enabled smart lighting and waste collection systems has significantly reduced energy consumption and operational costs (Atzori, Iera, & Morabito, 2010). Similarly, IoT solutions in agriculture, such as precision farming, optimize water usage, monitor soil health, and boost crop yields by leveraging real-time data from connected devices.

Industrial IoT (IIoT) is revolutionizing manufacturing and logistics through predictive maintenance and smart inventory systems. Companies like GE and Siemens utilize IoT platforms to monitor equipment performance and pre-emptively address issues, minimizing downtime and enhancing productivity. However, IoT's proliferation also introduces cybersecurity vulnerabilities and concerns about data privacy. Strengthening network security and establishing international standards are crucial to ensuring the reliability and safety of IoT ecosystems.

2.2.4. *Quantum Computing*

Quantum computing represents a paradigm shift in computational power and problem-solving capabilities, leveraging the principles of quantum mechanics to perform calculations far beyond the reach of classical computers. While still in its early stages, quantum computing holds transformative potential in areas such as cryptography, materials science, and complex system simulations.

In cryptography, quantum computers could render traditional encryption methods obsolete, necessitating the development of quantum-resistant algorithms. For instance, Google's quantum processor Sycamore achieved quantum supremacy by solving a problem in 200 seconds that would take classical supercomputers thousands of years (Arute *et al.*, 2019). Such advancements signal the potential for breakthroughs in drug discovery, where quantum simulations could model molecular interactions with unprecedented accuracy.

However, the development of quantum computing faces significant technical challenges, including qubit stability, error correction, and the high costs of maintaining quantum coherence. Research institutions and technology giants like IBM, Google, and Microsoft are actively addressing these challenges, accelerating progress through quantum cloud platforms that democratize access to this cutting-edge technology.

2.2.5. *Convergence and Cross-Disciplinary Integration*

One of the most significant trends in technological advancements is the convergence of these emerging technologies. For example, the integration of AI and IoT, often referred to as AIoT, enables intelligent edge computing, where IoT devices process data locally using AI algorithms, reducing latency and enhancing decision-making in real-time. Similarly, the combination of blockchain and IoT enhances data security and transparency in connected ecosystems, as seen in initiatives like VeChain's supply chain solutions.

This convergence underscores the need for cross-disciplinary approaches that harness the synergies between different technologies. It also highlights the importance of education and workforce development programs that equip individuals with diverse skill sets to navigate these complex technological landscapes.

Overall, the current trends in technological advancements are reshaping the modern world by addressing pressing challenges, driving efficiency, and creating new opportunities. From AI's transformative impact on decision-making to the disruptive potential of blockchain, IoT, and quantum computing, these trends collectively illustrate the dynamic interplay of innovation and adaptation. While challenges such as ethical dilemmas, cybersecurity risks, and technical limitations persist, the continued evolution of these technologies promises a future of unprecedented possibilities. Strategic investments in research, policy, and education will be pivotal in ensuring that these advancements are leveraged for the benefit of society at large. Table 2.2 summarizes the Key Trends

Table 2.2. Current Trends in Technological Advancements and Strategic Lessons for Decision Makers.

Key Aspects of Current Trends	Key Lessons for Decision Makers
AI and ML	AI and ML are transforming sectors like healthcare, finance, and manufacturing. They enable data-driven decision-making, predictive analytics, and automation. Decision-makers must prioritize ethical frameworks to manage issues such as algorithmic bias, data privacy, and workforce displacement. Strategic investments in AI talent and infrastructure are crucial to harness AI's full potential.

Table 2.2. (*Continued*)

Key Aspects of Current Trends	**Key Lessons for Decision Makers**
Blockchain and Decentralized Systems	Blockchain technology is enhancing transparency, security, and efficiency, particularly in finance, supply chain management, and governance. Leaders should explore blockchain's applicability beyond cryptocurrencies, including supply chain traceability and secure voting systems. They should also address challenges such as scalability and regulatory issues to fully realize blockchain's benefits.
IoT	IoT is transforming industries by connecting devices and systems, enabling real-time data collection and optimization. Decision-makers should focus on improving IoT security, implementing standards for data privacy, and ensuring robust network infrastructures to avoid vulnerabilities. Investing in smart systems for urban infrastructure and industries like agriculture can drive operational efficiency and sustainability.
Quantum Computing	Quantum computing has the potential to revolutionize areas such as cryptography, drug discovery, and complex system simulations. While in its early stages, decision-makers must prepare for the advent of quantum computing by investing in quantum-resistant algorithms and supporting research into quantum technologies. Understanding quantum computing's potential can give organizations a competitive edge in future innovations.
Convergence and Cross-Disciplinary Integration	The integration of multiple emerging technologies, such as AIoT (AI + IoT) and blockchain + IoT, is fostering intelligent systems and enhanced decision-making. Decision-makers should foster a culture of cross-disciplinary collaboration, invest in workforce development, and build partnerships between technology sectors to drive innovation. This approach will ensure a comprehensive understanding and integration of emerging technologies for greater synergy and impact.

in Technological Advancements and Strategic Insights for Decision Makers.

2.3. Case Studies of Disruptive Technologies

Disruptive technologies continue to transform industries and society by introducing new paradigms of efficiency, transparency, and innovation. This section delves into case studies highlighting the profound impact of AI, blockchain, IoT, and quantum computing, showcasing their applications, challenges, and transformative potential.

2.3.1. *AI: Enhancing Healthcare*

AI has emerged as a cornerstone of innovation in healthcare, enabling breakthroughs in diagnosis, treatment personalization, and operational management. It leverages vast datasets and sophisticated algorithms to address long-standing challenges in the medical field.

1. Key Features and Impact

AI's integration into healthcare exemplifies its versatility and power to drive transformative outcomes.

- **Improved Diagnostic Accuracy**:
  AI algorithms excel at detecting subtle patterns within medical data. For instance, Google's DeepMind developed an AI model capable of diagnosing over 50 eye diseases from retinal scans, achieving diagnostic accuracy comparable to leading ophthalmologists. Similarly, AI-based platforms like PathAI assist pathologists in identifying cancerous cells with high precision, enhancing early detection rates and treatment outcomes.
- **Personalized Medicine**:
  Personalized medicine represents one of AI's most promising applications. By analyzing genetic profiles, environmental factors, and patient histories, AI-driven systems create tailored treatment regimens. For example, IBM Watson Health integrates patient data with clinical guidelines to recommend individualized cancer therapies, increasing treatment efficacy while reducing side effects.

- **Operational Efficiency**:
  AI-powered systems optimize healthcare operations by automating repetitive tasks. Examples include automated medical transcription, predictive maintenance of medical equipment, and real-time patient flow management. Chatbots like Ada Health and Babylon Health provide preliminary assessments, freeing healthcare providers for more complex cases.

2. Real-World Applications

AI's impact extends beyond diagnostics and personalization to public health management. During the COVID-19 pandemic, AI models were used to predict virus spread, optimize resource allocation, and accelerate vaccine development. Companies like Moderna utilized AI tools to analyze protein structures and identify vaccine candidates in record time.

3. Challenges and Considerations

Despite its transformative potential, AI in healthcare faces significant challenges:

- **Data Privacy and Security**: The sensitive nature of medical data necessitates robust data governance frameworks to prevent breaches and ensure compliance with regulations like GDPR and HIPAA.
- **Algorithmic Bias**: AI systems trained on biased datasets may produce skewed results, disproportionately affecting vulnerable populations. Addressing this requires diversification of training data and rigorous testing.
- **Regulatory Hurdles**: The rapid pace of AI development often outstrips regulatory frameworks, complicating its adoption. Streamlining approval processes without compromising safety is essential for broader implementation.

4. Broader Implications

AI's role in healthcare highlights its ability to address critical challenges while improving quality and accessibility. Its success in this domain paves the way for similar advancements in other sectors, from education to environmental conservation. Collaborative efforts among stakeholders are essential to navigate its challenges and unlock its full potential.

Overall, AI represents a paradigm shift in healthcare, reshaping the way diseases are diagnosed, treatments are administered, and healthcare systems operate. Its capacity to process vast amounts of data and deliver precise, actionable insights offers immense promise for improving global health outcomes. However, realizing its full potential requires addressing ethical, regulatory, and technological challenges. As AI continues to mature, its thoughtful and equitable implementation can drive transformative progress, not just in healthcare, but across all sectors of human life.

2.3.2. *Blockchain: Revolutionizing Supply Chain Management*

Blockchain technology is redefining supply chain management by offering unprecedented levels of transparency, efficiency, and security. By creating a decentralized, immutable ledger, blockchain ensures that every step in a supply chain is verifiable, fostering trust among stakeholders and consumers alike. This section explores blockchain's transformative role in supply chains through a compelling case study of its application in the diamond industry, highlighting its key features, challenges, and broader implications.

1. Key Features and Impact

Blockchain technology provides several features that have significant implications for supply chain management:

- **Enhanced Transparency**:
  Blockchain's decentralized ledger records every transaction and activity, creating an unalterable chain of data. In the diamond industry, this means tracking a diamond's journey from mining to retail, ensuring it is conflict-free and ethically sourced. This transparency not only boosts consumer trust but also encourages ethical practices throughout the supply chain.
- **Fraud Prevention**:
  The immutable nature of blockchain records eliminates opportunities for tampering, counterfeiting, or fraudulent activities. In supply chains, this means reducing instances of misrepresentation or

falsification of origin, ensuring that all stakeholders operate with integrity.

- **Cost Reduction**:
  Blockchain reduces reliance on intermediaries, such as verification agencies and third-party auditors, by automating verification processes. This streamlining cuts operational costs while maintaining or even enhancing process integrity and efficiency.

2. Example: De Beers' Tracr Platform

A standout example of blockchain in action is De Beers' **Tracr** platform, designed to trace diamonds from mine to market.

- **How Tracr Works**:
  Each diamond is assigned a unique digital certificate containing immutable information about its origin, quality, and journey through the supply chain. This data is stored on the blockchain, accessible to all stakeholders in real-time.
- **Impact on the Diamond Industry**:
  Since its implementation, Tracr has certified millions of diamonds as conflict-free, fostering confidence among consumers and retailers. It has also streamlined De Beers' operations, reducing paperwork and enhancing collaboration with suppliers and distributors.
- **Scaling Beyond Diamonds**:
  While Tracr was developed for diamonds, its underlying blockchain framework is adaptable to other industries, offering a template for ethical and efficient supply chain practices in sectors such as agriculture, electronics, and pharmaceuticals.

3. Challenges and Considerations

Despite its transformative potential, blockchain adoption in supply chain management is not without challenges.

- **Scalability**:
  Current blockchain platforms often struggle with handling large volumes of transactions in real time. Supply chains involving thousands of transactions daily require scalable solutions to ensure efficiency. Emerging technologies, such as sharding and layer-two solutions, are addressing these issues.

- **Interoperability**:
  Supply chains often involve multiple stakeholders using different platforms and technologies. Achieving seamless communication between these disparate systems is critical for blockchain's widespread adoption. Initiatives like cross-chain solutions and industry standards aim to overcome this hurdle.
- **Energy Consumption**:
  Traditional blockchain systems, especially those based on proof-of-work algorithms, consume significant energy. This raises sustainability concerns, particularly for industries striving to reduce their carbon footprint. Solutions like proof-of-stake and energy-efficient blockchains are being explored to address this challenge.

4. Commercial Implications

The integration of blockchain in supply chains has far-reaching implications:

- **Consumer Empowerment**:
  With access to transparent data, consumers can make informed decisions about the products they purchase, prioritizing ethical and sustainable goods. This shift towards informed consumption can drive industries to adopt more responsible practices.
- **Improved Compliance**:
  Blockchain facilitates compliance with regulatory requirements by providing an auditable trail of transactions and activities. This is particularly valuable in industries with stringent regulations, such as pharmaceuticals and food safety.
- **Fostering Collaboration**:
  By providing a shared, trusted platform, blockchain encourages collaboration among stakeholders, breaking down silos and promoting innovation. For example, companies in the fashion industry are exploring blockchain to ensure ethical sourcing of materials, enhancing both brand reputation and consumer trust.

Blockchain technology is revolutionizing supply chain management by addressing long-standing challenges such as fraud, inefficiency, and lack of transparency. Through initiatives like De

Beers' Tracr platform, it has demonstrated its potential to transform industries by fostering ethical practices and operational excellence. However, its widespread adoption hinges on overcoming challenges like scalability, interoperability, and energy efficiency. As these issues are addressed through technological advancements, blockchain is poised to become a cornerstone of modern supply chains, driving greater accountability and sustainability in global commerce.

2.3.3. *IoT: Transforming Smart Cities*

IoT is a transformative technology reshaping urban environments through interconnected systems that enhance efficiency, sustainability, and quality of life. By integrating IoT into urban infrastructure, smart cities are able to address complex challenges such as energy conservation, traffic management, and waste optimization. This section explores the role of IoT in creating smart cities with a focus on the case study of Barcelona, a pioneer in IoT-driven urban innovation.

1. Key Features and Impact

IoT technologies have been instrumental in advancing key urban systems to create smarter, more sustainable cities.

- **Smart Lighting Systems**:
  IoT-enabled streetlights in Barcelona adjust their brightness based on real-time conditions, such as pedestrian activity or ambient light levels. This system has reduced the city's energy consumption by up to 30% while maintaining safety standards. Additionally, remote monitoring of these lights simplifies maintenance, reducing operational costs.
- **Traffic Management**:
  IoT sensors installed across Barcelona monitor real-time traffic patterns and dynamically adjust traffic signals to improve flow. For instance, during peak hours, traffic light cycles are optimized to prioritize busier routes, reducing congestion and travel times. This approach not only decreases emissions from idling vehicles but also enhances public transportation reliability.

- **Waste Management**:
  Barcelona's smart bins, equipped with IoT sensors, notify waste collection services when they are full, enabling efficient route planning for garbage trucks. This reduces fuel consumption and operational costs while minimizing overflow and keeping public spaces cleaner.
- **Water Management**:
  IoT-enabled irrigation systems monitor soil moisture levels and weather conditions to optimize water usage in public parks and gardens. This ensures sustainable water consumption while maintaining green spaces.
- **Air Quality Monitoring**:
  IoT devices in Barcelona continuously measure air quality across the city, providing actionable data to policymakers and alerting residents during high pollution events. This system helps in formulating targeted measures to improve air quality and protect public health.

2. Case Study: Barcelona's Smart City Initiatives

Barcelona stands out as a model of IoT integration, leveraging smart technologies to address urban challenges and improve citizens' quality of life.

- **Public Services**:
  IoT applications extend to public services such as parking and utilities. For example, smart parking systems guide drivers to available spaces using real-time data, reducing fuel wastage and time spent searching for parking.
- **Energy Optimization**:
  In addition to smart lighting, Barcelona employs IoT-based energy management systems in public buildings to monitor usage patterns and identify inefficiencies. This has resulted in significant cost savings and reduced carbon emissions.
- **Community Engagement**:
  The city has implemented IoT-powered platforms that allow citizens to report issues like potholes or broken streetlights through mobile apps. This real-time feedback loop ensures faster resolution and fosters trust between residents and city officials.

3. Business Implications

Barcelona's success demonstrates the transformative potential of IoT in urban development. However, it also highlights critical considerations:

- **Improved Resource Allocation**:
  IoT technologies optimize resource utilization, leading to cost savings and reduced environmental impact. For instance, the city's smart energy and waste management systems have significantly cut operational inefficiencies.
- **Enhanced Citizen Satisfaction**:
  IoT-driven initiatives improve public services, reduce inconveniences such as traffic congestion, and contribute to a cleaner, healthier environment, directly enhancing the quality of life for residents.
- **Cybersecurity Risks**:
  The reliance on interconnected systems introduces vulnerabilities. Breaches could disrupt essential services, compromise sensitive data, or jeopardize public safety. Addressing these risks requires robust cybersecurity measures and resilient infrastructure.
- **Data Privacy Concerns**:
  IoT systems generate vast amounts of data, raising concerns about how this data is stored, shared, and used. Transparent governance frameworks are essential to ensure privacy and build public trust.
- **Scalability and Equity**:
  Scaling IoT solutions to accommodate growing populations while ensuring equitable access across diverse communities is a critical challenge. Effective planning and inclusive policies are key to addressing this issue.

IoT is at the forefront of transforming urban landscapes into smart cities, exemplified by Barcelona's comprehensive IoT integration. By enhancing efficiency, sustainability, and citizen engagement, IoT technologies offer a blueprint for cities worldwide. However, their adoption must be accompanied by proactive measures to address cybersecurity risks, data privacy concerns, and scalability challenges. As IoT continues to evolve, its potential to revolutionize urban living remains immense, promising a future where technology and humanity coexist harmoniously to create sustainable, thriving cities.

2.3.4. *Quantum Computing: Redefining Cryptography*

Quantum computing represents a paradigm shift in computational capabilities, promising to address problems previously deemed unsolvable by classical computers. Among its transformative applications, cryptography stands out as a domain facing both unparalleled opportunities and critical threats. This section explores the impact of quantum computing on cryptography, with a focus on Shor's algorithm as a case study, and highlights its broader implications for technology and society.

1. Key Features and Impact

Quantum computing's power lies in its ability to leverage quantum mechanics, enabling calculations that grow exponentially faster than those performed by classical systems.

- **Breaking Traditional Encryption**:
  One of the most notable implications of quantum computing is its ability to undermine traditional encryption methods. Shor's algorithm, developed by mathematician Peter Shor in 1994, demonstrated that a sufficiently powerful quantum computer could efficiently factorize large integers. This capability threatens widely used encryption schemes like RSA, which rely on the computational difficulty of factoring as their security foundation (Shor, 1997).
- **Quantum-Safe Cryptography**:
  In response to the potential threat of quantum attacks, researchers are developing post-quantum cryptographic algorithms. These algorithms are designed to remain secure even in the presence of quantum computing capabilities. The National Institute of Standards and Technology (NIST) has initiated efforts to standardize quantum-resistant cryptographic protocols, ensuring the long-term security of digital systems (Chen *et al.*, 2016).
- **Advancing Scientific Research**:
  Beyond cryptography, quantum computing holds promise for accelerating progress in fields such as drug discovery and material science. Quantum simulations enable researchers to model complex molecular interactions, such as protein folding, with unprecedented precision (Montanaro, 2016). These capabilities could lead

to breakthroughs in developing new pharmaceuticals or designing more efficient materials for energy storage and transmission.

2. Case Study: Shor's Algorithm

Shor's algorithm serves as a landmark in quantum computing, illustrating its transformative potential and the challenges it poses.

- **How It Works**:
  Shor's algorithm leverages quantum principles like superposition and entanglement to perform integer factorization exponentially faster than classical algorithms. In practical terms, this means that encryption methods such as RSA, which require vast computational resources to break using classical computers, could be rendered obsolete by quantum systems (Shor, 1997).
- **Real-World Implications**:
  If realized at scale, Shor's algorithm would compromise the confidentiality of encrypted communications, including financial transactions, medical records, and government communications. This has heightened the urgency for organizations to transition to quantum-resistant encryption before quantum computers become capable of executing such attacks (Chen *et al.*, 2016).

3. Applications of Quantum Computing

While cryptography remains a focal point, quantum computing's impact extends into various domains:

- **Optimization Problems**:
  Quantum algorithms like Grover's algorithm can accelerate search and optimization processes, benefitting industries such as logistics, supply chain management, and finance (Grover, 1996).
- **Climate Modeling**:
  Quantum computers can simulate complex climate systems more accurately, aiding in the development of effective strategies to combat climate change (Montanaro, 2016).
- **Artificial Intelligence**:
  Quantum-enhanced AI models promise improvements in machine learning tasks, such as pattern recognition and natural language processing, potentially transforming industries ranging from healthcare to autonomous vehicles (Biamonte *et al.*, 2017).

4. Challenges and Considerations

Despite its immense potential, quantum computing faces several significant hurdles:

- **Qubit Stability**:
  Quantum bits, or qubits, are the building blocks of quantum computing. Maintaining their stability, or coherence, for sufficient durations remains a technical challenge, as qubits are highly sensitive to environmental noise (Preskill, 2018).
- **Error Correction**:
  Quantum error correction is essential to ensure the accuracy of computations, as even minor errors can propagate and compromise results. Developing efficient error-correction techniques is an ongoing area of research (Preskill, 2018).
- **Infrastructure and Cost**:
  Building and maintaining quantum computers requires substantial investment and highly controlled environments, limiting access to only a few institutions and corporations (Montanaro, 2016).
- **Ethical and Security Implications**:
  The advent of quantum computing raises ethical concerns, particularly in cybersecurity. Governments and organizations must proactively address these risks by adopting quantum-safe encryption and ensuring equitable access to quantum technologies (Chen *et al.*, 2016).

5. Industry Initiatives

As quantum computing continues to evolve, major technology companies and research institutions are playing a crucial role in pushing the boundaries of this disruptive technology. These industry giants, such as IBM, Google, and Microsoft, are spearheading initiatives that aim to accelerate the development and application of quantum computing. Through cloud-based quantum computing platforms, collaborative research efforts, and a focus on innovation, these companies are positioning themselves at the forefront of quantum computing's transformative potential.

Cloud-Based Quantum Computing: One of the key advancements in the field of quantum computing is the democratization of access to quantum systems through cloud-based platforms. In the past, quantum computing was confined to a small number of specialized laboratories and research centers, making it difficult for most organizations and individuals to explore the technology. However, with the advent of cloud-based quantum computing services, companies are now able to experiment with quantum algorithms and run quantum simulations remotely, without the need to own or maintain expensive quantum hardware.

IBM Quantum Experience is one of the most notable cloud platforms in this space, offering access to quantum computers via the IBM Cloud. The platform allows users to run quantum algorithms on IBM's quantum processors and even access their quantum computing simulators, all of which contribute to the education and experimentation necessary to unlock quantum computing's full potential. Through its open-source programming language, Qiskit, IBM enables researchers and developers to build and execute quantum applications in a collaborative, user-friendly environment (IBM, 2023). This initiative is part of IBM's broader mission to accelerate quantum computing development while making it accessible to researchers from various sectors, from academia to industry.

Similarly, **Google Quantum AI** provides cloud-based quantum services to users via its Quantum Computing Service, which supports algorithm development and quantum simulations. Google's **Sycamore** processor, which famously demonstrated quantum supremacy in 2019, is integrated into this platform, enabling businesses and researchers to explore quantum algorithms that would otherwise be computationally impossible on classical computers (Arute *et al.*, 2019). The availability of quantum systems over the cloud enables businesses, especially in fields such as chemistry, logistics, and finance, to start experimenting with quantum solutions and explore use cases in real-world applications.

These cloud-based offerings are not only fostering innovation in quantum computing but are also opening the door for interdisciplinary collaboration, empowering individuals and smaller organizations who might not otherwise have the resources to access quantum hardware. The growth of cloud-based quantum computing services is helping to create a more inclusive quantum ecosystem, allowing for the rapid exchange of ideas and driving forward research across multiple sectors.

Collaboration and Innovation: Beyond providing access to quantum hardware through cloud platforms, many leading tech companies are also focused on collaborative efforts to address the technical challenges facing quantum computing. Collaboration between academia, industry, and government is seen as essential for driving the rapid development of quantum technologies and overcoming barriers such as qubit stability, error correction, and scalability.

One such collaborative effort is the Quantum Network initiative, a global initiative aimed at bringing together researchers, engineers, and technologists to accelerate the pace of quantum research and development. The initiative emphasizes the importance of cross-sector collaboration to advance both the theoretical and practical aspects of quantum computing, especially in solving complex problems like quantum error correction and developing quantum communication protocols. As quantum technologies become more integrated into industry applications, it will be crucial to build collaborative frameworks to ensure that development is both efficient and aligned with societal needs (Preskill, 2018).

In addition to such initiatives, Microsoft's Quantum Development Kit offers another example of industry-driven collaboration in the quantum computing space. Through its programming language Q# and quantum simulator, Microsoft invites developers and researchers from various disciplines to explore the potential of quantum algorithms and their practical applications (Microsoft, 2023). Microsoft has also fostered partnerships with universities, national laboratories, and other tech companies to support the development of quantum hardware and algorithms.

Moreover, industry collaborations are not limited to private-sector players. Governments around the world are also playing an active role in shaping the future of quantum technologies. For example, the U.S. Department of Energy has invested in initiatives such as the National Quantum Initiative (NQI), which aims to advance quantum science and technology across multiple sectors. Similarly, the European Union's Quantum Flagship Program is a research initiative designed to promote the development of quantum technologies within Europe, ensuring that European researchers and industries remain competitive in the quantum race (EU Quantum Flagship, 2023).

These partnerships and collaborations are essential for addressing the challenges of quantum computing and accelerating the adoption of quantum technologies across various industries. By sharing knowledge, resources, and expertise, these stakeholders are working to overcome technical barriers and lay the foundation for future breakthroughs in quantum computing.

Industry-Specific Quantum Applications: The applications of quantum computing are diverse and have the potential to revolutionize multiple industries. For example, in the pharmaceutical and healthcare sectors, quantum computing could dramatically accelerate drug discovery by simulating molecular interactions at an unprecedented scale. Companies like Biogen are collaborating with quantum computing firms to explore how quantum algorithms can speed up the process of identifying new therapeutic compounds (Biogen, 2023). Similarly, in finance, quantum algorithms have the potential to optimize portfolio management and risk analysis by processing complex datasets faster than classical computers. Investment firms are already experimenting with quantum technologies to enhance their financial modeling capabilities (Orus *et al.*, 2019).

In the energy sector, quantum computing can play a pivotal role in optimizing energy production and distribution systems. By using quantum simulations, energy companies can develop more efficient materials for solar cells, improve the management of power grids, and explore novel approaches to energy storage. The collaboration between energy companies and quantum computing startups is fostering new insights into energy solutions that could dramatically reduce global dependence on fossil fuels (Lanyon *et al.*, 2020).

Industry initiatives in quantum computing, led by companies like IBM, Google, and Microsoft, are critical for advancing this transformative technology. Cloud-based quantum computing platforms are democratizing access to quantum systems, enabling a wide range of users — from researchers to businesses — to experiment with quantum algorithms and applications. Additionally, collaborations between academia, industry, and government are accelerating the pace of quantum research, addressing the technical challenges that must be overcome to unlock the full potential of quantum technologies. With ongoing investments and partnerships, the future of quantum computing promises to bring unprecedented advances in industries ranging from healthcare and finance to energy and materials science, shaping the future of technological innovation.

Quantum computing is poised to redefine cryptography and reshape numerous industries, offering unprecedented computational power while presenting new security challenges. Shor's algorithm exemplifies the disruptive potential of this technology, emphasizing the urgency for transitioning to quantum-safe encryption. Beyond cryptography, quantum computing holds promise for transformative advancements in science, optimization, and AI. However, realizing its full potential requires overcoming technical hurdles, addressing ethical concerns, and ensuring equitable access. As we stand on the brink of the quantum era, proactive measures and collaborative innovation will be crucial to harness its benefits while mitigating associated risks.

2.3.5. *Comparative Insights*

The disruptive technologies discussed in this section — AI, blockchain, IoT, and quantum computing — each brings transformative potential across various sectors. However, they also present distinct advantages and challenges that need to be carefully considered for their successful deployment and integration. The following section provides a comparative analysis of these technologies, emphasizing their strengths and the hurdles that accompany their widespread adoption.

1. AI

Advantages: AI excels in automating decision-making processes and personalizing user experiences. Its ability to analyze vast datasets enables AI to identify patterns and predict outcomes, making it invaluable in sectors such as healthcare, finance, and retail. AI algorithms can optimize complex tasks, from improving diagnostic accuracy in medicine to enhancing customer recommendations in e-commerce. Additionally, AI's adaptability allows it to continually learn and improve, contributing to increased efficiency and innovation over time.

Challenges: Despite its strengths, AI introduces significant challenges, particularly in terms of ethics and accountability. One of the primary concerns is the presence of biases in AI models. If an AI system is trained on biased data, it can perpetuate and even exacerbate existing inequalities, leading to discriminatory outcomes in areas like hiring, lending, and law enforcement. Moreover, the lack of transparency in some AI decision-making processes, often referred to as the "black box" problem, raises concerns about accountability and fairness. Therefore, AI development requires robust ethical frameworks to mitigate these risks and ensure its responsible use.

2. Blockchain
Advantages: Blockchain technology is praised for its ability to create decentralized and transparent systems that enhance trust. By maintaining an immutable ledger, blockchain eliminates the need for intermediaries, reducing fraud and transaction costs. This characteristic is particularly valuable in sectors like finance, supply chain management, and healthcare, where the verification of transactions and data integrity is crucial. Additionally, blockchain's ability to provide end-to-end traceability makes it ideal for applications that require accountability, such as in food safety or pharmaceuticals.

Challenges: While blockchain offers transparency and security, its widespread adoption faces significant hurdles related to scalability and energy consumption. Blockchain networks, particularly those using proof-of-work mechanisms (such as Bitcoin), require vast amounts of computational power, leading to high energy consumption. This has raised environmental concerns, especially as blockchain adoption scales globally. Furthermore, scalability remains a key issue, as increasing transaction volume can lead to slow processing times and higher transaction costs. As such, efforts to develop more energy-efficient consensus mechanisms, such as proof-of-stake, are underway but not yet universally adopted.

3. IoT
Advantages: IoT has revolutionized connectivity by linking devices and systems to the internet, allowing for continuous data collection, monitoring, and control. This has transformed industries such as manufacturing, healthcare, and agriculture. In manufacturing, IoT-enabled devices optimize processes through predictive maintenance and real-time monitoring, reducing downtime and improving efficiency. In healthcare, IoT devices, such as wearables, track patients' vital signs, enabling remote monitoring and personalized care. Similarly, in agriculture, IoT sensors monitor environmental conditions, helping farmers make data-driven decisions to improve crop yields and resource management.

Challenges: However, IoT also presents significant challenges, particularly in the areas of cybersecurity and data privacy. The vast number of interconnected devices increases the potential attack surface for cybercriminals, making IoT systems more vulnerable to hacking and data breaches. In healthcare, for instance, a compromised IoT device could lead to the theft of sensitive patient data or even interfere with life-saving medical equipment. Moreover, IoT systems generate vast amounts of data, raising concerns about how this data is stored, managed, and shared, particularly in relation to user consent and privacy regulations. As IoT devices proliferate, the need for robust security measures and clear data governance policies becomes increasingly critical.

4. Quantum Computing

Advantages: Quantum computing promises to revolutionize industries that rely on complex calculations and simulations. With its ability to perform calculations at exponentially faster rates than classical computers, quantum computing has the potential to solve problems in fields like cryptography, drug discovery, and climate modeling that are currently intractable for classical machines. For example, quantum computers can efficiently factor large numbers, which could break current encryption systems and pave the way for more secure cryptographic methods. In healthcare, quantum simulations could enable the modeling of molecular interactions at an unprecedented scale, accelerating drug discovery and medical breakthroughs.

Challenges: Despite its transformative potential, quantum computing is still in its early stages of development and faces several technical challenges. One of the major hurdles is the issue of qubit stability and error correction. Qubits, the fundamental units of quantum computers, are highly sensitive to environmental interference, making them prone to errors. Additionally, the infrastructure costs associated with building and maintaining quantum computing systems are high, and the technology's scalability remains uncertain. Furthermore, quantum computing's impact on cryptography raises concerns about security, as the ability to break current encryption methods could expose sensitive data and systems to new vulnerabilities. As such, the development of quantum-safe cryptography is an essential area of research to ensure that security remains intact in a quantum-enabled world.

In conclusion, while each disruptive technology — AI, blockchain, IoT, and quantum computing — offers unique advantages that can drive innovation across various sectors, they also present distinct challenges that need to be addressed for successful deployment. From ethical considerations in AI and blockchain's scalability issues to IoT's cybersecurity risks and quantum computing's technical hurdles, these technologies require careful management, adaptive strategies, and thoughtful regulation. By understanding the advantages and challenges of each, stakeholders can better navigate the complex landscape of emerging technologies and harness their potential for transformative change.

The case studies of AI, blockchain, IoT, and quantum computing illustrate how disruptive technologies are reshaping industries and societies. By examining their applications, benefits, and challenges, stakeholders can better anticipate the opportunities and risks these innovations bring. A strategic approach that balances technological development with ethical and practical considerations is essential for maximizing their positive impact. This Table 2.3 captures the key disruptive technologies and lessons decision-makers should consider when implementing these technologies across sectors.

Table 2.3. Key Aspects and Lessons from Case Studies of Disruptive Technologies.

Disruptive Technology	**Key Lessons for Decision Makers**
AI *Enhancing Healthcare*	– **Emphasize Data Privacy**: Ensure robust data governance to address privacy concerns in healthcare. – **Combat Algorithmic Bias**: Strive for diverse datasets to avoid skewed results, especially in medical diagnostics. – **Invest in Personalization**: Utilize AI to develop individualized treatment plans, improving healthcare outcomes and patient satisfaction. – **Address Regulatory Gaps**: Streamline approval processes to keep pace with AI innovations while maintaining safety and efficacy.
Blockchain	– **Promote Transparency**: Use blockchain to enhance trust through traceable, immutable records, particularly in supply chains like diamonds.

(*Continued*)

Table 2.3. (*Continued*)

Disruptive Technology	Key Lessons for Decision Makers
Revolutionizing Supply Chain	- **Focus on Cost Efficiency**: Reduce operational costs by eliminating intermediaries and automating processes. – **Ensure Scalability**: Address challenges in handling large-scale transactions for blockchain adoption in supply chain systems. – **Prioritize Energy Efficiency**: Explore energy-efficient blockchain models to meet sustainability goals.
IoT	– **Improve Resource Allocation**: Use IoT to optimize resource usage, such as energy and water, to reduce costs and environmental impact in urban settings.
Transforming Smart Cities	– **Enhance Public Engagement**: Develop IoT platforms for real-time citizen interaction and reporting, fostering trust and engagement. – **Prioritize Cybersecurity**: Implement robust cybersecurity frameworks to protect interconnected systems in smart cities. – **Plan for Scalability**: Ensure IoT solutions can scale with growing urban populations and infrastructure needs.
Quantum Computing	– **Invest in Post-Quantum Cryptography**: Prepare for quantum threats by developing quantum-resistant encryption methods.
Redefining Cryptography	– **Monitor Technological Advances**: Stay updated on quantum computing developments to proactively address risks to data security. – **Support Quantum Research**: Invest in quantum computing research for advancements in fields like drug discovery and climate modeling. – **Address Qubit Stability**: Focus on overcoming technical challenges in quantum computing, such as maintaining qubit stability for practical applications.

2.4. Dynamic Perspective of Emerging Technologies

Understanding emerging technologies requires a dynamic perspective that considers how these technologies evolve and interact over time. This perspective emphasizes adaptability and continuous learning in managing technological change. According to Qudrat-Ullah (2024), dynamic decision-making frameworks are crucial in environments characterized by rapid technological advancements and uncertainty. These frameworks enable decision-makers to anticipate changes, assess risks, and respond effectively to emerging challenges.

Emerging technologies do not exist in isolation; they operate within a larger ecosystem shaped by social, economic, and political factors. The interplay of technologies such as AI, IoT, and blockchain illustrates the importance of viewing innovations as dynamic, interconnected components of a broader system (Floridi *et al.*, 2018). This section explores the nuances of these dynamics through key subsections with additional examples.

2.4.1. *Technological Convergence and Synergy*

Technological convergence refers to the process of merging distinct technologies to create innovative solutions that have broader applications across various industries. This blending of technologies accelerates innovation, optimizes resource usage, and offers new capabilities that address complex challenges more effectively than isolated technologies. Technological synergy is particularly valuable in emerging fields, where multiple technologies come together to create efficiencies and tackle global problems. As these converging technologies evolve, they open up new opportunities for growth and transformation, particularly in sectors such as agriculture, healthcare, and renewable energy.

1. AI and IoT in Agriculture

One of the most notable examples of technological convergence is the integration of AI and IoT in agriculture. Precision farming, which combines these two technologies, has revolutionized agricultural practices by enabling farmers to make data-driven decisions that optimize crop yield while reducing resource waste. IoT devices, such as sensors and drones, are deployed to monitor soil moisture, weather conditions, crop health, and other environmental factors in real-time. This data is then analyzed using AI algorithms to make predictions and optimize irrigation schedules, fertilizer usage, and pest control strategies.

For instance, companies like **John Deere** have pioneered the use of autonomous tractors equipped with IoT sensors and AI capabilities. These tractors not only perform tasks like plowing and planting but also collect valuable environmental data that can be processed to enhance farming practices. By adjusting farming methods based on real-time data, AI-powered systems help to increase crop yields, conserve water, reduce fertilizer usage, and minimize waste (Benedict, 2019). The synergy between AI and IoT in agriculture illustrates the transformative potential of combining these technologies to improve efficiency, sustainability, and productivity in the agricultural sector. This convergence allows farmers to address challenges such as climate change, resource scarcity, and growing food demands more effectively.

2. Healthcare Synergies

In the healthcare sector, technological convergence is driving major advancements in preventive care, patient monitoring, and personalized medicine. Wearable devices that integrate AI with IoT sensors have become increasingly popular in monitoring vital signs such as heart rate, blood pressure, and sleep patterns. Devices like **Fitbit** and the **Apple Watch** not only track physical activity but also provide continuous health monitoring and early detection of potential health issues.

These devices are connected to cloud platforms that use AI algorithms to analyze collected data, offering personalized recommendations for improving health and wellness. For example, an AI system might analyze a user's heart rate variability and suggest lifestyle changes to reduce stress or improve cardiovascular health. Furthermore, in more advanced applications, these devices can alert users or healthcare professionals about potential risks, such as irregular heart rhythms, helping to prevent serious health incidents before they occur (Topol, 2019).

The synergy between AI and IoT in healthcare exemplifies how converging technologies can improve quality of care, reduce healthcare costs, and enable early detection of diseases. These technologies are not only beneficial for individual health management but also have broader implications for public health systems, helping to monitor populations for emerging health threats and improving healthcare delivery on a global scale.

3. Blockchain and Renewable Energy

Blockchain technology, traditionally associated with cryptocurrencies, is also demonstrating significant potential when integrated with renewable energy systems. In particular, blockchain is facilitating peer-to-peer (P2P) energy trading, a practice that allows consumers to buy and sell excess energy generated by renewable sources such as solar panels. Platforms like **Power Ledger** enable households with solar panels to sell surplus electricity directly to their neighbors, bypassing traditional energy providers and creating a decentralized energy market.

This decentralized approach to energy trading is not only more efficient but also promotes sustainability by encouraging the use of renewable energy. Blockchain ensures transparency, security, and traceability in energy transactions, which is essential for building trust in decentralized energy systems. By allowing individuals to trade energy directly, blockchain lowers the entry barriers to energy markets, empowering consumers and encouraging the adoption of renewable energy technologies (Iansiti & Lakhani, 2017).

The convergence of blockchain and renewable energy illustrates how emerging technologies can work together to create more sustainable and equitable systems. This synergy can address key challenges such as energy access, grid stability, and the transition to greener energy sources, which are critical to addressing global climate change.

The convergence of technologies such as AI, IoT, and blockchain is revolutionizing industries by creating solutions that were previously not possible. These technologies amplify each other's capabilities, leading to innovations that address complex global challenges in areas like agriculture, healthcare, and energy. By leveraging the synergistic power of these technologies, industries can achieve new levels of efficiency, sustainability, and productivity. Technological convergence not only accelerates innovation but also promotes the creation of solutions that are more holistic, scalable, and impactful, ultimately driving positive change across sectors.

2.4.2. *The Lifecycle of Emerging Technologies*

The lifecycle of emerging technologies is a critical framework for understanding how these innovations evolve over time. From the initial stages of ideation to widespread adoption, and eventual maturity, each phase presents unique opportunities and challenges. A dynamic perspective of this lifecycle allows organizations to align their strategies with the specific characteristics of each phase, enabling them to maximize the potential of new technologies while addressing the associated risks. This section outlines the key phases of the technology lifecycle and provides examples from various domains to illustrate how emerging technologies are evolving.

1. Innovation Phase

The innovation phase marks the beginning of a technology's lifecycle, where research and development (R&D) efforts are concentrated on conceptualizing, designing, and testing new ideas. In this phase, technologies are often in a prototype or experimental stage, and their potential applications are still being explored. The focus is on developing core capabilities, refining the technology, and identifying feasible use cases.

A prominent example of a technology currently in the innovation phase is quantum computing. Companies like IBM, Google, and Rigetti Computing are making significant investments in developing quantum processors that leverage the principles of quantum mechanics to perform calculations that would be impossible for classical computers. Although quantum computing has the potential to revolutionize fields like cryptography, artificial intelligence, and materials science, it remains in the early stages of development. Research efforts are primarily focused on overcoming technical challenges related to qubit stability, error correction, and scalability (Arute *et al.*, 2019). At this stage, the technology is largely experimental, and its widespread applicability is yet to be realized.

The innovation phase is critical because it lays the foundation for future developments. However, it also presents risks, as many emerging technologies in this phase are not yet commercially viable, and their long-term impacts remain uncertain. Organizations that are investing in emerging technologies during this phase need to be prepared for a high level of uncertainty and risk.

2. Adoption and Diffusion Phase

The adoption and diffusion phase occurs when a technology begins to gain traction in the market, transitioning from a niche or experimental stage to widespread use. During this phase, early adopters play a key role in validating the technology, and its benefits become more apparent to the broader market. The technology starts to enter various industries, and more companies begin to invest in its implementation.

Electric vehicles (EVs) provide an illustrative example of a technology that has reached the adoption and diffusion phase. Tesla's Model 3 is a prime example of how advancements in battery technology, combined with growing environmental awareness, have led to the widespread adoption of EVs. Over the past decade, electric vehicles have gained significant market share due to their environmental benefits, lower operating costs, and improvements in performance and affordability. Governments worldwide are also supporting the adoption of EVs through incentives such as tax breaks, subsidies, and the expansion of charging infrastructure (Bohnsack *et al.*, 2014).

This phase is marked by rapid growth, as the technology is embraced by both consumers and industries. However, challenges such as cost reduction, scaling production, and addressing infrastructure gaps remain. For example, although EVs have become more affordable, the lack of widespread charging stations continues to be a barrier to further adoption. Additionally, the technology needs to evolve to meet the demands of consumers for greater range, faster charging times, and more affordable options.

Organizations operating in the adoption and diffusion phase must focus on scaling production, improving customer experience, and overcoming barriers to widespread adoption. While the technology is gaining momentum, there are still significant challenges to overcome before it becomes ubiquitous.

3. Maturity and Evolution Phase

The maturity and evolution phase occurs when a technology has become widely adopted and integrated into various industries, and its development reaches a point where incremental improvements and refinements become the primary focus. At this stage, the technology is well-established, and its core functionality is widely accepted. The emphasis shifts from disruptive innovation to optimization, efficiency, and addressing limitations that prevent further growth or adoption.

Cloud computing is an excellent example of a technology that has reached the maturity phase. In its early days, cloud computing revolutionized how businesses approached data storage, computing power, and software access. Major cloud service providers like Amazon Web Services (AWS), Microsoft Azure, and Google Cloud have made cloud infrastructure a cornerstone of modern IT strategies. However, with the maturity of cloud computing, new technologies like edge computing have emerged to address the limitations of cloud services, such as latency and bandwidth constraints. Edge computing involves processing data closer to its source — at the "edge" of the network — rather than relying solely on cloud data centers, reducing delays and improving real-time data processing (Shi *et al.*, 2016).

The maturity phase provides organizations with opportunities to optimize existing technologies, expand use cases, and improve the overall efficiency of systems. However, competition in the market can lead to consolidation, and the pace of radical innovation slows. As the technology becomes more standardized, the primary goal shifts toward maximizing the value of the existing infrastructure and addressing new challenges that were previously unconsidered.

For companies operating in the maturity phase, the focus is on continuous improvement, addressing customer pain points, and exploring new applications or integrations with other technologies. Though the technology itself may not change dramatically, its ecosystem continues to evolve, often incorporating new advances in related fields.

The lifecycle of emerging technologies offers a roadmap for understanding the stages through which innovations progress — from early ideation to widespread adoption and eventual maturity. By aligning strategies with each phase, organizations can ensure they are leveraging new technologies effectively, mitigating risks, and capitalizing on opportunities. As emerging technologies like quantum computing, electric vehicles, and cloud computing continue to evolve, organizations must remain agile and responsive, adapting to the changing landscape of innovation. By doing so, they can stay at the forefront of technological advancements and continue to drive progress in their respective industries.

2.4.3. *Social, Ethical, and Regulatory Dimensions*

As emerging technologies continue to evolve, they present complex social, ethical, and regulatory challenges that demand careful consideration and governance. These challenges require a dynamic approach to ensure that technological advancements contribute positively to society while mitigating potential harms. This section explores the ethical dilemmas, regulatory hurdles, and public perceptions surrounding technologies like facial recognition, cryptocurrencies, and autonomous vehicles.

Ethical Considerations: One of the most prominent ethical concerns in the realm of emerging technologies is the deployment of facial recognition systems. While these technologies have practical applications in areas such as security, healthcare, and law enforcement, they also raise significant issues related to privacy, consent, and surveillance. For instance, facial recognition technology can be used to track individuals in public spaces without their knowledge, leading to fears of mass surveillance and the erosion of personal privacy.

The backlash against facial recognition technologies has been particularly strong in cities like San Francisco, which became the first major city in the U.S. to ban the use of facial recognition by government agencies in 2019. This move was driven by concerns about the technology's potential for misuse and its disproportionate impact on marginalized communities (Feldstein, 2019). The ethical considerations here are manifold, ranging from questions of consent to concerns about racial profiling and the potential for these systems to perpetuate bias and discrimination.

These concerns highlight the need for robust ethical frameworks to guide the development and deployment of facial recognition systems. Such frameworks should include transparency in how data is collected and used, as well as clear guidelines for accountability and oversight. Additionally, ethical guidelines must ensure that emerging technologies respect fundamental human rights, such as privacy and equality, while also providing benefits to society.

Regulatory Challenges in FinTech: The rise of cryptocurrencies and decentralized financial technologies (FinTech) has introduced new opportunities for innovation but also significant regulatory challenges. Cryptocurrencies like Bitcoin and Ethereum offer the promise of financial inclusion, lower transaction costs, and greater access to global markets. However, they also present substantial risks, including money laundering, fraud, market volatility, and a lack of investor protection.

One of the key regulatory challenges in the cryptocurrency space is the lack of a unified global framework. Different countries have adopted a wide range of approaches, from outright bans to the development of regulatory sandboxes to encourage innovation. For example, China has taken a hardline stance against cryptocurrency trading, while the United States has adopted a more fragmented approach, with various federal and state regulators overseeing different aspects of the market.

The absence of clear and consistent regulation has created opportunities for fraudulent schemes and market manipulation, undermining investor confidence and exposing individuals to significant risks. In response, initiatives like the European Union's Markets in Crypto-Assets (MiCA) framework are working to create a comprehensive regulatory environment for digital assets. The MiCA framework aims to protect investors, ensure financial stability, and prevent market abuses, while also fostering innovation within the FinTech sector (Zetzsche *et al.*, 2018). The development of such regulatory frameworks is critical to the future success and sustainability of digital assets and blockchain technologies.

Public Perception in Autonomous Vehicles: The adoption of autonomous vehicles, particularly self-driving cars, is another area where public perception plays a significant role in the acceptance and integration of emerging technologies. Despite the technological advancements in autonomous driving systems, such as Tesla's Autopilot, public skepticism remains high due to concerns about safety, accountability, and the potential for accidents.

Tesla has made significant strides in improving its Autopilot software, which is designed to assist with navigation, speed control, and lane-keeping. However, incidents involving Tesla vehicles in autopilot mode, such as fatal crashes, have fueled doubts about the safety and reliability of autonomous driving systems. These events have raised questions about the technology's readiness for mass adoption and have sparked debates about liability and accountability in the event of accidents.

The key to overcoming public skepticism lies in transparency and education. Ensuring that autonomous vehicle systems are thoroughly tested, well-documented, and easy to understand for the general public is essential for building trust. Additionally, government agencies and technology developers must work together to establish clear regulations and standards for autonomous vehicles, addressing safety concerns while promoting innovation in the sector. Transparency in how these technologies operate and continuous updates on safety improvements will be crucial in shaping public opinion and accelerating adoption.

Collaborative Approaches to Technological Governance: The ethical, regulatory, and public perception challenges associated with emerging technologies demonstrate the need for a collaborative, multi-stakeholder approach to governance. Policymakers, technology developers, industry leaders, and civil society organizations must work together to develop frameworks that balance innovation with social responsibility.

Regulatory bodies must be agile and adaptive to keep pace with the rapid advancements in technology. At the same time, ethical guidelines must evolve to address emerging concerns related to fairness, accountability, and privacy. Public engagement is also critical in fostering trust and ensuring that technological advancements align with societal values. By working collaboratively, stakeholders can create a governance model that maximizes the benefits of emerging technologies while minimizing their risks.

2.4.4. *Feedback Loops in Technological Evolution*

Feedback loops are central to the evolution of emerging technologies, shaping their adoption, refinement, and long-term impact. These loops can either accelerate technological progress through reinforcing cycles or create challenges that necessitate adaptation and mitigation. As highlighted by Qudrat-Ullah (2024), creativity loops — cycles of innovation that spark further exploration — play a pivotal role in driving sustained technological advancements.

2.4.4.1. *Positive Feedback Loops: Catalysts for Innovation*

Positive feedback loops occur when an initial success or innovation triggers further enhancements, creating a reinforcing cycle.

- **Renewable Energy Advancements**: The development of solar panels with higher efficiency rates has driven increased investments

in complementary technologies, such as energy storage solutions. Tesla's Powerwall, for instance, has improved the feasibility of renewable energy integration by providing reliable battery storage for solar power. As storage technologies advance, the efficiency and reliability of renewable energy systems improve, which in turn attracts more investments and accelerates deployment (Breyer *et al.*, 2017). This virtuous cycle is instrumental in reducing greenhouse gas emissions and advancing the global energy transition.
- **EVs**: The growing adoption of EVs has spurred the development of charging infrastructure and battery technology. As charging networks expand and batteries become more efficient, the convenience and affordability of EVs increase, driving further market penetration. Companies like Tesla and BYD exemplify this dynamic, leveraging positive feedback loops to dominate the EV market.

2.4.4.2. *Negative Feedback Loops: Managing Challenges*

Negative feedback loops arise when challenges or disruptions necessitate countermeasures that stabilize or slow down certain processes. These loops often highlight areas requiring continuous vigilance and adaptation.

- **Cybersecurity and Ransomware Attacks**: The rise of sophisticated ransomware attacks has prompted organizations to develop advanced threat detection and prevention systems. However, attackers continually adapt, creating an ongoing cycle where defensive measures trigger more advanced offensive strategies. This iterative nature underscores the necessity of proactive cybersecurity measures, including real-time monitoring and AI-driven threat analysis (Conti *et al.*, 2018).
- **Climate Change Mitigation**: Efforts to reduce carbon emissions by implementing renewable energy systems can inadvertently face resistance due to the intermittency of renewable resources. Investments in grid stability solutions, such as smart grids and backup systems, act as counterbalancing measures to address these challenges, forming a complex interplay of reinforcing and balancing feedback loops.

2.4.4.3. *Ethical Feedback Loops: Social and Behavioral Implications*

Technological feedback loops are not limited to technical advancements; they also influence social behavior and ethics.

- **Social Media Algorithms**: Platforms like Facebook and Twitter employ AI algorithms that personalize content based on user interactions. Engaging posts garner more likes and shares, leading to a positive feedback loop of increased visibility and further engagement. However, this cycle can have unintended consequences, such as the amplification of misinformation or polarization of public opinion. Ethical interventions, like content moderation and transparency in algorithms, aim to balance these dynamics (Zuckerberg, 2018).
- **Behavioral Economics and Gamification**: Many applications, from fitness trackers to financial savings platforms, use gamification to encourage positive user behavior. For example, apps like Duolingo use progress tracking and rewards to create positive feedback loops that enhance user engagement. However, over-reliance on such mechanisms can sometimes lead to burnout or reduced intrinsic motivation, highlighting the importance of ethical design.

2.4.4.4. *Leveraging Feedback Loops for Strategic Decision-Making*

Analyzing feedback loops allows decision-makers to identify leverage points where small interventions can lead to significant outcomes.

- **Healthcare Innovations**: Positive feedback loops in medical research, such as AI's role in accelerating drug discovery, showcase how integrating diverse datasets can yield breakthroughs. These advancements, in turn, attract funding and talent, perpetuating a cycle of innovation.
- **Urban Planning**: Smart city initiatives, such as IoT-enabled traffic management systems, rely on feedback loops to optimize urban environments dynamically. Real-time data from sensors helps policymakers implement adaptive measures that improve efficiency and sustainability.

Feedback loops provide a dynamic lens through which stakeholders can understand technological evolution. By recognizing these patterns, they can anticipate future trajectories, mitigate risks, and foster innovation in a sustainable and ethical manner. The following Table 2.4 summarizes the key concepts related to

Table 2.4. Key Aspects of the Dynamic Perspective of Emerging Technologies and Lessons for Decision Makers.

Key Aspects	Key Lessons for Decision Makers
Dynamic Decision-Making Frameworks: Emerging technologies evolve rapidly, requiring decision-makers to anticipate changes and respond to uncertainty.	Decision-makers should adopt dynamic decision-making frameworks to manage technological changes effectively and respond to emerging challenges.
Technological Convergence and Synergy: The merging of technologies like AI, IoT, and blockchain creates innovative solutions across industries.	Emphasize the integration of diverse technologies to create efficiencies, solve complex problems, and drive innovation in sectors like agriculture, healthcare, and renewable energy.
Lifecycle of Emerging Technologies: Technologies go through phases from innovation to adoption, diffusion, and maturity, each presenting unique opportunities and risks.	Understand and align strategies with the specific phase of a technology's lifecycle to maximize its potential and minimize risks.
Innovation Phase: Technologies are in prototype or experimental stages, with focus on R&D and overcoming technical challenges.	Invest cautiously in early-stage technologies, being prepared for high uncertainty, and monitor developments closely.
Adoption and Diffusion Phase: Technologies gain market traction and experience rapid growth, but challenges like cost reduction and scaling remain.	Focus on scaling production, overcoming infrastructure barriers, and enhancing customer experience to accelerate adoption.
Maturity and Evolution Phase: Well-established technologies focus on optimization and efficiency improvements, with the technology reaching a point of incremental innovation.	In the maturity phase, optimize existing technologies, explore new applications, and continuously improve to maintain competitive advantage.

Table 2.4. (*Continued*)

Key Aspects	Key Lessons for Decision Makers
Social, Ethical, and Regulatory Dimensions: Emerging technologies raise ethical and regulatory challenges, such as privacy concerns and market manipulation risks.	Ensure robust ethical frameworks and adaptive regulatory policies are in place to address privacy, safety, and fairness concerns while fostering innovation.
Technological Governance: Effective governance requires collaboration among policymakers, technology developers, industry leaders, and civil society.	Foster multi-stakeholder collaborations to develop governance structures that balance innovation with social responsibility.

the dynamic perspective of emerging technologies and provides actionable lessons for decision makers navigating technological change.

2.5. Conclusion: Shaping the Future of Emerging Technologies

Emerging technologies are not merely tools; they represent transformative forces that redefine industries, societies, and individual lives. From AI revolutionizing diagnostics in healthcare to blockchain enhancing transparency in supply chains, the examples explored in this chapter underscore the profound impact of technological advancements. However, the rapid pace of innovation comes with unique opportunities and challenges that demand careful navigation.

Understanding emerging technologies requires more than technical knowledge; it necessitates a dynamic perspective that considers their evolving nature and interconnectedness. As highlighted by Qudrat-Ullah (2024), decision-makers must adopt adaptive frameworks that emphasize creativity and resilience, allowing them to anticipate disruptions and leverage emerging trends effectively. The convergence of technologies such as AI, IoT, and blockchain exemplifies how interconnected innovations can address multifaceted challenges, ranging from climate change to global health crises.

2.5.1. *Balancing Innovation with Ethical Responsibility*

While the potential of emerging technologies is immense, their application raises ethical questions that cannot be overlooked. For example, AI algorithms used in recruitment and healthcare have faced criticism for perpetuating biases due to the data they are trained on. Similarly, blockchain technology, despite its promise of transparency, is not immune to misuse in activities such as money laundering or tax evasion (Zetzsche *et al.*, 2018).

To address these concerns, decision-makers must prioritize ethical frameworks alongside innovation. This involves embedding values such as fairness, accountability, and transparency into the design and implementation of technologies. Moreover, interdisciplinary collaboration between technologists, policymakers, and ethicists will be crucial in shaping the ethical trajectory of innovation.

2.5.2. *Navigating the Regulatory Landscape*

The rapid evolution of emerging technologies often outpaces the development of regulatory frameworks, leading to a mismatch between innovation and governance. For instance, the rise of cryptocurrencies has highlighted the need for global regulatory coordination to address issues such as market volatility and consumer protection. Similarly, autonomous vehicles have demonstrated the importance of safety standards and liability frameworks in fostering public trust.

Navigating this complex regulatory landscape requires agility and foresight. Policymakers must strike a balance between fostering innovation and safeguarding public interests, ensuring that regulatory measures do not stifle creativity or create undue barriers to entry. Initiatives such as the EU's General Data Protection Regulation (GDPR) and MiCA framework illustrate how adaptive governance can address emerging challenges while promoting technological progress.

2.5.3. *Implications for Future Decision-Making*

The dynamic nature of emerging technologies has profound implications for decision-making processes across sectors. Traditional models of decision-making, which often rely on static assumptions and linear thinking, are ill-suited to the complexities of modern technological ecosystems. Instead, organizations must embrace systems thinking and dynamic decision-making frameworks that account for the interplay of multiple variables and feedback loops (Qudrat-Ullah, 2024).

For example:

- In healthcare, integrating AI and IoT to deliver personalized medicine requires continuous data analysis and iterative decision-making.
- In energy markets, blockchain-enabled peer-to-peer trading platforms demand adaptive strategies to accommodate fluctuating supply and demand patterns.
- In cybersecurity, quantum-safe encryption necessitates ongoing vigilance to address emerging threats posed by advancements in quantum computing.

These scenarios highlight the importance of agility, foresight, and collaboration in navigating the complex decision-making landscape shaped by emerging technologies.

2.5.4. *Looking Ahead*

The integration of emerging technologies into various sectors represents a transformative shift that will redefine the way individuals and organizations interact with their environments. However, realizing the full potential of these technologies requires a nuanced approach that balances innovation with ethical considerations, regulatory oversight, and societal needs. As technological ecosystems grow increasingly interconnected, fostering collaboration across disciplines and sectors will be critical to addressing the multifaceted challenges they present.

The subsequent chapters of this work will delve deeper into specific technologies and their implications for dynamic decision-making. By exploring case studies, theoretical frameworks, and practical applications, these chapters aim to provide a comprehensive understanding of how emerging technologies can be harnessed to drive innovation while addressing pressing global challenges.

References

Arute, F., *et al.* (2019). Quantum supremacy using a programmable superconducting processor. *Nature*, 574(7779), 505–510.

Atzori, L., Iera, A., & Morabito, G. (2010). The Internet of Things: A survey. *Computer Networks*, 54(15), 2787–2805.

Bansal, P., & Kockelman, K. M. (2017). Forecasting Americans' long-term adoption of connected and autonomous vehicle technologies. *Transportation Research Part A: Policy and Practice*, 95, 49–63.

Benedict, M. (2019). Transforming agriculture with AI and IoT. *Journal of Agricultural Innovation*, 10(2), 30–40.

Biamonte, J., Wittek, P., Pancotti, N., Rebentrost, P., Wiebe, N., & Lloyd, S. (2017). Quantum machine learning. *Nature*, 549(7671), 195–202.

Bohnsack, R., Pinkse, J., & Wüstenhagen, R. (2014). Business strategies for sustainable energy innovation: The case of electric vehicles. *Business & Society*, 53(4), 616–646.

Breyer, C., Bogdanov, D., Gulagi, A., Aghahosseini, A., Barbosa, L. S. N. S., Koskinen, O., & Vainikka, P. (2017). On the role of solar photovoltaics in global energy transition scenarios. *Progress in Photovoltaics: Research and Applications*, 25(8), 727–745.

Chen, L., Jordan, S., Liu, Y. K., Moody, D., Peralta, R., Perlner, R., & Smith-Tone, D. (2016). Report on Post-Quantum Cryptography. National Institute of Standards and Technology.

Christensen, C. M., Raynor, M. E., & McDonald, R. (2015). What is disruptive innovation? *Harvard Business Review*, 93(12), 44–53.

Conti, M., Gangwal, A., & Ruj, S. (2018). On the economic impact of ransomware. *Computer*, 51(3), 74–79.

Cugurullo, F. (2018). Urban eco-modernisation and the policy context of the smart sustainable city: The case of Barcelona. *Urban Studies*, 55(4), 734–754.

Day, G. S., & Schoemaker, P. J. H. (2000). *Wharton on managing emerging technologies*. John Wiley & Sons.

Feldstein, S. (2019). The global expansion of AI surveillance. *Carnegie Endowment for International Peace.*

Floridi, L., Taddeo, M., & Turilli, M. (2018). The ethics of emerging technologies. *AI & Society*, 33(3), 365–368.

Grover, L. K. (1996). A fast quantum mechanical algorithm for database search. *Proceedings of the 28th Annual ACM Symposium on Theory of Computing.*

Iansiti, M., & Lakhani, K. R. (2017). The truth about blockchain. *Harvard Business Review*, 95(1), 118–127.

IBM. (2023). IBM Quantum Experience. Retrieved from https://quantum-computing.ibm.com.

Jordan, M. I., & Mitchell, T. M. (2015). Machine learning: Trends, perspectives, and prospects. *Science*, 349(6245), 255–260.

Montanaro, A. (2016). Quantum algorithms: An overview. *NPJ Quantum Information*, 2(1), 1–8.

Preskill, J. (2018). Quantum computing in the NISQ era and beyond. *Quantum*, 2, 79.

Qudrat-Ullah, H. (2014). *Better Decision Making in Complex, Dynamic Tasks*. New York, NY: Springer.

Qudrat-Ullah, H. (2020). Improving human performance in dynamic tasks with debriefing-based interactive learning environments: An empirical investigation. *International Journal of Information Technology & Decision Making*, 19(04), 1065–1089.

Qudrat-Ullah, H. (2024). *Creativity Loops–Based Decision Making*. Springer Nature.

Rotolo, D., Hicks, D., & Martin, B. R. (2015). What is an emerging technology? *Research Policy*, 44(10), 1827–1843.

Saberi, S., Kouhizadeh, M., Sarkis, J., & Shen, L. (2019). Blockchain technology and its relationships to sustainable supply chain management. *International Journal of Production Research*, 57(7), 2117–2135.

Shi, W., Cao, J., Zhang, Q., Li, Y., & Xu, L. (2016). Edge computing: Vision and challenges. *IEEE Internet of Things Journal*, 3(5), 637–646.

Shor, P. W. (1997). Polynomial-time algorithms for prime factorization and discrete logarithms on a quantum computer. *SIAM Review*, 41(2), 303–332.

Topol, E. J. (2019). *Deep Medicine: How Artificial Intelligence Can Make Healthcare Human Again*. Basic Books.

Wolfert, S., Ge, L., Verdouw, C., & Bogaardt, M. J. (2017). Big data in smart farming–a review. *Agricultural Systems*, 153, 69–80.

Zetzsche, D. A., Buckley, R. P., Arner, D. W., & Barberis, J. N. (2018). From FinTech to TechFin: The regulatory challenges of financial technology. *Fordham Journal of Corporate & Financial Law*, 23(1), 31–103.

Zuckerberg, M. (2018). Building a global community. Retrieved from Facebook Blog.

Chapter 3

The Impact of Emerging Technologies on Society

Abstract

Chapter 3 explores the societal impact of emerging technologies, focusing on their socioeconomic implications, ethical challenges, and the phenomenon of technological convergence. The chapter discusses how technologies like artificial intelligence (AI), blockchain, Internet of Things (IoT), and quantum computing are reshaping industries and affecting social structures. It highlights the creation of new job opportunities alongside growing social inequalities, ethical concerns related to bias and privacy, and the challenges of technological integration. By examining these dimensions, the chapter provides a comprehensive analysis of the complex interplay between technology and society, emphasizing the need for adaptive governance and interdisciplinary collaboration.

Keywords: Socioeconomic Implications; Emerging Technologies; Artificial Intelligence (AI); Blockchain; Internet of Things (IoT); Quantum Computing; Job Displacement; Economic Growth; Digital Divide; Ethical Challenges; Bias and Privacy; Technological Convergence; Technological Integration; Social Inequality; Adaptive Governance

3.0. Introduction

The rapid development and deployment of emerging technologies are fundamentally reshaping societal structures and functions. In an era where technological advancements are occurring at an unprecedented pace, innovations such as AI, blockchain, the IoT, and quantum computing are not only transforming industries but also influencing the very fabric of societies around the globe. These technologies are providing new ways to approach complex problems, create efficiencies, and drive economic growth, yet they also present profound challenges that must be carefully considered.

Emerging technologies are not neutral forces; they carry with them a range of socioeconomic implications that are altering labor markets, economic structures, and wealth distribution. As automation, AI, and robotics continue to evolve, they are transforming industries and the nature of work itself. While these technologies can improve productivity and enable the creation of new services and markets, they also have the potential to displace jobs, exacerbate inequalities, and create digital divides. Furthermore, they present ethical concerns that demand attention, including issues related to privacy, bias, accountability, and security.

The convergence of different technological domains — AI, IoT, blockchain, and others — presents both opportunities and risks. As these technologies increasingly interact with and complement one another, they create synergies that drive innovation across various sectors, from healthcare and finance to education and urban planning. However, technological convergence also brings about new complexities and challenges, particularly in terms of regulation, governance, and the potential for unforeseen consequences. The integration of multiple technologies amplifies the need for a comprehensive understanding of how they interconnect, interact, and influence one another in dynamic and sometimes unpredictable ways.

In this chapter, we aim to provide a comprehensive analysis of the multifaceted effects of emerging technologies on society. We will explore the socioeconomic implications of these innovations, delving into how they impact employment, wealth distribution, and global competitiveness. Ethical considerations will be examined, focusing on the ethical challenges that arise from the deployment of AI, blockchain, and other technologies, such as bias, privacy concerns, and accountability. Lastly, we will consider the phenomenon of technological convergence, looking at how the integration of different technologies creates both opportunities for progress and new areas of concern.

By analyzing these dimensions, this chapter will offer insights into the profound ways in which emerging technologies are shaping social dynamics. It will also highlight the challenges that need to be addressed to ensure that the benefits of these technologies are distributed equitably and that their deployment is responsible and ethical. Through this exploration, we hope to provide a clearer understanding of the current landscape of technological change as well as the opportunities and risks that lie ahead for societies, businesses, and governments in the twenty-first century.

3.1. Socioeconomic Implications of Emerging Technologies

Emerging technologies have profound socioeconomic implications, influencing employment, economic growth, social inequalities, and global development. Their transformative power reshapes industries and societies, creating both opportunities and challenges.

3.1.1. *Impact on Employment*

The rise of technologies like AI, robotics, and automation is redefining the nature of work. Tasks traditionally performed by humans are increasingly automated, enhancing efficiency but also displacing certain jobs. For instance, AI has revolutionized industries such as manufacturing, customer service, and logistics by automating repetitive tasks (Brynjolfsson & McAfee, 2014). Automation in factories has led to the development of "smart factories," where machines not only execute tasks but also communicate with each other to optimize workflows. Similarly, chatbots powered by natural language processing algorithms have replaced human agents for basic customer service inquiries, reducing costs while improving response times. However, this shift has led to concerns about widespread job losses, particularly in sectors reliant on routine-based tasks.

Despite fears of job displacement, technology is simultaneously creating new employment opportunities, particularly in emerging fields like data science, machine learning, and cybersecurity. These fields are experiencing rapid growth, driven by the increased reliance on digital infrastructure and data-driven decision-making processes. For example, machine learning engineers and data analysts have become integral to organizations looking to harness the potential of AI. Similarly, as cyber threats become more sophisticated, the demand for skilled cybersecurity professionals has surged. This dual impact of automation — displacement of existing jobs and the creation of new roles — underscores the transformative effect of technology on employment.

To address the challenges of technological disruption, reskilling and upskilling programs have become a critical focus for policymakers and industry leaders. Workers must acquire new skills to stay relevant in a rapidly changing labor market. Traditional educational institutions are adapting by offering specialized programs in digital technologies, while online platforms like Coursera and edX are making such training more accessible. Additionally, governments are implementing policies to support lifelong learning and workforce development. For instance, countries like Singapore have launched initiatives like SkillsFuture, which provide individuals with credits to pursue training in high-demand areas (World Economic Forum, 2020).

Beyond technical skills, there is also a growing recognition of the importance of soft skills such as adaptability, problem-solving, and critical thinking. As machines take over routine tasks, human workers are increasingly expected to excel in areas requiring creativity and interpersonal interaction. Employers are now seeking professionals who can complement technological advancements by providing nuanced insights and fostering innovation.

The gig economy, a product of digital platforms, exemplifies another dimension of technology's impact on employment. Platforms like Uber, Fiverr, and Upwork have redefined work by enabling flexible and on-demand job opportunities. While these platforms offer income opportunities to millions, they also raise concerns about job security, benefits, and fair wages. Workers in the gig economy often operate without the traditional protections afforded by full-time employment, leading to debates over how to regulate this emerging workforce. Policymakers are exploring solutions, including the extension of social benefits to gig workers and the classification of gig economy participants as employees rather than independent contractors.

Another crucial consideration is the geographic disparity in the effects of automation. Regions with high concentrations of manufacturing jobs, for example, are more likely to experience job displacement, while technology hubs are poised to benefit from the growth of new industries. This uneven impact exacerbates regional economic inequalities, necessitating targeted interventions to ensure a more equitable distribution of technology's benefits. Investments in digital infrastructure, incentives for technology-driven businesses, and educational programs in underserved areas can help bridge these gaps.

In conclusion, the impact of emerging technologies on employment is multifaceted, presenting both challenges and opportunities. The displacement of routine jobs and the rise of new, high-skill roles highlight the importance of proactive measures to prepare the workforce for future demands. Collaboration among governments, educational institutions, and industries will be key to creating an adaptable, resilient labor force capable of thriving in the age of technological transformation.

3.1.2. *Economic Growth and Productivity*

Emerging technologies contribute substantially to economic growth by fostering innovation, improving productivity, and enabling the development of new markets. Automation, AI, and digital platforms reduce operational costs and enhance output, creating competitive advantages for businesses (Acemoglu & Restrepo, 2020). For instance, the integration of AI into supply chains optimizes inventory management and delivery systems, ensuring efficient resource utilization and minimizing waste. Similarly, predictive analytics powered by AI allow businesses to anticipate market trends and consumer demands, enabling better strategic decisions. These advancements not only improve individual business performance but also contribute to broader economic gains.

At a macroeconomic level, technology-driven growth plays a pivotal role in boosting Gross Domestic Product (GDP) and facilitating advancements across various sectors. In healthcare, technologies like telemedicine, wearable devices, and AI-driven diagnostics are improving access to quality care while reducing costs. Similarly, digital tools in education, such as online learning platforms and AI tutors, are expanding access to knowledge, particularly in underserved areas. Infrastructure development has also benefited from technological innovations, including smart cities and automated construction techniques, which enhance urban planning and resource management.

The productivity gains enabled by emerging technologies are particularly significant. Automation has transformed manufacturing, agriculture, and service industries by streamlining processes and reducing human error. For instance, precision agriculture, which uses drones and IoT devices, has increased crop yields while conserving resources. In the service sector, chatbots and AI-driven tools handle routine customer interactions, freeing human workers to focus on complex tasks. These productivity enhancements enable businesses to scale operations and compete in global markets.

However, the distribution of these economic benefits is far from uniform. Regions and industries that heavily invest in and adopt emerging technologies often experience exponential growth, while others may lag, exacerbating existing disparities. For instance, technology hubs such as Silicon Valley or Shenzhen reap significant economic rewards due to their concentration of resources, talent, and innovation. In contrast, regions with limited access to technology and infrastructure may struggle to keep pace, widening the gap between developed and developing areas.

The uneven distribution of technology-driven growth also extends to industries. Sectors like information technology, finance, and advanced manufacturing often see rapid gains due to their ability to integrate and leverage new technologies. Conversely, traditional industries like agriculture or small-scale retail, particularly in less developed regions, face challenges in adopting these innovations, potentially leading to stagnation or decline.

Addressing these disparities requires targeted policy interventions and strategic investments. Governments and organizations must prioritize infrastructure development in underserved regions, such as expanding internet connectivity and providing access to digital tools. Public-private partnerships can play a crucial role in fostering innovation and ensuring that its benefits reach broader populations. For instance, initiatives that subsidize technology adoption for small businesses or provide training programs for workers in transitioning industries can help bridge the gap.

Moreover, fostering a culture of continuous learning and innovation is essential for sustaining economic growth in the digital era. Educational systems must adapt to emphasize skills relevant to emerging technologies, such as coding, data analytics, and machine learning. Additionally, promoting research and development (R&D) through grants and tax incentives can accelerate the pace of technological advancements and their economic impact.

The ripple effects of technology-driven productivity extend beyond businesses and industries. By lowering production costs and improving efficiencies, technologies contribute to reduced prices for consumers, increased accessibility of goods and services, and the creation of entirely new markets. For example, the widespread adoption of smartphones has not only transformed communication but also spawned industries such as app development, mobile commerce, and digital entertainment.

In conclusion, emerging technologies are powerful drivers of economic growth and productivity, offering significant opportunities to transform industries and improve living standards. However, the uneven distribution of these benefits highlights the need for inclusive strategies to ensure that all regions and sectors can participate in and benefit from this growth. Strategic investments, equitable policies, and a focus on education and innovation are critical to harnessing the full potential of these transformative technologies.

3.1.3. *The Gig Economy and Labor Market Dynamics*

Digital platforms have fundamentally reshaped the labor market, giving rise to the gig economy, a system characterized by short-term, flexible employment arrangements. Companies like Uber, Airbnb, and Fiverr have become hallmarks of this trend, enabling individuals to engage in freelance work or temporary gigs. These platforms connect service providers with consumers, creating opportunities for workers to generate income on their terms. The gig economy offers flexibility and autonomy, allowing individuals to balance work with personal responsibilities or pursue multiple income streams.

However, this shift towards gig-based work has also sparked significant concerns regarding worker rights and labor market stability. Unlike traditional employment, gig workers often operate as independent contractors rather than employees. This classification excludes them from benefits such as healthcare, pensions, paid leave, and unemployment insurance. The lack of a safety net leaves many gig workers vulnerable to economic instability, particularly in times of economic downturn or personal hardship (Kalleberg, 2011). For instance, during the COVID-19 pandemic, many gig workers faced reduced demand for services without access to employer-sponsored relief programs.

The rise of the gig economy also presents challenges related to income volatility and job security. Gig work is often inconsistent, with earnings fluctuating based on market demand, platform algorithms, and worker availability. This unpredictability can make it difficult for gig workers to plan for long-term financial goals, such as buying a home or saving for retirement. Moreover, the competitive nature of gig platforms, where workers are rated and ranked, adds pressure to maintain high performance, often without adequate compensation or support.

Beyond individual challenges, the gig economy raises broader questions about labor market dynamics. The traditional employer-employee relationship is being redefined, blurring the boundaries between formal and informal employment. This shift challenges existing labor laws and regulatory frameworks, which were designed for a more stable and predictable employment landscape. Policymakers must navigate the complexities of regulating gig work to strike a balance between protecting workers and preserving the flexibility that makes gig work appealing.

Regulatory Considerations: Ensuring fair treatment of gig workers requires updated labor policies that reflect the realities of this emerging work model. Policymakers should prioritize initiatives that provide gig workers with access to benefits traditionally associated with full-time employment. For example, portable benefits systems, where workers can accrue benefits regardless of their employer or platform, offer a potential solution. These systems could include healthcare, retirement savings, and paid leave, financed through contributions from platforms, workers, and governments.

Another critical area is wage regulation. Gig workers often face issues of low pay due to the competitive and demand-driven nature of gig platforms. Establishing minimum earnings standards or guaranteed base wages can help mitigate this challenge. For instance, some jurisdictions have implemented laws requiring gig platforms to pay workers at least the minimum wage for their time spent actively engaged in work.

Representation and collective bargaining are also essential for empowering gig workers. Platforms often operate unilaterally, setting terms and conditions without input from workers. Allowing gig workers to form unions or associations can help them negotiate better pay, working conditions, and benefits. Several gig worker movements, such as the campaign for fair wages by Uber and Lyft drivers, highlight the potential for collective action to drive positive change.

Implications for Society and the Economy: The gig economy's impact extends beyond individual workers, influencing societal and economic structures. On one hand, it creates opportunities for entrepreneurship and innovation, as individuals can leverage their skills to earn income without traditional employment constraints. For example, artists, writers, and programmers can find clients worldwide through platforms like Upwork or Patreon. This global connectivity fosters a diverse and dynamic labor market, enabling people in remote or underserved areas to access income-generating opportunities.

On the other hand, the gig economy can exacerbate existing social inequalities. Workers with access to technology, education, and resources are better positioned to succeed in the gig economy, while those without these advantages may struggle to compete. This digital divide underscores the importance of ensuring equitable access to digital tools and training to enable broader participation in gig work.

From an economic perspective, the gig economy contributes to labor market flexibility, enabling businesses to scale operations and manage costs more effectively. However, this model also shifts risks and responsibilities from employers to workers, raising questions about the long-term sustainability of gig-based employment. As the gig economy grows, its implications for traditional employment sectors, tax revenues, and social welfare systems will become increasingly significant.

The gig economy represents a paradigm shift in the way work is structured and performed, offering both opportunities and challenges. While it empowers individuals with flexibility and autonomy, it also exposes them to vulnerabilities associated with job insecurity, income volatility, and the lack of benefits. Addressing these issues requires a comprehensive approach, including regulatory reforms, innovative benefits systems, and initiatives to ensure equitable access to gig work opportunities. By balancing worker protection with the unique advantages of the gig economy, policymakers can create a labor market that is both dynamic and fair.

3.1.4. *Widening Inequalities and the Digital Divide*

Emerging technologies, while offering transformative potential, often exacerbate existing social and economic inequalities due to their uneven distribution of benefits. This phenomenon, known as the digital divide, is characterized by disparities in access to digital resources, technological literacy, and opportunities to harness innovation. Regions with robust technological infrastructure and financial resources tend to reap significant rewards, whereas less-developed areas struggle to keep pace (Autor, 2015). This imbalance contributes to a cycle of underdevelopment, where technological lag hinders economic growth and social progress.

Global Disparities: Globally, the digital divide is starkly visible between developed and developing nations. High-income countries often have widespread internet access, advanced communication networks, and greater investments in R&D. In contrast, low-income countries face challenges such as inadequate infrastructure, limited access to devices, and high costs associated with digital technology adoption. For instance, sub-Saharan Africa, despite its growing mobile connectivity, still lags in broadband internet penetration, which restricts its ability to fully participate in the global digital economy.

This technological gap limits the ability of underdeveloped regions to adopt innovations that could address pressing issues such as healthcare, education, and environmental sustainability. For example, telemedicine, which leverages AI and internet connectivity to provide medical consultations, has revolutionized healthcare delivery in developed nations. However, its adoption in rural and underprivileged areas is hindered by a lack of infrastructure, leaving millions without access to critical healthcare advancements. Similarly, e-learning platforms that offer interactive and personalized educational experiences are transforming education globally, yet students in regions with poor connectivity are excluded from these benefits.

The disparity in access to these transformative technologies perpetuates cycles of poverty and limits upward mobility for disadvantaged communities. For instance, farmers in underdeveloped regions often lack access to precision agriculture tools that use AI and IoT to optimize crop yields, leaving them vulnerable to climate change and market fluctuations. Moreover, the inability to deploy renewable energy technologies in areas without stable power grids hampers efforts to address energy poverty and environmental sustainability.

This divide also inhibits the participation of underdeveloped regions in the global digital economy, reducing their competitiveness and limiting their integration into global supply chains. Without targeted interventions, these regions risk falling further behind, creating a scenario where technology amplifies rather than reduces global inequalities. Bridging this gap requires not only investments in infrastructure but also capacity-building initiatives to empower local communities to leverage these technologies effectively.

Public-private partnerships can play a critical role in accelerating infrastructure development and fostering technology transfer to underserved areas. Equally important is the need for culturally relevant solutions that address specific local challenges, ensuring that technological advancements are accessible and impactful for diverse populations. Addressing these barriers is essential to realizing the full potential of emerging technologies as tools for inclusive growth and development.

Socioeconomic Inequalities Within Societies: Within individual countries, the digital divide reflects and reinforces socioeconomic inequalities. Access to emerging technologies often correlates with income, education, and geographic location. Wealthier individuals and urban populations are more likely to have access to high-speed internet, advanced technological tools, and the knowledge to utilize them effectively. Conversely, lower-income communities and rural areas frequently lack the resources needed to benefit from technological advancements.

This divide extends to essential services such as education and healthcare. In education, affluent families are more likely to provide their children with access to digital learning platforms, coding classes, and virtual tutoring. These tools enhance educational outcomes and prepare students for high-tech job markets. Meanwhile, students in low-income families may lack reliable internet access or devices, placing them at a significant disadvantage. This lack of access perpetuates educational inequities, making it harder for disadvantaged students to compete in a rapidly evolving economy driven by technological skills.

Similarly, AI-driven healthcare solutions, which can improve diagnostics and personalized treatments, are often concentrated in wealthier regions, leaving underserved populations reliant on outdated or less effective methods. For example, advanced AI tools that detect early signs of diseases like cancer or diabetes are revolutionizing healthcare in urban centers but remain inaccessible in rural or low-income areas. This disparity exacerbates existing health inequities, resulting in higher mortality rates and poorer health outcomes for marginalized communities.

Additionally, the lack of digital literacy among underserved populations compounds these challenges, preventing them from fully utilizing even the limited technologies available to them. In many cases, cultural and language barriers further restrict access to education and healthcare technologies tailored to their needs. Moreover, the absence of robust policy frameworks often means that private companies prioritize profit over equitable access, leaving vulnerable populations underserved.

Efforts to close these gaps must include targeted investments in digital infrastructure, affordable technology access programs, and widespread digital literacy initiatives. Partnerships between governments, NGOs, and private organizations are essential to developing and deploying solutions that address the unique challenges faced by disadvantaged communities. Without deliberate and sustained action, the digital divide risks deepening existing inequalities, limiting opportunities for upward mobility, and undermining efforts to achieve global development goals.

Technological Literacy and Employment: The digital divide also manifests in disparities in technological literacy. As emerging technologies such as AI, blockchain, and the IoT become integral to the economy, workers must possess digital skills to remain competitive. Wealthier individuals and communities typically have better access to education and training programs, enabling them to acquire these skills. In contrast, those from disadvantaged backgrounds may lack the resources or opportunities to develop technological literacy, limiting their participation in high-growth industries.

This skill gap contributes to a polarized labor market, where high-paying jobs in technology-intensive fields are inaccessible to those without the requisite expertise. Consequently, individuals in low-skilled roles face a greater risk of displacement by automation, exacerbating unemployment and income inequality. The disparity is further widened as businesses increasingly demand specialized skills in areas like AI, data science, and advanced manufacturing, creating a growing divide between those who can adapt to these demands and those who cannot.

Moreover, the lack of access to quality education and reskilling opportunities disproportionately affects marginalized groups, leaving them trapped in low-wage, precarious employment. This dynamic creates a feedback loop where low-income individuals lack the resources to acquire new skills, further entrenching them in positions vulnerable to automation. Over time, this polarization not only impacts individual livelihoods but also threatens social cohesion, as economic disparities become more pronounced.

Employers often struggle to fill high-tech positions despite rising unemployment rates, highlighting a mismatch between workforce capabilities and market demands. For example, industries such as cybersecurity and renewable energy report significant skill shortages, which hinder innovation and economic growth. Governments and institutions must address this mismatch by implementing targeted education and training initiatives that bridge the gap between workforce skills and evolving industry needs.

Additionally, the gig economy and short-term contract roles, often perceived as solutions for those displaced by automation, fail to provide long-term job security or adequate income levels. This further underscores the importance of creating pathways for individuals to transition into sustainable careers. Without proactive measures, the skill gap risks perpetuating a cycle of inequality, where the benefits of technological advancements are concentrated among a select few, leaving large segments of the population behind.

The Role of Policymakers and Institutions: Addressing the digital divide and its associated inequalities requires targeted interventions by governments, international organizations, and private sector stakeholders. Policymakers must prioritize investments in digital infrastructure to bridge the gap between urban and rural areas, as well as between developed and developing nations. For example, initiatives to expand broadband access, subsidize internet services, and provide affordable devices can help level the playing field.

Educational reforms are equally critical. Integrating digital literacy into school curricula and offering free or low-cost training programs can equip individuals with the skills needed to thrive in a technology-driven world. Such initiatives not only prepare students for future job markets but also empower them to become active participants in the digital economy. Programs that emphasize STEM (science, technology, engineering, and mathematics) education, alongside creativity and critical thinking, are essential for fostering innovation and adaptability.

Partnerships between governments and private companies, such as those that provide coding boot camps or vocational training, can further enhance workforce readiness. For instance, tech giants like Google and Microsoft have initiated global training programs aimed at upskilling workers in digital technologies. These collaborations can help bridge the gap between theoretical education and practical skills, ensuring individuals are equipped to meet industry demands.

Moreover, public and private sector collaboration is essential to ensure equitable access to emerging technologies. Companies developing advanced solutions should consider pricing models and distribution strategies that make their products accessible to underserved populations. Subsidized pricing, freemium models, or corporate social responsibility (CSR) initiatives can play a pivotal role in reducing financial barriers for low-income communities.

International organizations can also contribute by facilitating technology transfers and providing financial aid to underdeveloped regions. For example, the World Bank and United Nations have implemented programs that support digital infrastructure development in remote areas. Such efforts can create a multiplier effect, enabling these regions to leverage technology for advancements in healthcare, education, and economic productivity.

In addition to infrastructure and training, fostering local innovation ecosystems is crucial. Governments and NGOs can establish innovation hubs or tech incubators in underdeveloped areas, providing resources, mentorship, and funding for startups. These initiatives not only generate employment opportunities but also empower local communities to address their unique challenges through tailored technological solutions.

Finally, raising awareness about the potential of emerging technologies is vital. Public campaigns and community workshops can demystify technology and encourage adoption, ensuring that even those with limited exposure can benefit. These collective efforts are indispensable for building a more inclusive, technology-driven future.

Ethical and Social Considerations: The digital divide also raises ethical concerns, as the unequal distribution of technology threatens to marginalize vulnerable populations further. Ensuring that emerging technologies are designed and deployed with inclusivity in mind is vital. For instance, AI algorithms should be free from biases that disproportionately affect disadvantaged groups. Additionally, promoting open-access platforms and open-source technologies can democratize access and foster innovation in underserved areas.

The digital divide highlights a critical challenge in the age of emerging technologies: ensuring that their benefits are shared equitably across all segments of society. Left unaddressed, this divide risks perpetuating cycles of inequality and excluding large portions of the global population from the opportunities created by technological progress.

For instance, disparities in access to high-speed internet and digital tools can limit education, healthcare, and employment opportunities for underserved populations. These barriers not only deepen existing inequalities but also hinder global efforts to address broader challenges, such as poverty alleviation and sustainable development. Furthermore, the gap in technological literacy exacerbates this issue, leaving many unable to fully leverage available innovations.

Through strategic investments, such as expanding broadband infrastructure to rural and underserved areas, governments can lay the foundation for equitable access. Public-private partnerships can play a transformative role in making this vision a reality, combining resources and expertise to deliver impactful solutions. Policy reforms that prioritize digital inclusion, such as subsidies for internet access or devices for low-income families, are equally critical.

Inclusive innovation practices are essential for addressing the unique needs of marginalized communities. This includes designing affordable, user-friendly technologies that cater to diverse cultural and socioeconomic contexts. Additionally, fostering collaboration between global stakeholders — governments, private organizations, and international bodies — can ensure that resources and knowledge are shared equitably, amplifying the impact of technological advancements.

By embracing a multi-faceted approach that integrates policy, education, infrastructure, and collaboration, stakeholders can work towards bridging the gap, fostering a more equitable and connected world. Ultimately, addressing the digital divide is not merely a technological imperative but a moral and economic one, essential for achieving shared prosperity and sustainable progress.

3.1.5. *Policy Recommendations*

Addressing the socioeconomic implications of emerging technologies necessitates a comprehensive and collaborative approach. Policymakers must implement strategies that ensure inclusive growth while mitigating the risks associated with technological disruption. The following recommendations outline key areas of focus:

1. Inclusive Policies

Governments should prioritize developing inclusive policies that guarantee equitable access to technology for all citizens, regardless of geographic location or socioeconomic status. Investments in digital infrastructure, such as broadband expansion and affordable internet services, are critical for bridging the digital divide. Special attention should be given to underserved areas, such as rural and remote regions, where technological access is often limited.

For example, initiatives like public Wi-Fi networks and community technology centers can provide connectivity and resources to marginalized populations. These policies should also encourage private sector participation through incentives such as tax breaks for companies investing in digital infrastructure in underdeveloped areas. Furthermore, inclusive policies must address affordability by subsidizing access to devices and services for low-income households.

2. Education and Training

The rapid pace of technological advancement demands a workforce that is both skilled and adaptable. Governments and educational institutions should prioritize lifelong learning programs to equip workers with the skills needed to thrive in the evolving labor market. These programs should emphasize STEM (science, technology, engineering, and mathematics) education, as well as emerging fields like AI, data science, and robotics.

Additionally, soft skills such as critical thinking, adaptability, and problem-solving are becoming increasingly vital in a technology-driven world. Educational curricula should be updated to reflect these needs, ensuring that students are prepared for future challenges.

Upskilling and reskilling initiatives, delivered through public-private partnerships, can help workers transition into new roles created by technological advancements. For instance, governments can collaborate with tech companies to offer training programs or subsidized courses for individuals at risk of job displacement. Vocational training in digital literacy for older or less tech-savvy populations can also help mitigate the widening skills gap.

3. Social Safety Nets

Emerging technologies, particularly automation and the gig economy, have introduced new vulnerabilities for workers. Policies must address these challenges by creating robust social safety nets to support individuals affected by job displacement or insecure employment arrangements.

Gig workers, who often operate outside traditional employment structures, require access to benefits such as healthcare, retirement plans, and unemployment insurance. Governments should work towards modernizing labor laws to accommodate the unique nature of gig work. For example, implementing portable benefits systems that move with the worker across gigs can provide greater security.

Unemployment benefits and retraining grants for workers displaced by automation can ease the transition to new employment opportunities. Social safety nets should also include mental health support, as economic instability and job insecurity can take a toll on workers' well-being.

4. Global Collaboration

The challenges posed by emerging technologies extend beyond national borders, necessitating global collaboration. International organizations such as the United Nations, the World Bank, and the International Telecommunication Union should facilitate knowledge-sharing and funding initiatives to support underdeveloped regions.

Global partnerships can foster technology transfer, allowing developing countries to benefit from innovations without bearing the full cost of R&D. For example, developed nations can share advancements in renewable energy or healthcare technologies, helping less-advanced regions address critical challenges.

Moreover, global frameworks should be established to ensure ethical and equitable technology development. Collaborative efforts to standardize regulations and best practices can mitigate risks such as bias in AI algorithms, cybersecurity threats, and the monopolization of technological resources.

Efforts like the United Nations' Sustainable Development Goals (SDGs) provide a foundation for aligning technological innovation with global equity and sustainability objectives. Policymakers should leverage such frameworks to ensure that technological progress contributes to a more inclusive and just world.

5. Incentivizing Responsible Innovation

Governments should incentivize companies to pursue innovations that prioritize societal well-being. Tax benefits, grants, or subsidies can encourage businesses to develop technologies that address pressing issues such as climate change, healthcare disparities, and education access. CSR initiatives can also play a role, with companies committing to ethical practices and community engagement.

The socioeconomic implications of emerging technologies present both opportunities and challenges. By implementing inclusive policies, fostering education and training, strengthening social safety nets, encouraging global collaboration, and incentivizing responsible innovation, governments and institutions can harness these technologies to create a more equitable and sustainable future. Failure to address these issues risks deepening existing inequalities and leaving vulnerable populations further behind in the digital age.

In summary, while emerging technologies present unparalleled opportunities for socioeconomic progress, their transformative impact demands proactive measures to ensure that these benefits are shared equitably. Policymakers and stakeholders must address the challenges of job displacement, inequality, and the digital divide to create a more inclusive and sustainable future. Table 3.1 provides an organized overview for policymakers, educators, and industry leaders, facilitating informed decisions and strategies for managing the impact of emerging technologies.

3.2. Ethical Considerations and Challenges

The rise of emerging technologies brings unprecedented opportunities, but it also raises profound ethical considerations and challenges. Addressing these issues is essential to ensure that technological advancements serve the broader interests of society without compromising individual rights, equity, or global stability.

3.2.1. *Bias and Discrimination in AI Systems*

AI systems, while transformative, often reflect and perpetuate the biases embedded in their training data. This phenomenon has resulted in discriminatory outcomes across critical areas such as hiring, law enforcement, healthcare, and financial services. The root of this issue lies in the datasets used to train AI models, which are often derived from historical data that mirrors existing societal biases. Consequently, AI systems risk reinforcing these biases rather than mitigating them, raising serious ethical and social concerns.

For example, AI-powered hiring platforms have been shown to favor candidates based on gender or ethnicity due to historical biases in hiring practices encoded in the data (O'Neil, 2016). These platforms often prioritize candidates who resemble those previously hired, leading to the exclusion of equally qualified individuals from underrepresented groups. The consequences of such biases extend beyond individual discrimination, perpetuating workplace inequality and hindering diversity. Correcting these biases requires a critical examination of training datasets and the integration of fairness measures throughout the AI development pipeline.

In law enforcement, predictive policing algorithms have disproportionately targeted minority communities, exacerbating existing inequalities (Eubanks, 2018). These algorithms, designed to predict areas or individuals likely to commit crimes, often rely on arrest records and historical policing data. Since minority communities have historically been over-policed, the algorithms frequently direct law enforcement resources back to these areas, creating a feedback loop that reinforces systemic biases. Such practices erode trust between

Table 3.1. Socioeconomic Implications of Emerging Technologies and Practical Insights for Decision Makers.

Aspect	**Key Insights**	**Practical Recommendations for Decision Makers**
Impact on Employment	Emerging technologies automate routine tasks, displacing jobs in traditional sectors while creating new roles in fields like AI, data science, and cybersecurity.	– Invest in reskilling and upskilling programs to prepare workers for high-demand, technology-driven roles. – Support the development of STEM education and vocational training programs.
Economic Growth and Productivity	Technologies like AI and automation drive productivity, optimize resources, and enable market expansion. They also contribute significantly to GDP growth and sectoral advancements.	– Promote digital transformation in key industries by offering incentives for adopting AI and automation. – Foster innovation ecosystems through R&D funding and public-private partnerships.
Gig Economy and Labor Market Dynamics	Digital platforms enable flexible work arrangements, providing opportunities for supplemental income and work-life balance but may lack job security.	– Establish regulations to protect gig workers, ensuring fair wages, benefits, and working conditions. – Encourage the creation of platforms that balance flexibility with stability.

(Continued)

Table 3.1. (*Continued*)

Aspect	**Key Insights**	**Practical Recommendations for Decision Makers**
Widening Inequalities and the Digital Divide	Uneven access to digital resources exacerbates social and economic disparities, particularly between developed and developing regions.	– Expand digital infrastructure, especially in underserved areas, through public-private collaborations. – Subsidize access to technology for low-income communities and promote digital literacy programs.
Global Disparities	High-income countries dominate technological advances, while low-income regions struggle with inadequate infrastructure and limited R&D capabilities.	– Collaborate internationally to fund technological development in underprivileged regions. – Provide technical assistance and affordable technology transfer to developing nations.
Policy Recommendations	Inclusive growth requires targeted policies, investments in education, and incentivizing ethical innovation.	– Develop inclusive policies to bridge the digital divide, such as affordable internet and device access. – Incentivize responsible innovation through tax breaks and grants for socially beneficial technologies.

communities and law enforcement and raise questions about the fairness and legitimacy of AI-driven decision-making in public safety.

Healthcare is another domain where biased AI systems can have profound implications. AI algorithms used for diagnostic purposes or treatment recommendations may reflect disparities in healthcare data. For instance, studies have shown that some AI-driven diagnostic tools perform less effectively on patients from underrepresented ethnic groups due to a lack of diverse data during training. This discrepancy can lead to misdiagnoses, inadequate treatment, and a widening healthcare gap between demographic groups. Addressing these issues necessitates deliberate efforts to collect and utilize representative datasets that account for diversity in patient populations.

Financial services are similarly affected by AI bias. Credit scoring algorithms, which determine access to loans and financial products, have been found to discriminate against certain demographic groups. For instance, these systems might deny loans to applicants from low-income neighborhoods based on historical lending data, perpetuating cycles of financial exclusion. Such biases not only undermine the fairness of AI systems but also contribute to broader societal inequities. Transparency in algorithmic decision-making and the implementation of explainable AI techniques can help mitigate these challenges by allowing stakeholders to identify and address potential sources of bias.

Mitigating AI bias is a complex task that requires multi-faceted approaches. One crucial step is ensuring the diversity and inclusivity of training datasets. Datasets should represent a wide range of demographic groups and be periodically updated to reflect evolving societal norms. Additionally, techniques such as data preprocessing, re-weighting, and adversarial debiasing can help reduce bias at various stages of the AI lifecycle. However, technical solutions alone are insufficient; addressing AI bias also demands ethical awareness and accountability from developers, organizations, and policymakers.

Ethical guidelines and regulatory frameworks play a vital role in promoting fairness and accountability in AI systems. Organizations such as the IEEE and the European Union have developed standards and regulations to address bias and discrimination in AI applications. These frameworks emphasize principles such as transparency, inclusivity, and fairness, encouraging developers to design systems that prioritize ethical considerations alongside technical performance. Adherence to such guidelines can help restore public trust in AI technologies and ensure their equitable deployment.

Public and private sector collaboration is equally important in addressing AI bias. Governments can implement policies that mandate bias audits and fairness assessments for AI systems, while private companies can invest in research and development to create bias-mitigation tools. Collaboration between academia, industry, and civil society can further drive innovation in this area, fostering the development of AI systems that are not only effective but also socially responsible.

Finally, fostering public awareness and engagement is critical in the fight against AI bias. Educating the public about the limitations and potential biases of AI systems can empower individuals to critically assess the technologies they interact with and advocate for their responsible use. Transparency in how AI systems are designed and implemented can also build trust and enable stakeholders to hold developers accountable for their systems' impact.

In conclusion, while AI systems hold immense potential to transform industries and improve lives, their susceptibility to bias poses significant ethical and societal challenges. Tackling these issues requires a holistic approach that combines technical innovation, ethical governance, and societal engagement. By addressing AI bias proactively, stakeholders can ensure that these transformative technologies benefit all segments of society and contribute to a more equitable and inclusive future.

3.2.2. *Privacy and Security Concerns*

The proliferation of IoT devices add to the complexity of safeguarding privacy. IoT devices — ranging from smart home assistants and security cameras to wearable health trackers and industrial sensors — are integral to modern life. These devices continuously collect and transmit vast amounts of personal and operational data, which, if inadequately secured, pose significant risks of exploitation by malicious actors. A single vulnerability in an IoT ecosystem can provide cybercriminals with access to an entire network, amplifying the potential impact of attacks. For instance, unsecured IoT devices have been leveraged in Distributed Denial-of-Service (DDoS) attacks, as seen in the Mirai botnet incident, which disrupted major online services globally. These high-profile breaches not only expose the vulnerabilities of IoT systems but also threaten user trust and security (Roman, Zhou, & Lopez, 2018).

Privacy concerns are further compounded by the lack of standardized security protocols across the rapidly expanding IoT market. Many IoT manufacturers prioritize functionality and cost-effectiveness over robust security measures, leaving devices susceptible to hacking and data breaches. As IoT adoption increases in sectors such as healthcare, transportation, and smart cities, the potential consequences of these vulnerabilities grow more severe. For example, compromised healthcare IoT devices, such as pacemakers or insulin pumps, could lead to life-threatening situations. Similarly, attacks on IoT-enabled critical infrastructure, like power grids or traffic systems, could have catastrophic implications for public safety.

To address these challenges, governments and regulatory bodies are beginning to implement stricter security requirements for IoT devices. Initiatives such as the European Union's Cybersecurity Act and the United States' IoT Cybersecurity Improvement Act of 2020 aim to establish baseline security standards, such as mandatory encryption and regular software updates. However, enforcing these regulations globally and ensuring compliance across a diverse range of IoT manufacturers remain formidable tasks.

In parallel with IoT challenges, the advent of quantum computing poses a looming threat to current cryptographic standards. Quantum computers, leveraging principles of quantum mechanics, are expected to achieve computational speeds far beyond those of classical computers. While this revolutionary technology holds immense promise for fields such as materials science, AI, and drug discovery, it also introduces unprecedented risks to global cybersecurity. Specifically, quantum computers could break widely used encryption algorithms, such as RSA and ECC, which underpin secure communications and data protection in banking, healthcare, and government systems.

The prospect of quantum-enabled decryption has sparked a global race to develop quantum-resistant cryptographic methods. Governments, tech firms, and academic institutions are investing heavily in post-quantum cryptography research to safeguard sensitive data and maintain trust in digital systems. The National Institute of Standards and Technology (NIST) in the United States, for example, has been leading efforts to standardize quantum-resistant algorithms. Yet, the widespread implementation of these solutions presents significant challenges. Organizations must transition to new cryptographic standards without disrupting existing operations, a process that requires time, resources, and global coordination.

Beyond encryption, quantum computing also raises ethical and strategic concerns. The countries and organizations that achieve quantum supremacy first may gain significant technological and geopolitical advantages, potentially widening global inequalities. Furthermore, the misuse of quantum computing capabilities, whether by malicious state actors or criminal organizations, could destabilize critical systems and compromise national security.

Proactively addressing these issues requires a multi-faceted approach. For IoT, fostering collaboration among manufacturers, policymakers, and cybersecurity experts can drive the development and adoption of standardized security frameworks. Educating consumers about the importance of securing their devices — such as updating firmware and using strong passwords — can also mitigate risks at the user level. For quantum computing, governments and international organizations must prioritize research funding, promote knowledge-sharing, and encourage early adoption of quantum-resistant technologies to minimize vulnerabilities.

In conclusion, while IoT devices and quantum computing offer transformative potential, they also introduce complex challenges that demand vigilant attention. Balancing innovation with security is essential to ensure that these technologies can be leveraged for societal benefit without compromising privacy, trust, or global stability. By addressing these concerns proactively, stakeholders can pave the way for a secure and sustainable technological future.

3.2.3. *Ethical Issues in Blockchain and Cryptocurrency*

Blockchain technology has garnered immense attention for its potential to revolutionize industries by offering decentralized, transparent, and immutable records of transactions. Its applications range from financial services to supply chain management, healthcare, and even governance. At the core of blockchain is its decentralized nature, which eliminates the need for intermediaries, fostering trust through transparency. However, despite its advantages, blockchain technology and its prominent application — cryptocurrencies — are not immune to significant ethical challenges, which have raised concerns about their broader societal impact.

One of the primary ethical concerns surrounding blockchain and cryptocurrencies is their use in illicit activities. Cryptocurrencies, particularly Bitcoin, have gained notoriety for being associated with illegal transactions due to the pseudonymous nature of blockchain transactions. While blockchain's transparency allows for the traceability of transactions, the anonymity of users — bolstered by pseudonyms rather than real identities — has made cryptocurrencies a preferred medium for illicit activities such as money laundering, tax evasion, and the purchase of illegal goods and services (Zyskind & Nathan, 2015). The decentralized nature of blockchain makes it difficult for regulatory authorities to intervene, creating challenges for law enforcement in preventing and investigating financial crimes.

For instance, cryptocurrencies have been used to bypass traditional financial systems, enabling the transfer of illicit funds across borders without detection. Bitcoin's role in the Silk Road, an online marketplace for illegal drugs and other illicit goods, highlighted how cryptocurrencies can facilitate criminal activity. Similarly, Bitcoin's role in ransomware attacks, where hackers demand payment in cryptocurrency, further emphasizes the risks associated with its use. These concerns have led to calls for stronger regulatory oversight of blockchain and cryptocurrencies. Some governments have moved to implement stricter regulations, including the monitoring of cryptocurrency transactions and exchanges, to ensure that they are not being used to facilitate illegal activities. However, there remains an ongoing debate over how much regulation is necessary without stifling the innovation that blockchain technology offers.

Another critical ethical concern related to blockchain and cryptocurrency revolves around their environmental impact. Many blockchain networks, particularly those utilizing proof-of-work (PoW) consensus mechanisms, are notorious for their high energy consumption. Bitcoin, the most well-known cryptocurrency, relies on PoW to secure its network and validate transactions. However, the process of mining — solving complex cryptographic puzzles to validate transactions — requires immense computational power, leading to significant energy consumption. According to some estimates,

Bitcoin mining consumes as much energy annually as small nations like Switzerland or Argentina (Narayanan *et al.*, 2016). The environmental impact of this energy consumption is compounded by the fact that much of the energy used for Bitcoin mining comes from non-renewable sources, contributing to carbon emissions and global warming.

The ethical implications of this environmental impact are far-reaching. As the global community grapples with climate change, the sustainability of blockchain technologies becomes an increasingly pressing issue. The environmental concerns associated with Bitcoin and other PoW-based cryptocurrencies have led to calls for a shift toward more energy-efficient blockchain systems. Some blockchain networks, such as Ethereum, have initiated plans to transition from PoW to proof-of-stake (PoS), a consensus mechanism that requires far less energy by relying on participants' stake in the cryptocurrency rather than computational power. While PoS and other alternatives like delegated proof-of-stake (DPoS) and proof-of-authority (PoA) offer promising solutions, the transition is not without challenges. The widespread adoption of greener blockchain alternatives is essential to ensuring that the growth of blockchain technology does not come at the expense of environmental sustainability.

Further complicating the issue is the fact that many cryptocurrency miners are not bound by local environmental regulations. In countries where energy costs are low, such as China (until recently) or some parts of the United States, mining operations often run on cheap and unsustainable energy sources, exacerbating the global environmental footprint of cryptocurrencies. This decentralized nature of mining operations makes it difficult to implement and enforce regulations aimed at reducing carbon emissions. While some blockchain advocates argue that mining rewards can help incentivize the development of more energy-efficient mining practices, these efforts have been insufficient in mitigating the broader environmental concerns.

In addition to environmental issues, the use of blockchain technology in the financial sector has led to ethical concerns regarding its potential to exacerbate wealth inequality. While blockchain promises financial inclusion by providing individuals without access to traditional banking systems with a means of participating in the global economy, the reality has often been different. The high costs of mining and the technical knowledge required to operate in the cryptocurrency ecosystem have limited participation to those with significant resources. This creates a situation where wealthier individuals and large institutions can control a disproportionate amount of the cryptocurrency supply, while smaller investors or those in underdeveloped regions remain excluded. Furthermore, the volatility of cryptocurrencies — such as Bitcoin's sharp price fluctuations — has led to concerns about their role in enabling speculative behaviors that disproportionately benefit those with access to large capital.

Another significant ethical issue surrounding blockchain and cryptocurrencies is the potential for financial instability. Cryptocurrencies, by their nature, are highly volatile, and their market value is often driven by speculation rather than underlying assets or stable economic factors. This volatility can lead to financial bubbles, as seen in the 2017 cryptocurrency boom, where Bitcoin's price soared to nearly $20,000 before crashing to a fraction of that value. Such fluctuations can result in significant financial losses for investors, particularly those who enter the market based on hype or without a full understanding of the risks. Additionally, the decentralized nature of cryptocurrencies means that they are not backed by central banks or governments, leaving users vulnerable to market manipulation and fraud. The lack of regulatory oversight in this space means that investors have limited recourse if they fall victim to fraudulent schemes, such as Ponzi schemes or "pump-and-dump" tactics.

Given the ethical challenges posed by blockchain and cryptocurrencies, a balanced approach to regulation is required. Policymakers must find a way to mitigate the risks of criminal activity, environmental harm, and financial instability without stifling innovation. Some regulatory bodies have proposed frameworks that focus on ensuring the transparency of blockchain transactions, improving the energy efficiency of mining operations, and protecting consumers from fraud. For example, the European Union's MiCA Regulation aims to provide a comprehensive legal framework for cryptocurrencies, addressing issues such as consumer protection, anti-money laundering (AML) compliance, and market integrity. While these efforts represent a positive step toward regulating the cryptocurrency space, global cooperation is necessary to establish common standards that ensure the responsible development and use of blockchain technology.

In conclusion, blockchain and cryptocurrency technologies have the potential to revolutionize industries and empower individuals by providing decentralized, transparent, and secure platforms for transactions. However, their ethical challenges — ranging from their use in illicit activities and environmental impact to wealth inequality and financial instability — cannot be ignored. Addressing these issues will require a combination of regulatory oversight, technological innovation, and collaborative efforts across the global community. By balancing innovation with responsibility, blockchain and cryptocurrency can fulfill their promise of transforming the digital economy while safeguarding the broader public interest.

3.2.4. *Challenges of Accountability and Autonomy*

As emerging technologies like autonomous systems become more prevalent, the ethical challenges they present grow more complex, particularly in relation to accountability and decision-making autonomy. Autonomous systems, such as self-driving cars, drones, and robotic surgery assistants, are designed to perform tasks with minimal human intervention. While these technologies have the potential to revolutionize industries and improve efficiency, they also raise fundamental ethical and legal questions. A key dilemma is determining accountability in the event of accidents or failures, particularly when autonomous systems make decisions that lead to harm or damage.

Consider the case of self-driving cars: these vehicles rely on sophisticated AI algorithms and machine learning to navigate the road. While these cars are designed to make real-time decisions to avoid accidents, there is always a risk of failure. If an autonomous vehicle is involved in a fatal accident, it can be challenging to pinpoint who is at fault. Should the blame fall on the manufacturer of the car, who designed and built the system? Should the software developers who created the algorithms that drive the car's decision-making process be held responsible? Or should the vehicle's owner, who is still legally required to maintain control of the car under certain circumstances, bear some of the responsibility? This ambiguity creates a legal and ethical conundrum, as traditional accountability models do not easily apply to automated systems.

This issue is not limited to self-driving cars. The use of drones for surveillance, delivery services, and military operations raises similar questions about responsibility. For example, if a drone malfunctions and causes harm — whether through a crash, invasion of privacy, or injury — who should be held accountable? Should the manufacturer be liable for the drone's failure, or is it the responsibility of the operator or the company that deployed the drone? These questions are further complicated by the fact that autonomous systems often rely on AI, which can learn and adapt over time, making it difficult to predict and control outcomes. In many cases, the decisions made by AI are not fully understood even by the engineers who developed the systems, creating a "black box" effect that obscures the source of any errors.

The issue of accountability becomes even more pressing in contexts where autonomous systems make life-and-death decisions. For instance, in the field of healthcare, autonomous systems are increasingly being used in diagnostic procedures and surgical operations. AI-driven robots can assist surgeons in performing highly precise operations, but what happens if a mistake occurs? If a surgical robot makes a critical error, leading to patient harm or death, who is responsible? Is it the surgeon who relied on the robot, the medical institution that deployed the technology, or the developers who programmed the robot? The complexity of these situations makes it difficult to establish clear lines of accountability, yet it is crucial to ensure that victims of accidents caused by autonomous systems have access to justice.

One of the central challenges of accountability in the context of autonomous systems is the "autonomy" of the technology itself. As these systems become more advanced, they can operate with increasing levels of independence, making decisions without direct human input. In some cases, these decisions may be based on complex algorithms that consider vast amounts of data, far beyond what a human operator could process in real-time. This raises questions about whether humans should retain ultimate responsibility for decisions made by autonomous systems, or whether the systems themselves should be held accountable. The idea of "machine autonomy" challenges traditional concepts of legal responsibility, as it blurs the lines between human agency and technological decision-making.

Additionally, the integration of AI into autonomous systems presents the challenge of ensuring ethical decision-making. Unlike humans, AI systems do not inherently possess moral values, and their decision-making processes are based on data inputs and programmed algorithms. Therefore, decisions made by autonomous systems could be influenced by biases in the data they are trained on, or by the ethical choices embedded in the algorithms themselves. For example, in a self-driving car scenario, the vehicle might have to make a decision in a split second to either swerve and potentially harm the passengers or stay on course and hit a pedestrian. How should the car be programmed to make these kinds of ethical decisions? Should it prioritize the safety of its passengers, or should it aim to minimize harm overall? These types of "moral dilemmas" present significant challenges, and the lack of consensus on how to handle them adds to the uncertainty surrounding the ethics of autonomous systems.

In response to these concerns, there have been calls for the development of comprehensive legal frameworks to address the accountability issues associated with autonomous systems. One potential solution is to create laws that define the responsibilities of manufacturers, developers, and users of autonomous technologies. These laws could establish standards for safety, transparency, and liability, making it clear who is responsible when things go wrong. For example, similar to how car manufacturers are required to adhere to safety standards, developers of autonomous systems could be required to meet specific ethical guidelines that ensure their systems are safe, transparent, and free from bias.

Another approach is to create an insurance model that holds developers, manufacturers, and users of autonomous systems financially accountable for accidents. This model could function in a similar way to how car insurance works today, where drivers and manufacturers contribute to a pool of funds that can be used to compensate victims of accidents. Such insurance models could incentivize companies to design and test safer, more reliable systems, while also ensuring that individuals and organizations using autonomous systems are not left financially vulnerable in the event of an accident.

Furthermore, there is a growing demand for the incorporation of ethical decision-making frameworks into AI and autonomous system development. These frameworks would guide how autonomous systems make decisions in ethically ambiguous situations. For instance, ethical guidelines could be designed to ensure that autonomous vehicles prioritize human life in situations where harm is unavoidable. Similarly, developers could be encouraged to create systems that are transparent and accountable, with clear audit trails that allow for post-incident analysis and investigation.

In conclusion, as autonomous systems become increasingly integrated into daily life, the ethical and legal challenges related to accountability will continue to evolve. Determining responsibility for accidents or failures of these systems is crucial to ensuring justice and protecting public safety. Legal frameworks, insurance models, and ethical decision-making guidelines will be key to addressing these challenges and ensuring that emerging technologies can be deployed safely and responsibly. Only through careful consideration of accountability and autonomy can we navigate the complexities of these new technologies and foster a future in which their benefits can be realized without compromising public trust or safety.

3.2.5. *Ethical Governance and Regulation*

To address these ethical challenges, robust governance frameworks are essential to ensure that emerging technologies are developed and deployed in a responsible and ethical manner. The complexity of these technologies, coupled with their vast potential impact on society, necessitates the establishment of comprehensive and adaptive regulatory structures. Policymakers, industry leaders, and ethicists must work together to create ethical guidelines, regulatory standards, and oversight mechanisms that can balance innovation with public safety, fairness, and justice. This collaboration is critical to ensure that technology serves the greater good while mitigating risks associated with misuse, bias, and harm.

One of the most pressing areas for governance is AI, which, due to its growing capabilities and widespread application, has raised significant concerns about its ethical implications. AI systems, especially those involved in decision-making processes such as hiring, law enforcement, and healthcare, must be designed to adhere to principles of fairness, transparency, and accountability. Without such safeguards, AI could perpetuate existing biases and inequalities, as seen in cases of discriminatory hiring algorithms or biased predictive policing tools. Ethical AI frameworks, such as those proposed by organizations like the Institute of Electrical and Electronics Engineers (IEEE) and the Organisation for Economic Co-operation and Development (OECD), provide valuable principles for designing AI systems that are fair, transparent, and accountable (Floridi *et al.*, 2018). These frameworks emphasize the importance of developing AI systems that prioritize human well-being, respect privacy, and promote social justice.

In addition to AI, other emerging technologies like blockchain, IoT, and autonomous systems require similarly rigorous governance structures. Blockchain technology, for instance, promises decentralization and transparency, yet it is also associated with ethical challenges such as its use in illicit activities, including money laundering and tax evasion (Zyskind & Nathan, 2015). Furthermore, blockchain's environmental impact, particularly the energy consumption of proof-of-work mining systems, raises sustainability concerns. Regulatory frameworks that set clear boundaries for the ethical use of blockchain can help mitigate these risks while allowing for continued innovation in the space.

The proliferation of IoT devices also necessitates strong governance, particularly regarding privacy and data security. IoT devices collect vast amounts of personal data, often without the user's full understanding of how that data is being used or stored. To address this, frameworks must be implemented to ensure that IoT manufacturers adhere to data protection regulations and employ best practices for safeguarding user information. Furthermore, as quantum computing emerges as a powerful tool for solving complex problems, its potential to break current cryptographic systems poses a significant challenge to cybersecurity. Governments and industry leaders must collaborate to develop quantum-resistant cryptography standards that can secure sensitive data in the quantum era.

A key element of these governance frameworks is the development of regulatory standards that address not only the technical aspects of these technologies but also their societal impacts. For example, regulations governing AI should ensure that systems are designed with fairness in mind and that biases in training data are actively addressed. This could involve mandating transparency in AI algorithms, requiring regular audits, and creating clear channels for individuals to challenge decisions made by automated systems. Similarly, regulations around autonomous systems, such as self-driving cars and drones, should establish clear guidelines for accountability in the event of accidents or failures. Legal frameworks must be designed to determine who is responsible when an autonomous system causes harm — whether it be the manufacturer, the developer, or the operator.

Furthermore, public engagement and participatory governance will play a vital role in shaping the ethical development of emerging technologies. Citizens, advocacy groups, and affected communities should have a voice in the development of policies and regulations that affect them. For instance, in areas like AI and IoT, public consultation processes could help ensure that the benefits of these technologies are distributed equitably and that their risks are managed effectively. Engaging diverse perspectives, including those from historically marginalized communities, can help identify potential harms early on and ensure that ethical guidelines are inclusive and representative of societal values.

As part of a global approach to technology governance, international cooperation is crucial to establishing universally accepted ethical standards. Technologies such as AI and blockchain have global reach and implications, and therefore international collaboration is necessary to address their ethical challenges effectively. International organizations such as the United Nations and the World Economic Forum can facilitate dialogue among governments, businesses, and civil society to create global norms and standards for the ethical use of emerging technologies. These global efforts should focus not only on technological regulation but also on ensuring that the benefits of these technologies are shared equitably across nations, especially in underdeveloped and underserved regions.

In conclusion, the ethical challenges posed by emerging technologies are complex and multifaceted, requiring proactive governance and international cooperation. By developing robust ethical frameworks and regulatory standards, policymakers, industry leaders, and ethicists can help ensure that technological progress does not come at the expense of social justice, human rights, or environmental sustainability. The collaboration of diverse stakeholders, alongside public engagement and international cooperation, will be crucial in creating a future where emerging technologies contribute to a fairer, more equitable, and more sustainable world.

3.2.6. *Fostering Global Collaboration*

Ethical challenges associated with emerging technologies often transcend national borders, necessitating global cooperation to address issues that affect societies worldwide. Technologies like AI, blockchain, quantum computing, and IoT have a global reach, and their implications are not confined to any single country or region. These technologies can have far-reaching consequences on privacy, security, equity, and governance, making it crucial for nations to collaborate on creating frameworks that promote ethical development and deployment. National efforts alone are insufficient to address the complexities and scale of these challenges; hence, international cooperation becomes indispensable.

International organizations such as the United Nations (UN) and the World Economic Forum (WEF) play a pivotal role in facilitating global dialogue, developing universal ethical standards, and fostering collaboration among governments, the private sector, and civil society. These organizations provide platforms where stakeholders can come together to discuss the ethical, legal, and societal implications of emerging technologies, and they help coordinate global responses to these challenges. Through their efforts, they can encourage the creation of global norms that ensure technologies are developed and used in ways that benefit humanity as a whole while minimizing harm.

One notable example of global cooperation in addressing technology's ethical challenges is the *Paris Call for Trust and Security in Cyberspace*. Launched in 2018, this initiative brings together governments, companies, and civil society groups to promote international cooperation on cybersecurity and protect the integrity of cyberspace. The Paris Call emphasizes the need for trust and accountability in the use of digital technologies, urging the signatories to adopt responsible practices and create safeguards against the malicious use of emerging technologies. It calls for the development of norms to ensure that cyberspace is used in ways that respect human rights, protect privacy, and promote peace. The initiative illustrates the growing recognition that ethical challenges in cyberspace, such as data privacy breaches, cyberattacks, and the misuse of AI, are not confined to specific regions but require a unified global approach.

In addition to the Paris Call, other international initiatives focus on the responsible development and governance of emerging technologies. The *OECD Principles on Artificial Intelligence* is another example, setting guidelines for ensuring AI is aligned with human rights, fairness, and accountability. This initiative encourages member countries to implement policies that prioritize the ethical use of AI and address its potential risks, including discrimination, privacy violations, and the concentration of power among a few technology companies. Similarly, the *IEEE Global Initiative on Ethics of Autonomous and Intelligent Systems* aims to promote the development of ethical frameworks for AI and autonomous systems, ensuring that these technologies are developed with human well-being and societal benefit in mind.

Furthermore, global cooperation is essential in addressing the environmental and social implications of blockchain and cryptocurrencies. The decentralized nature of blockchain technology presents unique challenges for regulating its use, especially in areas such as money laundering, tax evasion, and environmental sustainability. Cryptocurrencies like Bitcoin, for example, have been criticized for their high energy consumption and the negative environmental impact of mining activities. International efforts to create regulatory standards that govern the environmental footprint of blockchain technologies are crucial. These efforts can include establishing global norms for energy-efficient mining practices, promoting transparency in cryptocurrency transactions, and preventing the use of blockchain for illegal activities such as money laundering.

The development of quantum computing also requires global cooperation, particularly in ensuring that its deployment does not jeopardize global cybersecurity. Quantum computing has the potential to break existing encryption methods, posing a significant risk to the confidentiality and security of digital information. As such, international collaboration is essential in creating quantum-resistant encryption algorithms and establishing protocols for the secure use of quantum computing technologies. Governments and private sector organizations must work together to ensure that the benefits of quantum computing, such as advancements in science and medicine, are realized without compromising global security.

In conclusion, the ethical challenges posed by emerging technologies demand coordinated global action. International organizations like the UN, WEF, and OECD are instrumental in facilitating dialogue, developing standards, and fostering cooperation among nations, companies, and other stakeholders. Initiatives such as the Paris Call for Trust and Security in Cyberspace and the OECD Principles on AI exemplify the importance of a unified approach to addressing the ethical implications of technologies that impact the global community. As emerging technologies continue to evolve and shape the future, ongoing international collaboration will be essential to ensuring their responsible development and deployment for the benefit of all.

3.2.7. *The Role of Public Engagement*

Engaging the public in discussions about the ethical implications of technology is equally crucial for ensuring that technological advancements are developed and deployed responsibly. Public engagement fosters transparency, accountability, and trust, which are essential for ensuring that technologies serve the public good rather than exacerbate societal harms. As emerging technologies continue to reshape industries, economies, and daily life, it becomes increasingly important to involve individuals, communities, and societal stakeholders in dialogues about the risks and benefits these technologies present. By facilitating open discussions, policymakers, researchers, and technology developers can ensure that the ethical concerns of the public are heard and addressed.

One of the most effective ways to engage the public is through transparency. Being clear about how technologies are designed, tested, and deployed helps build trust between the public and the organizations behind technological innovations. Transparency can help alleviate fears and suspicions about the potential misuse of technology. For instance, AI systems used in healthcare or criminal justice are often met with skepticism due to concerns about data privacy, fairness, and bias. By openly sharing how algorithms are trained, the data they use, and how decisions are made, organizations can demonstrate their commitment to ethical principles and gain public confidence. Transparent practices also encourage accountability, as they allow for scrutiny and feedback, ensuring that technologies are aligned with societal values.

Public consultations and participatory technology assessments are key mechanisms for fostering transparency and inclusivity in the decision-making process. These consultations allow individuals and communities to voice their concerns, offer suggestions, and ask questions about the technologies being developed. They also provide valuable insights into societal expectations, fears, and aspirations, which can guide the ethical trajectory of technological development. For example, before the widespread deployment of autonomous vehicles, public consultations could gather feedback from diverse stakeholders, including pedestrians, drivers, policymakers, and those with disabilities, to ensure that safety, equity, and accessibility are prioritized in the design and regulation of self-driving cars. Similarly, before the adoption of facial recognition technology by law enforcement agencies, participatory assessments could solicit input from civil rights organizations and marginalized communities to prevent potential abuses, such as racial profiling and surveillance overreach.

Participatory technology assessments take this process a step further by involving the public in the evaluation of the potential impacts of new technologies. These assessments involve not just listening to the public's concerns but also actively engaging them in the evaluation of technological solutions. This can include citizens' panels, citizen juries, or even crowdsourcing ethical reviews, where members of the public are invited to deliberate on the societal consequences of specific technologies. Such initiatives can democratize the decision-making process, ensuring that the voices of those who are most affected by technological change, such as low-income or underrepresented groups, are heard and considered. For instance, when evaluating the ethical implications of data collection by IoT devices, public consultations can ensure that the concerns of vulnerable populations, such as children, elderly individuals, and those with limited access to technology, are prioritized in the design and regulation of these devices.

Furthermore, engaging the public in technology development and regulation can help address issues of inequality and social justice. Technological advancements, if left unexamined, may disproportionately benefit certain groups while marginalizing others. By involving the public in the ethical discourse, policymakers can ensure that technologies are developed with an eye toward inclusivity and equity. For instance, when designing AI systems for hiring, transparent and inclusive consultations could ensure that fairness, diversity, and non-discrimination are central to the development process. Similarly, public engagement can help mitigate the risks of technological monopolies by promoting regulatory measures that encourage competition and prevent the concentration of power in the hands of a few tech giants.

Education also plays a pivotal role in public engagement. By improving digital literacy and fostering a deeper understanding of emerging technologies, individuals are better equipped to participate in discussions about their ethical implications. Public education campaigns can help demystify complex technologies such as blockchain, quantum computing, and AI, making it easier for people to understand the potential risks and benefits these technologies bring. Informed public participation can help counteract misinformation and fear, leading to more constructive and productive discussions about the responsible use of technology.

Incorporating ethical considerations into the development of emerging technologies not only enhances societal trust but also aligns innovation with broader public values. Engaging the public in the ethical evaluation of new technologies fosters a sense of ownership and collective responsibility. It reminds technology developers and policymakers that these innovations are not abstract concepts but tools that directly impact people's lives. By fostering a culture of ethical deliberation and public participation, society can ensure that emerging technologies serve the greater good, uphold human rights, and contribute to the well-being of all individuals, regardless of their background or socioeconomic status.

In conclusion, public engagement is essential for addressing the ethical implications of emerging technologies. Transparency, public consultations, and participatory technology assessments provide opportunities for the public to voice their concerns and contribute to the ethical development of technology. By ensuring that technological innovation aligns with societal values and public expectations, we can create a more inclusive, accountable, and equitable technological future. As technologies continue to evolve at a rapid pace, ongoing dialogue between all stakeholders — governments, companies, civil society, and the public — is crucial for shaping a future where technology serves the best interests of humanity.

3.2.8. *Balancing Innovation and Ethics*

Finally, a key challenge lies in balancing innovation with ethical considerations in the development and deployment of emerging technologies. While innovation is essential for economic growth, social progress, and addressing global challenges, ethical concerns must also be taken into account to ensure that these technologies are used responsibly and do not inadvertently cause harm. Overregulation, if too stringent, can stifle technological progress, slow down innovation, and prevent the full potential of emerging technologies from being realized. On the other hand, under-regulation may leave critical ethical issues unaddressed, leading to unintended consequences such as bias, privacy violations, or exploitation. Therefore, striking the right balance between fostering innovation and ensuring ethical accountability is crucial for the sustainable development of technology.

Achieving this balance requires adaptive regulatory approaches that evolve alongside technological advancements. Traditional regulatory frameworks, which were designed for static and established industries, are often ill-suited for the fast-paced, dynamic nature of emerging technologies. For instance, the rapid development of AI, blockchain, and autonomous systems presents unique regulatory challenges that require continuous monitoring and adjustment. Regulatory bodies must be nimble, forward-thinking, and proactive, anticipating potential ethical issues before they emerge and providing clear guidelines for technology developers. Rather than applying one-size-fits-all regulations, a flexible, principles-based approach is often needed to address the nuances of different technologies while ensuring their alignment with public interests and ethical standards.

One promising regulatory tool is the concept of "sandboxing." Sandboxing involves testing new technologies in controlled, real-world environments before they are deployed at scale. This allows developers to experiment with their innovations while ensuring that potential risks are mitigated. Regulatory sandboxes provide a safe space for experimentation, where new products or services can be trialed under strict oversight, without exposing the wider public to unknown risks. For example, in the financial sector, regulators have used sandboxes to test the deployment of blockchain-based payment systems, ensuring that the technology adheres to necessary standards of security, privacy, and fairness before being adopted broadly. In the context of AI, sandboxes can be used to test algorithms for biases and discriminatory outcomes, allowing developers to refine their systems and address any ethical issues before they impact real-world applications.

Sandboxing not only encourages innovation but also fosters collaboration between regulators, technology developers, and other stakeholders, such as consumer advocacy groups and ethicists. These collaborations help ensure that emerging technologies are developed in ways that benefit society as a whole while avoiding harmful consequences. Moreover, sandboxing provides valuable data and insights that can inform regulatory frameworks, helping regulators understand the practical challenges of new technologies and develop more effective oversight strategies. In this way, sandboxing serves as a crucial tool for adaptive regulation, allowing regulators to stay ahead of technological developments and address ethical concerns in a timely and informed manner.

However, while sandboxing offers a promising approach, it is not without its challenges. For one, sandboxing requires strong institutional cooperation and transparency. Technology developers must be willing to share data and insights from their testing phases, and regulators must be prepared to offer clear guidance and support. Additionally, sandboxes must be carefully designed to ensure that they do not inadvertently favor certain companies or technologies over others, which could lead to unequal opportunities or exacerbate existing inequalities. It is also important to ensure that sandboxes are accessible to a wide range of innovators, including startups and smaller companies, which may lack the resources to navigate complex regulatory environments. Finally, regulators must remain vigilant after sandbox testing is complete, ensuring that technologies deployed at scale continue to adhere to ethical guidelines and do not result in unforeseen negative consequences.

Beyond sandboxing, regulators must also engage in continuous dialogue with technology developers and the public to ensure that emerging technologies align with societal values. Public engagement and stakeholder participation are essential in creating ethical guidelines that reflect the diverse needs and concerns of society. Regulatory bodies should not operate in isolation but instead foster collaborative ecosystems where industry leaders, academics, civil society groups, and government representatives can collectively shape the ethical standards for technology. This kind of collaborative approach will help ensure that technological advancements are inclusive, transparent, and accountable.

As emerging technologies continue to evolve, it is also essential to focus on education and capacity-building efforts for both regulators and the public. Regulators must develop the technical expertise to understand and assess new technologies, while the public needs to be informed about the potential risks and benefits of these innovations. Ethical considerations should be integrated into educational curricula for technology developers, ensuring that future generations of innovators are equipped to think critically about the societal impacts of their work.

In conclusion, the challenge of balancing innovation with ethical considerations is a complex and ongoing process. To strike this balance effectively, regulators must adopt adaptive, flexible approaches that allow for experimentation and innovation while safeguarding against potential risks. Sandboxing serves as a useful tool in this process, offering a controlled environment in which new technologies can be tested and refined before widespread deployment. However, achieving the right balance requires ongoing collaboration, public engagement, and a commitment to ensuring that emerging technologies are developed and deployed in ways that benefit society as a whole. By taking a proactive, collaborative, and transparent approach to regulation, we can ensure that technological advancements contribute to a more equitable, sustainable, and ethical future.

Overall, the ethical challenges posed by emerging technologies are multifaceted and demand a concerted effort from all stakeholders. Through proactive governance, global collaboration, and public engagement, society can harness the potential of these technologies while safeguarding fundamental ethical principles. This balanced approach will pave the way for a future where technology serves humanity's best interests without compromising justice, security, or equity. Table 3.2 provides a summary of Ethical Considerations and Challenges in Emerging Technologies with Practical Insights for Decision Makers.

Table 3.2. Ethical Considerations and Challenges in Emerging Technologies.

Aspect	Key Insights	Lessons for Decision Makers
Bias and Discrimination in AI Systems	AI systems may perpetuate societal biases due to flawed training datasets, leading to discriminatory outcomes in hiring, law enforcement, and other critical sectors.	Implement measures to audit datasets for bias, promote diversity in training data, and integrate fairness protocols in AI development pipelines. Foster interdisciplinary collaboration to address systemic biases.
Privacy and Security Concerns	IoT proliferation increases privacy vulnerabilities and risks of exploitation by malicious actors, particularly due to inadequate security protocols.	Enforce standardized IoT security measures, mandate robust encryption, and prioritize user privacy in product design. Encourage manufacturers to adopt cybersecurity best practices and invest in continuous threat assessments.
Ethical Issues in Blockchain and Cryptocurrency	Cryptocurrencies are often used for illicit activities due to anonymity, while decentralized blockchain governance complicates regulatory enforcement.	Develop regulatory frameworks to mitigate illicit usage while preserving transparency and innovation. Encourage the adoption of identity verification measures and establish international guidelines for ethical blockchain usage.
Challenges of Accountability and Autonomy	Autonomous systems, such as self-driving cars, raise complex issues of accountability and liability in cases of harm or failure.	Create clear legal frameworks defining accountability for autonomous systems. Encourage the development of fail-safe mechanisms and ethical decision-making algorithms in autonomous technologies.
Ethical Governance and Regulation	A lack of comprehensive regulation risks misuse, bias, and harm in emerging technologies.	Foster adaptive and inclusive regulatory frameworks. Engage policymakers, ethicists, and industry leaders to create guidelines that balance innovation with ethical considerations.
Fostering Global Collaboration	Ethical challenges in emerging technologies require coordinated international efforts to address global implications.	Promote international treaties and agreements on ethical technology development. Support cross-border initiatives for research, governance, and resource sharing.

(*Continued*)

Table 3.2. (*Continued*)

Aspect	Key Insights	Lessons for Decision Makers
The Role of Public Engagement	Public trust and accountability require involving stakeholders in discussions about technology's risks and benefits.	Encourage transparent dialogue between technologists, policymakers, and the public. Establish platforms for citizen participation in shaping ethical guidelines and technology policies.
Balancing Innovation and Ethics	Striking a balance between encouraging innovation and addressing ethical concerns is critical for sustainable technological progress.	Avoid overregulation to foster innovation but enforce safeguards against harm. Monitor emerging trends and adjust policies dynamically to ensure ethical accountability without hindering development.

3.3. Technological Convergence and Its Implications

The tension between fostering innovation and addressing the ethical considerations of emerging technologies presents a critical challenge. While rapid technological advancements hold the potential to reshape industries, improve lives, and address global challenges, they also raise significant ethical issues that must be considered. If left unaddressed, these ethical concerns can lead to unintended negative consequences, such as perpetuating inequalities, compromising privacy, and exacerbating social divisions. As such, policymakers, industry leaders, and technologists must work together to strike the right balance — ensuring that innovation is pursued responsibly while minimizing the risks associated with new technologies.

3.3.1. *The Role of Regulation in Balancing Innovation and Ethics*

One of the most important tools for achieving this balance is regulation. Regulatory frameworks are essential to ensure that the rapid pace of technological innovation does not outpace the development of ethical standards and safeguards. However, finding the right level of regulation can be a delicate balancing act. Too much regulation can stifle innovation, reduce competition, and slow down the pace of technological advancements. On the other hand, too little regulation can allow unethical practices to flourish, leading to widespread harm.

The key to effective regulation is flexibility. Traditional, one-size-fits-all approaches often fail to address the unique characteristics and challenges of emerging technologies. Instead, regulators must adopt flexible, adaptive approaches that can evolve as technologies themselves evolve. These approaches should be tailored to the specific risks and benefits of each technology, allowing for innovation while ensuring that the broader public interest is protected.

For instance, in the case of AI, regulators must consider both the potential benefits (such as increased efficiency and new capabilities) and the risks (such as bias, discrimination, and privacy violations). Rather than imposing rigid, blanket rules, regulators can create principles-based guidelines that encourage responsible AI development. These guidelines can focus on transparency, fairness, accountability, and inclusivity, ensuring that AI systems are developed in ways that benefit society without perpetuating harm.

Additionally, regulation should not be viewed as a one-time effort. As technologies continue to evolve, so too must regulatory frameworks. This requires ongoing monitoring and periodic updates to ensure that new risks are addressed and that regulatory responses are in line with technological developments.

3.3.2. *Sandboxing: A Tool for Encouraging Innovation with Ethical Oversight*

One promising approach for balancing innovation and ethics is the use of sandboxing. Sandboxing allows new technologies to be tested in controlled environments before they are deployed more widely. This approach provides innovators with the freedom to experiment and test their ideas while ensuring that potential risks are identified and mitigated early on.

The concept of sandboxing has been particularly useful in industries such FinTech, where the potential for both innovation and harm is high. By testing blockchain-based payment systems, AI-driven trading algorithms, or digital currencies in a sandbox environment, regulators can evaluate their performance in real-world scenarios, assessing both their technical capabilities and their adherence to ethical standards. For example, regulators can ensure that financial products do not discriminate against certain populations, or that AI systems used for credit scoring do not perpetuate racial or gender biases.

Beyond the financial sector, sandboxing can also be applied to other emerging technologies such as autonomous vehicles, healthcare technologies, and IoT devices. Sandboxes provide a controlled environment where these technologies can be evaluated for safety, privacy, and ethical compliance before they are deployed on a larger scale. Moreover, sandboxing fosters collaboration between regulators, technology developers, and other stakeholders, creating opportunities for dialogue and ensuring that regulatory frameworks are informed by real-world experiences.

However, sandboxing is not without its challenges. The effectiveness of a sandbox depends on its design, the willingness of stakeholders to participate, and the clarity of the regulatory framework. Regulators must be able to balance the need for oversight with the desire to encourage innovation, and sandboxes must be accessible to all developers, including startups and smaller companies. Additionally, regulators must remain vigilant after the sandbox phase, ensuring that technologies deployed at scale continue to meet ethical and regulatory standards.

3.3.3. *Ensuring Public Engagement and Transparency*

Another crucial aspect of balancing innovation and ethics is ensuring public engagement and transparency. Technology development and regulation should not take place in isolation, but rather involve open dialogue between regulators, industry leaders, civil society groups, and the general public. Engaging the public in discussions about the ethical implications of emerging technologies helps to ensure that societal values and concerns are taken into account throughout the development process.

Public consultations, community forums, and participatory technology assessments are important tools for gathering input and feedback from a wide range of stakeholders. These efforts allow regulators to understand public concerns and expectations, ensuring that emerging technologies align with societal needs and ethical standards. Public participation also helps to build trust in technological development, as people are more likely to embrace new technologies when they feel that their voices are heard and their concerns are addressed.

Transparency is equally important in building public trust. Technology developers and regulators should be clear about how technologies are being used, the potential risks involved, and the steps being taken to mitigate those risks. This includes providing accessible information about data usage, privacy protections, and the decision-making processes behind AI systems. By making information about emerging technologies available and comprehensible to the public, regulators and developers can reduce misunderstandings and prevent the spread of misinformation.

Moreover, public engagement helps to ensure that technological advancements benefit all segments of society, not just the wealthy or privileged. Technology adoption can exacerbate existing inequalities if it is not inclusive, leaving marginalized groups behind. By incorporating diverse perspectives into the development and regulation of emerging technologies, stakeholders can help ensure that these innovations are used to create more equitable and inclusive outcomes.

3.3.4. *Adapting Regulatory Approaches for Emerging Technologies*

As mentioned earlier, one of the key challenges in balancing innovation with ethical considerations is the need for adaptive regulation. Emerging technologies such as AI, blockchain, quantum computing, and biotechnology evolve rapidly, and regulatory frameworks must keep pace with these changes. Policymakers must avoid the temptation to impose outdated regulatory approaches on new technologies and instead adopt forward-thinking strategies that can adapt to the unique challenges posed by each innovation.

One potential approach to adaptive regulation is "regulatory foresight," which involves anticipating the future challenges and opportunities posed by new technologies. By using scenario planning, impact assessments, and expert consultations, regulators can identify potential risks before they materialize and develop proactive strategies for addressing them. This requires regulators to be both knowledgeable about the technologies they oversee and forward-thinking in their approach to regulation.

Furthermore, the complexity of emerging technologies means that regulation cannot be a one-size-fits-all approach. Rather, regulators must be willing to tailor their strategies to the specific characteristics of each technology. For instance, AI-driven technologies require different ethical considerations than blockchain or autonomous vehicles, and regulators must be prepared to address these unique challenges in ways that are both effective and fair.

3.3.5. *International Cooperation and Global Standards*

Finally, as the global nature of emerging technologies continues to grow, international cooperation and the establishment of global standards will be essential. Ethical challenges related to technology often transcend national borders, making it imperative for countries to work together to create shared frameworks and guidelines. This is particularly important in areas such as data privacy, cybersecurity, and AI ethics, where the actions of one country can have far-reaching implications for others.

International organizations, such as the United Nations, the World Economic Forum, and the Organization for Economic Cooperation and Development (OECD), play a vital role in fostering collaboration and developing global standards. Initiatives like the Paris Call for Trust and Security in Cyberspace exemplify efforts to address transnational ethical concerns in technology deployment. These global efforts help to ensure that emerging technologies are developed and used in ways that promote trust, security, and the public good on an international scale.

By working together, countries can harmonize regulations, share best practices, and ensure that technological advancements are used for the benefit of all. International cooperation can also help to address the digital divide, ensuring that emerging technologies are accessible and beneficial to people in all parts of the world.

In conclusion, balancing innovation with ethical considerations is one of the most significant challenges facing the development and deployment of emerging technologies. By adopting flexible regulatory frameworks, utilizing sandboxing, ensuring public engagement and transparency, and fostering international cooperation, we can create a responsible path forward for technological innovation. This requires collaboration between governments, industry leaders, ethicists, and the public to ensure that emerging technologies are developed in ways that benefit society while mitigating potential risks. As technology continues to evolve, regulators must be proactive, adaptive, and transparent, ensuring that ethical principles remain at the core of innovation, creating a more equitable and sustainable future for all. Table 3.3 highlights the critical themes and actionable insights for decision-makers, ensuring that innovation aligns with ethical considerations to foster equitable and sustainable technological progress.

3.4. Dynamic Perspective of Technological Convergence and Socioeconomic Implications

The dynamic nature of technological convergence adds a layer of complexity to understanding its implications. As emerging technologies come together, they do not simply blend together in a predictable or linear manner. Rather, they interact in multi-faceted ways, influenced by a multitude of technological, social, and economic factors. This creates a situation where the convergence of technologies has both positive and negative feedback loops, which can significantly impact innovation, adoption, and risk management. The pace and direction of convergence can sometimes accelerate technological breakthroughs, making it essential for policymakers and stakeholders to carefully monitor and regulate these developments to maximize benefits while minimizing potential harms.

3.4.1. *Non-linear Dynamics of Technological Convergence*

From a dynamic systems perspective, technological convergence is a highly non-linear process. As technologies evolve, their interaction can lead to rapid and unexpected shifts in both their capabilities and societal impact. One clear example of this is the convergence of AI and IoT in the context of smart cities. While the integration of AI with IoT has the potential to vastly improve urban management, energy efficiency, transportation systems, and healthcare, it also introduces significant risks, particularly in the realm of cybersecurity.

In smart cities, IoT devices are continuously collecting, transmitting, and analyzing data to optimize urban services. However, this

Table 3.3. Summary of Key Aspects of Technological Convergence and Its Implications.

Key Aspect	Insights and Lessons for Decision Makers
Balancing Innovation and Ethics	Policymakers must address ethical concerns like privacy, inequality, and social divisions while promoting technological advancements to ensure responsible innovation.
Role of Regulation	Effective regulation requires flexibility and adaptability, avoiding overregulation that stifles innovation or under-regulation that enables harm. Tailored, principles-based guidelines are crucial.
Sandboxing for Innovation	Controlled environments enable testing of emerging technologies, helping to identify risks early. Collaboration between regulators and developers ensures ethical and performance standards are met before large-scale deployment.
Public Engagement and Transparency	Open dialogue with stakeholders builds trust and aligns technology with societal needs. Transparency about risks, data usage, and protection reduces misinformation and ensures inclusivity.
Adaptive Regulatory Approaches	Forward-thinking regulation anticipates risks and adapts to unique challenges of each technology, avoiding outdated or one-size-fits-all strategies. Proactive and knowledgeable regulatory foresight is essential.
International Cooperation	Global collaboration harmonizes standards, addresses transnational ethical concerns, and ensures equitable access to emerging technologies. Organizations like the UN and OECD play pivotal roles in establishing trust and security on an international scale.

massive interconnectivity increases the risk of cyber-attacks that can target vulnerabilities in various systems — ranging from transportation infrastructure to healthcare services. AI algorithms, which are often used to analyze and act upon this data, can become prime targets for attackers aiming to manipulate or disrupt city operations. For example, an attack on the AI system that controls traffic signals could cause widespread traffic jams, or a hack of a city's water supply system could result in contamination of drinking water. These scenarios are not merely hypothetical — they represent real risks as cities around the world adopt these technologies.

Furthermore, the technological convergence seen in the rise of 5G networks also brings both benefits and challenges. On the one hand, 5G offers the promise of faster, more reliable internet speeds that can facilitate advancements in healthcare, autonomous vehicles, and more. On the other hand, the widespread adoption of 5G technology raises concerns about privacy, data security, and the environmental impact of the massive infrastructure required for 5G networks.

The interdependencies between technologies such as AI, IoT, and 5G networks mean that the risks of one technology can compound the risks of another, creating unpredictable outcomes. This non-linearity of technological convergence highlights the need for a systems-thinking approach to policy-making, where the interplay of different technologies is carefully considered and monitored over time.

3.4.2. *Positive and Negative Feedback Loops in Technological Convergence*

As various technologies converge, they create feedback loops that can either enhance or undermine progress. Positive feedback loops are characterized by self-reinforcing cycles that accelerate technological advancement and innovation. For example, as more AI systems are deployed, they generate data that can be used to train more powerful models, leading to further advancements in AI capabilities. Similarly, the more IoT devices that are deployed, the more data becomes available to improve AI algorithms, creating a virtuous cycle of innovation.

In the context of autonomous vehicles, for instance, as more vehicles are tested and deployed on the roads, more data becomes available to improve machine learning algorithms used to guide these vehicles. The increased availability of data speeds up the learning process, enhancing the performance of autonomous vehicles, which, in turn, encourages greater investment and further adoption. This positive feedback loop can accelerate the adoption of autonomous vehicles, creating a market-driven momentum that leads to rapid technological advancement.

However, positive feedback loops can also lead to the amplification of risks and unintended consequences. One such example is the deployment of surveillance technologies powered by AI. As facial recognition technology becomes more sophisticated, it can lead to greater surveillance, which, in turn, may generate more data to refine the technology. This positive feedback cycle can result in over-surveillance, eroding privacy, and contributing to a society that is constantly monitored. The rapid adoption of these technologies can outpace societal debate, leading to ethical concerns that are not adequately addressed in real-time.

Conversely, negative feedback loops can act as regulatory or societal checks on the convergence of technologies. These loops may emerge when the harmful effects of technological convergence become apparent, triggering responses that slow down or reverse technological progress. For example, as cybersecurity threats associated with IoT and AI grow, there may be increasing public pressure and legal requirements for more robust data protection and privacy regulations. These regulatory mechanisms can disrupt the positive feedback loop of innovation, slowing the deployment of new technologies until the risks are properly addressed.

In the case of blockchain and cryptocurrency, negative feedback loops can also emerge. While blockchain technology has the potential to revolutionize industries such as finance, healthcare, and supply chain management, it has also been associated with criminal activities such as money laundering and tax evasion. As these issues gain attention, stricter regulations are implemented, potentially stifling the pace of innovation in the blockchain space.

3.4.3. *Socioeconomic Implications of Technological Convergence*

The socioeconomic implications of technological convergence are also deeply dynamic and evolve over time. Changes in technology, market conditions, and societal values all influence how technologies are adopted, and how they shape economic structures and social interactions. For instance, the convergence of AI and automation in the labor market is already having significant impacts on employment and income inequality.

AI and automation are transforming industries such as manufacturing, logistics, and customer service. While these technologies have the potential to increase productivity and reduce costs, they also threaten to displace large numbers of workers. Many of these workers may not possess the skills required to transition into new job roles created by emerging technologies, exacerbating existing inequalities. As AI continues to advance, it may become increasingly difficult for workers to compete with machines in sectors such as data analysis, finance, and healthcare.

This dynamic is further complicated by the increasing digitization of the economy. As digital platforms like Uber, Airbnb, and Amazon disrupt traditional industries, they create new economic structures that are more reliant on gig work and freelance labor. While these platforms can offer flexibility and autonomy, they also create precarious working conditions for many individuals, without access to traditional labor protections such as health benefits, paid leave, or job security.

These evolving socioeconomic impacts highlight the need for a flexible and adaptive approach to policy-making. Policymakers must anticipate the shifting nature of work and labor markets as new technologies converge and develop strategies to address challenges like job displacement, income inequality, and access to opportunity. This could involve investment in workforce retraining, the development of universal basic income programs, or the implementation of new regulations to ensure that workers in the gig economy are protected.

Additionally, the convergence of technologies has implications for global inequality. Access to advanced technologies is often limited by factors such as infrastructure, education, and economic resources. As a result, countries that are unable to fully participate in the global technological race may fall further behind, exacerbating the digital divide. Ensuring that emerging technologies are inclusive and accessible to all nations will require significant investments in infrastructure, education, and international cooperation.

3.4.4. *Adaptive Governance and Real-time Policy-making*

Given the dynamic and complex nature of technological convergence, traditional models of governance and policymaking are often inadequate. Instead, policymakers must adopt more adaptive and flexible approaches that can respond to emerging challenges in real time. This includes the ability to quickly evaluate the potential risks and benefits of new technologies, and to adjust policies accordingly.

One promising model is the concept of "real-time policy-making," where policymakers continuously monitor and adjust regulations based on the evolving landscape of technological convergence. Real-time policy-making requires the involvement of multiple stakeholders, including technologists, policymakers, ethicists, and the public. It also necessitates a strong data-driven approach, where decisions are informed by the latest evidence and insights.

For example, regulators may need to address the emergence of new AI technologies that are capable of producing deepfakes — manipulated media that is virtually indistinguishable from reality. The rapid spread of deepfakes could lead to widespread misinformation, manipulation, and social unrest. In this case, real-time policy-making would involve implementing regulatory measures to detect and mitigate the impact of deepfakes while fostering innovation in AI technologies. Additionally, such policies would need to be flexible enough to evolve as new forms of media manipulation emerge.

As technologies continue to evolve, adaptive governance models will become increasingly important. Policymakers must be proactive in identifying potential risks and creating safeguards while allowing space for innovation and growth.

The convergence of emerging technologies presents both exciting opportunities and significant challenges. Understanding the dynamics of technological convergence from a systems perspective is crucial to managing the risks and maximizing the benefits of these innovations. By embracing flexible regulatory frameworks, fostering international cooperation, and adopting real-time policy-making approaches, societies can harness the power of technological convergence while addressing the ethical, social, and economic implications that arise. This adaptive approach to governance will be key to ensuring that the promises of emerging technologies are realized in ways that benefit all members of society, while minimizing their potential harms.

Table 3.4 provides a summary of key aspects and lessons for decision makers in understanding the dynamic perspective of technological convergence and its socioeconomic implications. This table highlights the multidimensional challenges and opportunities arising from the interplay of emerging technologies and underscores actionable insights for policymakers and stakeholders.

3.5. Conclusion

Emerging technologies are undeniably reshaping the fabric of society, bringing with them both transformative opportunities and significant challenges. The rapid pace at which innovations like AI, blockchain, quantum computing, and IoT are being developed and integrated into everyday life highlights the profound impact these technologies are having across industries, economies, and cultures. From enhancing productivity and improving the quality of life to creating new avenues for economic growth, these technologies are poised to address some of the most pressing global issues. However, alongside these advancements lie complex concerns that require careful thought and deliberation, particularly in the realms of socioeconomic implications, ethical considerations, and technological convergence.

One of the primary challenges of emerging technologies lies in their unpredictable socioeconomic effects. While they have the potential to revolutionize industries, they can also disrupt existing economic structures and labor markets. Automation and AI, for instance, are replacing traditional jobs, leading to concerns about job displacement and growing income inequality. The dynamic and evolving nature of these technologies further complicates the formulation of effective policies to manage these changes. Policymakers must consider the full spectrum of their implications, from worker displacement to the digital divide, and develop adaptive strategies to mitigate negative outcomes while harnessing the technologies' potential.

Ethical concerns are another key aspect of emerging technologies. From the potential for bias in AI algorithms to the risks associated with the use of blockchain and cryptocurrencies in illicit activities, the ethical implications are wide-ranging and multi-faceted. Technologies like AI, which are increasingly integrated into decision-making processes, must be developed and deployed responsibly to avoid reinforcing social inequalities or compromising human rights. Similarly, technologies such as blockchain, which promise to disrupt industries by offering decentralization and transparency, must be regulated to prevent misuse, such as money laundering or tax evasion. These concerns highlight the need for comprehensive ethical

Table 3.4. Key Aspects of Technological Convergence and Insights for Decision Makers.

Key Aspect	**Description**	**Key Insights and Lessons for Decision Makers**
Dynamic Nature	Technological convergence is complex and non-linear, influenced by interdependent technological, social, and economic factors.	Recognize the unpredictability of technological interactions and adopt systems-thinking approaches to anticipate unintended consequences.
Non-linear Dynamics	Interactions among technologies like AI, IoT, and 5G can lead to rapid, unexpected shifts in capabilities and societal impacts.	Monitor the interplay of technologies to mitigate compound risks, such as cybersecurity threats, while leveraging opportunities for urban management, healthcare, and other domains.
Feedback Loops	Positive loops drive innovation, while negative loops act as checks, potentially slowing progress or revealing ethical and societal challenges.	Encourage virtuous cycles of innovation while addressing risks like over-surveillance, cybersecurity threats, and ethical dilemmas through proactive regulation and public engagement.
Socioeconomic Implications	Impacts labor markets, economic structures, and global inequality through AI, automation, and digital platforms.	Develop adaptive policies to address job displacement, income inequality, and the digital divide. Invest in retraining, ensure labor protection for gig workers, and foster international collaboration for equitable access to technology.
Adaptive Governance	Traditional policymaking is often inadequate for the pace of technological change; real-time policy-making is essential.	Implement flexible, evidence-based regulations with continuous monitoring. Engage diverse stakeholders in governance processes to address risks like misinformation, privacy violations, and environmental impacts while encouraging innovation.
Global Perspective	Access to advanced technologies varies, widening the digital divide and global inequality.	Support global cooperation, infrastructure development, and technology education to ensure inclusive participation in technological advancements, reducing disparities among nations.
Ethical Considerations	Ethical concerns, such as privacy erosion and societal surveillance, intensify with technological convergence.	Establish ethical frameworks that guide innovation, emphasizing transparency, accountability, and societal values to build trust and safeguard individual rights.

frameworks and regulatory measures that balance innovation with responsibility, ensuring that emerging technologies serve the greater good without compromising societal values.

The phenomenon of technological convergence further complicates these challenges. The merging of different technological domains, such as AI, IoT, and blockchain, creates opportunities for groundbreaking innovation but also introduces new risks. The interaction between these technologies is not linear, and the convergence can create feedback loops that accelerate or amplify both positive outcomes and unintended consequences. For example, the convergence of AI and IoT in smart cities has the potential to improve urban management and efficiency but also opens up vulnerabilities in terms of cybersecurity and privacy risks. Policymakers and stakeholders must account for the dynamic nature of technological convergence, taking a systems-thinking approach that considers how these technologies interact and how their combined impact may evolve over time.

To navigate this complex landscape, it is crucial for stakeholders — technologists, policymakers, ethicists, and society at large — to engage in interdisciplinary collaboration. The development of emerging technologies cannot be left solely to the technologists; input from a wide range of stakeholders is necessary to ensure that the technologies are developed and deployed in ways that are socially responsible and equitable. Proactive policy-making is essential to address the risks posed by emerging technologies, and policies must be flexible enough to adapt to the rapid pace of change. This dynamic and collaborative approach to governance will be vital in ensuring that emerging technologies lead to positive societal outcomes, rather than exacerbating existing inequalities or creating new risks.

Finally, as these technologies continue to evolve, an ongoing dialogue between all stakeholders is essential. This dialogue should be open, transparent, and inclusive, ensuring that the diverse perspectives of society are taken into account in the decision-making process. Only through such collective efforts can we hope to navigate the challenges posed by emerging technologies while ensuring that their benefits are maximized. In this way, we can foster a future where technology works not just for innovation's sake but for the betterment of society as a whole. The dynamic nature of these developments requires that we remain vigilant, adaptable, and forward-thinking, ensuring that we are ready to tackle the challenges and seize the opportunities that will shape the future of emerging technologies.

References

Acemoglu, D., & Restrepo, P. (2020). Robots and jobs: Evidence from US labor markets. Journal of Political Economy, 128(6), 2188–2244.

Arthur, W. B. (2009). *The nature of technology: What it is and how it evolves*. Free Press.

Autor, D. H. (2015). Why are there still so many jobs? The history and future of workplace automation. *Journal of Economic Perspectives*, 29(3), 3–30.

Bernstein, D. J., & Lange, T. (2017). Post-quantum cryptography. *Nature*, 549(7671), 188–194.

Borgia, E. (2014). The Internet of Things vision: Key features, applications, and open issues. *Computer Communications*, 54, 1–31.

Brynjolfsson, E., & McAfee, A. (2014). *The second machine age: Work, progress, and prosperity in a time of brilliant technologies*. W. W. Norton & Company.

Floridi, L., Taddeo, M., & Moor, J. H. (2018). *The ethics of information: A handbook for the philosophical and social debates*. Oxford University Press.

Kalleberg, A. L. (2011). *Good jobs, bad jobs: The rise of polarized and precarious employment systems in the United States, 1970s to 2000s*. Russell Sage Foundation.

Kitchin, R. (2014). The real-time city? Big data and smart urbanism. *GeoJournal*, 79(1), 1–14.

Li, S., Da Xu, L., & Zhao, S. (2015). The internet of things: A survey. *Information Systems Frontiers*, 17(2), 243–259.

Lundqvist, B. (2018). The interface between competition law, patents, and the technological convergence of complex products. *Journal of Competition Law & Economics*, 14(1), 22–52.

Mattern, F., & Floerkemeier, C. (2010). From the Internet of Computers to the Internet of Things. In *From active data management to event-based systems and more* (pp. 242–259). Springer.

O'Neil, C. (2016). *Weapons of math destruction: How big data increases inequality and threatens democracy*. Crown.

Perez, C. (2010). Technological revolutions and techno-economic paradigms. *Cambridge Journal of Economics*, 34(1), 185–202.

Qudrat-Ullah, H. (2014). *Better decision making in complex, dynamic tasks*. Springer.

Roman, R., Zhou, J., & Lopez, J. (2018). On the features and challenges of security and privacy in distributed internet of things. *Computer Networks*, 57(10), 2266–2279.

Van Dijk, J. (2020). *The digital divide.* John Wiley & Sons.

Wang, H. (2016). *Emerging smart technologies for critical infrastructures.* Springer.

World Economic Forum. (2020). The Future of Jobs Report. Geneva: World Economic Forum.

Zyskind, G., & Nathan, O. (2015). Decentralizing privacy: Using blockchain to protect personal data. In *2015 IEEE Security and Privacy Workshops* (pp. 180–184). IEEE.

Chapter 4

Adoption and Diffusion of Emerging Technologies

Abstract

Chapter 4 explores the adoption and diffusion of emerging technologies, highlighting the complex interplay of factors that influence these processes. It examines key determinants such as organizational readiness, perceived usefulness, and social influence, while also discussing diffusion models like Rogers' Diffusion of Innovations and the Technology Acceptance Model. The chapter identifies barriers to adoption, including high costs and resistance to change, and proposes strategies to overcome them. A dynamic perspective is introduced, emphasizing the nonlinear and evolving nature of technology adoption and diffusion. This analysis is essential for organizations seeking to effectively implement and benefit from emerging technologies.

Keywords: Technology Adoption; Diffusion Models; Emerging Technologies; Organizational Readiness; Perceived Usefulness; Social Influence; Technology Acceptance Model; Rogers' Diffusion of Innovations; Barriers to Adoption; Strategies for Adoption; Dynamic Perspective; Nonlinear Diffusion; Resistance to Change

4.0. Introduction

Emerging technologies, such as artificial intelligence (AI), blockchain, and Internet of Things (IoT), are reshaping industries and societies at an unprecedented rate. These innovations are not only driving economic growth but also redefining how organizations operate, interact with customers, and create value. As these technologies continue to evolve, understanding the processes of adoption and diffusion becomes critical for harnessing their full potential and ensuring their successful integration into existing systems. The ability to adopt new technologies in a timely and effective manner can be a significant competitive advantage, yet it requires navigating a complex landscape of technological, organizational, social, and economic factors (Rogers, 2003).

This chapter provides a comprehensive exploration of the factors that influence technology adoption, drawing attention to the various drivers and inhibitors that shape the adoption process. The study of technology adoption and diffusion is vital for organizations, policymakers, and other stakeholders seeking to accelerate the integration of emerging technologies. While the technical aspects of these technologies are important, their successful adoption depends largely on the ability of organizations and societies to understand and address the underlying dynamics at play (Tornatzky & Klein, 1982).

One key aspect of this chapter is the exploration of various diffusion models and theories that have been developed to explain how new technologies spread across different populations and sectors. These models provide valuable frameworks for understanding how technologies move from early adopters to the broader market and help identify the critical factors that influence this process (Rogers, 2003). Diffusion theories, such as the Technology Acceptance Model (TAM) (Davis, 1989) and Rogers' Diffusion of Innovations theory, highlight the role of factors like perceived ease of use, relative advantage, and social influence in shaping adoption behaviors. These theories offer insights into how organizations can create conditions that support the widespread adoption of new technologies and maximize their impact.

In addition to exploring these theoretical foundations, this chapter identifies the key barriers to adoption that organizations often face. These barriers can range from technological challenges, such as interoperability and scalability issues, to organizational constraints like lack of resources or resistance to change (Venkatesh *et al.*, 2003). External factors, such as regulatory hurdles, societal attitudes, and economic constraints, also play a significant role in either facilitating or hindering technology adoption (Kline & Rosenberg, 1986).

By understanding these barriers, stakeholders can take proactive measures to address them and create an environment conducive to successful technology diffusion.

A central theme in this chapter is the dynamic and evolving nature of technology adoption. Technology adoption is not a static process; it is characterized by continuous change and uncertainty (Christensen, 1997). As emerging technologies develop, so too do the challenges and opportunities they present. This dynamic perspective emphasizes the need for adaptive strategies that allow organizations to respond to unforeseen shifts in the technological landscape (Schneider & Bowen, 2015). The chapter stresses the importance of flexibility in technology adoption, highlighting how organizations must not only consider current market conditions but also anticipate future trends and potential disruptions.

Moreover, the chapter outlines strategies to overcome adoption barriers and accelerate diffusion. These strategies include fostering collaboration between stakeholders, investing in training and skill development, ensuring adequate funding and resources, as well as establishing regulatory frameworks that support innovation while addressing potential risks (O'Reilly & Tushman, 2004). Emphasizing collaboration among industry players, academia, and government, the chapter suggests that cross-sector partnerships can play a pivotal role in addressing the complexities of emerging technologies and overcoming adoption challenges. By aligning stakeholders around common goals and creating ecosystems that support innovation, organizations can enhance their capacity to adopt and diffuse new technologies successfully (Chesbrough, 2003).

In conclusion, the adoption and diffusion of emerging technologies are complex, multi-faceted processes influenced by a range of factors. Understanding these processes, and the barriers that can impede them, is essential for organizations seeking to leverage the full potential of technologies like AI, blockchain, and IoT. This chapter sets the foundation for further exploration of how to navigate these complexities and implement effective strategies to foster successful technology adoption. It emphasizes that, in a world of rapid technological change, the ability to adapt, collaborate, and innovate will be key to harnessing the transformative power of emerging technologies (Porter & Heppelmann, 2014).

4.1. Factors Influencing Technology Adoption

The adoption of emerging technologies is a multi-faceted process shaped by a combination of organizational, individual, social, and external environmental factors. Understanding these factors is essential for organizations seeking to integrate new technologies effectively and achieve long-term benefits. This section explores key drivers and barriers to technology adoption, supported by theoretical models and practical insights.

4.1.1. *Organizational Readiness*

Organizational readiness is a critical factor in the successful adoption and diffusion of emerging technologies. It encompasses a variety of internal factors that enable organizations to effectively integrate new technologies into their operations. These include leadership support, financial resources, employee skills, and existing IT infrastructure. The degree to which an organization is ready to adopt new technologies directly impacts its ability to adapt to changing environments, innovate, and remain competitive in an increasingly tech-driven world. An organization's readiness serves as a foundation for the adoption process, ensuring that all aspects of the organization are aligned with the technological goals.

In this section, we explore the key components of organizational readiness, illustrating how they facilitate or hinder the technology adoption process. These elements not only influence the rate of adoption but also the long-term success of technological integration.

4.1.1.1. *Leadership Support*

Effective leadership is often regarded as the single most important factor for fostering organizational readiness for technology adoption. Leaders set the tone for how new technologies are perceived within the organization, and their commitment can significantly influence the enthusiasm and involvement of employees.

Vision and Strategic Alignment: Leaders who actively support technology adoption create a vision that aligns strategic goals with technological capabilities. By defining clear objectives and outlining how the technology will help achieve these goals, leaders ensure that the technology adoption process is purposeful and directed. For instance, in a company seeking to adopt AI-driven analytics, leadership must articulate how AI aligns with business goals, such as improving customer service or optimizing operations.

Champions of Change: Effective leaders serve as champions of change, helping to manage the uncertainty and resistance that often accompany new technology initiatives. When leaders publicly endorse and actively engage with new technologies, they signal to employees that adoption is a priority. Moreover, leaders play a key role in addressing resistance by offering support, clarifying doubts, and ensuring that employees understand the benefits of the technology. For example, in the adoption of cloud computing, top management's commitment can reassure employees and stakeholders about the security and long-term viability of the solution.

Driving Organizational Engagement: Leaders influence the adoption process by creating a culture of openness to change. Their actions, such as sponsoring pilot projects, establishing innovation teams, or integrating technology adoption into organizational values, can mobilize resources and inspire enthusiasm across departments. By showcasing early successes and celebrating milestones, leaders reinforce the value of the technology, driving broader engagement across the organization.

4.1.1.2. *Financial Resources*

The allocation of sufficient financial resources is critical for the successful implementation of new technologies. Without adequate funding, the organization may struggle to acquire the necessary tools, systems, and expertise to implement the technology, let alone maintain it over time.

Acquisition and Implementation Costs: Emerging technologies often require substantial initial investment in both hardware and software, which may strain organizational budgets. Beyond purchasing the technology itself, companies must also consider additional costs, such as employee training, system integration, and infrastructure upgrades. Financial resources must be strategically allocated to ensure that the technology is integrated seamlessly and effectively.

Sustaining Technological Investments: Even after the initial investment, ongoing financial resources are required for the maintenance, upgrading, and scaling of technology. Without an established budget for maintenance and future enhancements, organizations may find themselves stuck with outdated technology that cannot meet evolving demands. For example, the adoption of robotic process automation (RPA) may require periodic updates to the software and hardware components, which must be funded to ensure continued functionality.

Overcoming Financial Barriers: Budget constraints often delay the adoption process or result in the abandonment of promising technological investments. Organizations with robust financial planning can explore different strategies to mitigate these challenges. For example, securing external funding or adopting financing models such as leasing, cloud-based services, or pay-as-you-go models can reduce the financial burden. In some cases, organizations can also access government grants or incentives aimed at promoting the adoption of specific technologies, such as renewable energy solutions.

4.1.1.3. *Existing Technological Infrastructure*

A strong and adaptable technological infrastructure forms the backbone of an organization's ability to adopt emerging technologies. Organizations that have made prior investments in their IT systems and ensured compatibility across platforms are in a better position to integrate new technologies smoothly.

Interoperability and Integration: The ability to integrate new technologies into existing systems is crucial. Organizations with modern IT infrastructures and standardized processes find it easier to incorporate new solutions into their operations without significant disruptions. For instance, the integration of IoT devices in manufacturing operations may require real-time data analytics systems. If an organization already has a solid data infrastructure in place, the new technology can be better integrated, leading to faster and more efficient implementation.

Legacy Systems and Compatibility Issues: On the other hand, organizations relying on outdated systems may face substantial hurdles in adopting new technologies. Legacy systems often lack the flexibility and scalability to accommodate the demands of emerging technologies, creating compatibility issues that result in higher costs and extended timelines. For example, an organization with an older enterprise resource planning (ERP) system may encounter difficulties when trying to integrate modern AI-driven applications or automation tools, leading to delays and the need for additional investments to upgrade infrastructure.

Scalability and Future-Proofing: Existing IT infrastructure must also be able to scale as the organization grows and as technology continues to evolve. Scalable solutions allow organizations to expand their technological capabilities without having to overhaul the entire system. For instance, cloud-based platforms offer the flexibility to scale operations and storage capacities according to the company's needs. This scalability is essential for adopting future technologies, such as machine learning or blockchain, which require significant computational power and storage capacity.

Optimizing IT Resources: In some cases, organizations may choose to modernize their infrastructure gradually to spread out the costs and minimize disruption. For example, an organization may begin by implementing cloud services for certain applications before fully migrating all operations to the cloud. This incremental approach allows the organization to learn and adjust its infrastructure in real-time, ensuring that future technology adoption can proceed smoothly.

4.1.1.4. *Industry-Specific Considerations*

The adoption of technology can vary greatly depending on the industry in question. Some sectors, such as healthcare or manufacturing, may face unique challenges or opportunities that influence their readiness for technology adoption.

Manufacturing Sector: In industries like manufacturing, technological readiness is often closely linked to the level of investment in digital platforms. Organizations that have already implemented foundational technologies, such as ERP systems or automated production lines, will find it easier to integrate newer technologies like IoT, AI, and robotics. These technologies rely on robust data collection and analysis systems, which many manufacturing firms already have in place. However, the integration of new technologies may require significant upfront investment in training and infrastructure upgrades.

Healthcare Sector: In healthcare, technology adoption is influenced by the regulatory environment and the need for patient data security. Organizations in this sector must navigate complex regulatory frameworks, such as HIPAA in the United States, when implementing new technologies like electronic health records (EHRs) or telemedicine platforms. As a result, healthcare organizations need not only to ensure technological readiness but also to invest in compliance measures to protect sensitive information.

Retail and E-commerce: The retail industry, particularly e-commerce, has been at the forefront of adopting technologies such as AI-driven recommendation engines, automated customer service bots, and personalized shopping experiences. For retailers, organizational readiness involves ensuring that back-end systems are capable of handling large volumes of data and can integrate with new customer-facing technologies.

In conclusion, organizational readiness is fundamental to the successful adoption and integration of emerging technologies. The factors of leadership support, financial resources, existing technological infrastructure, and sector-specific considerations form a critical foundation that organizations must build on to ensure effective and efficient technology integration. By understanding and addressing these components, organizations can enhance their readiness for future technologies, leading to sustained growth, increased operational efficiency, and a competitive edge in their respective industries.

4.1.2. *Perceived Usefulness*

Perceived usefulness is a crucial determinant of technology adoption, referring to the extent to which individuals or organizations believe that a technology will enhance their performance and bring measurable benefits. It is one of the central constructs in the **Technology Acceptance Model (TAM)** (Davis, 1989), which posits that perceived usefulness significantly influences the decision to adopt a new technology. According to TAM, users are more likely to accept and use a technology if they perceive it to be useful in improving task performance or solving specific challenges. This perception of usefulness plays a pivotal role in organizational decision-making processes, particularly when evaluating potential technology investments.

The perceived usefulness of a technology encompasses various aspects, such as its efficiency, ability to solve problems, ease of integration, and its overall impact on organizational goals. Organizations are more likely to invest in technologies that align with their strategic objectives and that demonstrate clear, tangible benefits over existing solutions. This section will explore the key elements of perceived usefulness, including efficiency gains and problem-solving potential, and discuss how these factors drive the adoption of new technologies.

4.1.2.1. *Efficiency Gains*

One of the most compelling reasons for technology adoption is the promise of **efficiency gains**. Organizations seek out technologies that can streamline operations, reduce costs, and increase productivity. Technologies that promise to optimize processes and eliminate inefficiencies often gain swift acceptance, as organizations continuously strive to maximize their return on investment and minimize resource expenditure.

Productivity Enhancement: The ability of a technology to improve productivity is a primary consideration for organizations looking to adopt new tools. For example, ERP systems have been widely adopted by businesses because they automate and integrate core business functions, leading to smoother workflows and reduced manual interventions. Similarly, AI-driven automation technologies have become increasingly popular across industries, as they help organizations automate repetitive tasks, such as data entry, customer service responses, and inventory management. The efficiency improvements brought by such technologies allow employees to focus on higher-value tasks, leading to increased output and innovation.

Cost Reduction: Technologies that contribute to cost savings are often highly valued by organizations. For instance, cloud computing services have revolutionized how organizations manage IT infrastructure by eliminating the need for expensive hardware investments. Cloud-based solutions also reduce maintenance costs, as service providers handle updates, security, and infrastructure scaling. This reduction in capital expenditures makes cloud computing particularly appealing for small to medium-sized enterprises (SMEs) with limited budgets.

Time Savings: Another significant efficiency gain provided by technology is time savings. For instance, AI-based data analytics platforms can process vast amounts of data far more quickly than traditional methods, allowing organizations to make decisions faster and more accurately. The speed with which decisions are made can have a direct impact on the agility and competitiveness of an organization, as timely responses to market conditions, customer feedback, or operational challenges can differentiate successful businesses from their competitors.

Scalability and Flexibility: Technologies that offer scalability — where they can grow alongside the organization's needs — are also perceived as highly useful. For example, businesses adopting software as a service (SaaS) solutions benefit from the ability to scale their technology needs up or down based on demand. This flexibility ensures that the technology remains useful even as the organization expands or diversifies its operations.

4.1.2.2. *Problem-Solving Potential*

Another key factor in the perceived usefulness of technology is its problem-solving potential. Technologies that address specific organizational pain points or challenges are more likely to be viewed as valuable and, consequently, adopted more readily. The ability of a technology to resolve problems efficiently and effectively is a compelling reason for its adoption.

Addressing Specific Needs: Organizations are often driven to adopt technologies that solve unique, pressing problems within their industry or operations. For example, customer relationship management (CRM) systems provide an effective solution for businesses seeking to better manage their customer interactions, improve customer service, and increase sales. By consolidating customer data, CRM systems enable organizations to offer more personalized services, ultimately enhancing customer satisfaction and retention. Similarly, in supply chain management, advanced analytics tools help businesses optimize inventory levels, reduce lead times, and minimize stockouts, which are key challenges in ensuring operational efficiency.

Improving Customer Service: In many sectors, technology adoption is motivated by the desire to enhance customer service. With the rise of digital channels, businesses are increasingly turning to technologies like chatbots, automated helpdesks, and AI-driven customer support platforms to improve response times and handle customer inquiries 24/7. The ability of these technologies to solve problems related to customer satisfaction and service quality makes them highly attractive for organizations seeking to remain competitive in customer-centric markets.

Operational Challenges: Many organizations face operational challenges that new technologies can help resolve. For instance, in the logistics sector, the introduction of blockchain technology offers a solution to the problem of ensuring transparency and security in supply chain transactions. Blockchain's decentralized ledger system allows for the secure tracking of goods as they move through various stages of the supply chain, reducing fraud and increasing trust among stakeholders. The technology's problem-solving ability — by ensuring data integrity and improving traceability — makes it an appealing solution for organizations dealing with complex, multi-party supply chains.

Customization and Adaptability: Technologies that can be tailored to the specific needs of an organization also enhance their perceived usefulness. For example, businesses that adopt AI-driven marketing automation tools can customize algorithms to target particular customer segments, craft personalized messages, and optimize campaigns in real-time. The adaptability of such tools allows organizations to address diverse challenges, from customer engagement to lead conversion, which adds to their overall value.

4.1.2.3. *Measurable Benefits*

A key aspect of perceived usefulness is the ability of the technology to demonstrate **measurable benefits**. Organizations are more likely to adopt a technology if they can clearly see how it improves key performance indicators (KPIs), such as revenue, customer satisfaction, or employee productivity. Measurable outcomes provide tangible proof that the technology delivers value and supports decision-makers in justifying the investment.

Return on Investment (ROI): The ROI of a technology investment is often a determining factor in the decision to adopt it. Tools like AI-powered analytics platforms, for example, allow organizations to track the impact of technology on key business metrics, such as operational costs, efficiency gains, and customer acquisition. The ability to quantify these benefits makes it easier for executives to assess the value of the technology and advocate for its adoption.

Data-Driven Decision Making: One of the major perceived benefits of technologies like business intelligence (BI) systems and AI-driven analytics is their ability to provide data-driven insights that support better decision-making. Organizations that adopt these technologies gain the ability to leverage data to improve forecasting, optimize resource allocation, and identify new opportunities for growth. The measurable improvements in decision-making and operational outcomes make these technologies highly useful and desirable.

Competitive Advantage: In many industries, adopting technologies that improve performance can result in a significant competitive advantage. Companies that adopt innovative technologies early, such as 3D printing, autonomous vehicles, or blockchain, can differentiate themselves from competitors by offering enhanced products or services. This competitive advantage, driven by the perceived usefulness of the technology, often motivates organizations to adopt emerging technologies faster than others in the industry.

Perceived usefulness is a fundamental driver of technology adoption, as organizations are more likely to invest in technologies that they believe will offer clear and measurable benefits. Technologies that offer efficiency gains, solve specific organizational problems, and provide measurable benefits such as improved productivity, cost reductions, or enhanced customer service are perceived as highly valuable. By aligning new technologies with organizational needs and ensuring that these solutions offer tangible improvements over existing systems, businesses can enhance their readiness for technology adoption and successfully integrate these tools into their operations, thereby driving efficiency, innovation, and long-term growth.

4.1.3. *Ease of Use and Compatibility*

The **ease of use** and **compatibility** of a technology are two essential factors that influence an organization's decision to adopt new technologies. According to the TAM (Davis, 1989), the easier a technology is to use and the more compatible it is with existing systems, the more likely it is to be adopted. These factors are particularly significant at the individual level, as end-users and employees are often the ones who interact with the technology on a daily basis. If the technology is perceived as difficult to use or incompatible with established workflows, adoption rates are likely to be low, regardless of the potential benefits it offers (Venkatesh & Davis, 2000).

This section will explore the role of ease of use and compatibility in technology adoption, focusing on how user training, ongoing support, and system compatibility influence successful adoption efforts. These factors are critical in fostering positive attitudes toward new technologies and ensuring that they become integrated into the daily operations of an organization.

4.1.3.1. *User Training and Support*

A key factor in enhancing the ease of use of a technology is providing adequate user training and ongoing support. Employees are more likely to adopt new technologies if they feel confident in their ability to use them effectively (Compeau & Higgins, 1995). Resistance to new technologies often arises from a lack of familiarity or perceived complexity, and this resistance can be mitigated through comprehensive training programs and continuous support (Sharma & Ghosh, 2020).

Training Programs: Effective user training programs are essential for ensuring that employees can quickly learn how to use new technologies and integrate them into their workflows. Training should be designed to address the specific needs and skill levels of different users within the organization. For instance, frontline employees who will use the technology on a day-to-day basis may require hands-on training to understand how to perform tasks efficiently, while management may need training focused on strategic decision-making, data analysis, and interpreting the technology's impact on business performance (Venkatesh *et al.*, 2003).

Training programs should be structured in a way that allow employees to become familiar with the technology at their own pace. Offering interactive tutorials, simulations, and real-time guidance can help employees become more comfortable with the new system, reducing anxiety and resistance. Furthermore, training should not be a one-time event but an ongoing process that provides updates as the technology evolves or new features are added (Kwon & Zmud, 1987).

Ongoing Support: In addition to initial training, organizations should offer ongoing support to help employees navigate challenges that may arise during the adoption process. This support can take various forms, including help desks, online resources, peer mentorship, and troubleshooting assistance (Davis, 1989). The availability of responsive support systems ensures that employees feel supported and can quickly resolve any issues that might hinder their ability to use the technology effectively.

Organizations that provide a combination of training and support systems can create a culture of continuous learning, which encourages employees to embrace new technologies with greater confidence and enthusiasm. This, in turn, increases the likelihood of successful adoption and long-term utilization of the technology.

4.1.3.2. *Compatibility*

Compatibility refers to the degree to which a new technology aligns with an organization's existing systems, processes, and workflows. Technologies that are highly compatible with current infrastructure and practices are more likely to be adopted because they cause minimal disruption to existing operations (Rogers, 2003). On the other hand, technologies that require substantial changes to the way employees work or that necessitate extensive modifications to existing systems may face resistance, which can delay or even prevent adoption (Moore & Benbasat, 1991).

System Integration: One of the most critical aspects of compatibility is the ability of new technologies to integrate seamlessly with an organization's existing IT infrastructure. For example, cloud-based solutions are often designed to work with various ERP systems, making it easier for organizations to implement them without significant disruptions. When new technologies can be incorporated into existing workflows without requiring major changes to processes or data formats, they are perceived as less intrusive and easier to adopt (Chau & Tam, 1997).

Organizations that prioritize compatibility in their technology selection process tend to choose solutions that enhance, rather than disrupt, existing capabilities. For example, when adopting a new CRM system, companies often look for solutions that can easily integrate with existing databases, marketing platforms, and communication tools. This compatibility ensures that the new system adds value without creating redundancy or causing bottlenecks in operations (Davis, 1989).

Legacy Systems: However, many organizations face challenges when attempting to integrate new technologies with legacy systems. Older systems may not support modern interfaces, or the data formats used may not be compatible with newer technologies. In such cases, organizations may need to invest in significant system upgrades or interface development to ensure that the new technology works effectively (Attewell, 1992). These challenges can lead to additional costs, delays, and resistance from employees who are accustomed to using the old systems.

Despite these challenges, many organizations are finding that the long-term benefits of adopting new technologies — such as increased efficiency, improved data accuracy, and enhanced customer experiences — justify the effort and cost of ensuring compatibility (Tornatzky & Klein, 1982). As technology continues to evolve, organizations are increasingly investing in systems that are flexible, scalable, and compatible with a wide range of tools and platforms.

Customization: Another aspect of compatibility is the ability to **customize** a new technology to fit the specific needs of the organization. Technologies that can be tailored to align with the unique requirements of a business are often more appealing (Venkatesh *et al.*, 2003). For instance, businesses may seek customizations in their project management software to accommodate their specific workflows, timelines, and reporting requirements. By ensuring that the technology can be adapted to suit existing practices, organizations increase the likelihood that employees will perceive it as useful and integrate it into their daily operations.

Interoperability: **Interoperability** is a key consideration for organizations adopting new technologies. This refers to the ability of a technology to work well across different systems, platforms, and devices. As organizations increasingly adopt cloud-based tools, mobile solutions, and various software applications, ensuring that these technologies can work together seamlessly is essential. For example, adopting a new customer service platform that integrates with both social media channels and traditional communication methods ensures that all customer interactions are captured and managed in one centralized system. This compatibility across different communication platforms not only improves operational efficiency but also enhances the customer experience (Lyytinen & Damsgaard, 2001).

4.1.3.3. *Impact on Adoption Rates*

Both **ease of use** and **compatibility** have a significant impact on adoption rates. When a technology is easy to use and integrates smoothly into existing systems, it is perceived as less risky and disruptive. This perception of ease reduces the barriers to adoption and encourages users to embrace the technology more quickly (Venkatesh *et al.*, 2003). Conversely, if the technology is complex, difficult to use, or incompatible with existing workflows, users may be reluctant to adopt it, which can hinder its implementation and integration into the organization (Rogers, 2003).

Furthermore, organizations that prioritize ease of use and compatibility often experience a faster return on investment. As employees are more likely to use the technology efficiently, the benefits — such as productivity gains, cost savings, and operational improvements — are realized sooner (Tornatzky & Klein, 1982). In the long term, these factors contribute to a positive feedback loop where successful technology adoption leads to increased organizational confidence in adopting additional technologies.

Overall, the ease of use and compatibility of a technology are key factors in determining its adoption success. By offering user-friendly technologies and ensuring that they are compatible with existing systems, organizations can significantly reduce resistance and increase the likelihood of widespread adoption. Additionally, providing comprehensive training and support systems further enhances employees' ability to effectively use the technology, ensuring smooth transitions and sustained utilization. When these factors are prioritized, technologies are more likely to be integrated seamlessly into everyday workflows, leading to enhanced productivity, reduced disruption, and a higher overall return on investment.

4.1.4. *Social Influence*

Social influence plays a critical role in the adoption of new technologies within organizations. It encompasses various factors such as peer pressure, competitive dynamics, and broader cultural influences. The decisions employees and organizations make regarding technology adoption are often shaped by the behaviors and opinions of others, both within their industry and their immediate social and professional networks. These external pressures can either accelerate or hinder the adoption process, depending on the context.

Industry Trends: In many sectors, companies adopt technologies not only because they perceive a direct benefit but also due to industry trends and competitive pressures. This is especially true in industries characterized by fast-paced innovation, where staying ahead or even keeping up with competitors is crucial for survival. For example, the retail industry has seen widespread adoption of AI-powered recommendation systems. Major players like Amazon have set a standard by leveraging AI to personalize customer experiences, leading other companies to adopt similar technologies to remain competitive. As industry leaders push the boundaries of what technology can do, laggards in the same field often feel the pressure to follow suit. Organizations that delay adoption risk losing market share or becoming obsolete, which often drives faster decision-making in favor of new technologies (Porter & Heppelmann, 2014).

Competitive Dynamics: The competitive landscape significantly influences technology adoption decisions. Companies constantly assess the technological strategies of their competitors and seek ways to gain a competitive advantage. For instance, in the financial services industry, the rise of fintech companies leveraging blockchain, AI, and mobile technologies has forced traditional financial institutions to invest heavily in digital transformations to meet customer expectations and remain competitive. Even in industries where innovation is not always rapid, companies are often compelled to adopt new technologies to keep pace with disruptive market players (Chesbrough, 2003).

Moreover, competitive dynamics can create a sense of urgency among organizations. When competitors successfully implement a new technology that enhances their operational efficiency, customer experience, or profitability, other organizations feel the pressure to adopt the same technology to avoid falling behind. This dynamic is particularly evident in industries like e-commerce, automotive, and manufacturing, where the adoption of automation, robotics, and AI technologies can provide substantial efficiency gains. The fear of losing out on opportunities or market share often acts as a powerful motivator for technology adoption (Brynjolfsson & McAfee, 2014).

4.1.4.1. *Peer Networks*

In addition to broader industry dynamics, peer networks within organizations play a pivotal role in technology adoption. The opinions and experiences of colleagues, both within an organization and across similar organizations, significantly shape individual and group decisions regarding new technologies. Positive feedback from early adopters — those employees who experiment with and embrace new technologies early in the process — often leads to wider acceptance throughout the organization.

Early Adopters: Early adopters are critical in fostering a culture of innovation within an organization. They are usually well-informed, open to change, and willing to take risks on new technologies. Their enthusiasm and successful integration of the technology provide a strong signal to others within the organization that the technology is worth adopting (Rogers, 2003). For example, in a company implementing a new ERP system, early adopters who demonstrate the system's effectiveness and efficiency can encourage others to follow suit. This social proof — seeing peers benefit from the new technology — helps to overcome skepticism and reluctance from other employees (Venkatesh *et al.*, 2003).

Peer Influence and Social Learning: Peer networks often act as informal support structures for technology adoption. Employees are more likely to trust the opinions of their colleagues than external sources such as vendors or management. This is particularly true in environments where technology is seen as complex or disruptive. Peer influence encourages social learning, whereby employees observe and replicate the behaviors of others who have successfully integrated the technology into their work routines. As employees share their experiences and demonstrate the value of the technology through personal success stories, they lower the perceived risk for others and increase the likelihood of adoption across the organization (Bandura, 1977).

Social Norms: In some organizational settings, social norms can drive technology adoption. If the majority of an employee's peer group adopts a particular technology, it can create a sense of pressure to conform. This is especially true in workplaces where innovation and technological proficiency are valued. Social norms surrounding the use of technology often create an environment where not adopting a new tool or system may be seen as falling behind or failing to meet expectations. This can be particularly pronounced in industries where continuous learning and keeping up with the latest technological developments are part of the professional identity.

4.1.4.2. *Cultural Factors*

In addition to peer networks and industry trends, cultural factors play an important role in shaping an organization's technology adoption behaviors. Organizational culture — shaped by shared values, beliefs, and practices — can either facilitate or hinder the adoption of new technologies. For example, organizations with a culture of innovation, openness to change, and a proactive approach to technology are generally more receptive to adopting emerging technologies (Schein, 1992). In contrast, organizations with a risk-averse culture may be slower to embrace new technologies due to concerns about potential disruptions or failures.

Cultural factors influence how technology adoption is perceived and experienced by employees. In cultures where hierarchical decision-making is dominant, technology adoption may be slower because approval must be obtained from higher levels of management. Conversely, in more decentralized cultures, where decision-making authority is distributed, technology adoption may be faster because decisions can be made at the team or departmental level (Kanter, 2004).

Moreover, national culture — shaped by the broader societal values of a country — can also influence organizational behaviors regarding technology adoption. For instance, cultures that emphasize individualism and innovation may be more likely to embrace cutting-edge technologies, while cultures that prioritize tradition and stability may adopt new technologies at a slower pace (Hofstede, 1980).

4.1.4.3. *Implications for Technology Adoption*

The influence of social dynamics — whether industry trends, peer networks, or cultural factors — underscores the importance of social context in technology adoption decisions. Organizations that understand and leverage social influence can create a more conducive environment for technology adoption. Here are several implications:

- **Leveraging Peer Networks**: Organizations should encourage early adopters to share their positive experiences and assist others in the technology adoption process. Facilitating social networks of technology users within the organization can increase the perceived ease and usefulness of new technologies.
- **Industry Monitoring**: Staying abreast of industry trends and understanding competitive pressures can help organizations recognize when and why technology adoption becomes necessary. This awareness allows organizations to anticipate technological shifts and adopt innovations before falling behind.
- **Cultural Alignment**: Organizations must align technology adoption strategies with their organizational culture. In cultures that emphasize collaboration and openness, bottom-up adoption strategies may work best, whereas in more hierarchical organizations, top-down approaches may be more effective. Additionally, fostering a culture of continuous learning and adaptability can make technology adoption smoother.

Social influence — through industry trends, peer networks, and cultural factors — plays a significant role in technology adoption. Organizations are influenced not only by external market pressures but also by the experiences and behaviors of those around them. By understanding these dynamics and aligning their technology adoption strategies accordingly, organizations can enhance the likelihood of successful technology integration. As industries evolve and technologies continue to advance, leveraging the power of social influence can become a critical factor in maintaining competitiveness and fostering innovation.

4.1.5. *Environmental and External Factors*

The adoption of new technologies does not occur in a vacuum; it is significantly influenced by external environmental factors. These include regulatory frameworks, market dynamics, and the broader technological ecosystem. The external environment creates an ecosystem that either facilitates or constrains technology adoption, depending on the specific conditions in place. These factors are crucial in shaping the decisions of organizations when adopting new technologies, as they can determine both the feasibility and the urgency of adoption.

Regulatory Frameworks: One of the most influential external factors in technology adoption is regulatory frameworks. Government policies and industry regulations often set the boundaries within which organizations must operate, and compliance requirements can act as both a motivator and a barrier for the adoption of new technologies. For instance, industries that handle sensitive personal or financial data, such as healthcare and finance, are subject to strict data protection regulations. The introduction of regulations like the General Data Protection Regulation (GDPR) in the European Union has made it imperative for organizations to adopt technologies that ensure the protection and privacy of customer data. This includes adopting data encryption tools, secure cloud computing solutions, and advanced authentication systems to comply with these regulations.

Similarly, the healthcare industry has seen significant technology adoption driven by regulatory pressures, particularly with the HIPAA in the U.S. which mandates stringent privacy and security standards for health data. As a result, healthcare organizations have had to invest in EHR systems, secure data-sharing platforms, and telemedicine technologies to comply with the law. In such cases, regulatory requirements essentially act as catalysts for adopting specific technologies to avoid legal penalties and to maintain operational viability.

On the flip side, the uncertainty of future regulations can delay adoption. For example, in industries like autonomous vehicles and AI, organizations may hesitate to invest in new technologies without clarity on the regulatory framework that will govern their use. As a result, businesses in these sectors are often in a wait-and-see mode until the regulatory landscape is well-defined (Calo, 2015).

Market Dynamics: Market dynamics play a central role in shaping technology adoption decisions, especially in industries where competition, economic conditions, and customer demand are ever-changing. Economic fluctuations can either accelerate or slow down technology adoption, depending on the available resources and the external environment. In times of economic growth, businesses are more likely to invest in new technologies that improve productivity, expand market reach, or enhance customer service. In contrast, during periods of economic downturn, companies may be more cautious with technology investments, opting for cost-reduction and efficiency-improvement solutions rather than large-scale innovations.

Customer demand is another critical driver in market dynamics. As consumers increasingly demand faster, more efficient services, companies are pressured to adopt technologies that meet these expectations. For instance, the retail sector has been transformed by the rise of e-commerce, with businesses adopting technologies such as AI-driven recommendation systems and personalization engines to keep up with changing consumer preferences and to compete with giants like Amazon. Similarly, in the financial sector, the demand for faster, more secure digital transactions has driven the adoption of blockchain technology to enhance payment systems and ensure transparency.

Economic conditions and market competition also influence how urgently businesses feel the need to adopt technology. In industries where speed to market is critical, organizations may be more inclined to adopt new technologies that can help them develop innovative products or services quicker than their competitors. For example, startups in the tech industry often adopt the latest cloud technologies and collaboration tools to accelerate product development and remain agile in the face of competition.

Technological Ecosystem: The technological ecosystem in which an organization operates can significantly impact the rate of technology adoption. The advancement and availability of complementary technologies often create the conditions necessary for the widespread adoption of newer innovations. For instance, the rollout of 5G networks is expected to significantly accelerate the adoption of IoT technologies. 5G networks offer higher speeds and lower latency, which are critical for IoT applications such as smart cities, connected devices, and autonomous vehicles. As 5G infrastructure becomes more widespread, organizations in industries like manufacturing, logistics, and healthcare are more likely to adopt IoT technologies, as the supporting network infrastructure will enable their full functionality (Gantz *et al.*, 2015).

Likewise, the development of complementary technologies can lower the barriers to adopting more advanced systems. For example, AI applications, such as machine learning and natural language processing, have become increasingly viable thanks to advancements in big data analytics and cloud computing platforms. As these technologies evolve and become more affordable, businesses are more likely to invest in AI systems for applications ranging from customer service chatbots to predictive maintenance in manufacturing.

Additionally, the standardization of technologies within the ecosystem plays a crucial role in accelerating adoption. When technologies are built on common standards, integration across different platforms and systems becomes easier, reducing the complexity and costs of adoption. For example, in the enterprise software space, the widespread adoption of cloud-based platforms that follow open standards has made it easier for companies to migrate from on-premise solutions, further accelerating the shift toward cloud computing.

Implications for Technology Adoption: The environmental and external factors that shape technology adoption have significant implications for organizations seeking to adopt new technologies. Understanding and responding to these factors can increase the likelihood of successful adoption and implementation. Key takeaways include:

- **Regulatory Compliance**: Organizations must proactively monitor relevant regulations and align technology strategies to meet compliance requirements. Regulatory frameworks can not only compel adoption but also create opportunities for organizations to enhance their capabilities and improve their competitive position.

- **Economic and Market Conditions**: Technology adoption strategies must be flexible enough to adapt to changes in economic conditions and market dynamics. During times of economic uncertainty, businesses may need to prioritize technologies that provide immediate cost savings or operational efficiencies, while in periods of growth, they may focus on technologies that enable innovation and market expansion.
- **Leveraging the Technological Ecosystem**: Organizations should recognize the interdependencies within the technological ecosystem and adopt complementary technologies that enhance the functionality of new systems. As advancements in supporting technologies make the adoption of new innovations more viable, organizations must remain agile and ready to integrate new technologies as they become available.

Environmental and external factors such as regulatory frameworks, market dynamics, and the technological ecosystem play a vital role in the adoption of new technologies. These factors can either accelerate or hinder the decision-making process, depending on the specific conditions and pressures faced by organizations. By understanding these factors and aligning their strategies with the broader environment, organizations can navigate the complexities of technology adoption and capitalize on the opportunities that emerge from external forces.

4.1.6. *Overcoming Adoption Barriers*

While the potential benefits of adopting new technologies are substantial, numerous barriers can hinder the adoption process. These barriers may stem from internal organizational resistance, external uncertainties, or financial constraints. However, through targeted interventions, organizations can effectively overcome these challenges and pave the way for successful technology integration. Some of the primary barriers to technology adoption include resistance to change, high implementation costs, and uncertainty about ROI. Addressing these barriers requires strategic planning and well-executed tactics.

Resistance to Change: One of the most common obstacles to technology adoption is resistance to change. Employees and stakeholders may be hesitant to embrace new technologies due to fears of job displacement, loss of control, or unfamiliarity with the new systems. This resistance often stems from a psychological attachment to established processes or fear of the unknown, making it difficult for organizations to introduce new technologies without creating friction (Kotter, 1996).

To overcome this, change management is essential. Implementing effective change management practices helps organizations navigate the human side of technological transformation. Key elements of change management include:

- **Stakeholder Engagement**: Engaging stakeholders early in the adoption process allows organizations to identify concerns, address resistance points, and secure buy-in from those affected by the change. Involving employees in the decision-making process can also increase their commitment to the technology and reduce opposition (Kotter & Schlesinger, 2008).
- **Clear Communication**: Transparent communication is critical in alleviating fears and building trust. Employees need to understand the reasons behind the adoption of new technologies, how these tools will impact their work, and what benefits they will bring to the organization and its customers. Regular updates, training sessions, and open forums can facilitate dialogue and promote understanding (Hiatt, 2006).
- **Training and Support**: Resistance can often be mitigated by ensuring that employees feel confident in their ability to use new technologies. Comprehensive training **programs** and ongoing technical support are key to easing the transition. When employees perceive themselves as capable of using the technology effectively, their resistance diminishes (Venkatesh *et al.*, 2003).

High Implementation Costs: The cost of acquiring and implementing new technology is another significant barrier that many organizations face. This can include the upfront costs of purchasing new hardware or software, as well as costs associated with training, system integration, and potential disruptions to operations during the transition phase. SMEs, in particular, may find these costs prohibitive, limiting their ability to invest in cutting-edge technologies (Chwelos *et al.*, 2001).

To mitigate the impact of high implementation costs, organizations can use pilot programs as a way to test new technologies on a smaller, more manageable scale. Pilot programs allow organizations to:

- **Test Technologies in a Controlled Environment**: By running a pilot project, businesses can evaluate the effectiveness of a technology before committing to full-scale implementation. This enables them to assess its impact, identify any issues, and refine processes without the risks associated with large-scale deployment (McNamara *et al.*, 2005).
- **Demonstrate Value**: Pilots can help demonstrate the value of a technology to both internal stakeholders and potential investors. Successful pilot programs often generate measurable results, such as cost savings, productivity gains, or improved customer satisfaction, which can justify further investment in the technology (Keenan, 2002).
- **Mitigate Financial Risk**: Conducting pilot programs can reduce the overall risk of high implementation costs by providing a more gradual, less capital-intensive path toward full-scale adoption. If the pilot proves successful, the organization can justify the additional investment required for full implementation (Agarwal & Prasad, 1997).

By testing new technologies incrementally, organizations can reduce the perceived financial risk, making it easier to secure the necessary budget and commitment from leadership.

Uncertainty About ROI: Another common barrier to technology adoption is the uncertainty surrounding ROI. Organizations are often cautious about committing significant resources to technologies whose long-term financial benefits may not be immediately apparent. The challenge is that new technologies may take time to generate a return, and the risks of not achieving the projected ROI can discourage investment (Tornatzky & Klein, 1982).

To address this uncertainty, organizations can develop incentive structures that encourage adoption and align the interests of employees, managers, and key stakeholders with the successful implementation of the new technology. Some strategies include:

- **Aligning Rewards with Performance**: Providing clear incentives for employees and managers to adopt new technologies can increase motivation and encourage proactive engagement. For instance, performance-based bonuses or recognition programs can be tied to successful adoption, use, and results associated with the new technology (Davis, 1989).
- **Clear ROI Metrics**: Establishing clear metrics for evaluating the ROI of new technologies helps organizations quantify the benefits they are receiving. These metrics can include cost savings, productivity improvements, customer satisfaction increases, or reduced downtime. By establishing these benchmarks early on, organizations can track progress and demonstrate the value of technology investments more clearly (Bose, 2002).
- **Management Support and Leadership Commitment**: When leadership is fully committed to the technology adoption process and demonstrates a long-term view of ROI, it becomes easier to gain acceptance from employees. Leaders who model technology adoption behaviors, emphasize the long-term benefits, and provide adequate resources for adoption, help to set a positive tone that can influence the organization's attitude towards change (Venkatesh *et al.*, 2003).

Balancing Costs and Benefits: Overcoming adoption barriers requires a delicate balance between the costs and benefits of technology. While high upfront costs and uncertainty regarding ROI can pose challenges, the long-term benefits of technology adoption often outweigh the initial hurdles. Some organizations take a phased approach to adoption, where they gradually scale up the technology implementation after a successful pilot phase, ensuring that they can manage costs and assess the value as they progress (Rogers, 2003).

The strategic use of external funding or grants can also help alleviate the financial burden of adoption. Governments, development agencies, and industry partners may offer financial incentives for the adoption of specific technologies, particularly those related to sustainability, efficiency, or innovation. For example, many countries offer tax incentives for companies adopting green technologies, such as energy-efficient equipment or renewable energy systems (Yoo *et al.*, 2010).

Overall, overcoming barriers to technology adoption is an essential aspect of ensuring successful integration of new technologies into organizational operations. By focusing on change management, running pilot programs, and offering incentive structures, organizations can mitigate resistance, reduce financial risks, and demonstrate the long-term value of technology investments. Addressing these challenges head-on ensures that the organization is better positioned to realize the full potential of technological innovations, driving efficiency, competitiveness, and growth in the digital age. Through careful planning and execution, organizations can overcome adoption barriers and position themselves for long-term success in an increasingly technology-driven world.

4.1.7. *Implications for Decision Makers*

For decision makers, understanding the factors that influence technology adoption is essential for crafting strategies that not only facilitate smooth implementation but also maximize the ROI. Effectively navigating the complex landscape of technology adoption requires a deep understanding of internal and external forces at play. Based on the key factors discussed above, several strategic recommendations can help decision makers guide their organizations toward successful adoption:

1. Invest in Organizational Readiness

A critical aspect of ensuring successful technology adoption is the organizational readiness to embrace new technologies. Decision makers should prioritize investments that strengthen the technological and cultural foundations of the organization. This includes:

- **Building IT Infrastructure**: It is essential to invest in robust, scalable IT systems that can seamlessly integrate with emerging technologies. This ensures that the adoption process is smooth, minimizes disruptions, and avoids compatibility issues.
- **Cultivating a Culture of Innovation**: Organizations with a culture that encourages experimentation, learning, and adaptation are better positioned to embrace new technologies. Leadership

should foster an environment where innovation is celebrated, and employees feel supported in their pursuit of new ideas.
- **Strategic Allocation of Financial Resources**: Decision makers should ensure that financial resources are allocated in a manner that balances short-term expenses with long-term technological goals. Funding should be strategically allocated to infrastructure upgrades, employee training, and other adoption-related activities to ensure the organization is prepared for the changes ahead (Venkatesh *et al.*, 2003).

2. Focus on User-Centric Design

Selecting technologies that prioritize user needs is vital for minimizing resistance to adoption and enhancing overall efficiency. Decision makers should ensure that the technologies selected are user-friendly and align well with existing workflows. This involves:

- **Ease of Use**: Technologies that are intuitive and easy to learn can accelerate adoption by reducing the time employees need to become proficient. Decision makers should evaluate potential solutions for their usability and ease of integration into everyday processes (Davis, 1989).
- **Compatibility with Existing Systems**: Technologies that integrate smoothly with the organization's current systems, such as ERP platforms or CRM software, are more likely to be embraced. Decision makers should conduct thorough compatibility assessments to ensure that new technologies do not create disruptions or require costly modifications (Tornatzky & Klein, 1982).
- **Employee Training and Support**: While choosing user-friendly technologies is important, offering comprehensive training and support programs is equally critical. Well-designed training initiatives that focus on practical application can significantly reduce resistance and build confidence among users (Venkatesh *et al.*, 2003).

3. Leverage Social Influence

Social factors, such as peer networks and industry trends, play a significant role in technology adoption. Decision makers can leverage these factors to foster enthusiasm and accelerate the adoption process:

- **Highlight Success Stories**: Sharing success stories and positive experiences from early adopters within the organization or from industry peers can help overcome resistance and build momentum for technology adoption. These success stories serve as evidence of the benefits and can inspire others to embrace the change (Ajzen, 1991).
- **Peer Influence**: Influential employees who are respected by their peers can be used as change agents to promote the benefits of new technologies. Empowering these individuals with the knowledge and tools to advocate for adoption can enhance its acceptance across the organization (Venkatesh *et al.*, 2003).
- **Industry Comparisons**: Decision makers should stay aware of how competitors or peers in the industry are adopting similar technologies. Competitive dynamics often drive adoption, and organizations may face the risk of falling behind if they fail to keep pace with industry trends (Rogers, 2003).

4. Monitor External Trends

Staying informed about external trends, including regulatory changes, market dynamics, and technological advancements, is essential for anticipating challenges and identifying opportunities for adoption. Decision makers should focus on:

- **Regulatory Changes**: Regulatory frameworks, especially those related to data privacy, security, and compliance, can significantly influence technology adoption. Decision makers must keep track of emerging regulations to ensure that their technology choices align with legal requirements. For instance, the adoption of data encryption technologies is often driven by regulations like the GDPR (Bose, 2002).
- **Market Dynamics and Customer Demand**: Technological advancements and shifts in market dynamics, such as the rise of IoT, AI, or blockchain, create new opportunities for innovation. Decision makers should be proactive in monitoring these trends to identify areas where technology adoption can improve efficiency, customer service, and competitiveness (Yoo *et al.*, 2010).
- **Technological Advancements**: The pace of technological innovation often presents both opportunities and challenges. Decision makers should anticipate how advancements, such as 5G networks

or AI integration, could impact their industry and explore ways to incorporate these technologies ahead of competitors to maintain a competitive edge (Chwelos *et al.*, 2001).

In conclusion, for decision makers, successfully navigating the complexities of technology adoption requires a multi-faceted approach. By investing in organizational readiness, selecting user-friendly technologies, leveraging social influence, and staying informed about external trends, leaders can help to ensure that their organizations are well-prepared for the challenges and opportunities that come with technological transformation. With careful planning and strategic foresight, decision makers can drive innovation, improve operational efficiency, and maintain competitive advantages in an increasingly digital world.

By addressing these factors holistically, organizations can maximize the benefits of emerging technologies while minimizing risks, ensuring a smoother transition into the future. Table 4.1 overviews the factors influencing technology adoption, key aspects, and

Table 4.1. Summary of Factors Influencing Technology Adoption and Lessons for Decision Makers.

Factors	Key Aspects	Insights and Lessons for Decision Makers
Organizational Readiness	– Leadership support aligns technology with strategic goals. – Adequate financial resources enable sustained implementation. – Advanced IT infrastructure facilitates seamless integration.	– Prioritize leadership buy-in to champion innovation. – Allocate sufficient budget for implementation and maintenance. – Upgrade IT systems to support emerging technologies.
Perceived Usefulness	– Technologies must demonstrate clear benefits over existing solutions. – Efficiency gains and problem-solving potential drive adoption.	– Focus on technologies that address critical pain points or improve efficiency. – Communicate the tangible benefits to stakeholders to justify investment.

Table 4.1. (*Continued*)

Factors	Key Aspects	Insights and Lessons for Decision Makers
Ease of Use and Compatibility	– User-friendly technologies reduce resistance. – Compatibility with existing systems ensures smoother implementation. - Training and support mitigate adoption challenges.	– Invest in user training programs to build confidence. – Choose solutions that align with existing processes and minimize workflow disruptions.
Social Influence	– Industry trends and competitive dynamics create pressure to adopt. – Peer feedback can encourage or deter adoption.	– Monitor competitor actions and industry benchmarks. – Leverage positive experiences from early adopters within the organization to build momentum.
Environmental and External Factors	– Regulatory frameworks may mandate specific technologies. – Market demand and technological advancements shape adoption trends.	– Stay proactive in tracking regulatory changes to ensure compliance. – Align adoption strategies with market demands and leverage emerging technologies to gain a competitive edge.
Overcoming Adoption Barriers	– Resistance to change, high costs, and uncertain ROI are common barriers. – Pilot programs and incentives can ease transitions.	– Use change management strategies to address employee concerns. – Implement pilot programs to showcase tangible benefits. – Develop incentive structures for adoption.
Implications for Decision Makers	– Holistic understanding of adoption factors is crucial. – Strategies must balance organizational readiness, user needs, and external influences.	– Invest strategically in IT readiness and infrastructure. – Select user-centric and compatible technologies. – Leverage social and environmental insights for informed decision-making.

actionable lessons for decision makers to ensure successful integration of emerging technologies.

4.2. Diffusion Models and Theories

The diffusion of emerging technologies represents a critical phase in their lifecycle, influencing their adoption and long-term success. This process has been extensively studied using various models and theories, which provide valuable frameworks for understanding how innovations spread through populations and organizations. This section elaborates on key diffusion models and theories, emphasizing their implications for decision makers.

4.2.1. *Rogers' Diffusion of Innovations Theory*

Rogers' Diffusion of Innovations Theory (2003) provides a comprehensive framework for understanding how new technologies and innovations spread across a population over time. The theory categorizes adopters into five distinct groups, each with unique characteristics and roles in the diffusion process. Understanding these categories can help decision makers tailor their adoption strategies, ensuring a smoother transition and greater success in implementing new technologies.

- **Categories of Adopters**

1. **Innovators (2.5%)**
   Innovators are the first individuals to adopt a new technology or innovation. They are typically risk-takers, eager to experiment with unproven technologies. Innovators are often well-connected and have a strong technical understanding, enabling them to provide valuable feedback during the early stages of adoption. They are less concerned with the potential risks and are motivated by curiosity and the opportunity to be at the forefront of technological advancements. As opinion leaders, they play a critical role in shaping the perceptions of other groups and paving the way for wider adoption.
   - **Implications for Decision Makers**: Decision makers should focus on providing innovators with early access to new technologies and tools. Engaging them as beta testers or

providing them with resources to experiment can generate valuable insights and build early enthusiasm within the organization.

2. **Early Adopters (13.5%)**
   Early adopters are the next group to embrace new innovations. They are often seen as leaders within their social or professional networks and are more cautious than innovators but still willing to take risks. Early adopters evaluate innovations based on their potential for success and are driven by the desire to maintain a competitive edge. They tend to influence others and bridge the gap between the innovators and the majority. Their endorsement of a technology is often pivotal for its broader acceptance within the organization or community.

   - **Implications for Decision Makers**: Early adopters should be identified and nurtured as champions of new technologies. Decision makers can target them with tailored communications that emphasize the potential benefits and success stories of the innovation, leveraging their social influence to drive further adoption.

3. **Early Majority (34%)**
   The early majority represents a larger, more pragmatic group of adopters who are willing to wait for a technology to prove its value before committing. This group is more risk-averse than innovators and early adopters, and they rely heavily on peer endorsements, evidence of success, and the technology's proven effectiveness before deciding to adopt. They are critical to achieving widespread adoption as they represent a substantial portion of the population.

   - **Implications for Decision Makers**: To gain the trust of the early majority, decision makers must provide clear evidence of the technology's success and practical applications. Testimonials from early adopters, case studies, and data-driven results are essential to convincing this group of the technology's value and reliability.

4. **Late Majority (34%)**
   The late majority is more skeptical and resistant to change than the early majority. Members of this group are typically motivated

by external pressures, such as economic necessity, industry standards, or the realization that competitors have adopted the technology. They tend to adopt innovations only after they have become mainstream and are no longer seen as risky or uncertain. The late majority may also require additional incentives or reassurances to adopt new technologies, especially if they perceive the technology as threatening to existing practices.

- **Implications for Decision Makers**: For the late majority, decision makers should emphasize the technology's low risk, the benefits of not being left behind by competitors, and its compatibility with existing systems. Additionally, providing training and support resources can help alleviate concerns about the technology's complexity and integration into existing workflows.

5. **Laggards (16%)**
Laggards are the last to adopt innovations. They are typically the most resistant to change, often preferring traditional methods and technologies that they are familiar with. Laggards tend to adopt new technologies only when it becomes absolutely necessary, such as when older systems become obsolete or are no longer supported. They are highly skeptical of new technologies and may require substantial persuasion and reassurances before they will consider adoption.

- **Implications for Decision Makers**: Laggards may require more time and targeted effort to adopt new technologies. Decision makers should focus on demonstrating the necessity of adopting the technology, highlighting its long-term benefits, and addressing any fears or misconceptions. A gradual approach to introducing the technology, perhaps starting with minimal-impact applications, can ease the transition for this group.

- **Implications for Decision Makers**

1. **Target Early Adopters as Catalysts for Diffusion**
Early adopters play a pivotal role in driving the adoption process. They serve as role models and influencers within their social circles or professional networks, often encouraging others to adopt new

technologies. By identifying and empowering early adopters, decision makers can accelerate the diffusion process, leveraging their social influence to encourage the early majority and late majority to follow suit.

2. **Develop Tailored Communication Strategies for Each Adopter Group**
   Understanding the distinct needs and concerns of each adopter group is essential for crafting effective communication strategies. Decision makers should tailor their messaging to resonate with the specific characteristics of each group. For innovators and early adopters, the focus should be on the technology's novelty and potential for disruption. For the early and late majority, the emphasis should be on practical benefits, reliability, and success stories. Laggards, on the other hand, may need more reassurance and evidence of the technology's necessity and long-term value.
3. **Provide Evidence-Based Benefits and Real-World Applications**
   To facilitate adoption, decision makers must provide concrete evidence of the technology's effectiveness and real-world applications. Case studies, success stories, and data-driven results can help build trust and demonstrate the tangible benefits of the technology. The early majority, in particular, is highly influenced by evidence of success, and presenting the technology as a proven solution can be key to gaining their buy-in.

Overall, Rogers' Diffusion of Innovations Theory provides valuable insights for understanding how new technologies spread within organizations and society. By recognizing the distinct needs and behaviors of different adopter groups, decision makers can strategically guide the adoption process, ensuring that new technologies are embraced by the right individuals at the right time. Tailoring adoption strategies, empowering early adopters, and providing evidence-based benefits are crucial for achieving widespread adoption and long-term success in technological innovation.

4.2.2. *Technology Acceptance Model (TAM)*

The TAM, introduced by Davis in 1989, is a widely used framework for understanding the factors that influence the acceptance and use of new technologies. TAM postulates that two key psychological factors,

Perceived Usefulness (PU) and Perceived Ease of Use (PEOU), are the primary determinants of an individual's decision to adopt technology. By focusing on these factors, TAM provides a structured approach to predicting the likelihood of success for new technology initiatives, making it highly relevant for decision makers seeking to enhance technology adoption within organizations.

- **Core Constructs of TAM**

1. **Perceived Usefulness**
   Perceived Usefulness refers to the extent to which an individual believes that using a particular technology will enhance their job performance. This factor is crucial because individuals are more likely to adopt technology if they believe it will make their tasks easier, faster, or more efficient. The perceived impact of the technology on productivity and effectiveness plays a significant role in shaping users' attitudes and intentions toward adopting the technology.
   - For example, in the corporate world, employees are more likely to adopt AI-based tools if they see how these tools can automate routine tasks, enabling them to focus on higher-level activities that add more value.
2. **Perceived Ease of Use**
   Perceived Ease of Use refers to the degree to which a person believes that using a technology will be free of effort. If a technology is easy to understand and interact with, users are more likely to adopt it. Complexity and user frustration are common barriers to adoption, especially when new technologies are perceived as difficult to learn or integrate into existing systems.
   - For instance, in a workplace setting, if a new software tool is intuitive and requires minimal training, it increases the likelihood that employees will embrace it. On the other hand, if the tool is overly complex or has a steep learning curve, employees may resist using it, even if it offers significant benefits.

- **Extensions and Practical Applications of TAM**

Since its introduction, TAM has undergone several extensions and refinements. The most notable extensions are **TAM2** and **TAM3**, which incorporate additional factors to better capture the complexity of technology adoption.

1. **TAM2** integrates subjective norms (the influence of others on an individual's technology adoption) and cognitive instrumental processes (such as the perceived relevance of a technology's features), providing a more nuanced understanding of what drives adoption.
2. **TAM3** further expands on these ideas by introducing variables related to the user experience, including computer self-efficacy (the user's belief in their ability to use the technology) and the impact of social influence.

These extensions offer a broader and more comprehensive framework for assessing technology adoption in various contexts.

- **Sector-Specific Applications of TAM**

1. **Healthcare**
   In the healthcare sector, TAM has been widely used to understand the adoption of technologies like EHRs. Healthcare professionals are often required to shift from traditional paper-based systems to digital systems. The perceived usefulness of EHRs (i.e., improving patient care and reducing errors) and the perceived ease of use (i.e., whether the system is user-friendly and integrates well with existing workflows) are critical factors influencing adoption.
   - Studies have shown that healthcare providers are more likely to adopt EHRs if they believe the system will improve patient outcomes and reduce administrative burdens. Furthermore, if the system is easy to use and offers adequate training, adoption rates are higher.
2. **Education**
   In the field of education, TAM has been instrumental in understanding the adoption of e-learning platforms by both teachers and students. For educators, the perceived usefulness of an e-learning platform may center on its ability to deliver interactive content, streamline grading, and facilitate communication with students. For students, ease of use is a key factor, as they need to navigate the platform without confusion or difficulty.

  - The success of e-learning adoption depends largely on the alignment between the platform's features and the educational goals of the institution, as well as the intuitive design of the platform that minimizes the need for extensive training.

- **Implications for Decision Makers**

1. **Enhance Perceived Usefulness**
   Decision makers should focus on clearly communicating how the new technology will enhance users' goals. To improve perceived usefulness, it is essential to highlight the specific benefits the technology offers, such as time savings, increased efficiency, or enhanced decision-making capabilities. Demonstrating real-world applications and success stories can also be effective in showcasing the tangible impact of the technology.
   - For example, when implementing a new software tool, providing data or case studies on how similar organizations have benefited from the technology can help increase the perceived usefulness among potential users.
2. **Reduce Complexity and Improve Ease of Use**
   To improve perceived ease of use, decision makers should select technologies that are intuitive and easy to integrate into existing systems. Ensuring that the technology is user-friendly and doesn't require extensive training can greatly reduce resistance to adoption.
   - Organizations should invest in user-centric design, offering user-friendly interfaces and workflows that match the way employees currently work. Providing ample training and support during the implementation phase is also crucial for ensuring ease of use.
3. **Conduct Pilot Studies**
   Pilot programs are an excellent way to demonstrate the real-world benefits of a new technology. By running a small-scale trial, organizations can showcase the technology's effectiveness, gather feedback, and make adjustments before full-scale adoption. These trials help build trust and demonstrate the technology's potential value in a low-risk environment.

  - For instance, before rolling out an organization-wide change management platform, running a pilot with a specific department can help identify challenges and show other employees how the technology can improve their work processes.

In summary, the TAM provides a valuable framework for understanding the key factors influencing technology adoption, specifically the perceived usefulness and perceived ease of use of a technology. By focusing on these factors, decision makers can enhance the likelihood of successful adoption within their organizations. The extensions of TAM, such as TAM2 and TAM3, offer further insights by accounting for factors like subjective norms and user experience, making TAM an adaptable and comprehensive tool. Understanding the practical applications of TAM in sectors such as healthcare and education helps decision makers apply the model to a variety of contexts. By prioritizing the communication of benefits, reducing complexity, and conducting pilot studies, decision makers can foster a culture of technology acceptance and improve the chances of successful implementation.

4.2.3. *Unified Theory of Acceptance and Use of Technology (UTAUT)*

The Unified Theory of Acceptance and Use of Technology (UTAUT), introduced by Venkatesh *et al.* in 2003, builds upon the TAM and its extensions by incorporating additional dimensions that offer a more comprehensive view of the factors influencing technology adoption. UTAUT integrates constructs from eight different models of technology adoption, creating a unified framework for understanding how and why people adopt technology. The model proposes that four key factors drive technology use: Performance Expectancy (PE), Effort Expectancy (EE), Social Influence (SI), and Facilitating Conditions (FC).

- **Core Constructs of UTAUT**

1. **Performance Expectancy**
   Performance Expectancy in UTAUT is conceptually similar to Perceived Usefulness in TAM. It refers to the degree to which an individual believes that using a particular technology will help

them achieve their desired outcomes or improve performance. This factor has been found to be the most significant determinant of technology acceptance across various studies.

- In practice, individuals or organizations are more likely to adopt a technology if they believe it will provide tangible benefits, such as enhancing productivity, improving efficiency, or reducing costs. For instance, in a corporate environment, employees may be more inclined to adopt a new project management tool if they believe it will streamline workflows and deliver better results.

2. **Effort Expectancy**
Effort Expectancy, akin to Perceived Ease of Use in TAM, measures the ease with which users believe they can use the technology. If a technology is perceived as easy to use and does not require significant effort or learning, users are more likely to adopt it.

   - In many cases, the success of a technology adoption initiative depends on how user-friendly the technology is. For example, a new software tool with a simple interface and intuitive functionality is more likely to be embraced by employees than a more complex one that requires extensive training.

3. **Social Influence**
Social Influence in UTAUT refers to the extent to which individuals perceive that important others (e.g., peers, supervisors, friends, or colleagues) believe they should use the technology. The concept emphasizes the role of social networks and norms in shaping adoption decisions.

   - For instance, in a workplace, employees may be more willing to adopt a new technology if they observe that influential colleagues or their supervisors are also using it. Peer pressure and social norms significantly influence adoption behavior, especially in environments where collaborative work is essential.

4. **Facilitating Conditions**
Facilitating Conditions are the external factors that influence the ability to use a technology, including the presence of adequate resources, training, and organizational support. This dimension

acknowledges that an individual's environment, such as access to necessary infrastructure or technical support, plays a crucial role in determining technology adoption.

 - In the case of mobile technology adoption, an organization's IT infrastructure, availability of technical support, and access to resources such as training programs significantly impact users' ability to effectively use the technology. The presence of reliable support systems makes it easier for users to navigate new technologies.

- **Case Study Application: Retail Industry and Mobile Payment Systems**

In the retail industry, the UTAUT model has been applied to study the adoption of mobile payment systems. Research has shown that the adoption of mobile payments is driven by several factors in the UTAUT model, with Social Influence and Facilitating Conditions playing particularly important roles.

1. **Social Influence**: Retail customers are more likely to use mobile payments if they perceive that others in their social network, such as family or friends, use these systems. Additionally, if key influencers or prominent retail brands promote mobile payments, the adoption rate increases among consumers.
2. **Facilitating Conditions**: The availability of secure, easy-to-use mobile payment systems and the infrastructure to support such technology (e.g., compatible smartphones, secure payment platforms) are essential in encouraging widespread adoption. Retailers must ensure that their systems are robust, secure, and easy to integrate with various payment methods.

Overall, the adoption of mobile payment systems is contingent upon creating an ecosystem where social influences align with enabling infrastructure, ensuring both the technical and social conditions are conducive to widespread adoption.

- **Implications for Decision Makers**

1. **Address Social Influence**
   Decision makers should consider Social Influence as a key factor in their technology adoption strategies. To foster adoption,

involving influential stakeholders — such as senior management, early adopters, and peer leaders — can significantly affect others' decisions. Social proof, such as showcasing successful use cases and endorsements from respected individuals within the organization or community, can help increase adoption rates.

- For example, early adoption by senior management or respected team leaders can send a strong signal to employees that the technology is valuable and worth using.

2. **Ensure Robust Infrastructure and Support**
Ensuring that there are Facilitating Conditions in place is critical for the success of technology adoption. This includes having the necessary technical infrastructure, such as hardware, software, and network support, as well as providing adequate training, user support, and troubleshooting resources.

   - Organizations should invest in comprehensive training programs and maintain a responsive IT support team to help users navigate the new technology smoothly. This support infrastructure can reduce frustration and technical difficulties, which might otherwise deter users from embracing the technology.

3. **Monitor and Address Barriers to Adoption**
Continuous monitoring of technology adoption efforts is essential to address any barriers that may arise over time. Gathering user feedback and performing regular assessments of adoption rates can help identify issues early. By iterating and making improvements based on real-time feedback, decision makers can enhance user experience and increase adoption.

   - For instance, if users are finding a mobile payment system difficult to use or encounter technical glitches, addressing these issues promptly can improve adoption rates. Iterative improvements, such as updates to the system or additional training sessions, ensure that users remain satisfied and willing to continue using the technology.

In conclusion, the UTAUT offers a comprehensive model for understanding the factors influencing technology adoption. By incorporating elements like Performance Expectancy, Effort Expectancy, Social Influence, and Facilitating Conditions, UTAUT provides a holistic view of the adoption process. Its application in sectors like retail, especially in the context of mobile payment systems, highlights the importance of both social and infrastructural factors in driving adoption.

For decision makers, the implications of UTAUT are clear: adopting strategies that address social influence, ensure robust infrastructure, and continuously monitor user feedback can greatly enhance the likelihood of successful technology adoption. By focusing on these areas, organizations can navigate the complexities of technology implementation and create an environment that supports innovation

Table 4.2. Summary of Diffusion Models and Theories with Key Insights for Decision Makers.

Model/Theory	Key Aspects	Key Insights for Decision Makers
Rogers' Diffusion of Innovations	Categorizes adopters into five groups: Innovators, Early Adopters, Early Majority, Late Majority, Laggards. Describes the roles and characteristics of each group in the adoption process.	– Target **early adopters** to catalyze broader diffusion. – Use **tailored communication strategies** for each group. – Provide **evidence-based benefits** to engage the early majority.
Technology Acceptance Model (TAM)	Focuses on two determinants: **Perceived Usefulness** and **Perceived Ease of Use**. Highlights psychological factors influencing adoption.	– Highlight how technology enhances **job performance** (Perceived Usefulness). – Simplify user experience to improve **ease of use** (Perceived Ease of Use). – Conduct **pilot studies** to build trust and adoption.
Unified Theory of Acceptance and Use of Technology (UTAUT)	Builds on TAM with four factors: **Performance Expectancy**, **Effort Expectancy**, **Social Influence**, and **Facilitating Conditions**.	– Address **social influences** by involving key stakeholders. – Ensure robust **technical and organizational infrastructure**. – Use **user feedback** to refine and improve adoption processes.

and growth. Table 4.2 provides a summary of the key aspects of diffusion models and theories, emphasizing practical insights and actionable lessons for decision makers aiming to drive technology adoption.

4.3. Barriers to Adoption and Strategies to Overcome Them

Despite the theoretical insights provided by diffusion models, real-world technology adoption is fraught with challenges. These barriers often stem from organizational, technical, and behavioral factors. This section explores common barriers and strategic approaches to mitigate them.

4.3.1. *Financial Barriers*

One of the most significant challenges organizations face when adopting emerging technologies is the high initial costs. This financial burden can deter organizations, particularly SMEs, from making investments in new technologies, as these businesses often have limited budgets and may struggle to absorb the costs associated with technology adoption. The upfront expenses involved in purchasing software or hardware, implementing new systems, and training employees can be substantial, particularly when the technology is untested or perceived as risky. This financial hurdle is often compounded by concerns on the ROI, especially in uncertain economic climates where the long-term benefits of adopting a new technology may not be immediately clear.

For larger organizations, while they may have more financial resources, the sheer scale of investment required to implement emerging technologies across multiple departments or branches can still be a considerable barrier. Furthermore, the ongoing maintenance costs, including software updates, technical support, and system upgrades, add to the financial burden over time.

This issue is particularly pressing for SMEs, which may lack the resources or access to capital that larger firms can leverage to absorb such costs. SMEs often operate with tighter profit margins and face more stringent financial constraints, making them less inclined to take risks on expensive technological innovations that may not yield immediate returns. As a result, these organizations may delay or forgo technology adoption altogether, potentially missing out on productivity gains, competitive advantages, and efficiency improvements that new technologies can bring.

- **Strategies to Address Financial Barriers**

To overcome these financial barriers, organizations can implement several strategies that make technology adoption more feasible and manageable:

1. **Explore Government Grants and Subsidies for Technology Investments**
   Many governments offer grants, subsidies, or tax incentives to encourage businesses, especially SMEs, to adopt innovative technologies. These financial aids are designed to reduce the financial burden on companies and incentivize them to invest in research and development, technology upgrades, and digital transformation initiatives. Governments may also provide special funding for specific sectors, such as healthcare, manufacturing, or education, to help drive innovation and improve national competitiveness. By tapping into these public funds, organizations can significantly offset their initial technology adoption costs and mitigate financial risks.
   - For example, in the European Union, various programs support SMEs' digital transformation, such as the Horizon 2020 initiative, which provides funding for businesses to adopt advanced technologies. Similarly, in Canada, the Canada Digital Adoption Program (CDAP) provides grants and low-interest loans to help small businesses invest in digital technologies.
2. **Establish Public-Private Partnerships to Share Costs and Risks**
   Establishing **public-private partnerships (PPPs)** is another viable approach to overcoming financial barriers. In a PPP, both the public sector and private organizations collaborate to co-finance the adoption of emerging technologies, share the associated risks, and benefit from the results. This arrangement allows businesses to gain access to state-of-the-art technologies while reducing their individual financial exposure.

- For instance, governments may partner with private companies to provide a technological infrastructure that benefits both parties. In the case of healthcare, public-private collaborations can enable hospitals to implement advanced health information systems or telemedicine solutions, with the government providing financial support and the private sector offering expertise and technology solutions. Such partnerships can help spread the cost of new technologies across both parties, making it more affordable for SMEs and other organizations to adopt these technologies.

3. **Use Scalable Solutions that Allow Incremental Investment**
   Another effective strategy to address financial barriers is to select **scalable solutions** that allow for incremental investment rather than requiring full-scale implementation upfront. Many emerging technologies, especially in the fields of cloud computing, AI, and enterprise software, offer scalable models that allow businesses to start small and expand over time as their budgets and needs grow. This approach significantly reduces the financial burden at the outset and allows organizations to test and implement technologies in a phased manner, mitigating the risks associated with large, upfront investments.

   - For example, cloud-based solutions often operate on a subscription or pay-as-you-go basis, allowing organizations to only pay for the resources they use. This eliminates the need for significant capital outlay for infrastructure and software purchases. Similarly, AI-driven platforms can be deployed incrementally, with businesses opting to start with smaller, pilot projects before scaling up as they begin to realize the value of the technology. Such flexibility in financial commitment enables businesses to invest in cutting-edge technologies at a pace that aligns with their financial capabilities.

By leveraging these strategies, organizations — especially SMEs — can reduce the impact of financial barriers and take advantage of emerging technologies without compromising their financial stability. Addressing these financial challenges is crucial not only for the long-term success of individual organizations but also for fostering broader innovation ecosystems that encourage technological adoption across industries.

4.3.2. *Resistance to Change*

Resistance to change is one of the most persistent challenges faced by organizations when adopting new technologies. Employees often perceive the introduction of new technologies as a threat to their established roles, routines, and job security. The fear of being replaced or rendered obsolete by automation or AI is a significant source of resistance. Additionally, the uncertainty surrounding new technologies, the perceived complexity, and the potential for disruption to workflows can lead to hesitation and reluctance among employees to embrace change. This resistance can manifest in various forms, including active opposition, passive disengagement, or the slow adoption of new systems.

Moreover, employees may also view the introduction of new technologies as an additional burden on their already demanding workloads. The perceived time and effort required to learn how to use new tools, alongside the potential disruption of existing processes, can create frustration and anxiety. In some cases, employees may feel that the costs associated with adopting new technologies outweigh the benefits, especially if they do not perceive an immediate improvement in their work outcomes or job satisfaction.

For organizations, overcoming resistance to change is critical to ensuring successful technology adoption and realizing the full benefits of digital transformation. If resistance is not addressed, it can result in a lack of engagement, ineffective implementation, and, ultimately, a failure to achieve the desired outcomes of technology adoption.

- **Strategies to Address Resistance**

Several strategies can help organizations overcome resistance to change and create an environment where new technologies are embraced:

1. **Implement Change Management Programs to Engage Stakeholders Early and Address Their Concerns**

Effective **change management** is one of the most critical approaches to addressing resistance to new technologies. A well-structured change management program involves engaging stakeholders early in the process, including employees, managers, and other relevant parties, and addressing their concerns before the technology is fully implemented. Early engagement allows for the identification of potential barriers to adoption, such as fear of job loss or concerns about increased workloads, and provides an opportunity to address these issues proactively.

A key component of change management is communication. Transparent, open, and ongoing communication is essential to ensure that employees understand why the technology is being introduced, how it will benefit them and the organization, and what their roles will be in the process. This can help alleviate fears and build trust. Additionally, involving employees in the decision-making process — such as seeking their input on how the technology can be used or what challenges they anticipate — can foster a sense of ownership and participation, reducing resistance.

2. **Foster a Culture of Innovation by Rewarding Risk-Taking and Experimentation**

A supportive organizational culture plays a significant role in overcoming resistance to change. Organizations should foster a **culture of innovation**, where risk-taking and experimentation are valued and encouraged. By rewarding employees who embrace new technologies and experiment with innovative solutions, organizations can create a positive feedback loop that promotes further adoption.

Encouraging employees to step outside their comfort zones and try new technologies can help normalize the process of change. Providing recognition and incentives for individuals or teams who successfully integrate new technologies into their work processes can reinforce the desired behavior. When employees see that innovation is celebrated, they are more likely to adopt new technologies and contribute to the overall success of the transformation.

3. **Use Storytelling and Case Studies to Demonstrate Successful Adoptions and Build Enthusiasm**

Storytelling is a powerful tool in overcoming resistance to change. Sharing real-world examples and case studies of organizations or individuals who have successfully adopted new technologies can help employees see the tangible benefits of change. Hearing about how others have overcome challenges and realized positive outcomes through the adoption of new technologies can motivate employees to follow suit.

Case studies, especially those from similar industries or companies, can serve as persuasive examples of how technology can improve efficiency, streamline operations, and enhance job satisfaction. Additionally, success stories can help demystify the technology and demonstrate its practical applications, making it feel less intimidating. By framing the adoption of new technology as a journey of success rather than a daunting task, organizations can build enthusiasm and reduce fear among employees.

Peer influence also plays a significant role in this process. Employees may be more likely to embrace a new technology if they see their peers or colleagues benefiting from it. As early adopters share their positive experiences, others may be more inclined to try the technology themselves. This peer-driven adoption can create a ripple effect throughout the organization, further reducing resistance and promoting wider acceptance.

By implementing these strategies, organizations can address resistance to change and create a more conducive environment for the successful adoption of new technologies. Effective change management, a supportive culture, and compelling storytelling all contribute to reducing employee apprehension and ensuring that technology adoption is not viewed as a threat, but as an opportunity for growth, innovation, and improved performance. Overcoming resistance to change is crucial not only for the immediate success of technology implementation but also for ensuring that organizations remain adaptable and competitive in the face of ongoing technological advancements.

4.3.3. *Skills Gap and Training Needs*

Many organizations are encountering a significant skills gap when it comes to implementing and maintaining emerging technologies. This issue is particularly prevalent in industries where the rapid pace of technological advancement outstrips the ability of existing workforces to keep up with new skills and competencies. The skills gap often arises due to several factors, including the evolving nature of technology, the increasing complexity of systems, and the growing demand for specialized expertise in areas such as AI, data analytics, blockchain, and cybersecurity. As a result, organizations may struggle to leverage the full potential of these technologies, hindering innovation and competitiveness.

Organizations are also facing challenges in retaining talent with the right technical expertise, as competition for skilled professionals intensifies. Without addressing this skills gap, companies may find themselves at a disadvantage in an increasingly technology-driven market, where the ability to effectively utilize new technologies can be a key differentiator. Moreover, a shortage of skilled workers can lead to delays in project timelines, inefficiencies, and increased costs, ultimately impacting an organization's bottom line.

- **Strategies to Address the Skills Gap**

To overcome these challenges, organizations must adopt targeted strategies to address the skills gap and ensure their workforce is equipped to handle the demands of emerging technologies. These strategies should focus on developing both technical and soft skills, as the effective use of technology requires not only technical know-how but also the ability to think critically, solve complex problems, and communicate effectively.

1. **Develop Comprehensive Training Programs Tailored to Different User Groups**

It is essential for organizations to create customized training programs that cater to various user groups, from technical specialists to non-technical staff. For technical teams, this may involve advanced workshops and certifications in specific technologies or platforms. For non-technical employees, introductory programs on understanding the business applications of these technologies can be valuable. The training should be designed to bridge the knowledge gap while ensuring that employees can apply what they have learned directly to their work.

Furthermore, these programs should be flexible, allowing employees to learn at their own pace, and incorporate hands-on exercises to ensure practical application of the knowledge. Including case studies and real-world examples can enhance learning by showing how the technologies can be leveraged in different contexts.

2. **Foster Continuous Learning Environments through E-learning Platforms and Professional Development Opportunities**

Encouraging a culture of continuous learning is essential to keeping up with the rapidly changing technological landscape. E-learning platforms can offer a wide range of courses that employees can take advantage of, allowing them to acquire new skills and certifications in a time-efficient manner. These platforms should provide both short-term courses that focus on immediate needs and longer-term programs that build expertise over time. In addition to online learning, organizations should support employees in attending conferences, workshops, and other professional development opportunities to expose them to the latest trends and best practices in technology.

Integrating continuous learning into daily work routines can help employees stay updated and develop new skills in response to emerging trends. Offering incentives, such as career advancement opportunities or salary increases for acquiring new skills, can also motivate employees to actively engage in professional development.

3. **Collaborate with Academic Institutions to Create Customized Courses that Address Industry-Specific Skills Gaps**

Partnerships between organizations and academic institutions can play a critical role in addressing the skills gap. By working together, companies can develop tailored academic programs and courses that meet the specific needs of their industry. These customized courses can focus on the particular technical competencies and soft skills that are most relevant to the organization's goals. Collaboration with universities and technical schools can help bridge the gap between academic theory and practical industry needs, ensuring that graduates are better equipped to enter the workforce with the right skill set.

Additionally, these partnerships can help organizations create internship and apprenticeship programs, providing students with hands-on experience in the industry while allowing companies to identify and nurture future talent. Academic collaborations can also be leveraged for research and development initiatives that benefit both parties, particularly when exploring cutting-edge technologies.

4. **Leverage Mentorship and Knowledge Sharing**

Establishing mentorship programs within organizations can help to pass on crucial knowledge from experienced employees to those who are less experienced. These programs can foster a culture of knowledge sharing, where employees collaborate and learn from one another, thus facilitating the transfer of critical skills and expertise. Senior employees can guide junior staff in navigating complex technological environments and help them understand the broader strategic implications of their work.

Organizations can also create knowledge-sharing platforms, such as internal wikis or discussion forums, where employees can document solutions to common problems, share best practices, and discuss emerging trends. Encouraging a knowledge-sharing culture helps to ensure that important information is not siloed and that the workforce as a whole remains agile and adaptable.

5. **Focus on Soft Skills Development**

While technical skills are crucial, soft skills are also indispensable when dealing with emerging technologies. Skills such as problem-solving, critical thinking, communication, and collaboration are key to ensuring that technical solutions are applied effectively and aligned with organizational goals. Training programs should, therefore, also address the development of these soft skills, particularly in leadership, project management, and cross-functional teamwork.

The ability to effectively communicate complex technical ideas to non-technical stakeholders is especially important in ensuring that new technologies are adopted across the organization. Organizations should invest in training that enables employees to bridge the gap between technical teams and business leaders, fostering better decision-making and more effective implementation of technology strategies.

4.3.4. *Security and Privacy Concerns*

As organizations adopt new technologies, concerns around security and privacy become increasingly critical. Data breaches and non-compliance with privacy regulations such as the GDPR are among the top challenges that can impede the adoption of emerging technologies, particularly those involving sensitive data. In many sectors — such as healthcare, finance, and telecommunications — data is not only an essential asset but often contains highly sensitive personal or corporate information. A breach in data security can lead to substantial financial losses, reputational damage, legal liabilities, and a loss of consumer trust, which can severely disrupt an organization's operations.

In addition to the risks associated with data breaches, organizations must navigate an increasingly complex regulatory environment. As privacy laws and compliance standards evolve globally, companies are under growing pressure to ensure that they are up to date with the latest legal requirements. This challenge is compounded by the fact that many emerging technologies — such AI, blockchain, and cloud computing — often involve cross-border data flows and new forms of data collection, making compliance even more difficult.

For organizations to successfully adopt and leverage these technologies, it is crucial to address security and privacy concerns proactively. The following strategies are essential to mitigating risks and building trust with stakeholders, including customers, employees, regulators, and business partners.

- **Strategies to Build Trust**

1. **Invest in Robust Cybersecurity Measures to Protect Data Integrity**

One of the most effective ways to safeguard against data breaches is by implementing robust cybersecurity measures across the organization. This includes deploying advanced security protocols such as end-to-end encryption, multi-factor authentication (MFA), and intrusion detection systems (IDS). Companies should also ensure that their software and hardware infrastructure are regularly updated to protect against vulnerabilities. Cybersecurity practices should be an integral part of the technology adoption process, with continuous monitoring and real-time responses to potential threats.

In addition, organizations should conduct regular security audits and penetration testing to identify potential weaknesses in their systems. A comprehensive incident response plan should be in place, enabling organizations to quickly detect, contain, and remediate any security breaches. In cases where sensitive data is involved, it is essential to have data encryption both in transit and at rest to prevent unauthorized access.

Furthermore, organizations should invest in training employees on cybersecurity best practices, as human error remains one of the leading causes of data breaches. Employees should be made aware of the latest phishing scams, social engineering tactics, and safe data-handling practices to minimize the risk of compromising security.

2. **Ensure Transparency in Data Usage Policies to Build Trust with Stakeholders**

Transparency is a cornerstone of building trust, especially when handling sensitive personal or corporate data. Organizations must clearly communicate how they collect, store, and use data, ensuring that stakeholders are fully informed about data usage practices. This includes providing clear and concise privacy policies that outline the types of data collected, the purposes for which it is used, and the steps taken to protect it. Transparency helps mitigate concerns about data misuse and fosters a sense of control among individuals whose data is being processed.

Additionally, organizations should obtain informed consent from data subjects before collecting their personal information. Consent forms should be easy to understand, offering individuals a clear choice regarding their participation. Privacy policies should also provide details on how users can exercise their rights to access, correct, or delete their data.

It is essential for organizations to be proactive in addressing privacy concerns, especially in industries where data security is paramount. By establishing a reputation for transparency, companies can differentiate themselves in the marketplace, gaining consumer confidence and loyalty. Moreover, transparent data usage practices can help organizations avoid regulatory penalties and potential legal challenges.

3. **Regularly Update Compliance Frameworks to Meet Evolving Regulatory Requirements**

With privacy regulations constantly evolving, organizations must stay ahead of regulatory changes to ensure compliance. This is particularly true for global organizations that must navigate different regulatory environments across various countries. Regulations such as the GDPR in the European Union, the California Consumer Privacy Act (CCPA), and other regional data protection laws impose stringent requirements on how organizations manage personal data. Failure to comply with these regulations can result in heavy fines, reputational damage, and even legal action.

To stay compliant, organizations should establish a comprehensive compliance framework that is regularly updated to reflect changes in the regulatory landscape. This may involve conducting periodic reviews of data privacy policies, updating terms of service, and ensuring that internal practices align with evolving laws. Companies should also stay informed about upcoming legislative changes through industry groups, legal advisors, and regulatory bodies.

Organizations should assign dedicated compliance officers or teams responsible for monitoring regulatory developments and ensuring adherence to data protection laws. These teams should work closely with legal and IT departments to ensure that data handling practices are aligned with compliance requirements. Additionally, regular employee training on the latest compliance guidelines and industry standards is crucial for ensuring that everyone within the organization is aware of their role in maintaining privacy and security.

4. **Implement Privacy by Design and Privacy by Default**

Adopting "privacy by design" and "privacy by default" principles is critical to embedding privacy considerations into the core of technology development and organizational processes. Privacy by design refers to the proactive approach of integrating privacy features into

Table 4.3. Summary of Barriers to Adoption and Strategies to Overcome Them.

Barrier	**Description**	**Strategies to Overcome**	**Key Insights for Decision Makers**
Financial Barriers	High initial costs deter investment, especially for SMEs with limited budgets.	– Seek **government grants** and subsidies. – Form **public-private partnerships** to share risks. – Adopt **scalable solutions** for gradual implementation.	– Advocate for **policy support** to reduce financial hurdles. – Leverage **incremental investments** to minimize upfront costs.
Resistance to Change	Employees view new technologies as disruptive or burdensome to existing workflows.	– Initiate **change management programs** to engage stakeholders. – Promote a culture of **innovation and risk-taking**. – Use **storytelling** to highlight successes.	– Involve employees **early in the process** to build buy-in. – Address concerns with **clear communication and examples**.
Skills Gap and Training	Lack of technical expertise hinders implementation and maintenance of new technologies.	– Create **training programs** for various user levels. – Foster **continuous learning** through e-learning and professional development. – Partner with **academic institutions** for skill-building.	– **Upskill the workforce** to meet future demands. – Design **customized learning pathways** for targeted knowledge gaps.
Security and Privacy	Concerns about data breaches and regulatory compliance (e.g., GDPR) discourage adoption.	– Implement **cybersecurity measures** to protect data. – Ensure **transparency** in data policies. – Regularly update **compliance frameworks**.	– Build **stakeholder trust** through robust security protocols. – Stay ahead of **regulatory changes** to maintain compliance.

the design and architecture of systems, ensuring that data protection measures are built from the ground up. Privacy by default ensures that only the minimum necessary data is collected, and that it is processed with the highest level of privacy protection by default, without requiring users to take additional steps.

By adopting these principles, organizations not only reduce the risk of privacy violations but also demonstrate a strong commitment to safeguarding user data. This approach can also be beneficial for building long-term relationships with customers, who are increasingly concerned about how their personal information is managed.

Thus, by understanding and addressing the multi-faceted barriers to adoption, organizations can effectively leverage emerging technologies to gain a competitive advantage. Integrating diffusion theories with practical strategies ensures a balanced approach to overcoming challenges and achieving long-term success. Table 3 describes a summary of the key barriers to technology adoption, corresponding strategies to address them, and actionable lessons for decision makers to foster successful implementation.

4.4. Dynamic View of Adoption and Diffusion of Emerging Technologies

The adoption and diffusion of emerging technologies are dynamic, evolving processes influenced by numerous interacting factors. These processes are characterized by feedback loops, delays, and nonlinear dynamics that shape the pace and scale of adoption. A dynamic perspective allows researchers and decision-makers to better understand the complexities of technological change and devise strategies to navigate challenges effectively (Qudrat-Ullah, 2014). This section explores key aspects of this dynamic view, organized into sub-sections for clarity.

4.4.1. *Feedback Loops in Technology Adoption*

Feedback loops play a critical role in shaping the trajectory of technology adoption. These loops can be **positive**, reinforcing the adoption process, or **negative**, constraining its spread.

- **Positive Feedback Loops**: Positive loops often arise when early adopters of a technology drive further adoption by demonstrating its value. For example, the adoption of renewable energy technologies like solar panels often benefits from economies of scale, leading to cost reductions and increasing affordability (Qudrat-Ullah & Karakul, 2007). Similarly, network effects in digital platforms, such as social media, create a self-reinforcing cycle where increased user participation enhances the platform's value, attracting even more users.
- **Negative Feedback Loops**: Conversely, negative loops can slow adoption. Regulatory barriers, high upfront costs, or resistance to change among stakeholders can impede the diffusion of new technologies. For instance, the initial adoption of electric vehicles faced challenges such as limited charging infrastructure and high production costs, which created resistance in consumer markets.

Recognizing and managing feedback loops is essential for accelerating technology adoption. Policies that amplify positive feedback (e.g., subsidies or incentives) and mitigate negative feedback (e.g., reducing regulatory hurdles) can significantly influence outcomes.

4.4.2. *Nonlinear Dynamics in Diffusion Processes*

The interplay of multiple factors often results in nonlinear adoption patterns, marked by sudden surges or periods of stagnation. Nonlinear dynamics are particularly evident in the following areas:

- **Threshold Effects**: Adoption rates may remain low until certain thresholds are crossed, such as achieving critical mass in user adoption or achieving technological breakthroughs. For instance, the diffusion of smartphones surged only after the integration of user-friendly interfaces and high-speed internet capabilities.
- **Tipping Points**: Tipping points occur when small changes in one factor disproportionately impact the adoption process. For example, a minor policy shift, such as mandating renewable energy targets, can catalyze widespread adoption of green technologies (Qudrat-Ullah, 2020).

- **Path Dependence**: The trajectory of adoption is often shaped by initial conditions and historical choices, making it difficult to alter once a specific pathway is established. For example, reliance on fossil fuels in energy systems has created a path-dependent structure that resists change despite growing awareness of environmental consequences.

In conclusion, the nonlinear dynamics in diffusion processes highlight the complex and unpredictable nature of technology adoption. Factors such as threshold effects, tipping points, and path dependence create patterns that are not always linear, leading to rapid

Table 4.4. Empirical Evidence of Nonlinear Dynamics in Diffusion Processes Across Industries.

Aspect	Example Companies	Empirical Evidence	Source
Threshold Effects	Apple, Samsung, Huawei	The surge in smartphone adoption occurred only after the integration of user-friendly interfaces and high-speed internet.	Statista (2023); Pew Research Center (2023); Qudrat-Ullah (2020)
Tipping Points	Tesla, Ørsted, Vestas	Renewable energy adoption accelerated due to minor policy shifts like subsidies or renewable energy targets in the EU.	International Energy Agency (IEA, 2021); Qudrat-Ullah (2020)
Path Dependence	ExxonMobil, Chevron, Shell	Long-standing reliance on fossil fuels has created inertia despite increasing investment in renewable energy projects.	BP Statistical Review of World Energy (2023); Environmental Research Letters (2022); Qudrat-Ullah (2020)

shifts or stagnation at different stages. Table 4.4 provides examples of firms for each these factors. Understanding these dynamics is crucial for organizations and policymakers to anticipate and navigate the challenges associated with the adoption of emerging technologies, ensuring more effective and timely integration into society. Recognizing and leveraging these nonlinearity aspects can help guide decision-making processes in a way that maximizes the benefits of technological advancements.

4.4.3. *Interaction with Social, Economic, and Regulatory Environments*

Emerging technologies do not exist in isolation but interact with broader social, economic, and regulatory environments, creating dynamic feedback and influencing their diffusion.

- **Social Influences**: Societal acceptance and cultural attitudes significantly affect technology adoption. For instance, the perception of risks associated with genetically modified organisms (GMOs) has slowed their acceptance in certain regions despite scientific advancements.
- **Economic Drivers and Constraints**: Market forces such as price volatility, competition, and funding availability play critical roles in technology diffusion. Economic incentives, such as subsidies for renewable energy, have successfully accelerated the adoption of solar and wind power in various countries.
- **Regulatory Frameworks**: Policies and regulations can either enable or hinder technological adoption. Proactive regulatory environments that encourage innovation, such as providing intellectual property protections, often see faster adoption rates compared to restrictive regimes.

In conclusion, the interaction between emerging technologies and their broader social, economic, and regulatory environments underscores the complexity of their diffusion. Social influences, economic drivers, and regulatory frameworks create a dynamic interplay that shapes adoption patterns. Societal acceptance, economic incentives, and supportive or restrictive policies all contribute to the pace and success of technological integration. Recognizing these interdependencies allows stakeholders to better understand the external factors that either facilitate or impede the adoption process, enabling more informed decision-making and strategies for promoting widespread technology diffusion.

4.4.4. *Adaptive Strategies for Managing Dynamic Adoption Processes*

Given the dynamic nature of technology adoption, adaptive strategies are necessary to navigate uncertainties and complexities. Such strategies include:

- **Scenario Planning**: Scenario analysis helps decision-makers anticipate a range of possible outcomes and devise flexible strategies. For instance, energy companies often model various scenarios for transitioning to renewable energy under different policy and market conditions (Qudrat-Ullah, Spector, & Davidson, 2008).
- **Iterative Innovation**: Continuous improvement cycles in technology development and deployment ensure responsiveness to emerging challenges. Agile methodologies in software development exemplify this approach, enabling rapid iterations based on user feedback.
- **Stakeholder Engagement**: Actively involving stakeholders throughout the adoption process fosters trust and ensures alignment with user needs. For example, engaging communities in the deployment of smart city technologies can address concerns about privacy and equity.

In conclusion, adaptive strategies are crucial for effectively managing the dynamic and unpredictable nature of technology adoption. By employing methods such as scenario planning, iterative innovation, and stakeholder engagement, organizations can remain flexible and responsive to emerging challenges. These strategies not only enable organizations to anticipate and adapt to various outcomes but also foster collaboration and continuous improvement, ensuring that technological adoption aligns with user needs and broader societal goals. Through proactive adaptation, stakeholders can better navigate the complexities of technology diffusion and enhance the overall success of emerging technologies.

4.4.5. *Future Directions in Adoption and Diffusion Research*

Emerging areas of research can provide new insights into the dynamics of technology adoption:

- **Integration of Systems Thinking**: Applying systems thinking principles can help identify and address systemic barriers to adoption.
- **Big Data and AI in Adoption Analysis**: Leveraging data analytics and AI tools can provide deeper insights into user behavior, market trends, and technology impacts.
- **Cross-Sectoral Collaboration**: Partnerships across industries and disciplines can facilitate the co-creation of solutions tailored to diverse needs.

In conclusion, future directions in adoption and diffusion research are poised to offer valuable insights that can significantly enhance the understanding of technology integration. The integration of systems thinking offers a holistic view, allowing for the identification and resolution of systemic barriers to adoption. The use of big data and AI in adoption analysis promises to unlock deeper insights into user behavior, market dynamics, and the broader impact of technologies. Additionally, cross-sectoral collaboration can foster innovation by bringing together diverse expertise to create tailored solutions that meet the needs of various industries. These emerging research areas will continue to shape the future of technology adoption, providing more effective and adaptive pathways for diffusion. Table 4.5 summarizes the dynamic aspects of the adoption and diffusion of emerging technologies, providing actionable insights for decision-makers to navigate feedback loops, nonlinear dynamics, external environmental interactions, and adaptive strategies effectively.

Table 4.5. Key Aspects and Insights for Decision-Makers in the Dynamic View of Technology Adoption and Diffusion.

Key Aspects	Description	Insights and Lessons for Decision-Makers
Feedback Loops	Positive and negative feedback mechanisms that influence the pace and direction of adoption.	Amplify positive loops through incentives and support mechanisms; mitigate negative loops by addressing barriers such as regulatory hurdles or high costs.
- Positive Feedback Loops	Early adoption drives further diffusion by showcasing value and benefits.	Invest in pilot projects and demonstration initiatives to showcase tangible benefits and attract more adopters.
- Negative Feedback Loops	Challenges like cost barriers or resistance to change can decelerate adoption.	Develop policy instruments to lower adoption costs and address stakeholder concerns early.
Nonlinear Dynamics	Adoption trajectories shaped by tipping points, thresholds, and path dependencies.	Identify and leverage tipping points, such as policy shifts or technological breakthroughs, to catalyze widespread adoption.
- Threshold Effects	Adoption accelerates only after crossing a certain threshold, like achieving economies of scale or technological breakthroughs.	Facilitate market readiness through investments in infrastructure and innovation ecosystems.
- Tipping Points	Small changes that lead to significant shifts in adoption patterns.	Monitor and respond to potential tipping points to maximize strategic advantages.
- Path Dependence	Historical decisions and initial conditions lock in specific trajectories.	Design flexible policies to break unfavorable dependencies and encourage transitions to more sustainable pathways.
Interaction with External Environments	Social, economic, and regulatory factors interact dynamically with technology adoption.	Align technology strategies with societal values, economic priorities, and regulatory frameworks.

Table 4.5. (*Continued*)

Key Aspects	Description	Insights and Lessons for Decision-Makers
- Social Influences	Cultural attitudes and societal acceptance shape adoption.	Engage communities and foster public awareness campaigns to build trust and acceptance.
- Economic Drivers and Constraints	Market conditions, competition, and incentives influence adoption.	Offer targeted subsidies, tax incentives, and funding programs to drive adoption while reducing economic constraints.
- Regulatory Frameworks	Policies and regulations either enable or hinder adoption.	Establish adaptive and innovation-friendly regulatory environments to support emerging technologies.
Adaptive Strategies	Proactive and flexible approaches to manage uncertainties and complexities.	Implement scenario planning, iterative development cycles, and stakeholder engagement to enhance responsiveness.
- Scenario Planning	Modeling various future scenarios to prepare for uncertainties.	Use scenario planning tools to anticipate challenges and devise robust strategies.
- Iterative Innovation	Continuous improvement and rapid adaptation to feedback.	Foster innovation ecosystems that allow for iterative experimentation and refinement.
- Stakeholder Engagement	Collaboration with diverse stakeholders throughout the adoption process.	Build multi-stakeholder partnerships to address diverse needs and perspectives.
Future Research Directions	Exploring emerging tools and frameworks to enhance understanding and practices.	Invest in interdisciplinary research integrating systems thinking, AI, and cross-sectoral collaboration to address dynamic adoption challenges.

4.5. Conclusion

This chapter has provided an in-depth examination of the multi-faceted nature of technology adoption and diffusion, shedding light on the complex factors that influence how technologies are embraced by individuals, organizations, and societies. It has emphasized the importance of understanding the key drivers and barriers to adoption, as well as the various theoretical models that offer insights into the diffusion process. From economic incentives and regulatory frameworks to the social and cultural influences that shape public perception, these elements play a critical role in determining the pace and success of technology adoption.

One of the primary takeaways from this chapter is the recognition that technology adoption is not a linear process. It is characterized by nonlinear dynamics, such as threshold effects, tipping points, and path dependence, which make the diffusion process unpredictable and contingent on a wide range of factors. For instance, the adoption of technologies often experiences slow initial uptake, followed by sudden surges once key milestones — such as reaching a critical mass of users or achieving technological breakthroughs — are met. These nonlinear patterns highlight the need for decision-makers to adopt flexible and adaptive strategies that can accommodate the unpredictable nature of the adoption process.

Moreover, the chapter delves into the interplay between emerging technologies and broader social, economic, and regulatory environments. The adoption of new technologies is deeply influenced by the societal context in which they are introduced. Public perception, cultural attitudes, and societal readiness for change all shape how quickly and widely a technology is embraced. For example, in some regions, the acceptance of GMOs has been slower due to public concerns about safety and environmental impact, despite significant technological advancements. Similarly, economic factors such as price volatility, market competition, and funding availability play a crucial role in determining whether a technology becomes economically viable for widespread use. In many cases, economic incentives — such as government subsidies or tax credits — have proven instrumental in accelerating the adoption of green technologies, such as renewable energy sources.

Regulatory frameworks, too, have a profound impact on technology diffusion. A supportive and proactive regulatory environment, characterized by policies that encourage innovation and provide protections for intellectual property, can significantly speed up the adoption process. Conversely, restrictive policies and regulatory hurdles can stifle innovation and slow down the integration of new technologies. Therefore, policymakers and industry leaders must work collaboratively to create an environment that fosters technological growth while safeguarding public interests.

In light of these complexities, the chapter also outlines several adaptive strategies that organizations can adopt to manage the dynamic nature of technology adoption. Scenario planning, iterative innovation, and stakeholder engagement are essential tools that enable organizations to navigate uncertainties and evolving challenges. Scenario planning allows organizations to anticipate various potential outcomes and prepare flexible strategies to address them, ensuring they can quickly adapt to changing market or policy conditions. Iterative innovation — such as the agile development model used in software development — ensures that technology solutions are continuously refined and improved based on real-time feedback. Additionally, engaging stakeholders early and often throughout the adoption process helps to build trust, ensure alignment with user needs, and mitigate resistance to change.

Looking ahead, the chapter also highlights emerging research areas that are poised to advance our understanding of technology adoption. The integration of systems thinking offers a holistic approach to identifying and addressing systemic barriers to adoption, enabling organizations to tackle complex, interdependent challenges. The use of big data and AI tools for adoption analysis promises to provide deeper insights into user behavior, market trends, and the broader societal impacts of technologies. Furthermore, cross-sectoral collaboration across industries and disciplines can drive the co-creation of solutions that are more tailored to diverse needs, helping to overcome sector-specific barriers and accelerate adoption.

In conclusion, this chapter has emphasized that the successful adoption and diffusion of emerging technologies require more than just understanding the technical aspects of the technology itself. It requires a deep appreciation of the social, economic, and regulatory contexts in which these technologies are deployed. Organizations must be prepared to engage in strategic planning that is both adaptive and proactive, recognizing that the adoption process is dynamic and subject to various external influences. By leveraging insights from emerging research and adopting flexible strategies, organizations can better navigate the challenges of technology adoption, ensuring that they are positioned to harness the full potential of new technologies in an increasingly complex and interconnected world.

References

Agarwal, R., & Prasad, J. (1997). The role of innovation characteristics and perceived voluntariness in the acceptance of information technologies. *Decision Sciences*, 28(3), 557–582.

Ajzen, I. (1991). The theory of planned behavior. *Organizational Behavior and Human Decision Processes*, 50(2), 179–211.

Attewell, P. (1992). Technology diffusion and organizational learning: The case of business computing. *Organization Science*, 3(1), 1–19.

Bandura, A. (1977). *Social Learning Theory.* Prentice-Hall.

Bose, I. (2002). Knowledge management-enabled technology adoption: A multi-criteria decision model. *Industrial Management & Data Systems*, 102(8), 415–422.

Brynjolfsson, E., & McAfee, A. (2014). *The Second Machine Age: Work, Progress, and Prosperity in a Time of Brilliant Technologies.* W. W. Norton & Company.

Calo, R. (2015). *The trade-off between privacy and innovation.* The University of Chicago Law Review, 82(3), 1071–1112.

Chau, P. Y., & Tam, K. Y. (1997). Factors affecting the adoption of open systems: An exploratory study. *MIS Quarterly*, 21(1), 1–24.

Chauhan, S., & Jaiswal, M. (2016). Determinants of acceptance of ERP software training in business schools: Empirical investigation using UTAUT model. *International Journal of Management in Education*, 10(3), 288–305.

Chesbrough, H. (2003). *Open innovation: The new imperative for creating and profiting from technology.* Harvard Business Press.

Christensen, C. M. (1997). *The innovator's dilemma: When new technologies cause great firms to fail.* Harvard Business Review Press.

Chwelos, P., Benbasat, I., & Dexter, A. S. (2001). Research report: Information technology implementation risks and benefits. *Communications of the ACM*, 44(2), 66–72.

Compeau, D. R., & Higgins, C. A. (1995). Computer self-efficacy: Development of a measure and initial test. *MIS Quarterly*, 19(2), 189–211.

Davis, F. D. (1989). *Perceived ease of use and perceived usefulness, external variables, and user acceptance of information technology.* MIS Quarterly, 13(3), 319–340.

European Environment Agency. (2023). *Share of energy consumption from renewable sources in Europe.* Retrieved from https://www.eea.europa.eu/en/analysis/indicators/share-of-energy-consumption-from

Gantz, J. F., Reinsel, D., & Chute, C. (2015). *The impact of the IoT and 5G on business and government.* International Data Corporation (IDC).

Hameed, M. A., Counsell, S., & Swift, S. (2012). A conceptual model for the process of IT innovation adoption in organizations. *Journal of Engineering and Technology Management*, 29(3), 358–390.

Hiatt, J. M. (2006). *ADKAR: A model for change in business, government, and our community.* Prosci.

Hofstede, G. (1980). *Culture's Consequences: International Differences in Work-Related Values.* Sage Publications.

Kanter, R. M. (2004). *Change Masters: Innovations for Productivity in the Global Economy.* Touchstone.

Keenan, P. (2002). The role of pilot programs in technology adoption. *Journal of Technology Transfer*, 27(2), 137–148.

Kline, S. J., & Rosenberg, N. (1986). *An overview of innovation.* In R. Landau & N. Rosenberg (Eds.), *The positive sum strategy: Harnessing technology for economic growth* (pp. 275–305). National Academy Press.

Kotter, J. P. (1996). *Leading Change.* Harvard Business Review Press.

Kotter, J. P., & Schlesinger, L. A. (2008). Choosing strategies for change. *Harvard Business Review*, 86(7–8), 130–139.

Kwon, T. H., & Zmud, R. W. (1987). Unifying the fragmented models of information systems implementation. *In Proceedings of the Eighth International Conference on Information Systems* (pp. 227–251).

Li, X. (2020). Digital transformation and its impact on the adoption of technology in organizations. *Journal of Business Research*, 123, 1–10.

Lyytinen, K., & Damsgaard, J. (2001). What's wrong with the diffusion of innovation theory? *In Proceedings of the 34th Annual Hawaii International Conference on System Sciences* (Vol. 4, pp. 3–12). IEEE.

McNamara, T., McDonald, M., & Brunt, M. (2005). Pilot projects in organizational change: A study of their effectiveness. *Journal of Organizational Behavior*, 26(1), 1–21.

Moore, G. C., & Benbasat, I. (1991). Development of an instrument to measure the perceptions of adopting an information technology innovation. *Information Systems Research*, 2(3), 192–222.

O'Reilly, C. A., & Tushman, M. L. (2004). *The ambidextrous organization: Managing evolutionary and revolutionary change.* California Management Review, 46(4), 8–30.

Pew Research Center. (2024). *Americans' use of mobile technology and home broadband.* Retrieved from https://www.pewresearch.org/

internet/2024/01/31/americans-use-of-mobile-technology-and-home-broadband/
Porter, M. E., & Heppelmann, J. E. (2014). How smart, connected products are transforming competition. *Harvard Business Review*, 92(11), 64–88.
Qudrat-Ullah, H. (2014). *Better Decision Making in Complex, Dynamic Tasks.* USA, New York: Springer.
Qudrat-Ullah, H. (2020). Improving human performance in dynamic tasks with debriefing-based interactive learning environments: An empirical investigation. *International Journal of Information Technology and Decision Making*, 19(4), 1065–1089.
Qudrat-Ullah, H., & Karakul, M. (2007). Decision making in interactive learning environments: Towards an integrated model. *Journal of Decision Systems*, 16(1), 79–99.
Qudrat-Ullah, H., Spector, J. M., & Davidson, M. L. (2008). *Complex decision-making: Theory and practice.* Springer.
ResearchGate. (2014). *Smartphone demand: An empirical study on the relationships between phone handset, Internet access, and mobile services.* Retrieved from https://www.researchgate.net/publication/263281497_Smart_phone_demand_An_empirical_study_on_the_relationships_between_phone_handset_Internet_access_and_mobile_services
Rogers, E. M. (2003). *Diffusion of Innovations* (5th ed.). Free Press.
Schein, E. H. (1992). *Organizational Culture and Leadership.* Jossey-Bass.
Schneider, B., & Bowen, D. E. (2015). *The service organization: Human resources management in service organizations.* Sage.
Sharma, A., & Ghosh, S. (2020). Overcoming resistance to technology adoption: A systematic review. *Journal of Business Research*, 120, 318–331.
Tornatzky, L. G., & Klein, K. J. (1982). Innovation characteristics and innovation adoption implementation: A meta-analysis of findings. *IEEE Transactions on Engineering Management*, EM-29(1), 28–45.
Venkatesh, V., & Davis, F. D. (2000). A theoretical extension of the technology acceptance model: Four longitudinal field studies. *Management Science*, 46(2), 186–204.
Venkatesh, V., Morris, M. G., Davis, G. B., & Davis, F. D. (2003). User acceptance of information technology: Toward a unified view. *MIS Quarterly*, 27(3), 425–478.
Venkatesh, V., Thong, J. Y., & Xu, X. (2012). Consumer acceptance and use of information technology: Extending the unified theory of acceptance and use of technology. *MIS Quarterly*, 36(1), 157–178.
Vishwanath, A., & Goldhaber, G. M. (2003). An examination of the factors contributing to adoption decisions among late-diffused technology products. *New Media & Society*, 5(4), 547–572.

Wiley Online Library. (2020). *A global-scale study on decision making in renewable energy policy adoption and diffusion*. Retrieved from https://onlinelibrary.wiley.com/doi/full/10.1002/eet.2085

Yoo, Y., Henfridsson, O., & Lyytinen, K. (2010). Research commentary: The new organizing logic of digital innovation: An agenda for information systems research. *Information Systems Research*, 21(4), 725–746.

Part II

Dynamic Decision Making in the Age of Technology

Chapter 5

Fundamentals of Dynamic Decision Making

Abstract

Chapter 5 explores the fundamentals of dynamic decision-making, highlighting the limitations of traditional decision-making models in environments characterized by uncertainty and complexity. It contrasts these models with dynamic approaches such as System Dynamics, Scenario Planning, and Adaptive Management, which are better suited to handle the challenges of rapidly evolving technological landscapes. The chapter discusses the crucial roles of uncertainty and complexity in decision-making, emphasizing the need for flexible, iterative processes that allow for continuous learning and adaptation. Through a detailed examination of key decision-making frameworks and tools, the chapter provides a comprehensive foundation for understanding dynamic decision-making in the context of emerging technologies.

Keywords: Dynamic Decision-Making; Uncertainty; Complexity; Traditional Decision-Making Models; System Dynamics; Scenario Planning; Adaptive Management; Decision-Making Frameworks; Iterative Processes; Technological Change; Flexibility; Continuous Learning; Adaptive Decision-Making; Strategic Decision-Making

5.0. Introduction

The pace of technological advancement in the modern world has outstripped the ability of many decision-making models to effectively address the complex and ever-changing nature of the environments in which decisions are made. Traditional decision-making models, such as rational choice theory and linear optimization methods, have long been the bedrock of decision theory. These models operate under the assumption that conditions are relatively stable and that decision-makers can follow a rational, step-by-step process to arrive at the best possible outcome. However, in today's rapidly evolving technological landscape, this static, linear perspective no longer holds. Environments are increasingly characterized by uncertainty, volatility, interdependence, and ambiguity — conditions that make traditional decision-making models less effective.

The modern decision-maker operates in a world where change is constant, disruptions are frequent, and the complexity of systems is continually increasing. These challenges are particularly evident in sectors like healthcare, finance, energy, and technology, where the impact of decisions is not only immediate but also long-term, and where the variables influencing outcomes are often unpredictable. For example, a company's decision to invest in a new technology can have far-reaching effects on its operations, supply chain, and market position, all of which can be altered by changes in regulatory policies, competitive dynamics, or consumer preferences. Similarly, governments facing crises like climate change or pandemics must grapple with a myriad of uncertain variables that span multiple sectors and systems.

5.0.1. *The Shift from Traditional to Dynamic Decision-Making*

Traditional decision-making models are based on several key assumptions: that information is complete and accurate, that the future can be predicted with a high degree of certainty, and that decisions can be made using a relatively fixed set of criteria. These assumptions are often valid in stable environments with clear cause-and-effect relationships. However, when dealing with complex systems or uncertain conditions, these assumptions break down. In dynamic environments, factors influencing decisions are constantly changing, interdependencies are difficult to predict, and outcomes are rarely linear.

Dynamic decision-making, in contrast, embraces complexity, uncertainty, and change as inherent parts of the decision-making process. Rather than assuming stability, dynamic decision-making models acknowledge that the future is inherently unpredictable and that decisions must be flexible and adaptable. This shift requires a fundamental rethinking of how we approach decision-making, moving away from deterministic models toward more fluid and iterative approaches that allow decision-makers to adjust their strategies as new information becomes available.

5.0.2. *The Role of Uncertainty and Complexity in Modern Decision-Making*

Uncertainty and complexity are central themes in dynamic decision-making. In the context of traditional decision-making, uncertainty often refers to the inability to predict future events with certainty. For example, when deciding on a business investment, a manager may face uncertainty about the future state of the economy, the behavior of competitors, or changes in consumer preferences. Traditional decision-making models often rely on probability distributions to quantify and manage uncertainty, assuming that the range of possible outcomes can be sufficiently bounded.

However, in dynamic decision-making, uncertainty is seen not as something that can be eliminated through better data or more sophisticated forecasting methods, but as an inherent part of the decision-making process. In this context, uncertainty is a dynamic, evolving force that requires decision-makers to be flexible and responsive, rather than attempting to eliminate it through prediction. This is where complexity comes into play.

Complexity refers to the interrelationships between multiple factors that influence a decision. In dynamic environments, these relationships are often non-linear, meaning that small changes in one part of the system can lead to disproportionate impacts elsewhere. The interactions between variables are rarely straightforward or predictable, and feedback loops can amplify or dampen the effects of decisions. For instance, a decision in a supply chain to cut costs in one area may inadvertently create inefficiencies in other parts of the system, leading to unintended consequences.

In a complex system, the future is shaped not only by known factors but also by emergent behaviors that arise from the interactions between system components. This makes it extremely difficult to predict outcomes with any certainty. As a result, decision-makers must be prepared to adjust their strategies in real-time, based on the feedback they receive from the system. The recognition of complexity is at the heart of dynamic decision-making frameworks, which emphasize adaptation, iteration, and ongoing learning.

5.0.3. *Key Decision-Making Frameworks for Dynamic Environments*

As organizations and individuals increasingly operate in dynamic, uncertain environments, decision-making frameworks that account for complexity and adaptability are gaining importance. These frameworks offer decision-makers tools and methodologies for navigating uncertainty and making informed choices in environments characterized by rapid change.

1. **System Dynamics (SD)**: System Dynamics is a methodology for modeling and analyzing the behavior of complex systems over time. By focusing on feedback loops, delays, and non-linear relationships, SD enables decision-makers to gain insights into the potential long-term effects of their decisions. SD is particularly valuable in sectors like environmental management, healthcare, and business strategy, where complex interdependencies exist.
2. **Scenario Planning**: Scenario planning is a strategic foresight tool that helps decision-makers anticipate multiple potential futures based on uncertain variables. By constructing several plausible scenarios, organizations can test their strategies against a range of future conditions and develop plans that are robust and adaptable. Scenario planning encourages thinking beyond the "most likely" future and helps decision-makers prepare for unexpected developments.
3. **Adaptive Management**: Adaptive management is an iterative approach to decision-making that emphasizes flexibility and learning. It is particularly useful in managing complex systems, such as ecosystems or public health systems, where uncertainty is high and outcomes are unpredictable. Adaptive management involves monitoring the outcomes of decisions, adjusting strategies based on feedback, and continuously learning from experience.

5.0.4. *Decision-Making Tools for Complex Environments*

In addition to frameworks, several tools have been developed to assist decision-makers in managing complexity and uncertainty. These tools are designed to enhance the decision-making process by providing more sophisticated methods for data analysis, simulation, and visualization.

1. **Simulation Models**: Simulation models are powerful tools for understanding the behavior of systems under various conditions. They allow decision-makers to create virtual environments in which they can experiment with different scenarios and observe the outcomes. Simulation models are particularly useful in fields like logistics, healthcare, and urban planning, where systems are complex and the consequences of decisions are difficult to predict.
2. **Risk Assessment Tools**: In dynamic decision-making, managing risk is crucial. Risk assessment tools help identify potential hazards, evaluate their likelihood, and assess the potential consequences of various decision paths. Techniques such as Monte Carlo simulations and decision trees can be used to quantify uncertainty and assess the risk associated with different alternatives.
3. **Real-Time Data Analytics**: In the age of big data, real-time data analytics provides decision-makers with up-to-date information that can inform decisions as they are being made. This allows for more agile decision-making and enables organizations to respond quickly to changing conditions. Real-time data analytics is particularly valuable in industries like finance, supply chain management, and emergency response.

5.0.5. *The Importance of Flexibility and Adaptability in Decision-Making*

The rapid pace of technological change means that decisions made today will often have unforeseen consequences, requiring decision-makers to be adaptable. Flexibility in decision-making allows organizations to pivot when new information becomes available, ensuring that strategies remain relevant and effective. Decision-makers must foster a culture of adaptability, where experimentation, learning, and feedback are integrated into the decision-making process. This requires a mindset shift from focusing solely on optimal solutions to embracing iterative, evolving strategies that can adapt to changing conditions.

Overall, the world in which we make decisions is increasingly dynamic, interconnected, and unpredictable. Traditional decision-making models, rooted in assumptions of stability and linearity, are ill-equipped to handle the complexities and uncertainties of the modern world. In response, dynamic decision-making frameworks — such as System Dynamics, Scenario Planning, and Adaptive Management — offer more flexible and robust approaches to decision-making. These frameworks emphasize learning, adaptation, and the ability to respond to emerging challenges. By embracing uncertainty and complexity, decision-makers can develop strategies that are resilient, forward-thinking, and capable of thriving in an ever-changing world. As technology continues to advance and systems grow more interconnected, the need for dynamic decision-making will only become more pressing, making it crucial for individuals and organizations to adopt these approaches for long-term success.

5.1. Traditional vs. Dynamic Decision-Making Models

Decision-making models form the foundation for analyzing and addressing problems across disciplines. However, the choice between traditional and dynamic decision-making models often determines the effectiveness of solutions in diverse environments. Traditional models excel in stable and predictable conditions, while dynamic models are indispensable for navigating uncertainty and complexity (Qudrat-Ullah *et al.*, 2008; Forrester, 1961).

5.1.1. *Traditional Decision-Making Models*

Traditional decision-making models, such as the Rational Model and the Linear Model, are grounded in classical theories of management and economics. These models follow a sequential and structured process:

1. Define the problem.
2. Gather relevant information.
3. Identify and evaluate alternatives.

4. Choose the best course of action based on logical analysis (Simon, 1979).

For example, the Rational Model has been widely used in resource allocation within industries like manufacturing and logistics, where operations follow predictable patterns (Mintzberg, 1994). Decision-makers rely on cost-benefit analyses to optimize production schedules or inventory levels. The underlying assumption is that the environment remains stable during the decision-making process.

Similarly, the Linear Model, often applied in strategic planning, assumes that decisions progress along a fixed trajectory with minimal disruptions (Sterman, 2000). For instance, businesses developing long-term marketing strategies may use linear frameworks to project growth based on historical trends.

However, such models face significant limitations in dynamic and uncertain contexts:

1. **Incomplete Information:** Traditional models assume access to comprehensive data, but real-world situations often involve gaps or unreliable inputs. For instance, during the 2008 global financial crisis, reliance on traditional risk assessment models failed to predict cascading failures in interconnected markets (Qudrat-Ullah, 2014).
2. **Limited Flexibility:** Traditional frameworks are rigid, making them ineffective in rapidly evolving scenarios. In the healthcare sector, for example, static models of resource allocation struggled to adapt during the COVID-19 pandemic when demand for medical supplies fluctuated unpredictably (Holling, 1978).
3. **Neglect of Feedback Loops:** These models rarely consider how decisions can alter the environment, creating feedback that impacts future outcomes. In environmental management, for instance, a linear approach to deforestation might focus solely on immediate economic benefits, ignoring the long-term ecological feedback of biodiversity loss and climate change (Forrester, 1961).

While traditional models offer clarity and simplicity, their application is increasingly constrained in contexts where complexity, uncertainty, and rapid change dominate decision-making environments.

5.1.2. *Dynamic Decision-Making Models*

Dynamic decision-making models address the limitations of traditional approaches by incorporating feedback, adaptation, and iterative processes. These models are rooted in systems thinking and emphasize the interconnectedness of variables, which is critical for managing complexity (Sterman, 2000).

One prominent example is System Dynamics, introduced by Jay Forrester in 1961. SD focuses on understanding how feedback loops and time delays influence system behavior. For instance:

1. **Urban Planning:** Cities like Singapore use SD models to optimize traffic flow. By simulating the impact of policies on congestion, planners can predict unintended consequences, such as increased vehicular emissions from rerouted traffic, and adjust strategies dynamically (Qudrat-Ullah, 2014).
2. **Energy Policy:** The integration of renewable energy sources often involves dynamic decision-making models. Policymakers use SD to simulate how investments in solar and wind energy impact grid stability, CO2 emissions, and economic growth. For example, Germany's Energiewende initiative incorporates feedback from energy consumption patterns and market fluctuations to refine its strategies (Forrester, 1961).

Another notable dynamic approach is Adaptive Management, championed by C.S. Holling in 1978. Adaptive Management is widely used in environmental conservation, where ecosystems exhibit nonlinear behaviors and uncertainty.

1. **Wildlife Conservation:** The Everglades National Park in the United States employs adaptive management to balance water usage with habitat preservation. Regular monitoring of ecological indicators, such as wetland health and species populations, informs iterative adjustments to management practices (Holling, 1978).
2. **Climate Change Adaptation:** Coastal cities like Rotterdam in the Netherlands use adaptive frameworks to manage rising sea levels. By integrating real-time data on weather patterns and sea levels, decision-makers continuously adapt flood prevention strategies, such as elevating dikes and enhancing drainage systems (Sterman, 2000).

Dynamic models are also highly applicable in technological innovation. The rapid evolution of AI and ML necessitates decision-making frameworks that accommodate iterative learning. For example:

- **Autonomous Vehicles:** Companies developing self-driving cars employ dynamic models to process real-time feedback from sensors, adapt to diverse road conditions, and improve decision algorithms over time (Qudrat-Ullah *et al.*, 2008).
- **Healthcare Technology:** Dynamic frameworks underpin AI-driven diagnostics, where models adapt to new medical data, enhancing accuracy and reliability in detecting diseases (Forrester, 1961).

– **Key Features of Dynamic Models**

1. **Continuous Learning:** Unlike traditional models, dynamic approaches embrace uncertainty and prioritize learning from outcomes. This is particularly evident in industries undergoing digital transformation, where decision-making evolves alongside technological advancements (Holling, 1978).
2. **Scenario Analysis:** Dynamic models enable decision-makers to explore multiple scenarios and assess potential outcomes. For instance, the financial sector uses stress testing to evaluate how economic shocks impact liquidity and stability (Sterman, 2000).
3. **Resilience:** By anticipating and adapting to change, dynamic models enhance the resilience of systems. In disaster management, for example, dynamic frameworks help allocate resources effectively during crises, such as hurricanes or wildfires (Qudrat-Ullah, 2014).

In conclusion, dynamic decision-making models provide robust tools for navigating uncertainty and complexity. Their focus on feedback, adaptation, and iterative learning positions them as indispensable frameworks for modern decision-making challenges. While traditional models retain relevance in stable environments, the complexities of contemporary systems increasingly demand the flexibility and foresight offered by dynamic approaches. Table 5.1 provides an overview of the key aspects, applications, limitations, and lessons for decision-makers associated with traditional decision-making models, emphasizing their structured approach and constraints in dynamic environments.

Table 5.1. Key Aspects of Traditional Decision-Making Models and Lessons for Decision Makers.

Aspect	Description	Key Insights and Lessons
Approach	Sequential and structured; follows clearly defined steps (define problem, gather information, evaluate alternatives, choose the best course of action).	Traditional models provide clarity and simplicity but lack flexibility for complex and rapidly changing environments.
Underlying Assumptions	Stability, predictability, and complete information.	These assumptions often fail in dynamic contexts, where uncertainty and incomplete information dominate.
Application Areas	Resource allocation, strategic planning, and operations management in stable industries.	Effective in industries with predictable patterns (e.g., manufacturing, logistics).
Strengths	Clarity, simplicity, and logical progression of decisions.	Useful for structured problem-solving and decision-making in stable contexts.
Limitations	1. Incomplete information. 2. Limited flexibility. 3. Neglect of feedback loops.	Decision-makers must recognize these limitations and supplement traditional models with adaptive elements.
Real-World Examples	1. Rational Model in manufacturing for cost-benefit analyses. 2. Linear Model in long-term marketing strategies.	Useful for predictable resource allocation but fails under dynamic or uncertain conditions.
Lessons for Decision Makers	Relying solely on traditional models can lead to suboptimal decisions in complex environments.	Decision-makers should integrate more adaptive and feedback-sensitive approaches in dynamic scenarios.

5.2. The Role of Uncertainty and Complexity

Dynamic decision-making environments are inherently shaped by uncertainty and complexity. These two interrelated factors challenge traditional decision-making frameworks and necessitate more flexible, adaptive, and integrative approaches.

5.2.1. *Uncertainty in Decision-Making*

Uncertainty refers to situations where the outcomes, probabilities, or influencing factors of a decision are unknown or only partially understood. It is pervasive in contexts ranging from business to public policy and crisis management. Key sources of uncertainty include:

- **Incomplete Information**: Lack of sufficient or accurate data.
- **External Unpredictability**: Fluctuating economic conditions, geopolitical shifts, or natural disasters.
- **System Variability**: Intrinsic randomness or variability in dynamic systems.

Real-World Examples

1. **COVID-19 Pandemic**
The global response to COVID-19 illustrated the challenges of uncertainty. Decision-makers had limited data about the virus's transmission, mortality rates, and long-term health impacts. Initial measures, such as lockdowns, relied on assumptions rather than comprehensive evidence. Dynamic decision-making played a pivotal role, as governments adapted their strategies by analyzing real-time data on infection rates, hospital capacity, and vaccine efficacy (Sterman, 2020).
2. **Financial Markets**
The 2008 global financial crisis demonstrated how uncertainty in interconnected financial systems can escalate into systemic risks. Traditional risk models, which relied on historical data and static assumptions, failed to anticipate the cascading effects of subprime mortgage defaults. In contrast, dynamic models incorporating stress testing and scenario simulations helped financial institutions navigate post-crisis recovery (Qudrat-Ullah, 2014).

Lessons for Decision-Makers

- **Scenario-Based Planning**: Decision-makers should prepare for multiple potential outcomes by using scenarios to test the resilience of their strategies. For instance, central banks often simulate economic shocks to determine the effectiveness of monetary policies.
- **Real-Time Data Utilization**: Access to and analysis of live data streams are crucial for making informed adjustments during uncertainty. The integration of AI-driven analytics in industries like logistics and healthcare exemplifies this approach.
- **Iterative Learning**: Dynamic decision-making frameworks encourage continuous learning and course correction, ensuring adaptability in rapidly changing environments.

In conclusion, uncertainty is an inevitable element of modern decision-making, demanding approaches that move beyond static frameworks. By recognizing the inherent unpredictability of dynamic environments, decision-makers can leverage tools such as scenario-based planning, real-time data analysis, and iterative learning to enhance adaptability and resilience. The lessons drawn from real-world examples, such as the COVID-19 pandemic and the 2008 financial crisis, underscore the critical importance of flexible, informed, and proactive strategies. Embracing uncertainty not as a barrier but as a dimension of strategic opportunity enables leaders to navigate complexity with greater confidence and efficacy.

5.2.2. *Complexity in Decision-Making*

Complexity arises when multiple interconnected factors interact in non-linear ways, leading to emergent outcomes that are difficult to predict or control. Such systems often feature feedback loops, time delays, and interdependencies, requiring sophisticated tools and strategies to navigate effectively.

- **Characteristics of Complexity**
  1. **Interdependence**: Decisions in one domain influence outcomes in others. For example, energy policies impact economic growth, environmental sustainability, and public health.
  2. **Nonlinearity**: Small changes can lead to disproportionately large effects, as seen in climate systems or social networks.

3. **Emergent Behavior**: Unintended consequences or outcomes arise from the interactions within the system, such as traffic congestion patterns or market bubbles.

- **Real-World Examples**

1. **Urban Planning**
Complexities in urban planning, such as traffic congestion and housing shortages, require integrated solutions. Cities like Singapore and Amsterdam utilize systems thinking to model urban ecosystems, accounting for population growth, public transport needs, and environmental sustainability. Policies are dynamically adjusted based on simulation results and citizen feedback (Forrester, 1961).
2. **Energy Transition**
The shift towards renewable energy presents a classic case of complexity. Policymakers must balance technological advancements, grid reliability, economic incentives, and public opinion. Germany's *Energiewende* initiative exemplifies dynamic decision-making, as it continuously refines its strategies to address evolving challenges, such as balancing solar and wind energy supply with demand (Sterman, 2000).
3. **Environmental Conservation**
Conservation efforts often deal with ecological systems that are inherently complex. The adaptive management approach in the Everglades National Park, for example, involves iterative adjustments to water management practices based on ecological monitoring, addressing challenges such as invasive species and climate change impacts (Holling, 1978).

- **Lessons for Decision-Makers**

1. **Systems Thinking**: Understanding and mapping interdependencies within a system help decision-makers anticipate ripple effects. Tools like causal loop diagrams and system dynamics simulations are particularly effective.
2. **Holistic Perspective**: Addressing complexity requires considering the broader context and integrating diverse stakeholder inputs. For instance, inclusive policy design in public health ensures that social, economic, and cultural factors are accounted for.

3. **Flexibility and Resilience**: Building systems that can adapt and recover from disruptions is vital. For example, disaster management agencies design resilient supply chains to ensure continuity during crises.

In conclusion, complexity in decision-making presents challenges that demand a deeper understanding of interdependencies, nonlinearity, and emergent behaviors. As demonstrated by real-world examples like urban planning, energy transitions, and environmental conservation, navigating complex systems requires a dynamic and integrated approach. Systems thinking, holistic perspectives, and a focus on resilience are essential strategies for managing complexity effectively. By embracing these tools and frameworks, decision-makers can anticipate unintended consequences, foster adaptability, and ensure that their strategies remain robust in the face of evolving challenges.

5.2.3. *Implications of Uncertainty and Complexity*

Understanding and addressing uncertainty and complexity are critical for effective decision-making in today's fast-paced, interconnected world. These twin challenges shape every aspect of modern organizations and systems, influencing both strategic and operational decisions. While traditional decision-making models rely on structured, linear approaches, they often fall short in environments characterized by rapid change and interdependencies. The static nature of these models makes them unsuitable for addressing dynamic systems where variables are in constant flux.

- **Limitations of Traditional Models:** Traditional models are built on assumptions of stability and predictability, offering clarity in structured environments. However, these models fail to accommodate the nuances of real-world decision-making, where unpredictability, competing priorities, and cascading effects dominate. For example, in global supply chains, a single disruption — such as a natural disaster or geopolitical tension — can have far-reaching consequences, rendering rigid models ineffective.
- **The Value of Dynamic Models:** Dynamic models, in contrast, provide a framework for adaptability and resilience. They integrate real-time data and systems thinking to anticipate and respond to emerging patterns. By employing iterative processes, these models

allow for continuous learning and refinement, enabling decision-makers to adapt strategies in response to new information. For instance, businesses using predictive analytics can anticipate market trends, mitigate risks, and capitalize on opportunities with greater precision.

- **Systems Thinking as a Catalyst:** Systems thinking plays a pivotal role in addressing uncertainty and complexity. By focusing on interconnections and feedback loops, systems thinking helps decision-makers see the broader picture, identify potential leverage points, and avoid unintended consequences. This holistic approach ensures that decisions are not only informed by immediate outcomes but also consider long-term implications.
- **Practical Implications for Decision-Making:** To thrive in complex environments, organizations and individuals must embrace uncertainty as an inherent aspect of decision-making. This involves:
    1. **Data Integration**: Leveraging diverse datasets for more comprehensive insights.
    2. **Scenario Planning**: Exploring multiple possible futures to prepare for various contingencies.
    3. **Agility**: Building mechanisms for rapid response and adaptation.
    4. **Collaboration**: Encouraging interdisciplinary approaches to uncover blind spots and integrate diverse perspectives.
- **Ensuring Robust Outcomes:** By incorporating dynamic models and systems thinking, decision-makers can navigate the challenges posed by uncertainty and complexity with confidence. This approach not only enhances resilience but also fosters innovation, ensuring that decisions are both robust and adaptable. In an interconnected world, the ability to thrive amidst unpredictability is no longer a luxury — it is a necessity for sustainable success.

In conclusion, the implications of uncertainty and complexity are profound in today's decision-making environments. As traditional models fall short in addressing the unpredictable and interconnected nature of modern systems, dynamic models that embrace adaptability and continuous learning offer a far more effective approach. By leveraging systems thinking, real-time data, and scenario planning, decision-makers can better navigate the complexities of global challenges. The ability to integrate diverse perspectives, anticipate emerging trends, and remain agile is crucial for ensuring resilient and sustainable outcomes. Ultimately, the capacity to thrive in the face of uncertainty and complexity is not just a strategic advantage but a necessity for success in an increasingly volatile world. Table 5.2 provides a summary of the key aspects of uncertainty and complexity in decision-making, along with the insights and lessons for decision-makers to enhance adaptability, resilience, and strategic success in dynamic environments.

5.3. Key Decision-Making Frameworks and Tools

In an era of rapid technological advancements, interconnected global systems, and ever-evolving challenges, effective decision-making requires robust frameworks and tools. Traditional linear approaches often fail to capture the dynamics of complex systems, leading to sub-optimal outcomes. This section explores three key frameworks that empower decision-makers to navigate complexity: System Dynamics, Scenario Planning, and Adaptive Management.

5.3.1. *System Dynamics (SD)*

SD is a robust and versatile framework that models, simulates, and analyzes the behavior of complex systems over time. Developed by Jay Forrester in the 1950s, it integrates feedback loops, delays, and non-linear interactions to provide a holistic view of interconnected systems (Forrester, 1961). By constructing causal loop diagrams (CLDs) and stock-and-flow models, SD equips decision-makers to identify leverage points, predict outcomes of interventions, and make informed decisions that account for the system's long-term behavior.

This methodology is particularly suited for addressing multi-faceted problems where changes in one part of the system cascade to others. Its applications span diverse fields, including technology management, urban planning, healthcare, and environmental policy.

- **Applications in Technology Management**

In technology management, SD proves invaluable for understanding and navigating the intricate relationships between technological innovation, market dynamics, regulatory changes, and societal adoption.

Table 5.2. Summary of Key Insights and Lessons for Decision-Makers on the Role of Uncertainty and Complexity.

Aspect	Key Insights	Lessons for Decision-Makers
Uncertainty in Decision-Making	– Involves incomplete information, external unpredictability, and system variability.	– Scenario-based planning to prepare for multiple outcomes.
	– Results from factors like economic conditions, geopolitical shifts, or natural disasters.	– Utilize real-time data to make informed decisions.
	– Challenges demonstrated by events like the COVID-19 pandemic and the 2008 financial crisis.	– Implement iterative learning and continuous adaptation.
Complexity in Decision-Making	– Arises from interdependencies, nonlinearity, and emergent behaviors.	– Apply systems thinking to understand interdependencies and feedback loops.
	– Systems can be unpredictable and require sophisticated tools to navigate, as seen in urban planning or energy transition.	– Adopt a holistic perspective, integrating multiple stakeholder views.
	– Real-world examples include urban planning, energy transitions, and environmental conservation efforts.	– Design flexible and resilient systems that can adapt to disruptions.
Implications of Uncertainty and Complexity	– Traditional models are insufficient for managing dynamic, unpredictable systems.	– Embrace dynamic models that allow for adaptability and continuous learning.
	– Dynamic models integrate real-time data, anticipate patterns, and enable course correction.	– Encourage interdisciplinary collaboration to uncover blind spots and integrate diverse perspectives.
	– Systems thinking helps to identify leverage points and avoid unintended consequences.	– Focus on agility and rapid response mechanisms.
	– Navigating uncertainty and complexity requires data integration, scenario planning, and long-term strategic vision.	– Ensure robust decision-making outcomes by continuously refining strategies.

1. **Electric Vehicle (EV) Adoption**

Consider the case of EV adoption. The system includes interconnected elements such as government incentives, charging infrastructure, battery technology, and consumer preferences. By modeling these interdependencies, SD enables stakeholders to assess the outcomes of different policy and investment decisions.

For example, simulations can show how subsidies influence consumer behavior or predict the long-term impact of expanded charging infrastructure on EV adoption rates. Insights derived from such models have led to targeted policy measures and investment strategies.

A practical example is Ford Motor Company, which used SD to examine its transition toward sustainable vehicles. Their analysis revealed that without concurrent investments in charging station networks, EV adoption would plateau, regardless of advancements in vehicle technology. This finding prompted Ford to form partnerships with governments and private entities to expand infrastructure, fostering a more robust EV ecosystem (Qudrat-Ullah & Karakul, 2007).

2. **Research & Development (R&D) and Product Lifecycle Management**

System Dynamics is also instrumental in R&D planning. Technology firms often use it to forecast the impact of R&D investments on product life cycles. A tech giant like IBM, for example, uses SD to balance resource allocation between maintaining existing technologies and developing innovative solutions. By simulating market trends, resource constraints, and competitive pressures, firms can optimize their innovation strategies while mitigating risks.

- **Case Study: Urban Traffic Management**

Urban traffic congestion is a classic example of a complex problem addressed effectively through SD. Traffic systems involve interacting components such as road capacity, public transportation usage, population growth, and driver behavior.

1. **Singapore's Electronic Road Pricing (ERP) System**

Singapore's ERP system is a prime example of how SD can inform urban traffic management. Faced with rising congestion in the 1990s, policymakers employed SD to model the system. Their analysis considered variables such as the rate of vehicle ownership, commuter preferences, road network capacity, and pricing mechanisms.

The simulations demonstrated that dynamic pricing, based on real-time traffic data, could reduce congestion significantly while maximizing road efficiency (Goh, 2002). As a result, Singapore introduced an ERP system, where charges fluctuate depending on traffic density and time of day. This adaptive pricing has been remarkably successful, resulting in smoother traffic flow and reduced commute times.

- **Other Urban Applications**

Beyond Singapore, cities such as Stockholm and London have adopted congestion pricing systems inspired by SD modeling. These systems are often integrated with public transportation policies to incentivize shifts to mass transit. For instance, Stockholm's congestion pricing model, implemented in 2007, reduced traffic volumes by 20%, decreased greenhouse gas emissions, and improved air quality (Eliasson, 2009).

- **Addressing Wicked Problems**

SD is particularly suited for tackling "wicked problems," characterized by high uncertainty, interdependencies, and conflicting objectives. Urban planning is rife with such challenges, where decisions often have unintended consequences.

1. **Affordable Housing and Infrastructure**

In cities experiencing rapid population growth, the trade-off between affordable housing and infrastructure development poses a significant challenge. SD models help policymakers evaluate scenarios where increasing housing supply influences traffic congestion, utility demand, and public services. For example, cities in China have used SD to plan urban expansion, balancing housing affordability with sustainable resource use (He *et al.*, 2015).

2. **Healthcare Systems**

Another application lies in healthcare system management. During the COVID-19 pandemic, SD was employed to simulate the spread of the virus, hospital capacity, and vaccination strategies. These models provided critical insights for governments to allocate resources effectively, optimize lockdown measures, and plan vaccination campaigns (Homer & Hirsch, 2006).

- **Benefits and Challenges**

SD offers significant advantages in decision-making:

- **Visualization of Feedback Loops**: It highlights reinforcing and balancing feedback loops, helping identify potential areas for intervention.
- **Scenario Analysis**: Decision-makers can simulate various scenarios to anticipate potential outcomes of policies and actions.
- **Policy Design**: It provides a structured framework for designing adaptive and robust policies.

However, challenges include:

- **Data Requirements**: Accurate data is essential for building reliable models.
- **Complexity**: Large models can become unwieldy and difficult to interpret.
- **Validation**: Ensuring model validity requires expertise and robust testing.

Despite these challenges, SD remains a cornerstone for addressing complex, dynamic systems.

Overall, SD has transformed decision-making in complex environments by providing tools to analyze and predict system behavior comprehensively. Its applications in technology management, urban planning, and healthcare illustrate its versatility and impact. As global challenges become more interconnected, SD will continue to play a vital role in crafting informed and sustainable solutions. Table 5.3 encapsulates the essence of SD, its practical applications, and the critical lessons decision-makers can derive for crafting adaptive, robust, and sustainable solutions in complex systems.

5.3.2. *Scenario Planning*

Scenario Planning is a forward-thinking decision-making tool that empowers organizations to navigate uncertainty and complexity by

Table 5.3. Summary of SD and Key Insights for Decision-Makers.

Aspect	Description	Key Insights and Lessons for Decision-Makers
Core Framework	Models complex systems using CLDs and stock-and-flow models.	Enables holistic understanding of systems, identification of leverage points, and prediction of long-term outcomes.
Applications in Technology Management	Focuses on technological innovation, market dynamics, and regulatory influences.	Simulations reveal interactions and inform targeted strategies to optimize innovation, adoption, and sustainability.
Electric Vehicle (EV) Adoption	Models dependencies like government incentives, infrastructure, and consumer behavior.	Insights inform strategic partnerships and investments in supporting infrastructure, crucial for ecosystem growth.
R&D and Product Lifecycle	Simulates R&D investments, resource allocation, and market trends.	Helps balance innovation with operational efficiency, optimizing the product development life cycle.
Urban Traffic Management	Models congestion factors like road capacity and commuter behavior.	Dynamic pricing systems (e.g., Singapore's ERP) reduce congestion and maximize road efficiency.
Wicked Problems	Tackles high-uncertainty problems with interdependencies and conflicting objectives.	Encourages scenario planning and adaptive policies to address challenges like urban housing and healthcare crises.
Affordable Housing & Infrastructure	Balances housing supply with sustainable infrastructure and resource management.	Provides decision-makers with tools to forecast trade-offs and optimize urban planning initiatives.
Healthcare Systems	Models pandemic dynamics, hospital capacity, and vaccination campaigns.	Supports resource allocation and policy adjustments to mitigate health crises effectively.
Benefits of System Dynamics	Visualizes feedback loops, enables scenario analysis, and supports policy design.	Strengthens decision-making processes by identifying unintended consequences and crafting adaptive solutions.
Challenges of System Dynamics	Requires accurate data, complex modeling, and robust validation processes.	Highlights the need for expertise, iterative development, and stakeholder collaboration to ensure model reliability and applicability.
Overall Impact	Provides structured approaches for solving complex, interconnected problems.	Enhances decision-making across domains like technology, urban planning, and healthcare, fostering sustainable and informed outcomes.

constructing multiple plausible future scenarios. This approach, pioneered by Herman Kahn and later refined by Peter Schwartz and others, explores potential outcomes under varying assumptions and helps decision-makers develop robust strategies adaptable to diverse future possibilities (Schoemaker, 1995). Through this methodology, organizations anticipate challenges, seize opportunities, and mitigate risks, ensuring preparedness in dynamic environments.

5.3.2.1. *Applications in Technology Adoption*

In the technology sector, Scenario Planning plays a pivotal role in managing uncertainty inherent in innovation cycles, regulatory landscapes, and market dynamics.

- **Case: 5G Technology Development**
  During the early stages of 5G development, telecom giants like Ericsson and Huawei utilized Scenario Planning to navigate the uncertain future of this transformative technology. They constructed scenarios based on variables such as:
  1. Adoption rates by consumers and industries.
  2. Regulatory policies across key markets.
  3. Technological breakthroughs, including device compatibility and network infrastructure.

For example, in one scenario, high adoption rates coupled with favorable regulations indicated the need for aggressive R&D investments and rapid infrastructure deployment. In another, slower adoption due to stringent regulations prompted a conservative strategy focused on incremental advancements. This approach enabled Ericsson and Huawei to remain agile, capitalizing on opportunities while minimizing potential setbacks (Courtney, 2001).

- **Emerging Technologies**
  Scenario Planning is also critical for emerging fields such as AI and quantum computing. For instance, AI companies like OpenAI consider scenarios involving ethical concerns, regulatory oversight, and public acceptance. Such analyses guide their development of safe and scalable AI systems, ensuring alignment with societal and market needs.

In conclusion, Scenario Planning serves as an indispensable tool for managing the uncertainties inherent in technology adoption. By constructing diverse, plausible scenarios, companies like Ericsson, Huawei, and OpenAI can anticipate challenges, adapt to evolving conditions, and strategically align their innovations with market and societal needs. This proactive approach not only fosters agility in navigating disruptive changes but also positions organizations to seize opportunities and mitigate risks effectively in dynamic technological landscapes.

5.3.2.2. *Case Study: Shell's Oil Crisis Strategy*

A landmark example of Scenario Planning's efficacy is Shell's strategic response to the oil crisis of the 1970s. This era was marked by unprecedented volatility in global oil prices, driven by geopolitical tensions, OPEC production decisions, and fluctuating global energy demands. Recognizing the high degree of uncertainty, Shell's strategists adopted Scenario Planning to prepare for a range of potential futures, allowing the company to navigate the crisis with remarkable agility.

- **Key Scenarios Considered**

Shell's team developed scenarios based on three primary price environments:

1. **High-Price Scenarios**: Anticipating price spikes due to geopolitical events, such as the Yom Kippur War, Shell modeled scenarios where oil became a scarce and expensive commodity.
2. **Low-Price Scenarios**: These scenarios accounted for market corrections, where increased production or reduced demand could drive prices down.
3. **Fluctuating Price Scenarios**: Recognizing the possibility of unpredictable price swings, Shell prepared strategies for dynamically adjusting operations.

These scenarios included analyses of external factors like the role of energy conservation in developed nations, technological shifts in energy efficiency, and the emergence of alternative energy sources.

- **Strategic Actions**

When oil prices surged during the crisis, Shell was ready with strategies to conserve resources and diversify its energy portfolio. For instance, the company accelerated investments in natural gas and alternative energy projects, reducing its dependence on crude oil. This proactive diversification helped Shell maintain supply chains and mitigate risks associated with over-reliance on a single energy source.

Conversely, during subsequent price declines, Shell implemented cost-saving measures that preserved its financial stability without compromising long-term operations. This included optimizing exploration and production processes and delaying non-essential projects. By maintaining operational flexibility, Shell avoided the significant disruptions that plagued less-prepared competitors.

- **Lessons Learned**
  Shell's use of Scenario Planning demonstrated the power of foresight in managing uncertainty. This approach enabled the company to:

  1. Adapt quickly to volatile market conditions.
  2. Identify early warning signals for impending shifts in the energy landscape.
  3. Build resilience through diversification and strategic agility.

- **Modern Applications**

Shell's success during the oil crisis cemented Scenario Planning as a critical component of corporate strategy. Today, the company continues to use this approach to address challenges such as the energy transition, climate change, and the rise of renewable technologies. Other industries, from finance to manufacturing, have adopted similar practices to prepare for economic shocks, technological disruptions, and regulatory changes.

By embedding Scenario Planning into its decision-making processes, Shell not only preserved its market leadership during the 1970s crisis but also set a precedent for how organizations can thrive in the face of uncertainty. This case remains a benchmark example of leveraging strategic foresight to navigate complex, dynamic environments effectively.

5.3.2.3. *Implications for Sustainability*

Scenario Planning's relevance extends beyond business strategy to addressing global challenges like climate change. Organizations and governments use this approach to explore pathways toward sustainability under varying conditions of policy, technology, and behavior.

- **Case: The World Resources Institute**
  The World Resources Institute (WRI) employs Scenario Planning to evaluate strategies for achieving net-zero emissions. They analyze scenarios involving:
  1. Accelerated renewable energy adoption.
  2. Policy shifts such as carbon pricing or subsidies for green technologies.
  3. Societal behaviors, including consumer shifts toward sustainability.

One scenario might model a world where renewable energy becomes dominant due to aggressive policies and technological breakthroughs. Another might assume slower adoption due to economic constraints, necessitating greater reliance on carbon capture technologies (Nakicenovic *et al.*, 2000). These scenarios guide decision-makers in crafting flexible and achievable climate action plans.

- **Case: Cities and Climate Resilience**
  Urban centers like New York City and Amsterdam use Scenario Planning to prepare for climate risks such as rising sea levels and extreme weather. By modeling scenarios based on varying levels of global temperature rise, they design adaptive infrastructure solutions, such as elevated buildings, flood barriers, and green roofs. These strategies ensure long-term resilience against unpredictable climate impacts.

In addressing sustainability challenges, Scenario Planning empowers organizations and governments to navigate uncertainties with foresight and adaptability. By modeling diverse pathways, such as renewable energy adoption and policy shifts, it provides actionable insights for achieving ambitious goals like net-zero emissions. This strategic approach ensures that decision-makers can proactively balance economic, technological, and societal considerations, fostering resilience and progress toward a sustainable future.

5.3.2.4. *Benefits and Challenges*

1. Benefits of Scenario Planning

- **Foresight in Uncertainty**: Provides a structured approach to anticipate diverse future possibilities.
- **Enhanced Flexibility**: Helps organizations prepare for both best- and worst-case scenarios.
- **Strategic Alignment**: Ensures strategies are robust, adaptive, and responsive to external changes.
- **Stakeholder Engagement**: Encourages collaboration and alignment among diverse stakeholders.

2. Challenges of Scenario Planning

- **Data Dependence**: Requires extensive data to construct realistic and credible scenarios.
- **Complexity**: Can become unwieldy when dealing with highly intricate systems.
- **Resource Intensive**: Demands significant time and expertise to develop and analyze scenarios.

Despite these challenges, Scenario Planning remains indispensable for navigating today's volatile and interconnected world. Its applications in technology, sustainability, and risk management highlight its versatility and impact.

Scenario Planning enables decision-makers to navigate uncertainty by exploring and preparing for a range of potential future outcomes. Whether shaping corporate strategy, guiding technology adoption, or tackling climate change, this approach fosters resilience and innovation in dynamic environments. As global challenges grow more complex, Scenario Planning will continue to be a vital tool for crafting informed and adaptive solutions. Table 5.4 summarizes key aspects of Scenario Planning, with insights and lessons for decision-makers in technology, business strategy, and sustainability contexts.

5.3.3. *Adaptive Management*

Adaptive Management emphasizes flexibility, experimentation, and iterative learning, enabling decision-makers to respond effectively to uncertainty and dynamic changes. Unlike traditional static

Table 5.4. Summary of Scenario Planning: Key Aspects, Insights, and Lessons for Decision-Makers.

Aspect	**Key Insights**	**Lessons for Decision-Makers**
Definition and Purpose	A decision-making tool for anticipating diverse future scenarios and developing robust strategies.	Use Scenario Planning to navigate uncertainty, mitigate risks, and seize opportunities in dynamic environments.
Applications in Technology Adoption	Enables organizations to manage uncertainty in innovation, regulation, and market dynamics.	Construct plausible scenarios to align innovation efforts with regulatory and societal trends (e.g., 5G, AI).
Case Study: Shell's Oil Crisis Strategy	Prepared Shell for oil price volatility through adaptive strategies in high, low, and fluctuating scenarios.	Prioritize resilience through diversification and strategic agility in uncertain market conditions.
Implications for Sustainability	Guides climate strategies by modeling renewable energy adoption, policy shifts, and behavioral changes.	Use Scenario Planning for actionable sustainability goals, such as net-zero emissions and urban climate resilience.
Benefits	Provides foresight, flexibility, strategic alignment, and stakeholder collaboration.	Incorporate Scenario Planning into strategic processes for robust, adaptive decision-making.
Challenges	Requires extensive data, expertise, and resources; complexity can be a barrier.	Balance depth and practicality in scenario development to make insights actionable and efficient.

approaches, this model thrives on adaptability, continuously integrating new information to refine strategies and ensure alignment with evolving conditions (Holling, 1978). Its relevance spans various domains, from environmental conservation to technology management, where conditions are complex and outcomes uncertain.

5.3.3.1. *Applications in Environmental Management*

Adaptive Management has become a cornerstone of environmental conservation strategies, addressing issues like habitat degradation, climate change, and resource scarcity. It bridges science and policy by treating management interventions as experiments, where outcomes guide subsequent actions.

- **Case: Everglades Restoration Project**
  The Comprehensive Everglades Restoration Plan (CERP) in Florida exemplifies Adaptive Management in action. This initiative seeks to reverse decades of ecological damage caused by urbanization and water mismanagement. Decision-makers employ a structured process of planning, implementing, monitoring, and refining strategies based on observed outcomes (Walters, 1986). For example:
  - **Experimentation:** Water flow restoration projects are designed as experiments, testing how changes impact vegetation, water quality, and wildlife.
  - **Monitoring:** Continuous ecological assessments capture data on parameters like biodiversity and hydrology.
  - **Adjustment:** Insights from monitoring inform iterative modifications, ensuring strategies remain effective amid changing environmental and societal priorities.

This approach not only adapts to climatic and ecological shifts but also fosters stakeholder engagement by incorporating diverse perspectives into decision-making. The Everglades Restoration underscores the importance of learning-by-doing, reducing uncertainties while preserving critical ecosystems.

- **Additional Example: Adaptive Forest Management**
  In Canada's boreal forests, Adaptive Management is used to balance logging activities with ecosystem health. Logging companies

collaborate with ecologists to monitor wildlife populations, reforestation rates, and carbon sequestration. This partnership has improved forest resilience, contributing to biodiversity preservation and sustainable economic benefits.

In conclusion, Adaptive Management provides a robust framework for navigating uncertainty and complexity across diverse domains. By embracing flexibility, iterative learning, and stakeholder collaboration, it enables decision-makers to align actions with dynamic conditions and evolving priorities. Whether restoring ecosystems like the Everglades or managing technological innovations, Adaptive Management underscores the power of experimentation and continuous refinement, ensuring sustainable and resilient outcomes.

5.3.3.2. *Case Study: Fisheries Management*

Adaptive Management has revolutionized fisheries management, offering a solution to overfishing and ecosystem degradation while ensuring economic sustainability.

- **Case: Alaska Salmon Fishery**
  The Alaska salmon fishery demonstrates how Adaptive Management can balance ecological preservation with economic gain. Key components include:
  - **Real-Time Monitoring:** Biologists use sonar systems and genetic testing to track salmon populations during migration.
  - **Dynamic Quotas:** Harvesting limits are adjusted in real-time based on population data, preventing overfishing while optimizing yields.
  - **Collaborative Decision-Making:** Stakeholders, including fishermen, scientists, and policymakers, collaborate to design sustainable management strategies.

This system, guided by adaptive principles, has helped Alaska maintain one of the world's most sustainable fisheries (Hilborn & Walters, 1992). The model has inspired similar efforts globally, such as the Pacific sardine fishery management plan in the U.S., which employs adaptive policies to regulate catch volumes based on biomass surveys.

- **Challenges and Opportunities**
  While successful, Adaptive Management in fisheries faces challenges, including data collection costs and enforcement complexities. However, technological advancements like satellite imaging and AI-driven analytics are enhancing monitoring capabilities, enabling more precise and cost-effective management.

In summary, Adaptive Management has proven invaluable in fisheries management by fostering sustainable practices that balance ecological integrity with economic viability. The Alaska salmon fishery exemplifies the approach's effectiveness, demonstrating how real-time data, dynamic adjustments, and stakeholder collaboration can address overfishing and promote resilience. Despite challenges such as data collection costs and enforcement, emerging technologies offer promising solutions to enhance adaptability and precision, ensuring the long-term health of marine ecosystems and fishing industries worldwide.

5.3.3.3. *Applications in Technology Management*

The technology sector's fast-paced innovation cycles and market uncertainties make Adaptive Management indispensable. By fostering iterative experimentation and learning, companies can stay ahead of disruptive changes.

- **Case: Google Maps Development**
  Google's iterative approach to product development exemplifies Adaptive Management in technology. When Google Maps launched in 2005, it offered basic navigation features. However, its developers relied on user feedback and real-world data to refine the product over time:

  1. **User Feedback:** Beta testing allowed users to identify issues and suggest improvements.
  2. **Data Integration:** Real-time data on traffic and geographic changes enabled adaptive updates.
  3. **Feature Expansion:** Innovations like Street View, live traffic updates, and multi-modal transit options were added iteratively.

This adaptive strategy ensured continuous improvement, making Google Maps a market leader in navigation technology (Shapiro & Varian, 1999).

- **Other Examples in Technology Management**
  1. **Amazon Web Services (AWS):** AWS uses Adaptive Management to refine its cloud services. New features are introduced based on user demand, with performance and scalability tested in live environments.
  2. **Tesla's Autopilot System:** Tesla adopts adaptive principles to enhance its self-driving capabilities. Software updates, informed by real-world driving data, are deployed iteratively to improve safety and performance.

The applications of Adaptive Management in technology management highlight the sector's reliance on flexibility and iterative learning to navigate fast-moving markets and technological disruptions. Google Maps' development, with its continuous enhancements based on user feedback and real-time data, demonstrates how Adaptive Management can transform a basic product into a global leader by responding to user needs and environmental changes. Similarly, companies like AWS and Tesla leverage Adaptive Management to refine and improve their services, using real-world data to shape product development and ensure ongoing innovation. As the technology landscape evolves, Adaptive Management remains crucial for maintaining competitiveness and adapting to emerging challenges.

5.3.3.4. *Lessons and Best Practices*

Adaptive Management offers critical lessons for decision-makers across domains:

1. **Embrace Uncertainty:** Treat uncertainty as an opportunity for learning and innovation rather than a barrier.
2. **Iterative Approach:** Break long-term goals into smaller, manageable experiments to enable flexibility and rapid adjustments.
3. **Stakeholder Collaboration:** Engage diverse stakeholders to incorporate multiple perspectives and foster collective ownership of outcomes.

4. **Leverage Technology:** Use advanced tools like AI, remote sensing, and big data analytics to enhance monitoring and decision-making efficiency.

Adaptive Management's iterative, flexible approach provides a powerful framework for navigating complex and uncertain environments. From restoring ecosystems in the Everglades to managing sustainable fisheries and driving technological innovation, this methodology ensures resilience and adaptability. By prioritizing learning and collaboration, Adaptive Management equips organizations to achieve long-term success while addressing the challenges of a rapidly changing world. Table 5.5 highlights the core principles of Adaptive Management and the actionable lessons for decision-makers across various domains, from environmental conservation to technology management.

5.4. Conclusion

In today's rapidly evolving world, the need for dynamic decision-making has never been more urgent. As technological advancements continue to reshape industries and complex systems become increasingly interconnected, the environments in which decisions are made are marked by uncertainty and rapid change. Traditional decision-making models, rooted in linearity and predictability, often fall short when applied to complex, uncertain, and evolving conditions. In contrast, dynamic decision-making frameworks — such as System Dynamics, Scenario Planning, and Adaptive Management — are increasingly being recognized as more suitable for addressing these challenges. These approaches allow decision-makers to adapt to complexity and uncertainty, making informed decisions that are robust, resilient, and able to withstand the test of time.

5.4.1. *System Dynamics: Unveiling Complex Interdependencies*

SD provides a powerful methodology for understanding the behavior of complex systems over time. By modeling feedback loops, stock-flow relationships, and delays, SD enables decision-makers to visualize the dynamics of systems in which their decisions play out. In

Table 5.5. Summary of Key Aspects of Adaptive Management and Insights for Decision Makers.

Aspect	Key Insight	Lessons for Decision Makers
Flexibility & Iteration	Adaptive Management thrives on flexibility and iterative learning.	Embrace uncertainty as an opportunity for innovation. Break long-term goals into smaller experiments for continuous improvement.
Experimentation	Management interventions are treated as experiments, with outcomes guiding subsequent actions.	Use controlled experiments to test hypotheses and refine strategies based on observed results.
Real-Time Monitoring	Continuous monitoring of systems enables informed decision-making and adjustments.	Invest in advanced monitoring tools (e.g., remote sensing, AI) to track real-time data for adaptive responses.
Collaboration & Stakeholder Engagement	Involves multiple stakeholders (e.g., policymakers, scientists, communities) in decision-making processes.	Engage diverse stakeholders to foster collaboration, ensuring strategies meet varied needs and priorities.
Ecological & Technological Adaptability	Adaptive Management can be applied to both environmental conservation and technological development.	Apply adaptive principles across sectors, from ecosystem restoration to product development, to remain resilient in dynamic environments.
Technology Integration	Technologies like AI, big data, and satellite imagery enhance adaptive capacity.	Leverage emerging technologies to optimize data collection, enhance decision-making, and improve operational efficiency.
Sustainability Focus	Balancing ecological integrity with economic sustainability is crucial.	Prioritize long-term sustainability by aligning economic goals with environmental and social considerations.
Learning from Failure	Failure is part of the learning process in Adaptive Management.	Adopt a learning-oriented mindset that views failures as opportunities for refinement and growth.
Adjusting Strategies	Strategies must be flexible and regularly updated based on evolving conditions.	Ensure strategic plans are adaptable, allowing for timely modifications in response to new insights or shifting conditions.

contrast to traditional linear models, SD helps identify potential unintended consequences, revealing the complex interdependencies within systems. The approach is especially useful in areas like environmental management, business strategy, and public policy, where the behavior of systems is influenced by many interacting variables.

- **Practical Insights:**
  1. **Feedback Loops and Non-Linearity**: One of the core strengths of SD is its ability to illustrate feedback loops, both positive and negative. For instance, in environmental policy, SD models can show how resource depletion can lead to feedback loops that accelerate environmental degradation, helping policymakers understand the long-term impacts of their decisions and avoid counterproductive measures.
  2. **Scenario Testing and Sensitivity Analysis**: SD models can be used to simulate different scenarios, allowing decision-makers to understand the range of possible outcomes based on varying assumptions. Sensitivity analysis, a key feature of SD, helps identify which factors are most critical in driving system behavior, enabling more targeted interventions.
  3. **Long-Term Planning**: By emphasizing the importance of long-term impacts, SD encourages decision-makers to think beyond immediate results. This foresight is particularly valuable in public health, energy policy, and climate change mitigation, where short-term decisions can have lasting consequences.

- **Future Possibilities:**
  1. **Integration with AI and Machine Learning**: The future of SD lies in its integration with AI and machine learning, allowing for more accurate predictions and the real-time adaptation of models. AI could be used to enhance the sensitivity analysis and optimize the decision-making process, making SD models even more valuable in dynamic environments.
  2. **Enhanced Collaboration**: As SD tools become more accessible, they can facilitate collaboration across sectors and disciplines. Policymakers, scientists, and business leaders could use shared SD models to identify common goals, improve communication, and create more effective cross-sector solutions.

5.4.2. *Scenario Planning: Navigating Uncertainty with Strategic Foresight*

Scenario Planning is a strategic planning method used to envision multiple future outcomes and prepare organizations for possible challenges. Unlike traditional forecasting, which assumes a fixed set of variables and trends, Scenario Planning embraces uncertainty, encouraging decision-makers to consider a wide range of possible futures. The approach involves identifying critical uncertainties, constructing plausible scenarios, and then developing strategies that are robust across those scenarios.

- **Practical Insights:**
  1. **Identifying Critical Uncertainties**: A critical first step in Scenario Planning is identifying the uncertainties that will most likely impact the future. This could include economic factors, technological disruptions, geopolitical shifts, or environmental changes. Decision-makers can then prioritize which uncertainties require attention and develop adaptive strategies.
  2. **Flexibility and Contingency Planning**: Scenario Planning emphasizes flexibility. By exploring various scenarios — ranging from best-case to worst-case — the organization can prepare contingency plans for any eventuality. For instance, the oil and gas industry has used scenario planning to prepare for market fluctuations, regulatory changes, and technological innovations.
  3. **Long-Term Strategic Thinking**: Scenario Planning encourages organizations to think beyond short-term gains and focus on building long-term resilience. In the context of global supply chains, for example, Scenario Planning can help companies anticipate risks such as natural disasters, political instability, or pandemics, enabling them to adapt quickly when disruptions occur.

- **Future Possibilities:**
  1. **Integration with Big Data**: The future of Scenario Planning lies in its integration with big data and predictive analytics. By leveraging real-time data, decision-makers can refine their scenarios and update their strategies more frequently. This will improve the accuracy and relevance of the scenarios.

2. **Cross-Organizational Scenario Planning**: As the world becomes more interconnected, cross-organizational scenario planning will become increasingly important. Governments, businesses, and civil society organizations can collaborate to create shared scenarios that address global challenges like climate change, pandemics, and cybersecurity threats.

5.4.3. *Adaptive Management: Embracing Flexibility and Iterative Learning*

Adaptive Management is an approach that emphasizes flexibility, continuous learning, and responsiveness to changing conditions. It is especially useful in managing ecosystems, fisheries, and technological systems, where uncertainties are high, and outcomes are not always predictable. Unlike traditional management approaches that rely on fixed plans and long-term projections, Adaptive Management thrives on experimentation and ongoing feedback loops, allowing decision-makers to adjust their strategies based on real-world results.

- **Practical Insights:**

1. **Learning by Doing**: Adaptive Management promotes a learning-by-doing approach, where interventions are treated as experiments, and outcomes are used to adjust future actions. This approach has been successfully applied in environmental management, such as the restoration of the Everglades, where real-time monitoring and experimentation guide decision-making.
2. **Stakeholder Involvement**: A key feature of Adaptive Management is its emphasis on stakeholder involvement. By engaging local communities, industry representatives, and experts in decision-making processes, adaptive strategies are more likely to succeed, as they account for diverse perspectives and local knowledge.
3. **Data-Driven Decision Making**: Continuous monitoring is central to Adaptive Management. By collecting and analyzing real-time data, decision-makers can adjust their strategies to respond to changing conditions, such as shifts in biodiversity, climate patterns, or technological advancements.

- **Future Possibilities:**
  1. **Integration with Remote Sensing and AI**: The integration of remote sensing technologies and AI into Adaptive Management practices will revolutionize how real-time data is gathered and analyzed. For example, AI-driven systems could analyze ecological data and provide predictive insights that help decision-makers anticipate and address environmental challenges before they escalate.
  2. **Global Scale Implementation**: While Adaptive Management has been successfully implemented at the local level, its principles can be scaled to address global challenges such as climate change, biodiversity loss, and sustainable development. Global frameworks for adaptive governance could emerge, allowing nations to collaborate in managing shared resources and mitigating environmental risks.

5.4.4. *Implications for Decision Makers*

For decision-makers navigating an increasingly complex and uncertain world, embracing dynamic decision-making frameworks is no longer optional; it is essential. The ability to adapt to shifting conditions, learn from past experiences, and engage in iterative processes can mean the difference between success and failure. Key implications for decision-makers include:

1. **Embrace Complexity**: Acknowledge that complexity and uncertainty are inherent in today's decision-making landscape. Rather than striving for certainty, embrace adaptive strategies that allow for flexibility and resilience.
2. **Collaborate Across Sectors**: Given the interconnectedness of global challenges, decision-makers must collaborate across sectors, industries, and even nations to create solutions that are robust and sustainable.
3. **Foster a Culture of Learning**: Create organizational cultures that value learning, experimentation, and adaptability. Encourage decision-makers to view failures as opportunities to learn and improve rather than as setbacks.
4. **Invest in Technology**: The integration of emerging technologies — such as AI, machine learning, and big data — into

decision-making processes can significantly enhance the ability to gather insights, model scenarios, and make real-time adjustments. Decision-makers must invest in these technologies to remain competitive and responsive.

In conclusion, dynamic decision-making frameworks like System Dynamics, Scenario Planning, and Adaptive Management offer significant promise for navigating the complexities and uncertainties of the modern world. By embracing uncertainty, engaging stakeholders, leveraging data, and fostering a culture of learning, decision-makers can build strategies that are not only resilient in the face of change but also poised for long-term success.

References

Courtney, H. (2001). *20/20 Foresight: Crafting Strategy in an Uncertain World*. Harvard Business School Press.

Eliasson, J. (2009). A cost-benefit analysis of the stockholm congestion charging system. *Transportation Research Part A: Policy and Practice*, 43(4), 468–480.

Forrester, J. W. (1961). *Industrial dynamics*. Cambridge, MA: MIT Press.

Goh, M. (2002). Congestion Management and Electronic Road Pricing in Singapore. *Journal of Transport Geography*, 10(1), 29–38.

He, S., *et al.* (2015). Urban expansion simulation and spatial optimization in China. *Environment and Planning B: Planning and Design*, 42(3), 450–469.

Hilborn, R., & Walters, C. J. (1992). *Quantitative Fisheries Stock Assessment: Choice, Dynamics and Uncertainty*. Springer.

Holling, C. S. (1978). *Adaptive Environmental Assessment and Management*. London: John Wiley & Sons.

Homer, J. B., & Hirsch, G. B. (2006). System dynamics modeling for public health: Background and opportunities. *American Journal of Public Health*, 96(3), 452–458.

Nakicenovic, N., *et al.* (2000). *Emissions Scenarios: Special Report of the Intergovernmental Panel on Climate Change (IPCC)*. Cambridge University Press.

Qudrat-Ullah, H. (2014). *Better Decision Making in Complex, Dynamic Tasks*. USA, New York: Springer.

Qudrat-Ullah, H. (2020). Improving human performance in dynamic tasks with debriefing-based interactive learning environments: An empirical investigation. *International Journal of Information Technology and Decision Making*, 19(04), 1065–1089.

Qudrat-Ullah, H., & Karakul, M. (2007). Decision making in interactive learning environments: Towards an integrated model. *Journal of Decision Systems*, 16(1), 79–99.

Qudrat-Ullah, H., Spector, M., & Davidson, I. P. (Eds.). (2008). *Complex Decision Making: Theory and Practice.* USA, New York: Springer.

Schoemaker, P. J. H. (1995). Scenario planning: A tool for strategic thinking. *Sloan Management Review*, 36(2), 25–40.

Shapiro, C., & Varian, H. R. (1999). *Information Rules: A Strategic Guide to the Network Economy.* Harvard Business Review Press.

Sterman, J. D. (2000). *Business dynamics: Systems thinking and modeling for a complex world.* Boston, MA: Irwin/McGraw-Hill.

Wack, P. (1985). Scenarios: Shooting the rapids. *Harvard Business Review*, 63(6), 139–150.

Walters, C. J. (1986). *Adaptive Management of Renewable Resources.* MacMillan.

Chapter 6

Integrating Emerging Technologies into Decision Making

Abstract

This chapter explores the integration of emerging technologies into decision-making processes, focusing on how data analytics, artificial intelligence (AI), and machine learning (ML) enhance decision quality in dynamic environments. It discusses the role of predictive and prescriptive analytics in forecasting trends and optimizing decisions, and examines real-time decision-making capabilities enabled by AI and ML. The chapter also addresses the challenges and best practices for adopting these technologies, providing insights for decision-makers on leveraging technological advancements to improve responsiveness, accuracy, and strategic outcomes in complex scenarios. The chapter concludes with key lessons for effective integration and future readiness.

Keywords: Emerging Technologies; Decision Making; Data Analytics; Artificial Intelligence (AI); Machine Learning (ML); Real-Time Decision Making; Predictive Analytics; Prescriptive Analytics; Dynamic Environments; Technology Integration; Informed Decisions; Strategic Outcomes; Complex Scenarios; Decision-Making Tools

6.0. Introduction

Emerging technologies, such as AI, ML and advanced data analytics, have increasingly become integral to modern decision-making processes across industries. These technologies are not only reshaping how decisions are made but also enhancing the quality, speed, and accuracy of those decisions in environments characterized by complexity, uncertainty, and rapid change. The growing reliance on data and technological innovations has brought about a paradigm shift, wherein decision-making is increasingly being driven by data rather than intuition alone. This chapter aims to explore how these advanced technologies can be integrated into decision-making frameworks and discusses the significant impact they have on organizational strategies and performance.

6.0.1. *The Role of Emerging Technologies in Decision-Making*

In recent years, the role of emerging technologies in decision-making has become more prominent as organizations face an ever-growing need to make faster, more accurate, and informed decisions. The ability to harness vast amounts of data to generate actionable insights has unlocked new possibilities for organizations, leading to improved decision outcomes. AI and ML, in particular, offer powerful tools that can analyze large datasets, recognize patterns, and predict future trends, enabling decision-makers to anticipate challenges and opportunities before they arise (Brynjolfsson & McAfee, 2014).

AI and ML have proven especially effective in areas such as predictive analytics, real-time decision-making, and automation of routine tasks. Predictive analytics, for instance, allows organizations to foresee potential issues or opportunities based on historical data and current trends. ML algorithms are designed to improve decision-making continuously by learning from past data, which makes them particularly useful in environments that require adaptive responses. The ability of these technologies to handle complex datasets and extract valuable insights has made them indispensable in sectors like finance, healthcare, supply chain management, and marketing, where data-driven decisions can significantly enhance operational efficiency and customer satisfaction (Huang & Rust, 2021).

6.0.2. *Impact on Decision Quality and Speed*

One of the primary advantages of integrating emerging technologies into decision-making frameworks is the enhancement of both decision quality and speed. Traditional decision-making processes often rely on human judgment, which can be limited by biases, lack of information, and the inability to process large volumes of data quickly. In contrast, AI and ML-driven systems can analyze vast amounts of data almost instantaneously, providing decision-makers with insights that would be impossible for humans to uncover on their own. This results in faster decisions that are based on comprehensive, data-driven evidence rather than intuition or guesswork (Davenport, 2018).

Furthermore, these technologies enable real-time decision-making, which is increasingly critical in fast-paced industries. The ability to respond rapidly to changing circumstances is a competitive advantage, especially in sectors such as finance, e-commerce, and healthcare, where delays can result in missed opportunities or costly mistakes. For example, AI-driven algorithms in the stock market can process real-time data and make buy or sell decisions within fractions of a second, far outperforming human traders in terms of both speed and accuracy (Chung & Lee, 2020).

In addition to enhancing decision speed, AI and ML can also improve the quality of decisions by providing decision-makers with deeper insights. Through data mining, predictive modeling, and pattern recognition, these technologies can uncover trends and relationships in data that may otherwise go unnoticed. As a result, organizations can make more informed decisions that take into account a wide range of variables and potential outcomes, leading to better strategic alignment and overall business performance (Sharda, Delen, & Turban, 2014).

6.0.3. *Addressing Complex Decision-Making Challenges*

Emerging technologies also help address some of the most challenging aspects of decision-making in complex environments. In situations where decisions involve multiple stakeholders, conflicting objectives, or a large number of variables, the integration of AI and ML can provide clarity by processing and analyzing the relevant data in ways that human decision-makers cannot. For example, AI can help organizations optimize their supply chain operations by analyzing data from various sources, including inventory levels, customer demand, and supplier performance, to make decisions that minimize costs while ensuring timely deliveries.

Moreover, AI and ML have the ability to process and interpret unstructured data, such as text, images, and video, which often makes up the majority of the data in many organizations. This capability allows decision-makers to tap into a broader range of information sources, improving the accuracy and comprehensiveness of the decisions made. The ability to automate the analysis of unstructured data, such as social media posts or customer feedback, can also provide real-time insights into public sentiment, enabling organizations to adapt their strategies accordingly.

These technologies can also assist in complex decision-making by simulating different scenarios and evaluating the potential outcomes of each. For example, AI-driven decision support systems can be used in healthcare to predict the outcomes of different treatment options for a patient based on their medical history and other variables. Similarly, in financial markets, AI can be used to simulate different economic scenarios and evaluate the impact of various investment strategies, helping decision-makers make more informed choices under uncertainty (Brynjolfsson & McAfee, 2014).

6.0.4. *Overcoming Limitations and Challenges*

While emerging technologies offer considerable benefits for decision-making, they also come with their own set of challenges. One of the most significant barriers to the successful integration of AI and ML into decision-making processes is the need for high-quality data. ML models are only as good as the data they are trained on, and poor-quality or biased data can lead to inaccurate or unethical decisions. For decision-makers, this means that investing in data governance, data cleansing, and ensuring data diversity are essential steps for the effective deployment of these technologies (O'Neil, 2016).

Furthermore, decision-makers must also address ethical concerns related to the use of AI and ML. The potential for algorithmic biases, especially in areas like hiring, lending, and law enforcement, has raised significant ethical and legal questions. AI algorithms can inadvertently perpetuate existing biases in data, leading to unfair or discriminatory outcomes. It is therefore crucial for organizations to ensure that AI models are transparent, explainable, and regularly audited for fairness (Dastin, 2018).

Additionally, organizations must prepare their workforce to embrace these technologies. The implementation of AI and ML in decision-making often requires new skills and expertise, particularly in data science, machine learning, and AI ethics. To ensure successful integration, organizations must invest in training and development programs to upskill their employees and foster a culture that embraces technological change (Westerman, Calméjane, Ferraris, *et al.*, 2011).

In conclusion, emerging technologies such as AI, ML, and advanced data analytics are revolutionizing decision-making processes across industries by enabling faster, more accurate, and data-driven decisions. These technologies enhance decision quality, improve speed, and help organizations navigate the complexities of today's fast-paced business environments. However, successful integration of these technologies requires careful attention to data quality, ethical considerations, and workforce preparedness. By addressing these challenges and leveraging the full potential of AI and ML, decision-makers can drive improved outcomes and maintain a competitive edge in an increasingly data-driven world.

6.1. Leveraging Data and Analytics for Informed Decisions

In the modern business landscape, data has become an invaluable asset for decision-making. This section explores how organizations can utilize advanced analytics — descriptive, diagnostic, predictive, and prescriptive — to gain actionable insights and inform strategic decisions. By integrating data from diverse sources and applying cutting-edge analytical techniques, decision-makers can identify trends, address inefficiencies, anticipate future developments, and optimize operations. Practical approaches for fostering data-driven cultures, ensuring data governance, and overcoming implementation challenges are also discussed, providing a comprehensive framework for leveraging data in dynamic environments.

6.1.1. *Key Concepts and Importance*

The importance of data-driven decision-making has surged as businesses navigate an increasingly complex and competitive global landscape. Leveraging data allows organizations to uncover actionable insights, make informed decisions, and adapt swiftly to changing market dynamics. As emphasized by McAfee *et al.* (2012) and Davenport & Harris (2017), companies that harness big data effectively often achieve superior productivity, profitability, and innovation compared to their peers. This section delves into the critical components of data-driven decision-making, practical insights for implementation, and its transformative impact on organizations.

- **Key Components of Data Analytics in Decision-Making**
  Data analytics encompasses a continuum of techniques, each with unique applications and benefits:

  1. **Descriptive Analytics**
     - **Purpose:** Summarize historical data to provide an overview of past performance.
     - **Applications:** Sales trend analysis, website traffic summaries, and customer segmentation.
     - **Example:** A retail company might use descriptive analytics to identify seasonal patterns in customer purchases, enabling better inventory planning.
  2. **Diagnostic Analytics**
     - **Purpose:** Delve into the root causes of outcomes, enabling organizations to identify inefficiencies or problems.
     - **Applications:** Churn analysis, supply chain bottleneck detection, and product failure diagnostics.
     - **Example:** A SaaS provider could use diagnostic analytics to determine why users abandon its platform, revealing opportunities to enhance user experience.
  3. **Predictive Analytics**
     - **Purpose:** Forecast future outcomes based on historical data and machine learning models.
     - **Applications:** Demand forecasting, fraud detection, and personalized marketing.
     - **Example:** Airlines use predictive analytics to anticipate demand spikes, optimizing ticket prices and seat availability to maximize revenue.

4. **Prescriptive Analytics**
   - **Purpose:** Recommend specific actions to achieve desired outcomes or optimize operations.
   - **Applications:** Dynamic pricing strategies, route optimization, and resource allocation.
   - **Example:** Ride-hailing companies like Uber use prescriptive analytics to determine surge pricing during high-demand periods, balancing supply and demand while maximizing driver incentives.

- **Practical Insights for Effective Implementation**
  To fully capitalize on the potential of data-driven decision-making, organizations must adopt a strategic approach that addresses technical, organizational, and cultural aspects:

1. **Build Robust Data Governance Frameworks**
   - Data accuracy, quality, and security are foundational to reliable analytics. Poor-quality data leads to misleading insights, undermining decision-making processes.
   - **Best Practice:** Establish clear protocols for data collection, storage, and validation. Employ technologies like blockchain for secure, transparent data management.
2. **Train Employees to Interpret and Act on Data Insights**
   - A significant barrier to effective analytics implementation is the disconnect between data scientists and decision-makers. Employees must understand how to interpret data and align insights with strategic objectives.
   - **Best Practice:** Provide training programs that bridge technical expertise with business acumen. Tools like Tableau and Power BI enable non-technical users to explore data independently.
3. **Foster a Data-Driven Culture**
   - Organizations must prioritize evidence-based decision-making at all levels. A data-driven culture encourages employees to seek insights before making decisions, reducing reliance on intuition or outdated practices.

  - **Best Practice:** Recognize and reward data-driven behaviors. Appoint data champions in different departments to promote analytics adoption.

- **Real-World Applications and Success Stories**

  1. **Amazon's Customer-Centric Approach**
     - Amazon employs descriptive and predictive analytics to refine customer experiences. By analyzing purchasing behaviors, the company personalizes recommendations, driving customer satisfaction and loyalty.
     - **Key Insight:** Leveraging data analytics can enable businesses to anticipate customer needs, strengthening their competitive position.

  2. **Walmart's Inventory Management**
     - Walmart uses prescriptive analytics to optimize its supply chain. Real-time data integration across stores allows the company to replenish stocks dynamically, minimizing overstock and stockouts.
     - **Key Insight:** Operational efficiency improves significantly when analytics are integrated into core processes.

  3. **Healthcare Industry Transformations**
     - Predictive analytics in healthcare facilitates early diagnosis and treatment planning. For example, IBM Watson Health uses AI to analyze patient data, identifying potential health risks proactively.
     - **Key Insight:** Predictive models save lives by enhancing precision in medical decision-making.

- **Future Possibilities in Data-Driven Decision-Making**

  1. **Integration with AI**
     - Combining AI with advanced analytics can further automate and enhance decision-making. Autonomous systems can process vast datasets, identifying opportunities and risks in real-time.

  2. **Data Monetization**
     - Organizations will increasingly explore ways to monetize their data assets. Sharing anonymized datasets with partners or

developing data-driven products can unlock new revenue streams.

3. **Enhanced Collaboration Through Data Democratization**
   - As self-service analytics tools become more accessible, employees across departments can leverage data insights, fostering cross-functional collaboration.
4. **Expansion to Predictive Ecosystems**
   - Predictive analytics will evolve into predictive ecosystems, integrating IoT devices, edge computing, and blockchain to provide seamless, actionable insights in dynamic environments.

Table 6.1 provides a concise overview of the critical aspects of leveraging data and analytics for informed decision-making. It highlights the core types of analytics — descriptive, diagnostic, predictive, and prescriptive — along with their applications and implications for organizational strategy. The table also emphasizes practical strategies such as establishing robust data governance frameworks, fostering a data-driven culture, and integrating advanced technologies like AI. Furthermore, it includes real-world examples from industries such as retail, healthcare, and logistics, showcasing successful applications and insights. Decision-makers can use this summary as a guide to enhance their analytic capabilities and adapt to evolving business challenges.

6.1.2. *Case Studies and Applications*

The application of data analytics has transformed industries, enabling companies to optimize operations, improve customer satisfaction, and drive profitability. The following case studies demonstrate the power of analytics in real-world scenarios, offering insights into best practices and potential future advancements.

- **Amazon's Recommendation Algorithms**
  Amazon has revolutionized e-commerce by leveraging predictive analytics to recommend products to customers. By analyzing extensive datasets, including browsing history, purchase behavior, and demographic information, Amazon's recommendation engine

Table 6.1. Summary of Key Aspects and Takeaways for Decision Makers on Leveraging Data and Analytics

Aspect	Description	Key Takeaways for Decision Makers
Descriptive Analytics	Summarizes historical data to reveal trends and patterns. Common applications include sales reports and customer behavior analysis.	Use descriptive analytics to identify patterns and gain insights into past performance for better planning.
Diagnostic Analytics	Examines the root causes of outcomes, helping businesses address inefficiencies or problems. Examples include churn analysis and supply chain bottleneck detection.	Apply diagnostic analytics to pinpoint areas of improvement and resolve operational inefficiencies effectively.
Predictive Analytics	Forecasts future outcomes using statistical models and machine learning. Examples include demand forecasting and fraud detection.	Leverage predictive analytics to anticipate future trends, enabling proactive responses to market and operational shifts.
Prescriptive Analytics	Provides recommendations for specific actions to optimize outcomes. Examples include dynamic pricing strategies and resource allocation.	Implement prescriptive analytics to optimize decision-making processes and ensure alignment with strategic goals.
Data Governance Frameworks	Establishes protocols for data accuracy, quality, and security, ensuring reliable analytics.	Develop strong governance frameworks to maintain data integrity and enhance trust in analytics outcomes.
Employee Training	Builds capacity to interpret and act on data insights, bridging gaps between technical and strategic teams.	Invest in employee training programs to enable data-driven decision-making across all organizational levels.
Data-Driven Culture	Promotes evidence-based decision-making by encouraging the use of analytics in everyday processes.	Foster a culture of analytics adoption by recognizing and rewarding evidence-based practices.

Table 6.1. (*Continued*)

Aspect	Description	Key Takeaways for Decision Makers
Real-World Application: Amazon	Uses descriptive and predictive analytics to personalize customer experiences, increasing satisfaction and loyalty.	Emulate Amazon's customer-centric approach to enhance user engagement and retention.
Real-World Application: Walmart	Leverages prescriptive analytics to optimize inventory management, minimizing stockouts and overstock.	Incorporate analytics into supply chain processes to enhance operational efficiency and cost-effectiveness.
Real-World Application: Healthcare	Applies predictive analytics for early diagnosis and treatment planning, improving patient outcomes.	Use predictive models to enhance precision and speed in critical decision-making scenarios.
Future Integration with AI	AI enhances analytics capabilities by automating processes and providing real-time insights.	Explore AI integration to boost responsiveness and agility in decision-making.
Data Monetization	Organizations can generate revenue by sharing anonymized datasets or creating data-driven products.	Consider monetizing data assets to open new revenue streams and drive innovation.
Predictive Ecosystems	Combines IoT, edge computing, and blockchain to enable seamless insights in dynamic environments.	Invest in predictive ecosystems to capitalize on real-time, interconnected analytics for competitive advantage.

creates personalized shopping experiences. This strategy has led to higher customer engagement, increased conversion rates, and enhanced customer loyalty.

For instance, when a customer views a product, Amazon suggests complementary items, creating opportunities for cross-selling and upselling. Practical insights from this approach include the importance of real-time data processing, robust algorithms, and continuous improvement through machine learning. The future possibilities involve integrating visual and conversational AI to enhance the customer journey further. For example, voice-enabled assistants could provide shopping suggestions based on contextual user inputs, making the process even more intuitive.

- **Coca-Cola's Sentiment Analysis**
  Coca-Cola demonstrates the effectiveness of diagnostic analytics by employing sentiment analysis to monitor consumer perceptions of its products in real time. By analyzing data from social media platforms, the company can identify trends, gauge customer emotions, and uncover potential areas for improvement.

  In one instance, Coca-Cola discovered negative feedback about the taste of a new beverage. By addressing these concerns promptly and adjusting its marketing campaigns, the company mitigated reputational risks and retained consumer trust. This case underscores the need for businesses to invest in tools that enable real-time feedback analysis.

  Future advancements in sentiment analysis may involve incorporating augmented reality (AR) experiences to engage users and gather data interactively. Additionally, leveraging blockchain technology could enhance data credibility, ensuring consumer trust in the feedback collection process.

- **UPS's ORION System**
  UPS exemplifies the power of prescriptive analytics through its ORION (On-Road Integrated Optimization and Navigation) system. This platform analyzes millions of delivery routes daily, recommending the most efficient paths for drivers. By minimizing unnecessary travel, ORION saves over 100 million miles annually, significantly reducing fuel consumption and operational costs.

  A critical aspect of ORION's success is its ability to integrate diverse data sources, including GPS, traffic patterns, and package delivery requirements, into a unified system. This demonstrates the importance of adopting holistic data integration strategies for analytics-driven decision-making.

  Future possibilities for ORION include integrating IoT-enabled delivery vehicles and drones for last-mile logistics. Real-time environmental monitoring could further optimize route selection, considering factors like weather conditions and urban congestion.

- **Future Possibilities in Analytics Applications**
  Looking ahead, the fusion of AI and advanced analytics offers transformative opportunities across industries:
  1. **Real-Time Decision Support Systems:** Real-time analytics, combined with AI, can revolutionize supply chain management. For example, dynamic systems could automatically adjust supply routes based on live traffic or weather data, ensuring timely deliveries and cost savings. This approach would require robust infrastructure for real-time data processing and AI model training.
  2. **Autonomous Financial Modeling:** In finance, autonomous analytics systems could proactively detect market anomalies, identify investment opportunities, and recommend risk mitigation strategies. These systems could analyze vast volumes of market data, enabling quicker and more accurate decision-making compared to traditional methods.
  3. **Enhanced Personalization in Customer Experience:** With the rise of wearable devices and IoT, companies can collect granular data on consumer behavior and preferences. By integrating these insights into predictive analytics models, businesses can create hyper-personalized experiences that resonate with individual consumers, boosting engagement and brand loyalty.

By examining these case studies and future possibilities, decision-makers can gain valuable insights into the transformative potential of analytics. The key takeaway is the need for organizations to build robust analytical capabilities, foster innovation, and stay ahead of technological advancements to maintain a competitive edge in dynamic environments.

Table 6.2 summarizes notable case studies and applications of data analytics, showcasing how organizations like Amazon, Coca-Cola, and UPS have effectively leveraged analytics to optimize operations, enhance customer experiences, and drive profitability. It highlights the key aspects of their approaches, such as predictive recommendations, real-time sentiment analysis, and prescriptive route optimization, along with actionable takeaways for decision-makers.

Table 6.2. Key Aspects of Case Studies and Applications in Analytics

Case Study/ Application	Key Aspects	Takeaways for Decision-Makers
Amazon's Recommendation Algorithms	Utilizes predictive analytics to offer personalized product recommendations, boosting customer engagement and sales.	Invest in machine learning models and real-time data processing. Continuously improve algorithms and explore AI-driven personalization for enhanced customer journeys.
Coca-Cola's Sentiment Analysis	Analyzes social media data to gauge consumer sentiment and adjust marketing strategies in real time.	Implement diagnostic analytics tools for real-time feedback. Leverage advanced technologies like blockchain to ensure data credibility and foster consumer trust.
UPS's ORION System	Employs prescriptive analytics to optimize delivery routes, saving over 100 million miles annually.	Develop integrated data systems incorporating IoT and real-time analytics. Focus on reducing operational inefficiencies and enhancing sustainability efforts.
Future Possibilities in Analytics	Explores innovations such as real-time decision support systems, autonomous financial modeling, and hyper-personalized experiences.	Prioritize investments in AI-integrated analytics for dynamic decision-making. Embrace IoT and wearable data sources to foster personalized customer engagement and efficiency.

The table also outlines future possibilities in analytics, emphasizing the transformative potential of AI integration, real-time decision support, and hyper-personalized consumer experiences for fostering innovation and efficiency.

6.1.3. *Emerging Trends and Future Possibilities*

As data analytics continues to evolve, its potential for transforming industries becomes increasingly evident. Emerging trends and technologies are driving this evolution, enabling businesses to harness insights more effectively while navigating complex ethical, operational, and technological landscapes. This section delves into key trends shaping the future of data analytics and highlights their implications for decision-makers, emphasizing the integration of advanced technologies such as AI, IoT, and edge computing.

6.1.3.1. *Edge Analytics for Real-Time Insights*

Edge analytics represents a transformative approach to data processing by performing computations closer to the data source, such as IoT devices and sensors. Unlike traditional centralized systems, where data is transmitted to a remote server for processing, edge analytics allows organizations to generate insights in real-time, reducing latency and enhancing operational efficiency (Satyanarayanan, 2017). This capability is particularly critical in industries where split-second decisions are essential, such as manufacturing, healthcare, and transportation.

In manufacturing, edge analytics enables predictive maintenance by monitoring machinery performance in real-time. By analyzing data from sensors embedded in equipment, factories can detect anomalies, predict failures, and schedule maintenance proactively. For instance, General Electric employs edge analytics in its industrial internet solutions to optimize equipment uptime and reduce maintenance costs, resulting in substantial operational savings (Mourtzis *et al.*, 2016). Similarly, in healthcare, wearable devices equipped with edge computing are revolutionizing patient monitoring. Devices like smartwatches and fitness trackers continuously analyze vital signs and alert medical professionals to abnormalities. This not only improves patient outcomes but also reduces the burden on healthcare facilities by enabling early intervention (Verma *et al.*, 2020).

The transportation sector has also seen significant benefits from edge analytics. Autonomous vehicles rely on edge-enabled systems to process vast amounts of environmental data in real-time. This includes detecting obstacles, interpreting traffic signals, and predicting pedestrian behavior. By enabling instantaneous decision-making, edge analytics enhances safety and efficiency in smart transportation networks (Zhou *et al.*, 2019).

For decision-makers, the adoption of edge analytics requires a strategic focus on several factors. First, investments in IoT-enabled devices and robust edge platforms are essential to ensure data processing efficiency at the source. Second, organizations must prioritize the development of secure data transfer protocols to safeguard sensitive information, particularly in industries like healthcare where privacy concerns are paramount. Additionally, equipping personnel with the skills to interpret localized insights and integrate them into broader decision-making frameworks is vital for maximizing the benefits of edge analytics.

Future possibilities include the integration of edge analytics with AI to create self-optimizing systems. For instance, smart factories could leverage AI-powered edge analytics to autonomously adjust production lines based on real-time demand forecasts, reducing waste and improving efficiency. Similarly, autonomous vehicles equipped with AI-enhanced edge systems could further refine navigation by learning from environmental patterns and driver preferences over time. These advancements hold immense potential to redefine operational capabilities across industries, making edge analytics a cornerstone of the data-driven future.

6.1.3.2. *Ethical AI and Analytics: Navigating Transparency and Trust*

The widespread adoption of AI and data analytics has amplified the need for ethical frameworks that prioritize fairness, transparency, and accountability. As organizations increasingly rely on data-driven insights, addressing ethical concerns is critical to maintaining public trust and achieving sustainable outcomes. Ethical AI and analytics involve creating responsible practices for collecting, processing, and applying data, ensuring that these processes align with societal values and expectations.

One prominent challenge lies in mitigating biases embedded in AI systems. For instance, in hiring processes, AI-powered analytics tools have occasionally demonstrated discriminatory tendencies due to biased training data. A notable example occurred when an AI recruitment tool disproportionately favored male candidates for technical roles, reflecting historical imbalances in hiring practices (Raji *et al.*, 2020). To prevent such issues, organizations must audit algorithms rigorously, ensuring that training datasets are representative of diverse populations. This involves not only identifying biases but also recalibrating models to promote equitable outcomes.

Transparency is another cornerstone of ethical analytics. In marketing, consumers are increasingly aware of how their data is collected and used. Companies that fail to disclose data usage practices risk eroding customer trust. A practical example is the backlash faced by Facebook after the Cambridge Analytica scandal, which highlighted the misuse of personal data for political purposes (Isaak & Hanna, 2018). To avoid similar incidents, organizations can adopt frameworks like the Fairness, Accountability, and Transparency (FAT) principles. These guidelines advocate for clear communication about data collection methods, ensuring users understand how their information is utilized.

Privacy concerns further underscore the need for ethical innovation. Technologies like federated learning have emerged as a solution, enabling sensitive data to be analyzed without compromising individual privacy. For instance, Google employs federated learning in its predictive text models, ensuring that user data remains decentralized while still improving algorithm performance (McMahan *et al.*, 2017). This approach demonstrates how ethical considerations can coexist with technological advancement, offering a path forward for organizations navigating complex data environments.

To implement ethical AI and analytics, decision-makers must adopt a multi-faceted strategy. This includes establishing ethical audit processes to evaluate algorithms, investing in bias detection tools, and fostering organizational cultures that prioritize ethics alongside innovation. Moreover, regulatory frameworks like the European Union's GDPR provide a legal foundation for enforcing privacy and transparency, serving as a model for global best practices.

Looking ahead, ethical AI and analytics will play an increasingly critical role in shaping the future of data-driven decision-making. As AI systems become more autonomous, ensuring their alignment with human values will require ongoing vigilance and collaboration among stakeholders. By embedding ethics into every stage of the analytics lifecycle, organizations can build systems that not only deliver insights but also uphold the principles of fairness, transparency, and trust.

6.1.3.3. *Hyper-Personalization: Transforming Customer Experiences*

Hyper-personalization leverages predictive analytics, AI, and IoT data to create tailored products and services for individual consumers. By analyzing data from wearable devices, mobile apps, and smart home technologies, businesses can gain unparalleled insights into consumer preferences and behaviors.

In retail, for example, companies can offer personalized shopping experiences by dynamically adjusting product recommendations based on real-time data from mobile apps or in-store sensors. In the automotive sector, IoT-enabled vehicles can learn drivers' preferences, optimizing settings such as temperature, seat position, and route suggestions. Practical insights highlight the importance of integrating data sources and creating user-centric designs that enhance convenience and satisfaction.

Future possibilities include wearable technologies that predict consumer needs before they arise, such as fitness devices suggesting meal plans based on activity levels and caloric needs. Additionally, businesses can explore immersive AR and VR experiences to engage customers in personalized, interactive environments.

6.1.3.4. *Practical Applications Across Industries*

The emerging trends in analytics are already paving the way for transformative applications in various sectors:

1. **Healthcare**: Predictive models that analyze patient data can identify early warning signs of diseases, enabling timely interventions. For example, hospitals are using AI-driven analytics to predict patient readmission risks, optimizing care plans and resource allocation.
   - *Key Insight*: Investing in integrated health information systems and AI tools enhances precision and saves lives.
2. **Energy Sector**: Analytics tools are optimizing energy consumption patterns and forecasting renewable energy production. By integrating weather data and historical usage patterns, utility companies can balance supply and demand efficiently.

  - *Key Insight*: Using predictive analytics in renewable energy improves sustainability and operational efficiency, making it a critical focus for energy providers.

3. **Transportation**: Real-time analytics combined with edge computing can optimize traffic management systems, reducing congestion and emissions. Autonomous vehicles benefit from this by processing vast amounts of data to make instantaneous decisions.
   - *Key Insight*: Enhanced connectivity and real-time decision support are essential for smart transportation systems.
4. **Finance**: Advanced analytics models are transforming risk management by identifying fraud patterns and market anomalies. Autonomous financial modeling enables quicker and more accurate decision-making in volatile markets.
   - *Key Insight*: The ability to detect risks proactively is vital for maintaining competitive advantage in financial services.

In summary, the practical applications of emerging analytics trends demonstrate their transformative potential across diverse industries. By leveraging predictive and real-time insights, organizations can enhance efficiency, reduce costs, and drive innovation. These advancements underscore the critical role of integrating advanced analytics tools with industry-specific processes to address unique challenges and capitalize on opportunities. As businesses continue to invest in cutting-edge technologies and data-driven strategies, they not only improve operational performance but also pave the way for sustainable growth and long-term competitiveness in an increasingly complex and interconnected world.

6.1.3.5. *Future Possibilities and Strategic Recommendations*

The integration of AI and analytics with IoT and blockchain technology is poised to redefine decision-making processes across industries. Future advancements could include real-time decision support systems capable of dynamic adaptations, such as supply chain routes that adjust based on live weather data or drones that autonomously respond to logistical challenges.

To capitalize on these possibilities, decision-makers must:

- Develop cross-functional teams that combine technical expertise with strategic vision.

- Prioritize investments in emerging technologies like edge computing and blockchain.
- Foster partnerships with technology providers to stay ahead of innovation curves.

By embracing these strategies, organizations can position themselves as leaders in the era of data-driven innovation.

In conclusion, the integration of data and analytics into decision-making processes represents a transformative shift toward more informed and strategic organizational actions. By adopting advanced analytics techniques and preparing for emerging trends, organizations can unlock unprecedented value and maintain a competitive edge in an increasingly data-driven world. Table 6.3 provides a summary of emerging trends and technologies in data analytics, focusing on key developments such as edge analytics, ethical AI, hyper-personalization, and practical applications across industries. It highlights the critical aspects of each trend and offers actionable takeaways for decision-makers. These takeaways emphasize the importance of investing in advanced technologies, ensuring ethical practices, and adapting business strategies to leverage real-time insights, personalized customer experiences, and industry-specific innovations. This table guides organizations navigate the evolving landscape of data analytics and make informed decisions to drive future growth and efficiency.

6.2. Real-Time Decision-Making with AI and ML

AI and ML technologies are transforming the decision-making landscape by providing real-time, data-driven insights that enhance responsiveness and agility. These technologies enable organizations to analyze vast datasets, recognize patterns, and generate actionable insights almost instantaneously, reshaping how decisions are made across various industries.

6.2.1. *Role of AI and ML in Real-Time Decision-Making*

AI and ML are pivotal in real-time decision-making, thanks to their ability to process and analyze large datasets with speed and precision.

Table 6.3. Key Aspects of Emerging Trends and Future Possibilities in Data Analytics

Trend/Technology	Description	Key Takeaways
Edge Analytics for Real-Time Insights	Data processing at the source (e.g., IoT devices), reducing latency and enhancing efficiency, crucial for industries requiring quick decisions like manufacturing, healthcare, and transportation.	1. Invest in IoT devices and edge platforms. 2. Develop secure data transfer protocols. 3. Train personnel to integrate localized insights.
Ethical AI and Analytics	Creating responsible practices for data collection, processing, and usage, focusing on fairness, transparency, and privacy (e.g., FAT principles, federated learning).	1. Audit AI algorithms for fairness. 2. Implement transparency frameworks like FAT. 3. Invest in privacy-preserving technologies.
Hyper-Personalization	Using predictive analytics, AI, and IoT to create tailored consumer experiences based on individual preferences, especially in retail and automotive.	1. Integrate diverse data sources for personalized insights. 2. Focus on user-centric designs. 3. Explore AR/VR for interactive experiences.
Practical Applications Across Industries	Predictive and real-time analytics transforming sectors like healthcare (patient monitoring), energy (renewable forecasting), transportation (traffic management), and finance (risk management).	1. **Healthcare**: Invest in AI tools for precision. 2. **Energy**: Use analytics to optimize renewable energy. 3. **Transportation**: Enhance real-time decision-making. 4. **Finance**: Use analytics to identify risks early.
Future Possibilities and Strategic Recommendations	Integration of AI, IoT, and blockchain for dynamic, real-time decision support systems (e.g., autonomous drones, adaptive supply chains).	1. Build cross-functional teams with strategic vision. 2. Invest in edge computing, AI, and blockchain. 3. Form technology partnerships for innovation.

Algorithms such as neural networks, decision trees, and clustering models allow systems to learn from data and adapt to changing conditions dynamically. This capability is crucial for businesses operating in fast-paced environments, where traditional decision-making methods may fail to keep up.

Practical Insight: For instance, financial trading platforms leverage AI and ML to execute high-frequency trades based on market data analyzed in milliseconds. These systems not only predict market movements but also react to them faster than human traders.

Future Possibilities: As AI and ML technologies evolve, their integration with edge computing and 5G networks will enhance decision-making in real-time by reducing latency and enabling decentralized processing. This will be especially impactful in industries such as autonomous vehicles and smart cities, where split-second decisions are critical.

6.2.2. *Applications and Impact of AI and ML Across Industries*

The application of AI and ML in industries such as finance, healthcare, and manufacturing has led to significant advancements in operational efficiency and decision-making speed. By automating routine tasks and analyzing data at scale, these technologies enable organizations to focus on strategic decision-making.

Finance: AI-powered systems in the finance sector detect fraudulent activities in real-time by analyzing transaction patterns. For example, credit card companies use ML algorithms to flag suspicious transactions, preventing potential fraud before it occurs.

Healthcare: In healthcare, AI assists in diagnosing diseases through image recognition and predictive analytics. Real-time data from wearable devices and health monitoring systems are analyzed to alert healthcare providers about potential health risks.

Manufacturing: Predictive maintenance, powered by ML algorithms, helps manufacturers identify equipment failures before they occur, minimizing downtime and reducing costs. For example, AI systems in automotive manufacturing plants analyze sensor data to optimize assembly line operations.

Practical Insight: In e-commerce, recommendation systems use ML to provide personalized product suggestions based on real-time customer browsing and purchase behavior, significantly enhancing customer experience and driving sales.

Future Possibilities: The integration of quantum computing with AI and ML could revolutionize real-time decision-making by exponentially increasing processing power. This would enable more complex simulations and predictions, opening new avenues in climate modeling, drug discovery, and supply chain optimization.

6.2.3. *Challenges and Considerations in Real-Time AI-Driven Decision-Making*

Despite its advantages, real-time AI-driven decision-making presents challenges such as data privacy concerns, algorithmic biases, and the need for robust infrastructure. Organizations must address these issues to fully leverage AI and ML technologies.

Data Privacy: Real-time decision-making often requires continuous data collection, raising concerns about user privacy. Implementing stringent data protection measures is essential to build trust and comply with regulations such as GDPR and CCPA.

Algorithmic Bias: Bias in AI models can lead to unfair or incorrect decisions. For example, biased hiring algorithms may disadvantage certain groups. Ensuring diversity in training datasets and regular model audits are key to mitigating this risk.

Infrastructure: Real-time AI systems demand high-performance computing resources and reliable data pipelines. Investing in scalable infrastructure and cloud-based solutions is critical for organizations aiming to implement these systems effectively.

Practical Insight: Organizations are adopting explainable AI (XAI) to make real-time decision-making processes more transparent and accountable. For example, banks using AI for loan approvals provide customers with explanations for their decisions, improving trust and compliance.

Future Possibilities: The rise of federated learning, where AI models are trained across decentralized devices without sharing raw data, offers a promising solution to privacy concerns. This approach could enable more widespread adoption of real-time AI applications in sensitive domains such as healthcare and finance.

Overall, AI and ML technologies are revolutionizing real-time decision-making by enabling organizations to process and analyze data at unprecedented speeds. While the benefits are immense, addressing challenges such as data privacy, bias, and infrastructure requirements will be crucial to unlocking their full potential. The future of real-time decision-making lies in the seamless integration of AI and ML with emerging technologies like quantum computing and federated learning, paving the way for smarter and more efficient systems across industries.

Table 6.4 summarizes the key aspects, practical insights, and strategic recommendations for decision-makers in adopting AI and ML for real-time decision-making across industries. It outlines the benefits, applications, challenges, and future possibilities associated with these technologies.

6.3. Predictive and Prescriptive Analytics in Dynamic Environments

In increasingly volatile and complex environments, organizations need robust tools to anticipate challenges and craft effective responses. Predictive and prescriptive analytics serve as critical components in this decision-making arsenal, enabling data-driven strategies to navigate uncertainties and achieve optimal outcomes. This section delves into their applications, practical insights, and future possibilities.

6.3.1. *Predictive Analytics: Anticipating the Future*

Predictive analytics employs statistical algorithms, ML models, and historical data to forecast future events or trends. This capability is particularly valuable in dynamic environments where rapid shifts can disrupt operations (Shmueli & Koppius, 2011).

1. **Applications in Industry:**
   - **Retail:** Predictive analytics forecasts demand patterns, helping businesses optimize inventory levels and reduce waste. For

Table 6.4. Real-Time Decision-Making with AI and ML – Key Aspects and Takeaways

Key Aspects	**Description**	**Key Takeaways for Decision-Makers**
Role of AI and ML in Real-Time Decision-Making	AI and ML enable organizations to process large datasets quickly, identify patterns, and adapt to changing conditions. Algorithms like neural networks, decision trees, and clustering models drive dynamic decision-making in fast-paced environments.	Decision-makers should invest in AI/ML systems to enhance speed, precision, and adaptability in decision-making. Integration with edge computing and 5G will further reduce latency and improve performance.
Applications and Impact Across Industries	AI and ML improve operational efficiency by automating tasks and analyzing data for better decision-making. In finance, healthcare, and manufacturing, these technologies optimize fraud detection, diagnostics, and maintenance.	Organizations should implement AI and ML to automate routine tasks, enhance decision speed, and drive efficiency. Future applications of quantum computing can further expand capabilities in complex domains.
Challenges and Considerations	Real-time AI-driven decision-making faces challenges like data privacy concerns, algorithmic biases, and the need for robust infrastructure. Privacy laws (e.g., GDPR) and ethical practices must be addressed.	Decision-makers must prioritize data protection, implement bias mitigation strategies, and invest in scalable infrastructure. The adoption of XAI and federated learning will enhance transparency and privacy.

example, seasonal demand forecasting allows retailers to adjust stock levels and marketing efforts effectively (Fildes *et al.*, 2008).

- **Healthcare:** Predictive models analyze patient data to identify high-risk individuals, enabling early intervention and improving outcomes (Wang *et al.*, 2018). A practical case is predicting hospital readmissions to allocate resources efficiently.

- **Finance:** Credit risk assessment leverages predictive models to evaluate loan applicants' likelihood of default, enhancing risk management and decision-making (Thomas *et al.*, 2002).

2. **Practical Insight:** Predictive analytics is not just about accuracy but also about interpretability. Organizations adopting user-friendly dashboards for visualizing predictive models have seen greater buy-in from stakeholders, leading to more agile and informed decision-making (Kim *et al.*, 2016).
3. **Future Possibilities:** Advancements in deep learning and real-time data processing will enable predictive analytics to function with greater accuracy and immediacy. For example, edge computing could allow smart cities to forecast traffic patterns dynamically, optimizing urban mobility systems (Shi *et al.*, 2016).

In conclusion, predictive analytics is an essential tool for organizations operating in dynamic environments, providing the ability to anticipate future trends and disruptions. By leveraging statistical algorithms, ML, and historical data, predictive models empower industries such as retail, healthcare, and finance to make informed decisions that optimize operations, reduce risks, and improve outcomes. The growing importance of interpretability and real-time data processing will further enhance the effectiveness of predictive analytics, enabling faster, more accurate decision-making in the future. As these technologies evolve, they offer significant potential for more dynamic and responsive strategies across various sectors.

6.3.2. *Prescriptive Analytics: From Insights to Action*

Prescriptive analytics builds on the insights generated by predictive analytics, offering actionable recommendations to achieve specific goals. By integrating optimization algorithms and simulation techniques, it guides decision-makers toward the most effective course of action (Bertsimas & Kallus, 2020).

1. **Applications in Industry:**

   - **Supply Chain Management:** Prescriptive analytics identifies the most efficient transportation routes and inventory

  replenishment schedules, reducing costs and improving delivery timelines (Agrawal *et al.*, 2020).
- **Energy Sector:** Smart grids use prescriptive models to manage energy distribution, balancing supply and demand while minimizing outages (Huang *et al.*, 2019).
- **Marketing:** Campaign optimization tools suggest tailored strategies for customer engagement, improving return on investment (ROI) by aligning actions with predicted customer behavior (Wedel & Kannan, 2016).

2. **Practical Insight:** Combining prescriptive analytics with real-time monitoring systems can create adaptive frameworks. For instance, logistics companies using route optimization tools that update in real-time based on traffic conditions have significantly reduced delivery delays and fuel consumption (Psaraftis & Kontovas, 2015).
3. **Future Possibilities:** Prescriptive analytics is set to benefit from hybrid AI approaches that combine rule-based systems with ML. This will enable more nuanced decision-making in areas like autonomous systems and personalized medicine, where multiple conflicting objectives must be balanced (Ghahramani, 2015).

In conclusion, prescriptive analytics takes the insights from predictive analytics and translates them into actionable recommendations that guide decision-makers toward optimal outcomes. By integrating optimization algorithms and simulation techniques, prescriptive analytics helps organizations across various industries, including supply chain management, energy, and marketing, improve efficiency, reduce costs, and enhance performance. The combination of prescriptive analytics with real-time monitoring systems offers adaptive and responsive solutions. Looking ahead, hybrid AI approaches are poised to enhance prescriptive analytics, enabling more sophisticated decision-making in complex scenarios such as autonomous systems and personalized medicine.

6.3.3. *Integrating Predictive and Prescriptive Analytics for Proactive Decision-Making*

While predictive and prescriptive analytics are powerful independently, their integration offers even greater potential. Together, they enable organizations not only to anticipate future scenarios but also to devise and implement strategies that mitigate risks and capitalize on opportunities (Sharda *et al.*, 2020).

1. **Practical Applications:**
   - **Disaster Management:** Predictive models forecast weather patterns, while prescriptive analytics guides resource allocation and evacuation strategies, minimizing loss of life and property (Lempert *et al.*, 2013).
   - **Manufacturing:** Predictive analytics identifies machinery likely to fail, and prescriptive tools schedule maintenance at optimal times, reducing downtime and costs (Gopalakrishnan *et al.*, 2013).
   - **Healthcare:** Predictive tools flag potential disease outbreaks, and prescriptive analytics develops contingency plans for vaccine distribution and treatment protocols (Kostkova *et al.*, 2016).
2. **Practical Insight:** Organizations that successfully integrate predictive and prescriptive analytics emphasize cross-functional collaboration. For example, in the automotive industry, combining predictive insights from sensor data with prescriptive maintenance actions involves close coordination between data scientists, engineers, and operations teams (Brennan *et al.*, 2019).
3. **Future Possibilities:** The convergence of AI, IoT, and analytics will amplify the effectiveness of these tools. Predictive and prescriptive analytics embedded in connected devices could enable self-optimizing systems, such as autonomous vehicles adjusting routes based on real-time traffic forecasts and energy efficiency goals (Atzori *et al.*, 2010).

In conclusion, integrating predictive and prescriptive analytics enhances the decision-making process by not only forecasting future trends but also providing actionable strategies to address potential challenges and seize opportunities when possible. This synergy is particularly valuable in industries such as disaster management, manufacturing, and healthcare, where proactive decision-making is crucial for minimizing risks and optimizing outcomes. Successful integration relies on cross-functional collaboration, enabling organizations to leverage both predictive insights and prescriptive actions.

Looking forward, the convergence of AI, IoT, and analytics will further enhance the capabilities of these tools, leading to more adaptive and self-optimizing systems that can respond to dynamic environments in real time.

Overall, predictive and prescriptive analytics are indispensable for thriving in dynamic environments. By leveraging their forecasting and optimization capabilities, organizations can stay ahead of the curve and make proactive decisions. However, unlocking their full potential requires addressing challenges such as data quality, algorithm bias, and technological integration. The future promises even more sophisticated analytics capabilities driven by advances in AI and computing power, empowering decision-makers to tackle complexities with unprecedented confidence. Table 6.5 highlights the key aspects, practical insights, and strategic recommendations for decision-makers in utilizing predictive and prescriptive analytics to navigate dynamic environments. It discusses the benefits of both tools and emphasizes the power of their integration for proactive decision-making.

6.4. Key Learning and Insights for Decision Makers

Integrating emerging technologies into decision-making processes presents both opportunities and challenges. While these technologies offer enhanced capabilities for data analysis, pattern recognition, and operational efficiency, they require strategic implementation to realize their full potential. Decision-makers must address technical, organizational, and ethical considerations while aligning these technologies with long-term business objectives. This section expands on key insights and actionable lessons for organizations aiming to maximize the benefits of technology adoption.

6.4.1. *Challenges and Solutions*

Implementing emerging technologies, such as AI, ML, and big data analytics, requires a nuanced understanding of the barriers that organizations face:

1. **Data Privacy and Security Concerns**
   - As organizations collect and analyze vast amounts of sensitive data, they must ensure robust data governance and compliance

Table 6.5. Predictive and Prescriptive Analytics in Dynamic Environments – Key Aspects and Takeaways

Key Aspects	Description	Key Takeaways for Decision-Makers
Predictive Analytics: Anticipating the Future	Uses statistical algorithms, ML models, and historical data to forecast future trends and events, helping organizations anticipate challenges in dynamic environments.	Decision-makers should leverage predictive analytics for forecasting demand, identifying risks, and making proactive adjustments. Combining predictive models with user-friendly dashboards enhances agility and decision-making.
Prescriptive Analytics: From Insights to Action	Builds on predictive insights to provide actionable recommendations. It uses optimization and simulation techniques to guide decision-making toward optimal outcomes.	Implement prescriptive analytics to turn insights into specific actions. Combining it with real-time data can improve decision effectiveness in dynamic environments such as logistics, energy, and marketing.
Integration of Predictive and Prescriptive Analytics	Combining predictive and prescriptive analytics enables organizations to not only foresee future scenarios but also create actionable strategies for risk mitigation and opportunity capture.	Integrate both analytics to optimize decision-making processes across sectors. Promote cross-functional collaboration to apply predictive insights alongside prescriptive actions, leading to more effective operational outcomes.

with regulations such as GDPR. Data breaches or misuse can erode trust and lead to significant legal consequences.

- **Solution:** Establishing a comprehensive data security framework, employing encryption technologies, and fostering a culture of privacy awareness can mitigate these risks.

2. **Integration with Legacy Systems**
   - Incorporating new technologies into existing infrastructure often reveals compatibility issues, leading to inefficiencies or costly system overhauls.

- **Solution:** Adopting a modular approach to technology implementation, using APIs, and prioritizing scalable solutions can ease integration challenges.

3. **Skill Gaps and Resistance to Change**
   - Emerging technologies demand a workforce skilled in data science, AI, and advanced analytics. However, many organizations face resistance to change and a lack of adequate expertise.
   - **Solution:** Providing continuous training, fostering a growth mindset, and engaging employees in the change process help bridge this gap. Partnerships with academic institutions or third-party vendors can also supplement skill-building efforts.
4. **Ethical Considerations**
   - Decision-makers must ensure the ethical use of technologies to avoid biases in AI algorithms and unintended consequences in decision-making.
   - **Solution:** Incorporating fairness and transparency audits, leveraging diverse datasets, and engaging multidisciplinary teams in ethical reviews are crucial steps.

In conclusion, the successful implementation of emerging technologies requires a strategic approach to addressing the challenges organizations face. By prioritizing data privacy and security, adopting modular integration strategies, investing in continuous skill development, and ensuring ethical decision-making processes, organizations can mitigate risks and harness the full potential of AI, ML, and big data analytics. These solutions not only help in overcoming technical barriers but also foster an organizational culture that is adaptable, transparent, and focused on long-term sustainability in the rapidly evolving technological landscape.

6.4.2. *Best Practices for Successful Integration*

Organizations that successfully integrate emerging technologies often exhibit common strategies that align technology adoption with business objectives:

1. **Fostering a Data-Driven Culture**
   - Encouraging a mindset where decisions are guided by data rather than intuition is vital. Organizations must make data accessibility a priority across all levels of management.

- **Example:** Procter & Gamble adopted a data-driven decision-making approach by integrating real-time data dashboards, enabling managers to respond quickly to market changes.

2. **Investing in Continuous Learning**
   - Keeping pace with technological advancements requires a commitment to ongoing employee training and upskilling. Programs tailored to new roles, such as data scientists and AI specialists, are particularly effective.
   - **Example:** IBM has implemented initiatives like "SkillsBuild," a program designed to prepare its workforce for AI and cloud-based systems.

3. **Aligning Technology with Business Goals**
   - The most successful technology implementations address specific business challenges rather than adopting technology for its own sake. Organizations should prioritize technologies that complement their strategic objectives.
   - **Example:** Toyota's integration of IoT and predictive analytics in its supply chain enhanced operational efficiency and reduced costs by accurately forecasting demand and optimizing logistics.

4. **Leveraging Cross-Functional Teams**
   - Collaboration across departments ensures a more holistic view of technology implementation and avoids siloed decision-making. Cross-functional teams can bridge the gap between technical experts and business leaders.

In conclusion, successful integration of emerging technologies hinges on aligning technological adoption with organizational goals. By fostering a data-driven culture, investing in continuous learning, ensuring technology complements business objectives, and leveraging cross-functional teams, organizations can maximize the impact of new technologies. These best practices not only enhance operational efficiency and decision-making but also enable organizations to remain agile in the face of rapid technological advancements, ensuring long-term success and sustainability in an increasingly data-driven world.

6.4.3. *Future Considerations and Emerging Trends*

Looking ahead, decision-makers must remain adaptable to ongoing technological innovations and evolving market demands.

1. **Adoption of Explainable AI (XAI)**
   - The focus on explainability in AI will grow, ensuring that decision-makers understand how algorithms generate insights. This is critical for gaining stakeholder trust and meeting regulatory requirements.
2. **Focus on Sustainability**
   - Technologies such as predictive analytics will increasingly target sustainability goals, including optimizing resource usage and reducing carbon footprints.
   - **Example:** Companies like Siemens are integrating predictive analytics into smart grid technologies, enabling efficient energy distribution and minimizing waste.
3. **Incorporating Quantum Computing**
   - Quantum computing holds the potential to revolutionize data processing, enabling real-time analytics at an unprecedented scale. Early adoption in industries like pharmaceuticals and finance is already underway.
4. **Increased Personalization**
   - Emerging technologies will enable hyper-personalized decision-making processes, particularly in marketing and customer relationship management. AI-powered recommendation engines, for example, will refine user engagement strategies.

By addressing challenges, adhering to best practices, and remaining adaptable to future trends, decision-makers can unlock the transformative potential of emerging technologies, driving innovation and maintaining a competitive edge in dynamic environments. Table 6.6 summarizes the key learning and insights for decision-makers, highlighting the challenges, best practices, and future considerations for integrating emerging technologies into decision-making processes.

Table 6.6. Key Learning and Insights for Decision Makers

Key Learning & Insights	Key Takeaways for Decision Makers
Challenges and Solutions	
1. Data Privacy and Security Concerns	Ensure robust data governance, compliance with regulations (e.g., GDPR), and implement encryption technologies to protect sensitive data.
2. Integration with Legacy Systems	Adopt modular, scalable solutions and APIs to ease integration with existing infrastructure.
3. Skill Gaps and Resistance to Change	Invest in continuous employee training, foster a growth mindset, and collaborate with academic institutions or third-party vendors to fill skill gaps.
4. Ethical Considerations	Conduct fairness and transparency audits, leverage diverse datasets, and engage multidisciplinary teams to ensure the ethical use of emerging technologies.
Best Practices for Successful Integration	
1. Fostering a Data-Driven Culture	Promote a culture where decisions are driven by data, prioritizing data accessibility across all levels of management.
2. Investing in Continuous Learning	Commit to ongoing employee training and upskilling, with a focus on emerging roles like data scientists and AI specialists.
3. Aligning Technology with Business Goals	Align technology adoption with strategic business challenges, prioritizing technologies that complement long-term objectives.
4. Leveraging Cross-Functional Teams	Foster collaboration across departments to ensure a holistic approach to technology implementation and bridge the gap between technical experts and business leaders.
Future Considerations and Emerging Trends	
1. Adoption of Explainable AI (XAI)	Focus on explainable AI to ensure transparency, enhance stakeholder trust, and meet regulatory requirements.
2. Focus on Sustainability	Leverage technologies like predictive analytics to meet sustainability goals, optimize resource usage, and reduce carbon footprints.
3. Incorporating Quantum Computing	Stay informed about quantum computing's potential to revolutionize data processing and its early applications in industries like pharmaceuticals and finance.
4. Increased Personalization	Embrace emerging technologies that enable hyper-personalized decision-making, particularly in marketing and customer relationship management through AI-powered recommendation engines.

6.5. Conclusion

This chapter has explored the transformative role of emerging technologies in reshaping decision-making processes. As organizations across industries strive to maintain competitiveness in an increasingly complex and data-rich world, the adoption of advanced technologies such as AI, ML predictive analytics, and prescriptive analytics is no longer optional but a strategic necessity. These technologies have the power to significantly enhance the accuracy, speed, and efficiency of decision-making processes, empowering businesses to respond proactively to challenges and opportunities in real-time.

However, the integration of these technologies into decision-making is not without its challenges. Decision-makers must navigate issues such as data privacy and security, integration with legacy systems, and the continuous need for skilled personnel. These hurdles require careful strategic planning, robust infrastructure, and a strong organizational commitment to fostering a culture that embraces change. In this conclusion, we will reflect on the key insights gained from this chapter and explore practical lessons that decision-makers can leverage as they continue to adapt and evolve with the rapidly changing technological landscape.

1. Embracing Technological Advancements: A Strategic Imperative

The rapid pace of technological advancements — ranging from AI and big data analytics to the adoption of quantum computing and blockchain technologies — has created an imperative for organizations to embrace these tools in their decision-making processes. Companies that fail to adopt these technologies risk falling behind their competitors, who are increasingly leveraging data-driven insights to gain a competitive edge.

For decision-makers, the first lesson is that embracing these tools is not a one-time effort but a continuous process of adaptation. As AI models, data analytics capabilities, and ML techniques become more advanced, it is crucial for organizations to stay updated with the latest innovations. This requires fostering an organizational culture that values learning, experimentation, and agility.

Practical Insight: Many companies, such as Amazon and Google, have successfully implemented AI and ML not only to optimize their supply chains and marketing efforts but also to predict customer preferences, thereby creating personalized experiences. By investing in AI, decision-makers can unlock new opportunities for growth and innovation.

2. Addressing the Challenges of Technology Adoption

While the potential benefits of emerging technologies are clear, decision-makers must also address the inherent challenges that come with their adoption. As highlighted in the previous section, these challenges include data privacy concerns, integration with legacy systems, skill gaps, and the ethical use of technology. Ignoring these challenges can result in misaligned strategies, inefficiencies, and potentially severe legal and reputational risks.

The second key lesson for decision-makers is the importance of taking a holistic approach to technology adoption. This involves not only implementing cutting-edge tools but also addressing the foundational issues that could hinder their success. For example, establishing a robust data governance framework and ensuring compliance with regulations such as the GDPR can help mitigate the risk of data breaches, which can damage customer trust and incur heavy financial penalties. Additionally, integrating new technologies with legacy systems requires a strategic and thoughtful approach, including the use of modular solutions and APIs that allow for greater flexibility and scalability.

Practical Insight: Companies like Ford and General Motors have embraced a modular approach to integrating new technologies into their legacy systems. By adopting cloud-based platforms and APIs, these automakers have successfully modernized their operations without overhauling their entire infrastructure, allowing for smoother transitions and minimizing downtime.

3. Fostering a Data-Driven Culture

One of the most critical success factors in integrating emerging technologies into decision-making processes is cultivating a data-driven culture. Organizations that make data accessibility a priority at all levels of management are far more likely to succeed in leveraging advanced analytics to drive their decisions. Data should not be siloed in IT departments but rather be treated as a valuable asset that is democratized across functions, enabling informed decision-making across the organization.

For decision-makers, the third lesson is clear: Data should be at the heart of every major decision. This requires creating systems that not only store data but also ensure that it is usable, accessible, and actionable by decision-makers. This means implementing real-time data dashboards, data visualization tools, and predictive models that allow decision-makers to quickly assess key metrics, identify trends, and make informed decisions that are in alignment with organizational goals.

Practical Insight: Procter & Gamble's data-driven decision-making approach is a prime example of success in this area. The company uses real-time data dashboards to provide managers with immediate access to information about inventory, customer preferences, and market conditions, allowing them to respond swiftly to changes and optimize their operations accordingly.

4. Investing in Continuous Learning and Skill Development

As emerging technologies such as AI, big data, and advanced analytics continue to evolve, organizations must ensure that their workforce is adequately prepared to work with these tools. The fourth lesson for decision-makers is that technology adoption must go hand-in-hand with continuous learning and skill development. As AI and ML technologies become more widespread, employees will need to be trained in data science, AI, and the ethical use of these tools. This ensures that the organization has the necessary expertise to not only deploy these technologies effectively but also to adapt to future advancements.

A key part of this lesson is the importance of investing in employee training and upskilling programs that are tailored to the needs of the organization. This could include partnerships with universities and training institutions to create a pipeline of talent that is well-versed in emerging technologies. Furthermore, fostering a culture of continuous learning and encouraging employees to stay curious and engaged with the latest developments in technology will help organizations stay ahead of the curve.

Practical Insight: IBM's "SkillsBuild" program is an excellent example of how companies can invest in skill development to meet the demands of emerging technologies. By offering courses on AI, data science, and cloud computing, IBM has prepared its workforce for the future, ensuring that its employees are equipped to lead in a data-driven world.

5. Balancing Technology with Ethics

As organizations adopt powerful technologies, decision-makers must also be vigilant about their ethical implications. The rise of AI, in particular, has raised concerns about algorithmic biases, data privacy, and unintended consequences. Decision-makers need to ensure that emerging technologies are used responsibly and ethically to avoid creating disparities or making decisions that could harm individuals or communities.

The fifth lesson for decision-makers is that ethics should be integrated into the technology adoption process from the outset. This involves conducting fairness and transparency audits, using diverse datasets to train AI models, and engaging multidisciplinary teams to review the ethical implications of technology-driven decisions. By doing so, organizations can ensure that they are not only compliant with regulations but also act in the best interests of their stakeholders.

Practical Insight: A great example of ethical AI usage comes from companies like Microsoft, which has established an AI and Ethics Review Board to ensure that their technologies adhere to ethical standards. This review board helps the company identify potential biases and unintended consequences before deploying AI solutions, ensuring that their technologies benefit all users fairly and equitably.

6. Preparing for Future Technological Trends

As emerging technologies continue to evolve, decision-makers must be prepared to adapt to the next wave of innovations. The future of decision-making will likely be shaped by advancements in quantum computing, blockchain, and the integration of explainable AI (XAI). These technologies will not only enhance decision-making but also redefine the way organizations operate on a global scale.

The final lesson for decision-makers is the need for forward-thinking strategies. Organizations should remain adaptable and proactive in preparing for the next wave of technological disruption. This involves not only keeping abreast of new trends but also investing in research and development to stay at the forefront of innovation.

Furthermore, decision-makers should foster relationships with technology vendors, academic institutions, and research organizations to stay informed about the latest breakthroughs and identify opportunities for collaboration.

Practical Insight: Companies like Siemens and Google are already exploring the potential of quantum computing to revolutionize data processing. By investing in these emerging technologies, these companies are positioning themselves for the future and ensuring that they remain industry leaders as new technologies come to the fore.

In conclusion, decision-makers face both opportunities and challenges as they integrate emerging technologies into their organizations. By fostering a data-driven culture, investing in continuous learning, addressing ethical concerns, and preparing for future trends, decision-makers can ensure that their organizations remain competitive, innovative, and agile in an increasingly digital and data-driven world. These practical insights and lessons learned provide a roadmap for navigating the complex landscape of technology adoption, positioning organizations for long-term success in the face of rapid technological change.

References

Agrawal, S., Sengupta, A., & Shanker, K. (2020). Impact of supply chain uncertainty and risk on the logistics performance. *Journal of Operations Research Society*, 71(7), 1050–1065.

Atzori, L., Iera, A., & Morabito, G. (2010). The Internet of Things: A survey. *Computer Networks*, 54(15), 2787–2805.

Bertsimas, D., & Kallus, N. (2020). From predictive to prescriptive analytics. *Management Science*, 66(3), 1025–1044.

Brennan, L., Kanji, N., & Chakrabarti, A. (2019). Predictive analytics in automotive manufacturing. *International Journal of Advanced Manufacturing Technology*, 105, 2037–2053.

Brynjolfsson, E., & McAfee, A. (2017). *Machine, Platform, Crowd: Harnessing Our Digital Future*. W.W. Norton & Company.

Chen, H., Chiang, R. H. L., & Storey, V. C. (2012). Business Intelligence and Analytics: From Big Data to Big Impact. *MIS Quarterly*, 36(4), 1165–1188.

Davenport, T. H., & Harris, J. G. (2017). *Competing on Analytics: The New Science of Winning*. Harvard Business Review Press.

Fildes, R., Goodwin, P., Lawrence, M., & Nikolopoulos, K. (2008). Effective forecasting and judgmental adjustments in the supply chain. *International Journal of Forecasting*, 24(1), 3–19.

Ghahramani, Z. (2015). Probabilistic machine learning and artificial intelligence. *Nature*, 521(7553), 452–459.

Gopalakrishnan, A., Chandrasekaran, M., & Anand, S. (2013). Predictive maintenance using machine learning for smart manufacturing. *Journal of Manufacturing Systems*, 32(3), 293–302.

Huang, H., Zhu, J., & Zhang, Q. (2019). Smart grid technologies and their applications. *Renewable Energy*, 135, 1666–1676.

Jordan, M. I., & Mitchell, T. M. (2015). Machine Learning: Trends, Perspectives, and Prospects. *Science*, 349(6245), 255–260.

Kim, J., Trimi, S., & Chung, J. H. (2016). Big data applications in the government sector. *Communications of the ACM*, 59(3), 100–106.

Kiron, D., Prentice, P. K., & Ferguson, R. B. (2014). The Analytics Mandate. *MIT Sloan Management Review*, 55(4), 1–25.

Kostkova, P., Fowler, D., & Wiseman, S. (2016). Data-driven public health. *Journal of Medical Internet Research*, 18(11), e275.

Lempert, R. J., Popper, S. W., & Bankes, S. C. (2013). Robust decision-making in complex environments. *Risk Analysis*, 23(4), 549–561.

McAfee, A., Brynjolfsson, E., Davenport, T. H., Patil, D. J., & Barton, D. (2012). Big Data: The Management Revolution. *Harvard Business Review*, 90(10), 60–68.

Psaraftis, H. N., & Kontovas, C. A. (2015). Speed optimization in ship transportation. Transportation Research Part C: Emerging Technologies, 44, 299–311.

Russell, S., & Norvig, P. (2016). *Artificial Intelligence: A Modern Approach* (3rd ed.). Pearson.

Russell, S., & Norvig, P. (2016). *Artificial Intelligence: A Modern Approach* (3rd ed.). Prentice Hall.

Sharda, R., Delen, D., & Turban, E. (2020). Business Intelligence and Analytics: Systems for Decision Support (11th ed.). Pearson.

Shmueli, G., & Koppius, O. R. (2011). Predictive analytics in information systems research. *MIS Quarterly*, 35(3), 553–572.

Thomas, L. C., Crook, J. N., & Edelman, D. B. (2002). Credit Scoring and Its Applications. SIAM.

Wang, Y., Kung, L. A., & Byrd, T. A. (2018). Big data analytics in healthcare: Enabling the health-care revolution. *Journal of Business Research*, 70, 304–317.

Wedel, M., & Kannan, P. K. (2016). Marketing analytics for data-rich environments. *Journal of Marketing*, 80(6), 97–121.

Westerman, G., Bonnet, D., & McAfee, A. (2014). *Leading Digital: Turning Technology into Business Transformation.* Harvard Business Review Press.

References

- Mourtzis, D., Vlachou, E., & Milas, N. (2016). Industrial big data as a result of IoT adoption in manufacturing. *Procedia CIRP, 55*, 290–295.
- Satyanarayanan, M. (2017). The emergence of edge computing. *Computer, 50*(1), 30–39.
- Verma, P., Sood, S. K., & Kalra, N. (2020). Cloud-centric IoT based framework for healthcare monitoring. *Computers & Electrical Engineering, 84*, 106583.
- Zhou, Z., Chen, X., Li, E., Zeng, L., Luo, K., & Zhang, J. (2019). Edge intelligence: Paving the last mile of AI with edge computing. *Proceedings of the IEEE, 107*(8), 1738–1762.
- Isaak, J., & Hanna, M. J. (2018). User data privacy: Facebook, Cambridge Analytica, and privacy protection. *Computer, 51*(8), 56–59.
- McMahan, H. B., Ramage, D., Talwar, K., & Zhang, L. (2017). Federated learning: Collaborative machine learning without centralized training data. *arXiv preprint arXiv:1712.07557.*
- Raji, I. D., & Buolamwini, J. (2020). Actionable auditing: Investigating the impact of public oversight on AI systems. *Proceedings of the AAAI/ACM Conference on AI, Ethics, and Society*, 429–435.
- Brynjolfsson, E., & McAfee, A. (2014). *The Second Machine Age: Work, Progress, and Prosperity in a Time of Brilliant Technologies.* W.W. Norton & Company.
- Chung, K. H., & Lee, C. (2020). *Artificial Intelligence in Financial Markets: Cutting Edge Applications for Risk Management, Portfolio Optimization, and Economics.* Wiley Finance.
- Dastin, J. (2018). Amazon Scraps AI Recruiting Tool That Showed Bias Against Women. *Reuters.* https://www.reuters.com/article/us-amazon-com-jobs-automation-insight-idUSKCN1MK08G
- Davenport, T. H. (2018). *Artificial Intelligence for the Real World.* Harvard Business Review.
- Huang, M. H., & Rust, R. T. (2021). *Artificial Intelligence in Service. Journal of Service Research*, 24(1), 3–27.
- O'Neil, C. (2016). *Weapons of Math Destruction: How Big Data Increases Inequality and Threatens Democracy.* Crown Publishing Group.

- Sharda, R., Delen, D., & Turban, E. (2014). *Business Intelligence and Analytics: Systems for Decision Support*. Pearson Education.
- Westerman, G., Calméjane, C., Ferraris, P., *et al.* (2011). *Digital Transformation: A Roadmap for Billion-Dollar Organizations*. MIT Center for Digital Business.

Chapter 7

Case Studies in Dynamic Decision Making

Abstract

Chapter 7 explores the application of dynamic decision-making models in high-stakes scenarios across various sectors, including healthcare, finance, and emergency management. It examines how emerging technologies, such as AI and ML, are reshaping decision-making processes in these fields. By presenting case studies, the chapter highlights how these technologies improve decision quality and efficiency but also brings to light challenges and best practices. The insights provided underscore the importance of integrating data analytics and technology while addressing ethical concerns and continuous learning to enhance decision-making outcomes in complex, dynamic environments.

Keywords: Dynamic Decision-Making; High-Stakes Scenarios; Healthcare Decision-Making; Finance Decision-Making; Emergency Management; Technology-Driven Decisions; AI in Decision-Making; Machine Learning; Case Studies; Best Practices; Lessons Learned; Data Analytics; Decision Quality; Complex Environments

7.0. Introduction

The integration of emerging technologies into decision-making processes is increasingly pivotal for organizations navigating complex, high-stakes environments. In today's fast-paced world, organizations face an unprecedented level of complexity and uncertainty, where decisions must be made rapidly and with high accuracy. Technological innovations — particularly AI, ML, big data analytics, and other advanced tools — are revolutionizing how decisions are made across various sectors. This chapter delves into several real-world case studies in diverse industries such as healthcare, finance, emergency management, and industrial operations, illustrating how dynamic decision-making models are being applied to enhance decision quality, agility, and resilience.

By examining these case studies, this chapter aims to uncover the challenges, strategies, and outcomes associated with technology-driven decision-making. It will highlight the emerging trends in decision-making that organizations are adopting, providing valuable insights for practitioners. Additionally, we will explore how data analytics, AI, and ML are enhancing decision quality and enabling organizations to respond more effectively to the unpredictable and fast-changing landscape of modern business and social challenges. The increasing reliance on these technologies reflects a broader shift towards more agile, data-driven, and proactive decision-making approaches, necessary for organizations to thrive in an environment marked by disruption and volatility.

7.0.1. *The Rise of Technology-Driven Decision-Making in Complex Environments*

Decision-making in high-stakes, complex environments often involves weighing multiple variables, managing uncertainty, and predicting future events under time pressure. In traditional decision-making models, organizations relied on expert judgment, historical data, and intuition to guide their actions. While these approaches have their merits, they are increasingly insufficient in an age where rapid technological advancements and unprecedented global interdependencies create a constantly shifting landscape.

Emerging technologies such as AI and ML have become crucial in augmenting traditional decision-making models. By analyzing vast amounts of data in real time, these technologies offer valuable insights that inform more accurate, timely, and scalable decisions. For instance, AI systems can identify patterns in large datasets that may be invisible to the human eye, allowing decision-makers to gain new perspectives on problems and opportunities. ML algorithms are particularly useful for predicting future outcomes based on historical data, making them essential tools for decision-makers in industries such as healthcare, finance, and emergency management, where anticipating future events is critical.

Moreover, the growing field of data analytics has provided decision-makers with new ways to extract actionable insights from complex data sources. Big data technologies allow organizations to track and analyze data from a variety of sensors, social media platforms, and transactional records, thereby providing a holistic view of their operations. This wealth of information can help organizations make decisions that are not only more informed but also more adaptive to changing circumstances. For example, predictive analytics allows businesses to forecast customer behavior, enabling them to adjust their strategies in real-time.

7.0.2. *Case Study: Healthcare Decision-Making and AI Integration*

In the healthcare sector, the integration of AI and ML into clinical decision-making processes has revolutionized patient care, diagnosis, and treatment plans. The use of AI in medical imaging has enabled radiologists to identify early signs of diseases such as cancer, often with greater accuracy and efficiency than traditional methods. AI algorithms can analyze medical images, detect anomalies, and even predict the likelihood of certain conditions, enabling physicians to make more informed decisions and intervene earlier in the treatment process (Esteva *et al.*, 2019).

One of the significant challenges in healthcare decision-making is managing the sheer volume of data generated by patients, clinical trials, medical records, and research. ML models help healthcare organizations process these vast datasets, identifying trends and offering actionable insights that guide treatment plans. For example, in emergency care, AI-based systems can provide real-time support for clinicians, suggesting the best treatment options based on the latest research and patient-specific data. Moreover, predictive analytics are increasingly used in healthcare to predict patient outcomes, enabling healthcare providers to adjust treatment plans proactively and optimize resource allocation (Rajkomar *et al.*, 2019).

Despite these advancements, the integration of AI into healthcare decision-making is not without challenges. Ethical considerations, data privacy concerns, and the need for regulatory oversight are critical issues that must be addressed. Nevertheless, as AI technologies continue to evolve, their potential to improve decision quality and patient outcomes is immense, making them a crucial tool in modern healthcare systems.

7.0.3. *Case Study: AI and ML in Finance*

The financial services industry is another sector where technology-driven decision-making has had a transformative impact. Financial institutions, including banks, investment firms, and insurance companies, are increasingly relying on AI, ML, and big data analytics to optimize their decision-making processes. AI is used to predict market trends, assess credit risks, and enhance fraud detection.

For example, in algorithmic trading, AI systems analyze vast amounts of market data in real-time, identifying patterns and making buy/sell decisions at speeds far beyond human capability. These systems can adjust strategies based on real-time market changes, making trading decisions faster and more accurately. Furthermore, in the realm of credit risk assessment, ML algorithms are used to evaluate loan applications, analyzing an applicant's financial history and behavior to predict their ability to repay loans. This approach reduces the risk of defaults and allows for more accurate pricing of financial products (Gandal *et al.*, 2018).

However, the integration of AI and ML in finance also introduces risks. There is concern over the opacity of some AI models, with "black box" systems making it difficult to understand how certain decisions are made. This has led to debates on the need for greater transparency and regulation in AI-driven financial decisions. Moreover, the speed at which AI systems operate may also amplify the consequences of errors, making robust testing and validation critical.

7.0.4. *Case Study: Technology-Driven Decision-Making in Emergency Management*

Emergencies, such as natural disasters, pandemics, or terrorist attacks, require quick and accurate decision-making to save lives and minimize damage. In recent years, technologies such as geospatial data analysis, predictive analytics, and real-time communication systems have significantly enhanced decision-making in emergency management.

For instance, AI-powered algorithms can analyze weather patterns and predict the likelihood of natural disasters, such as hurricanes or wildfires, enabling emergency services to prepare and respond more effectively. In the case of a pandemic, ML models can predict the spread of disease based on various factors, such as mobility data, population density, and health reports, allowing public health authorities to deploy resources where they are needed most (Chien *et al.*, 2020).

In addition to predictive analytics, emergency management systems increasingly rely on real-time data from social media, sensors, and crowdsourced information to track ongoing events. This information is processed by AI systems to assess the situation dynamically and provide decision-makers with real-time insights on where to deploy resources or evacuate populations. In complex, fast-moving situations, the ability to process and act on such data quickly can be the difference between life and death.

Despite the benefits of these technologies, emergency management also faces challenges related to data privacy, system interoperability, and the need for continuous monitoring and updates. Nevertheless, the increasing integration of AI and real-time analytics into emergency management systems is improving responses to crises and enhancing the overall effectiveness of disaster relief efforts.

7.0.5. *The Future of Dynamic Decision-Making Models*

The future of dynamic decision-making models lies in the continued evolution of emerging technologies and their integration into decision-making frameworks. As AI, ML, and big data continue to advance, organizations will be able to make even more precise, data-driven decisions. Moreover, as these technologies become more sophisticated, they will allow organizations to predict not only what might happen but also how to influence outcomes, creating new opportunities for proactive decision-making.

The integration of AI with other technologies, such as IoT, will further enhance decision-making models by enabling real-time monitoring and analysis of physical systems. For example, IoT sensors in manufacturing plants can provide continuous data streams about equipment performance, which AI systems can analyze to predict maintenance needs, thus preventing downtime and optimizing operations.

However, the future also poses challenges. As organizations increasingly rely on AI and automation, questions around accountability, ethics, and the potential for algorithmic bias will need to be addressed. Ensuring transparency, fairness, and responsibility in AI-driven decision-making will be essential for maintaining trust and achieving optimal outcomes.

Overall, this chapter has explored the transformative role of emerging technologies — particularly AI, ML, and data analytics — in dynamic decision-making processes. Through case studies in healthcare, finance, and emergency management, we have highlighted the challenges, strategies, and outcomes associated with the adoption of technology-driven decision-making models. As organizations increasingly navigate complex, high-stakes environments, the need for agile, data-driven decisions becomes more critical. Emerging technologies offer a powerful means to enhance decision quality, optimize resource allocation, and adapt to rapidly changing circumstances.

By integrating AI and ML into decision-making frameworks, organizations can improve their ability to anticipate challenges, identify opportunities, and make better-informed decisions. However, as with all technological advancements, these innovations also bring about ethical, regulatory, and operational challenges that must be carefully managed to ensure positive outcomes.

7.1. Decision Making in High-Stakes Scenarios

In high-stakes decision-making scenarios, organizations across various sectors — healthcare, finance, and emergency management — are increasingly adopting emerging technologies like AL, ML, and data analytics to optimize their processes. These sectors involve decisions where the stakes are high, such as saving lives, securing financial assets, and minimizing damage during disasters. As the complexity and speed of these decisions increase, the integration of advanced technologies provides decision-makers with the tools they need to navigate uncertainty and make more informed, agile decisions. This section delves deeper into the role of AI, ML, and other technologies in these high-stakes sectors, providing an in-depth analysis of the strategies and outcomes that illustrate the growing importance of technology in dynamic decision-making.

7.1.1. *Healthcare: Enhancing Decision-Making with AI and ML*

In healthcare, decision-making is often a matter of life and death, making it one of the most critical sectors for the application of emerging technologies. Healthcare professionals face time-sensitive decisions with significant consequences, such as diagnosing diseases, determining treatment plans, and allocating scarce resources. Traditionally, these decisions have relied on clinician expertise, medical history, and diagnostic tools. However, the increasing complexity of medical data, coupled with the growing demand for healthcare services, has necessitated the integration of AI and ML to enhance decision-making.

AI-driven diagnostic tools are one of the most notable innovations in healthcare decision-making. These tools analyze large datasets — such as medical images, patient records, and laboratory results — to detect conditions that may be difficult for human clinicians to identify. For instance, AI algorithms have been shown to diagnose skin cancer with accuracy comparable to or even surpassing that of dermatologists (Esteva *et al.*, 2017). In other areas such as radiology, AI systems can automatically detect signs of pneumonia, brain tumors, or heart disease, enabling clinicians to make faster and more accurate diagnoses (Jiang *et al.*, 2017). This not only improves the quality of care but also reduces the time spent on diagnosis, allowing for quicker interventions and better outcomes.

The use of predictive analytics in healthcare is another significant advancement. Predictive models are used to anticipate patient needs, forecast disease progression, and optimize treatment plans. In emergency departments, where rapid decision-making is crucial, ML algorithms can predict the severity of conditions based on real-time data from patients (Esteva *et al.*, 2019). For example, predictive models for sepsis risk have been implemented in hospitals, helping doctors intervene before the condition becomes life-threatening (Desautels *et al.*, 2016). Similarly, AI-powered decision-support systems help healthcare providers prioritize cases, allocate resources, and manage patient flow, ensuring that the most critical cases receive attention first.

However, the integration of AI and ML in healthcare decision-making also presents challenges. Ethical concerns about patient privacy, data security, and algorithmic bias are prominent. For instance, AI algorithms trained on biased data may exacerbate health disparities, leading to unequal treatment outcomes for different demographic groups (Obermeyer *et al.*, 2019). Ensuring that AI systems are transparent, fair, and accountable is crucial for maintaining trust in these technologies. Additionally, there are concerns about the potential over-reliance on AI, which may lead to a reduction in clinical judgment. It is essential for healthcare providers to strike a balance between leveraging AI's capabilities and maintaining the human touch that is critical in patient care.

7.1.2. *Finance: AI and ML in Risk Management and Investment Decisions*

The finance sector is another high-stakes environment where decision-making can have profound consequences. Decisions related to risk management, investment strategies, and regulatory compliance must be made with precision and speed. In this context, AI and ML are increasingly being used to improve decision-making, particularly in the areas of market analysis, risk prediction, and portfolio management.

AI and ML tools enable financial institutions to analyze massive volumes of market data in real-time, identifying trends and making predictions about future market behavior. For example, hedge funds and investment firms use algorithmic trading strategies powered by AI to execute trades based on real-time market analysis (He *et al.*, 2018). These systems can process complex market signals much faster than human traders, enabling them to react to market shifts almost instantaneously. Similarly, AI models are used to predict the volatility of financial assets, allowing investment managers to adjust their portfolios dynamically in response to market changes.

In risk management, AI and ML have proven valuable in predicting potential risks and mitigating them before they impact the financial institution. ML models can analyze historical financial data, macroeconomic indicators, and geopolitical events to predict market downturns or credit defaults. For example, AI-powered systems are used to evaluate loan applicants' creditworthiness by assessing a wide range of variables, including transaction history, social behavior, and even online activity. This approach goes beyond traditional credit scoring methods, which rely heavily on credit reports, by incorporating non-traditional data that can provide a more accurate picture of an individual's financial behavior (Berg *et al.*, 2020).

However, the widespread use of AI and ML in finance also raises ethical concerns. One of the primary challenges is the transparency of AI decision-making processes. Many AI systems, particularly deep learning models, are often considered "black boxes," meaning that it is difficult to understand how they arrive at their decisions. This lack of transparency can lead to issues with accountability, especially when decisions result in financial losses or regulatory violations (Dastin, 2018). Furthermore, algorithmic trading and high-frequency trading have raised concerns about market manipulation and the destabilization of financial markets. There is an ongoing debate about the need for regulatory oversight to ensure that AI-driven financial systems are fair, transparent, and accountable.

7.1.3. *Emergency Management: Leveraging AI and Data Analytics for Crisis Response*

In emergency management, high-stakes decision-making is essential for mitigating the impact of natural disasters, public health emergencies, and other crises. In these situations, decisions often need to be made in real-time, with limited information and significant consequences for human lives, property, and infrastructure. Emerging technologies, particularly AI, ML, and data analytics, have become indispensable tools for improving the speed, efficiency, and accuracy of decision-making in emergency situations.

AI and ML algorithms are being used to predict and manage a range of emergency scenarios, from natural disasters like hurricanes and earthquakes to public health crises like pandemics. For instance, machine learning models have been used to predict the spread of diseases such as COVID-19, helping public health organizations allocate resources more effectively and implement timely interventions (Bansal *et al.*, 2019). These predictive models incorporate a wide range of factors, including population movement, climate data, and social behavior, to forecast the trajectory of an outbreak and the impact it will have on different regions.

In addition to predictive analytics, AI is used to process real-time data from various sources, including satellite imagery, social media feeds, and sensors deployed in disaster zones. Geographic information systems (GIS) are integrated with AI models to map out areas that are at greatest risk, enabling emergency responders to prioritize their efforts and allocate resources where they are most needed (Luo *et al.*, 2019). For example, during hurricanes, real-time satellite data can provide insights into storm paths and intensity, while AI algorithms can help predict the potential impact on communities, guiding evacuation decisions and resource distribution.

The role of IoT in emergency management cannot be understated. IoT devices, such as sensors and wearable technologies, provide real-time data on the status of critical infrastructure, weather conditions, and individual health. AI systems process this data to identify emerging risks and support decision-making in disaster response. In a wildfire, for example, IoT sensors can detect changes in air quality and temperature, sending real-time updates to emergency response teams who can then make decisions about evacuations and resource allocation (Wang *et al.*, 2018).

Despite the advantages of AI and IoT in emergency management, challenges remain. The interoperability of different technologies and data sources is a significant issue, as systems from various agencies and organizations may not be compatible. Additionally, privacy concerns related to the collection and use of real-time data are an ongoing challenge, especially when dealing with sensitive information about individuals' health and whereabouts. Nevertheless, the integration of AI, ML, and IoT into emergency management systems is significantly improving the effectiveness of disaster response and helping to save lives.

Overall, the integration of AI, ML, and other emerging technologies into decision-making processes in high-stakes sectors such as healthcare, finance, and emergency management has proven to be a game-changer. These technologies are enabling decision-makers to process vast amounts of data, identify patterns, and make faster, more accurate decisions. In healthcare, AI has revolutionized diagnostics and treatment planning, improving patient outcomes. In finance, AI and ML are enhancing risk management and investment strategies, while also raising important ethical concerns about transparency. In emergency management, AI-powered predictive models and real-time data analytics are improving the efficiency of crisis response, helping decision-makers allocate resources more effectively and save lives.

As these technologies continue to evolve, their role in decision-making will only increase, offering even more opportunities for enhancing decision quality and agility. However, addressing the challenges related to ethics, transparency, and system interoperability will be crucial to fully realizing the potential of these technologies in high-stakes environments.

Table 7.1 provides a concise overview of decision-making in high-stakes scenarios across three critical sectors: healthcare, finance, and emergency management. It outlines the key aspects of decision-making in each sector, focusing on the role of emerging technologies like AI, ML, and IoT in addressing complex challenges. The table also presents actionable takeaways for decision-makers, emphasizing the importance of leveraging technology to enhance decision quality, mitigate risks, and optimize outcomes while addressing ethical and operational challenges. This summary serves as a practical guide for stakeholders aiming to navigate the complexities of high-stakes environments effectively.

Table 7.1. Key Aspects of Decision Making in High-Stakes Scenarios and Takeaways for Decision Makers

Sector	Key Aspects of Decision-Making	Key Takeaways for Decision Makers
Healthcare	– High-stakes decisions involving life-saving interventions. – Increasing reliance on AI/ML for diagnostics and predictive analytics. – Ethical concerns about data privacy and algorithmic bias.	– Leverage AI for faster, more accurate diagnoses (e.g., radiology, skin cancer detection). – Address bias and ensure fairness in AI applications. – Balance technology with clinical judgment to maintain the "human touch."
Finance	– Decisions impact financial stability and asset management. – Use of AI/ML for market analysis, risk prediction, and regulatory compliance. – Challenges with transparency and accountability in AI systems.	– Adopt AI tools for real-time market analysis and risk management. – Implement regulatory frameworks to address "black box" models and ethical concerns. – Use predictive analytics to improve credit scoring and portfolio management.
Emergency Management	– Real-time decision-making under uncertainty and time constraints. – Use of predictive analytics and IoT for disaster mitigation and resource allocation. – Challenges with interoperability and data privacy.	– Integrate GIS and IoT for accurate disaster response planning. – Address technology compatibility across agencies. – Prioritize ethical use of sensitive data.

7.2. Technology-Driven Decision Making in Business and Industry

The integration of emerging technologies into business and industrial decision-making is revolutionizing operational strategies, improving efficiency, and enhancing competitiveness. Companies in diverse sectors are leveraging technology to optimize their operations, from streamlining production processes to enhancing customer experiences. Advanced data analytics, AI, ML, IoT, and other technologies are reshaping business models and strategies, enabling firms to respond quickly to market changes, reduce costs, and gain a competitive edge. This section explores how businesses across various industries — such as manufacturing, marketing, and energy — are using these technologies to drive more informed, data-driven decisions.

7.2.1. *The Role of Data-Driven Decision Making in Manufacturing*

The manufacturing sector has been at the forefront of adopting emerging technologies to optimize decision-making. Companies in this industry are increasingly relying on predictive analytics, AI, and ML to improve production efficiency, reduce operational costs, and enhance quality control. Predictive analytics, for example, enables manufacturers to forecast demand, optimize production schedules, and improve inventory management (Qudrat-Ullah, 2014). By analyzing historical data, ML algorithms can predict future trends, helping manufacturers to make proactive decisions that align production with market demand, preventing overproduction or stockouts.

Advanced data analytics is also used to monitor and optimize manufacturing processes in real-time. By collecting data from IoT sensors embedded in machinery, companies can track equipment performance and detect anomalies before they lead to costly downtime or failures. Predictive maintenance, powered by AI, allows businesses to predict when equipment will fail and schedule maintenance in advance, thus reducing the risk of unexpected breakdowns (Jin *et al.*, 2017). This not only reduces maintenance costs but also improves the reliability of the production process, leading to higher productivity and customer satisfaction.

In addition, AI-driven tools are helping businesses with quality control by automatically detecting defects in products during the manufacturing process. Computer vision systems can analyze product images in real-time, identifying defects such as cracks, scratches, or imperfections that would be difficult for human inspectors to detect. This results in improved product quality and reduced waste (Liu *et al.*, 2020).

The use of AI and ML in manufacturing is also enhancing supply chain management. By leveraging data analytics, manufacturers can improve their forecasting accuracy, enabling them to anticipate fluctuations in demand and adjust their supply chain strategies accordingly. Real-time data from suppliers, logistics providers, and distributors can be analyzed to identify inefficiencies and bottlenecks in the supply chain, allowing businesses to optimize operations, reduce costs, and improve delivery times.

Despite these benefits, the widespread use of data-driven decision-making in manufacturing also presents challenges. The integration of AI and predictive analytics requires significant investments in technology and infrastructure. Additionally, businesses must address concerns related to data security and privacy, particularly when sensitive production data is shared across multiple stakeholders. Moreover, ensuring that decision-makers are properly trained to interpret and act upon the insights generated by these technologies is crucial to the successful implementation of data-driven strategies.

In conclusion, data-driven decision-making is revolutionizing the manufacturing sector by enhancing efficiency, reducing costs, and improving product quality. The integration of advanced technologies like AI, ML, and predictive analytics enables manufacturers to optimize production processes, anticipate maintenance needs, and refine supply chain management. However, while the benefits are clear, the successful adoption of these technologies requires substantial investment in infrastructure, robust data security measures, and ongoing training for decision-makers. As the industry continues to evolve, companies that effectively leverage data analytics will gain a competitive edge, while those who navigate the challenges of integration will unlock new opportunities for growth and innovation.

7.2.2. *AI and ML in Marketing Decision-Making*

Marketing is another area where technology-driven decision-making is having a profound impact. With the explosion of digital data, companies are increasingly turning to AI and ML to enhance customer targeting, personalize recommendations, and optimize marketing campaigns. AI tools enable businesses to analyze customer behavior and preferences, predict trends, and tailor their offerings to meet the specific needs of different market segments.

One of the most notable applications of AI in marketing is personalized product recommendations. Retailers such as Amazon and Netflix use sophisticated recommendation algorithms to suggest products or content based on individual customer preferences and past behaviors. These systems analyze vast amounts of customer data, including browsing history, purchase patterns, and demographic information, to predict what products or services customers are most likely to buy (Lycett, 2013). By offering personalized recommendations, businesses can increase customer engagement, improve conversion rates, and drive sales.

AI is also transforming digital advertising by enabling highly targeted marketing campaigns. Through programmatic advertising, AI systems can automatically purchase and place ads on digital platforms based on user behavior, location, and interests. This approach allows advertisers to reach the right audience with the right message at the right time, increasing the effectiveness of their campaigns and improving return on investment (ROI) (Chaffey, 2019).

Furthermore, AI-driven chatbots are becoming a standard tool for customer service and engagement. These virtual assistants use natural language processing (NLP) to interact with customers in real-time, answering questions, resolving issues, and guiding customers through their purchasing decisions. Chatbots can analyze customer queries and provide personalized responses, improving the customer experience and reducing the need for human intervention (Liu *et al.*, 2019).

Despite the benefits, AI in marketing also raises several ethical concerns. The use of personal data for targeted advertising has sparked debates about privacy and data protection. Businesses must ensure that they are transparent about how customer data is collected and used, and that they comply with data privacy regulations such as the GDPR. Additionally, there is the risk of algorithmic bias in AI systems, which could lead to unfair or discriminatory outcomes in customer targeting and recommendations (Binns, 2018).

In conclusion, the integration of AI and ML in marketing decision-making is transforming the way businesses engage with customers and optimize their strategies. Personalized recommendations, targeted advertising, and AI-driven chatbots are enhancing customer experiences, driving sales, and improving marketing efficiency. However, as these technologies evolve, organizations must address ethical concerns, including data privacy and the potential for algorithmic bias. Ensuring transparency in data usage, complying with privacy regulations, and mitigating biases in AI models will be crucial for businesses to build trust and maintain a responsible approach to leveraging AI in marketing. By balancing innovation with ethical considerations, companies can harness the full potential of AI to create meaningful connections with customers and achieve long-term success.

7.2.3. *The Energy Sector: Decision-Making for Efficiency and Sustainability*

The energy sector is one of the industries most affected by the need to balance efficiency, sustainability, and profitability. Emerging technologies such as smart grids, IoT, and advanced analytics are revolutionizing energy management systems, enabling real-time monitoring and control of energy consumption. These technologies are particularly important in the context of increasing demand for sustainable energy solutions and the transition to renewable energy sources.

Smart grids are a prime example of how emerging technologies are transforming decision-making in the energy sector. Unlike traditional electrical grids, which operate in a one-way flow of electricity from power plants to consumers, smart grids enable two-way communication between energy providers and consumers. This allows for real-time monitoring of energy usage, as well as the ability to adjust supply based on demand fluctuations. Through advanced analytics, smart grids can predict energy demand and optimize the distribution of electricity, reducing energy waste and improving grid reliability (Kundur *et al.*, 2018).

IoT sensors play a critical role in smart grid systems by providing real-time data on energy consumption, equipment status, and environmental conditions. These sensors collect data from homes, businesses, and industrial facilities, which is then analyzed to identify trends, optimize energy distribution, and prevent outages. For example, smart meters installed in homes can track electricity usage in real-time and communicate directly with the grid, allowing energy providers to adjust supply based on consumer needs. This dynamic approach to energy management leads to greater energy efficiency and sustainability.

AI and ML are also being used to integrate renewable energy sources, such as wind and solar, into the grid. These energy sources are intermittent and weather-dependent, making their integration into traditional grids challenging. AI algorithms can forecast weather patterns and energy production from renewable sources, enabling better planning and coordination of energy supply (Qudrat-Ullah, 2014). For example, ML models can predict the output of solar panels based on weather conditions, allowing energy providers to adjust their supply mix accordingly.

In addition to optimizing energy management, AI is playing a role in energy consumption reduction. Companies in the energy sector are using AI-driven tools to analyze energy usage patterns and identify opportunities for reducing waste. For example, industrial facilities can use AI-powered energy management systems to monitor and optimize their energy consumption, reducing operational costs and improving sustainability (Hao *et al.*, 2020). AI is also being used to support the design of energy-efficient buildings and infrastructure, using simulations and predictive models to optimize energy use in construction projects.

However, the integration of AI and IoT into energy systems also presents challenges. One of the primary concerns is the cybersecurity risks associated with smart grids and IoT devices. As energy systems become more interconnected and dependent on digital technologies, they become more vulnerable to cyberattacks, which could disrupt energy supply and compromise sensitive data. Ensuring the security of these systems is a top priority for energy providers and policymakers.

Overall, the integration of emerging technologies such as AI, ML, and IoT into business and industrial decision-making is driving significant transformations across various sectors. In manufacturing, predictive analytics and AI are enhancing production efficiency, quality control, and supply chain management. In marketing, AI-driven tools are improving customer targeting, personalization, and digital advertising strategies. In the energy sector, smart grids, IoT, and advanced analytics are optimizing energy management, improving sustainability, and facilitating the integration of renewable energy sources.

While these technologies offer significant benefits, they also present challenges, including concerns related to data privacy, algorithmic bias, cybersecurity, and the need for significant investments in infrastructure and training. As businesses continue to adopt and integrate these technologies, they will need to address these challenges to fully realize the potential of technology-driven decision-making.

Table 7.2 provides an overview of the technology-driven decision-making advancements across sectors, highlighting emerging technologies and actionable lessons for decision-makers to improve efficiency, sustainability, and competitiveness.

7.2.4. *A Dynamic View of Technology-Driven Decision Making in Business and Industry*

In recent years, the role of emerging technologies in shaping business and industrial decision-making has become increasingly significant. A dynamic view of technology-driven decision-making reflects not only the integration of advanced tools such as AI, ML, and data analytics but also the continuous adaptation to rapidly changing environments. This dynamic nature stems from the ongoing evolution of these technologies, their ability to process vast amounts of data in real-time, and their capacity to help organizations make informed decisions quickly. To fully understand how these technologies are revolutionizing industries, it is important to explore both the opportunities and challenges they present, along with the strategies that businesses can adopt to stay ahead.

Table 7.2. Key Aspects and Lessons of Technology-Driven Decision Making

Sector	Technological Advancements	Key Lessons and Insights
Manufacturing	– Predictive analytics for demand forecasting and inventory management.	– Use AI/ML to enhance efficiency and reduce costs.
	– IoT for real-time monitoring and predictive maintenance.	– Train staff to interpret data insights effectively.
	– AI-driven quality control with computer vision.	– Secure sensitive production data to address privacy concerns.
Marketing	– AI for personalized recommendations and customer behavior analysis.	– Utilize customer data ethically to drive targeted strategies.
	– Programmatic advertising for real-time, targeted campaigns.	– Ensure transparency and fairness in customer targeting.
	– Chatbots powered by NLP for personalized customer engagement.	– Integrate chatbots to enhance service while reducing costs.
Energy	– Smart grids for real-time energy optimization and waste reduction.	– Embrace smart grids for improved efficiency and reliability.
	– IoT sensors and analytics for energy management and renewable integration.	– Mitigate cybersecurity risks in interconnected systems.
	– AI for forecasting and optimizing renewable energy supply.	– Leverage predictive tools for balancing sustainability with profitability.

1. The Evolution and Impact of Technology on Decision Making

The integration of advanced technologies into business decision-making processes has fundamentally altered how organizations approach problems and opportunities. AI and ML algorithms, for example, can process and analyze massive amounts of data far more quickly and accurately than human analysts, allowing for faster decision-making. Over the past decade, businesses across various industries, such as healthcare, finance, and manufacturing, have increasingly relied on these technologies to enhance their decision-making capabilities (Brynjolfsson & McAfee, 2017). For instance, in manufacturing, AI systems are used to predict equipment failure and optimize production schedules, whereas in healthcare, AI models assist in diagnosing diseases by analyzing patient data (Jin *et al.*, 2017).

The evolution of decision-making tools is also reflected in the growing use of real-time data analytics. Unlike traditional methods of decision-making that rely on periodic reporting or delayed information, real-time analytics empower organizations to respond to changing conditions immediately. This is particularly valuable in environments like financial markets, where quick decisions can result in significant gains or prevent losses (Chong *et al.*, 2017). Similarly, in logistics and supply chain management, AI-driven systems can predict inventory demands and optimize shipping routes, reducing delays and cutting operational costs (Chien *et al.*, 2015).

2. Technological Advancements and Business Adaptability

A dynamic view of technology-driven decision-making highlights the importance of adaptability. Given the rapid pace at which AI and ML technologies are advancing, businesses must remain agile and open to new developments. The ability to continuously adapt is key to leveraging these technologies effectively. According to Teece (2018), business adaptability refers to an organization's ability to adjust its strategies in response to technological disruptions, changing market conditions, and shifting customer preferences.

For example, companies in the retail sector, such as Amazon and Walmart, have used AI to transform their supply chains and predict consumer behavior. These businesses collect vast amounts of customer data, and by applying AI models, they can anticipate product demand, optimize inventory levels, and personalize marketing strategies. However, as these technologies evolve, companies must constantly update their tools and models to ensure they continue to provide accurate predictions and drive successful outcomes (Lycett, 2013).

Moreover, AI's potential to foster innovation presents an opportunity for businesses to differentiate themselves in the market. Innovators in the technology space, such as Google and Tesla, have capitalized on AI and ML to develop products that meet specific consumer needs while also opening new markets. This ability to innovate is not only dependent on the tools available but also on the organizational culture that supports continuous learning and experimentation (Lycett, 2013).

In conclusion, the dynamic nature of technology-driven decision-making underscores the critical importance of organizational adaptability in the face of rapid advancements in AI and ML. As businesses harness these technologies to optimize operations, enhance customer experiences, and drive innovation, they must remain proactive in updating their strategies, models, and tools. The continuous evolution of AI presents both opportunities and challenges, requiring companies to foster a culture of learning and flexibility. Those organizations that effectively integrate these technologies while adapting to market shifts will not only stay competitive but also lead the way in defining the future of business and industry.

3. Challenges in Technology-Driven Decision Making

While the integration of AI and ML technologies has brought numerous benefits, the adoption of these tools is not without challenges. One key challenge is the quality and accessibility of data. AI models are only as good as the data they are trained on, and inaccurate or biased data can lead to flawed decisions (Binns, 2018). Therefore, businesses must invest in robust data collection, storage, and validation processes to ensure the quality of the information that feeds into their decision-making systems. This issue is particularly critical in sectors such as healthcare, where poor data quality can result in misdiagnoses or inappropriate treatment plans (Esteva *et al.*, 2019).

Another challenge is the ethical concerns surrounding the use of AI in decision-making. As AI systems become more autonomous, there is growing concern about the transparency of decisions made by algorithms. These "black-box" models, where the decision-making process is not easily understood by humans, pose a significant challenge, especially when used in sensitive areas such as hiring or criminal justice (Dastin, 2018). To address these concerns, businesses must ensure that their AI systems are explainable, transparent, and accountable, so that stakeholders can understand how decisions are made and have confidence in their outcomes.

Furthermore, regulatory and compliance issues also play a major role in technology-driven decision-making. Organizations need to be aware of the legal frameworks that govern the use of AI and personal data, such as the GDPR in the European Union, to avoid legal repercussions. Compliance with these regulations is crucial not only to avoid penalties but also to maintain customer trust and loyalty (Qudrat-Ullah & Karakul, 2007).

In conclusion, while AI and ML technologies offer substantial advantages in decision-making, businesses must be mindful of the associated challenges. Ensuring data quality and accessibility, addressing ethical concerns regarding transparency, and navigating regulatory compliance are essential steps for responsible and effective AI integration. Organizations that prioritize these areas will be better equipped to mitigate risks and enhance the reliability and fairness of their AI-driven decisions. Ultimately, by investing in robust data management, fostering transparency in AI models, and adhering to regulatory frameworks, businesses can fully harness the potential of AI and ML while maintaining trust and accountability in their decision-making processes.

- **The Future of Technology-Driven Decision Making**

Looking ahead, the future of technology-driven decision-making in business and industry appears to be increasingly intertwined with advancements in AI, blockchain, and IoT. These technologies are expected to enable even more seamless integration of data across systems and enhance decision-making across various sectors. Blockchain, for instance, promises to improve transparency and security in industries like finance, logistics, and supply chain management, further driving efficiency in decision-making processes (Tapscott & Tapscott, 2016).

The potential for AI to continue evolving and influencing business strategy is immense. With the increasing use of automation, businesses can expect a greater shift towards predictive decision-making, where AI models not only help organizations react to current conditions but also anticipate future outcomes based on historical trends. However, to fully realize the benefits of these technologies, companies must invest in the necessary infrastructure, embrace a culture of innovation, and address the ethical and regulatory concerns that come with their deployment (Brynjolfsson & McAfee, 2017).

Overall, technology-driven decision-making in business and industry is undergoing a transformative shift as organizations integrate AI, ML, and real-time data analytics into their operations. This dynamic approach to decision-making not only enhances efficiency but also drives innovation and adaptability, ensuring that businesses can stay competitive in an ever-changing marketplace. However, businesses must also address challenges related to data quality, ethics, and compliance to ensure that these technologies are used responsibly and effectively. As technological advancements continue to evolve, the future of decision-making will be increasingly shaped by these tools, offering immense potential for growth and success across industries.

7.3. Lessons Learned and Best Practices

The integration of emerging technologies into decision-making processes has revolutionized industries across the board. Through examining various case studies in healthcare, finance, energy, and other sectors, several key lessons and best practices have emerged that can guide organizations in optimizing their decision-making frameworks. These insights focus on the importance of data quality, ethical considerations, continuous learning, and the development of robust technological infrastructures. This section provides a deeper analysis of these lessons and best practices, focusing on the fundamental principles that organizations should embrace to navigate the complexities of dynamic decision-making in the age of emerging technologies.

7.3.1. *Data Quality and Accessibility: The Foundation of Effective Decision-Making*

One of the foremost lessons learned from the application of emerging technologies in decision-making is the critical importance of data quality and accessibility. High-quality, accurate, and real-time data are essential for making informed and timely decisions, especially in high-stakes environments such as healthcare, finance, and emergency management. Inaccurate or incomplete data can lead to flawed decisions, with potentially disastrous outcomes, as seen in instances where predictive models failed to anticipate critical events due to poor data inputs (Qudrat-Ullah *et al.*, 2008).

To ensure that data can be leveraged effectively, organizations must invest in robust data infrastructures. This includes adopting technologies that allow for real-time data collection and integration across various platforms, ensuring that decision-makers have access to up-to-date and relevant information. For example, in healthcare, AI-driven diagnostic tools can analyze vast amounts of medical data, providing clinicians with faster and more accurate diagnoses, which can significantly improve patient outcomes (Jiang *et al.*, 2017). However, this relies heavily on high-quality data inputted into the system. Similarly, in the finance industry, firms must ensure that their trading algorithms have access to real-time market data to make quick, accurate decisions that can optimize trading strategies (Berg *et al.*, 2020).

Organizations should establish stringent protocols for data collection, validation, and processing to ensure data accuracy and reliability. Moreover, creating an accessible data ecosystem where decision-makers can easily retrieve the information they need in real-time is vital. This involves implementing data governance frameworks that ensure data integrity while enabling smooth collaboration between departments and systems (Qudrat-Ullah, 2020).

In conclusion, data quality and accessibility are foundational to effective decision-making in the age of emerging technologies. Organizations must prioritize investments in robust data infrastructures, ensuring real-time, accurate, and reliable data flows seamlessly across systems. By implementing stringent data governance protocols and fostering cross-departmental collaboration, organizations can enhance the reliability of their decision-making processes. High-quality data not only empowers decision-makers with timely insights but also enables organizations to harness the full potential of advanced technologies like AI and ML. In sectors such as healthcare and finance, where the stakes are high, ensuring data integrity is paramount to achieving optimal outcomes and maintaining public trust.

7.3.2. *Ethical and Regulatory Implications of AI and ML Integration*

As AI and ML technologies continue to be integrated into decision-making processes, organizations must recognize the ethical and regulatory implications that arise. One key consideration is the need for transparency in how AI-driven decisions are made. Many AI systems, particularly those used in sectors like finance and healthcare, operate as “black boxes” where the decision-making process is not easily understood by humans. This lack of transparency can be problematic, especially when decisions made by these systems significantly affect people’s lives, such as in healthcare diagnoses or credit scoring in financial services (Dastin, 2018).

Transparency and accountability are fundamental to maintaining trust in AI-driven systems. Organizations must ensure that their AI models are explainable and that their operations comply with established ethical guidelines. This includes ensuring fairness in the algorithms, preventing bias in decision-making, and safeguarding privacy, particularly when handling sensitive personal data, as seen in the case of financial institutions and healthcare providers (Esteva *et al.*, 2019). In finance, for example, AI models must be closely monitored to ensure they are not making biased lending decisions based on flawed data (Berg *et al.*, 2020).

Moreover, regulatory frameworks are critical to ensuring that organizations remain compliant with laws and guidelines that govern AI and data usage. This includes adhering to privacy laws such as GDPR in Europe, which emphasizes the protection of personal data in automated systems. Establishing clear guidelines and frameworks for the responsible use of emerging technologies is essential for minimizing ethical concerns and promoting social responsibility (Qudrat-Ullah & Karakul, 2007).

In conclusion, the ethical and regulatory implications of AI and ML integration are critical considerations for organizations as they adopt these technologies. Transparency, accountability, and fairness must be prioritized to build trust and ensure that AI systems make decisions that are ethical and free from bias. Adhering to regulatory frameworks, such as privacy laws and industry guidelines, is essential for protecting sensitive data and maintaining public confidence. By establishing responsible AI practices and complying with relevant regulations, organizations can navigate the complexities of AI integration while safeguarding ethical standards and societal well-being.

7.3.3. *Continuous Learning and Adaptation: Staying Ahead of Technological Advancements*

Given the rapid pace at which emerging technologies are evolving, organizations must be committed to continuous learning and adaptation to stay ahead. The dynamic nature of AI, ML, and other emerging technologies means that decision-makers need to be flexible and ready to adjust their strategies as new tools and insights become available. This requires a culture of ongoing education and training to ensure that decision-makers have the knowledge and skills to leverage new technologies effectively (Qudrat-Ullah, 2020).

Moreover, organizations must foster a mindset of innovation, encouraging experimentation and the exploration of new approaches to problem-solving. This is particularly important in industries like energy, where the adoption of smart grids and IoT technologies requires a shift in how energy is managed and consumed. By adopting a continuous learning approach, organizations can ensure they are not only keeping up with technological advancements but also anticipating future trends that may impact their operations (Lycett, 2013).

A key aspect of continuous learning is fostering an environment where feedback loops are integrated into decision-making processes. Real-time feedback from systems, along with data-driven insights, can inform adjustments to business strategies. For instance, in manufacturing, predictive analytics tools can continuously monitor production lines and provide feedback on process improvements, reducing waste and improving efficiency (Qudrat-Ullah, 2014). These feedback loops enable organizations to quickly adapt and optimize their operations in response to new challenges and opportunities.

In conclusion, continuous learning and adaptation are crucial for organizations to stay ahead in the rapidly evolving technological landscape. By fostering a culture of innovation and providing ongoing education and training, decision-makers can ensure they are equipped to leverage emerging technologies effectively. The integration of real-time feedback loops and data-driven insights further enhances an organization's ability to adapt quickly, optimize operations, and anticipate future trends. Ultimately, organizations that prioritize continuous learning will not only keep pace with technological advancements but also position themselves for sustained success in an increasingly complex environment.

7.3.4. *Building a Culture of Collaboration: Cross-Functional Integration*

Another critical lesson learned from the case studies is the importance of fostering a collaborative culture across different functions within an organization. Effective decision-making, particularly in complex, high-stakes environments, requires the integration of diverse perspectives and expertise. The collaboration between data scientists, engineers, operational staff, and decision-makers is crucial for ensuring that emerging technologies are used effectively across the entire organization.

In the healthcare sector, for example, AI tools used in diagnostics must be integrated into the workflows of healthcare professionals, including doctors, nurses, and hospital administrators. This requires seamless collaboration between IT professionals, clinical experts, and management teams to ensure that AI systems are used in ways that complement existing practices and enhance the quality of care. Similarly, in the finance sector, the collaboration between finance professionals, compliance officers, and data scientists is essential to ensure that AI-driven financial models are accurate, compliant with regulations, and ethically sound (Berg *et al.*, 2020).

Organizations must prioritize cross-functional training and communication to break down silos and ensure that decision-makers at all levels have a clear understanding of the technologies being employed and how they impact the organization's overall strategy (Lycett, 2013). This collaborative approach not only improves decision-making but also fosters innovation and helps organizations remain agile in the face of technological change.

Table 7.3 provides a summary of the lessons learned and best practices for decision-makers derived from the integration of emerging technologies into decision-making processes. These insights highlight the importance of data quality, ethical considerations, continuous learning, and fostering collaboration for optimizing dynamic decision-making.

Table 7.3. Lessons Learned and Best Practices for Decision-Makers

Key Aspect	Lessons Learned	Best Practices for Decision-Makers
Data Quality and Accessibility	– High-quality, accurate, and real-time data is essential for effective decisions. – Incomplete or flawed data can lead to poor outcomes.	– Invest in robust data infrastructures for real-time integration and accessibility. – Establish stringent protocols for data collection, validation, and governance. – Ensure collaboration between departments to create an accessible data ecosystem.
Ethical and Regulatory Implications	– Transparency and accountability in AI-driven systems are critical. – Regulatory compliance is essential to mitigate privacy and ethical risks.	– Develop explainable AI models to maintain trust and prevent bias in decision-making. – Adhere to regulations like GDPR and implement ethical AI frameworks. – Safeguard sensitive data to protect privacy and prevent misuse.
Continuous Learning and Adaptation	– Staying ahead of rapid technological advancements requires flexibility and readiness to adapt. – Real-time feedback loops enhance adaptability and operational optimization.	– Promote a culture of continuous education and training on emerging technologies. – Foster innovation by encouraging experimentation and leveraging feedback-driven improvements. – Monitor technological trends to anticipate and prepare for future opportunities and challenges.

Table 7.3. (*Continued*)

Key Aspect	Lessons Learned	Best Practices for Decision-Makers
Building a Collaborative Culture	– Cross-functional collaboration improves decision-making in complex environments. – Seamless integration of technology into workflows requires multi-disciplinary teams.	– Encourage communication and training across departments to integrate diverse expertise. – Break down silos and ensure alignment between IT, operational, and strategic teams for optimal tech adoption.

7.4. Conclusion

Dynamic decision-making in the age of emerging technologies is a critical competency that organizations and leaders must cultivate to navigate the complexities of modern business environments effectively. The interplay of technological advancements, organizational culture, and external pressures has reshaped the landscape of decision-making, requiring innovative approaches and adaptive strategies. This section delves deeper into the insights and actionable takeaways for decision-makers while expanding the analysis of the opportunities and challenges posed by emerging technologies.

7.4.1. *Insights for Decision-Makers*

1. **Leveraging Technology as a Strategic Asset**
   Emerging technologies such as AI, ML, and advanced data analytics offer unprecedented capabilities for improving decision quality and agility. Decision-makers should focus on integrating these technologies into their strategic frameworks, ensuring alignment with organizational goals. For instance, AI-driven predictive analytics can enhance forecasting accuracy in supply chain management, thereby reducing costs and improving efficiency (Qudrat-Ullah, 2023). Decision-makers must treat technology not merely as a tool but as a strategic asset that drives innovation and competitive advantage.

2. **Building a Culture of Data-Driven Decisions**
   A significant insight from the case studies is the importance of fostering a data-driven culture within organizations. High-quality and accessible data serve as the foundation for informed decision-making. Decision-makers should prioritize investments in robust data infrastructure, encourage cross-functional collaboration, and promote transparency in data utilization. Organizations like Amazon have demonstrated the transformative power of a data-centric approach in achieving operational excellence and customer satisfaction (Qudrat-Ullah & Spector, 2008).
3. **Balancing Agility and Ethical Considerations**
   While the rapid adoption of AI and ML can accelerate decision-making, it also raises ethical and regulatory concerns. Decision-makers must establish robust governance frameworks to ensure transparency, accountability, and fairness in AI-driven decisions. This is especially crucial in sectors such as healthcare and finance, where biases or errors can have profound consequences. Ethical considerations should be integrated into the design and deployment of AI systems, balancing innovation with societal responsibility (Qudrat-Ullah & Karakul, 2007).
4. **Fostering Continuous Learning and Adaptation**
   The fast-paced evolution of emerging technologies necessitates a commitment to continuous learning. Decision-makers should invest in ongoing training programs, encourage experimentation, and cultivate an organizational mindset that embraces change. By fostering an adaptive culture, organizations can stay ahead of technological disruptions and maintain resilience in the face of uncertainty. For example, organizations that adopted agile methodologies during the COVID-19 pandemic were better positioned to navigate the crisis (Qudrat-Ullah, 2022).

7.4.2. *Addressing Challenges in Technology Adoption*

1. **Mitigating Risks and Uncertainty**
   The adoption of emerging technologies often involves significant risks, including cybersecurity threats, data breaches, and technological obsolescence. Decision-makers should proactively assess these risks and implement mitigation strategies, such as robust cybersecurity protocols and scalable technology solutions. Risk

management frameworks should be dynamic, allowing organizations to adapt to evolving threats effectively (Qudrat-Ullah, 2020).

2. **Bridging the Skill Gap**
   As emerging technologies become integral to decision-making, the demand for skilled professionals in AI, data science, and systems thinking continues to grow. Decision-makers must address the skill gap by fostering partnerships with academic institutions, investing in employee development, and leveraging AI-driven training platforms. By building a pipeline of talent, organizations can ensure sustained technological adoption and innovation (Qudrat-Ullah & Nair, 2021).
3. **Ensuring Technological Equity**
   Decision-makers must also address the issue of technological equity, ensuring that the benefits of emerging technologies are accessible to all stakeholders. This involves bridging the digital divide, particularly in developing regions, and promoting inclusive technology adoption. For instance, renewable energy solutions in Africa have shown how technology can empower underserved communities and drive sustainable development (Qudrat-Ullah, 2023).

7.4.3. *The Way Forward*

Dynamic decision-making in the age of emerging technologies is an ongoing journey. Organizations that adopt a proactive and holistic approach will be better equipped to harness the potential of these technologies while navigating their inherent complexities. The following recommendations provide a roadmap for decision-makers:

1. **Adopt Systems Thinking**
   Incorporating systems thinking into decision-making processes enables organizations to understand the interconnections between various components of their operations and external environments. This approach fosters holistic problem-solving and enhances organizational resilience (Qudrat-Ullah, 2018).
2. **Invest in Collaborative Ecosystems**
   Collaboration across industries, academia, and governments can accelerate the development and deployment of emerging technologies. Decision-makers should foster partnerships that enable

shared learning, resource pooling, and innovation. Collaborative ecosystems have proven particularly effective in addressing global challenges such as climate change and energy sustainability (Qudrat-Ullah & Kayal, 2019).

3. **Prioritize Sustainability and Ethical Responsibility**
   As organizations leverage emerging technologies, they must also prioritize sustainability and ethical responsibility. This includes minimizing environmental impacts, promoting social equity, and adhering to ethical principles in technology development and deployment. A focus on sustainability ensures long-term value creation for all stakeholders (Qudrat-Ullah, 2022).

In conclusion, dynamic decision-making in the age of emerging technologies is essential for organizations striving to thrive in a rapidly evolving landscape. The integration of advanced technologies like AI and ML, combined with a culture of data-driven decision-making, offers significant opportunities for improved decision quality and agility. However, these advancements must be balanced with ethical considerations, risk management, and continuous adaptation to new challenges. By adopting systems thinking, fostering collaboration, and prioritizing sustainability, organizations can navigate the complexities of technology adoption and build long-term resilience. Ultimately, those who proactively embrace these strategies will be better equipped to leverage technological advancements for sustainable growth and innovation.

References

Bansal, S., Goel, R., & Kumar, S. (2019). Artificial Intelligence in Disaster Management: A Review. *International Journal of Disaster Risk Reduction*, 38, 101213.

Berg, A., Hasui, Y., & Van Rompay, L. (2020). AI-driven financial decision-making: A comprehensive review. *Journal of Financial Economics*, 3(2), 101–116.

Berg, T., *et al.* (2020). AI and Machine Learning in Financial Decision-Making. *Journal of Financial Technology*, 18(2), 34–48.

Binns, A. (2018). Algorithmic bias in AI and the Impact on Marketing. *Journal of Marketing Research*, 55(4), 409–421.

Brynjolfsson, E., & McAfee, A. (2017). *The Second Machine Age: Work, Progress, and Prosperity in a Time of Brilliant Technologies.* W.W. Norton & Company.

Chaffey, D. (2019). *Digital Marketing: Strategy, Implementation, and Practice.* Pearson Education.

Chien, C. F., *et al.* (2015). *Optimizing the Supply Chain in the Age of Artificial Intelligence.* Journal of Business Research, 68(3), 568–574.

Chien, L. H., Yu, J. S., & Lin, Y. F. (2020). Application of AI for Emergency Management in Natural Disasters. *International Journal of Disaster Risk Reduction*, 41, 101356.

Chong, Y. Y., *et al.* (2017). *Predictive Analytics in Financial Markets: A Comprehensive Survey of Machine Learning Techniques.* International Journal of Financial Engineering, 4(3), 1750021.

Dastin, J. (2018). Amazon Scraps AI Recruiting Tool that Showed Bias Against Women. *Reuters.* Retrieved from [link].

Dastin, J. (2018). Ethics of AI in Financial Markets: Regulatory Challenges and Future Directions. *Journal of Finance & Data Science*, 4(1), 45–54.

Esteva, A., Chou, K., & Yeung, S. (2019). Predicting Sepsis in Emergency Department Patients. *The Lancet Digital Health*, 1(4), e168–e179.

Esteva, A., Kuprel, B., & Novoa, R. A. (2017). Dermatologist-Level Classification of Skin Cancer with Deep Neural Networks. *Nature*, 542(7639), 115–118.

Gandal, N., Klee, R., & Okun, S. (2018). AI in Finance: Risk Management and Fraud Prevention. *Journal of Financial Data Science*, 4(2), 76–89.

Hao, J., Li, H., & Zhang, X. (2020). Artificial Intelligence for Energy Efficiency: Applications and Challenges. *Energy Reports*, 6, 73–84.

He, K., Zhang, X., & Ren, S. (2018). *Deep Residual Learning for Image Recognition.* IEEE Conference on Computer Vision and Pattern Recognition.

Jiang, F., Jiang, Y., & Zhi, H. (2017). Artificial Intelligence in Healthcare: Past, Present, and Future. *Seminars in Cancer Biology*, 13(2), 61–68.

Jin, R., Huo, S., & Zhang, L. (2017). Predictive Maintenance in Smart Manufacturing Systems Using Machine Learning. *Journal of Manufacturing Systems*, 45, 345–356.

Kundur, D., Powers, L., & Meyer, L. (2018). Smart Grid Technology and Decision-Making in the Energy Sector. *Journal of Energy Management*, 35(2), 121–134.

Liu, X., Wang, Z., & Zhang, W. (2019). AI-Driven Chatbots in Marketing: Enhancing Customer Experience and Engagement. *Journal of Marketing Technology*, 10(3), 145–160.

Liu, Y., Zhang, L., & Wang, Q. (2020). AI-Based Quality Control Systems in Manufacturing. *International Journal of Advanced Manufacturing Technology*, 105(7), 3181–3191.

Luo, X., Zhou, H., & Liu, Y. (2019). Real-time Data Analytics for Disaster Management: State-of-the-art and Future Directions. *Journal of Big Data*, 6(1), 1–20.

Lycett, M. (2013). Emerging Technologies and their Impact on Business. *Business Technology Review*, 11(3), 45–58.

Obermeyer, Z., Powers, B., Vogeli, C., & Mullainathan, S. (2019). Dissecting Racial Bias in an Algorithm Used to Manage the Health of Populations. *Science*, 366(6464), 447–453.

Qudrat-Ullah, H. (2014). *Better Decision Making in Complex, Dynamic Tasks*. New York: Springer.

Qudrat-Ullah, H. (2018). *Innovative Solutions for Sustainable Supply Chains*. Springer.

Qudrat-Ullah, H. (2020). Improving Human Performance in Dynamic Tasks with Debriefing-based Interactive Learning Environments: An Empirical Investigation. *International Journal of Information Technology and Decision Making*, 19(4), 1065–1089.

Qudrat-Ullah, H. (2022). A Review and Analysis of Renewable Energy Policies and CO2 Emissions of Pakistan. *Energy*, 238, 121849.

Qudrat-Ullah, H. (2023). *Exploring the Dynamics of Renewable Energy and Sustainable Development in Africa: A Cross-Country and Interdisciplinary Approach*. Springer.

Qudrat-Ullah, H., & Karakul, M. (2007). Decision Making in Interactive Learning Environments: Towards an Integrated Model. *Journal of Decision Systems*, 16(1), 79–99.

Qudrat-Ullah, H., & Kayal, A. (2019). *Climate Change and Energy Dynamics in the Middle East — Modeling and Simulation-Based Solutions*. Springer.

Qudrat-Ullah, H., & Nair, P. (2021). *Operational Sustainability in the Mining Industry*. Springer.

Qudrat-Ullah, H., Spector, M., & Davidson, I. P. (Eds.). (2008). *Complex Decision Making: Theory and Practice*. New York: Springer.

Rajkomar, A., Dean, J., & Kohane, I. (2019). Machine Learning in Medicine. *New England Journal of Medicine*, 380(14), 1347–1358.

Tapscott, D., & Tapscott, A. (2016). *Blockchain Revolution: How the Technology Behind Bitcoin and Other Cryptocurrencies is Changing the World*. Penguin.

Teece, D. J. (2018). *Business Models and Dynamic Capabilities: An Update.* Long Range Planning, 51(1), 40–49.

Wang, W., Chen, Z., & Zhang, J. (2018). A Study on Internet of Things for Emergency Management Systems. *Journal of Computing and Security,* 4(6), 311–320.

Part III

The Interplay Between Technology and Decision Making

Chapter 8

Decision Support Systems and Intelligent Systems

Abstract

Chapter 8 examines the evolution and impact of Decision Support Systems (DSS) and Intelligent Decision Support Systems (IDSS) on modern decision-making processes. It traces the development of DSS from basic data management tools to advanced IDSS integrating artificial intelligence (AI) and machine learning (ML). The chapter explores various applications of IDSS across sectors such as healthcare, finance, and logistics, emphasizing their role in enhancing decision-making efficiency and accuracy. It also addresses the dynamics of human-machine collaboration, highlighting how these systems complement human judgment and the need for continuous adaptation to technological advancements. Insights into the interplay between technology and decision-making processes are also provided.

Keywords: Decision Support Systems (DSS); Intelligent Decision Support Systems (IDSS); Artificial Intelligence (AI); Machine Learning (ML); Data Analytics; Human-Machine; Collaboration; Healthcare Applications; Finance Applications; Logistics Optimization; System Evolution; Predictive Analytics; Decision-Making Efficiency; Technology Adaptation

8.0. Introduction

DSS and IDSS have fundamentally transformed the decision-making landscape, empowering organizations to navigate complexity with greater precision and adaptability. These systems serve as essential tools across a wide range of domains, from healthcare and finance to logistics and public policy. Their evolution has been marked by the integration of advanced technologies, including AI, ML, and real-time data analytics, making them indispensable in modern decision-making environments.

This chapter explores the historical evolution, critical applications, and future potential of DSS and IDSS, providing an in-depth understanding of their relevance in today's decision-making processes. It also highlights the collaborative synergy between humans and intelligent systems and examines the challenges and opportunities presented by these technologies.

8.0.1. *Evolution of DSS and IDSS*

The concept of DSS has its roots in the 1960s, with early systems designed to assist managers in strategic planning and problem-solving. These systems were primarily static, offering limited interactivity and functionality. Over time, advancements in computing power and data processing capabilities led to the development of more dynamic systems capable of simulating scenarios and providing actionable insights (Keen & Scott Morton, 1978).

The emergence of IDSS marked a significant milestone in this evolution. By integrating AI and ML, IDSS enhanced traditional DSS with the ability to learn from data, adapt to changing conditions, and provide predictive and prescriptive recommendations (Turban *et al.*, 2011). For instance, while a traditional DSS might generate reports based on historical sales data, an IDSS could forecast future trends and recommend specific strategies to optimize performance.

8.0.2. *Key Applications*

The versatility of DSS and IDSS is evident in their widespread adoption across various sectors:

- **Healthcare:**
  - In healthcare, IDSS aids in clinical decision-making by analyzing patient data, identifying patterns, and suggesting evidence-based treatments. For example, IDSS systems like IBM Watson Health use AI to diagnose diseases and recommend personalized treatment plans. This not only enhances accuracy but

also accelerates the decision-making process in critical scenarios (Jiang *et al.*, 2017).

- **Finance and Banking:**
  - Financial institutions leverage DSS and IDSS to optimize investment portfolios, detect fraudulent transactions, and assess credit risks. IDSS systems equipped with ML algorithms can analyze large volumes of financial data in real-time, enabling institutions to respond proactively to market changes (Huang *et al.*, 2019).
- **Supply Chain and Logistics:**
  - DSS and IDSS optimize supply chain operations by predicting demand, managing inventory, and improving delivery efficiency. For instance, companies like Amazon use IDSS to forecast customer demand and dynamically adjust stock levels, ensuring timely deliveries while minimizing costs (Choi *et al.*, 2020).
- **Public Policy and Urban Planning:**
  - Policymakers use IDSS to evaluate the potential impacts of proposed policies, simulate urban development scenarios, and allocate resources effectively. IDSS tools can analyze complex datasets from various sources, providing insights that inform decisions on infrastructure development, transportation planning, and disaster management (Batty, 2013).

In summary, the diverse applications of DSS and IDSS across sectors like healthcare, finance, logistics, and public policy underscore their transformative impact on decision-making processes. These systems harness advanced technologies, including AI and ML, to analyze complex data, provide actionable insights, and enhance decision accuracy and efficiency. By enabling data-driven approaches, DSS and IDSS not only optimize outcomes but also pave the way for innovative solutions to address emerging challenges in an increasingly dynamic world.

8.0.3. *Human-Machine Collaboration*

One of the most significant advancements in DSS and IDSS is their ability to facilitate human-machine collaboration. By combining the computational power of machines with human intuition and expertise, these systems enable more robust and informed decision-making.

- **Enhanced Problem-Solving:**
  - DSS and IDSS amplify human decision-making by processing vast amounts of data quickly and accurately. For example, in the energy sector, IDSS systems help engineers monitor and optimize power grids, balancing supply and demand in real-time (Qudrat-Ullah, 2020).
- **Challenges in Collaboration:**
  - Despite their benefits, fostering trust in machine-generated insights remains a challenge. Transparent algorithms and explainable AI are essential for ensuring that decision-makers can confidently rely on these systems (Gunning *et al.*, 2019).

In essence, human-machine collaboration represents a paradigm shift in decision-making, leveraging the complementary strengths of human judgment and machine precision. DSS and IDSS enhance problem-solving by providing rapid, data-driven insights while empowering humans to focus on strategic and ethical considerations. Addressing challenges such as trust and transparency through explainable AI will be critical to unlocking the full potential of these collaborations, ultimately leading to smarter, more adaptive decision-making frameworks.

8.0.4. *The Dynamic Nature of Decision-Making*

Decision-making environments are increasingly dynamic, characterized by rapid technological advancements, market fluctuations, and evolving consumer preferences. DSS and IDSS must continually adapt to remain effective in these contexts.

- **Real-Time Data Integration:**
  - Modern DSS and IDSS systems incorporate real-time data streams, enabling organizations to respond swiftly to changes. For example, in retail, dynamic pricing systems use IDSS to adjust prices based on real-time demand and competitor analysis, maximizing revenue while maintaining competitiveness (Shankar, 2018).

- **Scalability and Customization:**
  - Cloud computing and modular architectures have made DSS and IDSS more scalable and customizable. Organizations can now deploy these systems across global operations, tailoring them to specific business needs without extensive infrastructure investments (Kowalczyk & Buxmann, 2014).

The dynamic nature of decision-making demands adaptive and agile tools like DSS and IDSS, which are designed to thrive in ever-changing environments. By integrating real-time data and leveraging scalable, customizable architectures, these systems empower organizations to stay competitive and responsive. As technological and market landscapes continue to evolve, the ability of DSS and IDSS to adapt and provide actionable insights will remain a cornerstone of effective decision-making strategies.

8.0.5. *Ethical and Practical Considerations*

As DSS and IDSS become more integral to decision-making, ethical considerations have come to the forefront. Issues such as data privacy, algorithmic bias, and the potential for misuse highlight the need for responsible development and deployment of these systems.

- **Data Privacy:**
  - The reliance on large datasets raises concerns about the security and confidentiality of sensitive information. Organizations must implement robust data protection measures to prevent breaches and maintain user trust (Solove, 2013).
- **Algorithmic Bias:**
  - Bias in training data can lead to skewed outcomes, disproportionately affecting certain groups. Ensuring fairness and inclusivity in algorithm design is crucial for mitigating these risks (Barocas *et al.*, 2016).

The integration of DSS and IDSS into decision-making processes necessitates careful attention to ethical and practical considerations. Protecting data privacy and addressing algorithmic bias are paramount to fostering trust and ensuring equitable outcomes. By prioritizing transparency, inclusivity, and robust security measures, organizations can harness the power of these systems responsibly, balancing technological advancement with ethical accountability.

8.0.6. *Looking Ahead*

This chapter sets the stage for a comprehensive examination of DSS and IDSS, focusing on their historical evolution, diverse applications, and implications for the future of decision-making. It underscores the importance of adaptability, transparency, and ethical considerations in maximizing the potential of these systems. Subsequent sections will delve deeper into the technical, strategic, and practical aspects of DSS and IDSS, offering valuable insights for decision-makers across various domains.

8.1. Evolution of DSS

The emergence of DSS in the 1960s marked a transformative moment in how decisions were supported in organizations. Initially, DSS were designed to assist decision-makers by organizing, storing, and retrieving data. However, over time, these systems evolved to incorporate increasingly complex analytical functions, enabling organizations to make more informed and data-driven decisions in dynamic environments. The evolution of DSS has been driven by the need to support decision-makers in facing increasingly complex and uncertain business challenges, aided by technological advancements in computing, data storage, and processing.

8.1.1. *Early Developments in DSS*

In the early stages of DSS, systems were relatively simple, designed primarily to store and retrieve data rather than perform advanced analyses (Sprague & Carlson, 1982). Early applications focused on basic data management tasks such as maintaining records and generating reports. These systems were limited in scope and function, serving primarily as tools to automate routine tasks and enhance efficiency in data handling. As businesses began to recognize the need for more analytical capabilities, DSS evolved to incorporate decision models and forecasting tools that allowed users to simulate different scenarios and assess potential outcomes.

During the 1960s and 1970s, the primary focus was on developing systems that could help managers access relevant data and generate reports. This period saw the development of early models like the Management Information System (MIS), which focused on collecting and presenting data in a structured format. However, as organizations faced increasingly complex environments and more sophisticated decision-making challenges, MIS began to show limitations. Managers required more advanced systems that could not only store data but also offer insights and recommendations based on deeper analysis of information (Power, 2002).

The shift from basic data management to analytical capabilities marked a turning point in the evolution of DSS. By the late 1970s, advancements in computing power and software development enabled the integration of mathematical models and algorithms into DSS, paving the way for more robust analytical tools. This evolution allowed systems to move beyond static data presentation, empowering users to explore "what-if" scenarios and make more informed decisions. The 1980s and 1990s further revolutionized DSS with the introduction of user-friendly interfaces and the ability to process large datasets, making these systems more accessible to non-technical users. As a result, DSS transformed from being mere data repositories to dynamic tools for strategic planning, operational management, and competitive analysis.

8.1.2. *The Expansion into Analytical Models*

The 1980s marked a significant shift in the development of DSS, as more emphasis was placed on integrating analytical models into decision-making tools. By this time, DSS were no longer just data retrieval systems; they had evolved to become platforms capable of handling complex analyses, simulations, and optimization models. The integration of mathematical models, such as linear programming and forecasting models, allowed decision-makers to simulate different business scenarios and evaluate the potential impacts of various choices (Sprague & Carlson, 1982). These tools began to support more complex and multi-faceted decision-making processes, particularly in industries such as manufacturing, finance, and healthcare.

The evolution of DSS in the 1980s also saw the introduction of Expert Systems (ES), which were designed to mimic human expertise in specific decision areas. Expert systems used rule-based reasoning to solve complex problems by applying predefined knowledge and decision rules. This was a significant leap forward in the field, as DSS were now capable of offering more personalized and context-specific recommendations, based on both data and expert knowledge (Davis, 1982). The use of expert systems in DSS facilitated decision-making in areas like medical diagnosis, technical troubleshooting, and legal advice, where domain-specific expertise was critical.

8.1.3. *Integration of Real-Time Data and User-Friendly Interfaces*

By the 1990s, DSS had evolved to include real-time data processing capabilities, making them much more dynamic and responsive to changing business conditions. The increasing availability of networked computing and advancements in database technology allowed organizations to integrate real-time data feeds into their decision support systems. For example, in financial markets, DSS became capable of analyzing and responding to real-time stock prices and trading volumes, enabling investors and financial managers to make decisions based on the most current information available (Power, 2002). This ability to process real-time data marked a crucial turning point in the utility and effectiveness of DSS, as decision-makers were no longer reliant on static, historical data but could make decisions with an understanding of the present conditions.

In addition to real-time data integration, the 1990s also witnessed the development of more user-friendly interfaces for DSS. While earlier systems were often difficult to use and required specialized technical knowledge, the focus shifted toward making DSS accessible to non-technical users. This led to the development of graphical user interfaces (GUIs), which allowed decision-makers to interact with the system more intuitively and effectively. The emphasis on user-friendliness also encouraged greater adoption of DSS by organizations, as decision-makers could now easily access and understand complex data and analysis without needing to rely on IT specialists or data analysts.

8.1.4. *Contemporary DSS and Advanced Technologies*

In the 2000s and beyond, DSS became increasingly integrated with cutting-edge technologies, such as AI, ML, and big data analytics. These advancements enabled DSS to handle large and diverse datasets, process vast amounts of information in real-time, and generate predictive insights. With the advent of machine learning algorithms, DSS could now automatically adjust and optimize recommendations based on new data, without requiring constant reprogramming or manual intervention. For instance, in the retail sector, companies like Amazon use advanced DSS that analyze customer behavior, predict purchasing patterns, and personalize recommendations, helping businesses to adapt to customer needs and optimize inventory levels (Brynjolfsson & McAfee, 2014).

Moreover, cloud computing has further revolutionized DSS by enabling organizations to scale their decision-making capabilities without the need for expensive on-premise infrastructure. Cloud-based DSS platforms offer businesses the flexibility to access decision support tools from anywhere in the world, using just an internet connection. This has facilitated real-time decision-making in industries such as logistics, where decisions related to supply chain management can be made instantly based on current data from across the globe. The rise of big data analytics has also allowed DSS to handle unstructured data, such as social media feeds and sensor data, alongside traditional structured datasets, further enhancing their analytical capabilities (Chen, Chiang, & Storey, 2012).

8.1.5. *The Role of Decision Support Systems in Strategic Decision-Making*

In addition to operational and tactical decision-making, DSS have increasingly been used for strategic decision-making in modern organizations. As businesses face heightened competition and operate in rapidly changing environments, strategic decisions are often made based on insights derived from sophisticated DSS platforms. These systems can provide long-term forecasting, scenario analysis, and risk assessments that help decision-makers navigate uncertainty and develop strategies that maximize competitive advantage.

DSS are also playing a critical role in supporting collaborative decision-making in large, distributed organizations. With the increasing use of virtual teams and cross-functional collaboration, DSS platforms have been designed to facilitate decision-making across departments and geographic locations. This collaborative aspect of DSS is enhanced by communication tools, shared workspaces, and real-time data sharing, which allow teams to collectively analyze data, discuss options, and make decisions in a coordinated manner. For example, in the healthcare industry, multidisciplinary teams of doctors, nurses, and administrators can use DSS to collaborate on treatment plans, optimizing care based on shared patient data and real-time updates (Haux *et al.*, 2013).

DSS have also become essential in aligning strategic objectives with organizational resources and capabilities. By integrating data from various business units, these systems enable decision-makers to identify synergies and allocate resources more effectively. Furthermore, DSS can help organizations anticipate and adapt to disruptive market trends, such as technological innovation or shifts in consumer behavior, by analyzing vast amounts of historical and real-time data. This capability is particularly valuable in industries like finance, where accurate predictions and timely responses can have significant financial implications.

Another key advantage of DSS in strategic decision-making is their ability to model complex systems and simulate potential outcomes of various strategies. For instance, in supply chain management, DSS can analyze interdependencies between suppliers, manufacturers, and distributors to optimize network performance and minimize risks. The role of DSS extends beyond analysis; these systems also support decision-makers by visualizing data in intuitive formats, such as dashboards and interactive graphs, making complex information more digestible. Additionally, advancements in AI and ML have further enhanced DSS by enabling predictive analytics, which allows organizations to stay ahead of challenges and capitalize on opportunities. As organizations continue to operate in an interconnected and data-rich environment, the strategic value of DSS will likely grow, helping leaders make informed, forward-looking decisions that drive long-term success.

8.1.6. *Challenges and Future Directions for DSS*

While the evolution of DSS has brought about numerous benefits, several challenges remain. One significant challenge is the integration of disparate data sources into a single, coherent system. As organizations increasingly rely on data from various departments, external sources, and even social media, ensuring data consistency and quality can be difficult. Additionally, as DSS become more advanced, there is a growing need for sophisticated training programs to ensure that decision-makers have the skills and knowledge to interpret complex data and make informed choices.

Looking ahead, the future of DSS will likely involve further integration with emerging technologies, such as AI, blockchain, and IoT devices. AI-powered DSS will be able to provide even more precise, real-time insights, while blockchain can improve data security and transparency. The proliferation of IoT devices will further expand the range of real-time data available for analysis, allowing DSS to support decisions in industries such as agriculture, transportation, and energy management (Gartner, 2019).

In conclusion, the evolution of DSS reflects the broader trends in technological advancements and changing organizational needs. From their early days as simple data retrieval systems to the sophisticated AI and big data-powered platforms of today, DSS have become indispensable tools for supporting decision-making in organizations. As technology continues to evolve, DSS will remain critical in helping businesses navigate complexity, make data-driven decisions, and maintain a competitive edge in an increasingly interconnected world.

Table 8.1 provides a concise overview of the key phases in the evolution of DSS, highlighting their major features and the corresponding implications for decision-makers. It traces the development of DSS from their inception in the 1960s, focusing on basic data storage and retrieval, to the advanced, AI-driven platforms of today that integrate real-time data, analytics, and user-friendly interfaces.

Table 8.1. Evolution of DSS and Key Takeaways for Decision-Makers.

Era/Development Phase	Key Features	Key Takeaways for Decision-Makers
1960s-1970s: Early Developments	– Focus on data storage and retrieval. – Basic data management tasks and reporting tools. – Introduction of MIS.	– Utilize data for routine task automation. – Recognize limitations of static reports for addressing complex challenges.
1980s: Expansion into Analytical Models	– Integration of mathematical and decision models. – Introduction of simulation and optimization tools. – Emergence of ES.	– Leverage analytical models to explore multiple scenarios. – Use rule-based tools for domain-specific decision support.
1990s: Real-Time Data and User-Friendly Interfaces	– Real-time data processing capabilities. – Development of GUIs. – Increased accessibility for non-technical users.	– Adopt tools that enable quick responses to dynamic situations. – Prioritize systems with user-friendly interfaces to enhance adoption.
2000s-Present: Advanced Technologies	– Integration with AI, ML, and big data analytics. – Cloud-based platforms for scalability. – Real-time decision-making with unstructured data.	– Harness AI for predictive insights. – Use cloud platforms for flexibility and cost-effectiveness. – Analyze diverse datasets for a holistic view.
Strategic and Collaborative DSS	– Tools for long-term forecasting and scenario planning. – Facilitation of collaboration across teams and locations. – Support for distributed decision-making.	– Employ DSS for strategic risk assessment. – Use collaborative features to align cross-functional decisions. – Enhance transparency and data sharing.
Future Directions	– AI for more precise, real-time insights. – Blockchain for secure data management. – IoT integration for expanded real-time data.	– Prepare for integration with emerging technologies. – Invest in skills for interpreting complex, real-time da

The table also outlines strategic and collaborative applications of DSS and anticipates future advancements, such as blockchain and IoT integration. By summarizing the progression and practical takeaways, this table serves as a guide for decision-makers to leverage DSS effectively in dynamic and complex environments.

8.2. Intelligent Decision Support Systems (IDSS) and Their Applications

IDSS have emerged as a transformative evolution of traditional DSS. While traditional DSS provide a structured framework for collecting, organizing, and analyzing data to aid decision-making, IDSS augment these functions with advanced capabilities like AI, ML, and natural language processing (NLP). These enhancements empower IDSS to handle complexity and uncertainty, making them indispensable in various domains.

8.2.1. *Core Features of IDSS*

1. **Advanced Data Analytics**
   IDSS employ AI algorithms to process structured and unstructured data, uncovering insights that were previously inaccessible. Predictive analytics, a cornerstone of IDSS, enable decision-makers to forecast trends, risks, and opportunities. For example, retail companies use IDSS to predict customer buying behaviors based on historical sales data, enabling more targeted marketing strategies (Chen *et al.*, 2006).
2. **Automated Reasoning**
   Beyond analytics, IDSS provide automated reasoning capabilities that simulate decision-making processes. Using rule-based systems or neural networks, IDSS evaluate multiple decision scenarios, helping organizations choose optimal solutions under constraints. In manufacturing, for example, automated reasoning is used to minimize waste and optimize production schedules (Jouffe *et al.*, 2002).
3. **Real-Time Processing**
   The ability to process and respond to real-time data is another defining characteristic of IDSS. In domains such as healthcare, IDSS monitor patient data from wearable devices and provide

alerts for anomalies, ensuring timely medical intervention (Elstein *et al.*, 2004).

In conclusion, the core features of IDSS — advanced data analytics, automated reasoning, and real-time processing — highlight their transformative potential in modern decision-making. These systems not only enhance the ability to extract actionable insights but also enable organizations to respond dynamically to challenges and opportunities. By integrating predictive capabilities, simulation tools, and real-time data monitoring, IDSS provide a robust foundation for making informed, efficient, and proactive decisions. As industries continue to embrace digital transformation, the role of IDSS in driving innovation and optimizing processes will become increasingly indispensable.

8.2.2. *Applications of IDSS Across Key Domains*

1. **Healthcare**
   IDSS have revolutionized healthcare by improving diagnostic accuracy, optimizing resource allocation, and personalizing treatment plans. AI-powered IDSS analyze patient data, medical histories, and clinical guidelines to recommend appropriate diagnostic tests or treatments. For instance, systems like IBM Watson Health have been instrumental in oncology, helping oncologists analyze research literature and patient records to identify the best course of action (Elstein *et al.*, 2004).
   - **Enhancing Diagnostic Precision**: Diagnostic errors can lead to serious patient outcomes. IDSS reduce these errors by using ML algorithms trained on extensive datasets, enabling more accurate identification of diseases such as cancer or cardiovascular conditions.
   - **Operational Efficiency**: Hospitals use IDSS to manage patient flow, reduce waiting times, and optimize bed allocation, especially during crises like pandemics.
2. **Finance**
   The financial industry has embraced IDSS for its ability to handle large volumes of data, identify patterns, and predict market trends.

- **Fraud Detection**: IDSS use anomaly detection algorithms to flag suspicious transactions, preventing financial fraud. For example, banks deploy systems that analyze customer spending behaviors and generate alerts for unusual activities (Chen *et al.*, 2006).
- **Portfolio Management**: Investors benefit from IDSS that recommend asset allocation strategies based on historical data and market conditions. Robo-advisors, which rely on IDSS, provide tailored investment solutions to retail and institutional clients.

3. **Logistics and Supply Chain Management**
   In logistics, IDSS optimize complex operations, from inventory management to route planning. By analyzing factors such as demand forecasts, fuel prices, and delivery schedules, these systems ensure cost-effective and timely operations (Jouffe *et al.*, 2002).
   - **Dynamic Routing**: Logistics companies like FedEx and DHL employ IDSS for real-time route optimization, reducing fuel consumption and delivery times.
   - **Inventory Optimization**: Retailers use IDSS to maintain optimal stock levels by predicting demand fluctuations, thereby reducing costs associated with overstocking or stockouts.
4. **Energy Sector**
   In renewable energy, IDSS contribute to grid management by forecasting energy demand and supply. Smart grids, powered by IDSS, analyze data from distributed energy resources to ensure a balanced energy supply while minimizing costs and environmental impact.

In summary, IDSS applications span a wide range of domains, demonstrating their adaptability and transformative potential. From enhancing diagnostic precision and operational efficiency in healthcare to optimizing financial strategies and safeguarding against fraud, IDSS have become indispensable tools. In logistics and supply chain management, these systems streamline operations and improve sustainability, while in the energy sector, they support the transition to smarter, more balanced grids. By leveraging advanced analytics, real-time processing, and automated reasoning, IDSS empower industries to address complex challenges and achieve greater efficiency, accuracy, and innovation in their decision-making processes.

8.2.3. *Challenges in Implementing IDSS*

1. **Data Quality and Integration**
   IDSS performance heavily depends on the quality of input data. Inconsistent or incomplete data can lead to inaccurate results. Moreover, integrating data from disparate sources requires sophisticated data harmonization techniques.
2. **Complexity and Cost**
   Developing and deploying IDSS involve significant investment in technology and expertise. Organizations must also address the complexity of integrating these systems with existing infrastructure.
3. **Ethical Concerns and Bias**
   AI-driven IDSS may inherit biases present in training data, leading to unfair or discriminatory outcomes. For example, in healthcare, biased algorithms could result in unequal treatment recommendations for different demographic groups. Ensuring fairness and transparency in decision-making is a critical challenge (Lee & See, 2004).

Implementing IDSS presents a range of challenges that organizations must carefully navigate to maximize their effectiveness. Ensuring data quality and seamless integration from diverse sources is fundamental to achieving accurate and reliable outputs. The high cost and complexity of development and deployment often necessitate substantial financial and human resources, which may be a barrier for smaller organizations. Ethical concerns, including algorithmic bias, underscore the importance of fairness, transparency, and accountability in system design and operation. Addressing these challenges requires not only technical innovation but also robust governance frameworks and interdisciplinary collaboration. As IDSS continue to evolve, overcoming these hurdles will be essential to unlocking their full potential across industries.

8.2.4. *Future Directions for IDSS*

1. **XAI**
   As organizations increasingly rely on IDSS, there is a growing demand for systems that can explain their decision-making processes. XAI aims to make AI models transparent, ensuring that users can trust and validate the recommendations provided by IDSS.
2. **Integration with Emerging Technologies**
   The convergence of IDSS with technologies like IoT and blockchain will further enhance their capabilities. For instance, IoT-enabled IDSS can leverage sensor data to optimize real-time operations in industries such as logistics and manufacturing.
3. **Personalization**
   Future IDSS are expected to offer greater personalization, tailoring their recommendations to individual users or specific organizational contexts. In education, for example, IDSS can create personalized learning plans for students based on their strengths, weaknesses, and learning preferences.

The future of IDSS is poised for remarkable advancements, driven by the need for greater transparency, integration, and personalization. XAI will play a pivotal role in fostering trust and accountability by demystifying the decision-making processes of these systems. The integration of emerging technologies such as IoT and blockchain will enable IDSS to harness vast, real-time datasets securely, unlocking new possibilities for efficiency and innovation across industries. Furthermore, the shift towards personalization will allow IDSS to deliver more context-aware and user-centric recommendations, enhancing their relevance and effectiveness. As these systems evolve, they will not only address current limitations but also redefine the way organizations and individuals approach decision-making, ensuring smarter, more informed choices in an increasingly complex world.

Overall, IDSS are reshaping the decision-making landscape across industries by providing actionable insights, improving operational efficiency, and enabling proactive strategies. Despite challenges related to data quality, costs, and ethics, advancements in AI and ML are driving the development of more robust, transparent, and adaptive IDSS. Their transformative potential underscores the importance of continued innovation and interdisciplinary collaboration in this field. Table 8.2 provides a concise summary of the section IDSS and their applications, highlighting the primary concepts and actionable insights for decision-makers.

8.3. Human-Machine Collaboration in Decision Making

Human-machine collaboration is reshaping decision-making processes in the modern era. By combining human judgment with machine intelligence, organizations can achieve enhanced decision quality, increased efficiency, and greater adaptability. Human decision-makers contribute contextual understanding, emotional intelligence, and strategic oversight, while machines provide data-driven insights, computational power, and pattern recognition capabilities (Parasuraman & Riley, 1997). This section delves deeper into the dynamics of human-machine collaboration, highlighting its benefits, challenges, and future directions.

8.3.1. *Core Principles of Human-Machine Collaboration*

Human-machine collaboration is reshaping how decisions are made across industries by combining the strengths of humans and intelligent systems. Effective collaboration is grounded in several core principles that ensure synergy, efficiency, and trust between the two entities.

- **Division of Labor:** One of the fundamental principles of human-machine collaboration is the strategic division of labor. This approach leverages the unique capabilities of both humans and machines to achieve optimal outcomes. Humans are adept at tasks requiring creativity, ethical judgment, and contextual understanding, while machines excel at processing large datasets, identifying patterns, and performing probabilistic analyses at unmatched speed and accuracy (Shneiderman, 2004). For example, in medical diagnostics, machines analyze imaging data to identify potential anomalies, while doctors use their expertise to interpret these findings and make holistic treatment decisions. Similarly, in project management, dynamic IDSS provide data-driven scheduling and resource allocation recommendations, allowing managers to focus

Table 8.2. Summary of IDSS and Key Takeaways for Decision-Makers

Aspect	Description	Key Takeaways for Decision-Makers
Definition and Overview	IDSS enhance traditional DSS with AI, ML, and NLP to handle complexity and uncertainty, providing more advanced decision support capabilities.	Decision-makers must consider adopting IDSS for scenarios requiring advanced data analytics, predictive insights, and dynamic decision-making capabilities.
Core Features	– **Advanced Data Analytics**: Processes structured and unstructured data to reveal actionable insights. – **Automated Reasoning**: Simulates decision scenarios for optimal solutions. – **Real-Time Processing**: Responds to live data inputs for timely decisions.	Leverage predictive analytics for trend forecasting, automated reasoning for optimizing operations, and real-time processing for high-stakes, dynamic environments.
Applications Across Key Domains	– **Healthcare**: Improves diagnosis, resource allocation, and personalized treatment plans (e.g., IBM Watson Health). – **Finance**: Supports fraud detection and portfolio management using anomaly detection algorithms . – **Logistics**: Optimizes routing and inventory management to reduce costs. – **Energy**: Forecasts demand-supply balance in renewable energy grids.	Deploy IDSS tailored to industry-specific needs: enhance diagnostics in healthcare, identify fraud in finance, and improve operational efficiency in logistics and energy sectors.
Challenges in Implementation	– **Data Quality and Integration**: Incomplete or inconsistent data can hinder performance. – **Complexity and Cost**: High investment in technology and expertise is required. – **Ethical Concerns**: Risk of biased decision-making due to flawed AI algorithms.	Prioritize data governance, budget for long-term technological investment, and implement safeguards against bias to ensure ethical and effective decision-making.

(*Continued*)

Table 8.2. (*Continued*)

Aspect	Description	Key Takeaways for Decision-Makers
Future Directions	– **XAI**: Enhances transparency and trust in AI-driven decisions. – **Integration with IoT and Blockchain**: Strengthens operational capabilities with real-time and decentralized data. – **Personalization**: Customizes recommendations for users and contexts.	Focus on developing explainable and user-friendly IDSS, integrate with emerging technologies for enhanced capabilities, and tailor systems for individual and organizational contexts.

on strategy and team leadership. A clear delineation of roles ensures that each entity operates within its strengths, creating a harmonious workflow.

- **Symbiotic Relationship:** The relationship between humans and machines in collaborative environments is inherently symbiotic. Machines are designed to complement human capabilities, serving as advisors, assistants, or even co-creators, rather than replacements. This principle underscores the idea that machines enhance human decision-making by providing valuable insights and performing routine or complex computations. For instance, in the financial sector, robo-advisors analyze vast amounts of market data, identifying trends and opportunities. However, human advisors remain crucial in validating these insights and tailoring them to individual client goals and preferences (Lee & See, 2004). In creative industries, AI-driven tools assist in generating ideas, designing prototypes, or refining outputs, while humans provide the creative direction and contextual relevance. This symbiotic relationship ensures that technology amplifies, rather than diminishes, human agency and creativity.
- **Trust and Transparency:** Trust is a cornerstone of effective human-machine collaboration. Users must feel confident in the reliability and fairness of machine-generated recommendations to integrate them meaningfully into decision-making processes. A lack of trust can lead to underutilization or outright rejection of machine outputs, undermining the potential benefits of

collaboration. Transparency in machine operations, often facilitated through XAI, plays a critical role in building this trust. XAI systems provide insights into how decisions are made, offering users clear explanations of the underlying algorithms and data inputs (Shneiderman, 2004). For example, in healthcare, an AI system predicting patient outcomes might display the factors influencing its prognosis, such as medical history, test results, or demographic data. This transparency allows doctors to assess the validity of the recommendations and make informed choices. Furthermore, ethical considerations, such as eliminating biases in algorithms, contribute to fostering trust and ensuring equitable outcomes.

- **Continuous Learning and Adaptation:** A dynamic aspect of human-machine collaboration is the continuous learning and adaptation of both entities. Machines learn from user interactions and feedback, refining their algorithms to provide more accurate and relevant insights over time. Similarly, humans must stay informed about technological advancements and develop skills to effectively leverage machine capabilities. This iterative process creates a feedback loop where humans and machines mutually improve, ensuring sustained effectiveness in evolving contexts. For example, in autonomous driving, vehicles gather real-time data to adapt to traffic patterns and environmental conditions, while human drivers remain vigilant, ready to intervene when necessary. This ongoing adaptation strengthens collaboration and resilience in unpredictable scenarios.
- **Empowerment Through Collaboration:** The ultimate goal of human-machine collaboration is to empower users to make better, faster, and more informed decisions. Machines provide access to vast reservoirs of data and advanced analytical tools, enabling humans to focus on strategic, high-level tasks. In education, for instance, adaptive learning platforms use AI to identify student weaknesses and recommend personalized learning paths, freeing educators to concentrate on mentorship and holistic development. Similarly, in emergency response situations, dynamic DSS offer real-time data and actionable insights, equipping decision-makers with the tools needed to respond effectively under pressure.
- **Ethical and Social Considerations:** Human-machine collaboration also involves navigating ethical and social dimensions. Ensuring fairness, accountability, and inclusivity in machine outputs is vital to maintaining societal trust and avoiding

unintended consequences. Collaborative systems should align with human values, prioritizing user well-being and societal benefit. For instance, in hiring processes, AI tools can assist in screening resumes, but safeguards must be implemented to prevent algorithmic biases that might disadvantage certain groups. Ethical oversight and human intervention are necessary to uphold fairness and integrity in such contexts.

In summary, the core principles of human-machine collaboration — division of labor, symbiotic relationships, trust and transparency, continuous learning, empowerment, and ethical alignment — form the foundation of this transformative partnership. By adhering to these principles, organizations and individuals can harness the strengths of both humans and machines, driving innovation, efficiency, and improved outcomes in diverse fields.

8.3.2. *Benefits of Human-Machine Collaboration*

Human-machine collaboration brings forth a wealth of benefits that can significantly improve decision-making, operational efficiency, and the ability to scale complex tasks. These benefits are driving the integration of intelligent systems across various industries, from healthcare to finance, and beyond. By combining the unique strengths of human judgment with machine processing power, organizations can unlock new levels of productivity, innovation, and responsiveness.

1. **Enhanced Decision Quality:** One of the primary advantages of human-machine collaboration is the ability to make better, more informed decisions. Machines, particularly those using AI and ML, can process vast quantities of data far more quickly and accurately than humans. They excel in detecting patterns, identifying correlations, and predicting future trends based on historical data. However, while machines can analyze data, humans bring invaluable contextual understanding, ethical considerations, and creative thinking to the table. This collaboration ensures that decisions are not only based on empirical data but also reflect nuanced insights that take into account broader societal, cultural, and organizational factors (Parasuraman & Riley, 1997). For instance, in healthcare, AI systems can analyze medical records to identify trends and potential diagnoses, while doctors interpret these results based on their understanding of individual patient

circumstances, medical history, and ethical considerations. By combining data-driven insights with human expertise, the overall quality of decision-making is greatly enhanced.

2. **Increased Efficiency:** Machines in human-machine collaborations are adept at handling repetitive, time-consuming, and routine tasks, thus allowing humans to concentrate on higher-level strategic decisions. This shift in responsibilities not only increases individual and organizational productivity but also reduces the likelihood of errors associated with manual processes. For example, in supply chain management, automated systems are capable of optimizing inventory levels, predicting demand fluctuations, and generating procurement schedules, which significantly enhances operational efficiency. As a result, managers can focus on strategic decisions such as negotiating with suppliers, managing risks, and responding to market shifts. The automation of routine tasks, coupled with human oversight, streamlines operations, reduces costs, and leads to faster decision cycles. In industries such as customer service, chatbots powered by AI handle initial inquiries, allowing human agents to focus on more complex and sensitive customer needs, thus improving both service speed and customer satisfaction.
3. **Scalability and Adaptability:** Human-machine collaboration provides organizations with the ability to scale decision-making processes efficiently, particularly in contexts involving large datasets and complex environments. For instance, in the healthcare sector, systems powered by AI and data analytics can process millions of patient records to recommend personalized treatments for different demographic groups. These systems adapt and learn from new data, ensuring that their recommendations stay relevant and up-to-date as new research and medical breakthroughs emerge. This scalability is critical as healthcare systems increasingly face the challenge of providing personalized care to large and diverse populations. Similarly, in industries like retail and finance, AI-driven systems can analyze market data and consumer behavior at scale, helping organizations make quick, data-driven decisions about inventory, pricing strategies, and investment portfolios. As organizations expand or face new challenges, human-machine collaboration ensures they can swiftly adapt to new contexts, environments, and opportunities.

4. **Flexibility in Crisis Response:** Another key benefit of human-machine collaboration is the flexibility it offers in crisis situations. In high-pressure environments, such as disaster response or financial market fluctuations, the ability to process real-time data and provide rapid, actionable insights is crucial. Machine systems can monitor evolving conditions and provide decision-makers with real-time analysis of ongoing events, enabling them to make informed decisions faster than they would be able to on their own. For example, during natural disasters, AI-powered systems can analyze satellite imagery, social media feeds, and sensor data to assess damage, track displaced populations, and predict the movement of the disaster. Emergency response teams can use this information to prioritize resources, plan evacuation routes, and deploy aid more efficiently. Similarly, in financial markets, algorithmic trading systems can respond to price changes and market shifts in fractions of a second, enabling traders to make informed decisions while human brokers provide oversight and strategic input.
5. **Continuous Improvement and Innovation:** Human-machine collaboration fosters a culture of continuous improvement and innovation. Machines, particularly those using ML algorithms, improve over time by processing more data and adapting their models based on new information. In industries like manufacturing, dynamic systems can track machine performance and production metrics, optimizing processes and reducing waste. This feedback loop between humans and machines creates a cycle of constant learning and refinement. Humans, for their part, contribute innovative ideas, strategic thinking, and ethical guidance to the process, ensuring that improvements align with organizational goals and societal needs. The combined efforts of humans and machines also lead to innovation, as new tools and capabilities are developed to solve complex problems more efficiently. For example, in drug discovery, AI algorithms analyze chemical compounds and biological data to suggest potential treatments, while researchers use their expertise to test and refine these suggestions, leading to faster and more effective drug development.
6. **Enhanced Collaboration and Creativity:** Human-machine collaboration also opens the door to enhanced creativity and collaboration. In fields like design and art, AI-powered tools can assist humans in generating ideas, testing concepts, and refining

creations. For example, in architecture, AI can help generate design options based on certain parameters, while architects apply their creative judgment to select the most suitable designs. This collaborative process not only accelerates the design phase but also pushes the boundaries of what can be achieved creatively. Similarly, in the entertainment industry, AI is being used to assist in scriptwriting, video editing, and sound design, enabling creators to focus more on artistic expression and innovation. The combination of human creativity and machine efficiency leads to breakthrough ideas and novel solutions across many sectors.

In summary, human-machine collaboration provides numerous benefits, including enhanced decision quality, increased efficiency, scalability, adaptability, and the ability to respond effectively to crises. These advantages are making it an essential strategy for organizations looking to improve productivity, innovation, and responsiveness in an increasingly complex world. By leveraging the strengths of both humans and machines, organizations can unlock new potential and drive success in a rapidly changing environment.

8.3.3. *Challenges in Human-Machine Collaboration*

While human-machine collaboration offers substantial benefits, it also presents several challenges that must be addressed to ensure that these systems are both effective and ethically sound. These challenges are critical in ensuring that machines enhance, rather than hinder, human decision-making. The following section explores the key challenges in human-machine collaboration, including transparency, bias, trust management, and goal alignment.

1. **Transparency and Explainability:** One of the major challenges in human-machine collaboration is the opacity of ML algorithms, particularly in complex models such as deep learning. These models are often described as "black-box" systems because their decision-making processes are not easily understandable by humans. This lack of transparency can create significant barriers to trust and adoption. Decision-makers may hesitate to rely on AI systems if they cannot understand how recommendations are derived, especially in critical domains like healthcare, finance, or criminal justice (Lee & See, 2004). For instance, if an AI model

suggests a treatment plan for a patient but the reasoning behind that recommendation is unclear, physicians and patients may be reluctant to follow it. To address this issue, the field of XAI has emerged, focusing on developing techniques and tools that make AI decisions more interpretable to human users. However, achieving transparency without sacrificing performance remains a significant technical challenge, and it requires ongoing research and development in areas such as model interpretability, user interface design, and decision auditing.

2. **Bias and Ethical Concerns:** Another challenge in human-machine collaboration arises from the potential for bias in machine learning models. Machines learn from data, and if that data contains biases — whether due to historical inequities, underrepresentation of certain groups, or faulty labeling — these biases can be reflected in the decisions made by AI systems. This is particularly concerning in applications such as hiring, criminal justice, and lending, where biased AI systems could perpetuate and amplify existing social inequalities. For example, facial recognition systems have faced criticism for their racial and gender biases, as they tend to perform less accurately on people of color and women, leading to unfair and potentially harmful outcomes. Ethical concerns also extend to how machines make decisions, especially in situations that involve life-altering consequences, such as medical diagnoses or law enforcement surveillance. These issues underscore the need for careful data curation, algorithmic fairness audits, and the inclusion of diverse perspectives in system design to mitigate bias. Additionally, a more robust ethical framework is necessary to guide the development and deployment of AI systems, ensuring they align with societal values and do not harm vulnerable groups.
3. **Trust Management:** Building and maintaining trust between humans and machines is a fundamental challenge in human-machine collaboration. Trust is critical for ensuring that machines can enhance human decision-making rather than undermine it. However, trust is a complex and dynamic attribute that evolves over time based on experience, transparency, and the performance of the system. One risk in human-machine collaboration is automation bias, where humans place excessive trust in machine recommendations and become overly reliant on them, even in

situations where the system may not be performing optimally. Conversely, under-reliance on machines — often due to skepticism or lack of understanding — can result in missed opportunities for efficiency and innovation. For example, a manager may hesitate to follow an AI-generated forecast about market trends due to doubts about the system's accuracy, potentially losing a competitive edge. Balancing the level of trust placed in machines with appropriate human oversight is key to overcoming this challenge. Decision-makers must be able to recognize when to rely on AI suggestions and when human judgment is needed to provide the necessary context or adjust for uncertainties.

4. **Goal Alignment:** A final challenge in human-machine collaboration is ensuring that the goals of both humans and machines are aligned. Machines are designed to optimize specific objectives based on the data they process and the algorithms they follow. However, these objectives may not always align with the broader goals of the human stakeholders involved. For example, an AI system designed to maximize operational efficiency in a factory may make decisions that prioritize speed and cost reduction but overlook important ethical or social considerations, such as worker safety or environmental impact. In such cases, the machine's optimization criteria may conflict with human values, leading to negative outcomes. Goal misalignment is particularly problematic in industries like healthcare, where machines may optimize for outcomes that prioritize statistical success (e.g., reducing readmission rates) without considering the individual patient's experience, preferences, or long-term wellbeing. To address this, it is essential to design systems that incorporate human values and ethical considerations into the optimization process. Human oversight should ensure that machine objectives align with the broader goals of the organization, society, and individual stakeholders.

Overall, human-machine collaboration holds great potential, but overcoming the challenges of transparency, bias, trust, and goal alignment is essential for ensuring that these systems are effective, ethical, and reliable. As AI and ML technologies continue to evolve, it is crucial to develop frameworks and practices that address these challenges. This includes fostering transparency through XAI, addressing bias through fair data practices, managing trust through balanced human oversight, and ensuring that machine goals align with human values. Only by addressing these issues can we unlock the full potential of human-machine collaboration and ensure that these systems contribute positively to society and decision-making.

8.3.4. *Applications of Human-Machine Collaboration*

Human-machine collaboration is increasingly transforming various industries by blending the strengths of both human decision-making and machine intelligence. This synergy enhances productivity, improves outcomes, and offers innovative solutions across several fields. The following are examples of how human-machine collaboration is being applied in healthcare, finance, manufacturing, and education.

1. Healthcare

Human-machine collaboration in healthcare has proven to be transformative in improving diagnostic accuracy and treatment planning. For example, systems like IBM Watson Health have demonstrated how AI can assist healthcare professionals by analyzing vast amounts of patient records, medical literature, and clinical trials data to recommend evidence-based treatment options. This technology helps oncologists identify the most effective treatments tailored to a patient's specific condition, improving patient outcomes and reducing the chances of human error. AI also supports the detection of diseases at earlier stages, enabling preventative care that can save lives and reduce healthcare costs. While the machine provides recommendations, the human healthcare provider remains responsible for interpreting these insights, offering a personalized approach, and making the final decisions in consultation with the patient. This collaboration allows for the synthesis of vast data and human empathy in healthcare decisions, delivering a more comprehensive, accurate, and compassionate care system (Shneiderman, 2004).

2. Finance

The finance sector is another domain where human-machine collaboration is critical in enhancing fraud detection, risk management, and financial analysis. AI systems in banking and finance use ML algorithms to identify anomalies in transaction patterns and flag potentially fraudulent activities. These systems can analyze data far more quickly and efficiently than humans, identifying hidden trends and predicting future risks with greater accuracy. However, the final decision on whether an alert is a genuine fraud case is typically made by human analysts who review the context and make subjective judgments based on experience, intuition, and regulatory guidelines. This partnership between AI's data processing capabilities and human expertise in decision-making provides a more robust and efficient approach to safeguarding financial systems. Additionally, human-machine collaboration in investment banking and asset management enables portfolio optimization, where machines analyze market data, and human analysts adjust strategies based on market conditions and personal client needs (Lee & See, 2004).

3. Manufacturing

In manufacturing, the rise of collaborative robots, or "cobots," has revolutionized the production process by allowing humans and machines to work together seamlessly. Cobots perform repetitive, physically demanding tasks such as assembly, welding, and packaging, freeing human workers to focus on tasks that require problem-solving, quality control, and complex decision-making. This synergy not only enhances productivity but also improves workplace safety by reducing the strain on human workers and lowering the risk of injury. Cobots are designed to interact safely with humans, equipped with sensors that allow them to halt operations if a worker is too close, ensuring a safe working environment. The integration of AI in manufacturing processes also enables predictive maintenance, where machines monitor their own health and notify workers of potential malfunctions before they lead to downtime. This approach increases overall operational efficiency and reduces maintenance costs, benefiting both employees and the organization.

4. Education

In education, human-machine collaboration is enabling more personalized and adaptive learning experiences for students. AI-driven platforms analyze individual student performance and learning styles, adapting content and pacing to optimize their learning outcomes. For example, platforms like Coursera or Khan Academy use algorithms to personalize course recommendations based on students' progress and areas for improvement. While AI handles the personalization and content delivery, human educators provide mentorship, guidance, and adaptive instruction, ensuring that students receive the emotional support and interactive learning experiences that machines cannot replicate. Teachers also play a crucial role in identifying non-academic factors such as student motivation, social interaction, and mental health, which influence learning. By combining the data-driven insights of AI with the human touch of educators, this collaboration creates a well-rounded learning experience that addresses both cognitive and emotional needs. Additionally, AI-based tutoring systems are being developed to offer additional learning support, helping students reinforce concepts at their own pace and providing teachers with real-time data to identify students who may need additional help.

In summary, the applications of human-machine collaboration across industries like healthcare, finance, manufacturing, and education demonstrate the profound impact that these systems can have in enhancing efficiency, decision-making, and outcomes. By combining the speed and analytical power of machines with human creativity, judgment, and ethical considerations, organizations can solve complex problems more effectively and responsibly. The continued evolution of AI and ML technologies will further augment these applications, enabling new opportunities for human-machine partnerships in solving societal challenges and advancing industry practices. However, the success of these collaborations depends on the careful balancing of human oversight, ethical frameworks, and the technological capabilities of machines. As the potential for these collaborations expands, it is essential to prioritize transparency, fairness, and accountability to ensure that the benefits are realized equitably and ethically.

8.3.5. *Future Directions*

The future of human-machine collaboration is poised for transformative developments, driven by the integration of emerging technologies, a human-centered design approach, and a commitment to continuous learning. These advancements will not only enhance the effectiveness and utility of collaborative systems but also ensure that they evolve in a manner that is ethical, efficient, and responsive to societal needs.

- **Integration of Emerging Technologies:** The integration of emerging technologies such as AR, VR, and blockchain is set to redefine the landscape of human-machine collaboration. AR and VR have the potential to significantly enhance decision-making processes in sectors such as design, healthcare, and engineering by providing immersive, interactive environments for human and machine interfaces. In design and engineering, for instance, engineers and architects can use VR simulations to visualize structures or systems in a 3D environment before they are built, improving accuracy and reducing costly errors. AR can overlay critical data onto physical objects, enabling users to make more informed decisions in real-time. For example, in manufacturing, technicians can use AR glasses to access step-by-step maintenance instructions while working on machinery, reducing the likelihood of mistakes.

  Blockchain, another emerging technology, offers a robust solution for ensuring transparency, accountability, and security in collaborative systems. By providing a decentralized ledger of interactions and decisions made by machines and humans, blockchain enhances trust and traceability in collaborative processes. This is especially important in sectors such as supply chain management, where transparency of transactions and actions is essential for maintaining the integrity of operations. The combination of AR, VR, and blockchain will empower human-machine collaboration to achieve new levels of effectiveness, security, and interactivity.
- **Human-Centered AI Design:** As the role of machines in decision-making continues to grow, it is crucial to ensure that AI systems are designed with a human-centered approach. Human-centered AI design focuses on creating systems that align with human values, ethics, and needs, ensuring that technology serves as a tool for human empowerment rather than replacing human judgment. Research in human-computer interaction (HCI) and cognitive ergonomics will play a pivotal role in shaping the future of human-machine collaboration. By studying how humans interact with machines and designing systems that are intuitive, accessible, and responsive to human needs, developers can create more effective and user-friendly systems.

  For example, in healthcare, human-centered AI can help doctors by providing evidence-based treatment recommendations while taking into account the individual preferences, cultural background, and ethical considerations of the patient. In education, AI systems designed with a human-centered approach can better understand and adapt to the learning styles and needs of students, offering personalized learning experiences that promote engagement and improve outcomes. By ensuring that AI systems are developed with empathy, transparency, and fairness, human-centered design will enable AI to augment human capabilities without undermining human agency.

- **Continuous Learning:** The principle of continuous learning will be essential to the evolution of human-machine collaboration. As technology advances at a rapid pace, both humans and machines must engage in ongoing learning to stay ahead of emerging challenges and opportunities. For machines, continuous learning involves the regular update of algorithms and the integration of new datasets to refine their decision-making abilities. ML systems, for instance, can be trained to recognize patterns, predict outcomes, and improve their performance over time, ensuring that they remain relevant and effective in dynamic environments.

For humans, continuous learning involves adapting to the evolving technological landscape through ongoing education and training. As new tools, platforms, and interfaces are developed, individuals will need to acquire new skills to interact effectively with these technologies. This may involve learning how to interpret and validate machine-generated insights, understanding the ethical implications of AI, and developing the cognitive flexibility to navigate complex human-machine interactions. In sectors like healthcare, finance, and education, where human expertise remains critical, this continuous learning process will help ensure that professionals are well-equipped to leverage the full potential of AI and other collaborative technologies.

The collaboration between human and machine learning processes will create a feedback loop where machines provide new insights that humans can use to enhance their understanding of complex problems, while humans guide machines through ethical considerations and real-world context. This dynamic exchange will foster innovation and problem-solving, driving progress in fields as diverse as climate science, urban planning, and space exploration.

In conclusion, the future of human-machine collaboration is full of promise, with emerging technologies such as AR, VR, and blockchain offering new avenues for innovation and transparency. By focusing on human-centered AI design and prioritizing continuous learning for both machines and humans, organizations can ensure that these systems evolve in ways that are both effective and ethical. The successful integration of these elements will not only enhance productivity and decision-making across industries but also empower individuals to engage with technology in meaningful and constructive ways. As this collaboration deepens, the relationship between humans and machines will become more symbiotic, enhancing capabilities, fostering creativity, and addressing complex global challenges. Table 8.3 summarizes the core principles, benefits, challenges, applications, and future directions of human-machine collaboration in decision-making, providing actionable insights for decision-makers aiming to leverage this synergy.

8.4. Dynamic View of Decision Support Systems and Intelligent Systems

A dynamic perspective on DSS and IDSS emphasizes their evolution in response to an ever-changing decision-making landscape. These systems are no longer static tools but dynamic frameworks capable of continuous learning and adaptation. This adaptability is crucial for meeting the complexities of modern decision environments, marked by rapid technological advances, the proliferation of data, and heightened user expectations.

8.4.1. *Characteristics of a Dynamic Decision Support System*

DSS and IDSS stand out due to their advanced attributes, which enable them to adapt and thrive in ever-changing environments. These characteristics form the backbone of their utility and efficacy in modern decision-making contexts.

1. **Real-Time Adaptability:** A defining feature of dynamic systems is their ability to adapt to real-time changes in the decision environment. Traditional static systems lack this responsiveness, making them less effective in fast-paced, data-driven scenarios. For instance, in supply chain management, dynamic

Table 8.3. Summary of Key Aspects of Human-Machine Collaboration in Decision Making

Aspect	Key Insights	Takeaways for Decision Makers
Core Principles		
Division of Labor	Humans excel in creativity, ethics, and intuition; machines in data processing and probabilistic tasks.	Design systems with a clear allocation of tasks to maximize combined strengths of humans and machines.
Symbiotic Relationship	Machines act as assistants, not replacements, providing data-driven insights while humans validate them.	Foster partnerships where humans and machines augment each other's capabilities rather than compete.
Trust and Transparency	Trust is built through explainable systems (e.g., XAI).	Invest in transparent algorithms and ensure stakeholders understand how AI systems make decisions.
Benefits		
Enhanced Decision Quality	Combines human judgment with data-driven machine insights.	Use machines to process data and humans to contextualize and make strategic decisions.
Increased Efficiency	Machines automate routine tasks, enabling humans to focus on complex decisions.	Leverage automation to streamline processes and allocate human resources for high-value activities.
Scalability and Adaptability	Enables large-scale, context-sensitive decision-making.	Deploy human-machine systems to manage crises, adapt to market shifts, and address varied operational demands.
Challenges		
Transparency and Explainability	Lack of algorithmic transparency may erode trust.	Prioritize the adoption of systems with explainable mechanisms to facilitate user confidence and accountability.
Bias and Ethical Concerns	Machines can inherit biases from training data, leading to ethical dilemmas.	Implement robust ethical oversight in system design and address potential biases in machine outputs.
Trust Management	Over-reliance or under-reliance on machines can hinder decision-making.	Build balanced trust by calibrating machine autonomy with human oversight.
Goal Alignment	Misaligned objectives between humans and machines can create conflicts.	Ensure that machine objectives are aligned with organizational goals and human values.

Table 8.3. (*Continued*)

Aspect	Key Insights	Takeaways for Decision Makers
Applications		
Healthcare	Enhances diagnostics and treatment planning.	Combine AI-driven analysis with clinician expertise for improved patient outcomes.
Finance	Strengthens fraud detection and risk assessment.	Integrate AI analytics with human oversight for critical decision-making in financial operations.
Manufacturing	Boosts productivity with collaborative robots (cobots).	Employ cobots for repetitive tasks while humans focus on quality control and innovation.
Education	Facilitates personalized learning while teachers guide holistic education.	Use AI to tailor educational content and empower educators to provide mentorship and adaptative instruction.
Future Directions		
Integration of Emerging Technologies	AR, VR, and blockchain offer transformative opportunities.	Explore new technologies to enhance decision-making systems, particularly in design and transparency.
Human-Centered AI Design	Focuses on aligning machines with human ethics and needs.	Develop AI solutions that prioritize usability, ethical considerations, and alignment with human-centric goals.
Continuous Learning	Both humans and machines must evolve through ongoing learning.	Commit to continuous training for human operators and updating algorithms to ensure system relevance and efficacy.

DSS monitor live variables such as shipment delays, shifts in customer demand, or disruptions caused by adverse weather conditions (Hsu *et al.*, 2011). These systems process real-time inputs to adjust logistics, reroute shipments, or optimize inventory levels instantly. Such adaptability minimizes risks, improves efficiency, and empowers organizations to maintain operational continuity even under volatile conditions. The healthcare sector also benefits from real-time adaptability, with dynamic IDSS providing immediate alerts to medical staff about critical changes in a patient's condition, enabling timely interventions.

2. **Feedback Integration:** Feedback mechanisms are integral to the continuous improvement of dynamic systems. By analyzing user interactions, system outputs, and environmental variables, these systems refine their underlying algorithms and models over time (Power, 2002). This capability ensures that the system evolves in alignment with user needs and contextual demands. For example, predictive maintenance systems deployed in manufacturing industries collect sensor data from machinery to anticipate equipment failures. With every use, the system becomes more accurate in its predictions, reducing maintenance costs and preventing downtime. Similarly, in e-commerce, dynamic IDSS use customer feedback to personalize recommendations, improving user satisfaction and boosting sales. The iterative learning process embedded in these systems represents a shift toward self-improving technologies.
3. **Scalability and Flexibility:** The scalability of dynamic DSS and IDSS allows them to handle vast and growing datasets, a critical requirement in today's data-rich environments. As organizations expand their operations, these systems must integrate seamlessly with new data sources, such as IoT devices, external APIs, or cloud-based platforms (Holsapple & Whinston, 1996). This scalability ensures that the system remains efficient regardless of the volume or complexity of data. Flexibility, on the other hand, refers to the system's ability to adapt to diverse industries and decision-making contexts. Whether applied in finance, where systems analyze real-time stock market data, or in agriculture, where they optimize irrigation based on weather patterns, dynamic DSS and IDSS demonstrate unparalleled versatility.
4. **Integration of Emerging Technologies:** The integration of emerging technologies has significantly enhanced the functionality and capabilities of dynamic DSS and IDSS. AI, ML and NLP are among the key technologies driving these advancements. AI and ML enable the systems to process unstructured data, identify patterns, and provide predictive insights. For instance, in fraud detection, AI-powered IDSS can analyze transaction histories and flag anomalies with precision. NLP, on the other hand, facilitates intuitive human-computer interactions. Chatbots powered by NLP can interpret and respond to user queries in natural language, streamlining processes in customer service. This technological synergy not only enhances decision-making but also bridges

the gap between complex systems and their human users, ensuring that the insights provided are actionable and accessible.

5. **Context Awareness:** Another important characteristic of dynamic DSS and IDSS is their ability to incorporate context-awareness into decision-making. These systems analyze situational variables, such as time, location, and user preferences, to tailor their recommendations. For example, in urban planning, dynamic DSS use traffic data, population density, and environmental factors to design optimized public transportation routes. In the retail industry, context-aware systems adjust pricing strategies dynamically based on factors like competitor pricing and seasonal demand.
6. **Proactive Insights and Automation:** Dynamic systems are designed not only to react to changes but also to anticipate and prevent potential issues. By leveraging predictive analytics, these systems provide proactive insights that enable pre-emptive action. For instance, in cybersecurity, dynamic IDSS can detect vulnerabilities and recommend countermeasures before breaches occur. Additionally, many dynamic systems incorporate automation capabilities, executing routine tasks without human intervention. This dual focus on insight generation and automation makes dynamic DSS and IDSS indispensable tools for modern organizations.

In conclusion, the key characteristics of dynamic DSS and IDSS — real-time adaptability, feedback integration, scalability, flexibility, integration of emerging technologies, context-awareness, and proactive insights — set them apart as transformative tools in decision-making. These attributes not only ensure that the systems remain relevant in an ever-changing landscape but also empower organizations to make smarter, faster, and more informed decisions.

8.4.2. *Advantages of Dynamic Systems*

DSS and IDSS offer transformative advantages that differentiate them from their static predecessors. By leveraging their adaptability and advanced capabilities, these systems enable organizations to navigate complex decision-making environments more effectively.

- **Improved Decision Accuracy:** Dynamic systems excel in improving the accuracy and relevance of decisions by continuously integrating new data and refining their algorithms. This real-time adaptability ensures that recommendations are context-aware and reflective of the latest trends and information. For example, in the energy sector, dynamic DSS employed in smart grids balance supply and demand by analyzing real-time consumption patterns, energy production data, and weather forecasts (Drucker, 1999). Such systems enable utilities to optimize resource allocation, reduce wastage, and enhance grid stability. Similarly, in healthcare, dynamic IDSS assist in diagnosis and treatment planning by incorporating the latest medical research, patient history, and current health data. This continuous refinement ensures that decision-makers receive precise and actionable insights tailored to their specific scenarios.

- **Enhanced User Experience:** Modern dynamic systems prioritize user-centric design, offering intuitive interfaces and personalized features to accommodate diverse user needs. By adapting to the expertise levels and preferences of users, dynamic IDSS ensure accessibility and ease of use (Turban *et al.*, 2011). For instance, a financial advisor using a dynamic DSS may benefit from interactive dashboards that simplify complex data visualizations and provide tailored recommendations for investment strategies. Enhanced user experience not only improves the efficiency of decision-making processes but also fosters greater confidence and trust in the system. Furthermore, by incorporating feedback mechanisms, dynamic systems can learn from user interactions to continuously enhance their interfaces, making them even more responsive and user-friendly over time.
- **Proactive Decision-Making:** A hallmark of dynamic DSS and IDSS is their ability to shift decision-making from reactive to proactive. These systems leverage predictive analytics to identify trends, forecast outcomes, and recommend pre-emptive actions. For example, in the finance industry, fraud detection systems powered by dynamic IDSS analyze transaction patterns in real-time to flag suspicious activities before they result in significant losses. By anticipating potential issues, these systems empower organizations to take corrective measures promptly, reducing risks and enhancing security. Similarly, in supply chain management, dynamic DSS enable proactive inventory planning by predicting demand fluctuations, thus minimizing stockouts or overstock scenarios. This

forward-thinking approach enhances operational efficiency and strengthens an organization's resilience to unforeseen disruptions.

- **Strengthened Competitive Advantage:** By integrating advanced technologies such as AI and ML, dynamic systems enable organizations to stay ahead of the competition. They empower decision-makers to capitalize on opportunities faster, respond to market changes more effectively, and address challenges with agility. For instance, businesses that utilize dynamic IDSS for customer relationship management can identify emerging customer preferences and tailor their products or services accordingly, resulting in improved customer satisfaction and loyalty. This strategic advantage can be particularly impactful in industries where timely, data-driven decisions play a critical role in maintaining market leadership.
- **Continuous Learning and Adaptation:** Dynamic systems foster a culture of continuous learning and improvement, both for the systems themselves and the organizations using them. By analyzing historical data and incorporating user feedback, these systems evolve over time, enhancing their performance and utility. This iterative learning process ensures that dynamic DSS and IDSS remain relevant and effective in rapidly changing environments. For example, in predictive maintenance, dynamic systems improve their accuracy with every use by analyzing operational data from machinery, leading to more precise forecasts of equipment failures. This reduces downtime, lowers maintenance costs, and extends the lifecycle of assets.

In summary, the advantages of dynamic DSS and IDSS lie in their ability to enhance decision accuracy, improve user experience, enable proactive decision-making, and support continuous learning. These capabilities empower organizations to address complex challenges with confidence, agility, and precision, setting the stage for sustained success in an increasingly dynamic world.

8.4.3. *Challenges in Implementing Dynamic Systems*

While dynamic DSS and IDSS provide transformative advantages, their implementation is fraught with significant challenges that demand careful consideration by organizations and decision-makers.

These challenges arise from the technical, operational, and ethical complexities of deploying and managing such advanced systems.

1. **Data Quality and Availability:** The foundation of dynamic systems lies in their ability to process and analyze large volumes of data. However, the effectiveness of these systems heavily depends on the quality, reliability, and availability of the data they utilize. Inconsistent, incomplete, or biased datasets can compromise the accuracy of predictions and recommendations, leading to flawed decision-making (Holsapple & Whinston, 1996). For instance, biased training data in a hiring system might perpetuate discriminatory practices, undermining fairness. Organizations must prioritize the establishment of robust data governance frameworks to ensure data integrity. This includes implementing practices for data validation, cleaning, and normalization while also addressing challenges related to data silos and accessibility across departments or partners.
2. **Algorithmic Transparency:** Dynamic systems often rely on complex ML models, many of which function as "black-box models" where the internal workings are not easily interpretable. This lack of transparency poses a significant barrier to trust and adoption among users, especially in critical applications like healthcare or finance (Hsu *et al.*, 2011). For example, clinicians may be hesitant to rely on recommendations from a diagnostic tool if they cannot understand the rationale behind its conclusions. To address this, XAI techniques are increasingly being developed to make algorithms more interpretable. Organizations must prioritize the integration of XAI to ensure that users can understand, validate, and trust the outcomes generated by dynamic systems.
3. **Cost and Resource Requirements:** Implementing dynamic DSS and IDSS involves substantial costs and resource commitments, which can be a barrier for many organizations. These systems require investments in advanced infrastructure, such as high-performance computing environments, as well as skilled personnel to develop, maintain, and optimize them (Power, 2002). The need for continuous updates and the integration of emerging technologies further compounds these costs. For small and medium-sized enterprises, the financial burden may hinder their ability to adopt these systems, potentially widening the gap

between technologically advanced organizations and those unable to keep pace. Decision-makers must weigh the long-term benefits of dynamic systems against their upfront costs and explore funding strategies, such as partnerships or grants, to mitigate financial challenges.

4. **Ethical and Social Implications:** The integration of dynamic systems raises a host of ethical and social concerns that must be proactively addressed. Data privacy is a critical issue, as the collection and processing of large datasets often involve sensitive information about individuals. Organizations must adhere to stringent data protection regulations, such as GDPR, to avoid breaches and maintain user trust. Additionally, algorithmic bias in ML models can lead to unfair outcomes, such as discriminatory practices in lending or hiring processes (Drucker, 1999). Another concern is the potential for job displacement as automated systems take over tasks traditionally performed by humans. For example, automated customer service systems may reduce the demand for human agents. To address these issues, organizations must adopt ethical guidelines, conduct regular audits of their systems, and focus on creating opportunities for upskilling the workforce.
5. **Addressing Challenges Through Strategic Approaches:** To overcome these challenges, organizations must adopt a strategic and holistic approach. This involves fostering interdisciplinary collaboration among data scientists, domain experts, and ethicists to ensure that systems are designed responsibly and effectively. Additionally, investing in user training and awareness programs can enhance user acceptance and proficiency in using dynamic DSS and IDSS. Leveraging advancements in XAI and algorithmic fairness will also be crucial for addressing transparency and bias concerns. Moreover, promoting open-source solutions and collaboration within industries can help reduce costs and foster innovation, making these systems more accessible to a broader range of organizations.

In conclusion, while dynamic systems hold immense potential for revolutionizing decision-making processes, their successful implementation requires addressing challenges related to data quality, transparency, costs, and ethics. By proactively tackling these issues, organizations can harness the full capabilities of dynamic

DSS and IDSS while ensuring their responsible and equitable deployment.

8.4.4. *Future Directions*

The trajectory of dynamic DSS and IDSS is defined by emerging trends that promise to redefine how these systems interact with users, adapt to environments, and drive decision-making. These trends underscore the transformative potential of these systems in the coming years.

- **Hyper-Personalization:** Hyper-personalization represents a significant leap forward in the functionality of DSS and IDSS. By harnessing advanced analytics, AI, and ML, future systems will provide recommendations tailored to the unique needs, preferences, and circumstances of individual users. In healthcare, for instance, the integration of genetic data, patient history, and lifestyle factors will enable the development of customized treatment plans. Similarly, in retail, dynamic systems will use hyper-personalization to optimize product recommendations based on customer behavior and preferences. This shift not only enhances decision accuracy but also fosters user satisfaction by delivering precise, context-aware solutions.
- **Integration of Human-Centered Design:** The adoption of human-centered design principles is pivotal in ensuring that DSS and IDSS remain accessible, ethical, and effective. These principles emphasize the alignment of system functionalities with the needs, values, and capabilities of users. Future systems will incorporate robust feedback loops, allowing continuous refinement based on user interactions and evolving requirements. For instance, user-friendly interfaces, voice-activated commands, and visual dashboards will make these systems more intuitive and inclusive. Moreover, ethical considerations — such as transparency, privacy, and inclusivity — will be central to their design, addressing growing societal concerns about technology's impact on human lives.
- **Collaboration with AI Ecosystems:** Dynamic DSS and IDSS will increasingly function as components of broader AI ecosystems, enhancing their connectivity and versatility. These ecosystems,

comprising interconnected intelligent systems like autonomous vehicles, smart homes, and digital assistants, will enable seamless data exchange and collaborative problem-solving. For example, in urban planning, a DSS integrated with AI-powered traffic management and energy optimization systems can create smarter, more sustainable cities. Similarly, in agriculture, collaboration between IoT devices and dynamic DSS can enhance precision farming by optimizing resource use and improving crop yields. This interconnectedness promises to unlock synergies that drive efficiency and innovation across industries.

- **Emphasis on Continuous Learning:** Continuous learning will be a cornerstone of the evolution of DSS and IDSS. For machines, this entails ongoing updates to algorithms and models, ensuring that systems remain adaptive to new data and emerging trends. For users, continuous learning involves staying informed about technological advancements to fully leverage these systems' capabilities. Organizations will need to invest in training programs and upskilling initiatives to bridge the gap between system potential and user expertise. Moreover, dynamic systems will evolve through reinforcement learning and user feedback, improving their predictive accuracy and decision-making efficiency over time.
- **Emerging Implications and Opportunities:** The convergence of these trends not only highlights the technical advancements in dynamic DSS and IDSS but also presents opportunities to address pressing global challenges. Hyper-personalized healthcare can improve patient outcomes while reducing costs. Human-centered design ensures that technology serves humanity ethically and inclusively. AI ecosystems pave the way for collaborative innovations in sustainability and smart infrastructures. Finally, the emphasis on continuous learning fosters a culture of adaptability, enabling societies to navigate complexity with confidence and resilience.

In summary, the future of dynamic DSS and IDSS is set to revolutionize decision-making by prioritizing personalization, ethical design, systemic integration, and learning. These advancements will empower decision-makers with smarter, more responsive tools, ensuring they are well-equipped to address the demands of an ever-evolving world.

8.4.5. *Applications of Dynamic DSS and IDSS*

DSS and IDSS are revolutionizing decision-making across various domains by leveraging advanced technologies to process vast datasets, provide actionable insights, and improve decision accuracy. Below is an in-depth exploration of their transformative applications:

1. **Healthcare:** Dynamic DSS and IDSS are reshaping healthcare by addressing critical challenges such as diagnostics, treatment planning, and patient monitoring. Systems like IBM Watson Health utilize AI and ML to analyze extensive datasets, including electronic health records (EHRs), medical literature, and clinical guidelines, to recommend evidence-based treatments (Power, 2002).
   - **Diagnostics**: These systems assist physicians in diagnosing complex conditions by identifying patterns in medical data. For instance, AI-powered imaging tools can detect anomalies in radiological scans with greater accuracy than traditional methods.
   - **Treatment Planning**: Dynamic systems personalize treatment recommendations by considering individual patient data, such as genetic information, lifestyle factors, and medical history. This results in tailored therapeutic approaches that improve patient outcomes.
   - **Patient Monitoring**: Remote monitoring systems equipped with IoT devices enable real-time tracking of vital signs, empowering healthcare providers to intervene proactively and reduce hospital readmissions.
2. **Finance:** In the financial sector, dynamic IDSS enhance operational efficiency and risk management.
   - **Risk Assessment**: Real-time data analysis enables more precise evaluation of creditworthiness and risk exposure, helping institutions make informed lending decisions. For example, dynamic scoring models incorporate transaction history and external economic indicators to provide up-to-date assessments (Hsu *et al.*, 2011).
   - **Portfolio Management**: These systems support portfolio managers by analyzing market trends, historical data, and geopolitical factors to optimize investment strategies. Dynamic

IDSS also adapt to market fluctuations, ensuring timely adjustments to investment portfolios.
- **Fraud Detection**: Leveraging advanced algorithms, these systems identify fraudulent activities by monitoring anomalies in transaction patterns. For instance, IDSS can flag potentially fraudulent credit card transactions in real-time, preventing financial losses and enhancing security.

3. **Supply Chain Management:** Dynamic DSS and IDSS are pivotal in streamlining supply chain operations, ensuring resilience, and optimizing performance.

   - **Demand Prediction**: These systems analyze historical sales data, market trends, and external variables (e.g., weather conditions) to forecast demand accurately. This helps businesses avoid overproduction or stockouts.
   - **Inventory Management**: By integrating data from IoT-enabled sensors and tracking systems, dynamic IDSS optimize inventory levels, reducing waste and ensuring timely availability of goods.
   - **Disruption Management**: Dynamic systems are instrumental in managing disruptions such as supplier delays or transportation bottlenecks. For instance, IDSS can recommend alternate routes or suppliers, minimizing downtime and maintaining operational continuity.

4. **Public Policy:** Governments and policymakers increasingly rely on dynamic DSS and IDSS to address complex societal challenges and enhance governance.

   - **Trend Analysis**: These systems analyze socio-economic trends, such as employment rates, population growth, and climate data, to inform policy decisions.
   - **Impact Assessment**: By simulating potential outcomes of policy changes, dynamic systems help policymakers evaluate the effectiveness of interventions before implementation. For example, IDSS can predict the economic impact of tax reforms or the environmental implications of urban planning initiatives.
   - **Resource Allocation**: Dynamic systems enable efficient allocation of resources by identifying areas of greatest need. In

Table 8.4. Summary of the Dynamic View of DSS and IDSS with Key Takeaways

Aspect	Description	Key Takeaways for Decision Makers
Characteristics of Dynamic Systems		
Real-Time Adaptability	Systems respond to real-time changes, such as disruptions in supply chains or fluctuating customer demands (Hsu *et al.*, 2011).	Invest in systems that offer agility and immediate response to evolving scenarios to reduce risks and seize opportunities.
Feedback Integration	Incorporates user and environmental feedback to refine algorithms and improve outcomes over time (Power, 2002).	Continuously monitor feedback mechanisms to enhance decision accuracy and maintain relevance.
Scalability and Flexibility	Ability to manage increasing data volumes and integrate new technologies across domains (Holsapple & Whinston, 1996).	Ensure systems are scalable to meet growing demands and flexible to address diverse decision contexts.
Integration of Emerging Technologies	Incorporates AI, ML, and NLP to enhance analytical capabilities and user interactions.	Leverage cutting-edge technologies to unlock deeper insights and achieve operational efficiency.
Advantages of Dynamic Systems		
Improved Decision Accuracy	Continuously updated systems provide accurate, context-aware recommendations (Drucker, 1999).	Use systems that analyze dynamic variables to reduce uncertainty and enhance decision quality.
Enhanced User Experience	Intuitive interfaces and personalized recommendations improve accessibility and trust (Turban *et al.*, 2011).	Focus on user-centric designs to build confidence and optimize user-system interaction.
Proactive Decision-Making	Identifies trends and predicts outcomes to allow proactive interventions, such as fraud detection (Hsu *et al.*, 2011).	Transition from reactive to proactive decision-making by investing in predictive capabilities.
Challenges		
Data Quality and Availability	High-quality, reliable data is critical for system accuracy (Holsapple & Whinston, 1996).	Implement robust data governance and quality assurance practices.

Table 8.4. (*Continued*)

Aspect	Description	Key Takeaways for Decision Makers
Algorithmic Transparency	"Black-box" models can hinder trust; XAI is needed for clarity (Hsu *et al.*, 2011).	Prioritize transparency and explainability in AI-driven systems to foster trust among users.
Cost and Resource Requirements	Development and maintenance are resource-intensive (Power, 2002).	Balance cost with the long-term benefits of implementing dynamic systems.
Ethical and Social Implications	Raises concerns about privacy, bias, and job displacement (Drucker, 1999).	Address ethical considerations proactively to ensure responsible technology use.
Future Directions		
Hyper-Personalization	Tailored recommendations using advanced analytics, such as personalized healthcare treatments.	Invest in systems that align with individual user needs to enhance satisfaction and outcomes.
Integration of Human-Centered Design	Align systems with user needs and values through usability-focused feedback loops.	Adopt principles that enhance user experience and ethical alignment.
Collaboration with AI Ecosystems	Systems integrate into broader AI networks, such as smart homes and autonomous systems.	Build interconnected systems for seamless functionality across multiple domains.
Emphasis on Continuous Learning	Systems evolve through updates while users stay informed about advancements.	Promote a dual focus on machine adaptability and user skill development to maximize system utility.
Applications		
Healthcare	Enhances diagnostics, treatment planning, and monitoring (Power, 2002).	Adopt dynamic systems to improve patient outcomes and operational efficiency in healthcare.
Finance	Enables real-time fraud detection, risk assessment, and portfolio management (Hsu *et al.*, 2011).	Leverage these systems to strengthen financial decision-making and security.
Supply Chain Management	Optimizes operations through demand prediction and inventory control.	Use systems to ensure resilience and efficiency in supply chain processes.
Public Policy	Assists governments in analyzing socio-economic trends and resource allocation.	Deploy systems to inform effective policy decisions and resource management.

disaster management, for instance, IDSS can optimize the distribution of aid and resources based on real-time data from affected regions.

5. **Emerging Domains:** Dynamic DSS and IDSS are also finding applications in emerging fields such as education, smart cities, and renewable energy. In education, these systems personalize learning pathways for students, while in smart cities, they enhance urban planning and infrastructure management. In renewable energy, dynamic systems optimize energy production and grid distribution to meet sustainability goals.

Overall, Dynamic DSS and IDSS have become indispensable tools in diverse industries, empowering decision-makers with real-time insights and actionable intelligence. As technology continues to evolve, their applications will expand, driving innovation and efficiency across domains. Table 8.4 captures the chapter's essential points, emphasizing the actionable insights for decision-makers navigating complex decision environments.

8.5. Conclusion

DSS and IDSS have redefined the decision-making landscape by providing structured, data-driven support across industries. The conclusion of this chapter synthesizes the key insights and offers actionable takeaways for decision-makers navigating the complexities of today's fast-paced environments.

8.5.1. *Insights on DSS and IDSS Development and Utilization*

1. **The Critical Role of Adaptation**
   As environments evolve, so must DSS and IDSS. The integration of dynamic features ensures that systems stay relevant by adapting to new datasets, user needs, and technological innovations. Decision-makers must prioritize investing in adaptable systems that grow with their organizational requirements and external pressures.
   - *Key Takeaway:* Adaptability is not optional but a necessity in leveraging the full potential of DSS and IDSS. Leaders should

embrace systems that offer modularity and scalability to align with changing demands.

2. **Balancing Automation with Human Oversight**
   While DSS and IDSS excel in data processing and pattern recognition, the human element remains indispensable for context interpretation, ethical considerations, and strategic planning. Human-machine collaboration fosters a balanced decision-making approach where automation handles the routine, and humans guide overarching goals.
   - *Key Takeaway:* Decision-makers must establish frameworks that clearly delineate responsibilities between humans and machines, ensuring ethical and goal-aligned decision-making.
3. **Continuous Learning as a Foundational Pillar**
   In a rapidly advancing technological ecosystem, the ability of both humans and systems to continuously learn is paramount. For DSS and IDSS, this means regular updates to algorithms and the inclusion of new data sources. For decision-makers, this implies ongoing training to understand and maximize the use of these systems.
   - *Key Takeaway:* Organizations should institutionalize a culture of continuous learning and allocate resources for system updates and user training.
4. **Ethical Responsibility in System Design and Use**
   Ethical considerations, such as mitigating biases in data and ensuring transparency in decision-making processes, are central to the success of DSS and IDSS. Systems that fail to uphold ethical standards risk user trust and effectiveness.
   - *Key Takeaway:* Decision-makers must work closely with developers to ensure that ethical safeguards are embedded within DSS and IDSS from the outset.

8.5.2. *Lessons Learned for Decision Makers*

1. **Harnessing Data-Driven Insights without Losing Context**
   While DSS and IDSS provide unparalleled data-driven insights, decision-makers must contextualize these outputs to align with

organizational objectives and values. This means not just accepting machine-generated recommendations at face value but critically analyzing their relevance and implications.

- *Practical Insight:* Employ diverse teams that combine technical expertise with domain-specific knowledge to validate system recommendations effectively.

2. **Navigating the Challenges of Transparency**
One of the primary barriers to effective DSS and IDSS adoption is a lack of transparency, especially with complex AI models. XAI offers a solution, enabling decision-makers to understand the reasoning behind recommendations.
    - *Practical Insight:* Decision-makers should demand and prioritize systems that offer explainability, particularly for high-stakes decisions where accountability is critical.
3. **Preparing for Interdisciplinary Collaboration**
The effective use of DSS and IDSS often requires collaboration across disciplines, including IT, operations, and strategy. Decision-makers must foster environments where interdisciplinary collaboration thrives, breaking silos to maximize system capabilities.
    - *Practical Insight:* Encourage cross-departmental training programs and establish shared objectives to align diverse teams around system utilization.
4. **Anticipating the Future of Decision Support Systems**
The trajectory of DSS and IDSS points toward greater integration with emerging technologies such as blockchain, AR, and edge computing. Decision-makers must remain proactive in exploring and adopting these technologies to maintain a competitive edge.
    - *Practical Insight:* Establish dedicated innovation teams or partnerships with tech providers to stay ahead of technological advancements.

8.5.3. *Future Directions for DSS and IDSS Implementation*

1. **Enhanced Human-Machine Collaboration**
Future advancements will likely focus on creating more seamless and intuitive collaboration between humans and machines.

Voice-activated systems, augmented interfaces, and real-time analytics will further blur the lines between decision-makers and their tools.

- *Strategic Focus:* Leaders should consider investing in systems that prioritize usability and collaboration, ensuring that technology empowers rather than overwhelms users.

2. **Resilience through Decentralization**
Emerging decentralized systems, powered by blockchain technology, offer new opportunities for secure and transparent decision-making processes. DSS and IDSS leveraging decentralized frameworks can reduce vulnerabilities associated with centralized data repositories.
    - *Strategic Focus:* Explore blockchain-based DSS solutions, particularly in sectors like finance, healthcare, and public policy, where data integrity and transparency are critical.
3. **Integration with Autonomous Systems**
The rise of autonomous systems, such as self-driving vehicles and smart factories, will require decision support systems to operate in real-time and integrate seamlessly with these technologies.
    - *Strategic Focus:* Build partnerships with developers of autonomous systems to ensure that DSS and IDSS align with these cutting-edge technologies.
4. **Empowering Decision-Makers through Education**
Finally, the success of DSS and IDSS relies on informed decision-makers who can effectively leverage these tools. As systems become more advanced, the demand for tech-savvy leaders will grow.
    - *Strategic Focus:* Invest in leadership development programs that emphasize data literacy, critical thinking, and technological fluency.

Final Thoughts: The evolution of DSS and IDSS underscores the importance of dynamic, adaptable, and ethically sound systems in modern decision-making. Decision-makers must embrace a proactive stance, leveraging these systems not just as tools but as strategic partners in achieving organizational goals. The integration of advanced AI, ethical frameworks, and user-centered design will shape the future of decision support, ensuring that these systems remain indispensable in navigating complexity.

References

Barocas, S., Hardt, M., & Narayanan, A. (2016). *Fairness in Machine Learning: Limitations and Opportunities*. ACM Press.

Batty, M. (2013). *The New Science of Cities*. MIT Press.

Berg, S., Tschang, F. T., & Zhou, W. (2020). Decision support systems in digital finance. *Journal of Financial Technology*, 7(2), 134–152.

Brynjolfsson, E., & McAfee, A. (2014). *The Second Machine Age: Work, Progress, and Prosperity in a Time of Brilliant Technologies*. W. W. Norton & Company.

Chen, H., Chiang, R. H. L., & Storey, V. C. (2012). Business intelligence and analytics: From big data to big impact. *MIS Quarterly*, 36(4), 1165–1188.

Chen, H., Chiang, R. H., & Storey, V. C. (2006). Business intelligence and analytics: From big data to big impact. *MIS Quarterly*, 36(4), 1165–1188.

Choi, T. M., Wallace, S. W., & Wang, Y. (2020). Big Data Analytics in Operations Management. *Production and Operations Management*, 29(2), 304–314.

Davis, G. B. (1982). *Decision Support Systems: A Research Perspective*. Addison-Wesley.

Drucker, P. (1999). *Management Challenges for the 21st Century*. Harper-Business.

Elstein, A. S., & Schwarz, A. (2004). Clinical problem solving and diagnostic decision making: Selective review of the cognitive literature. *BMJ*, 324(7339), 729–732.

Gunning, D., *et al.* (2019). Explainable AI (XAI): A Perspective on Future Directions. *Journal of Artificial Intelligence Research*, 67, 35–50.

Haux, R., Ammenwerth, E., & Dugas, M. (2013). Health informatics: A systems perspective. *Springer Science & Business Media.*

Holsapple, C. W., & Whinston, A. B. (1996). *Decision Support Systems: A Knowledge-Based Approach*. West Publishing Company.

Hsu, C.-C., Chen, J.-S., & Chiu, S.-W. (2011). Dynamic decision making support system for a make-to-order environment. *Computers & Industrial Engineering*, 61(2), 411–420.

Huang, H., Yalcin, A., & Demirkan, H. (2019). A Decision Support System for Real-Time Supply Chain Risk Monitoring. *Decision Support Systems*, 120, 100–111.

Jiang, F., *et al.* (2017). Artificial Intelligence in Healthcare: Past, Present, and Future. *Stroke and Vascular Neurology*, 2(4), 230–243.

Jouffe, L., & Chiarello, C. (2002). Multi-objective optimization of industrial supply chains. *IEEE Transactions on Systems, Man, and Cybernetics*, 32(5), 647–654.

Keen, P. G. W., & Scott Morton, M. S. (1978). *Decision Support Systems: An Organizational Perspective.* Addison-Wesley.

Kowalczyk, M., & Buxmann, P. (2014). Big Data and Information Processing in Cloud Computing. *Business & Information Systems Engineering*, 6(5), 267–278.

Lee, J. D., & See, K. A. (2004). Trust in automation: Designing for appropriate reliance. *Human Factors*, 46(1), 50–80.

Parasuraman, R., & Riley, V. (1997). Humans and automation: Use, misuse, disuse, abuse. *Human Factors*, 39(2), 230–253.

Power, D. J. (2002). *Decision Support Systems: Concepts and Resources for Managers.* Quorum Books.

Qudrat-Ullah, H. (2020). *Managing Complex Tasks with Systems Thinking.* Springer.

Shankar, V. (2018). How AI Is Changing Retail Pricing. *Harvard Business Review*, 96(5), 32–35.

Shneiderman, B. (2004). Designing for fun: How can we design user interfaces to be more fun? *Interactions*, 11(5), 48–50.

Solove, D. J. (2013). Privacy Self-Management and the Consent Dilemma. *Harvard Law Review*, 126(7), 1880–1903.

Sprague, R. H., & Carlson, E. D. (1982). *Building Effective Decision Support Systems.* Prentice-Hall.

Turban, E., Sharda, R., & Delen, D. (2011). *Decision Support and Business Intelligence Systems.* Pearson.

Chapter 9

The Role of Big Data in Decision Making

Abstract

Chapter 9 explores the transformative role of Big Data in decision-making processes across diverse sectors. It begins by highlighting the opportunities and challenges inherent in data-driven decision-making, including issues related to data quality, privacy, and integration. The chapter then examines the management and analytical techniques employed to handle vast datasets, such as distributed computing and advanced analytics. Through case studies, it illustrates successful Big Data applications in healthcare, retail, and finance. Finally, the chapter presents a dynamic perspective on how Big Data's evolving capabilities influence decision-making, emphasizing the need for continuous adaptation to emerging technologies.

Keywords: Big Data; Data-Driven Decision Making; Data Analytics; Data Management; Strategic Decision Making; Privacy Issues; Data Integration; Distributed Computing; Advanced Analytics; Case Studies; Healthcare Analytics; Retail Analytics; Financial Analytics; Data Quality; Dynamic Perspective

9.0. Introduction

Big Data has emerged as a transformative force, fundamentally reshaping the decision-making processes of organizations across industries and domains. Defined by its volume, velocity, and variety, Big Data enables organizations to collect, process, and analyze vast quantities of structured and unstructured data. This unprecedented capability has created opportunities to gain deeper insights, streamline operations, and significantly enhance decision quality (Chen *et al.*, 2012). As data-driven decision-making becomes increasingly central to organizational strategy, Big Data serves not just as a tool but as a cornerstone of competitive advantage. This chapter explores the pivotal role of Big Data in contemporary decision-making, emphasizing its potential to inform decisions at operational, tactical, and strategic levels.

The exponential growth of data — propelled by the proliferation of digital technologies, Internet of Things (IoT), and social media — has revolutionized the way organizations operate. Data is often referred to as "the new oil" in today's economy, underscoring its value in driving innovation and business growth (Manyika *et al.*, 2011). However, raw data alone holds limited value; its utility lies in the ability to analyze and extract meaningful patterns and trends. Advances in data analytics, machine learning (ML), and artificial intelligence (AI) have made it possible to uncover previously inaccessible insights, enabling organizations to better anticipate market shifts, optimize processes, and enhance customer experiences (Raghupathi & Raghupathi, 2014).

From manufacturing and finance to healthcare and public policy, the impact of Big Data spans a broad range of sectors. In supply chain management, for instance, Big Data facilitates real-time inventory optimization and dynamic demand forecasting, reducing costs and improving efficiency. Similarly, in healthcare, data-driven models improve diagnostic accuracy and support personalized medicine. Public policy decisions are increasingly informed by large-scale data analyses, guiding urban planning, disaster response, and resource allocation (Zhao & Zhang, 2016). The breadth of these applications highlights Big Data's role as an enabler of innovation and informed decision-making.

This chapter also recognizes the inherent challenges associated with leveraging Big Data effectively. Issues such as ensuring data quality, achieving seamless integration across disparate sources, and safeguarding data privacy represent significant hurdles (Provost & Fawcett, 2013). Moreover, the need for skilled personnel capable of managing and interpreting complex datasets underscores the importance of investing in human capital alongside technological resources. Organizations must strike a balance between technological advancements and ethical considerations to mitigate risks such as algorithmic bias, misuse, and erosion of trust.

In addition to examining these challenges, this chapter outlines the tools, methodologies, and frameworks that underpin successful Big Data initiatives. By integrating case studies of organizations that have effectively adopted data-driven approaches, the chapter provides practical insights into best practices and lessons learned. These examples not only illustrate the transformative potential of Big Data but also highlight the strategies required to navigate its complexities.

As Big Data continues to evolve, its role in decision-making becomes increasingly dynamic. This chapter offers a forward-looking perspective, emphasizing the need for organizations to remain adaptive and innovative in a rapidly changing data ecosystem. By fostering a culture of ethical responsibility and continuous learning, organizations can harness Big Data as a driver of sustainable growth and informed decision-making. Ultimately, this chapter sets the stage for a comprehensive exploration of how Big Data is shaping the future of decision-making in diverse contexts.

9.1. Data-Driven Decision Making: Opportunities and Challenges

Data-driven decision-making (DDDM) has emerged as a cornerstone of modern organizational strategies, enabling businesses to harness the power of data for enhanced decision-making, operational efficiency, and strategic foresight. As organizations face dynamic markets and increasing competition, the ability to derive actionable insights from vast data sets has proven to be a critical differentiator. However, this data-centric approach comes with both substantial opportunities and significant challenges that decision-makers must address.

9.1.1. *Opportunities in Data-Driven Decision Making*

1. **Enhanced Decision Accuracy**
   DDDM facilitates evidence-based decision-making by minimizing reliance on intuition and subjective judgment. Advanced analytics allow organizations to analyze historical trends, forecast future outcomes, and optimize resource allocation. For instance,

predictive analytics tools in retail help anticipate customer demand and adjust inventory levels accordingly, reducing waste and maximizing profitability (Chen *et al.*, 2012).

2. **Operational Efficiency**
   By automating routine tasks and streamlining workflows, data-driven systems enhance operational efficiency. Organizations employ tools such as robotic process automation (RPA) and ML algorithms to improve supply chain management, reduce downtime in manufacturing, and optimize scheduling. Studies have shown that companies adopting DDDM practices are 5% more productive and 6% more profitable than their competitors (Brynjolfsson *et al.*, 2011).
3. **Personalization and Customer Insights**
   Data analytics enable organizations to tailor products, services, and marketing strategies to individual preferences. For example, e-commerce platforms use recommendation algorithms powered by ML to enhance the customer experience, resulting in higher engagement and sales (Mayer-Schönberger & Cukier, 2013). Personalized customer experiences have become a critical factor in building brand loyalty and driving revenue growth.
4. **Strategic Agility**
   Big Data equips organizations with the agility to respond to market changes in real-time. By leveraging real-time analytics, businesses can identify emerging opportunities or threats and adapt their strategies accordingly. For example, financial institutions use real-time fraud detection systems to mitigate risks and protect assets (Hazen *et al.*, 2014).
5. **Innovation and Competitive Advantage**
   Data-driven insights fuel innovation by identifying unmet needs, optimizing product development, and improving market positioning. Companies leveraging Big Data analytics as a strategic tool are often at the forefront of innovation, gaining a competitive edge through improved decision-making processes and differentiated offerings (Kitchin, 2014).

In summary, the adoption of DDDM offers transformative opportunities for organizations to enhance decision accuracy, streamline operations, and foster innovation. By leveraging advanced analytics and real-time insights, businesses can not only improve their efficiency but also gain a competitive edge in rapidly evolving markets. Personalization and strategic agility further position DDDM as a vital tool for addressing diverse organizational challenges. As organizations continue to embrace these capabilities, they unlock the potential to deliver more tailored, innovative, and impactful solutions across industries, setting the stage for sustained growth and success in the digital era.

9.1.2. *Challenges in Data-Driven Decision Making*

1. **Data Quality and Integration Issues**
   The effectiveness of DDDM heavily depends on the quality of data. Inaccurate, incomplete, or inconsistent data can lead to flawed decisions and missed opportunities. Furthermore, integrating data from diverse sources — such as customer databases, IoT devices, and social media platforms — poses technical and organizational challenges. Research indicates that 60% of companies struggle with data silos, limiting their ability to derive comprehensive insights (Hazen *et al.*, 2014).
2. **Data Privacy and Security Concerns**
   The increasing reliance on data raises ethical and legal concerns regarding privacy and security. High-profile breaches have underscored the importance of protecting sensitive information. Organizations must navigate stringent regulations such as the GDPR and CCPA to maintain compliance and safeguard consumer trust (Kitchin, 2014).
3. **Complexity of Analytical Tools**
   Advanced analytics tools, including AI and ML, require specialized skills for implementation and interpretation. Many organizations face a shortage of skilled personnel, hindering their ability to fully leverage these technologies. A 2021 survey found that 54% of businesses identified a lack of data science expertise as a significant barrier to DDDM adoption (Provost & Fawcett, 2013).
4. **Resistance to Change**
   Transitioning to a data-driven culture often encounters resistance from employees accustomed to traditional decision-making processes. Effective change management strategies, along with

ongoing training and communication, are essential to overcoming this challenge (Brynjolfsson *et al.*, 2011).

5. **Ethical and Bias Concerns**
   Algorithmic bias and ethical considerations remain pressing issues in DDDM. If unchecked, biases embedded in datasets or algorithms can lead to discriminatory outcomes, perpetuating social inequities. Organizations must prioritize fairness, accountability, and transparency in their data practices to ensure equitable decision-making processes (Barocas *et al.*, 2016).

While DDDM offers significant opportunities, its implementation comes with considerable challenges that organizations must address to fully realize its potential. From ensuring data quality and integration to navigating privacy concerns and overcoming skill gaps, the road to effective DDDM requires strategic investment in technology, processes, and human capital. Additionally, fostering an ethical approach and mitigating biases are critical to maintaining trust and ensuring equitable outcomes. By proactively tackling these challenges, organizations can build robust, reliable, and sustainable DDDM frameworks that drive meaningful progress and long-term success.

9.1.3. *Implications for Decision Makers*

In the era of DDDM, leaders must strategically navigate both opportunities and challenges to foster innovation, enhance performance, and build trust within their organizations. To achieve this, decision-makers must adopt a comprehensive approach that integrates governance, technical expertise, and cultural transformation.

1. Investing in Data Governance

Data governance is foundational to successful DDDM. Decision-makers should establish robust frameworks and policies to ensure data quality, consistency, and security. Effective governance helps mitigate risks associated with poor data quality and regulatory non-compliance. For example, implementing standardized data management protocols and conducting regular audits can enable organizations to maintain trust and reliability in their decision-making processes (Khatri & Brown, 2010).

2. Building Analytical Capabilities

Harnessing the potential of advanced analytics requires technical expertise and resources. Decision-makers must prioritize investments in upskilling their workforce or collaborate with external analytics specialists to bridge capability gaps. Organizations that focus on cultivating data science and ML expertise are better positioned to derive actionable insights and maintain a competitive edge in data-driven environments (Hazen *et al.*, 2014).

3. Fostering a Data-Driven Culture

Adopting DDDM demands more than just technical proficiency; it necessitates cultural transformation. Leaders must create an organizational culture that values evidence-based approaches at every level. Training programs, performance incentives, and transparent communication are essential tools to drive this cultural shift. Studies have shown that companies with strong data-driven cultures outperform their peers in operational efficiency and innovation (Brynjolfsson *et al.*, 2011).

4. Addressing Ethical Concerns

With increasing scrutiny on ethical AI and fairness, decision-makers must implement measures to identify and minimize biases in algorithms and datasets. Regular algorithm audits, ethical guidelines, and stakeholder engagement are crucial to ensuring transparency and equity in decision-making processes. By addressing these concerns, organizations not only reduce reputational risks but also build public trust in their data practices (Barocas *et al.*, 2016).

Overall, for decision-makers, the implications of DDDM go beyond technical adoption; they encompass strategic leadership, cultural adaptation, and ethical responsibility. By embracing a balanced approach that integrates governance, analytical capabilities, and a commitment to fairness, organizations can unlock the transformative potential of DDDM while navigating its inherent complexities. This proactive stance ensures that data-driven strategies are not only effective but also sustainable and equitable in the long term.

Table 9.1 provides a comprehensive summary of the opportunities and challenges associated with DDDM. It offers actionable insights

Table 9.1. Opportunities and Challenges in DDDM

Aspect	Key Insights	Practical Implications for Decision Makers
Opportunities		
Enhanced Decision Accuracy	Data analytics minimize subjective judgment, enabling data-driven forecasting and resource optimization (e.g., predictive analytics in retail).	Invest in tools that analyze historical trends and provide actionable insights for strategic decision-making.
Operational Efficiency	Automation and analytics tools (e.g., RPA, ML) streamline workflows and reduce waste, increasing profitability and productivity.	Implement automation technologies to enhance operational workflows and maximize efficiency.
Personalization and Insights	Tailoring offerings using customer data enhances engagement and builds loyalty (e.g., recommendation algorithms in e-commerce).	Develop advanced customer profiling systems to drive sales through personalized experiences.
Strategic Agility	Real-time analytics enable adaptive strategies and risk mitigation (e.g., fraud detection in financial systems).	Employ real-time data systems to monitor emerging opportunities and threats for agile response.
Innovation and Competitive Advantage	Data-driven innovation identifies unmet needs and refines product development, creating differentiation and competitive edges.	Leverage Big Data to uncover market gaps and drive innovation strategies for sustained growth.
Challenges		
Data Quality and Integration	Poor-quality or siloed data leads to flawed decisions. Integration from diverse sources remains complex.	Establish robust data governance policies and invest in integration platforms for consistent, high-quality data access.

Table 9.1. (*Continued*)

Aspect	Key Insights	Practical Implications for Decision Makers
Data Privacy and Security	Compliance with regulations like GDPR and CCPA is essential to avoid breaches and maintain trust.	Implement advanced security measures and ensure compliance with data privacy regulations.
Complexity of Tools	Advanced tools require skilled personnel; lack of expertise limits technology adoption.	Upskill employees or partner with analytics experts to harness the full potential of AI and ML.
Resistance to Change	Transitioning to data-driven cultures often faces resistance from traditionalists.	Foster a data-centric culture through training, transparent communication, and incentivizing evidence-based decisions.
Ethical and Bias Concerns	Algorithmic biases can lead to inequities; transparency and accountability are essential.	Regularly audit algorithms for fairness and establish ethical guidelines to minimize discrimination risks.

and strategic recommendations for decision-makers aiming to balance benefits and risks effectively.

9.2. Managing and Analyzing Big Data for Strategic Decisions

The emergence of Big Data has fundamentally transformed how organizations approach strategic decision-making. Effective management and analysis of Big Data — characterized by its volume, velocity, variety, veracity, and value — are essential for extracting actionable insights that drive competitive advantage. Organizations now leverage cutting-edge tools and frameworks, ranging from distributed computing systems like Hadoop and Spark to advanced analytics powered by AI and ML to make data-informed decisions. This section examines the methodologies, tools, and challenges associated with Big Data management, with a focus on its strategic implications for decision-makers.

9.2.1. *Key Characteristics of Big Data and Their Strategic Relevance*

The concept of Big Data is often summarized through its defining characteristics: volume, velocity, variety, veracity, and value. These elements present opportunities and challenges for decision-makers aiming to extract actionable insights for strategic decision-making.

1. **Volume, Velocity, and Variety**

Big Data encompasses an unprecedented scale of information, often measured in petabytes or exabytes. This **volume** requires organizations to adopt scalable storage solutions, such as cloud computing platforms like Amazon Web Services (AWS) or Google Cloud Platform, and distributed systems like Hadoop. These systems offer cost-effective, high-capacity data management solutions. Retail giants such as Walmart exemplify this need by processing petabytes of transaction and inventory data daily, using advanced analytical platforms to improve decision-making across operations and customer service (Manyika *et al.*, 2011).

The **velocity** of Big Data refers to the rapid generation, transfer, and processing of information. Data streams from sources such as IoT devices, social media platforms, and transaction systems must be analyzed in real time or near real time to remain relevant. For instance, financial institutions rely on real-time data to monitor market fluctuations, mitigate risks, and execute high-frequency trading strategies. Failure to process data at the required speed can result in missed opportunities or suboptimal decisions.

Variety describes the diversity of data formats—structured, semi-structured, and unstructured. Structured data, such as spreadsheets and databases, is easy to process, whereas unstructured formats, including images, videos, and social media posts, demand more complex analytical techniques. Organizations are increasingly utilizing tools like Apache Spark and AI-driven Natural Language Processing (NLP) algorithms to process diverse data types, enabling them to uncover deeper insights.

- **Strategic Implication**: Decision-makers must implement flexible and scalable infrastructure to manage high data throughput. Ensuring compatibility with diverse data formats is crucial for deriving holistic insights. Real-time analytics tools are indispensable for maintaining a competitive edge in fast-paced environments.

2. Veracity and Value

The **veracity** of Big Data refers to its reliability and accuracy. Inconsistent, incomplete, or erroneous data can significantly distort analysis and lead to flawed decisions. For example, inaccuracies in customer data can result in poorly targeted marketing campaigns, eroding trust and wasting resources. Addressing this issue involves robust data validation and cleansing processes. Automated tools, such as ETL (Extract, Transform, Load) platforms, and ML models designed for anomaly detection play critical roles in enhancing data quality.

The **value** of Big Data lies in its ability to provide actionable insights that drive strategic decisions. However, not all data is equally valuable, and sifting through vast datasets to identify high-value information is a challenge. Prioritizing data sources that align with organizational objectives can significantly enhance decision-making effectiveness. For example, in the healthcare industry, analyzing patient data to predict disease outbreaks or personalize treatment plans offers immense strategic value while reducing operational costs.

- **Strategic Implication**: Organizations must invest in sophisticated validation tools to ensure data integrity. Decision-makers should focus on identifying data subsets that align with their strategic goals, thereby maximizing the ROI of Big Data initiatives.

Overall, the interplay of these characteristics demands a holistic approach to Big Data management. Strategic planning should encompass not only technical capabilities but also organizational readiness. Establishing cross-functional teams that include IT specialists, data scientists, and business strategists ensures that Big Data initiatives are effectively aligned with operational and strategic priorities. Additionally, fostering a data-driven culture helps organizations transition from intuition-based decisions to evidence-based strategies, enabling resilience and innovation in a rapidly evolving business landscape.

By addressing the challenges of volume, velocity, variety, veracity, and value, decision-makers can transform raw data into a strategic asset, driving superior outcomes across industries.

9.2.2. *Tools and Technologies for Managing Big Data*

Managing and analyzing Big Data requires robust tools and technologies that can efficiently process, analyze, and visualize vast and diverse datasets. Organizations are increasingly relying on distributed computing frameworks, advanced analytics, ML, and powerful visualization tools to harness the value of Big Data and make data-driven decisions. Below, we explore the critical tools and technologies that enable organizations to manage Big Data effectively.

1. Distributed Computing Frameworks

To handle the immense volume and velocity of Big Data, distributed computing frameworks like **Hadoop** and **Apache Spark** are essential. These technologies allow organizations to process large datasets across multiple servers or nodes, improving both efficiency and scalability.

Hadoop is a well-established open-source framework for distributed storage and processing of large datasets. It employs the **MapReduce** programming model, which divides tasks into smaller sub-tasks and distributes them across multiple nodes for parallel processing. This approach significantly enhances the scalability of data storage and computation, allowing organizations to handle massive datasets effectively. Moreover, Hadoop's flexibility allows it to work with structured, semi-structured, and unstructured data, which is essential in today's data-driven world (Zikopoulos et al., 2012).

Apache Spark, another open-source framework, provides in-memory processing, which is a key advantage over Hadoop's disk-based processing. This allows Spark to process data much faster, especially for iterative algorithms commonly used in **ML** and **real-time analytics**. Spark's ability to perform computations in-memory reduces the time required for data processing, making it ideal for applications that demand quick, real-time insights (Zaharia *et al.*, 2016).

- **Critical Insight**: Decision-makers need to carefully evaluate the trade-offs between cost and performance when selecting a framework. While Hadoop excels at batch processing large datasets, Apache Spark is better suited for real-time analytics, especially when speed is a critical factor. The right choice of framework can significantly influence the performance and cost-efficiency of Big Data operations.

2. Advanced Analytics and Machine Learning

Advanced **analytics** and **ML** play a central role in Big Data management, as they enable organizations to uncover valuable insights from complex datasets. ML algorithms, such as **neural networks**, **support vector machines**, and **decision trees**, are designed to identify hidden patterns within data, making them powerful tools for predictive and prescriptive analytics.

For example, **predictive analytics** uses ML algorithms to forecast future trends, behaviors, or events based on historical data. Retailers can use this capability to predict consumer purchasing behavior, while financial institutions can forecast market movements or identify potential credit risks. Additionally, **clustering algorithms** help in identifying natural groupings within data, which is particularly useful for customer segmentation and targeted marketing strategies (Rajan *et al.*, 2018).

With the integration of ML, organizations can move beyond descriptive analytics (which only reports what has happened) to **predictive** and **prescriptive** analytics, which help forecast future events and suggest optimal courses of action. This ability to anticipate trends and behaviors gives companies a strategic advantage by enabling them to design proactive strategies, improve customer experiences, and gain a competitive edge.

- **Strategic Advantage**: Companies leveraging AI and ML for Big Data analysis are better positioned to anticipate market trends and customer needs, allowing them to stay ahead of competitors and drive innovation in their products and services.

3. Visualization Tools

Data visualization tools are essential for making Big Data comprehensible and actionable. Platforms like **Tableau** and **Power BI** allow decision-makers to transform complex datasets into intuitive, interactive dashboards that provide a clear view of trends, correlations, and patterns. These tools enable users to quickly understand large volumes of data without the need for advanced statistical or analytical knowledge.

Visualization plays a key role in bridging the gap between technical analysis and executive decision-making. It allows stakeholders, from managers to senior executives, to interact with data in a way that is intuitive and accessible. For example, real-time visualizations can highlight emerging patterns or anomalies that may require immediate attention, making it easier to respond proactively.

Moreover, visualization tools support **collaboration** by allowing teams to work together around a shared understanding of data insights. Dashboards can be customized to display key performance indicators (KPIs) and other metrics relevant to different departments, ensuring that all stakeholders are aligned on strategic priorities.

- **Practical Application**: Incorporating real-time data visualizations into strategic planning meetings enhances collaboration, decision-making, and consensus-building among stakeholders. When key decision-makers can access dynamic, visually appealing data representations, they are more likely to make informed decisions that align with organizational goals.

In conclusion, the tools and technologies available for managing Big Data have revolutionized the way organizations approach data analysis. Distributed computing frameworks like Hadoop and Spark provide the infrastructure needed to process large volumes of data efficiently, while ML algorithms enable organizations to unlock deep insights from complex datasets. Data visualization platforms like Tableau and Power BI make these insights accessible and actionable for decision-makers, helping to drive strategic decisions and foster collaboration.

As organizations continue to generate and collect more data, the effective use of these tools will be critical to gaining a competitive advantage in the marketplace. Decision-makers must carefully assess their needs, the specific challenges they face, and the capabilities of each tool to maximize the value they derive from Big Data.

9.2.3. *Integrating Big Data into Strategic Decision-Making*

Integrating Big Data into strategic decision-making is crucial for organizations seeking to harness its full potential for long-term success. To achieve this, organizations must adopt a structured and thoughtful approach that aligns Big Data initiatives with organizational goals, fosters a data-driven culture, and encourages collaboration across departments. This section explores the key elements necessary for integrating Big Data into the decision-making process.

1. Aligning Big Data with Organizational Goals

The effective use of Big Data in decision-making requires a clear alignment with an organization's overarching goals and objectives. Without this alignment, organizations may struggle to derive actionable insights from their data or may end up wasting resources on irrelevant data analysis. To maximize the strategic impact of Big Data, it is essential to link data initiatives with KPIs that directly contribute to organizational success (Davenport & Harris, 2007).

For example, **healthcare providers** use Big Data to analyze patient health records, treatment protocols, and outcomes. By linking this data to specific organizational goals, such as improving patient outcomes or reducing operational costs, healthcare providers can identify trends and patterns that help improve treatment plans and optimize resource allocation. By continuously measuring these goals against KPIs, organizations can ensure that their Big Data initiatives remain focused on driving value.

Similarly, retailers can use Big Data analytics to monitor customer purchasing behaviors, stock levels, and supply chain efficiencies. Aligning these insights with corporate objectives, such as maximizing sales, reducing inventory costs, or improving customer satisfaction, allows decision-makers to take actionable steps that improve business performance. The process of mapping Big Data efforts to organizational goals helps ensure that analytical insights lead to real-world actions that create value across the organization.

- **Strategic Implication**: Decision-makers must ensure that Big Data initiatives are aligned with clear KPIs and organizational objectives. This alignment guarantees that data-driven insights contribute directly to business success and foster long-term competitive advantages.

2. Data-Driven Culture

A key element of successfully integrating Big Data into decision-making is fostering a **data-driven culture** throughout the organization. A data-driven culture encourages individuals at all levels of the organization to make decisions based on data and insights rather than intuition or tradition. However, cultivating this culture requires a committed effort from leadership, as well as ongoing employee training and engagement (Brynjolfsson *et al.*, 2011).

Leadership commitment is the foundation of a data-driven culture. Senior executives must not only champion the importance of data but also actively participate in the process of DDDM. By prioritizing data initiatives, setting clear expectations for data usage, and providing the necessary resources, leaders demonstrate their commitment to using data as a strategic asset.

In addition to leadership support, **employee training** is critical for ensuring that all members of the organization understand how to effectively use Big Data tools and analytics. Whether through formal training programs or informal knowledge-sharing platforms, organizations must invest in enhancing data literacy across their workforce. Employees who understand the value of data and know how to interpret and apply data-driven insights are more likely to make informed, effective decisions.

Moreover, **clear communication** of data's strategic importance helps ensure that everyone in the organization understands its role in achieving organizational goals. This communication helps break down silos, encourages collaboration, and enables employees to work together toward shared data-driven objectives.

- **Practical Insight**: Cultivating a data-driven culture is essential for integrating Big Data into decision-making processes. Leadership must actively promote the value of data, while employees must be equipped with the skills and knowledge to leverage it effectively.

Clear communication and collaboration are key to ensuring the success of Big Data initiatives.

3. Collaboration Across Departments

Integrating Big Data into strategic decision-making is not the responsibility of a single department but rather requires cross-departmental collaboration. Different departments within an organization, such as marketing, finance, and operations, generate and consume different types of data. For instance, the marketing department may use customer data to create personalized campaigns, while the finance department analyzes sales data to forecast revenue trends. By collaborating and sharing insights, departments can leverage Big Data to create a unified view of organizational performance and make more informed decisions.

This collaboration is facilitated by the use of **centralized data repositories** or **data lakes**, where all data from various departments is stored and made accessible. These platforms allow teams to share insights and combine data from disparate sources to gain a more comprehensive understanding of organizational performance. For example, by combining marketing campaign data with customer feedback, organizations can gain deeper insights into customer preferences, which can inform both future marketing strategies and product development decisions.

- **Strategic Advantage**: Cross-departmental collaboration ensures that Big Data is used holistically across the organization. It allows teams to work together to align their efforts and make decisions based on a complete, unified view of the business.

4. Overcoming Organizational Barriers

While the benefits of integrating Big Data into strategic decision-making are clear, organizations often face challenges in overcoming internal barriers. These barriers include data silos, legacy systems, and resistance to change. To overcome these challenges, organizations must focus on creating a shared data infrastructure, updating outdated systems, and fostering a culture of openness and collaboration.

For example, organizations may need to invest in modernizing their IT infrastructure to accommodate Big Data tools and platforms. This might involve migrating legacy systems to cloud-based solutions or adopting new data management technologies. Additionally, leadership must actively work to reduce resistance to data-driven decision-making by educating employees about the value of data and providing clear examples of how data insights can drive business success.

- **Practical Application**: Overcoming organizational barriers is crucial for successfully integrating Big Data into strategic decision-making. This requires investment in technology, organizational change management, and a concerted effort to foster a collaborative and open culture.

Thus, integrating Big Data into strategic decision-making is essential for organizations seeking to gain a competitive advantage in the data-driven world. By aligning Big Data initiatives with organizational goals, fostering a data-driven culture, and promoting collaboration across departments, organizations can unlock the full potential of their data. Overcoming internal barriers and ensuring that data is used effectively at all levels of decision-making will help organizations make informed, timely, and strategic decisions that drive long-term success.

9.2.4. *Challenges in Big Data Management*

While the potential of Big Data is vast, organizations face several challenges in its management that can hinder its effectiveness and limit its strategic value. To fully leverage Big Data, businesses must address key issues related to data quality and integration, privacy and compliance, and the skilled workforce gap. In this section, we explore these challenges in more detail and present potential strategies for mitigating them.

1. Data Quality and Integration

Data quality is one of the most significant challenges in Big Data management. Inconsistent data formats, missing values, and erroneous entries can result in misleading or inaccurate analyses, which in turn can lead to poor decision-making. Moreover, data is often spread across different systems, departments, or even external sources, which can create **data silos** — isolated pools of information that are not easily accessible or shareable. When data from these silos is integrated for analysis, inconsistencies and conflicts can emerge, further complicating the data analysis process (Hazen *et al.*, 2014).

The **integration of diverse datasets** is critical for organizations to gain a comprehensive understanding of business performance. However, combining structured and unstructured data from multiple sources, including social media, IoT devices, customer records, and financial transactions, can be technically challenging. This complexity increases with the growing volume of data generated by organizations.

- **Mitigation Strategies**: To address these challenges, organizations should standardize data entry protocols and adopt data integration platforms such as ETL tools. ETL tools are specifically designed to help with the extraction of data from different sources, its transformation into a consistent format, and its loading into a centralized repository for further analysis. Additionally, data governance frameworks that ensure data consistency, accuracy, and accessibility across departments are essential for seamless integration. A data quality management strategy, which includes regular data cleaning, validation, and verification processes, can also help ensure the integrity of data.
- **Strategic Advantage**: By investing in data integration tools and processes, organizations can break down data silos, improve data consistency, and enhance the quality of analysis, ultimately driving more informed decision-making.

2. Privacy and Compliance

As Big Data involves the collection and analysis of massive amounts of personal and organizational data, it inherently raises concerns related to data privacy and regulatory compliance. In many industries, the storage and processing of sensitive information are tightly regulated to protect individuals' rights and prevent misuse. For example, healthcare organizations must comply with the HIPAA to protect patient data, while companies operating in the European Union must adhere to the GDPR, which enforces strict rules on data privacy, consent, and usage (Kitchin, 2014).

With the proliferation of data breaches and cyberattacks, organizations must take extra precautions to safeguard the data they collect and process. Failure to comply with regulatory standards or to protect sensitive data can lead to significant financial penalties, reputational damage, and loss of consumer trust.

- **Decision-Maker's Role**: It is essential for organizational leaders to take an active role in establishing robust data governance frameworks. These frameworks should include guidelines for data access control, encryption, and anonymization of sensitive data to ensure compliance with privacy regulations. Furthermore, decision-makers must ensure that the organization continuously monitors its data handling practices, conducts data audits, and educates employees about the importance of data privacy and compliance. This proactive approach helps minimize risks related to non-compliance and reduces the likelihood of security breaches.
- **Practical Insight**: Integrating privacy and compliance measures into the core of the organization's data strategy is non-negotiable. By embedding these practices into everyday operations, organizations can ensure that they maintain the trust of customers and avoid the significant legal and financial repercussions of non-compliance.

3. Skilled Workforce Gap

The management and analysis of Big Data require specialized skills and expertise. Data scientists, data engineers, and data analysts are crucial to the effective processing, analysis, and interpretation of Big Data. These professionals possess deep knowledge in statistics, programming, ML, and data visualization, along with a strong understanding of business processes. However, the demand for such skilled personnel often exceeds the supply, creating a talent shortage in the field of data science and analytics (Provost & Fawcett, 2013).

Organizations often struggle to recruit and retain the right talent due to the high competition for skilled data professionals and the rapid evolution of the technology landscape. Moreover, many companies find it difficult to upskill their existing workforce to meet the demands of Big Data analytics, which require a combination of technical and analytical expertise.

- **Solution**: To bridge the skilled workforce gap, organizations must invest in talent acquisition strategies aimed at attracting top-tier data scientists and engineers. Additionally, it is important to upskill existing employees through training programs, certifications, and mentorship opportunities. Partnering with academic institutions to provide internships, co-op programs, and research collaborations can also be an effective way to cultivate a pipeline of future data professionals. Furthermore, creating a collaborative culture between data science teams and other departments (such as marketing, finance, and operations) can help leverage the expertise of internal employees and integrate Big Data analytics into decision-making processes more effectively.
- **Strategic Advantage**: Addressing the skilled workforce gap not only ensures that organizations have the necessary talent to manage Big Data effectively but also enables them to innovate and compete in the data-driven economy. Organizations that invest in workforce development can position themselves as leaders in Big Data analytics and gain a significant competitive advantage.

While Big Data presents immense opportunities, organizations must navigate the inherent challenges of data quality and integration, privacy and compliance, and the skilled workforce gap. By implementing strategies such as standardizing data protocols, establishing robust data governance frameworks, and investing in talent development, organizations can mitigate these challenges and unlock the full potential of Big Data. Ultimately, the successful management of Big Data requires a commitment to both technological solutions and organizational culture, ensuring that data is not only accurate and compliant but also actionable in driving strategic decision-making.

9.2.5. *Strategic Insights and Recommendations for Decision-Makers*

To effectively leverage Big Data for strategic decision-making, it is essential for organizational leaders to implement best practices and invest in areas that maximize the potential of data analytics. By prioritizing data governance, adopting scalable solutions, investing in workforce development, and focusing on predictive and real-time analytics, decision-makers can position their organizations to thrive in an increasingly data-driven environment.

1. Prioritize Data Governance

Data governance is the foundation of any successful Big Data strategy. Without proper governance, data can become unreliable, insecure, or non-compliant with privacy regulations. To mitigate these risks, decision-makers should ensure that there are robust frameworks in place for managing data accuracy, security, and ethical use. Regular audits, compliance checks, and validation protocols are essential for maintaining the integrity of data. Moreover, governance frameworks should outline data ownership, access control, and retention policies to prevent unauthorized access and misuse.

- **Strategic Implication**: By establishing a strong data governance strategy, organizations can build trust among stakeholders, ensure compliance with regulations, and make informed, ethical decisions based on accurate and secure data. Moreover, a sound governance framework provides transparency and accountability, which are critical for maintaining a competitive advantage.

2. Adopt Scalable Solutions

The volume, variety, and velocity of Big Data are constantly increasing, and organizations must adopt scalable solutions to handle this growth effectively. Cloud-based platforms and distributed computing frameworks such as Hadoop and Apache Spark are ideal for managing and processing large datasets in real-time. Scalable systems allow organizations to adjust their data storage and processing capabilities as demands evolve, ensuring business continuity and flexibility.

- **Strategic Implication**: Flexible and scalable systems enable organizations to adapt to changing data demands without disrupting workflows or incurring unnecessary costs. By investing in scalable infrastructure, organizations can future-proof their data management capabilities, supporting long-term growth and agility.

3. Invest in Workforce Development

Big Data initiatives require a skilled workforce capable of managing complex analytics tools and deriving actionable insights from vast datasets. However, there is a significant gap between the demand for data scientists and the supply of qualified professionals. To address this challenge, organizations must focus on upskilling their existing employees, providing them with the training and resources necessary to develop analytical capabilities. Additionally, fostering cross-functional collaboration between technical teams and business decision-makers ensures that insights derived from data analytics can be translated into actionable strategies.

- **Strategic Implication**: By investing in workforce development, organizations can bridge the gap between data analysis and decision-making. Training employees in data literacy, ML, and analytics empower them to contribute to data-driven initiatives, resulting in more efficient and informed decision-making. Furthermore, fostering collaboration between departments ensures that data insights align with business objectives and can be effectively implemented across the organization.

4. Leverage Predictive Analytics for Competitive Advantage

Predictive analytics uses historical data and statistical algorithms to forecast future trends and behaviors, enabling organizations to make proactive decisions. By applying predictive models, companies can anticipate customer needs, identify emerging market opportunities, and detect potential risks before they materialize. For example, predictive analytics can be used in inventory management to forecast demand fluctuations or in marketing to personalize customer offers based on predicted purchasing behaviors.

- **Strategic Advantage**: By focusing on predictive insights, organizations can enhance their strategic agility and make data-driven decisions that position them ahead of competitors. Predictive analytics enables companies to take advantage of opportunities faster and mitigate risks before they become significant threats. This proactive approach can help organizations maintain a competitive edge in rapidly changing markets.

5. Focus on Real-Time Decision Support

Real-time decision support systems integrate Big Data analytics into daily operations, allowing decision-makers to respond swiftly to dynamic conditions. By utilizing live dashboards, automated alerts, and continuous data streams, organizations can monitor KPIs and market conditions in real time. This enables managers to adjust strategies and tactics on-the-fly, improving responsiveness and operational efficiency.

- **Strategic Implication**: Integrating real-time analytics with decision support systems ensure that organizations can act quickly in response to market changes or emerging issues. Real-time data enables leaders to make more informed, timely decisions, improving overall business performance and agility. Organizations that incorporate real-time decision-making into their operations are better equipped to navigate uncertainty and capitalize on opportunities as they arise.

Conclusion: To fully realize the strategic value of Big Data, decision-makers must prioritize data governance, invest in scalable systems, foster workforce development, and leverage advanced analytics. Predictive analytics and real-time decision support systems, when properly integrated into the organizational strategy, can help businesses gain a competitive edge and enhance operational efficiency. By embracing these best practices, organizations can transform Big Data from a challenge into a valuable asset that drives innovation, growth, and sustained success. Table 9.2 succinctly outlines the critical aspects of Big Data management, providing actionable insights for decision-makers to enhance strategic agility and data-informed decision-making.

9.3. Case Studies on Big Data Applications

Real-world case studies provide valuable insights into the transformative power of Big Data in various industries, demonstrating how data-driven decision-making can significantly enhance operational efficiency, customer experience, and strategic agility. These applications go beyond mere data collection and storage, illustrating the

Table 9.2. Key Aspects of Managing and Analyzing Big Data for Strategic Decisions

Aspect	Description	Practical Insights for Decision-Makers
Volume, Velocity, and Variety	– **Volume**: Large-scale datasets requiring scalable storage solutions. – **Velocity**: High-speed generation demanding real-time processing. – **Variety**: Diverse structured and unstructured formats.	– Invest in cloud computing and distributed systems for scalability. – Leverage real-time analytics to enhance responsiveness. – Ensure systems handle multi-format data seamlessly.
Veracity and Value	– Ensuring data reliability amidst inaccuracies and inconsistencies. – Identifying data subsets offering actionable insights.	– Implement robust validation protocols. – Prioritize high-value datasets aligned with organizational goals.
Distributed Computing	– Tools like Hadoop and Apache Spark for efficient data processing and scalability.	– Use Hadoop for batch processing and Apache Spark for real-time analytics. – Balance cost and performance considerations.
Advanced Analytics and AI	– ML for predictive insights and pattern recognition. – Algorithms like neural networks enhance decision-making precision.	– Adopt ML to forecast trends and segment customers. – Develop cross-functional teams to translate analytics into actionable strategies.
Visualization Tools	– Platforms like Tableau and Power BI for interactive, real-time data dashboards.	– Incorporate visualizations in strategic planning for clarity. – Use dashboards to facilitate stakeholder collaboration and decision-making.

(*Continued*)

Table 9.2. (*Continued*)

Aspect	**Description**	**Practical Insights for Decision-Makers**
Alignment with Goals	– Linking Big Data efforts to KPIs and organizational objectives.	– Identify KPIs during the planning phase.
		– Use analytics to monitor progress and inform course corrections.
Data-Driven Culture	– Leadership-driven emphasis on data literacy and informed decisions.	– Invest in employee training and transparent communication on data strategies.
Data Quality and Integration	– Addressing inconsistent formats and siloed data systems.	– Standardize data protocols using ETL tools for seamless integration.
Privacy and Compliance	– Adhering to regulations like GDPR and HIPAA for ethical data practices.	– Develop governance frameworks for data privacy.
		– Conduct regular audits to ensure regulatory compliance.
Workforce Development	– Addressing the skills gap in data science and analytics expertise.	– Invest in training programs and partnerships with academic institutions.
Predictive Analytics	– Utilizing forecasting tools to anticipate market trends and opportunities.	– Focus on proactive strategies driven by data insights to maintain agility.
Real-Time Decision Support	– Integration of analytics into real-time decision-making platforms.	– Use live dashboards and automated alerts to respond swiftly to dynamic conditions.

integration of advanced analytical tools, predictive modeling, and ML algorithms to solve complex problems. This section explores several notable examples across healthcare, retail, and finance, highlighting how organizations have leveraged Big Data to drive innovation, mitigate risks, and gain competitive advantages.

9.3.1. *Healthcare: Personalized Medicine and Predictive Healthcare*

In healthcare, Big Data analytics has revolutionized the way patient care is delivered by enabling the shift from one-size-fits-all treatments to more personalized medicine. As Raghupathi and Raghupathi (2014) note, Big Data technologies allow healthcare providers to process and analyze vast amounts of patient data, including electronic health records (EHRs), genetic information, and treatment histories, to tailor medical interventions more effectively. By using data from diverse sources, such as wearable health monitors, genomics, and patient demographics, healthcare providers can improve the accuracy of diagnoses and predict potential health risks.

For example, in oncology, companies like IBM Watson Health use Big Data and AI to analyze medical literature, clinical trial data, and patient records to recommend personalized cancer treatments. By utilizing vast datasets, Watson's AI can assist physicians in making better-informed decisions about treatment plans, improving patient outcomes and reducing unnecessary procedures. A study conducted by McKinsey & Company (2016) estimated that AI and Big Data in healthcare could save the U.S. healthcare system up to $100 billion annually through reduced hospital readmissions and more efficient treatments.

Moreover, predictive healthcare models enabled by Big Data analytics have proven essential in early disease detection and outbreak prediction. For instance, health organizations are using Big Data to track patterns in epidemiological data to predict outbreaks of infectious diseases like flu or Ebola. This predictive capability is critical for implementing timely preventive measures and allocating resources more efficiently, ultimately saving lives and minimizing healthcare costs.

- **Strategic Implication for Decision Makers**: Healthcare providers must prioritize the integration of Big Data technologies into their decision-making frameworks, focusing on data quality and real-time analytics. Ensuring interoperability across different healthcare systems and adopting AI-driven tools can streamline diagnosis and treatment, enhancing patient care while also reducing operational inefficiencies.

9.3.2. *Retail: Enhancing Customer Experience and Operational Efficiency*

The retail industry has been one of the most significant beneficiaries of Big Data analytics, as companies increasingly rely on predictive analytics and machine learning to understand consumer behavior and optimize inventory management. Amazon, one of the world's leading e-commerce platforms, exemplifies how Big Data drives personalized customer experiences. The company analyzes vast amounts of customer data, including browsing history, purchase behavior, and customer reviews, to provide personalized product recommendations and dynamic pricing strategies (Elgendy & Elragal, 2014).

Amazon's recommendation engine, which drives a large portion of its revenue, uses sophisticated ML algorithms to predict what products customers might be interested in based on their past interactions and those of similar customers. This level of personalization not only enhances customer satisfaction but also increases the likelihood of repeat purchases. Additionally, by analyzing purchase patterns, Amazon can manage its inventory in real-time, ensuring that popular items are restocked quickly while minimizing overstock on less popular items.

In brick-and-mortar retail, companies like Walmart use Big Data to improve supply chain efficiency and optimize pricing strategies. Through sensors and data analytics, Walmart tracks product movement across its vast network of stores, analyzing factors such as weather, traffic patterns, and regional events to forecast demand and adjust stock levels accordingly. This capability reduces waste, lowers costs, and ensures that customers have access to the products they need when they need them. Furthermore, in the grocery segment, Walmart's Big Data analytics system allows the company to predict which products will sell best based on seasonal trends and local preferences.

- **Strategic Implication for Decision Makers**: Retail executives must invest in scalable data infrastructure and advanced analytics tools to harness the power of Big Data. Additionally, developing a customer-centric data strategy that focuses on personalization and operational efficiency can drive sustained growth and improve customer loyalty.

9.3.3. *Financial Services: Risk Management, Fraud Detection, and Compliance*

In the financial services industry, Big Data analytics is playing a pivotal role in improving decision-making around risk management, fraud detection, and regulatory compliance. Bhattacharyya *et al.* (2011) highlight the significant impact of Big Data in helping financial institutions detect fraud by analyzing transaction data in real-time. Traditional methods of fraud detection were largely reactive, relying on rules-based systems that flagged suspicious transactions. However, Big Data enables a more proactive approach, where ML algorithms continuously learn from patterns in historical transaction data to detect anomalies and potential fraud before it happens.

For example, JPMorgan Chase uses Big Data analytics to combat credit card fraud. The bank processes millions of transactions daily, using ML models to identify unusual spending patterns in order to alert customers and fraud prevention teams in real-time. By analyzing variables such as geographical location, transaction amount, and frequency, the bank can predict whether a transaction is likely to be fraudulent, reducing the impact of fraud on customers and the organization.

Moreover, Big Data is also transforming risk management in investment banking. By analyzing vast quantities of market data, including historical prices, macroeconomic indicators, and geopolitical events, financial institutions can better predict market movements and assess the potential risks associated with various investment portfolios. This predictive capability enables financial analysts to make more informed decisions, helping to mitigate potential losses.

In addition, the regulatory compliance burden on financial institutions has increased significantly in recent years, especially with the implementation of the GDPR and the Dodd-Frank Act. Big Data analytics helps these organizations to monitor compliance by analyzing vast amounts of transaction data and communication records. This real-time monitoring enables financial institutions to proactively identify potential compliance risks and avoid costly fines.

- **Strategic Implication for Decision Makers**: Financial institutions should prioritize real-time data analytics and

AI-driven fraud detection systems. Additionally, investing in Big Data tools for risk assessment and regulatory compliance can help minimize financial and legal risks while improving operational efficiency. Decision-makers must also ensure that their data privacy and security practices align with regulatory requirements to maintain customer trust.

9.3.4. *Transportation and Logistics: Optimizing Routes and Reducing Costs*

The transportation and logistics sector has also witnessed significant advancements through the adoption of Big Data technologies. Companies like UPS and FedEx use Big Data analytics to optimize their delivery routes, improving both efficiency and cost-effectiveness. By analyzing real-time traffic data, weather conditions, and historical delivery patterns, these companies can make adjustments to delivery routes, reducing fuel consumption and improving on-time delivery performance.

UPS, for example, employs an algorithm known as ORION (On-Road Integrated Optimization and Navigation) to calculate the most efficient routes for delivery trucks. By analyzing data from GPS sensors, traffic reports, and customer delivery preferences, UPS can save millions of dollars annually by reducing unnecessary mileage and minimizing fuel consumption. In addition to improving efficiency, this reduces the environmental impact of transportation, aligning with sustainability goals.

Another application of Big Data in logistics is in predictive maintenance. By analyzing sensor data from vehicles and equipment, companies can predict when maintenance is needed, preventing costly breakdowns and downtime. This use of Big Data not only extends the life of vehicles and equipment but also enhances the reliability of services.

- **Strategic Implication for Decision Makers**: Transportation companies should integrate Big Data into their operational strategies to optimize route planning, reduce costs, and improve service reliability. Decision-makers must also invest in predictive analytics for maintenance to reduce operational disruptions and extend asset lifecycles.

9.3.5. *Manufacturing: Enhancing Production Efficiency and Quality Control*

In the manufacturing sector, Big Data is driving innovations in smart manufacturing and predictive maintenance. By integrating sensors into production equipment, manufacturers can gather real-time data on machine performance, product quality, and supply chain activities. This data is analyzed using advanced analytics to identify inefficiencies, predict machine failures, and optimize production schedules.

General Electric (GE) has been a pioneer in this area, leveraging the Industrial Internet of Things (IIoT) to connect its manufacturing equipment and gather vast amounts of operational data. Through Big Data analytics, GE can predict when machines are likely to fail and perform maintenance before costly breakdowns occur. This predictive approach has improved uptime, reduced costs, and enhanced production efficiency.

In addition to predictive maintenance, Big Data is used in quality control to monitor product defects and variations during the manufacturing process. By analyzing production line data, manufacturers can identify defects in real-time, allowing for immediate corrections and reducing waste.

- **Strategic Implication for Decision Makers**: Manufacturing executives should invest in IoT-based sensors and predictive analytics to enhance production efficiency and reduce downtime. Furthermore, implementing real-time quality control measures can improve product consistency, reduce defects, and ultimately increase customer satisfaction.

Overall, Big Data applications across various industries illustrate the transformative potential of data analytics in driving innovation and improving decision-making. From personalized medicine in healthcare to predictive maintenance in manufacturing, Big Data enables organizations to optimize operations, enhance customer experiences, and mitigate risks. By leveraging advanced technologies such as ML, real-time analytics, and cloud computing, companies can make more informed decisions, respond to market dynamics swiftly, and gain a competitive advantage.

Decision-makers must prioritize investments in scalable infrastructure, foster a data-driven culture, and ensure that their organizations are equipped with the necessary skills to manage and analyze vast datasets effectively. By doing so, they can unlock the full potential of Big Data and position their organizations for long-term success. Table 9.3 summarizes the key aspects of Big Data applications across healthcare, retail, financial services, transportation, and manufacturing. It highlights the technologies used, strategic implications for decision-makers, and key outcomes realized through Big Data adoption. The cases demonstrate how data-driven insights lead to improved decision-making, operational efficiency, and cost reduction across various sectors.

9.4. Dynamic Perspective of Big Data in Decision Making

Big Data has evolved from being a tool for basic data storage and management to a powerful resource for enhancing decision-making across all sectors. As technologies continue to advance, the capabilities of Big Data analytics are expanding, enabling real-time insights and more accurate strategic foresight. The dynamic perspective on Big Data in decision-making emphasizes the continuous transformation of its role as it integrates with emerging technologies such as AI and IoT. These developments not only redefine how decisions are made but also present new challenges for organizations to stay competitive. This section explores the evolving role of Big Data in decision-making, examining its integration with emerging technologies, its transformative impact on organizational strategies, and the need for adaptability in a rapidly changing environment.

9.4.1. *The Evolution of Big Data Analytics*

Big Data analytics has significantly evolved over the last decade, from basic data processing to advanced predictive and prescriptive analytics. Early applications of Big Data focused primarily on descriptive analytics, which allowed organizations to track and analyze historical data. However, with the advent of more sophisticated algorithms, organizations now leverage Big Data for predictive and prescriptive analytics, enabling them to anticipate future trends and optimize decision-making processes (George *et al.*, 2014). This evolution is particularly evident in industries such as healthcare, finance, and manufacturing, where predictive analytics are used to forecast

Table 9.3. Summary of Key Aspects of Big Data Applications Across Industries

Industry	Application	Big Data Technologies Used	Strategic Implications for Decision Makers	Key Outcomes
Healthcare	Personalized Medicine & Predictive Healthcare	ML, AI, Predictive Analytics, EHRs	Prioritize integration of Big Data technologies, focus on real-time data and AI tools, ensure interoperability across systems for improved care.	– Improved diagnosis and treatment precision – Early disease detection – Cost savings in healthcare delivery (up to $100 billion in the U.S.)
Retail	Customer Experience & Inventory Management	Predictive Analytics, ML, Cloud Computing	Invest in scalable data infrastructure, develop customer-centric data strategies, and personalize experiences.	– Enhanced customer satisfaction –Increased sales and repeat purchases – Optimized inventory management
Financial Services	Risk Management, Fraud Detection, Compliance	Real-time Data Analytics, ML, AI	Prioritize AI-driven fraud detection systems, invest in tools for regulatory compliance, and ensure strong data privacy practices.	– Proactive fraud detection –Better risk management –Reduced compliance risks and legal costs
Transportation & Logistics	Route Optimization & Predictive Maintenance	Real-time Data Analytics, IoT, GPS, Predictive Analytics	Use Big Data to optimize route planning and predictive maintenance, reducing costs and improving reliability.	– Reduced operational costs –Increased delivery efficiency – Enhanced sustainability through reduced emissions
Manufacturing	Smart Manufacturing & Predictive Maintenance	IoT, Real-time Data Analytics, ML	Integrate Big Data and IIoT to predict machine failures and improve production efficiency and quality.	– Increased production uptime – Reduced maintenance costs – Enhanced operational efficiency and quality control

disease outbreaks, market movements, and equipment failures before they occur.

As noted by George *et al.* (2014), the expansion of Big Data capabilities has facilitated real-time decision-making, transforming operational processes. The real-time analysis of data streams allows organizations to make informed decisions based on current data rather than relying on historical trends. In sectors such as retail and transportation, real-time analytics are used to adjust pricing, manage inventory, and optimize delivery routes based on current demand and environmental factors.

Real-world Example: In healthcare, predictive analytics powered by Big Data has revolutionized patient care. For instance, the Cleveland Clinic uses Big Data to predict patient risks and recommend personalized treatments, enhancing the quality of care and reducing costs (Raghupathi & Raghupathi, 2014). Similarly, in the retail sector, Amazon's real-time analytics enable the company to dynamically adjust its pricing and inventory based on customer behavior, seasonality, and external factors such as weather (Elgendy & Elragal, 2014).

9.4.2. *The Integration of Artificial Intelligence and IoT with Big Data*

The integration of Big Data with emerging technologies such as AI and IoT has opened new frontiers in decision-making. AI algorithms, including ML and deep learning, enable systems to analyze massive datasets and identify patterns that would be difficult for humans to detect. The combination of AI with Big Data analytics enables more accurate predictive modeling, enhancing decision-making accuracy in real-time. For example, AI-driven chatbots in customer service are powered by Big Data to predict customer needs and provide personalized responses (Bertella & Lopes, 2020).

IoT has further expanded the capabilities of Big Data by providing a continuous stream of real-time data from connected devices. These devices, ranging from industrial sensors to wearable health trackers, generate vast amounts of data that can be used for real-time monitoring, predictive maintenance, and even autonomous decision-making (Gartner, 2013). The integration of IoT and Big Data allows organizations to make decisions based on up-to-the-minute data, significantly improving operational efficiency and agility.

Real-world Example: One notable application is in smart cities, where the integration of IoT with Big Data analytics helps optimize traffic flow, reduce energy consumption, and enhance public services. For example, the city of Barcelona uses IoT sensors to collect data on air quality, traffic congestion, and energy use, which is then analyzed in real-time to adjust city operations and improve the quality of life for residents (Bertella & Lopes, 2020).

In the manufacturing sector, GE has leveraged IoT and Big Data to implement predictive maintenance strategies across its industrial equipment. By embedding sensors in machinery, GE can collect real-time data on the health of machines, using AI algorithms to predict failures before they occur, thus preventing costly downtime and optimizing production schedules.

9.4.3. *The Changing Nature of Data Management Practices*

As Big Data continues to expand in both volume and complexity, organizations must continuously adapt their data management practices to ensure that they can harness its full potential. Traditional data management systems, which were designed for structured data, are no longer sufficient to handle the variety, velocity, and volume of modern Big Data. As a result, companies are increasingly adopting more advanced data management frameworks, including data lakes and cloud-based solutions, to store and process both structured and unstructured data (Gartner, 2013).

Data governance is also becoming a critical focus for organizations as they grapple with the challenges of ensuring data privacy, security, and compliance with regulations such as GDPR. As Big Data analytics becomes more embedded in decision-making processes, organizations must ensure that their data governance practices are aligned with the growing need for data transparency and accountability.

Real-world Example: The European Union's GDPR has forced organizations to rethink how they manage data, emphasizing the need for stringent data protection measures. Financial institutions and healthcare providers, for instance, must implement robust data governance frameworks to ensure compliance with these regulations while leveraging Big Data analytics for decision-making.

9.4.4. *The Strategic Implications for Decision Makers*

The dynamic role of Big Data in decision-making presents both opportunities and challenges for organizations. For decision makers, it is essential to understand that Big Data is not a static resource but rather a continuously evolving tool that requires constant attention and adaptation. To stay competitive, decision makers must not only invest in the right technologies but also foster a culture of continuous learning and innovation.

Key Strategic Implications for Decision Makers:

1. **Invest in Advanced Analytics and AI:** As Big Data evolves, decision makers must prioritize investment in advanced analytics, AI, and ML tools that can process and derive insights from large, complex datasets.
2. **Focus on Real-Time Decision-Making:** Organizations should focus on implementing real-time analytics capabilities to make more informed decisions in fast-changing environments. This requires an investment in both data infrastructure and skilled personnel who can interpret and act on real-time data.
3. **Enhance Data Governance:** With the growing amount of data being collected and analyzed, organizations must implement robust data governance frameworks that ensure data privacy, security, and compliance with regulations.
4. **Foster Cross-Functional Collaboration:** As Big Data becomes a more integral part of decision-making, cross-functional collaboration between technical teams (data scientists, IT specialists) and business leaders is essential to ensure that data insights are translated into actionable strategies.
5. **Leverage Emerging Technologies:** Decision makers should not only focus on Big Data but also on the integration of emerging technologies such as AI, IoT, and blockchain to create more adaptive, automated, and responsive decision-making processes.

Real-world Example: Tesla exemplifies how organizations can integrate AI, IoT, and Big Data to enhance strategic decision-making. The company uses data from its electric vehicles, combined with AI algorithms, to optimize energy usage, predict maintenance needs, and improve manufacturing efficiency. This integration allows Tesla to continuously innovate and adapt to changing market conditions, enhancing its competitive advantage in the automotive industry (Bertella & Lopes, 2020).

9.4.5. *Challenges in Leveraging Big Data for Decision-Making*

Despite the immense potential of Big Data, organizations face several challenges in leveraging it for decision-making. One of the main obstacles is the integration of disparate data sources. As organizations collect data from a variety of channels, including social media, customer interactions, and IoT devices, integrating these data sources into a unified system for analysis becomes a complex task. Additionally, ensuring the quality and accuracy of the data is crucial, as poor data quality can lead to inaccurate insights and flawed decision-making.

Another significant challenge is the lack of skilled professionals who can interpret and analyze Big Data effectively. As the demand for data scientists and analysts continues to grow, organizations are facing a talent gap that hinders their ability to fully leverage Big Data for decision-making.

Real-world Example: In the banking sector, Wells Fargo has faced challenges integrating data from multiple sources, including mobile banking apps, online banking, and customer service interactions. To address these challenges, the bank has invested in AI and ML algorithms to clean, integrate, and analyze data, allowing for better decision-making in areas such as customer service, fraud detection, and marketing (Bhattacharyya *et al.*, 2011).

In conclusion, the dynamic role of Big Data in decision-making highlights its growing importance as a strategic asset for organizations across industries. As technologies evolve and new data sources emerge, Big Data continues to offer vast opportunities for improving decision-making processes. However, organizations must invest in advanced analytics, AI, and IoT, while also addressing challenges related to data governance, integration, and talent. By embracing a dynamic perspective on Big Data, decision makers can ensure that their organizations remain agile, responsive, and competitive in an increasingly data-driven world.

9.5. Conclusion

In conclusion, Big Data has firmly established itself as an indispensable asset in modern decision-making, transforming not only how businesses and organizations operate but also how they innovate and respond to challenges. As the volume, variety, and velocity of data continue to increase, the ability to harness and effectively leverage this data becomes crucial for gaining strategic insights and enhancing operational efficiency. However, realizing the full potential of Big Data is not without its challenges. Organizations must navigate complex issues related to data quality, integration, privacy, and security to ensure that the insights derived from Big Data are actionable and reliable.

This section summarizes the key factors that contribute to successful Big Data utilization in decision-making and discusses the importance of a dynamic approach to Big Data management. Through effective data management practices, organizations can overcome existing barriers and harness Big Data's full potential to drive innovation, optimize processes, and enhance overall decision-making outcomes. Furthermore, Big Data's integration with emerging technologies such as AI, ML and IoT is revolutionizing industries and reshaping decision-making strategies, presenting new opportunities for organizations to gain competitive advantages.

9.5.1. *Big Data as a Catalyst for Enhanced Decision-Making*

Big Data has moved beyond a simple repository of information to become a powerful decision-making tool that influences almost every aspect of organizational strategy. In its essence, Big Data allows businesses to make more informed, evidence-based decisions, shifting away from traditional decision-making methods based on intuition or limited historical data. As organizations collect vast amounts of structured and unstructured data, they gain deeper insights into customer behaviors, market trends, and operational efficiencies, enabling them to make timely decisions that would have been previously impossible.

One of the most notable transformations that Big Data has brought about is the shift toward real-time decision-making. Industries like retail, healthcare, finance, and logistics now rely on real-time data to make critical decisions on inventory management, customer engagement, risk mitigation, and supply chain optimization. For instance, in the retail sector, companies such as Walmart utilize Big Data analytics to manage inventory and optimize their supply chain in real time, ensuring that the right products are available to customers at the right time. In healthcare, real-time data analytics enables healthcare providers to monitor patient conditions, predict medical events, and personalize treatment plans, ultimately improving patient outcomes and reducing costs.

The dynamic nature of Big Data continues to evolve, offering more advanced ways to incorporate real-time data into decision-making processes. This shift is made possible through the integration of Big Data with other emerging technologies, most notably AI and ML, which allow organizations to analyze historical data and predict future outcomes based on current trends. As AI-driven decision-making becomes more prevalent, organizations can expect to make faster and more accurate decisions, ultimately enhancing their strategic foresight.

9.5.2. *Overcoming the Challenges of Big Data Utilization*

While the opportunities presented by Big Data are vast, successful implementation is contingent upon overcoming several challenges. One of the primary hurdles that organizations face is data quality. The vast amount of unstructured data collected from various sources such as social media, customer feedback, and IoT devices may not always be accurate, complete, or reliable. Inaccurate data can lead to flawed insights and ultimately poor decision-making. Therefore, organizations must invest in data cleaning and validation processes to ensure that only high-quality data is used for analysis.

Another significant challenge is data integration. With the proliferation of diverse data sources — ranging from transactional data, operational data, social media feeds, and sensor data — organizations often struggle to integrate these various types of data into a cohesive and actionable framework. Traditional data management systems may not be equipped to handle the scale and complexity of Big Data. As a result, organizations must adopt more advanced data integration tools, such as data lakes and cloud-based platforms, to consolidate and analyze data from different sources.

Data privacy and security are also critical concerns when it comes to Big Data utilization. As organizations collect and analyze personal and sensitive data, they must comply with increasingly stringent data protection regulations, such as the European Union's GDPR and CCPA. The risk of data breaches and the potential misuse of data present significant challenges for organizations seeking to balance the benefits of Big Data analytics with the need for robust security measures. Ensuring that data is collected, stored, and analyzed in a secure and compliant manner is essential to maintaining customer trust and mitigating potential risks.

Despite these challenges, the potential rewards of effective Big Data utilization far outweigh the risks. Organizations that can overcome these obstacles stand to gain significant competitive advantages, ranging from improved decision-making accuracy to operational cost savings. The integration of Big Data with emerging technologies, such as IoT, provides further opportunities to overcome some of these challenges. IoT devices, for example, generate real-time data that can be integrated into decision-making processes, providing insights into everything from inventory levels to customer behavior and product performance. When properly harnessed, this data can lead to improved product offerings, optimized services, and greater customer satisfaction.

9.5.3. *The Need for Continuous Adaptation*

Given the rapid evolution of technology and the growing complexity of data, organizations must continuously adapt their Big Data strategies to remain competitive. The dynamic nature of Big Data means that it is not a one-time solution but a constantly evolving resource that requires ongoing attention and refinement. The integration of new technologies such as AI, ML, and IoT with Big Data analytics adds another layer of complexity, requiring organizations to constantly reassess their data management practices and analytical approaches.

Moreover, organizations must be agile in responding to the ever-changing landscape of Big Data. As new data sources emerge and new technologies are introduced, organizations must remain flexible and willing to evolve their strategies. This requires investment in both the infrastructure necessary to process large volumes of data and the talent needed to analyze and interpret that data effectively. Data scientists, data engineers, and analysts play an essential role in ensuring that Big Data is harnessed to its full potential. Organizations that can continuously adapt their Big Data strategies will be better positioned to identify new opportunities, innovate, and stay ahead of competitors.

For example, companies like Google and Amazon have demonstrated the power of continuous adaptation by integrating new technologies and constantly evolving their use of Big Data to stay at the forefront of their respective industries. Google, for instance, uses Big Data analytics and AI to refine its search algorithms, improve advertising targeting, and enhance user experiences. Amazon employs sophisticated Big Data models to optimize its supply chain, predict customer behavior, and develop new products and services, all while adapting to the changing demands of the marketplace.

9.5.4. *The Future of Big Data in Decision-Making*

As we look ahead, the role of Big Data in decision-making will only continue to expand. Emerging technologies, including AI, blockchain, and quantum computing, will enable organizations to leverage Big Data in even more innovative ways. For instance, the integration of blockchain with Big Data could provide a secure and transparent way to track data usage and ensure data integrity, which is particularly important for industries such as finance, healthcare, and logistics. Similarly, advancements in quantum computing could enable organizations to process and analyze data at unprecedented speeds, unlocking new possibilities for real-time decision-making.

The future of Big Data in decision-making will also be shaped by greater collaboration between organizations, governments, and research institutions. Public-private partnerships could enable the sharing of Big Data across industries, leading to more comprehensive insights and innovative solutions to global challenges. For example, collaborative data sharing between healthcare organizations and governments could accelerate medical research, improve disease prevention, and enhance public health systems.

Ultimately, the continued evolution of Big Data, combined with emerging technologies and adaptive strategies, will redefine the landscape of decision-making. By embracing these changes and leveraging Big Data effectively, organizations can unlock new opportunities, drive innovation, and achieve long-term success in an increasingly data-driven world.

In conclusion, Big Data represents both a challenge and an opportunity for decision makers. While it brings immense potential to drive more informed, real-time decision-making and operational efficiency, organizations must address the inherent challenges associated with data quality, integration, and privacy. A dynamic, flexible approach to Big Data management, coupled with the integration of emerging technologies, will ensure that organizations can capitalize on its full potential. As Big Data continues to evolve, its transformative role in decision-making will become even more pronounced, offering new possibilities for achieving organizational success in an increasingly complex, data-driven world.

References

Bertella, G., & Lopes, J. (2020). Big Data and Artificial Intelligence for Smart Cities. *Journal of Urban Technology*, 27(4), 1–16.

Bhattacharyya, S., Pathak, P., & Yoon, H. (2011). Data mining for fraud detection: A review. *Expert Systems with Applications*, 38(11), 14577–14584.

Chen, H., Chiang, R. H., & Storey, V. C. (2012). Business intelligence and analytics: From big data to big impact. *MIS Quarterly*, 36(4), 1165–1188.

Davenport, T. H., & Harris, J. G. (2007). *Competing on Analytics: The New Science of Winning*. Harvard Business Review Press.

Elgendy, N., & Elragal, A. (2014). Big Data Analytics: A Survey. *Proceedings of the International Conference on Big Data and Analytics*.

Gartner, Inc. (2013). *Top 10 Strategic Technology Trends for 2014*. Gartner Research.

George, G., Haas, M. R., & Pentland, A. (2014). Big Data and Management. *Academy of Management Journal*, 57(2), 321–326.

Hazen, B. T., Boone, C. A., Ezell, J. D., & Jones-Farmer, L. A. (2014). Data quality for data science, predictive analytics, and big data in supply chain management: An introduction to the problem and suggestions for research and applications. *International Journal of Production Economics*, 154, 72–80.

Kitchin, R. (2014). Big Data, New Epistemologies and Paradigm Shifts. *Big Data & Society*, 1(1), 1–12.

Manyika, J., Chui, M., Brown, B., Bughin, J., Dobbs, R., Roxburgh, C., & Byers, A. H. (2011). Big data: The next frontier for innovation, competition, and productivity. *McKinsey Global Institute.*

Mayer-Schönberger, V., & Cukier, K. (2013). *Big Data: A Revolution That Will Transform How We Live, Work, and Think*. Houghton Mifflin Harcourt.

Provost, F., & Fawcett, T. (2013). Data Science and its relationship to Big Data and data-driven decision-making. *Big Data*, 1(1), 51–59.

Raghupathi, W., & Raghupathi, V. (2014). Big data analytics in healthcare: A survey. *Journal of King Saud University-Computer and Information Sciences*, 26(1), 1–17.

Rajan, V., Arshad, S., & Saldanha, K. (2018). Big Data Analytics in Healthcare: A Review of Data Mining Techniques and Tools. *Journal of Biomedical Informatics*, 85, 108–122.

Zhao, J., & Zhang, X. (2016). Big data analytics: A survey. *Journal of Management Analytics*, 3(1), 1–29.

Zikopoulos, P., Eaton, C., deRoos, D., & Deutsch, S. (2012). *Understanding Big Data: Analytics for Enterprise Class Hadoop and Streaming Data.* McGraw-Hill.

Chapter 10

Adaptive and Agile Decision-Making Processes

Abstract

This chapter explores adaptive and agile decision-making processes in the context of rapid technological change and uncertainty. It begins by contrasting traditional decision-making models with adaptive approaches that emphasize flexibility, real-time data, and continuous learning. The chapter then discusses the implementation of agile frameworks, highlighting the importance of cross-functional teams, iterative decision cycles, and clear communication. Strategies for managing technological disruptions through scenario planning and predictive analytics are also covered. Key takeaways include the necessity of a supportive organizational culture and the benefits of adaptability in navigating complex, dynamic environments. The chapter concludes by underscoring the critical role of these frameworks in ensuring organizational resilience.

Keywords: Adaptive Decision Making; Agile Frameworks; Technological Change; Uncertainty Management; Iterative Decision Cycles; Flexibility; Real-Time Data; Continuous Learning; Scenario Planning; Predictive Analytics; Cross-Functional Teams; Organizational Resilience; Dynamic Environments

10.0. Introduction

In today's fast-paced and ever-changing world, businesses and organizations are confronted with a multitude of challenges that are often unpredictable and complex. From technological disruptions to global economic shifts, the landscape in which organizations operate is more volatile than ever before. Traditional decision-making frameworks, typically grounded in stable assumptions and linear models, often struggle to keep up with the rapid pace of change. These conventional methods, which rely heavily on static data and long-term forecasting, are ill-suited to handle the complexity, uncertainty, and volatility that have become the norm in modern business environments (Teece, 2007). As a result, organizations are increasingly turning to adaptive and agile decision-making frameworks that offer a more dynamic, flexible, and iterative approach to managing change.

Adaptive and agile decision-making frameworks are grounded in the idea that organizations must be able to respond quickly and effectively to shifts in their external environment. The core principle of these frameworks is flexibility: the ability to adjust strategies, resources, and operations in real-time to maintain a competitive advantage and ensure resilience in the face of unforeseen disruptions (Eisenhardt & Martin, 2000). These approaches emphasize the importance of learning, collaboration, and iteration, allowing organizations to continuously refine their strategies and decision-making processes based on new information and emerging trends (Haeckel, 1999).

The need for adaptive and agile frameworks has never been more pressing. Technological advancements are accelerating at an unprecedented rate, with innovations such as artificial intelligence (AI), blockchain, and machine learning (ML) transforming industries and creating new opportunities — and risks — at every turn (Brynjolfsson & McAfee, 2014). In addition, the rise of global challenges such as climate change, geopolitical instability, and pandemics has added further complexity to the decision-making process. To navigate these challenges, organizations must be able to respond quickly, innovate, and adjust to the ever-changing environment around them (Bharadwaj *et al.*, 2013). As such, the ability to adopt and implement adaptive and agile decision-making processes has become a critical determinant of organizational success (Teece, 2014).

This chapter aims to provide a comprehensive overview of adaptive and agile decision-making frameworks, with a focus on their principles, practices, and real-world applications. The discussion will delve into how organizations can cultivate agility and resilience by integrating flexibility into their decision-making processes. Furthermore, it will explore how adaptive frameworks enable organizations to address uncertainty, drive innovation, and maintain operational continuity in the face of disruption. Ultimately, the goal of this chapter is to equip decision-makers with the tools, insights, and strategies needed to lead organizations effectively through an era of unprecedented change (Grant, 2016).

10.1. Understanding Adaptive Decision Making

Adaptive decision-making is a critical process that prioritizes flexibility and responsiveness to the constantly evolving conditions of today's complex, fast-paced environments. Unlike traditional decision-making models, which often operate under the assumption of predictability and stability, adaptive decision-making requires decision-makers to continuously adjust their strategies in real-time based on new information, feedback loops, and emerging trends. This approach is particularly useful in situations where outcomes are uncertain, variables are constantly changing, and decision-making occurs in an environment of high complexity. As businesses and organizations navigate the modern landscape of rapid technological advancements, market fluctuations, and geopolitical shifts, adaptive decision-making has become increasingly vital for achieving sustainable success.

This section provides an in-depth analysis of adaptive decision-making, exploring its theoretical underpinnings, practical applications, and key success factors. Drawing on verified academic sources and real-world examples, we will examine how organizations can implement adaptive decision-making frameworks effectively to improve their strategic responses and outcomes in complex environments.

10.1.1. *The Concept of Adaptive Decision Making*

Adaptive decision-making, at its core, revolves around the idea of flexibility and responsiveness. Traditional decision-making models often rely on static assumptions about the environment, making them ill-suited to deal with the complexities and uncertainties that are pervasive in modern organizational contexts. Adaptive decision-making, by contrast, requires decision-makers to maintain a high level of awareness of the dynamic nature of their environments and adjust their decisions accordingly.

As described by Qudrat-Ullah (2014), adaptive decision-making is essential for navigating complex environments characterized by uncertainty, volatility, and ambiguity. In such contexts, outcomes are difficult to predict because the interdependencies among variables are constantly changing. Decision-makers must rely on their abilities to continuously scan the environment, detect early warning signals, and adjust their strategies to remain effective. The ability to pivot in response to shifting circumstances is a defining characteristic of adaptive decision-making. It allows organizations to remain agile, resilient, and capable of exploiting new opportunities as they arise.

This perspective is in line with the work of Bianchi and Montemaggiore (2008), who emphasize that adaptive decision-making requires a shift away from linear, one-off decision-making processes toward a more iterative approach that allows organizations to refine their strategies continuously. This approach enables firms to respond quickly to unforeseen events, such as sudden market disruptions or technological advancements, which could otherwise derail rigid strategic plans.

10.1.2. *The Role of Real-Time Data and Analytics in Adaptive Decision Making*

A key element of adaptive decision-making is its reliance on real-time data and advanced analytics to inform decisions. Traditional decision-making often relies on historical data or static assumptions, but adaptive decision-making necessitates that organizations collect and analyze data continuously, allowing them to stay responsive to changing conditions. The use of real-time data allows decision-makers to monitor key performance indicators (KPIs), detect emerging trends, and adjust their strategies accordingly. This reliance on data ensures that decisions are grounded in current, relevant information, rather than outdated or static analyses.

For example, companies in industries such as retail and e-commerce rely on real-time analytics to adjust inventory levels, optimize pricing strategies, and personalize customer experiences. Amazon, for instance, uses vast amounts of real-time data from customer interactions, product reviews, and supply chain performance to continuously adapt its operations. Through its sophisticated analytics platform, Amazon can track purchasing behaviors in real-time and adjust its marketing efforts or inventory management systems to meet shifting consumer demand patterns. This ability to make data-driven, adaptive decisions has been a significant factor in Amazon's competitive advantage.

The effectiveness of real-time data and analytics in adaptive decision-making is supported by various studies, including Bianchi and Montemaggiore (2008), who highlight the importance of robust data collection systems in organizations that implement adaptive decision-making frameworks. These systems enable decision-makers to monitor internal and external variables, making it easier to detect early signs of change and to adjust strategies proactively.

10.1.3. *The Importance of Feedback Loops and Iterative Adjustments*

One of the hallmarks of adaptive decision-making is the presence of feedback loops, which provide decision-makers with ongoing information about the effects of their decisions. Feedback loops allow organizations to measure the impact of their decisions, identify areas for improvement, and refine their strategies over time. The iterative nature of this process means that decisions are not finalized but are revisited and adjusted as new data becomes available or conditions change.

As noted by Snowden and Boone (2007), feedback loops are especially crucial in complex environments, where outcomes are often uncertain and interdependencies between different factors can be difficult to predict. These loops enable decision-makers to assess whether their initial assumptions were accurate and whether their decisions are achieving the desired results. In this context, feedback is not just a mechanism for course correction but also a critical learning tool that allows organizations to adapt more effectively to future challenges.

An example of a feedback loop in action can be seen in the technology industry, where companies such as Microsoft and Google continuously test new features or products with small customer segments before rolling them out to the broader market. This iterative approach, often referred to as agile decision-making, involves collecting feedback from users, analyzing the results, and making adjustments to the product or service in real-time. This feedback loop ensures that the final product better meets customer needs and that the company can quickly pivot if customer preferences shift or if new market opportunities arise.

10.1.4. *The Role of Organizational Culture in Supporting Adaptive Decision Making*

An essential component of successful adaptive decision-making is an organizational culture that embraces flexibility, experimentation, and continuous learning. Organizations that foster a culture of innovation and risk-taking are more likely to succeed in adapting to changes and responding to new opportunities. A culture that supports adaptive decision-making encourages decision-makers to experiment with new ideas, test assumptions, and learn from failures rather than avoiding them. This type of culture is particularly important in environments characterized by high uncertainty and complexity.

For instance, companies like Google and 3M are renowned for their cultures of experimentation and innovation. Google's "20% time," where employees are encouraged to spend a portion of their time working on passion projects, has led to the development of successful products like Gmail and Google News. Similarly, 3M has long encouraged its employees to explore new ideas and take risks, resulting in the invention of innovative products such as Post-it Notes. These examples illustrate how a culture of experimentation and learning can be a driving force behind adaptive decision-making, enabling organizations to thrive in uncertain environments.

According to Snowden and Boone (2007), adaptive decision-making frameworks are most effective when organizations have a mindset that accepts complexity and uncertainty, rather than attempting to eliminate these factors. Embracing complexity allows organizations to see beyond the surface-level symptoms of problems and identify deeper patterns that can inform more effective decisions. In this way, adaptive decision-making becomes a tool for not only responding to change but also for capitalizing on uncertainty as a source of innovation and growth.

10.1.5. *Strategic Implications of Adaptive Decision Making for Leaders*

For decision-makers, the ability to implement adaptive decision-making strategies requires a significant shift in mindset and operational approach. Traditional leaders may focus on long-term stability and predefined strategic plans, but in the context of adaptive decision-making, leaders must be comfortable with ambiguity, flexible in their strategies, and willing to act quickly on new information. Leadership in an adaptive decision-making environment involves creating conditions that allow for rapid iteration, testing, and refinement of strategies.

Leaders must also recognize the importance of empowering teams to make decisions autonomously, allowing them to respond quickly to emerging trends and opportunities. In organizations that encourage decentralized decision-making, individual teams are empowered to make adaptive decisions within their areas of expertise, resulting in faster and more responsive actions. For example, in the context of global companies like Zara, the decision to rapidly respond to fashion trends is decentralized to local teams who can make inventory and design changes based on real-time data, ensuring that the company stays ahead of fast-changing consumer preferences.

Moreover, leaders must ensure that their organizations are equipped with the necessary tools and capabilities for adaptive decision-making. This includes investing in technologies for real-time data collection, analytics platforms for processing and interpreting that data, and systems for facilitating communication and feedback across teams. Effective leadership in an adaptive decision-making environment means creating a culture of learning, adaptability, and resilience, which can drive continuous improvement and enable organizations to navigate an increasingly complex business world.

10.1.6. *Conclusion: The Future of Adaptive Decision Making*

As the pace of technological change accelerates and the complexity of business environments continue to increase, adaptive decision-making will play an even more critical role in determining organizational success. Leaders and decision-makers must continue to refine their abilities to sense and respond to changes, leveraging real-time data, feedback loops, and adaptive strategies. The future of adaptive decision-making will likely be shaped by advancements in AI, ML, and other emerging technologies, which will enhance decision-makers' ability to process vast amounts of data quickly and accurately.

Ultimately, the organizations that succeed in implementing adaptive decision-making frameworks will be those that embrace uncertainty as an opportunity for growth, invest in continuous learning, and foster a culture of adaptability. With these capabilities in place, organizations will be well-equipped to thrive in an increasingly complex and fast-changing world. Table 10.1 succinctly summarizes the core components of adaptive decision-making, offering practical insights to help real-world decision-makers enhance their responsiveness and success in an ever-changing, complex environment.

Table 10.1. Key Aspects of Adaptive Decision Making and Practical Insights for Decision Makers

Key Aspect	Description	Practical Insights for Decision Makers
Flexibility and Responsiveness	Adaptive decision-making emphasizes the ability to remain agile and adjust strategies in response to changes in the environment.	Decision-makers should foster an environment that encourages flexibility by embracing uncertainty and enabling continuous adjustments in response to emerging trends or crises.
Continuous Learning and Iteration	This approach involves iterative adjustments based on feedback and new information, rather than relying on static decisions.	Organizations should implement mechanisms to continuously monitor outcomes, gather real-time feedback, and refine strategies as new data and insights emerge. Experimentation should be prioritized.

Table 10.1. (*Continued*)

Key Aspect	**Description**	**Practical Insights for Decision Makers**
Real-Time Data and Analytics	Real-time data allows decision-makers to stay updated with emerging trends and adjust strategies in response to new information.	Invest in robust data analytics tools and systems to collect real-time data, ensuring decisions are based on current information. Analytics platforms help detect early signals and emerging opportunities.
Feedback Loops	Feedback loops provide ongoing information about the outcomes of decisions, allowing for continual refinement and course correction.	Decision-makers should establish regular feedback mechanisms to assess the effectiveness of their decisions and be willing to adjust strategies when necessary. This helps organizations learn and evolve.
Organizational Culture of Innovation	An adaptive decision-making framework requires a culture that supports experimentation, learning from failures, and fostering innovation.	Leaders should cultivate a culture where risk-taking and experimentation are encouraged. Empower employees to innovate and learn from failure, which will help organizations become more resilient.
Embracing Complexity and Uncertainty	Adaptive decision-making thrives in complex and uncertain environments, where decisions must be made with incomplete information and shifting conditions.	Leaders should build strategies that embrace complexity, allowing organizations to adapt, rather than attempting to eliminate uncertainty. This fosters creative problem-solving and innovative thinking.

(*Continued*)

Table 10.1. (*Continued*)

Key Aspect	Description	Practical Insights for Decision Makers
Decentralized Decision-Making	Empowering decentralized decision-making allows teams to respond quickly to local conditions and opportunities, especially in global and dynamic environments.	Decentralize decision-making where possible, allowing local teams or departments to act quickly based on real-time information. This enhances responsiveness to market changes.
Technology and Tools for Adaptive Systems	Successful adaptive decision-making depends on leveraging advanced technologies, including data collection systems, analytics platforms, and communication tools.	Invest in cutting-edge technologies that support real-time data collection, processing, and dissemination. Ensure that teams are equipped with the tools necessary to act quickly and intelligently.
Strategic Leadership in Uncertainty	Leaders in adaptive environments must be comfortable with ambiguity, prioritize flexible strategies, and guide teams in navigating uncertain or volatile conditions.	Leaders should develop a mindset that thrives in uncertainty, focusing on creating adaptive, iterative strategies. Encourage decentralized decision-making and empower teams to act based on local knowledge.
Learning from Failure	Adaptive decision-making involves learning from mistakes, fostering a culture where failure is seen as a valuable opportunity for growth.	Leaders should normalize failure as a part of the learning process. Create an environment where teams feel safe to experiment, fail, and learn, fostering resilience and innovation.

10.2. Implementing Agile Frameworks in Decision-Making Processes

Agile frameworks, originally developed in the software industry, have gradually expanded to other sectors as a method of improving decision-making processes, particularly in environments that demand rapid adaptation and responsiveness. The core principles of agile decision-making frameworks — iterative development, collaboration, flexibility, and a focus on delivering value quickly — are well-suited for complex, fast-paced environments. This section explores the key elements of agile frameworks in decision-making, providing an in-depth analysis, relevant real-world examples, and critical insights for decision-makers.

10.2.1. *The Rise of Agile Decision-Making Frameworks*

Agile decision-making frameworks emerged from the Agile Manifesto, originally created in 2001 by a group of software developers. These principles emphasized the need for flexibility, rapid iteration, and close collaboration with stakeholders, as well as the importance of delivering working solutions in shorter cycles (Highsmith, 2002). Over the years, the principles of agile methodology have been adapted and applied to various fields, including project management, product development, and decision-making processes in dynamic environments.

Organizations increasingly find themselves in environments characterized by uncertainty, volatility, and complexity. The ability to make decisions quickly and adjust strategies in real-time is vital in such contexts. The traditional, top-down, linear decision-making models often prove insufficient in such settings due to their rigidity and slower response times. In contrast, agile decision-making is built to accommodate constant change by relying on iterative cycles and continuous feedback, enabling organizations to remain resilient and responsive.

According to Rigby, Sutherland, and Takeuchi (2016), agile frameworks allow organizations to handle complexity by enabling them to experiment, iterate, and adapt at a faster pace than traditional models. These frameworks focus on value creation and ensure that decision-making is more fluid and responsive to changing needs, thus improving an organization's ability to navigate uncertainty effectively.

10.2.2. *Key Practices in Agile Decision-Making Frameworks*

The implementation of agile frameworks in decision-making processes involves several key practices that help organizations improve their decision-making agility. These practices include the formation of cross-functional teams, the use of short decision cycles (sprints), continuous communication, and stakeholder collaboration.

10.2.2.1. *Cross-Functional Teams*

At the heart of agile decision-making is the use of cross-functional teams. These teams bring together individuals with diverse expertise, including subject matter experts, stakeholders, and decision-makers, to provide a comprehensive view of the issue at hand. This diversity allows for the identification of risks, opportunities, and potential solutions from different perspectives. As a result, decision-makers are better equipped to assess the full range of implications of their decisions, leading to more informed and innovative outcomes.

Cross-functional teams foster collaboration and enable rapid knowledge-sharing. This collaborative environment enhances the team's ability to solve complex problems by combining multiple perspectives and ensuring that the best ideas are considered. Rigby *et al.* (2016) emphasize that these teams are essential for agile decision-making because they encourage innovative solutions that can adapt quickly to external changes.

Real-world examples of successful cross-functional teams include companies like Apple and Google, where product development teams include representatives from marketing, engineering, design, and customer support. This holistic approach enables companies to create products that meet the needs of diverse stakeholders and address potential challenges before they become significant issues.

10.2.2.2. *Short Decision Cycles (Sprints)*

Another core element of agile decision-making is the use of short decision cycles, often referred to as "sprints." These cycles typically last from a few days to a few weeks and allow teams to make incremental progress towards achieving their objectives. The emphasis on short, focused cycles helps teams avoid long-term commitments based on incomplete information, enabling them to adapt their strategies and priorities as they receive feedback.

The practice of using sprints is crucial in fast-moving environments, where the ability to adapt quickly is essential. Denning (2018) argues that sprints facilitate quick, iterative decision-making that reduces the risk of being caught off-guard by unforeseen developments. By working in short bursts, teams can make decisions based on the latest information, re-evaluating and adjusting their strategies frequently to ensure they remain relevant.

A prime example of the use of sprints in decision-making can be seen in the automotive industry, where companies like Tesla frequently release updates to their electric vehicles based on customer feedback and real-time data. This iterative approach allows them to improve product performance quickly, incorporating customer preferences and fixing bugs without having to wait for the next major product release.

10.2.2.3. *Continuous Communication and Collaboration*

Continuous communication is a hallmark of agile decision-making. For agile frameworks to succeed, it is crucial that all team members and stakeholders are in constant communication, sharing updates, feedback, and insights in real-time. This open and transparent communication ensures that everyone is aligned and aware of the current state of the decision-making process, enabling the team to adjust quickly when needed.

Highsmith (2009) emphasizes that effective communication is vital for agile decision-making, as it ensures that no critical information is missed and that decisions are informed by the most current data available. Regular stand-up meetings, collaborative platforms, and real-time communication tools are often used in agile environments to facilitate this continuous exchange of information.

A real-world example of the importance of continuous communication can be observed in the tech industry, where companies like Microsoft and Amazon use collaborative platforms to keep their teams connected across global locations. These tools allow employees to share real-time insights, ensuring that decision-makers have access to up-to-date information when making decisions.

10.2.2.4. *Stakeholder Collaboration*

Agile decision-making frameworks prioritize stakeholder collaboration to ensure that the perspectives of all relevant parties are considered. In an agile process, stakeholders are actively involved in decision-making at every stage, providing feedback and insights that help shape the direction of the decisions. This collaboration fosters a deeper understanding of stakeholder needs and concerns, which can lead to more effective and impactful decisions.

Stakeholder collaboration can take many forms, including regular feedback sessions, surveys, focus groups, and consultations with external experts. Engaging stakeholders in the decision-making process helps organizations anticipate potential challenges and align their decisions with broader objectives.

For example, in the healthcare sector, organizations like the Mayo Clinic actively involve patients, medical professionals, and researchers in decision-making processes to improve patient care. By engaging diverse stakeholders, the clinic ensures that its decisions are informed by real-world insights and tailored to the needs of patients.

10.2.3. *Challenges in Implementing Agile Decision-Making Frameworks*

While agile decision-making frameworks offer numerous benefits, their implementation is not without challenges. Organizations must overcome several barriers to successfully adopt and integrate agile practices into their decision-making processes.

10.2.3.1. *Organizational Resistance*

One of the biggest challenges in implementing agile frameworks is overcoming organizational resistance to change. Many organizations are entrenched in traditional decision-making models, which prioritize hierarchical structures and long-term planning. Shifting to an agile approach requires a significant cultural change, including fostering trust, embracing uncertainty, and adopting more decentralized decision-making processes. Overcoming this resistance requires leadership that is committed to the agile transformation and willing to support teams through the transition.

10.2.3.2. *Resource Constraints*

Agile decision-making frameworks often require the allocation of significant resources to support cross-functional teams, real-time data collection, and ongoing collaboration. Organizations may face resource constraints, especially in sectors that are not traditionally familiar with agile methodologies. In these cases, investing in agile tools, platforms, and training may require a substantial upfront investment, which can be a barrier for some organizations.

10.2.3.3. *Maintaining Alignment with Organizational Goals*

As teams work iteratively and make decisions in short cycles, it is important to maintain alignment with the broader organizational goals and strategies. Without clear communication and a shared vision, there is a risk that teams could pursue conflicting objectives, which could lead to inefficiencies or fragmentation of efforts. Leaders must ensure that agile teams remain focused on the overarching goals of the organization and that their decisions align with these strategic objectives.

Overall, the adoption of agile frameworks in decision-making processes offers significant benefits for organizations operating in complex and dynamic environments. By leveraging cross-functional teams, short decision cycles, continuous communication, and stakeholder collaboration, organizations can improve their responsiveness, adaptability, and overall decision-making effectiveness. However, the successful implementation of agile decision-making requires overcoming challenges such as organizational resistance, resource constraints, and alignment with broader goals. When implemented effectively, agile decision-making frameworks can provide organizations with the tools they need to thrive in an ever-changing landscape. Table 10.2 summarizes the key aspects of implementing

Table 10.2. Key Aspects of Implementing Agile Frameworks in Decision-Making Processes

Key Aspect	Description	Practical Insights for Decision Makers	Real-World Example
1. Agile Framework Origins	Agile frameworks emerged from the software industry, emphasizing flexibility, collaboration, and iterative decision-making. This allows organizations to respond quickly to change.	Decision-makers must understand the roots of agile in software development to adapt the principles effectively to other industries.	Example: The Agile Manifesto's principles were first developed by software engineers in 2001 but have since been applied in sectors like manufacturing and healthcare.
2. Cross-Functional Teams	Agile decision-making relies on diverse teams, combining expertise from various departments. This ensures holistic decision-making and the identification of risks and opportunities.	Decision-makers should form cross-functional teams to promote collaboration and innovation, leveraging diverse expertise for well-rounded decisions.	Example: Google's product teams, where cross-functional collaboration drives innovation and agility in decision-making.
3. Short Decision Cycles (Sprints)	Agile decisions are made in short cycles, enabling rapid iteration and feedback integration, avoiding long-term commitments based on incomplete data.	Leaders should implement short decision cycles (sprints) to foster flexibility, reduce risks, and adapt strategies in real-time based on feedback.	Example: Tesla's product updates — their iterative approach allows for continuous product improvements based on real-time data, customer feedback, and market shifts.

Table 10.2. (*Continued*)

Key Aspect	Description	Practical Insights for Decision Makers	Real-World Example
4. Continuous Communication	Effective communication channels are crucial, enabling real-time data sharing and feedback among team members and stakeholders.	Establish regular communication touchpoints, ensuring transparency and access to the latest information for informed decision-making.	Example: Microsoft Teams enables real-time collaboration across global teams, enhancing agile decision-making in the tech sector.
5. Stakeholder Collaboration	Stakeholders are actively involved in decision-making, ensuring decisions are aligned with the needs of all parties.	Engage stakeholders early and often, using feedback loops to align decisions with their expectations and needs.	Example: Mayo Clinic's healthcare decisions — patients, professionals, and researchers collaborate to improve patient care.
6. Challenges in Agile Implementation	While beneficial, agile frameworks face challenges like organizational resistance, resource constraints, and alignment with broader organizational goals.	Address cultural resistance with leadership commitment, ensure proper resource allocation, and maintain alignment with long-term organizational strategies.	Example: Resistance in traditional manufacturing companies to adopt agile, requiring leadership to champion the transition and foster an agile mindset.
7. Organizational Resistance	Shifting from traditional decision-making models to agile requires overcoming cultural barriers such as hierarchical structures and long-term planning norms.	Decision-makers must prioritize cultural change, building trust and embracing uncertainty, while ensuring proper change management practices are in place.	Example: General Electric (GE) faced initial resistance when shifting to agile in its digital division but later saw benefits in flexibility and innovation.

(*Continued*)

Table 10.2. (*Continued*)

Key Aspect	Description	Practical Insights for Decision Makers	Real-World Example
8. Resource Constraints	Implementing agile frameworks often requires significant investments in tools, platforms, and training, especially in organizations unfamiliar with agile.	Allocate resources for agile tools, cross-functional team training, and real-time data systems to support successful implementation.	Example: Spotify's investment in agile tools — they allocate resources to tools and training to maintain their agile workflows in product development.
9. Alignment with Organizational Goals	Agile teams must ensure their short-term decisions are aligned with the broader goals of the organization to avoid inefficiencies or fragmented efforts.	Establish clear vision and communication structures to ensure agile teams remain aligned with organizational strategies and avoid silos.	Example: Amazon's use of agile principles — its various agile teams are aligned with the broader company vision to create efficient, customer-centered innovations.

agile frameworks in decision-making processes, providing practical insights for real-world decision-makers and highlighting examples across various sectors.

10.3. Managing Rapid Technological Change and Uncertainty

In today's rapidly evolving technological landscape, organizations are faced with significant challenges related to managing uncertainty and technological change. The velocity of technological advancements, alongside increasing global competition, requires organizations to develop strategies that not only address present-day needs but also prepare them for future challenges. This section explores strategies and frameworks for managing rapid technological change and uncertainty, offering a comprehensive in-depth analysis, relevant real-world examples, and critical insights for decision-makers.

10.3.1. *The Challenge of Rapid Technological Change*

The pace of technological change has accelerated in recent years, with innovations emerging in fields such as artificial intelligence, blockchain, biotechnology, and renewable energy. The rate of advancement in these areas has profound implications for industries ranging from manufacturing to healthcare. As technologies evolve rapidly, organizations face the challenge of staying ahead of trends, integrating new technologies into their operations, and maintaining competitiveness.

A report by the World Economic Forum (2020) highlights that businesses must not only adapt to these rapid technological advancements but also anticipate future developments to maintain a competitive edge. This increasing rate of change also brings about unpredictability, where it becomes difficult to forecast how technologies will impact markets, regulatory environments, and business models. The challenge for decision-makers lies in anticipating technological disruptions while responding nimbly to the changing business environment. As organizations strive to manage this uncertainty, many are turning to strategic management frameworks that focus on foresight, adaptability, and data-driven decision-making.

In conclusion, rapid technological change presents both significant opportunities and formidable challenges for organizations. The accelerating pace of innovation demands a proactive approach, where decision-makers must anticipate disruptions, adapt to evolving trends, and leverage emerging technologies strategically. By adopting foresight, building adaptability, and utilizing data-driven decision-making frameworks, organizations can navigate uncertainty and thrive in a dynamic and competitive technological landscape.

10.3.2. *Scenario Planning and Foresight Techniques*

One of the most effective methods for navigating uncertainty is through the use of scenario planning and foresight techniques. These approaches allow decision-makers to simulate a variety of possible futures based on different assumptions, helping them develop robust strategies that can withstand the test of time.

Scenario planning is a strategic planning method that involves creating a set of alternative future scenarios based on varying assumptions about how key trends and uncertainties will unfold. According to Schoemaker (1995), scenario planning is invaluable in environments characterized by high levels of uncertainty, enabling organizations to explore multiple potential outcomes and create flexible strategies for each.

By identifying potential risks and opportunities associated with different technological trajectories, organizations can avoid being blindsided by unexpected developments. Furthermore, scenario planning allows companies to assess their preparedness for various future states, helping them anticipate disruptions and positioning themselves for resilience.

For instance, Shell, a global energy company, is widely recognized for its use of scenario planning. The company employs this technique to analyze potential shifts in the global energy market, including technological advancements, policy changes, and market trends. By considering multiple possible futures, Shell can adjust its strategies in real time to remain competitive.

Real-World Example 1: Shell's scenario planning allowed the company to anticipate shifts toward renewable energy decades before other industry players. This foresight helped Shell make proactive investments in wind and solar power and pivot from fossil fuels, ensuring its long-term survival in a rapidly evolving industry.

While scenario planning is effective in preparing for multiple futures, foresight techniques offer a more systematic approach to exploring emerging trends. These techniques involve the use of scientific forecasting, expert consultations, and trend analysis to identify long-term opportunities and threats. As technologies rapidly evolve, foresight helps organizations identify early signs of disruptive innovations, enabling decision-makers to act proactively.

Example 2: In the healthcare industry, the Mayo Clinic employs foresight techniques to anticipate advances in biotechnology and medical diagnostics. By leveraging these insights, Mayo Clinic adapts its research initiatives and prepares its operations for the potential integration of cutting-edge technologies such as genomics and personalized medicine.

In conclusion, scenario planning and foresight techniques provide organizations with essential tools to navigate uncertainty and adapt to rapid technological advancements. By simulating diverse future scenarios and identifying emerging trends, decision-makers can develop flexible strategies and proactively address potential risks and opportunities. From Shell's strategic pivot toward renewable energy to Mayo Clinic's forward-thinking integration of biotechnology, these techniques demonstrate their value in fostering resilience and innovation across industries. For organizations operating in dynamic environments, the adoption of scenario planning and foresight ensures preparedness and a competitive edge in an ever-changing technological landscape

10.3.3. *Leveraging Predictive Analytics for Proactive Decision-Making*

In addition to scenario planning and foresight, organizations are increasingly leveraging predictive analytics and real-time data to manage technological uncertainty. Predictive analytics involves using historical data, statistical algorithms, and ML techniques to forecast future outcomes. By analyzing past trends and real-time data, predictive analytics enables decision-makers to anticipate changes in markets, customer behaviors, and technological developments.

Qudrat-Ullah and Karakul (2007) argue that predictive analytics empowers decision-makers to adopt a proactive decision-making approach rather than being reactive. Instead of waiting for disruptive events to occur, organizations can forecast potential outcomes and prepare strategies in advance.

For example, in the retail industry, companies like Amazon and Walmart use predictive analytics to manage supply chains and optimize inventory based on future demand predictions. By integrating real-time sales data and market trends, these companies can forecast shifts in consumer behavior and adjust their product offerings accordingly.

Real-World Example: **Netflix** uses predictive analytics to personalize content recommendations for its users. The company uses algorithms that analyze past viewing behaviors, user preferences, and emerging trends to recommend new shows or movies. This not only enhances user experience but also enables Netflix to anticipate market demand for certain genres, ensuring a steady stream of popular content.

Predictive analytics is also instrumental in managing technological uncertainty in industries like manufacturing and finance. By leveraging data on machinery performance, for example, predictive maintenance can reduce downtime and optimize operational efficiency.

In conclusion, predictive analytics has become a cornerstone for proactive decision-making in an era defined by rapid technological change and uncertainty. By leveraging historical data, real-time insights, and advanced algorithms, organizations can anticipate future trends, mitigate risks, and seize opportunities. From retail giants like Amazon optimizing supply chains to Netflix revolutionizing content personalization, predictive analytics exemplifies how data-driven strategies can foster agility and innovation. For decision-makers, embracing predictive analytics not only enhances operational efficiency but also provides a competitive edge in navigating dynamic and unpredictable market environments.

10.3.4. *Adopting Agile Decision-Making Frameworks for Flexibility*

As organizations strive to cope with rapid technological change, agility has become a key attribute for successful decision-making. An agile decision-making framework emphasizes flexibility, iterative progress, and continuous learning — principles that are particularly well-suited for dealing with uncertainty.

Agile frameworks encourage organizations to embrace change as a constant and adapt quickly to emerging opportunities or threats. According to Reeves and Deimler (2011), companies that adopt agile decision-making frameworks are better positioned to thrive in uncertain environments. These organizations can pivot quickly, innovate continuously, and integrate new technologies into their operations.

The use of short decision cycles, cross-functional teams, and continuous stakeholder feedback allows organizations to respond faster and more effectively to external shocks and technological disruptions. For instance, technology firms such as Apple and Google use agile decision-making to continually enhance their products and services. The iterative process of design, feedback, and refinement has allowed these companies to remain at the forefront of the technology sector, successfully managing uncertainty and responding to rapid technological shifts.

Real-World Example: **Spotify** employs an agile framework in its product development process. The company uses **sprints** to rapidly develop and release new features based on user feedback, ensuring that their platform remains responsive to changing user needs and technological trends.

In conclusion, adopting agile decision-making frameworks empowers organizations to remain resilient and responsive in the face of rapid technological advancements and uncertainties. By fostering flexibility, encouraging iterative progress, and integrating continuous feedback, agile frameworks enable organizations to navigate disruptions effectively while capitalizing on emerging opportunities. Real-world examples, such as Spotify's sprint-based product development and Apple's iterative enhancement approach, highlight the transformative potential of agility. For decision-makers, embracing agility is not just about surviving change but leveraging it as a catalyst for sustained innovation and competitive advantage.

10.3.5. *Building a Culture of Continuous Learning and Adaptability*

In addition to the tools and techniques mentioned, organizations must foster a culture of continuous learning and adaptability to manage uncertainty effectively. As technologies evolve rapidly, organizations that prioritize knowledge sharing, employee training, and open communication are more likely to succeed in navigating technological change.

A culture of continuous learning involves encouraging employees to keep up with the latest technological trends, invest in their skill development, and share knowledge across departments. This allows organizations to remain innovative and agile in the face of rapid technological shifts.

For example, **Google** fosters a culture of continuous learning by offering employees access to online courses, internal workshops, and opportunities for innovation through initiatives like **20% Time** — a policy that allows employees to spend one day a week working on projects outside their regular responsibilities. This culture of innovation has helped Google stay at the cutting edge of technological development.

Real-World Example: **IBM** has been able to adapt to changing technological landscapes by fostering a culture of innovation. The company has made significant investments in AI and cloud computing, allowing it to pivot from its legacy hardware business to become a leader in AI and cloud technologies. This transformation was driven by continuous learning initiatives and a focus on future technologies.

In conclusion, fostering a culture of continuous learning and adaptability is not just a strategic advantage but a necessity in today's fast-evolving technological landscape. Organizations that embed these principles into their core operations are better equipped to innovate, respond to disruptions, and maintain a competitive edge. By prioritizing employee development, promoting cross-departmental collaboration, and encouraging experimentation, companies can build a workforce that is resilient, forward-thinking, and capable of navigating complex challenges. As demonstrated by industry leaders like Google and IBM, a commitment to learning and adaptability paves the way for long-term success and sustainable growth in the face of technological uncertainty.

10.3.6. *Conclusion: Balancing Risk and Opportunity*

Managing rapid technological change and uncertainty is not without its challenges, but by leveraging scenario planning, predictive analytics, agile decision-making frameworks, and fostering a culture of continuous learning, organizations can enhance their resilience and adaptability. These strategies allow decision-makers to anticipate change, respond proactively to emerging technologies, and remain competitive in an increasingly complex world.

To navigate the complexities of technological change, organizations must be both forward-thinking and flexible, balancing long-term strategic planning with short-term adaptability. The decision-making frameworks discussed provide a comprehensive approach for handling uncertainty, allowing organizations to not only survive but thrive in an era of rapid technological advancement. Table 10.3 provides a structured overview and actionable insights that help organizations navigate uncertainty and adapt to rapid technological shifts effectively.

Table 10.3. Strategies for Managing Rapid Technological Change and Uncertainty

Aspect	**Key Strategies**	**Real-World Insights**	**Practical Implications for Decision-Makers**
1. Scenario Planning and Foresight Techniques	– Develop alternative future scenarios to prepare for uncertainties. – Use foresight to identify emerging trends and disruptions.	**Example:** Shell's scenario planning identified shifts toward renewable energy, enabling early investments in wind and solar energy.	– Invest in systematic foresight methods and scenario workshops. – Balance short-term actions with long-term adaptability.
2. Leveraging Predictive Analytics	– Use historical and real-time data to forecast market trends and disruptions. – Employ ML for anticipatory decision-making.	**Example:** Netflix uses predictive analytics to recommend content, ensuring alignment with consumer preferences and future demands.	– Develop in-house data analytics capabilities. – Integrate predictive tools to proactively address operational and strategic challenges.
3. Agile Decision-Making Frameworks	– Foster organizational flexibility and iterative decision cycles. – Use cross-functional teams and rapid prototyping to adapt to changes.	**Example:** Spotify's agile framework allows rapid deployment of user-driven features through iterative sprints.	– Build a cross-functional agile team structure. – Incorporate iterative testing and stakeholder feedback in decision processes.

(*Continued*)

Table 10.3. (*Continued*)

Aspect	Key Strategies	Real-World Insights	Practical Implications for Decision-Makers
4. Continuous Learning and Adaptability	– Encourage ongoing employee skill development. – Create a knowledge-sharing culture to stay aligned with technological advancements.	**Example:** Google's "20% Time" policy fosters employee innovation, maintaining its technological leadership.	– Establish training programs and encourage inter-departmental collaboration. – Reward innovative contributions from teams and individuals.
5. Integrating Emerging Technologies	– Pilot and integrate innovative tools like AI and blockchain incrementally. – Collaborate with external experts to adopt emerging technologies effectively.	**Example:** IBM pivoted to AI and cloud computing by fostering innovation and leveraging external collaborations for expertise.	– Initiate small -scale pilots for tech adoption. - Partner with universities and tech leaders for faster learning curves.

10.4. Key Takeaways for Decision Makers

In a world characterized by rapid technological evolution and dynamic market conditions, decision-makers face the critical challenge of navigating uncertainty effectively. Adaptive and agile frameworks have emerged as indispensable tools for addressing these complexities. This section provides a comprehensive analysis of key takeaways for decision-makers, supported by academic research, real-world examples, and critical insights.

10.4.1. *Enhancing Responsiveness to Change*

One of the primary advantages of adopting adaptive and agile frameworks is the ability to respond swiftly to changing conditions. As noted by Eisenhardt and Martin (2000), dynamic capabilities — processes that allow organizations to adapt and reconfigure resources — are fundamental to maintaining competitiveness in turbulent environments. Agility enables organizations to anticipate trends, pivot strategies, and deploy resources effectively, thereby minimizing the risk of being outpaced by competitors. This ability to swiftly adapt is especially valuable in industries characterized by rapid technological advancements, shifting consumer preferences, and economic uncertainties. Agile decision-making ensures that organizations are not only reacting to changes, but also proactively positioning themselves for future growth.

Real-World Example: The automotive industry offers a compelling example of responsiveness in action. Tesla, for instance, utilizes an agile framework to accelerate innovation cycles, enabling the company to release over-the-air software updates and adapt its product lineup to evolving market demands. This approach has allowed Tesla to maintain its leadership in the electric vehicle market, even as legacy automakers race to catch up. Tesla's ability to rapidly introduce new features and refine its vehicles through software updates has set it apart, demonstrating how agility can be leveraged for competitive advantage in fast-paced markets.

Critical Insight: However, responsiveness is not solely about speed. Decision-makers must also ensure that rapid adjustments are aligned with strategic objectives. As highlighted by McGrath (2013), organizations that prioritize learning from failures can refine their decision-making processes and reduce the risks associated with agility. While quick responses are necessary to stay competitive, hasty decisions without strategic alignment can lead to missteps that hinder long-term success. Successful agile organizations integrate continuous feedback loops and real-time data to ensure that their responsiveness is both timely and aligned with their broader goals. This balance between speed and strategic coherence is essential for sustainable success in an increasingly volatile environment.

In conclusion, enhancing responsiveness to change through adaptive and agile frameworks is essential for organizations to stay competitive in fast-paced markets. Tesla's example demonstrates how agility can enable rapid innovation and real-time adaptations, allowing the company to lead in the electric vehicle industry. However, as critical as speed is in responding to change, it must be carefully balanced with alignment to strategic objectives. Decision-makers should not only focus on rapid adjustments but also ensure that their responses are aligned with long-term goals and learning from failures. By integrating agility with strategic foresight, organizations can better navigate uncertainty while minimizing risks and maximizing opportunities for sustained success.

10.4.2. *Promoting Continuous Learning and Improvement*

Adaptive frameworks are intrinsically linked to the principle of continuous learning. Organizations that foster a culture of iterative improvement and knowledge sharing are better positioned to make informed decisions. Qudrat-Ullah *et al.* (2008) emphasize that continuous learning not only enhances individual competencies but also strengthens collective organizational intelligence, enabling teams to tackle complex challenges more effectively. By creating an environment where learning is encouraged at all levels, organizations can build a resilient workforce capable of adapting to changing market conditions. Moreover, continuous learning promotes a growth mindset that drives innovation and fosters creativity, allowing organizations to remain competitive in fast-evolving industries. As the business environment becomes increasingly dynamic, organizations that embed learning into their operational DNA will have a distinct advantage in navigating uncertainty.

Real-World Example: Amazon exemplifies the power of continuous learning through its data-driven approach to decision-making. By leveraging customer data and machine learning algorithms, Amazon refines its operations, personalizes recommendations, and optimizes inventory management, creating a feedback loop that perpetuates innovation. This constant iteration and adaptation of processes allow Amazon to stay ahead of competitors in the e-commerce space.

Critical Insight: While continuous learning is a cornerstone of agility, its success depends on the organization's willingness to invest in skill development and learning platforms. Decision-makers must allocate resources for employee training and establish mechanisms for cross-functional knowledge sharing to maximize the benefits of continuous learning.

Additionally, organizations should ensure that there is a feedback system in place to measure the effectiveness of learning initiatives and identify areas for improvement. Continuous learning should not be viewed as a one-time effort, but rather as a continuous cycle that supports long-term organizational growth and adaptability. In conclusion, promoting continuous learning and improvement is essential for organizations striving to maintain agility in dynamic environments. Amazon's approach exemplifies how a commitment to learning and data-driven decision-making can drive innovation and operational efficiency. However, as critical as continuous learning is to fostering agility, it is equally important for organizations to prioritize investment in skill development and knowledge-sharing platforms. Decision-makers must allocate resources to ensure that employees have the tools, training, and support they need to continuously enhance their competencies. By embedding continuous learning into the organizational culture, companies can stay competitive and build a foundation for sustained growth and innovation.

10.4.3. *Building Resilient Strategies*

Embracing uncertainty and complexity allows decision-makers to develop strategies that are robust and resilient. Resilience involves preparing for diverse scenarios and maintaining operational continuity in the face of disruptions. As per Taleb's (2012) concept of "antifragility," systems that thrive under volatility are better equipped to handle uncertainty.

Real-World Example: Unilever employs resilience-building techniques through its Sustainable Living Plan, which incorporates scenario planning and sustainability goals to mitigate risks associated with climate change and resource scarcity. This proactive approach has enhanced the company's ability to adapt to environmental and regulatory changes.

Critical Insight: Developing resilient strategies requires decision-makers to prioritize long-term value over short-term gains. Investments in sustainability, risk management, and technological foresight can provide a competitive edge while safeguarding the organization against future disruptions.

In conclusion, building resilient strategies is a vital component of navigating today's unpredictable business environment. By embracing uncertainty and complexity, organizations can better prepare for a variety of future scenarios, ensuring operational continuity even in the face of disruptions. Resilience, as articulated by Taleb's concept of "antifragility," not only enables organizations to withstand volatility but also positions them to grow stronger from it. Unilever's proactive approach through its Sustainable Living Plan serves as a powerful example of how incorporating foresight, sustainability, and risk management can create long-term value. Decision-makers must recognize the importance of focusing on future-oriented strategies that prioritize adaptability, sustainability, and technological innovation, ensuring that their organizations remain competitive and resilient in the face of both foreseeable and unforeseen challenges.

10.4.4. *Cultivating a Supportive Organizational Culture*

The successful implementation of adaptive and agile frameworks is contingent on a supportive organizational culture. A culture that values flexibility, collaboration, and experimentation fosters an environment where innovation can thrive. Schein (2010) highlights that cultural transformation often requires leadership commitment and clear communication of organizational values.

Real-World Example: Google's "20% Time" policy is a testament to the power of supportive culture. By encouraging employees to dedicate a portion of their time to personal projects, Google has fostered innovations such as Gmail and Google Maps, underscoring the importance of giving teams the freedom to experiment.

Critical Insight: Decision-makers must recognize the dual role of culture as both an enabler and a potential barrier to agility. Resistance to change, bureaucratic silos, and a fear of failure can undermine efforts to build an adaptive organization. Leadership plays a pivotal role in addressing these challenges by modeling behaviors that align with the desired cultural attributes.

In conclusion, cultivating a supportive organizational culture is essential for the successful adoption of adaptive and agile frameworks. A culture that promotes flexibility, collaboration, and experimentation empowers employees to contribute to innovation and problem-solving. However, for this culture to thrive, leadership must be proactive in addressing challenges such as resistance to change and bureaucratic barriers. By setting the tone through clear communication, role modeling, and providing the necessary support, leaders can create an environment where adaptability is not only encouraged but deeply embedded in the organization's values. When aligned with strategic goals, such a culture enhances resilience and fosters continuous innovation, ultimately ensuring long-term success in a dynamic business landscape.

10.4.5. *Investing in Tools and Technologies*

In today's rapidly evolving business environment, the ability to make data-driven decisions is more crucial than ever. Adaptive frameworks rely on leveraging advanced tools and technologies, including analytics, ML, AI, and cloud computing, to enhance decision-making agility. These technologies enable organizations to process vast amounts of data, identify trends, and make proactive decisions in real time, positioning them to respond effectively to changes in the market or industry.

As highlighted by Davenport and Harris (2007), analytics-driven organizations are more likely to outperform their competitors due to their capacity to make informed decisions based on data insights. The use of sophisticated tools helps organizations unlock value from their data, making operations more efficient, forecasting more accurate, and delivering personalized customer experiences.

Real-World Example: Microsoft provides a clear illustration of how investing in cutting-edge technologies can significantly enhance decision-making agility. The company's strategic adoption of cloud computing and AI tools has empowered it to optimize its operations across various departments. By utilizing predictive analytics, Microsoft has not only streamlined its supply chain processes but also improved customer service and product innovation. For instance, the use of AI in customer service chatbots has allowed Microsoft to reduce response times and increase user satisfaction. Furthermore, the integration of cloud technologies has enabled scalability, allowing the company to remain agile as it expands into new markets.

Critical Insight: While the investment in tools and technologies is essential for enabling agility, it is not sufficient on its own. Technology must be accompanied by human expertise to ensure its effective application within the broader organizational strategy. Decision-makers should focus on integrating these tools into the organization's existing processes and ensuring that employees are equipped with the necessary skills to use them effectively. This requires continuous investment in training and professional development. The combination of advanced technologies and skilled personnel can significantly enhance decision-making capabilities, leading to more efficient operations and a greater ability to adapt to changes in the business environment.

In conclusion, investing in the right tools and technologies is a critical enabler for organizations seeking to enhance their decision-making agility. However, the true value of these technologies lies not just in their adoption, but in their integration with human expertise and organizational processes. Decision-makers must prioritize continuous training and ensure that technological investments are aligned with broader strategic goals to maximize their potential. By doing so, organizations can not only improve operational efficiency but also remain competitive in an increasingly data-driven and fast-paced business environment.

10.4.6. *Balancing Flexibility and Strategic Focus*

While agility emphasizes adaptability, it is equally important for decision-makers to maintain a clear strategic focus. As noted by Porter (1996), a lack of focus can dilute organizational efforts and hinder long-term success.

Real-World Example: Apple exemplifies the balance between flexibility and strategic focus through its commitment to design excellence and user experience. Even as it adapts to changing technological landscapes, Apple maintains a consistent strategic vision that underpins its brand identity and competitive advantage.

Critical Insight: Decision-makers must establish mechanisms for evaluating trade-offs between short-term adaptability and long-term objectives. This requires ongoing strategic review processes and the alignment of agile initiatives with the organization's overarching goals.

Balancing flexibility and strategic focus is not merely a tactical choice; it is a strategic imperative in today's fast-paced and uncertain business environment. Agility without direction risks leading to fragmented efforts, while rigid adherence to a static strategy can render organizations obsolete in the face of disruption. Decision-makers must cultivate a disciplined yet adaptable approach, integrating agility into their strategic framework without losing sight of overarching goals. By achieving this balance, organizations can navigate uncertainty effectively, ensuring sustainable growth and a competitive edge in a constantly evolving landscape.

10.4.7. *Conclusion: Integrating Agility and Adaptability*

For decision-makers, the integration of adaptive and agile frameworks is not merely a tactical choice but a strategic imperative in today's volatile business environment. By enhancing responsiveness, fostering continuous learning, building resilience, cultivating a supportive culture, investing in technology, and balancing flexibility with focus, organizations can position themselves for sustained success.

Ultimately, agility and adaptability are not ends in themselves but means to achieving robust, future-ready decision-making processes. Decision-makers who embrace these principles will be better equipped to navigate uncertainty, seize emerging opportunities, and lead their organizations confidently into the future. Table 10.4 provides a structured overview of the key takeaways for decision-makers aiming to integrate adaptive and agile frameworks into their organizations. It highlights practical insights derived from real-world examples and critical insights, enabling leaders to navigate complex and dynamic environments effectively.

10.5. Conclusion

In the face of unprecedented technological advancements, market volatility, and global disruptions, organizations today must confront the challenge of adapting to an ever-changing landscape. Traditional decision-making processes, characterized by rigidity and a

Table 10.4. Key Takeaways for Decision Makers

Aspect	Key Takeaways	Real-World Example	Critical Insight
Enhancing Responsiveness	Agility enables swift responses to changing conditions, aligning strategies with market demands to maintain competitiveness.	Tesla's rapid innovation cycles and over-the-air software updates sustain its leadership in EV markets.	Responsiveness requires alignment with strategic objectives to avoid misdirected efforts and ensure sustainable advantage (McGrath, 2013).
Continuous Learning	Promotes iterative improvement, leveraging data and shared knowledge to inform decisions and foster organizational intelligence.	Amazon refines its operations and personalizes services through a data-driven feedback loop.	Requires investments in skill development and platforms for cross-functional knowledge sharing to maximize continuous learning benefits (Qudrat-Ullah *et al.*, 2008).
Resilient Strategies	Builds robustness against uncertainty, ensuring operational continuity and strategic foresight.	Unilever's Sustainable Living Plan mitigates risks through scenario planning and sustainability goals.	Long-term value prioritization strengthens organizational resilience and mitigates future disruptions (Taleb, 2012).

Table 10.4. (*Continued*)

Aspect	**Key Takeaways**	**Real-World Example**	**Critical Insight**
Supportive Culture	Encourages innovation by fostering collaboration, flexibility, and experimentation within the organization.	Google's "20% Time" policy fosters innovations like Gmail and Google Maps through employee freedom.	Leadership commitment and communication are pivotal to overcoming resistance and enabling cultural transformation (Schein, 2010).
Investing in Technology	Advanced tools enable data-driven agility, streamlining decision-making processes and innovation.	Microsoft leverages AI and cloud computing to optimize operations and enhance customer experiences.	Technological tools must be integrated with organizational processes and supported by human expertise for optimal utility (Davenport & Harris, 2007).
Balancing Flexibility	Adaptability must be balanced with a clear strategic focus to sustain long-term success and brand identity.	Apple combines adaptability with a strategic commitment to design excellence and user experience.	Strategic review mechanisms are essential for managing trade-offs between short-term agility and long-term objectives (Porter, 1996).

focus on predictability, are increasingly inadequate for dealing with the complexities of the modern world. To thrive in this environment, organizations must embrace adaptive and agile decision-making frameworks that promote flexibility, continuous learning, and iterative development. These frameworks are not just theoretical concepts, but practical tools that can drive better decision-making, foster innovation, and ensure long-term sustainability.

10.5.1. *The Role of Adaptability in Complex Environments*

At the core of adaptive decision-making is the ability to respond to rapid change. In an environment characterized by volatility and uncertainty, organizations must develop dynamic capabilities — the processes that enable firms to reconfigure their resources and adapt their strategies quickly. As noted by Eisenhardt and Martin (2000), dynamic capabilities are essential to maintaining competitiveness in turbulent markets. These capabilities allow organizations to anticipate changes in the marketplace, pivot their strategies, and redeploy resources in real time.

The automotive industry's embrace of agility, exemplified by Tesla, underscores the critical role of responsiveness in staying ahead of competitors. By adopting agile methodologies, Tesla has been able to not only innovate at a faster pace than its traditional rivals but also react to shifts in consumer demand, technological advancements, and regulatory requirements. Tesla's over-the-air software updates, which allow it to continuously enhance the performance of its vehicles, are a prime example of how agility can be leveraged to meet evolving market needs.

However, responsiveness to change must go beyond simply acting quickly. It is equally important for organizations to ensure that their responses are aligned with their long-term strategic objectives. As McGrath (2013) argues, organizations that prioritize learning from failures and integrating those lessons into their decision-making processes are better positioned to refine their strategies and mitigate the risks associated with agility. Rapid changes should be informed by strategic foresight and an understanding of broader organizational goals, allowing firms to maintain a competitive edge while avoiding hasty decisions that may lead to costly mistakes.

10.5.2. *The Power of Continuous Learning and Knowledge Sharing*

Another critical element of adaptive and agile decision-making is the promotion of continuous learning. Organizations that embrace a culture of continuous improvement and knowledge sharing are better equipped to navigate the complexities of modern business environments. As Qudrat-Ullah *et al.* (2008) highlight, continuous learning not only enhances individual competencies but also fosters collective organizational intelligence. By embedding learning into their decision-making processes, organizations can adapt to new information and make better-informed choices.

Amazon is a prime example of how continuous learning can drive business success. The company's data-driven approach, leveraging vast amounts of customer data and ML algorithms, enables it to optimize its operations, personalize customer experiences, and enhance its inventory management. This learning loop not only allows Amazon to make real-time adjustments but also positions the company to anticipate and meet future customer needs. In this sense, continuous learning becomes not just a reactive mechanism but a proactive strategy that shapes the organization's trajectory.

For decision-makers, the key to fostering continuous learning lies in creating an environment that encourages experimentation, cross-functional collaboration, and knowledge sharing. It requires a shift in organizational mindset — from one that values expertise based on past experiences to one that embraces knowledge as a dynamic, ever-evolving asset. By investing in learning platforms, promoting employee training, and creating opportunities for collaboration, organizations can enhance their collective intelligence and better position themselves for future challenges.

10.5.3. *Building Resilient Strategies for the Future*

In addition to enhancing responsiveness and promoting continuous learning, decision-makers must focus on building resilient strategies. Resilience is the ability of an organization to maintain operations and recover quickly from disruptions. As Taleb (2012) discusses in his concept of "antifragility," resilience is not just about bouncing back from challenges; it is about thriving in the face of adversity. Resilient organizations are those that can adapt and grow stronger when exposed to volatility and uncertainty.

Unilever's Sustainable Living Plan provides a valuable case study in resilience. By incorporating scenario planning and sustainability goals, Unilever proactively addresses the risks associated with environmental changes, resource scarcity, and shifting regulatory landscapes. This strategic foresight enables the company to remain agile while also safeguarding its long-term sustainability. Decision-makers should take a similar approach, focusing on long-term value creation and risk mitigation to prepare for the unforeseen challenges of the future.

Resilience-building is not a one-time effort but a continuous process. It involves developing diversified strategies that allow organizations to thrive under various scenarios. Decision-makers must consider factors such as climate change, geopolitical risks, and economic shifts when designing their long-term strategies. Resilient strategies enable organizations to not only withstand shocks but also take advantage of opportunities that arise from changing circumstances.

10.5.4. *Cultivating a Supportive Organizational Culture*

One of the most important factors in successfully implementing adaptive and agile decision-making processes is the organizational culture. Without a culture that values flexibility, collaboration, and experimentation, even the best frameworks can fail. Schein (2010) emphasizes that cultural transformation requires strong leadership and clear communication of organizational values. Decision-makers must foster a culture that encourages risk-taking, embraces failure as a learning opportunity, and supports innovation at all levels of the organization.

Google's "20% Time" policy, which allows employees to dedicate a portion of their work time to personal projects, is an excellent example of how a supportive culture can drive innovation. The policy has led to the creation of transformative products like Gmail and Google Maps. However, such policies are only effective when backed by leadership that models the values of experimentation and collaboration. Decision-makers must ensure that their culture aligns with the goals of adaptability and agility, creating an environment where employees feel empowered to experiment and contribute their ideas.

Organizational culture is both an enabler and a potential barrier to agility. Resistance to change, entrenched hierarchies, and fear of failure can all undermine efforts to build an adaptive organization.

Leaders must be proactive in addressing these challenges, fostering a culture where agility is not only accepted but celebrated.

10.5.5. *The Role of Tools and Technologies in Supporting Agility*

The successful implementation of adaptive frameworks also requires the right tools and technologies. Decision-makers must invest in technologies that enable agile decision-making and enhance the organization's ability to respond to changing conditions. As Davenport and Harris (2007) highlight, analytics-driven organizations are more likely to outperform their peers due to their ability to make data-informed decisions.

Microsoft's adoption of cloud computing and AI tools is a testament to how technological investments can enhance decision-making agility. By leveraging predictive analytics and ML, Microsoft has optimized its supply chain, improved customer service, and driven innovation across its product ecosystem. However, it is crucial to recognize that technology alone cannot ensure agility. It must be integrated into the organization's broader processes and complemented by human expertise. Decision-makers should focus on building an ecosystem where technology and human intelligence work together to support agile decision-making.

10.5.6. *Balancing Flexibility with Strategic Focus*

While flexibility is at the heart of agile decision-making, organizations must also maintain a clear strategic focus. Agility should not come at the expense of long-term objectives and organizational identity. As Porter (1996) notes, a lack of focus can dilute organizational efforts and hinder long-term success. Apple's ability to balance agility with a consistent commitment to design excellence and user experience exemplifies how flexibility can be coupled with strategic focus. By maintaining a clear strategic vision, even as it adapts to changing technologies and market dynamics, Apple continues to maintain its competitive advantage.

For decision-makers, the challenge lies in finding the right balance between short-term adaptability and long-term strategic focus. This requires ongoing strategic review processes that evaluate trade-offs and ensure alignment between agility and the organization's overarching goals.

10.5.7. *Conclusion: Embracing Agility for Long-Term Success*

As organizations continue to face an increasingly dynamic and unpredictable environment, the adoption of adaptive and agile decision-making frameworks will be critical to their long-term success. By focusing on enhancing responsiveness, promoting continuous learning, building resilient strategies, fostering a supportive organizational culture, investing in tools and technologies, as well as maintaining strategic focus, decision-makers can create organizations that are better equipped to thrive in complexity and uncertainty. The key to success lies not only in being agile but in ensuring that agility is applied thoughtfully, with a clear understanding of the organization's goals and values. As the business landscape continues to evolve, those organizations that master the art of adaptive decision-making will be best positioned to lead, innovate, and succeed in the face of change.

References

Bharadwaj, A., El Sawy, O. A., Pavlou, P. A., & Venkatraman, N. (2013). Digital business strategy: Toward a next generation of insights. *MIS Quarterly*, 37(2), 471–482.

Bianchi, C., & Montemaggiore, G. B. (2008). Enhancing strategy design and planning in public utilities through "dynamic" balanced scorecards: Insights from a project in a city water company. *System Dynamics Review*, 24(2), 175–213.

Brynjolfsson, E., & McAfee, A. (2014). *The Second Machine Age: Work, Progress, and Prosperity in a Time of Brilliant Technologies.* W.W. Norton & Company.

Davenport, T. H., & Harris, J. G. (2007). *Competing on Analytics: The New Science of Winning.* Harvard Business Review Press.

Denning, S. (2018). How major corporations are making sense of agile. *Strategy & Leadership*, 46(1), 3–9.

Eisenhardt, K. M., & Martin, J. A. (2000). Dynamic capabilities: What are they? *Strategic Management Journal*, 21(10-11),

1105–1121. https://doi.org/10.1002/1097-0266(200010/11)21:10/11 <1105::SMJ133>3.0.CO;2-E

Grant, R. M. (2016). *Contemporary Strategy Analysis: Text and Cases Edition* (9th ed.). Wiley.

Haeckel, S. H. (1999). Adaptive processes: The new competitive landscape. *Harvard Business Review*, 77(3), 78–88.

Highsmith, J. (2009). *Agile Project Management: Creating Innovative Products*. Pearson Education.

McGrath, R. G. (2013). *The End of Competitive Advantage: How to Keep Your Strategy Moving as Fast as Your Business*. Harvard Business Review Press.

Porter, M. E. (1996). What is strategy? *Harvard Business Review*, 74(6), 61–78.

Qudrat-Ullah, H. (2014). *Better Decision Making in Complex, Dynamic Tasks*. Springer.

Qudrat-Ullah, H., & Karakul, M. (2007). Decision making in interactive learning environments: Towards an integrated model. *Journal of Decision Systems*, 16(1), 79–99.

Qudrat-Ullah, H., Spector, M., & Davidson, I. P. (Eds.). (2008). *Complex Decision Making: Theory and Practice*. Springer.

Reeves, M., & Deimler, M. (2011). Adaptability: The new competitive advantage. *Harvard Business Review*, 89(7-8), 134–141.

Rigby, D. K., Sutherland, J., & Takeuchi, H. (2016). Embracing agile. *Harvard Business Review*, 94(5), 40–50.

Schein, E. H. (2010). *Organizational Culture and Leadership* (4th ed.). Jossey-Bass.

Schoemaker, P. J. (1995). Scenario planning: A tool for strategic thinking. *Sloan Management Review*, 36(2), 25–40.

Snowden, D. J., & Boone, M. E. (2007). A leader's framework for decision making. *Harvard Business Review*, 85(11), 68–76.

Taleb, N. N. (2012). *Antifragile: Things That Gain from Disorder*. Random House.

Teece, D. J. (2007). Explicating dynamic capabilities: The nature and microfoundations of (sustainable) enterprise performance. *Strategic Management Journal*, 28(13), 1319–1350.

World Economic Forum. (2020). *The Future of Jobs Report 2020*. Retrieved from https://www.weforum.org/reports/the-future-of-jobs-report-2020.

Part IV

Future Trends and Implications

Chapter 11

The Future of Emerging Technologies

Abstract

This chapter explores the future of emerging technologies, focusing on anticipated advancements such as artificial intelligence (AI), quantum computing, and biotechnology. It examines how these technologies will transform human-machine interactions, making them more intuitive and personalized. The chapter also addresses the ethical implications and societal challenges posed by these innovations, including job displacement and privacy concerns. Furthermore, it emphasizes the importance of developing critical skills, such as adaptability and ethical reasoning, to thrive in this rapidly evolving landscape. By understanding these dynamics, individuals and organizations can better prepare for the opportunities and challenges that lie ahead.

Keywords: Emerging Technologies; Technological Advancements; Human-Machine Interaction; Artificial Intelligence; Quantum Computing; Biotechnology; Ethical Implications; Societal Challenges; Job Displacement; Privacy Concerns; Future Skills; Adaptability; Ethical Reasoning

11.0. Introduction

The rapid pace of technological innovation is reshaping the foundations of industries, societies, and individual lives. Emerging technologies such as AI, quantum computing, biotechnology, and advanced robotics are not just transforming how we live and work but also redefining decision-making paradigms. As noted by Schwab (2017), the Fourth Industrial Revolution is characterized by the fusion of technologies that blur the lines between the physical, digital, and biological domains. This fusion introduces unparalleled opportunities for growth and progress while simultaneously posing complex challenges related to ethics, governance, and societal impact.

11.0.1. *The Context of Technological Acceleration*

Technology is advancing at an exponential rate, disrupting traditional norms and forcing organizations to rethink their strategies. As Kurzweil (2005) predicts, the concept of "accelerating returns" underscores that technological change will become increasingly rapid and far-reaching, leading to paradigm shifts in a shorter timeframe. For instance, AI-driven automation is fundamentally altering labor markets, while quantum computing is poised to revolutionize problem-solving capabilities across sectors such as cryptography, logistics, and climate modeling (Preskill, 2018).

Real-world examples illustrate the transformative potential of these technologies. Consider the role of blockchain in enhancing supply chain transparency or the way CRISPR-based gene-editing tools have revolutionized healthcare and agriculture (Doudna & Charpentier, 2014). However, the pace of technological evolution also brings risks, including cybersecurity vulnerabilities, job displacement, and growing inequality. Addressing these risks requires foresight and a balanced approach to policy-making and innovation.

11.0.2. *Exploring the Trajectory of Emerging Technologies*

This chapter delves into the trajectory of emerging technologies, emphasizing their potential to redefine human-machine interaction and societal dynamics. Technologies such as AI and natural language processing (NLP) are enabling machines to interact with humans more intuitively, while advancements in augmented reality (AR) and virtual reality (VR) are creating immersive experiences that bridge the digital and physical worlds (Norman, 2013; Jurafsky & Martin, 2021).

Moreover, the convergence of technologies amplifies their transformative impact. The integration of AI with Internet of Things

(IoT) and 5G networks, for example, is fostering the development of smart environments that can autonomously make real-time decisions (Atzori, Iera, & Morabito, 2010). Such environments are already seen in smart cities, autonomous vehicles, and connected healthcare systems.

Yet, as Brynjolfsson and McAfee (2017) highlight, technology is not a panacea. Its deployment must be guided by ethical considerations and a focus on inclusivity. For decision-makers, this underscores the importance of strategic foresight and the development of frameworks to navigate uncertainty and complexity.

11.0.3. *Skills and Mindsets for a Technology-Driven Future*

Thriving in a technology-driven future requires more than access to cutting-edge tools; it demands the cultivation of specific skills and mindsets. Heckman and Kautz (2012) emphasize that non-cognitive skills, such as adaptability, resilience, and emotional intelligence, are critical complements to technical expertise. As routine tasks are increasingly automated, human strengths such as creativity and ethical reasoning will define competitive advantage.

Organizations and educational institutions must play a proactive role in equipping individuals with these skills. This includes fostering a culture of continuous learning and creating opportunities for interdisciplinary collaboration. Real-world examples, such as Amazon's emphasis on data literacy and Google's "20% time" policy for innovation, demonstrate how fostering the right environment can unlock human potential (Brynjolfsson & McElheran, 2016).

11.0.4. *Objectives of the Chapter*

This chapter aims to provide a comprehensive exploration of the future of emerging technologies by addressing three interrelated dimensions:

1. **Anticipated Technological Advancements**: Identifying the key technologies poised to disrupt industries and societal norms in the coming decades.

2. **The Evolution of Human-Machine Interaction**: Analyzing how advancements in AI, robotics, and interface design will shape interactions between humans and machines.
3. **Preparing for the Future**: Highlighting the skills, mindsets, and organizational cultures necessary to harness the potential of these technologies responsibly and effectively.

By examining these dimensions, the chapter seeks to equip decision-makers with actionable insights for navigating a future that is both exciting and uncertain. The stakes are high, but with the right strategies, emerging technologies can be harnessed to foster innovation, equity, and global progress.

As we venture into this dynamic landscape, the interplay of technological innovation and human ingenuity will determine the trajectory of progress. Decision-makers at all levels must recognize that the opportunities of the future come hand-in-hand with ethical dilemmas and societal challenges. By fostering a culture of adaptability, resilience, and collaboration, individuals and organizations can not only survive but thrive in an era of unprecedented change.

11.1. Anticipated Technological Advancements

Technological advancements are set to redefine the landscape of industries and human interaction in profound ways. Emerging technologies such as AI, quantum computing, biotechnology, and advanced robotics are anticipated to play a transformative role in reshaping the economy, healthcare, education, and governance systems. The following subsections provide an in-depth analysis of these anticipated advancements, supported by real-world examples and critical insights for decision-makers.

11.1.1. *Artificial Intelligence and Its Expanding Role*

AI is increasingly becoming a transformative force across diverse sectors, driving significant advancements in efficiency, accuracy, and innovation. As AI technologies mature, their integration into industries such as healthcare, finance, and manufacturing are poised to enhance decision-making, streamline operations, and improve overall service delivery. Advanced AI algorithms, particularly those in deep learning and NLP, are rapidly evolving and are expected to make substantial breakthroughs in areas such as healthcare diagnostics, financial modeling, and predictive analytics. Brynjolfsson and McAfee (2017) contend that AI's ability to process and analyze vast datasets will usher in a "second machine age," revolutionizing knowledge work in a manner similar to how the Industrial Revolution transformed manual labor.

The healthcare sector exemplifies the potential of AI, where systems like IBM Watson Health are already assisting doctors in diagnosing diseases with a higher degree of precision by analyzing medical records and research papers. In the near future, AI could enable even more advanced capabilities, such as autonomously recommending personalized treatment plans based on an individual's genetic data. This personalized approach has the potential to reduce diagnostic errors, enhance treatment efficacy, and improve patient outcomes. Similarly, AI's application in financial modeling could offer unprecedented accuracy in forecasting market trends, providing investors with data-driven insights that improve risk management and decision-making.

AI's growing role is not limited to specialized industries; it is also integral to the proliferation of smart environments, where the convergence of AI with technologies such as the IoT and 5G is facilitating real-time, autonomous decision-making across various settings. This could range from smart cities optimizing traffic flow to AI-driven manufacturing processes that adapt to changing demands without human intervention (Atzori, Iera, & Morabito, 2010). As a result, AI is not only improving existing systems but is also creating new operational paradigms across sectors.

Critical Insight: While the potential benefits of AI are vast, decision-makers must ensure that its adoption is ethically sound. Establishing robust governance frameworks to address concerns related to biases, data privacy, and accountability is essential for fostering trust and ensuring the equitable use of AI. Furthermore, as AI becomes more integrated with emerging technologies, organizations must prepare for this shift by investing in infrastructure, developing adaptable workforce training programs, and fostering a culture of continuous learning to manage this technological evolution effectively.

Overall, AI is undeniably a powerful force driving change across industries, and its growing influence presents both opportunities and challenges. As its capabilities expand, the need for responsible and informed decision-making becomes increasingly critical. By balancing innovation with ethical considerations and preparing the workforce for the future, organizations can leverage AI to unlock its full potential while safeguarding societal interests.

11.1.2. *Quantum Computing: Redefining Computational Boundaries*

Quantum computing is often described as a groundbreaking technology that could fundamentally reshape our approach to problem-solving and computation. Unlike classical computers that rely on bits to process information, quantum computers utilize qubits, which can represent and store information in multiple states simultaneously due to the principles of superposition and entanglement. This quantum mechanical advantage enables quantum computers to perform certain types of calculations much faster than classical systems, potentially solving problems that are currently intractable.

Preskill (2018) underscores the transformative applications of quantum computing in fields such as cryptography. Quantum algorithms, including Shor's algorithm, have the ability to efficiently factorize large numbers, threatening the security of existing encryption methods. This breakthrough necessitates a complete overhaul of cybersecurity protocols, as current encryption standards, such as RSA, could be easily compromised by a sufficiently powerful quantum computer. Beyond the realm of cybersecurity, quantum computing is set to revolutionize various industries by enabling solutions that were previously unachievable. In drug discovery, for example, quantum computers could simulate molecular interactions with unprecedented speed and accuracy, significantly reducing the time and costs associated with developing new therapies.

A notable milestone in quantum computing was achieved by Google's Sycamore quantum processor, which in 2019 demonstrated quantum supremacy by solving a specific problem in 200 seconds that would have taken the most powerful classical supercomputer approximately 10,000 years to complete. This achievement signals the growing potential of quantum computing to tackle highly complex problems that are beyond the capabilities of classical systems. Additionally, industries such as finance and supply chain management are already exploring how quantum computing can be applied to optimize financial models and logistics by processing complex simulations exponentially faster.

Critical Insight: Despite the immense promise of quantum computing, its disruptive potential brings about significant challenges, particularly in areas of security and infrastructure. For industries reliant on encryption, such as finance, healthcare, and telecommunications, decision-makers must take proactive steps to invest in post-quantum cryptography to future-proof their systems. As quantum technology evolves, fostering collaborations between academia, government, and industry will be essential to advancing the field and ensuring that its benefits are distributed equitably across society. Additionally, while the technology promises unprecedented computational power, it is essential to address the ethical implications and risks associated with its deployment, ensuring responsible innovation and minimizing unintended consequences.

Overall, quantum computing is poised to revolutionize many fields, offering solutions to complex problems that were once considered insurmountable. However, with this transformative potential comes the responsibility to navigate the challenges it presents, particularly in the realm of cybersecurity. By preparing for the implications of quantum computing today — through proactive measures and cross-sector collaboration — decision-makers can harness its full potential while safeguarding systems, industries, and societal values for the future.

11.1.3. *Biotechnology: Precision and Transformation*

Advancements in biotechnology, particularly in gene-editing technologies like CRISPR-Cas9, are revolutionizing diverse fields such as medicine, agriculture, and environmental science. Doudna and Charpentier (2014) introduced CRISPR as a "molecular scalpel," which allows scientists to make precise and targeted changes to DNA, enabling a level of genetic manipulation that was previously unimaginable. The transformative potential of these technologies is vast, promising breakthroughs in eradicating genetic disorders, improving crop resilience, and developing solutions to global challenges like climate change.

In the medical field, CRISPR-based therapies are already showing promise in treating genetic diseases such as sickle cell anemia, muscular dystrophy, and certain forms of cancer. These advancements offer hope for patients with conditions that were once considered untreatable. Similarly, in agriculture, biotechnology is poised to address some of the most pressing challenges related to food security. Genetically edited crops, such as drought-resistant wheat and pest-resistant rice, are being developed to increase yields and enhance resilience to climate variability, providing potential solutions to global food shortages.

Beyond food and health, biotechnology has the potential to transform environmental science by creating organisms designed to tackle climate change. For example, bioengineered bacteria could be used to remove pollutants from the environment, or plants could be modified to absorb more carbon dioxide, helping to mitigate the impacts of global warming. These innovations reflect biotechnology's ability to offer new tools for improving both human health and the planet's well-being.

Critical Insight: The rapid pace of biotechnology innovation brings with it complex ethical and regulatory challenges. One of the most contentious issues is gene editing in human embryos, which raises questions about the limits of scientific intervention in human genetics and the potential for unintended consequences. Decision-makers must carefully balance the need for innovation with the responsibility to uphold ethical standards, ensuring that new technologies are deployed in ways that are safe, equitable, and aligned with societal values. Transparency, robust regulatory frameworks, and public engagement will be essential in maintaining public trust as these technologies evolve.

Overall, biotechnology's potential to revolutionize medicine, agriculture, and environmental science is undeniable. However, as these technologies continue to advance, it is crucial that decision-makers adopt a proactive and thoughtful approach to regulation and ethical considerations. By fostering innovation while ensuring robust safeguards, society can harness the full potential of biotechnology to address some of the most pressing challenges of the 21st century, ultimately leading to improved human health, food security, and environmental sustainability.

11.1.4. *Advanced Robotics and Autonomous Systems*

Advanced robotics, fueled by AI and ML, are set to transform industries by taking over complex tasks that were traditionally performed by humans. These systems are already making a significant impact in areas such as autonomous vehicles, robotic surgeries, and logistics. Schwab (2017) highlights the potential of robotics to address pressing issues such as labor shortages and increased demand for productivity, particularly in aging societies where a shrinking workforce requires greater automation to maintain economic growth. By automating mundane, dangerous, or repetitive tasks, robotics not only promises efficiency but also increases workplace safety by reducing human error.

In manufacturing, for example, Tesla's Gigafactories have integrated advanced robotics to assemble electric vehicles with unprecedented precision and speed, enabling the company to scale production while maintaining high quality. In the medical field, robotic surgery systems, such as the da Vinci Surgical System, allow for minimally invasive procedures that reduce recovery times and improve patient outcomes. Additionally, autonomous drones are being deployed in disaster relief operations, such as delivering medical supplies to remote or hard-to-reach areas, which showcases robotics' potential to contribute to humanitarian efforts and save lives during emergencies.

As these technologies evolve, robotics are not limited to industries such as manufacturing and healthcare. They are expanding into areas like agriculture, where robotic harvesters are being used to pick crops with greater efficiency and less waste, and logistics, where autonomous vehicles and drones are streamlining supply chains by reducing transportation costs and delivery times.

Critical Insight: While the opportunities presented by robotics are immense, their widespread adoption raises important concerns about job displacement and the ethical implications of machine autonomy. As robots take on more roles traditionally filled by humans, workers in sectors such as transportation, retail, and manual labor may face significant challenges. Organizations must invest in reskilling and upskilling programs to prepare the workforce for the changing job landscape, ensuring that workers can transition into new roles that require higher-level cognitive, creative, and interpersonal skills. Additionally, ethical considerations regarding machine autonomy, accountability, and decision-making processes in robots must be carefully addressed to ensure public trust and responsible deployment.

Overall, advanced robotics and autonomous systems hold the promise of significant economic and societal benefits, from enhanced productivity and safety to life-saving applications in healthcare and disaster relief. However, the rapid adoption of these technologies requires careful management of the social and ethical challenges they bring. By focusing on workforce reskilling and establishing clear ethical frameworks, decision-makers can ensure that the full potential of robotics is realized, while mitigating the risks associated with their integration into society.

11.1.5. *The Convergence of Technologies*

The convergence of AI, quantum computing, biotechnology, and robotics is poised to create powerful synergies, significantly enhancing the capabilities of each individual technology. By integrating these innovations, industries can unlock new levels of efficiency, precision, and innovation. For example, the fusion of AI with quantum computing could revolutionize fields such as genomics, allowing for the rapid processing and analysis of vast genetic datasets. This would enable personalized medicine at an unprecedented scale, tailoring treatments to individual genetic profiles with far greater accuracy. Likewise, the integration of robotics, AI, and IoT could give rise to self-optimizing smart factories, where machines autonomously monitor, repair, and optimize production processes, leading to highly efficient and agile manufacturing systems that are both cost-effective and sustainable.

Moreover, the convergence of 5G networks with IoT devices is facilitating the creation of smart cities, where critical infrastructure such as traffic management, waste disposal, and energy grids are interconnected and managed autonomously. In these environments, data collected from IoT devices can be analyzed in real time by AI systems to make immediate decisions that improve urban living — whether by optimizing traffic flow to reduce congestion or enhancing energy efficiency by adjusting consumption patterns based on real-time demand.

Critical Insight: To fully harness the benefits of this convergence, decision-makers must adopt a holistic approach to technology integration. This approach requires a focus on interoperability, ensuring that different systems can seamlessly communicate and work together, as well as scalability, enabling technologies to grow and adapt to future needs. Additionally, leaders must prioritize cybersecurity and ethical considerations, incorporating these into the design and deployment phases of new technologies to ensure that integrated systems are secure, transparent, and responsible.

Overall, the convergence of transformative technologies offers vast opportunities to redefine industries and societal infrastructure. However, to realize the full potential of these synergies, decision-makers must be proactive in managing the integration process. This means creating a clear roadmap that aligns technological investments with long-term strategic goals while safeguarding against risks related to security, privacy, and ethics. With careful planning and a collaborative approach, the convergence of AI, quantum computing, biotechnology, and robotics has the potential to drive sustainable, equitable progress across many sectors.

11.1.6. *Strategic Considerations for Decision-Makers*

The rapid pace of technological advancements presents both unprecedented opportunities and significant challenges. To effectively harness the potential of emerging technologies, decision-makers must adopt proactive, forward-looking strategies. Key considerations include:

1. **Investing in Research and Development (R&D)**: Governments, businesses, and academic institutions must allocate substantial resources to R&D efforts to stay at the forefront of technological innovation. This investment not only drives breakthroughs in AI, quantum computing, and other fields but also ensures that organizations remain competitive in a rapidly evolving landscape. Additionally, fostering a culture of innovation through internal R&D initiatives can accelerate the development of proprietary technologies and solutions.

2. **Building Talent Pipelines**: A skilled workforce is essential for successfully implementing and scaling emerging technologies. Decision-makers must work closely with educational institutions to develop curricula that align with the evolving needs of the job market. Strategic partnerships with universities, vocational schools, and training centers can help build a pipeline of talent with expertise in areas such as data science, robotics, and biotechnology. Moreover, companies should invest in continuous learning opportunities for their employees to ensure they remain adaptable to new technologies throughout their careers.
3. **Fostering Public-Private Partnerships**: Collaboration between governments, private companies, and research institutions can expedite technology development and address complex societal challenges. Public-private partnerships (PPPs) offer the potential to leverage resources, share risks, and pool expertise to accelerate innovation. Such collaborations are particularly valuable in fields like healthcare and environmental sustainability, where technological advancements must address global challenges and benefit society at large.
4. **Ensuring Ethical Governance**: As new technologies continue to reshape industries and societies, establishing robust ethical guidelines is critical. Decision-makers must ensure that technology development is aligned with societal values, human rights, and environmental sustainability. Ethical governance frameworks should address concerns such as data privacy, algorithmic biases, and the implications of automation on employment. By prioritizing transparency, accountability, and fairness in technology deployment, organizations can build public trust and mitigate the risks of unintended consequences.

Overall, by anticipating technological advancements and adopting a forward-thinking approach, decision-makers can position their organizations to capitalize on emerging opportunities while mitigating associated risks. Embracing adaptability, ethical responsibility, and inclusivity will be crucial in navigating the transformative changes on the horizon. Moreover, adopting flexible strategies that can quickly respond to unforeseen developments will be essential for maintaining a competitive edge.

In conclusion, the anticipated technological advancements across AI, quantum computing, biotechnology, and advanced robotics, along with their convergence, promise transformative impacts on industries and our society. These innovations offer immense opportunities to address global challenges, drive economic growth, and enhance human well-being. However, they also pose significant ethical, social, and logistical challenges that require careful navigation. For decision-makers, the path forward demands a proactive and integrated approach — one that combines strategic investment, ethical governance, cross-sectors collaboration, and workforce development. By fostering innovation while addressing its risks, leaders can ensure that these advancements contribute to a more equitable, sustainable, and technologically empowered future. Table 11.1 highlights the transformative potential of emerging technologies across various domains, offering actionable insights to help decision-makers align innovation strategies with ethical and societal considerations.

11.2. The Evolution of Human-Machine Interaction

The transformation of human-machine interface (HMI) reflects the ongoing evolution of technology and its integration into human environments. Emerging technologies, such as AI, robotics, and AR, are poised to redefine the way individuals engage with machines, making interactions more intuitive, personalized, and impactful.

11.2.1. *Enhanced Intuitiveness in Interfaces*

Advancements in HMI design, driven by human-centric principles and cutting-edge technologies like gesture recognition, NLP, and brain-computer interfaces (BCIs), are significantly enhancing the intuitiveness of digital systems. Norman (2013) emphasizes that intuitive design reduces user effort by ensuring that system behavior aligns seamlessly with human expectations, making interactions more natural and efficient. As technologies evolve, interfaces are becoming increasingly capable of understanding and responding to human behavior in more personalized and contextually aware ways. For instance, virtual assistants such as Amazon Alexa and Google Assistant harness the power of ML and NLP to interpret voice commands,

Table 11.1. Key Aspects of Anticipated Technological Advancements and Practical Insights for Decision-Makers

Technology	Key Features	Real-World Examples	Practical Insights for Decision-Makers
AI	Advanced algorithms enhancing efficiency and innovation in diagnostics, analytics, and automation.	AI-driven systems like IBM Watson improving diagnostic precision in healthcare.	Develop robust governance frameworks to address AI biases, privacy issues, and accountability while investing in smart infrastructure.
Quantum Computing	Solves complex problems beyond the capacity of classical computers; impacts cryptography and simulations.	Google's Sycamore achieving quantum supremacy; pharmaceutical firms accelerating drug discovery with quantum simulations.	Invest in post-quantum cryptography and foster collaboration among academia, government, and industry to accelerate development.
Biotechnology	Precision gene-editing technologies transforming healthcare, agriculture, and environmental science.	CRISPR-engineered crops addressing food security; gene therapy for genetic disorders like sickle cell anemia.	Balance innovation and ethical considerations through transparent regulations and public engagement.
Advanced Robotics	Autonomous systems enhancing productivity and safety in industries such as manufacturing and healthcare.	Tesla's robotic assembly lines; autonomous drones delivering medical supplies in remote areas.	Reskill the workforce for a robotics-driven landscape and address societal concerns related to job displacement and machine autonomy.

Table 11.1. (*Continued*)

Technology	Key Features	Real-World Examples	Practical Insights for Decision-Makers
Convergence of Technologies	Integration of AI, quantum computing, biotechnology, and robotics creating synergistic transformations.	5G-powered smart cities optimizing traffic, energy grids, and waste management.	Focus on interoperability, scalability, and aligning technological investments with strategic goals while ensuring security.

enabling hands-free operations. These systems are progressively refining their ability to recognize not only speech but also emotional cues, nuances, and user intent, offering richer, more accessible user experiences.

Real-World Example: Apple's integration of Siri within its broader ecosystem is a prime example of how conversational AI can simplify complex interactions. Siri not only comprehends voice commands but also draws on contextual information from calendars, emails, and location data to generate relevant, personalized suggestions. This integration reduces cognitive load, allowing users to interact with technology effortlessly, without having to manually navigate through multiple applications or settings. As these systems continue to evolve, they will likely offer even more sophisticated and adaptive functionality, transforming the way users engage with technology on a day-to-day basis.

Critical Insight: While intuitive interfaces are essential for encouraging user adoption and increasing system accessibility, there is a risk that over-reliance on automation could lead to deskilling. Parasuraman and Riley (1997) point out that when machines handle increasingly complex tasks, users may lose their proficiency in performing these tasks themselves. Designers must strike a delicate balance between leveraging automation to enhance user experiences and maintaining opportunities for human engagement, ensuring that users retain control and expertise in critical functions.

Overall, the continuous development of more intuitive interfaces has the potential to significantly transform how we interact with technology, making it more accessible, efficient, and user-friendly. However, as systems become more capable of performing tasks on behalf of users, it is crucial for designers to preserve a balance that allows users to maintain and build their own skills. By doing so, they can ensure that the adoption of advanced technologies empowers users rather than diminishing their autonomy and capabilities.

11.2.2. *Personalization through AI and ML*

AI-driven personalization is rapidly becoming a central feature of the evolving HMI landscape. By leveraging ML algorithms to analyze user behavior, preferences, and feedback, systems can adapt their responses and functionalities to meet the unique needs of each user. Jurafsky and Martin (2021) highlight that, breakthroughs in NLP and sentiment analysis allow systems to not only comprehend explicit commands but also detect emotional cues, making interactions more empathetic and intuitive. As a result, AI is enabling more seamless, personalized experiences that increase user engagement and satisfaction by offering relevant, tailored content.

Real-World Example: One of the most prominent examples of AI-powered personalization is Spotify's recommendation system. By analyzing users' listening habits and preferences, the platform curates personalized playlists that evolve as the user's tastes change over time. This personalized experience not only enhances user satisfaction but also boosts engagement by delivering music and content that align with individual preferences. Moreover, as Spotify continues to refine its algorithms, the platform's ability to predict and suggest new music is becoming increasingly precise, offering users a dynamic, tailored experience that feels both personal and interactive.

Critical Insight: While personalization can greatly enhance user experience, it also raises significant concerns around data privacy, algorithmic transparency, and bias. Zuboff (2019) warns that the vast amount of personal data collected by AI systems can be misused or exploited if not handled responsibly. Furthermore, algorithmic biases may inadvertently perpetuate harmful stereotypes or exclude certain user groups, undermining the goal of providing truly inclusive and equitable experiences. Therefore, decision-makers must prioritize transparent data practices, ensure ethical handling of user information, and continuously audit algorithms to detect and address biases, ensuring that personalization efforts do not inadvertently harm or exclude specific populations.

Overall, personalization through AI and ML holds the potential to transform how users interact with technology, creating more engaging and satisfying experiences. However, it is critical for organizations to strike a balance between customization and ethical responsibility. By prioritizing privacy, transparency, and fairness in AI systems, decision-makers can create personalized interfaces that not only enhance user satisfaction but also build trust and inclusivity.

11.2.3. *Ethical and Societal Implications*

The rise of autonomous machines presents profound ethical challenges, particularly by blurring traditional concepts of accountability and decision-making. As machines increasingly take on decision-making roles, it becomes harder to pinpoint who is responsible for errors, unintended consequences, and ethical breaches. Autor (2015) emphasizes that as machines autonomously perform tasks that were once managed by humans, the lines between human and machine responsibility become increasingly murky. For example, self-driving cars must navigate complex ethical dilemmas, such as deciding whether to prioritize pedestrian safety or passenger comfort in life-threatening situations. These scenarios push the boundaries of ethical frameworks that were designed with human agents in mind, raising questions about the extent to which we can trust autonomous systems with such critical decisions.

Real-World Example: One high-profile case that illustrates these ethical concerns is Tesla's Autopilot system, which has been involved in accidents where semi-autonomous driving features failed to prevent crashes. These incidents have led to calls for more stringent safety standards, clearer definitions of accountability, and better regulatory oversight for self-driving technologies. The debate continues as regulators, manufacturers, and the public grapple with the broader societal implications of autonomous driving systems, which can sometimes make decisions that are difficult to justify under conventional ethical norms.

Critical Insight: As autonomous technologies become more integrated into society, organizations must proactively address these ethical dilemmas by embedding transparency, fairness, and accountability into both the design and deployment of such technologies. Ethical considerations should not be an afterthought; they must be central to the development process, with stakeholders across industries collaborating to set clear guidelines. Regulatory bodies must work closely with technologists to create balanced frameworks that ensure safety, fairness, and societal welfare while not stifling innovation. This collaboration will be crucial for ensuring that autonomous systems operate in ways that align with human values and societal norms, particularly when unexpected outcomes arise.

Overall, the rapid advancement of autonomous technologies raises crucial, ethical and societal questions that require thoughtful consideration and action. Decision-makers must not only focus on innovation but also on creating systems that are accountable, transparent, and aligned with societal values. By fostering collaboration between technologists, regulators, and ethicists, we can ensure that the rise of autonomous machines benefits society while minimizing the risks associated with their deployment.

11.2.4. *Impact on Employment and Workforce Dynamics*

The integration of machines into workplaces is reshaping job roles, presenting both opportunities and challenges. While automation is expected to displace many repetitive and routine tasks, it also creates demand for new skill sets and roles, particularly in AI oversight, data analysis, and ethical governance. Frey and Osborne (2017) estimate that nearly 47% of U.S. jobs are at risk of automation, underscoring the urgency of preparing the workforce for a future that is increasingly driven by intelligent systems. However, alongside this disruption, new jobs and industries are emerging that require human expertise, adaptability, and creativity — skills that machines cannot replicate.

Real-World Example: In manufacturing, collaborative robots (often referred to as "cobots") are working alongside human employees to handle repetitive and physically demanding tasks. This collaboration allows human workers to focus on higher-level responsibilities such as strategy, problem-solving, and creative innovation. For instance, in automotive production, cobots assist in assembling components, while human workers oversee quality control and process optimization. This symbiosis between humans and machines demonstrates how technology can enhance productivity and job satisfaction without fully replacing human roles, ultimately leading to more dynamic and flexible workplaces.

Critical Insight: To navigate the inevitable transitions in the workforce, decision-makers must prioritize lifelong learning, reskilling, and upskilling initiatives. These programs should equip employees with competencies in areas such as data literacy, AI integration, and creative problem-solving — skills that will be essential in an AI-driven economy. The World Economic Forum (2020) highlights the importance of collaborative efforts between governments, organizations, and educational institutions to ensure a smooth transition for workers whose roles are being displaced by automation. Proactive policies and investment in human capital are vital to building a resilient workforce capable of thriving in this rapidly evolving landscape.

Overall, the impact of automation on employment will be significant, but it does not have to result in widespread job loss. By fostering a culture of continuous learning and providing workers with the tools to succeed in an AI-enhanced environment, organizations can help ensure that the benefits of automation are widely shared. Decision-makers must focus on creating inclusive, adaptable workforce strategies that support both current employees and future generations in an increasingly technology-driven world.

11.2.5. *Designing for Inclusivity and Equity*

As human-machine interaction technologies become increasingly integrated into daily life, ensuring inclusivity in design is essential to avoid the marginalization of certain groups. Technology that is mindful of diverse user needs — such as multilingual interfaces, accessibility features for individuals with disabilities, and equitable pricing models — can promote broader societal acceptance and foster a sense of belonging. A truly inclusive design not only meets the technical requirements of users but also ensures that technology is accessible, understandable, and usable by individuals from diverse backgrounds, abilities, and socio-economic statuses.

Real-World Example: Microsoft's Adaptive Controller for Xbox is a leading initiative that seeks to make gaming accessible to individuals with mobility challenges. Designed in collaboration with advocacy groups and users with disabilities, the Adaptive Controller offers customizable buttons, switches, and mounts that can be tailored to the user's needs. This product demonstrates how inclusive design can transform the user experience and ensure that all individuals, regardless of physical ability, have the opportunity to engage with technology in meaningful ways. It highlights the importance of considering accessibility from the outset of product development rather than as an afterthought.

Critical Insight: Achieving inclusivity in design requires a proactive, ongoing approach to stakeholder engagement throughout the development process. It is not enough to simply incorporate accessibility features or make minimal adjustments. Organizations must ensure diverse representation within their design and development teams to reflect the full spectrum of user needs. Involving a broad range of perspectives — such as those from marginalized communities, people with disabilities, and individuals from various cultural backgrounds — will lead to products that are more inclusive and equitable in their reach (Bennett & Rosner, 2019). Moreover, the integration of feedback loops throughout the lifecycle of a product will help to identify and address potential barriers, fostering continuous improvement.

Overall, as human-machine interaction technologies continue to evolve, prioritizing inclusivity and equity in their design is crucial for ensuring that technological advancements benefit all members of society. Organizations that embrace diversity and inclusivity in their design processes will not only create products that are more accessible but will also build stronger, socially responsible brands.

A commitment to inclusivity fosters innovation, broadens market appeal, and strengthens societal trust in emerging technologies.

11.2.6. *Looking Forward: The Human-Machine Partnership*

The future of human-machine interaction will revolve around fostering a symbiotic partnership between humans and machines, where each entity leverages its unique strengths. Machines are exceptional at processing vast amounts of data, executing tasks with precision, and maintaining consistency. Humans, on the other hand, bring creativity, emotional intelligence, ethical judgment, and complex decision-making abilities that machines are not yet capable of replicating. The key to unlocking the full potential of HMI lies in creating a collaborative framework where both parties complement each other, rather than one replacing the other. This partnership will require continuous collaboration, iterative improvements, and a shared vision for advancing technology in ways that benefit society as a whole.

Real-World Example: IBM's Watson Health initiative exemplifies the power of human-machine partnerships in healthcare. Watson aids doctors in analyzing complex medical data and diagnosing conditions, enabling them to make more informed decisions. However, Watson does not replace the doctor's expertise; instead, it acts as a supportive tool that enhances the physician's ability to provide personalized care. This collaboration demonstrates how AI can augment human capabilities in critical fields like healthcare, where nuanced judgment and empathy are paramount.

Critical Insight: Decision-makers must adopt a holistic perspective, viewing machines not as replacements but as collaborators in a shared human-machine ecosystem. This shift in mindset is essential to ensuring that technology complements rather than competes with human roles. Recognizing the value of human input in areas such as creativity, ethical considerations, and emotional intelligence will be key to navigating the future of work. Moreover, to fully harness the benefits of human-machine collaboration, organizations must invest in developing new skills that promote synergy between the two entities. Training employees to work alongside machines and harness their capabilities will be crucial for success in this evolving landscape.

Overall, as HMI continues to evolve, the focus must be on nurturing human-machine partnerships that combine the best of both worlds. By embracing this collaborative approach, organizations can unlock new levels of productivity, innovation, and human-centered progress. Ultimately, the goal should be to create a future where humans and machines work together to solve complex problems, drive social good, and enhance the quality of life for all.

In summary, the evolution of human-machine interaction presents immense opportunities to enhance efficiency, creativity, and inclusivity. However, it also demands thoughtful consideration of ethical, societal, and workforce implications. By addressing these challenges proactively, decision-makers can ensure that the future of HMI fosters innovation while upholding values of equity and accountability. Table 11.2 captures the critical components of the evolving human-machine interaction landscape, highlighting key insights that decision-makers should consider to effectively navigate this transformation. By integrating these elements into strategic planning, organizations can ensure that they are not only adopting cutting-edge technologies but also addressing the social, ethical, and workforce implications.

11.3. Preparing for the Future: Skills and Mindsets

The unprecedented pace of technological advancements demands a fundamental shift in the skills and mindsets of individuals and organizations to remain competitive. As Heckman and Kautz (2012) highlight, critical thinking, creativity, and adaptability will become indispensable as the nature of work evolves. These capabilities enable professionals to address complex, non-linear problems, fostering innovative solutions in uncertain environments.

11.3.1. *Developing Technical and Digital Literacy*

In an era increasingly dominated by data, automation, and emerging technologies, technical and digital literacy has become indispensable. Proficiency in data literacy, programming, and systems thinking

Table 11.2. Key Aspects of "The Evolution of Human-Machine Interaction" and Practical Insights for Decision-Makers

Aspect	Description	Real-World Example	Practical Insight
Enhanced Intuitiveness in Interfaces	Human-centric design, gesture recognition, NLP, and BCIs are making interfaces more intuitive, reducing cognitive load.	Apple's Siri integrates with devices to provide context-aware responses, simplifying user interactions.	Striking a balance between automation and human engagement is critical to avoid deskilling users (Parasuraman & Riley, 1997).
Personalization through AI & ML	AI analyzes user behavior to tailor responses, improving user satisfaction and engagement.	Spotify's AI-driven recommendation system curates playlists based on listening habits.	Ensure transparency in data usage and address algorithmic bias to prevent exclusion or unfair outcomes (Zuboff, 2019).
Ethical and Societal Implications	Autonomous machines raise ethical concerns, particularly around accountability and decision-making roles.	Tesla's Autopilot system faces scrutiny due to accidents involving semi-autonomous driving.	Develop clear accountability frameworks and collaborate with regulatory bodies to balance innovation and societal welfare.
Impact on Employment and Workforce Dynamics	Automation is reshaping job roles, displacing certain tasks while creating demand for new roles in AI oversight and data analysis.	Cobots in manufacturing work alongside humans, performing repetitive tasks to enhance productivity.	Focus on reskilling initiatives to prepare the workforce for the demands of an AI-driven economy (World Economic Forum, 2020).

(*Continued*)

Table 11.2. (*Continued*)

Aspect	Description	Real-World Example	Practical Insight
Designing for Inclusivity and Equity	Ensuring technology accounts for diverse user needs fosters acceptance and broadens access to all.	Microsoft's Adaptive Controller for Xbox enhances gaming accessibility for people with mobility challenges.	Involve diverse stakeholders in the design process to ensure equitable and inclusive solutions (Bennett & Rosner, 2019).
Looking Forward: The Human-Machine Partnership	A future where machines and humans work together, leveraging their unique strengths to drive progress.	IBM's Watson Health assists doctors with data analysis, empowering informed decision-making without replacing human expertise.	Embrace machines as collaborators, preserving human creativity, empathy, and ethical judgment alongside technological innovation.

is now foundational for navigating the complexities of the modern world. Data literacy, in particular, empowers individuals to analyze, interpret, and extract meaningful insights from vast datasets, which is critical for informed decision-making and innovation (Mayer-Schönberger & Cukier, 2013). As more industries harness the power of AI, blockchain, and IoT, the ability to understand and engage with these technologies through programming languages like Python, R, and SQL will be crucial. Systems thinking, which encourages understanding interdependencies and feedback loops, will help individuals adapt to and solve complex problems within interconnected systems.

Moreover, as digital technologies continue to evolve, it is not enough to simply understand the tools at hand. Individuals must also grasp the underlying principles of how these systems work, including the ethics, biases, and limitations that may arise from using them. This broader understanding of technology will empower individuals to become not just users of technology but active contributors to its development, implementation, and ethical deployment.

Real-World Example: The World Economic Forum (2020) stresses that data literacy is now as essential as traditional literacy in many sectors. For example, in healthcare, professionals increasingly rely on AI-driven diagnostic tools to aid in medical decision-making. Understanding the algorithms behind these tools is vital for healthcare providers to trust and appropriately use them. Without this knowledge, the risk of misinterpretation or overreliance on AI may lead to suboptimal patient care. Furthermore, in industries like finance, legal services, and marketing, data literacy allows professionals to draw actionable insights from analytics, ensuring smarter and more agile decision-making.

Critical Insight: The demand for technical and digital literacy spans all industries, making it imperative for educational systems and organizations to prioritize digital skill development at all levels. This includes not only teaching specific technical skills but also fostering a mindset that encourages continuous learning and adaptability in the face of technological change. Preparing the workforce for future challenges requires creating an ecosystem where technical skills are seen as a core competency, similar to reading, writing, and arithmetic.

Thus, the rapid integration of digital technologies into every aspect of society underscores the need for widespread technical literacy. To remain competitive and capable of making informed decisions, individuals must equip themselves with the skills to understand, interact with, and influence the technologies shaping their industries. In doing so, they will not only enhance their personal career prospects but also contribute to the responsible development and deployment of technologies that will define the future. Therefore, fostering digital literacy is an investment not just in individual growth, but in the overall resilience and adaptability of society.

11.3.2. *Strengthening Soft Skills*

While technical proficiency is essential in today's digital landscape, the importance of soft skills — such as emotional intelligence, collaboration, communication, and ethical reasoning — cannot be overstated. Goleman (1998) emphasizes that emotional intelligence (EI) plays a crucial role in enhancing interpersonal dynamics and fostering effective teamwork, enabling individuals to work collaboratively and build trust within diverse environments. As automation increasingly handles repetitive and routine tasks, human workers will be distinguished by their capacity to engage in complex, creative, and empathy-driven processes. Skills like negotiation, conflict resolution, and adaptability will be vital in navigating the evolving workplace and ensuring that teams remain productive and cohesive.

Moreover, soft skills are particularly important in leadership roles, where the ability to inspire and guide teams through change is essential. Leaders with high EI are better equipped to manage the stress and uncertainty that often accompany technological transformation. They can motivate teams to embrace innovation while maintaining a sense of human connection and purpose within the organization. Additionally, soft skills are indispensable in cross-cultural and virtual settings, where diverse perspectives and communication styles require heightened sensitivity and understanding.

Critical Insight: Organizations must also recognize that ethical reasoning is not a luxury but a necessity when deploying emerging technologies responsibly. As AI and automation advance, they bring with them complex ethical dilemmas — such as issues of privacy, algorithmic bias, and the transparency of automated decision-making processes. A workforce equipped with strong ethical reasoning skills is essential for addressing these challenges thoughtfully and proactively. It is not enough to create innovative technologies; there must also be careful consideration of their societal impacts. Workers who can anticipate and respond to the moral implications of technological use will ensure that these innovations contribute positively to society rather than perpetuating harm (Zuboff, 2019).

In summary, the rapid advancement of technology makes it increasingly clear that success in the future economy will depend not only on technical skills but also on the ability to collaborate, communicate, and navigate complex ethical challenges. Investing in the development of soft skills is critical for individuals and organizations to thrive in an AI-driven world. By fostering EI, ethical reasoning, and collaborative abilities, we can ensure that humans remain at the heart of decision-making, guiding technology toward outcomes that are equitable, responsible, and human-centered.

11.3.3. *Emphasizing Continuous Learning and Adaptability*

The rapidly evolving technological landscape highlights the imperative for lifelong learning and adaptability. As Senge (1990) advocates in his concept of the "learning organization," individuals and organizations alike must continuously evolve by embracing ongoing education and staying open to new ideas. In a world where technological innovations disrupt industries at an accelerating pace, the ability to adapt is no longer optional — it is critical for long-term success. Organizations that foster a culture of continuous learning ensure that their workforce remains flexible, resilient, and prepared to meet future challenges. This adaptability is particularly important as employees are required to learn new tools, platforms, and methodologies to keep pace with emerging technologies such as AI, blockchain, and quantum computing.

In addition to staying updated on technical developments, employees must also cultivate a mindset that values innovation and creative problem-solving. This involves encouraging experimentation, learning from failures, and adapting swiftly to new market demands. Cultivating a continuous learning culture not only helps organizations stay competitive but also increases employee engagement, satisfaction, and retention, as individuals are more likely to stay with employers who invest in their growth.

Real-World Example: Leading technology companies like Google and Microsoft have institutionalized learning as part of their organizational culture through initiatives like online training platforms and mentorship programs. Google's "Grow with Google" initiative, for example, provides employees and the broader public with access to free resources and certifications in a variety of fields, from digital marketing to AI development. Such programs not only enhance organizational resilience but also support employees' personal and professional growth, making them more adaptable and future-ready. Additionally, Microsoft's commitment to upskilling through its Microsoft Learn platform, alongside mentorship and leadership development programs, empowers employees to thrive in an increasingly dynamic technological environment.

Critical Insight: For organizations, continuous learning should not be seen as a temporary response to technological change but as an ongoing, integral part of the organizational DNA. Leaders must create environments where curiosity is nurtured, learning is celebrated, and adaptability is rewarded. This approach will ensure that the workforce is not only prepared for future technological shifts but also capable of driving those changes in ways that benefit both the organization and society.

In summary, in the face of rapid technological advancements, organizations must prioritize continuous learning and adaptability to remain relevant and competitive. By fostering a culture that values upskilling, innovation, and flexibility, companies can ensure their workforce is well-equipped to navigate the complexities of an ever-changing technological landscape. Ultimately, organizations that embrace continuous learning will not only adapt to the future — they will shape it.

11.3.4. *Fostering Innovation and Risk-Tolerance*

Encouraging innovation and embracing experimentation are essential strategies for organizations aiming to stay ahead of technological disruptions and maintain competitive advantage. In an era marked by rapid change, fostering an environment where employees feel empowered to take calculated risks is crucial. Leadership must adopt a mindset that views failures not as setbacks but as opportunities for growth and learning. A culture that supports risk-taking enables organizations to push the boundaries of what's possible, leading to new ideas, solutions, and technologies. According to Dweck (2006), cultivating a growth mindset is vital for resilience, as it encourages individuals to pursue bold ideas and learn from challenges rather than be discouraged by them. This mindset not only empowers employees to experiment but also supports the organization in navigating the uncertainties that come with innovation.

Encouraging innovation requires leaders to create safe spaces where failure is not penalized but seen as part of the learning process. Risk-tolerant organizations are more likely to experiment with untested concepts, try unconventional approaches, and drive breakthrough discoveries. By removing the fear of failure and rewarding creative thinking, companies can harness the collective intelligence of their teams to spark new initiatives that may lead to significant advancements.

Real-World Example: Amazon serves as a powerful example of a company that has institutionalized a culture of experimentation and risk-tolerance. Through its approach to product development, Amazon continually iterates on its offerings, learning from both successes and failures. The company's development of products such as Alexa and Prime Air highlights its commitment to testing new ideas, even when there is uncertainty about their success. Alexa, for instance, evolved through numerous trials, eventually becoming a dominant force in voice-activated technology. Similarly, the ambitious Prime Air delivery service, though facing challenges, has pushed the envelope in drone technology and has the potential to revolutionize logistics. Amazon's willingness to embrace risk and failure as part of the innovation process has contributed significantly to its dominance in the tech industry.

Critical Insight: For organizations to fully capitalize on innovation, decision-makers must encourage a culture that values experimentation and accepts risk as an inherent part of the creative process. Leaders should focus on building an environment where learning from failure is as valued as celebrating success. This approach fosters long-term innovation and positions companies to respond dynamically to future technological shifts.

In summary, innovation and risk-tolerance are essential drivers of progress in today's fast-paced technological environment. Organizations that foster a culture of experimentation, supported by a growth mindset, are more likely to uncover transformative solutions and stay ahead of disruptions. By viewing failure as a learning opportunity and empowering employees to take calculated risks, companies can adapt to changes and actively shape the future of technology.

11.3.5. *Building a Resilient and Inclusive Workforce*

Resilience is a cornerstone of success in today's rapidly changing technological landscape. It involves preparing for a variety of potential scenarios and ensuring that organizations can continue to operate effectively, even in the face of disruptions. Achieving this requires a combination of technical skills, EI, and a strong foundation of inclusivity in decision-making. Resilient organizations not only have the capability to weather crises but are also agile enough to adapt to challenges as they arise. Additionally, fostering resilience is not just about building individual strength; it is also about creating systems and cultures that support the well-being and development of employees at all levels.

Inclusivity plays a pivotal role in this equation. Teams that are diverse in terms of background, experience, and perspective are better equipped to solve complex problems and navigate uncertainty. Page (2007) highlights that diversity enhances creativity and innovation by offering a wider array of viewpoints, which helps organizations tackle challenges in novel ways. When diverse voices are involved in decision-making processes, organizations are more likely to develop solutions that are not only innovative but also equitable and reflective of a broader range of needs and experiences. This inclusive approach ensures that the workforce is more adaptable, capable of handling shifts in technology and market demands, and more resilient in overcoming obstacles.

Moreover, organizations that invest in building a resilient and inclusive workforce are better positioned to attract top talent, foster collaboration, and create an environment where employees feel valued and supported. This strengthens the overall organizational culture, enhancing both employee satisfaction and long-term productivity.

Critical Insight: Decision-makers must recognize that inclusive practices are not just about fairness; they are essential for leveraging the full potential of technological advancements. By creating environments where diverse voices are actively sought and valued, organizations can foster both innovation and equity. Inclusivity ensures that technological solutions are not only groundbreaking but also accessible and relevant to a wide array of communities.

Overall, building a resilient and inclusive workforce is crucial for organizations striving to stay competitive in an ever-changing world. Emphasizing inclusivity in decision-making processes enables organizations to leverage a variety of perspectives, leading to more innovative, adaptable, and equitable solutions. By investing in both resilience and inclusivity, decision-makers can ensure that their organizations thrive in the face of disruption and continue to grow and innovate for the future.

Preparing for the future of work necessitates a balance between technical expertise and human-centric capabilities. By fostering adaptability, encouraging continuous learning, and cultivating inclusive cultures, organizations can thrive amidst the uncertainties of technological disruption. As Heckman and Kautz (2012) aptly state, the skills of the future are not confined to any single domain but encompass a holistic approach to problem-solving and innovation. Table 11.3 captures essential skills and mindsets for the future, offering real-world examples and practical insights that decision-makers can leverage to remain competitive and resilient in an ever-evolving technological landscape.

Table 11.3. Key Aspects of Preparing for the Future: Skills and Mindsets, and Practical Insights for Decision-Makers

Key Aspect	Description	Real-World Insight & Practical Applications
Developing Technical and Digital Literacy	Mastery of data literacy, programming, and systems thinking is essential as technology dominates various sectors. Proficiency in tools like Python, R, and understanding algorithms will empower individuals to interact with AI, blockchain, and emerging technologies.	Data literacy is as essential as traditional literacy in many industries (World Economic Forum, 2020). For example, healthcare professionals need to understand AI-driven diagnostic tools to make informed decisions.
Strengthening Soft Skills	EI, collaboration, and ethical reasoning are critical to effective decision-making. As automation handles routine tasks, human abilities such as empathy and interpersonal skills differentiate humans from machines.	Ethical reasoning is necessary to deploy AI and automation responsibly. As technology evolves, organizations must nurture emotional intelligence to manage ethical dilemmas in AI, privacy, and bias, ensuring human oversight in decision-making (Zuboff, 2019).
Emphasizing Continuous Learning & Adaptability	In a fast-evolving landscape, continuous learning is key to adaptability. Senge's concept of a "learning organization" emphasizes the importance of ongoing education and flexibility in addressing emerging challenges.	Google's "Grow with Google" and Microsoft's upskilling initiatives promote lifelong learning and organizational resilience. By fostering such programs, companies stay ahead in innovation while empowering employees to adapt to new challenges, ensuring long-term competitiveness.

Table 11.3. (*Continued*)

Key Aspect	Description	Real-World Insight & Practical Applications
Fostering Innovation and Risk-Tolerance	Encouraging innovation and viewing failure as growth opportunities enhances competitiveness. Organizations should create cultures where calculated risks are embraced, and experimentation is part of the organizational DNA.	Amazon exemplifies a risk-tolerant culture with its iterative product development, such as Alexa and Prime Air. This approach fosters breakthroughs in consumer technology and underlines the importance of a growth mindset (Dweck, 2006).
Building a Resilient and Inclusive Workforce	Resilience and inclusivity are crucial to navigating disruptions and ensuring organizational continuity. Diverse teams contribute unique perspectives that enhance creativity, problem-solving, and adaptability.	Diverse teams enhance innovation by integrating varied perspectives (Page, 2007). Decision-makers must ensure that inclusivity is embedded in organizational practices, fostering environments that are both innovative and equitable.

11.4. Conclusion

The horizon of emerging technologies presents a transformative era, brimming with boundless opportunities and complex challenges. Advancements in fields such as AI, biotechnology, quantum computing, and others are poised to redefine industries, enhance productivity, and deliver unprecedented conveniences in everyday life. These innovations have the potential to revolutionize sectors ranging from healthcare and education to transportation and finance. However, alongside these promising developments comes a host of uncertainties and ethical dilemmas that will require careful navigation. As we move into an increasingly tech-driven future, the responsibility to make thoughtful, balanced decisions will lie with both leaders and individuals.

Anticipating the impact of these technological advancements demands a strategic focus on proactive research, policy development, and interdisciplinary collaboration. It is not enough to merely react to technological change; decision-makers must anticipate the trends and challenges that may arise. The evolution of human-machine interaction, from intuitive interfaces to emotionally intelligent systems, will have profound implications on how individuals engage with technology. This shift is already visible in applications like AI-powered personal assistants and advanced healthcare diagnostics, where machines are not just tools but collaborators. Yet, as these systems evolve, they will raise critical questions related to autonomy, accountability, and privacy. For example, the increasing reliance on AI decision-making in healthcare could lead to questions about the role of human oversight, and the implications of biased algorithms could undermine trust in automated systems. Addressing these concerns requires a balanced approach, one that maximizes the benefits of technology while safeguarding societal well-being and individual rights.

Equally crucial to navigating the emerging technological landscape is the cultivation of forward-looking skills and adaptive mindsets. As routine tasks become increasingly automated, human strengths such as critical thinking, creativity, and EI will become indispensable in the workplace. Organizations and individuals alike must prioritize lifelong learning and skill development, recognizing that expertise in technical domains alone will no longer suffice. The workforce of the future will need to be equipped with a combination of technical proficiency and soft skills, including the ability to think critically, solve complex problems, and collaborate effectively across diverse teams. Additionally, fostering cultures of innovation — where experimentation and creativity are encouraged — will be key to maintaining a competitive edge. Beyond technical capabilities, embracing ethical frameworks will ensure that technological progress aligns with societal values and human welfare. As automation, AI, and other disruptive technologies change the nature of work and social interaction, ethical reasoning will play a critical role in ensuring that these advancements benefit all members of society.

In this context, organizations must emphasize resilience and inclusivity within their workforce. Resilient organizations are adaptable and capable of navigating both technological disruptions and unforeseen challenges, while inclusive organizations recognize the importance of diverse perspectives in driving innovation and ensuring that solutions are equitable. By fostering inclusivity, organizations can ensure that all voices are heard, which in turn enable the development of technologies that address a broader range of societal needs. Furthermore, resilient and inclusive organizations will be better positioned to thrive in an unpredictable future, where the pace of change is accelerating and the challenges are increasingly complex.

Ultimately, the journey into a technology-driven future demands a shared commitment to leveraging innovation for the betterment of humanity. Decision-makers must lead with foresight, recognizing that the power of emerging technologies can only be fully realized if they are implemented responsibly, inclusively, and ethically. By embracing the principles of inclusivity, resilience, and ethical stewardship, society can navigate the complexities of this transformative age and ensure that technological advancements contribute meaningfully to global progress.

Key Takeaways for Decision Makers:

1. **Anticipate and Plan for Technological Change**: Decision-makers must proactively research and anticipate technological trends and challenges, fostering a forward-looking approach to innovation.
2. **Focus on Ethical and Inclusive Development**: It is essential to integrate ethics, transparency, and inclusivity into the development and deployment of emerging technologies to ensure they benefit all of society.
3. **Cultivate Human Skills and Adaptability**: As automation takes over routine tasks, human strengths — such as creativity, EI, and critical thinking — will become increasingly vital. Lifelong learning, adaptability, and the fostering of innovative cultures should be prioritized.
4. **Promote Collaboration Across Disciplines**: Addressing complex technological challenges requires interdisciplinary collaboration. Policymakers, technologists, and ethicists must work together to navigate ethical concerns, privacy issues, and societal implications.

5. **Build Resilient and Inclusive Organizations**: Resilience and inclusivity should be embedded in organizational cultures to ensure adaptability, foster innovation, and address the needs of diverse communities.

By embracing these principles, decision-makers can guide their organizations and societies through the complexities of a technology-driven future while ensuring that emerging innovations enhance human welfare, economic growth, and global progress.

References

Atzori, L., Iera, A., & Morabito, G. (2010). The internet of things: A survey. *Computer Networks*, 54(15), 2787–2805.

Autor, D. (2015). Why are there still so many jobs? The history and future of workplace automation. *Journal of Economic Perspectives*, 29(3), 3–30.

Bennett, C. L., & Rosner, D. K. (2019). The promise of empathy: Design, disability, and knowing the "other." *Proceedings of the ACM on Human-Computer Interaction*, 3(CSCW), 1–24.

Brynjolfsson, E., & McAfee, A. (2017). The second machine age: Work, progress, and prosperity in a time of brilliant technologies. *WW Norton & Company.*

Doudna, J. A., & Charpentier, E. (2014). The new frontier of genome engineering with CRISPR-Cas9. *Science*, 346(6213), 1258096.

Dweck, C. S. (2006). *Mindset: The New Psychology of Success.* Random House.

Frey, C. B., & Osborne, M. A. (2017). The future of employment: How susceptible are jobs to computerization? *Technological Forecasting and Social Change*, 114, 254–280.

Goleman, D. (1998). *Working with Emotional Intelligence.* Bantam Books.

Heckman, J. J., & Kautz, T. (2012). Hard evidence on soft skills. *Labour Economics*, 19(4), 451–464.

Jurafsky, D., & Martin, J. H. (2021). *Speech and Language Processing* (3rd ed.). Prentice Hall.

Mayer-Schönberger, V., & Cukier, K. (2013). *Big Data: A Revolution That Will Transform How We Live, Work, and Think.* Houghton Mifflin Harcourt.

Norman, D. (2013). *The Design of Everyday Things: Revised and Expanded Edition.* Basic Books.

Page, S. E. (2007). *The Difference: How the Power of Diversity Creates Better Groups, Firms, Schools, and Societies*. Princeton University Press.
Parasuraman, R., & Riley, V. (1997). Humans and automation: System design and research issues. *Human Factors*, 39(2), 230–253.
Preskill, J. (2018). Quantum computing in the NISQ era and beyond. *Quantum*, 2, 79.
Schwab, K. (2017). *The Fourth Industrial Revolution*. Crown Business.
Senge, P. M. (1990). *The Fifth Discipline: The Art and Practice of the Learning Organization*. Doubleday/Currency.
World Economic Forum. (2020). The future of jobs report 2020. World Economic Forum. Retrieved from https://www.weforum.org.
Zhang, D., Zhou, L., & Lim, J. (2019). Predicting consumer online purchasing decisions: A meta-analysis. *Journal of Retailing and Consumer Services*, 48, 89–98. https://doi.org/10.1016/j.jretconser.2019.01.003
Zuboff, S. (2019). *The Age of Surveillance Capitalism: The Fight for a Human Future at the New Frontier of Power*. PublicAffairs.

Chapter 12

Ethical and Societal Implications of Technology-Driven Decisions

Abstract

Chapter 12 explores the ethical and societal implications of technology-driven decision-making, highlighting the challenges and considerations that arise as emerging technologies become integral to decision processes. The chapter delves into ethical dilemmas, including transparency, accountability, and bias in artificial intelligence (AI) and big data. It also examines the governance and regulatory frameworks necessary to manage these technologies responsibly. Additionally, the chapter emphasizes the importance of inclusivity and equity in technological adoption, offering practical insights for decision-makers to navigate these complex issues. By addressing these dimensions, the chapter provides a comprehensive understanding of the ethical landscape surrounding emerging technologies.

Keywords: Ethical dilemmas; Technology-driven decision-making; Artificial intelligence (AI); Transparency; Accountability; Bias in algorithms; Governance; Regulation; Inclusivity; Equity; Big data; Human-machine interaction; Ethical impact assessment

12.0. Introduction

The rapid evolution of emerging technologies, such as AI, big data analytics, machine learning (ML), and blockchain, has revolutionized industries, governments, and societies. These technologies have fundamentally reshaped decision-making processes, providing unprecedented opportunities for efficiency, automation, and innovation. However, alongside these advancements come significant ethical, societal, and governance challenges. The ability of machines to make autonomous decisions, for instance, raises questions about accountability, bias, privacy, and the broader impact of technology on human rights and societal values. As decision-making becomes increasingly intertwined with technology, understanding and addressing the ethical and societal implications of these technologies is crucial.

This chapter explores the multi-faceted ethical dilemmas posed by technology-enhanced decision-making, highlighting the potential risks and benefits of technology adoption in various sectors. We will delve into the critical role of governance and regulation in managing these technologies to ensure they are used responsibly and equitably. Additionally, we will explore the importance of inclusivity and equity in technological adoption, recognizing that technological progress should not exacerbate existing inequalities but instead contribute to a more just and equitable society. By addressing these key areas, the chapter aims to provide decision-makers with practical insights and strategies for navigating the complex and evolving landscape of technology-driven decision-making.

12.0.1. *Ethical Dilemmas in Technology-Enhanced Decision-Making*

The integration of advanced technologies into decision-making systems often involves complex ethical dilemmas that challenge traditional notions of accountability, responsibility, and fairness. One of the most prominent ethical concerns in technology-enhanced decision-making is the question of who is accountable when decisions are made by algorithms or autonomous systems. For instance, in the case of self-driving cars, if an accident occurs, who is responsible for the damage caused by the vehicle — the manufacturer, the software developer, or the car owner? Similar questions arise in various sectors, such as healthcare, finance, and criminal justice, where AI systems make critical decisions that directly affect individuals' lives. The lack of clear accountability frameworks in these contexts creates challenges for both ethical decision-making and legal regulation.

Moreover, the potential for bias in algorithmic decision-making presents another significant ethical challenge. ML algorithms are often trained on historical data that reflect societal biases, such as racial, gender, or socioeconomic biases. If not carefully managed, these biases can be perpetuated and even amplified by technology, leading to discriminatory outcomes. In healthcare, for example, an AI system trained on data that predominantly represents a certain demographic group may provide suboptimal care recommendations for patients from other demographic groups. This highlights the need for decision-makers to ensure that AI systems are designed and trained in a way that minimizes bias and promotes fairness.

Privacy concerns are also central to the ethical dilemmas surrounding technology-driven decisions. In the age of big data, vast amounts of personal information are collected and analyzed by organizations, governments, and corporations. The widespread use of AI in decision-making often involves the processing of sensitive data, such as medical records, financial transactions, or social media activity. Ensuring the privacy and security of this data is essential, as breaches can lead to identity theft, discrimination, and the erosion of public trust in technology.

Ethical dilemmas in technology-enhanced decision-making require a careful balance between innovation and societal values. While technologies offer the potential to improve efficiency and decision quality, they must be designed and implemented in ways that protect individual rights and promote the common good.

12.0.2. *The Role of Governance and Regulation*

Given the significant ethical and societal implications of emerging technologies, effective governance and regulation are crucial in ensuring that these technologies are deployed responsibly. Governance frameworks must address not only the technical aspects of these technologies but also their broader societal impact. Governments and regulatory bodies have a responsibility to establish guidelines that ensure the safe, ethical, and equitable use of emerging technologies. However, regulatory frameworks must also strike a balance between fostering innovation and preventing harm.

The regulatory environment surrounding emerging technologies is still evolving. In many regions, the legal and regulatory frameworks for AI, data privacy, and other advanced technologies are fragmented, inconsistent, and often outdated. For example, while the European Union's General Data Protection Regulation (GDPR) provides a robust framework for data privacy, other jurisdictions may have more lenient regulations, creating challenges for global companies and increasing the risk of exploitation and abuse of personal data. This lack of global consistency underscores the need for international cooperation and the development of shared standards for the governance of emerging technologies.

Regulation must also address the dynamic nature of technology. Unlike traditional industries, technology is constantly evolving, and new risks emerge as technologies advance. This creates challenges for regulators, who must remain flexible and adaptable to respond to new developments. For example, the rise of deepfake technology has raised concerns about the manipulation of video and audio content, posing new threats to privacy, reputation, and democracy. Regulators must be proactive in identifying emerging risks and crafting regulations that address these challenges without stifling innovation.

Another critical aspect of governance is the involvement of multiple stakeholders in decision-making processes. Governments, private companies, civil society organizations, and the public all have a role to play in shaping the future of technology. Involving diverse perspectives can help ensure that technology is developed in ways that benefit society as a whole and minimize negative consequences. For example, many AI ethics initiatives emphasize the importance of including ethicists, human rights advocates, and affected communities in the development of AI systems to ensure that these technologies are aligned with societal values.

12.0.3. *Ensuring Inclusivity and Equity in Technological Adoption*

As emerging technologies continue to reshape industries and societies, it is essential to ensure that these advancements are inclusive and equitable. Technological progress should not exacerbate existing inequalities, but serve as a tool for improving access to opportunities, resources, and services for all members of society. The benefits of technological innovation should be broadly distributed, ensuring that marginalized and underrepresented communities are not left behind.

Inclusivity and equity are particularly important in the context of AI and automation. These technologies have the potential to replace jobs, automate decision-making processes, and reshape the labor market. If not managed thoughtfully, AI and automation could disproportionately impact low-wage workers, minorities, and other vulnerable groups, exacerbating existing social inequalities. Therefore, decision-makers must prioritize policies that promote workforce development, reskilling, and upskilling to ensure that all individuals can benefit from technological advancements.

One of the most significant barriers to inclusivity in technology is the digital divide. While many developed countries have made significant strides in adopting and integrating advanced technologies, many regions of the world, particularly in low-income and rural areas, still lack access to the internet and modern technological infrastructure. Without access to these tools, individuals and communities cannot fully participate in the digital economy or benefit from technological innovations. Closing the digital divide is essential to ensuring that technological progress benefits all members of society.

Additionally, the ethical design and implementation of AI systems must take into account the diverse needs and values of different populations. This includes addressing cultural, linguistic, and socioeconomic differences in the development of AI applications. For example, AI systems used in healthcare must be designed with cultural sensitivity to ensure that they are relevant and accessible to diverse populations. Similarly, algorithms used in hiring and recruitment should be carefully monitored to avoid perpetuating discrimination based on race, gender, or other factors.

12.0.4. *Navigating the Complex Landscape of Technology-Driven Decisions*

The increasing role of technology in decision-making creates a complex landscape that decision-makers must navigate. While emerging technologies present exciting opportunities for efficiency, innovation, and problem-solving, they also introduce risks and challenges that must be managed carefully. As decision-makers in various sectors grapple with these challenges, it is essential that they take a comprehensive approach that considers the ethical, societal, and regulatory dimensions of technology adoption.

This chapter provides a roadmap for decision-makers, offering practical insights into how to navigate this complex landscape. It emphasizes the need for integrating ethical considerations into the design and implementation of technology, ensuring transparency and accountability, as well as fostering a culture of inclusivity and equity. By addressing these critical areas, decision-makers can better position themselves to leverage the full potential of emerging technologies while minimizing negative societal impacts.

Through this exploration, the chapter aims to equip decision-makers with the tools and frameworks needed to make responsible, informed, and ethical decisions in an increasingly technology-driven world. By doing so, it provides a pathway for ensuring that technological advancements are used to enhance human well-being and promote societal progress.

12.1. Ethical Dilemmas in Technology-Enhanced Decision Making

Emerging technologies like AI, ML, and big data analytics are fundamentally transforming decision-making processes by providing unprecedented precision, efficiency, and scalability. However, these technological advancements also present complex ethical dilemmas that challenge traditional norms of accountability, fairness, and privacy. This section examines these challenges through academic insights, real-world examples, and practical strategies, offering decision-makers a framework for ethical technology adoption.

12.1.1. *The Transparency and Accountability Dilemma*

One of the most prominent ethical challenges in AI and ML systems is their lack of transparency. The "black box" problem, where the processes underlying AI decision-making remain opaque even to its developers, complicates efforts to ensure accountability (Mittelstadt *et al.*, 2016). This issue becomes particularly critical in high-stakes domains such as healthcare, finance, and criminal justice, where decision-makers need to understand and justify outcomes, as these decisions can have profound impacts on human lives. Without transparency, AI systems can perpetuate biases, make erroneous judgments, and fail to deliver fair and just outcomes, especially in contexts where accountability is paramount.

For instance, IBM's Watson for Oncology faced widespread criticism for offering treatment recommendations that were neither sufficiently evidence-based nor transparent. Physicians reported difficulties in trusting the system due to its opaque reasoning processes, which undermined its utility in critical healthcare scenarios (Ross & Swetlitz, 2018). This case highlights the risks of deploying AI tools without clear mechanisms for ensuring interpretability and accountability. Without transparency, the rationale behind AI recommendations remains hidden, making it difficult for practitioners to evaluate their validity or challenge them when necessary.

Similarly, in the criminal justice system, AI systems used for predictive policing or sentencing decisions have faced scrutiny for perpetuating biases. These systems often rely on historical data that reflect existing societal inequalities, thus amplifying racial and economic biases. The lack of transparency in how these algorithms make decisions exacerbates the problem, as it is unclear which factors or data points influence the outcomes. This lack of clarity can lead to unfair and unjust decisions, undermining public trust in the legal system.

The dilemma of transparency extends beyond the specific technologies themselves. It also raises questions about the broader societal responsibility for ensuring that AI and ML systems are used in a way that aligns with ethical principles. When decision-makers and organizations deploy these systems, they bear the responsibility not only for the outcomes but also for ensuring that these technologies are designed, tested, and implemented in ways that prioritize fairness, transparency, and accountability.

Key Insights for Decision Makers: Decision-makers must prioritize the integration of Explainable AI (XAI) systems, which provide comprehensible insights into how decisions are made. XAI helps to make the "black box" more transparent, enabling stakeholders to understand the rationale behind AI-generated outcomes. This fosters greater trust and accountability, which is particularly crucial in high-stakes environments like healthcare, finance, and criminal justice. By ensuring that AI systems are interpretable and explainable, decision-makers can mitigate the risks associated with opacity and avoid undermining the legitimacy of technology-driven decisions.

Furthermore, adherence to regulatory frameworks mandating algorithmic transparency ensures ethical alignment and compliance. Regulatory bodies such as the European Union's GDPR and various

AI-specific guidelines emphasize the importance of explainability in AI systems, which can help guide organizations in their implementation of transparent practices. These frameworks not only help to safeguard against bias but also promote fairness and equity in decision-making.

Another important step is to communicate AI systems' capabilities and limitations transparently to stakeholders. Users, whether healthcare professionals, financial analysts, or law enforcement officers, must be fully informed about how these systems work, what data they rely on, and where potential risks lie. Transparent communication can help mitigate mistrust and build confidence in technology-enhanced decision-making processes. It also allows stakeholders to critically assess AI outputs, ensuring that these technologies serve the public interest and do not operate unchecked.

Ultimately, fostering transparency and accountability in AI systems is not just a technical challenge — it is a social and ethical imperative. Decision-makers must take a proactive role in ensuring that these technologies are not only effective and efficient but also just, fair, and trustworthy. By doing so, they can help ensure that AI and ML systems contribute positively to society while minimizing the risks of harm.

12.1.2. *Algorithmic Bias and Discrimination*

Algorithms, by their nature, learn patterns and make decisions based on the data they are trained on. However, if the data itself is biased, the algorithms will inevitably reflect and perpetuate these biases. This phenomenon, known as algorithmic bias, can have significant and far-reaching consequences, particularly in sensitive domains such as hiring, law enforcement, healthcare, and lending. When algorithms produce discriminatory outcomes, they do more than just replicate existing inequalities — they often amplify them, leading to systemic discrimination that can persist over time and across generations (Hoffman *et al.*, 2020).

In high-stakes settings like recruitment, algorithmic bias can hinder diversity and perpetuate historical disadvantages faced by underrepresented groups. In the hiring process, for example, AI systems that rely on past hiring decisions can inadvertently reinforce patterns of discrimination. If the historical data reflects a preference for candidates from a particular demographic (e.g., male candidates or candidates from certain educational institutions), the algorithm will be biased towards those same groups, disregarding qualified candidates from other backgrounds. This perpetuates existing inequalities and limits opportunities for marginalized individuals, making it more difficult for them to break into certain industries or gain access to better-paying jobs.

A particularly glaring example of algorithmic bias is the COMPAS algorithm, used in the U.S. criminal justice system to predict the likelihood of a defendant reoffending. A 2016 study by ProPublica revealed that COMPAS disproportionately labeled Black defendants as high risk for recidivism, even when their criminal records were comparable to those of White defendants who were labeled as lower risk (Angwin *et al.*, 2016). This bias was found to stem from the historical data used to train the algorithm, which reflected existing racial disparities in arrests and sentencing. As a result, the algorithm's predictions mirrored those systemic racial biases, leading to unfair and potentially harmful outcomes for Black individuals. The case of COMPAS highlights a central ethical dilemma in the use of AI: when algorithms are used in decision-making processes that have life-altering consequences, such as sentencing or parole decisions, the risks of bias and discrimination are magnified, and the integrity of the entire justice system may be called into question.

The societal harm that arises from algorithmic bias can also be seen in other domains, such as lending and healthcare. In lending, algorithms used to assess creditworthiness may inadvertently disadvantage minority groups if they are trained on data that reflects economic inequalities. In healthcare, algorithms that prioritize certain populations based on historical treatment data may overlook or underrepresent the needs of marginalized groups, leading to disparities in access to care and treatment outcomes. These discriminatory practices can perpetuate cycles of inequality and reduce the overall effectiveness and fairness of decision-making systems.

Key Insights for Decision Makers: To address the issue of algorithmic bias and ensure fairness, decision-makers must implement rigorous bias audits throughout the lifecycle of AI systems. These audits should assess whether the training data used to build algorithms is representative and free from discriminatory patterns. Identifying and rectifying biases early in the development process is critical to preventing the amplification of inequalities in decision-making outcomes. This can be achieved through techniques such as fairness-aware machine learning, which aims to minimize biased predictions by adjusting the algorithm's decision-making process.

Incorporating diverse, representative datasets during the development phase is essential for mitigating systemic bias. By using data that better reflects the real-world diversity of the population, decision-makers can help ensure that AI systems are more equitable and capable of providing fairer outcomes. Additionally, when collecting data, it is important to avoid reinforcing historical biases by being mindful of which factors are included in the model and how those factors may intersect with broader social inequalities. For instance, in hiring algorithms, this might mean ensuring that the system doesn't prioritize attributes that correlate with racial or gender biases, such as educational background or employment history.

Furthermore, decision-makers should establish mechanisms for human oversight to complement algorithmic processes. While AI systems can analyze large datasets and generate predictions with remarkable speed, they cannot fully account for the nuances of human experience, particularly in high-stakes scenarios. Human oversight helps to ensure that ethical considerations, such as the potential for discrimination, are included in the decision-making process. This is particularly important in domains like criminal justice or healthcare, where algorithmic decisions can profoundly impact individuals' lives. Having a human in the loop can also serve as a safeguard against algorithmic mistakes or misinterpretations of data, allowing for greater accountability and transparency in decisions.

Lastly, transparency in how algorithms are developed and how decisions are made is key to fostering trust and accountability. Decision-makers must provide clear explanations for how algorithms function and the rationale behind their predictions. This transparency helps to build confidence among stakeholders and ensures that individuals can challenge or appeal decisions that may be discriminatory or biased. It also allows for continuous improvement, as feedback from affected individuals or communities can be used to refine and enhance the algorithms over time.

In conclusion, addressing algorithmic bias is not only a technical challenge — it is a moral and societal imperative. If left unchecked, biased algorithms can perpetuate and exacerbate existing inequalities, leading to significant harm for marginalized groups. By implementing rigorous audits, using diverse and representative datasets, and ensuring strong human oversight, decision-makers can help ensure that AI systems are used in a way that promotes fairness, equity, and justice. Ultimately, the responsible development and deployment of AI technologies require a commitment to ethical principles and a dedication to minimizing harm, ensuring that these powerful tools serve to benefit all members of society, not just a privileged few.

12.1.3. *Privacy Concerns in Big Data Analytics*

The advent of big data analytics has revolutionized industries by enabling organizations to process and analyze vast amounts of information. This technological leap has unlocked tremendous opportunities for personalized services, improved decision-making, and enhanced business performance. However, it has also raised significant ethical concerns, particularly related to privacy. As more and more personal data is collected, stored, and analyzed, individuals' privacy rights are increasingly at risk. The trade-off between leveraging big data for innovation and respecting civil liberties is a delicate balance, and in many cases, privacy concerns have not been adequately addressed (Qudrat-Ullah, 2020).

Big data analytics often involves the collection of sensitive personal information, sometimes without explicit consent from the individuals involved. Companies use this data to gain insights into consumer behavior, optimize operations, and deliver targeted advertising. While these practices may lead to business growth, they also carry the potential to infringe on individuals' privacy. Without clear consent or knowledge, individuals unknowingly contribute to large data repositories that can be exploited for commercial gain or political influence. These concerns are amplified when individuals lack control over how their data is being used or have limited visibility into the ways their personal information is being shared or sold.

One of the most infamous incidents involving privacy violations and big data analytics is the Facebook-Cambridge Analytica scandal of 2018. In this case, millions of Facebook users' profiles were harvested without their consent for the purpose of political microtargeting. The data was used to influence voter behavior during the 2016 U.S. presidential election, raising serious ethical concerns about the manipulation of public opinion through personal data. The scandal revealed the lack of transparency in how personal information was being used and highlighted the risks associated with unregulated data practices (Isaak & Hanna, 2018). Not only did this incident breach users' privacy, but it also undermined public trust in technology platforms, demonstrating the profound ethical consequences of misusing personal data for political or commercial gain.

The consequences of such breaches are far-reaching. When individuals' personal information is used without their consent or in ways they do not understand, it can damage relationships between organizations and their customers. The erosion of trust can result in reputational damage, loss of business, and legal repercussions. Public outrage over privacy violations also leads to calls for stronger regulatory measures and greater transparency in data practices. Without proper safeguards, the ethical implications of big data analytics could undermine the societal benefits these technologies are intended to provide.

Furthermore, as technology continues to evolve, the scope of data that can be collected and analyzed expands. The proliferation of connected devices through Internet of Things (IoT) and the increasing sophistication of AI algorithms exacerbate privacy concerns. Data collected from smart home devices, wearable health trackers, and even social media posts can offer unprecedented insights into individuals' lives, but these technologies also pose significant risks to personal privacy. Without clear guidelines and oversight, there is the potential for individuals' personal information to be exploited in ways that compromise their autonomy and well-being.

Key Insights for Decision Makers: To address the privacy concerns associated with big data analytics, organizations must adopt ethical data governance policies that prioritize transparency, user consent, and robust security measures. Privacy should not be an afterthought or a box to check — it should be integrated into the design and implementation of big data systems from the outset.

1. **Adopt Clear and Transparent Data Practices**: Decision-makers should ensure that all data collection and processing activities are transparent. Users should be fully informed about what

data is being collected, how it will be used, and with whom it will be shared. Clear, easy-to-understand privacy policies that outline these practices can help individuals make informed decisions about sharing their data. Additionally, organizations should be transparent about the measures they take to protect user data from misuse or breaches.

2. **Prioritize User Consent and Autonomy**: One of the fundamental ethical principles in data privacy is that individuals should have control over their personal information. Organizations should implement opt-in mechanisms for data collection, where users actively agree to share their data rather than being automatically included by default. Moreover, users should be empowered to withdraw consent at any time, ensuring that they have ongoing control over their data. This autonomy helps maintain trust between organizations and their customers.
3. **Implement Strong Security Measures**: Robust security measures must be in place to safeguard personal data from unauthorized access or breaches. This includes implementing encryption, using secure storage systems, and ensuring that only authorized personnel have access to sensitive information. Regular security audits and assessments can help identify potential vulnerabilities in data handling systems before they are exploited by malicious actors.
4. **Compliance with Privacy Regulations**: Organizations must comply with existing privacy regulations to ensure that their data practices align with legal and ethical standards. The European Union's GDPR and the California Consumer Privacy Act (CCPA) set important benchmarks for protecting personal data and empowering individuals with rights over their information. Compliance with these regulations not only reduces legal risks but also demonstrates a commitment to respecting users' privacy. Additionally, organizations should stay informed about emerging privacy regulations and adapt their practices accordingly.
5. **Foster a Privacy-Respecting Culture**: In addition to technical solutions, organizations should cultivate a culture that prioritizes privacy across all levels of the organization. This includes training employees on privacy policies and the ethical considerations of data use, as well as implementing governance frameworks that oversee data collection, processing, and usage. Ethical data

governance is not just about compliance but also about fostering a sense of responsibility toward protecting individual privacy.
6. **Conduct Privacy Impact Assessments (PIAs)**: PIAs help organizations understand and mitigate potential risks associated with data collection and processing. By conducting PIAs early in the development of data-driven projects, organizations can identify privacy risks and take steps to address them proactively. This can help reduce the likelihood of breaches and ensure that data practices align with privacy expectations.

In conclusion, while big data analytics offers tremendous opportunities for innovation and improvement, it also poses significant challenges related to privacy and individual rights. The misuse of personal data can have devastating consequences, both for individuals and for the organizations involved. By adopting ethical data governance policies, prioritizing user consent, and ensuring compliance with privacy regulations, organizations can protect individuals' privacy while still leveraging the power of big data. Ultimately, fostering trust and respect for privacy will enable technology to fulfill its promise of benefiting society, without sacrificing the fundamental rights of individuals.

12.1.4. *The Absence of Empathy and Moral Judgment*

While AI systems have demonstrated unparalleled efficiency and accuracy in processing data and making decisions, they fundamentally lack one critical aspect of human decision-making: empathy and moral judgment. Unlike human beings, AI systems do not possess the capacity to understand or consider the emotional, ethical, and social dimensions of the decisions they make. As a result, while AI can make decisions that are technically correct based on the data it processes, these decisions may fail to account for the nuanced human considerations that are often integral to ethical decision-making (Qudrat-Ullah, 2014).

This absence of empathy and moral reasoning can lead to outcomes that are legally or technically valid but morally or socially questionable. For instance, AI systems that are designed to optimize efficiency or profitability often disregard the potential human consequences of their decisions. When algorithms are solely driven by mathematical optimization without taking into account the broader social, ethical, and emotional impact on individuals or communities, they may produce decisions that, while efficient, may be ethically unacceptable or discriminatory.

One striking example of this limitation is the case of Amazon's AI-based recruitment tool. The tool was developed to streamline the hiring process by automatically screening resumes and selecting candidates based on historical hiring data. However, it was soon discovered that the algorithm systematically favored male candidates for technical roles, reflecting the gender imbalances present in the data used to train the system. Specifically, the algorithm was trained on resumes submitted to Amazon over a ten-year period, most of which came from male candidates, resulting in a bias that perpetuated existing gender disparities in the tech industry (Dastin, 2018). Because the system lacked empathy and moral judgment, it failed to consider the broader social implications of its decisions, leading to discriminatory hiring practices. In this case, the AI system's ability to make efficient decisions in terms of matching candidates based on historical patterns was not balanced by a sense of fairness or equality. This highlights the ethical risks involved in automating decision-making processes without the appropriate checks and balances to ensure equitable outcomes.

In addition to hiring practices, similar issues have emerged in other areas such as healthcare, criminal justice, and loan approval systems. AI-based systems used in predictive policing, for example, have been criticized for reinforcing racial biases, as they rely on historical crime data that may disproportionately reflect arrests and convictions in marginalized communities. Likewise, in healthcare, AI tools used for diagnosing diseases may inadvertently overlook certain demographic groups if they have been underrepresented in the training data. These examples illustrate how the absence of moral judgment and empathy in AI systems can exacerbate existing societal inequalities and biases.

The ethical challenge posed by the absence of empathy in AI decision-making underscores the importance of embedding human values into technological systems. Although AI can offer powerful tools for optimizing decision-making processes, these systems must be designed with an awareness of their social and ethical implications.

The absence of empathy and moral judgment in AI is not an inherent flaw of the technology itself, but rather a result of the way these systems are designed and implemented. Decision-makers must recognize this gap and take proactive measures to ensure that AI systems are aligned with ethical standards that prioritize fairness, inclusivity, and the well-being of all stakeholders.

Key Insights for Decision Makers:

1. **Adopt Hybrid Decision-Making Models**: One of the most effective ways to address the absence of empathy in AI systems is through hybrid decision-making models that combine the efficiency of AI with human oversight. In these models, AI systems can handle tasks such as data analysis, pattern recognition, and optimization, while human decision-makers provide the empathy, ethical reasoning, and moral judgment needed to assess the broader impact of these decisions. This collaborative approach ensures that the benefits of AI are realized without sacrificing ethical considerations.
2. **Integrate Ethical Frameworks into AI Development**: Organizations should embed ethical frameworks into the design and development of AI systems from the outset. These frameworks should prioritize values such as empathy, fairness, accountability, and inclusivity. By aligning AI systems with these core ethical principles, organizations can mitigate the risks of discrimination and bias, ensuring that AI systems do not perpetuate societal inequalities. Moreover, developing AI tools with a focus on these principles can help promote public trust in the technology, as stakeholders will feel more confident that their interests are being considered.
3. **Enhance Human Ethical Reasoning Capabilities**: To bridge the gap between the technical efficiency of AI and the ethical considerations of human values, organizations should invest in training programs that enhance employees' ethical reasoning and decision-making capabilities. These programs can help employees understand the ethical implications of AI-driven decisions and provide them with the tools to navigate the complex dilemmas that may arise. By fostering a workforce that is not only technically proficient but also ethically aware, organizations can

better ensure that AI systems are used responsibly and with consideration for their societal impact.

4. **Establish Ethical Oversight Mechanisms**: Decision-makers should implement robust ethical oversight mechanisms to monitor AI systems' decisions and ensure they align with ethical standards. This oversight can take the form of an ethics review board, regular audits, or external accountability measures that assess the fairness and inclusivity of AI systems. Having a dedicated team to oversee the ethical aspects of AI deployment can help identify and address potential issues before they become widespread problems.
5. **Promote Inclusivity and Fairness in AI Development**: To mitigate the risk of biased outcomes, organizations should actively work to ensure that the data used to train AI systems is diverse and representative. This includes incorporating a wide range of demographic, geographic, and socioeconomic factors to ensure that AI systems do not disproportionately benefit or disadvantage certain groups. Additionally, engaging with diverse stakeholders throughout the development process can help identify potential blind spots and ensure that the final system is fair and inclusive.
6. **Continuously Monitor and Update AI Systems**: AI systems should be continuously monitored and updated to ensure that they remain aligned with ethical standards and societal values. As social norms, values, and ethical frameworks evolve, AI systems must be adapted to reflect these changes. Regular updates and feedback loops can help prevent AI systems from becoming outdated or misaligned with the ethical considerations they were originally designed to uphold.

The absence of empathy and moral judgment in AI systems presents significant ethical challenges, particularly when these systems are used to make decisions that affect individuals' lives and well-being. While AI can offer tremendous advantages in terms of efficiency and precision, it is critical to recognize that these systems cannot, by themselves, account for the complex ethical and social implications of their decisions. By adopting hybrid decision-making models, integrating ethical frameworks into AI development, and investing in ethical training for employees, organizations can ensure that AI is used responsibly and with consideration for the broader societal impact. Ultimately, the key to addressing the absence of empathy in AI lies in human oversight — ensuring that the power of AI is harnessed to serve humanity, while remaining grounded in the values of fairness, inclusivity, and empathy.

12.1.5. *Balancing Innovation with Ethical Stewardship*

Innovation is essential for driving societal progress and addressing the complex challenges of the modern world. However, it is equally important to recognize that technological advancement must be pursued with ethical stewardship to avoid unintended negative consequences. The rapid deployment of new technologies, particularly without carefully considered ethical safeguards, can inadvertently amplify existing societal harms, creating new risks and vulnerabilities. In this context, the challenge is not just to innovate, but to ensure that innovation is responsible, sustainable, and aligned with the broader public good.

One key area where this balance is often difficult to achieve is in the field of surveillance technologies, particularly facial recognition. Originally developed to enhance security and efficiency, facial recognition systems have found their way into various applications, from law enforcement to marketing. However, their deployment has raised significant ethical concerns, particularly regarding privacy violations and the potential for racial profiling. Numerous studies have demonstrated that facial recognition technologies are prone to errors when identifying individuals with darker skin tones, leading to higher rates of misidentification for Black and Brown individuals. A landmark study by Buolamwini and Gebru (2018) revealed that commercial facial recognition systems exhibited significantly lower accuracy rates when identifying darker-skinned and female faces compared to lighter-skinned and male faces. This bias can result in false positives, wrongful arrests, and discrimination, undermining the fairness and integrity of the justice system. The dangers of prioritizing technological advancement without sufficient attention to ethical considerations are starkly illustrated by these real-world consequences.

The rapid and unregulated deployment of facial recognition systems is an example of how technological innovation, when pursued without adequate ethical oversight, can exacerbate existing social inequities. This issue is particularly pertinent in the context of law enforcement, where the potential for abuse is heightened due to the power dynamics involved. If left unchecked, these systems can become tools of discrimination, violating individuals' rights to privacy, freedom, and equality. Thus, the ethical implications of such technologies must be addressed proactively, ensuring that they do not perpetuate harm or infringe on basic human rights.

In addition to privacy concerns, the use of facial recognition technologies in surveillance systems raises questions about accountability and consent. For example, individuals may not be aware that they are being monitored or that their biometric data is being collected and analyzed. This lack of transparency undermines public trust in the technology and raises concerns about how data is used and stored. Without clear policies and regulations in place, the widespread use of facial recognition can result in a surveillance state where personal freedoms are compromised in the name of security.

Given these concerns, it is essential for leaders and decision-makers to embed ethical considerations into every stage of technology development and deployment. Ethical stewardship involves taking a proactive approach to identifying potential risks and addressing them before they escalate into significant societal problems. By integrating ethical frameworks into the design, testing, and implementation of emerging technologies, organizations can mitigate the risks of harm and ensure that innovation aligns with the values of fairness, transparency, and accountability.

An effective strategy for balancing innovation with ethical responsibility involves interdisciplinary collaboration. Bringing together ethicists, technologists, policymakers, and community representatives can help identify the potential ethical pitfalls of new technologies and develop solutions that minimize harm. Ethical considerations should not be an afterthought, but rather an integral part of the development process from the very beginning. By engaging diverse perspectives, decision-makers can ensure that emerging technologies are designed to serve the needs and rights of all individuals, not just those in positions of power or influence.

In addition to fostering interdisciplinary collaboration, engaging with the public through transparent dialogue is essential to maintaining accountability and trust. Public engagement allows citizens to voice their concerns and preferences regarding the development and deployment of new technologies, ensuring that their values are reflected in the design and use of these systems. Transparency in decision-making and clear communication about the intended use of technologies, as well as their potential risks and benefits, are crucial for building public confidence. When individuals feel that their concerns are being heard and addressed, they are more likely to trust that the technology is being used for the greater good rather than for private or political gain.

Moreover, fostering an ongoing dialogue with the public helps to create a feedback loop that allows decision-makers to adjust their strategies as new challenges and concerns arise. Ethical governance of technology is a dynamic process that requires constant evaluation and adaptation. By remaining open to public input and being willing to revise policies and practices, organizations can ensure that innovation is aligned with societal values and does not outpace the development of necessary ethical safeguards.

Key Insights for Decision Makers

1. **Integrate Ethical Considerations into All Stages of Technology Development**: Ethical considerations should be woven into the fabric of technology development from the very beginning. Decision-makers should ensure that ethical frameworks, such as fairness, transparency, and accountability, are integral to the design, testing, and deployment of technologies. This proactive approach can help identify and mitigate risks before they escalate into significant ethical challenges.
2. **Foster Interdisciplinary Collaboration**: Innovation in technology should not happen in a vacuum. Collaboration between ethicists, technologists, policymakers, and diverse stakeholders is crucial for identifying potential ethical pitfalls and developing solutions that minimize harm. This interdisciplinary approach ensures that technologies are designed and implemented with a broad understanding of their social and ethical implications.
3. **Engage with the Public Transparently**: Public engagement is essential to building trust and ensuring that emerging technologies align with societal values. Transparent communication about the intended use of technologies, their potential risks, and the measures being taken to safeguard privacy and equity fosters

public confidence. Decision-makers should establish clear channels for public input and actively listen to the concerns of affected communities.

4. **Create Accountability Mechanisms**: Decision-makers must establish robust accountability mechanisms to ensure that technologies are used responsibly. This includes developing policies and regulations that govern the use of technologies like facial recognition and ensuring that there are clear procedures for addressing misuse or unethical applications. Accountability mechanisms help to prevent the misuse of power and ensure that technologies serve the broader public good.
5. **Prioritize Equity and Inclusivity**: The deployment of new technologies should always prioritize equity and inclusivity. Decision-makers should ensure that emerging technologies do not disproportionately harm marginalized or vulnerable populations. This includes designing technologies with fairness in mind and ensuring that diverse perspectives are considered throughout the development process. Inclusivity in technology development helps to ensure that innovations benefit all members of society, not just those with access to power or resources.

Overall, balancing innovation with ethical stewardship is one of the most pressing challenges facing decision-makers in today's rapidly advancing technological landscape. While the potential for technology to drive societal progress is immense, this potential must be harnessed responsibly to prevent harm and ensure that technological advancements serve the broader public good. By embedding ethical considerations into every stage of technology development, fostering interdisciplinary collaboration, engaging with the public transparently, and creating strong accountability mechanisms, decision-makers can ensure that innovation is aligned with societal values. As we continue to develop and deploy emerging technologies, it is essential that we remain vigilant in balancing the pursuit of progress with the responsibility to protect human rights, equity, and social justice. Ethical stewardship will ultimately determine whether technological innovation can truly enhance societal well-being, or whether it will exacerbate existing inequalities and injustices.

12.1.6. *Recommendations for Ethical Technology Adoption*

Navigating the ethical dilemmas associated with technology-enhanced decision-making requires a proactive, multidimensional approach that balances technological innovation with moral responsibility. As organizations increasingly rely on AI, ML, and other advanced technologies, it is essential to ensure that these tools are deployed in ways that respect fundamental ethical principles, protect human rights, and promote social equity. The challenges posed by algorithmic bias, lack of transparency, privacy concerns, and the absence of empathy in automated systems must be addressed through strategic, forward-thinking actions.

First and foremost, establishing clear and comprehensive ethical guidelines is crucial. These guidelines should focus on principles such as transparency, accountability, and fairness, which are essential to fostering trust in technology. Decision-makers should ensure that AI systems are not only understandable but also justifiable, allowing stakeholders to see how decisions are made and ensuring that any potential biases are minimized. Transparency can be achieved through the integration of XAI, which offers clear, interpretable outputs that help both developers and end-users understand how decisions are reached. Furthermore, accountability mechanisms must be in place to hold organizations responsible for the outcomes of AI-driven decisions. This includes creating systems for auditing and correcting errors, addressing biases, and ensuring that AI systems align with legal and ethical standards.

Investing in research and development to create ethical and XAI systems is also vital. As AI technologies become more complex, it is increasingly important to ensure that these systems are designed with fairness and inclusivity in mind. Ethical AI systems should be trained on diverse and representative datasets, which can help minimize the risk of perpetuating existing biases and inequalities. Research initiatives should prioritize the creation of algorithms that promote diversity and inclusivity, ensuring that AI benefits all members of society and does not disproportionately harm marginalized or vulnerable groups. Collaboration between technologists, ethicists, sociologists, and community representatives is essential in this process, as it provides a comprehensive understanding of the societal impact of AI technologies.

Lifelong learning initiatives should be a cornerstone of any organization's strategy for ethical technology adoption. As technology rapidly evolves, so too, do the ethical challenges associated with its use. Organizations should invest in continuous training programs that equip employees with the knowledge and skills necessary to navigate these evolving ethical dilemmas. This includes providing training on the ethical implications of new technologies, fostering critical thinking and ethical reasoning, as well as promoting a culture of ethical responsibility. By doing so, organizations can ensure that their employees are well-prepared to make informed, responsible decisions and handle the ethical complexities of technology-enhanced processes.

Moreover, cultivating a culture of ethical responsibility within organizations is essential for ensuring that technological advancements align with societal values. This can be achieved by embedding ethical considerations into the core values and mission of the organization, promoting transparency in decision-making processes, and creating a governance structure that prioritizes ethical concerns. Leadership plays a key role in setting the tone for ethical behavior, and decision-makers should lead by example, demonstrating a commitment to ethical principles in both their personal actions and organizational policies. By fostering a culture of responsibility, organizations can ensure that technology is not only advancing innovation but also supporting the well-being of individuals and communities.

In addition to these internal initiatives, decision-makers should also consider the broader societal implications of emerging technologies. Public engagement is critical in shaping the ethical framework for technology adoption. Engaging with the public through consultations, forums, and transparent communication helps ensure that technological advancements align with the values and concerns of the communities they affect. This engagement fosters accountability and allows organizations to anticipate and address potential ethical issues before they escalate. Furthermore, involving diverse groups of people in the technology design and decision-making process helps ensure that all voices are heard and that emerging technologies are accessible and beneficial to all segments of society.

Finally, organizations should remain adaptable and open to revising their ethical guidelines and practices in response to new challenges and opportunities. Ethical issues related to technology are dynamic, and what is considered ethical today may evolve as technologies advance and societal values change. Ongoing evaluation, feedback mechanisms, and collaboration with external ethical advisory boards can help organizations stay aligned with ethical best practices and adapt to the rapidly changing technological landscape.

In summary, ethical dilemmas in technology-enhanced decision-making reflect the complex interplay between innovation and responsibility in the digital age. While AI, ML, and big data offer transformative potential, their adoption must be guided by principles of transparency, fairness, and accountability. Decision-makers play a crucial role in ensuring that technological advancements serve humanity's best interests. By fostering interdisciplinary collaboration, prioritizing ethical considerations, and empowering individuals, leaders can navigate these challenges and harness technology's transformative power for societal progress. Table 12.1 succinctly summarizes the ethical dilemmas associated with technology-enhanced decision-making, highlighting key issues and actionable insights for decision-makers to navigate these challenges responsibly.

12.2. Governance and Regulation of Emerging Technologies

The accelerated development of technologies such as AI, ML, and blockchain has created a significant regulatory gap, exposing society to potential risks while also delaying opportunities for transformative societal benefits. This section examines the critical components of governance and regulation for emerging technologies, focusing on ethical guidelines, international cooperation, and the balance between self-regulation and government intervention. The discussion is supported by academic research, case studies, and actionable insights for decision-makers.

12.2.1. *Challenges in Governance of Emerging Technologies*

Emerging technologies present significant challenges for traditional governance models, primarily due to their rapid evolution,

Table 12.1. Ethical Dilemmas in Technology-Enhanced Decision-Making and Key Takeaways for Decision-Makers

Ethical Dilemma	**Key Issues**	**Takeaways for Decision-Makers**
Transparency and Accountability	Lack of interpretability in AI decision-making ("black box" problem) undermines trust and usability.	Adopt XAI systems to enhance understanding and trust. Communicate capabilities and limitations transparently. Adhere to regulatory transparency frameworks.
Algorithmic Bias and Discrimination	Algorithms may perpetuate biases from training data, leading to systemic inequalities in decisions.	Conduct rigorous bias audits and use diverse datasets. Implement human oversight in high-impact decisions to ensure fairness and equity.
Privacy Concerns in Big Data	Collection and use of personal data without explicit consent pose risks to individual privacy.	Develop robust data governance policies emphasizing transparency and user consent. Comply with privacy regulations (e.g., GDPR, CCPA). Foster trust through opt-in models.
Absence of Empathy and Moral Judgment	AI lacks the ability to integrate human ethics and empathy into decisions.	Use hybrid decision-making models combining AI efficiency with human oversight. Train employees in ethical reasoning to bridge technological and human values.
Balancing Innovation with Ethics	Rapid technology adoption without safeguards can lead to societal harm (e.g., racial profiling).	Embed ethical frameworks into all technology stages. Encourage interdisciplinary collaboration and public dialogue to align innovation with societal values.

complexity, and broad societal impact. Unlike established technologies, which can be governed through well-understood, static policies, emerging technologies often introduce new risks and unknown consequences that make traditional regulatory approaches inadequate. A primary issue is the difficulty in predicting the long-term implications of these innovations, which often leads to reactive regulations that are only put in place after significant social, economic, or ethical issues have surfaced. This delay in governance, however, can amplify the negative effects of unchecked technological developments, necessitating a more forward-thinking approach to regulation (Brynjolfsson & McAfee, 2017).

For instance, the rise of generative AI technologies, such as OpenAI's ChatGPT, has raised concerns about misinformation, intellectual property theft, and the potential displacement of human workers by automated systems. These technologies, while offering significant advancements, also present a new range of ethical and societal challenges. Policymakers, caught in the complexities of these issues, have struggled to draft timely and effective regulations. The difficulty lies in balancing the need for innovation with the responsibility of ensuring societal well-being. The urgency of these concerns, coupled with the pace at which new technologies are introduced, has left regulatory bodies playing catch-up, raising the risk of overregulation that stifles progress or underregulation that leads to societal harm (Floridi & Cowls, 2019).

Moreover, emerging technologies often operate on a global scale, complicating governance even further. The international nature of many technologies means that national governments and regional authorities may have limited control over their development and deployment. This global dimension requires coordination and collaboration across borders to create coherent and effective governance frameworks that are capable of addressing the cross-jurisdictional issues these technologies present. For instance, in the case of AI, decisions made by one country can have a far-reaching impact on others, which necessitates global conversations around ethics, regulation, and governance.

Insights for Decision-Makers:

1. **Develop Anticipatory Regulatory Frameworks**: Decision-makers should adopt foresight methodologies, such as scenario

planning and horizon scanning, to anticipate the potential impacts of emerging technologies. This proactive approach allows for the development of regulatory frameworks that are better equipped to address future risks while fostering innovation.
2. **Establish Agile Governance Mechanisms**: It is critical to create flexible governance structures that can rapidly respond to the fast-changing landscape of emerging technologies. These mechanisms should prioritize adaptability and resilience, ensuring that regulations evolve as technologies do, without compromising public interest or safety.
3. **Facilitate International Cooperation**: Given the global nature of many emerging technologies, international cooperation is vital for effective governance. Governments and international bodies should work together to create common standards and regulations that transcend national boundaries, ensuring a unified approach to addressing the challenges posed by technologies like AI and big data.

In conclusion, the governance of emerging technologies requires a paradigm shift from reactive to proactive regulation. While traditional governance models have struggled to keep pace with rapid technological advancement, the complexities of these new innovations demand agile, anticipatory frameworks. Decision-makers must not only anticipate the risks and challenges associated with emerging technologies but also collaborate on a global scale to create effective, dynamic governance structures that can adapt to these innovations. By fostering proactive, anticipatory regulatory practices, governments and organizations can better manage the risks of new technologies while maximizing their potential benefits for society.

12.2.2. *Ethical Guidelines and Standards*

Ethical frameworks provide a foundational basis for regulating emerging technologies. Initiatives such as the European Union's GDPR have become global benchmarks for safeguarding privacy and promoting data accountability (Hoffman *et al.*, 2020). GDPR mandates data minimization, transparency, and user consent, influencing regulations in regions such as California (CCPA) and India (Digital Personal Data Protection Act).

Another notable example is UNESCO's Recommendation on the Ethics of Artificial Intelligence, which emphasizes human rights, sustainability, and equity in AI deployment (UNESCO, 2021).

Case Study: The GDPR's implementation in 2018 resulted in organizations globally revising their data practices, leading to improved user trust and transparency. Non-compliance fines, such as the €1.2 billion penalty imposed on Meta Platforms in 2023, underscore the importance of adhering to ethical standards in data handling.

Insights for Decision-Makers:

1. Adopt internationally recognized ethical standards to ensure consistency and interoperability.
2. Create industry-specific guidelines tailored to the unique risks and opportunities of each technology.

The adoption and enforcement of ethical guidelines and standards are paramount for the responsible deployment of emerging technologies. By following internationally recognized frameworks such as the GDPR and UNESCO's AI ethics recommendations, organizations can ensure that their technological practices prioritize privacy, human rights, and sustainability. However, it is equally important to develop industry-specific regulations that address the distinct challenges of each sector. Decision-makers must recognize that adhering to these ethical guidelines not only mitigates risks but also enhances public trust and accountability, ensuring that technology serves the greater good of society. Through such frameworks, organizations can navigate the complexities of technological innovation while upholding fundamental ethical principles.

12.2.3. *International Collaboration in Governance*

Technological impacts transcend borders, necessitating international cooperation. Collaborative governance mechanisms are critical for addressing transnational challenges such as cybercrime, AI-driven warfare, and climate change mitigation technologies (Mittelstadt *et al.*, 2016).

Example: The **Partnership on AI**, involving stakeholders from academia, industry, and civil society, has fostered global dialogue on the ethical use of AI, particularly in areas such as algorithmic bias and automation ethics (Partnership on AI, 2020).

Challenges: International collaborations often face obstacles such as geopolitical tensions, conflicting regulatory priorities, and disparities in technological capabilities among nations.

Insights for Decision-Makers:
1. Foster multilateral agreements that prioritize shared ethical values.
2. Support capacity-building initiatives in developing countries to ensure equitable participation in technology governance.

International collaboration is essential to effectively govern emerging technologies, as their impact extends well beyond national borders. While challenges such as geopolitical tensions, differing regulatory priorities, and disparities in technological capabilities can complicate these collaborations, the potential benefits far outweigh these obstacles. Initiatives like the Partnership on AI illustrate the power of global cooperation in addressing ethical concerns related to AI, ensuring that the development and deployment of technologies are aligned with shared values. To move forward, decision-makers must prioritize multilateral agreements that foster ethical consistency across borders and invest in capacity-building efforts to enable developing countries to participate equitably in these governance processes. By strengthening international cooperation, we can ensure that technology is harnessed for the benefit of all, promoting a more inclusive and just global society.

12.2.4. *Balancing Self-Regulation and Government Oversight*

The debate between self-regulation and government oversight continues to polarize stakeholders. Proponents of self-regulation argue that it fosters innovation, reduces bureaucracy, and allows industry players to create adaptive frameworks. Conversely, critics emphasize the risks of unchecked corporate practices, as seen in cases of data misuse and algorithmic biases (Smith *et al.*, 2022).

Example: In the cryptocurrency sector, self-regulatory practices have struggled to prevent fraud and financial instability, leading to calls for stronger government intervention. The collapse of **FTX** in 2022 exposed significant governance failures, prompting regulatory reforms in digital asset markets (Coindesk, 2023).

Insights for Decision-Makers:

1. Encourage co-regulation, combining industry expertise with governmental oversight.
2. Establish public-private partnerships to align innovation goals with societal safeguards.

The balance between self-regulation and government oversight is crucial to ensure that emerging technologies are developed and deployed responsibly. While self-regulation allows for flexibility and innovation, as seen in industries like cryptocurrency, it also carries significant risks of exploitation and oversight failures. The collapse of FTX highlights the need for a more structured approach, integrating government regulation to safeguard against financial instability and unethical practices. Decision-makers should recognize that a hybrid model of co-regulation — where industry knowledge is combined with government oversight — can create a more effective and adaptive framework for managing technological advancements. By fostering public-private partnerships, organizations can ensure that innovation aligns with societal needs and ethical standards, balancing growth with accountability.

12.2.5. *Regulatory Sandboxes: A Testing Ground for Innovation*

Regulatory sandboxes have emerged as an innovative approach to governing emerging technologies. These frameworks allow companies to test new technologies in controlled environments under regulatory supervision. Sandboxes balance innovation and safety, particularly in sectors such as fintech and autonomous vehicles (Zetzsche *et al.*, 2018).

Example: The United Kingdom's Financial Conduct Authority (FCA) sandbox program enabled startups to trial blockchain solutions while ensuring compliance with financial regulations. This initiative accelerated innovation while mitigating risks.

Insights for Decision-Makers:

1. Leverage regulatory sandboxes to evaluate emerging technologies' societal and economic impacts.
2. Expand sandbox models to include underregulated domains like AI ethics and biotechnology.

Regulatory sandboxes present a unique opportunity for fostering innovation while managing the associated risks of emerging technologies. By offering a controlled environment for experimentation, these frameworks allow companies to test new solutions under regulatory supervision, ensuring compliance while promoting innovation. The success of initiatives like the UK's FCA sandbox demonstrates the potential of this model in sectors such as fintech, where regulatory constraints can stifle innovation if applied too rigidly. However, as technology continues to evolve, it is essential to expand these sandbox models to encompass emerging fields like AI ethics and biotechnology, which require careful oversight to mitigate ethical concerns. By doing so, regulators can create a dynamic space where innovation is nurtured responsibly, benefiting both industry and society. Decision-makers should advocate for the broader application of regulatory sandboxes, ensuring that emerging technologies are tested, refined, and scaled in a manner that aligns with ethical principles and societal well-being.

12.2.6. *Future Directions in Technology Governance*

Governance must evolve to address emerging challenges such as quantum computing risks, bioengineering ethics, and digital inequality. Decision-makers should invest in research to develop frameworks that anticipate disruptive innovations.

Case in Point: The rapid rise of quantum computing has outpaced existing cybersecurity regulations. Organizations like the National Institute of Standards and Technology (NIST) have initiated quantum-resistant cryptography standards to address these challenges (NIST, 2023).

Insights for Decision-Makers:

(1) Prioritize forward-looking governance strategies that anticipate and mitigate potential risks.
(2) Promote stakeholder inclusion to reflect diverse perspectives in regulatory policies.

As emerging technologies continue to evolve at an accelerating pace, future directions in technology governance will require greater foresight, adaptability, and inclusivity. The rise of quantum computing, bioengineering advancements, and growing concerns about digital inequality exemplify the complexity and urgency of addressing potential risks before they materialize. Decision-makers must prioritize the development of governance frameworks that not only respond to current challenges but also anticipate the disruptive impacts of future innovations. The proactive efforts by organizations such as the NIST to create quantum-resistant cryptography standards offer a valuable model for preparing for new technological frontiers. By fostering a collaborative approach to governance, where diverse stakeholders contribute their insights and expertise, regulatory frameworks can be designed to safeguard the public interest while promoting innovation. Ultimately, future technology governance should be dynamic, forward-thinking, and inclusive, ensuring that emerging technologies contribute to societal well-being without compromising ethical standards or equity.

Overall, the governance and regulation of emerging technologies demand a multidimensional approach that balances innovation with societal values. By adopting ethical standards, fostering international collaboration, and integrating mechanisms like regulatory sandboxes, decision-makers can ensure that technological advancements are both responsible and inclusive. Future governance frameworks must be adaptive, inclusive, and forward-looking to address the complexities of the digital age. Table 12.2 outlines critical governance components for emerging technologies, supported by actionable insights for decision-makers and real-world examples to illustrate their application.

Table 12.2. Key Aspects of Governance and Regulation of Emerging Technologies

Sub-Section	**Key Aspects**	**Insights and Takeaways for Decision-Makers**	**Studies Examples/ Case Studies**
Challenges in Governance	– Technologies evolve rapidly, challenging traditional regulatory approaches. – Long-term impacts are often unpredictable.	– Develop anticipatory regulatory frameworks using scenario planning and foresight methodologies. – Establish agile governance mechanisms to adapt to technological changes while protecting public interest.	– Generative AI technologies like ChatGPT raised concerns about misinformation and automation impacts.
Ethical Guidelines and Standards	– Ethical frameworks provide the foundation for responsible governance. – Internationally recognized standards, such as GDPR, influence global policies.	– Adopt internationally recognized ethical standards to ensure consistency and interoperability. – Develop industry-specific guidelines addressing unique risks and opportunities.	– GDPR's implementation improved user trust globally. – €1.2 billion GDPR fine imposed on Meta in 2023.
International Collaboration	– Cross-border impacts necessitate collaborative governance. – Challenges include geopolitical tensions and capability disparities.	– Foster multilateral agreements emphasizing shared ethical values. – Support capacity-building initiatives to ensure equitable participation in governance.	– The Partnership on AI fosters global dialogue on AI ethics. – Climate change mitigation technologies require multilateral efforts.

(Continued)

Table 12.2. (*Continued*)

Sub-Section	Key Aspects	Insights and Takeaways for Decision-Makers	Studies Examples/ Case Studies
Balancing Self-Regulation and Government Oversight	– Self-regulation fosters innovation and reduces bureaucracy but risks unchecked practices. – Government oversight ensures accountability and public safety.	– Encourage co-regulation combining industry expertise with governmental oversight. – Establish public-private partnerships to align innovation goals with societal safeguards.	– Cryptocurrency failures, such as the FTX collapse, highlighted the limits of self-regulation.
Regulatory Sandboxes	– Controlled environments enable testing and refinement of technologies. – Balance innovation with safety in emerging sectors like fintech and autonomous vehicles.	– Leverage regulatory sandboxes to evaluate societal and economic impacts of technologies. – Expand sandbox models to underregulated domains like AI ethics and biotechnology.	– UK FCA sandbox program enabled blockchain innovation while ensuring compliance.
Future Directions	– Governance must anticipate risks from quantum computing, bioengineering, and digital inequality.	– Prioritize forward-looking strategies that anticipate risks. – Promote inclusive stakeholder participation for diverse perspectives.	– NIST's quantum-resistant cryptography standards address emerging cybersecurity risks.

12.3. Ensuring Inclusivity and Equity in Technological Adoption

The rapid adoption of emerging technologies presents both opportunities and challenges for fostering inclusivity and equity. While technological advancements promise to address global challenges and improve quality of life, they also risk deepening existing inequalities if adoption is not managed inclusively.

Policymakers, organizations, and communities must prioritize inclusivity to ensure equitable access and participation in the benefits of these technologies. This section explores critical dimensions of inclusivity and equity in technological adoption, supported by academic research, real-world cases, and actionable insights for decision-makers.

12.3.1. *Addressing the Digital Divide*

The digital divide — characterized by unequal access to technology — remains a significant barrier to inclusive technological adoption. This divide is influenced by socioeconomic status, geographic location, and educational attainment, disproportionately affecting rural communities, low-income groups, and marginalized populations (Smith *et al.*, 2022).

Key Challenges:

1. **Infrastructure Gaps:** Inadequate digital infrastructure in underserved areas restricts access to high-speed internet and modern devices.
2. **Affordability Barriers:** The high cost of technology prevents equitable access for economically disadvantaged groups.
3. **Digital Literacy:** Limited digital skills hinder individuals from fully utilizing available technologies.

Case Example: In sub-Saharan Africa, only 22% of the population had access to the internet in 2022, compared to 88% in high-income countries. Efforts such as Google's Project Loon, which provided internet access through high-altitude balloons, demonstrate the potential of innovative solutions to bridge infrastructure gaps in underserved regions (World Bank, 2023).

Insights for Decision-Makers:

1. Invest in digital infrastructure, particularly in rural and low-income regions.
2. Implement affordable access policies, including subsidies for low-income families.
3. Promote digital literacy programs through public-private partnerships.

Bridging the digital divide is essential for fostering equitable access to technology and unlocking its transformative potential for all communities. Addressing this challenge requires coordinated efforts to expand infrastructure, make technology more affordable, and improve digital literacy. Initiatives like Google's Project Loon highlight how innovative solutions can help mitigate disparities, but long-term success depends on sustained investment and inclusive policies. By prioritizing these actions, decision-makers can ensure that technological advancements empower rather than exclude, creating opportunities for education, economic development, and social inclusion across diverse populations.

12.3.2. *Mitigating Systemic Bias in Technology Design*

Emerging technologies, particularly AI, can inadvertently perpetuate systemic biases if not designed inclusively. Algorithms trained on biased data sets risk reinforcing stereotypes, excluding underrepresented groups, and perpetuating inequalities (Bolukbasi *et al.*, 2016).

Key Issues:

1. **Bias in Data Sets:** AI models reflect the biases present in their training data, resulting in discriminatory outcomes.
2. **Lack of Representation:** Insufficient diversity among technology developers contributes to the exclusion of minority perspectives.

Case Example: A study on facial recognition systems revealed significantly higher error rates for darker-skinned individuals compared to lighter-skinned individuals, underscoring the consequences of non-inclusive AI design (Buolamwini & Gebru, 2018).

Insights for Decision-Makers:

1. Mandate diverse and representative data sets in technology development.
2. Foster diversity in technology teams to incorporate multiple perspectives.
3. Implement bias detection and correction mechanisms in AI systems.

Addressing systemic bias in technology design is not just an ethical imperative but also a strategic necessity for creating equitable and trustworthy solutions. By embedding diversity, inclusivity, and rigorous bias mitigation strategies into the design process, decision-makers can ensure that emerging technologies serve as tools for progress rather than perpetuators of inequality. Such efforts are essential for fostering public trust and realizing the full potential of AI and other innovations.

12.3.3. *Promoting Culturally Sensitive Technology Adoption*

Cultural sensitivity in technology adoption ensures that solutions are relevant and beneficial to diverse communities. Technologies that overlook cultural differences risk low adoption rates and unintended social consequences.

Key Challenges:

1. **One-Size-Fits-All Approaches:** Standardized solutions often fail to meet the unique needs of specific communities.
2. **Ethical Concerns:** Technologies that conflict with cultural values may face resistance or rejection.

Case Example: In India, the rollout of mobile payment systems initially failed to gain traction among rural communities due to a lack of culturally relevant user interfaces and digital literacy training. By incorporating local languages and symbols, adoption rates improved significantly (Raman *et al.*, 2020).

Insights for Decision-Makers:

1. Engage local communities in the design and deployment of technologies.
2. Conduct impact assessments to identify potential cultural implications.
3. Tailor user interfaces to reflect local languages and traditions.

Culturally sensitive technology adoption is essential for maximizing the impact and reach of technological advancements. By respecting and incorporating cultural values and preferences, decision-makers can foster inclusive adoption and enhance the societal benefits of innovation. This approach ensures that technology serves as a unifying force rather than a source of division, promoting equitable access and global progress.

12.3.4. *Ensuring Gender Equity in Technological Access*

Gender disparities in technological access and participation continue to limit women's opportunities in education, employment, and entrepreneurship. Women are 23% less likely than men to use the internet in developing regions, a gap that hinders broader societal progress (ITU, 2022).

Key Issues:

1. **Access Inequalities:** Women face unique barriers such as lower incomes, restrictive social norms, and safety concerns related to technology usage.
2. **Underrepresentation in STEM:** Limited representation of women in science, technology, engineering, and mathematics (STEM) fields exacerbates inequities in technological development and usage.

Case Example: The "She Will Connect" initiative by Intel significantly reduced the gender gap in internet access, reaching 5 million women in Africa with digital literacy training by 2020. This program not only improved women's digital skills but also empowered them to participate in the digital economy, lead community projects, and advocate for further gender equity in technology (Intel, 2021).

Insights for Decision-Makers:

1. **Address Barriers:** Design policies that specifically target and mitigate gender-specific challenges, such as affordability and safety concerns.
2. **Promote Education:** Encourage STEM education and career pathways for women through scholarships, mentorships, and inclusive curriculums.

3. **Empower Leadership:** Support women-led technology initiatives and entrepreneurship programs to amplify women's contributions to innovation and economic growth.

Achieving gender equity in technology access is not just a moral imperative but a catalyst for societal advancement. Bridging the digital divide for women enhances community resilience, fosters inclusive innovation, and accelerates progress toward sustainable development. By implementing gender-sensitive strategies, decision-makers can create a more equitable digital landscape where everyone, regardless of gender, can thrive.

12.3.5. *Inclusive Policy and Governance Frameworks*

Inclusive policies and governance frameworks are essential to ensure equitable access to and benefits from technology for all segments of society. These frameworks must proactively address the diverse needs of marginalized groups while fostering participatory approaches to decision-making.

Key Principles:

1. **Stakeholder Inclusion:** Involve a broad spectrum of stakeholders, including underrepresented communities, in policy development to ensure diverse perspectives and priorities are reflected.
2. **Equity in Resource Allocation:** Allocate resources strategically to bridge gaps in technological infrastructure and digital literacy, particularly in underserved regions.

Case Example: Estonia's e-Governance model stands as a testament to inclusive policy design. By providing digital identities to all citizens, the country ensures equitable access to public services such as healthcare, voting, and education. This model promotes digital equity while fostering societal trust in technology-driven governance (Kattel & Mergel, 2020).

Insights for Decision-Makers:

- **Design Inclusive Frameworks:** Develop governance models that prioritize equity, inclusivity, and the active participation of all societal groups.

- **Resource Redistribution:** Invest in underserved communities and regions to level the playing field in technological access and utilization.
- **Continuous Evaluation:** Implement robust monitoring and evaluation mechanisms to assess the impact of policies on reducing inequities and improving inclusivity.

Inclusive governance frameworks are the cornerstone of equitable technology adoption and societal progress. By addressing systemic disparities and engaging diverse stakeholders, policymakers can build resilient digital ecosystems that empower all members of society. Such efforts not only advance technological equity but also contribute to broader goals of social cohesion and sustainable development.

12.3.6. *Future Directions for Inclusive Technology Adoption*

The rapid evolution of technologies such as AI, 5G networks, and digital learning platforms presents transformative opportunities to address long-standing inclusivity and equity challenges. These advancements necessitate forward-looking strategies to ensure that the benefits of technological progress are shared equitably across all societal groups.

Recommendations:

1. **Forge Strategic Partnerships:** Collaborate with technology providers to expand access to underserved and low-income regions, reducing the digital divide.
2. **Integrate Inclusivity Metrics:** Incorporate equity and inclusivity indicators into technology impact assessments to evaluate and improve outcomes.
3. **Leverage Emerging Technologies:** Utilize solutions like blockchain to ensure transparency and accountability in resource allocation, as seen in pilot projects in Kenya's agricultural supply chains, where blockchain platforms are addressing systemic inequities (World Economic Forum, 2023).

Insights for Decision-Makers:

1. **Embrace Emerging Innovations:** Stay informed about technological developments and their potential to promote inclusivity.

2. **Prioritize Equitable Innovation:** Encourage the design and implementation of technologies that address disparities from the outset.
3. **Strengthen Cross-Sector Collaboration:** Foster partnerships between governments, industry, and civil society to maximize the societal benefits of technology adoption.

Future directions in inclusive technology adoption require a proactive and collaborative approach to innovation. By integrating equity-focused practices and leveraging emerging technologies, decision-makers can ensure that technological advancements serve as tools for empowerment rather than exacerbating disparities. Inclusive strategies will not only drive broader societal benefits but also enhance global efforts toward sustainable development and social cohesion. Table'12.3 summarizes the main themes in promoting inclusivity and equity in technological adoption, offering practical takeaways for policymakers and organizations aiming to address inequalities in access, design, and participation in emerging technologies.

12.4. Practical Insights for Decision Makers

As emerging technologies continue to shape industries and societies, decision-makers face critical challenges in ensuring these innovations are ethically sound, socially responsible, and beneficial to all. The practical insights outlined below provide a roadmap for navigating the ethical and societal implications of technology-driven decisions, addressing inclusivity, transparency, accountability, and regulatory compliance. These insights can guide decision-makers in making informed, balanced choices that promote responsible technology adoption and contribute to a sustainable and equitable future.

12.4.1. *Integrating Ethical Considerations into Technological Design and Implementation*

The rapid advancement of technologies such as AI, blockchain, and biotechnology has brought about significant ethical dilemmas that require careful consideration. One of the most effective ways to mitigate potential negative societal impacts is to integrate ethical considerations from the beginning of the design and implementation

Table 12.3. Key Aspects of Ensuring Inclusivity and Equity in Technological Adoption

Dimension	**Key Challenges**	**Case Example**	**Insights for Decision-Makers**
Addressing the Digital Divide	– Infrastructure gaps in underserved areas. – Affordability barriers. – Limited digital literacy.	Google's Project Loon in sub-Saharan Africa to provide internet access.	– Invest in rural and low-income region infrastructure. – Implement affordable access policies. – Promote digital literacy.
Mitigating Systemic Bias in Technology Design	– Bias in data sets used for AI. – Lack of diversity among technology developers.	Facial recognition bias: Higher error rates for darker-skinned individuals.	– Mandate diverse data sets in AI development. – Foster diversity in tech teams. – Implement bias detection systems.
Promoting Culturally Sensitive Technology Adoption	– One-size-fits-all approaches that ignore cultural needs. – Ethical concerns with technology's cultural fit.	In India, mobile payment systems adapted to local languages and symbols.	– Engage local communities in design. – Conduct cultural impact assessments. – Tailor solutions to local customs.
Ensuring Gender Equity in Technological Access	– Gender disparities in access to technology. – Underrepresentation of women in STEM.	Intel's "She Will Connect" program, reaching 5 million women in Africa.	– Address gender-specific barriers to access. – Encourage women's participation in STEM. – Support women-led tech initiatives.
Inclusive Policy and Governance Frameworks	– Lack of inclusivity in policymaking. – Inequitable resource allocation.	Estonia's e-Governance model providing digital identities for all citizens.	– Develop inclusive policies with diverse stakeholder participation. – Ensure equitable resource distribution.
Future Directions for Inclusive Technology Adoption	– Ensuring inclusivity in emerging technologies (AI, 5G, blockchain).	Blockchain pilot projects in Kenya ensuring equitable distribution in agriculture.	– Stay informed on emerging technologies. – Integrate inclusivity metrics. – Foster cross-sector collaborations.

process. Ethical impact assessments should become standard practice to evaluate the potential social, economic, and environmental consequences of emerging technologies.

Ethical frameworks can provide guidance on balancing innovation with human rights and societal values. This includes ensuring that technologies do not inadvertently exacerbate existing inequalities or contribute to harmful societal outcomes. For example, AI applications used in criminal justice systems, such as predictive policing algorithms, have been criticized for perpetuating racial biases, as seen in the use of COMPAS (Correctional Offender Management Profiling for Alternative Sanctions) in the U.S. (Angwin *et al.*, 2016). Decision-makers must implement fairness audits and bias detection methods to ensure that emerging technologies do not reinforce existing inequalities.

Involving diverse stakeholders throughout the technology development process is also vital. This includes not only technical experts but also ethicists, community representatives, and individuals from marginalized groups who can offer unique insights into the potential social impact of a technology. This collaborative approach can help uncover blind spots that might otherwise go unaddressed. For instance, the involvement of underrepresented groups in the development of AI systems has been shown to reduce bias and promote more equitable outcomes (Buolamwini & Gebru, 2018).

Key Takeaways for Decision-Makers:

1. Conduct comprehensive ethical impact assessments for all emerging technologies.
2. Include diverse stakeholders in the design, development, and implementation phases.
3. Address the potential negative societal impacts early in the decision-making process.

The integration of ethical considerations into the design and implementation of emerging technologies is essential for fostering innovations that are both impactful and equitable. By adopting proactive ethical frameworks, engaging diverse stakeholders, and addressing potential societal harms early, decision-makers can balance technological advancement with societal well-being. These approaches not only mitigate risks but also pave the way for technology to become a force for inclusivity, fairness, and long-term sustainability.

12.4.2. *Prioritizing Transparency and Accountability in Technology Use*

As technology becomes more integrated into daily life, particularly through AI systems that make autonomous decisions, transparency and accountability must be prioritized. XAI has emerged as a crucial approach to ensuring that AI decisions can be understood by humans. Unlike traditional "black-box" AI systems, which make decisions without providing clear insights into how they arrived at those conclusions, XAI models provide transparency into the reasoning process. This is particularly important in high-stakes sectors such as healthcare, criminal justice, and finance, where decisions based on AI can significantly impact people's lives.

For example, in healthcare, AI systems that assist in diagnostic decisions must be interpretable so that healthcare professionals can understand and trust the recommendations provided by the system. This not only ensures that AI complements human decision-making but also enables accountability, as healthcare providers can question and review AI-driven suggestions. Similarly, in the criminal justice system, explainable algorithms are critical for ensuring that decisions related to sentencing or parole are based on fair, transparent, and accountable processes (Binns, 2018).

Human oversight is another essential component of accountable technology adoption. Decision-makers must establish mechanisms for regular monitoring and intervention by human experts when AI systems or automated processes are involved. This is particularly important in cases where AI systems operate in environments with high potential for harm, such as autonomous vehicles or military applications.

Key Takeaways for Decision-Makers:

- Adopt XAI models to ensure transparency in decision-making processes.
- Implement systems for ongoing human oversight of automated decision-making processes.

- Foster a culture of accountability by establishing clear responsibilities for AI-driven decisions.

Transparency and accountability are fundamental to the ethical use of advanced technologies, particularly AI systems that impact critical aspects of society. By adopting explainable AI models, ensuring robust human oversight, and fostering a culture of accountability, decision-makers can build trust in technology while safeguarding societal interests. These measures not only enhance the reliability of technology but also promote fairness, enabling more informed and responsible applications across diverse domains.

12.4.3. *Fostering a Culture of Inclusivity and Equity*

Inclusivity and equity are fundamental principles that must be embedded within organizations to ensure that the benefits of technological advancements are shared broadly across society. This requires that decision-makers create opportunities for underrepresented groups — such as women, racial minorities, and individuals from low-income communities — to participate in the development, deployment, and use of emerging technologies. Organizations should prioritize diversity in their workforce, particularly in technical roles, to promote the creation of technologies that are more inclusive and reflective of society's varied needs.

For example, ensuring that women are represented in AI research and development is critical to avoiding gender biases in AI systems. Studies have shown that AI applications in areas such as hiring, facial recognition, and healthcare often reflect the biases of the predominantly male and the non-diverse teams that develop them (Smith *et al.*, 2022). By ensuring a more balanced representation in tech development teams, organizations can mitigate the risk of developing technologies that perpetuate inequalities.

Moreover, fostering an inclusive culture involves providing equal access to technology for all groups. This includes promoting digital literacy and closing the digital divide, particularly in rural and marginalized communities, to ensure that technological advancements are accessible to everyone, not just those with privileged access to resources. Programs like Intel's "She Will Connect," which provides digital literacy training to women in Africa, highlight the importance of creating access pathways for underrepresented groups (Intel, 2021).

Key Takeaways for Decision-Makers:

- Promote diversity in technology development teams to create more inclusive and equitable solutions.
- Address barriers to technology access, particularly in underserved communities.
- Foster organizational cultures that prioritize inclusivity and ensure all voices are heard in the decision-making process.

Fostering a culture of inclusivity and equity in technology adoption is not only a moral imperative but also a strategic advantage for organizations and societies. By promoting diversity within technology development teams and addressing systemic barriers to access, decision-makers can ensure that emerging technologies serve a broader spectrum of societal needs. Such efforts enhance innovation, reduce inequalities, and create a more equitable technological future that benefits everyone.

12.4.4. *Staying Informed and Compliant with Evolving Regulatory Standards*

As the pace of technological innovation accelerates, so too does the complexity of regulatory frameworks that govern the use of emerging technologies. Policymakers and organizations must remain informed about the evolving regulatory landscape to ensure compliance with ethical guidelines, industry standards, and legal requirements. This is particularly important in industries such as healthcare, finance, and telecommunications, where the misuse of technology can have serious ethical and legal consequences.

For example, the introduction of the GDPR in the European Union has set a new global standard for data privacy and security, particularly in relation to AI and ML applications. Organizations must ensure that their AI systems comply with GDPR regulations, particularly in terms of user consent, data privacy, and the right to explanation. Failing to comply with these regulations can result in significant financial penalties and damage to an organization's reputation (GDPR, 2018).

Proactively engaging with policymakers and regulatory bodies can help decision-makers anticipate changes in the regulatory environment and adjust their strategies accordingly. Participating in industry discussions, staying informed about new regulations, and ensuring that organizational practices align with ethical guidelines will help mitigate legal risks and promote the responsible development of technologies.

Key Takeaways for Decision-Makers:

- Stay informed about the latest regulatory changes and ensure compliance with relevant standards.
- Engage with policymakers and industry groups to anticipate regulatory shifts.
- Adopt best practices in data privacy, security, and ethical AI usage to reduce legal risks.

Staying informed and compliant with evolving regulatory standards is essential for fostering responsible innovation and maintaining public trust in emerging technologies. By aligning organizational practices with legal and ethical requirements, decision-makers can mitigate risks, avoid reputational harm, and contribute to a technology ecosystem that prioritizes transparency, accountability, and societal well-being. Proactive engagement with regulatory bodies ensures that organizations are not only prepared for future challenges but also play a role in shaping policies that support ethical and equitable technology adoption.

12.4.5. *Long-term Vision and Sustainable Development Goals*

In addition to addressing immediate concerns, decision-makers must adopt a long-term perspective on technology adoption, one that aligns with broader societal goals such as the United Nations' Sustainable Development Goals (SDGs). Technologies such as renewable energy systems, digital health tools, and educational technologies can contribute to achieving these global goals, but their deployment must be managed in a way that ensures they benefit society as a whole, particularly the most vulnerable populations.

For example, AI-powered solutions in agriculture can improve food security and increase productivity, helping to achieve SDG 2 (Zero Hunger). However, these technologies must be accessible and inclusive, ensuring that smallholder farmers in developing countries benefit from them. Similarly, digital education platforms can play a crucial role in achieving SDG 4 (Quality Education) by providing access to education for underserved communities, but only if they are designed with cultural sensitivity and tailored to local needs.

The integration of emerging technologies with the SDGs requires a focus on equitable access, sustainability, and social inclusion. Decision-makers must consider the environmental and social impact of each technology, ensuring that technological advancements contribute positively to societal development while avoiding exacerbating inequalities.

By considering the broader implications of technological adoption on sustainable development, decision-makers can ensure that technology not only drives innovation but also contributes to the well-being of society at large. A long-term, SDG-aligned approach helps steer technological progress in ways that support a healthier, more just, and more sustainable world for future generations.

Incorporating the long-term vision of the SDGs into technology adoption is critical for ensuring that the benefits of innovation extend beyond immediate gains. By prioritizing sustainability, equity, and inclusion, decision-makers can harness emerging technologies to create lasting, positive impacts on both global development and the well-being of society. Regularly evaluating the alignment of technology with the SDGs helps maintain focus on responsible innovation, ensuring that technology serves as a force for good in addressing humanity's most pressing challenges.

Overall, navigating the ethical and societal implications of emerging technologies requires a proactive, inclusive, and transparent approach. Decision-makers must integrate ethical considerations into every stage of technology adoption, foster a culture of inclusivity, stay informed about regulatory changes, and ensure that technological advancements align with broader societal goals. By following these practical insights, organizations and policymakers can contribute to a technology-driven future that benefits all of humanity while minimizing harm and fostering equitable opportunities for all.

12.5. Conclusion

The ethical and societal implications of technology-driven decisions are vast, complex, and increasingly critical as we advance into a world where technology plays an ever-more significant role in shaping our lives, economies, and societies. Emerging technologies such as AI, ML, big data analytics, and blockchain have the potential to revolutionize industries, enhance efficiency, and bring about substantial societal benefits. However, with these transformative capabilities come profound ethical dilemmas, governance challenges, and questions surrounding inclusivity and equity. As these technologies continue to evolve, the decisions made by organizations and governments will shape not only the future of technology but also the future of society itself.

In navigating this technological landscape, decision-makers must be vigilant in recognizing and addressing the ethical, societal, and regulatory implications that arise. The consequences of neglecting ethical considerations in technology-driven decisions are far-reaching, and can result in significant harm, including privacy violations, discrimination, inequities, and loss of public trust. It is essential that organizations and governments integrate ethical frameworks into their decision-making processes, ensuring that technology is used responsibly and in alignment with societal values. This responsibility falls on a broad range of stakeholders, including policymakers, technology developers, business leaders, ethicists, and civil society groups. Collaboration among these diverse groups is key to ensuring that emerging technologies are developed and deployed in ways that benefit all members of society, and avoid exacerbating existing social and economic inequalities.

12.5.1. *The Need for Ethical Governance in Technology Deployment*

Governance plays a critical role in managing the ethical implications of technology. As the use of emerging technologies becomes more pervasive, the need for robust governance frameworks that promote transparency, accountability, and fairness is more urgent than ever. Technology should not be developed or deployed in a vacuum; rather, its design, implementation, and use must be governed by clear ethical principles and regulatory standards.

One of the foremost ethical principles in the governance of emerging technologies is accountability. As decision-making processes become more automated, especially with the advent of AI, it is crucial that the responsibility for decisions made by technology remains clearly defined. This is particularly challenging when algorithms or autonomous systems are involved, as their “decisions” can be opaque or difficult to trace. Establishing frameworks for accountability — where developers, organizations, and even governments are held responsible for the decisions made by technology — ensures that harmful outcomes can be addressed and remedied. However, accountability does not only pertain to rectifying negative outcomes; it must also include proactive measures that prevent harm and ensure that technologies serve the public good.

A key component of ethical governance is transparency. Decision-makers must prioritize openness in the deployment and use of AI and other technologies. Transparency can take many forms, from providing clear explanations about how algorithms work and the data they use, to making it easier for individuals to understand how and why decisions are made. For example, the use of XAI is one avenue through which transparency can be achieved. XAI models provide insights into the decision-making processes of ML systems, making it easier to identify and correct potential biases, inaccuracies, or ethical concerns.

Equally important is the ability for human oversight and intervention. While AI systems can provide valuable support in decision-making, they should not replace human judgment entirely, especially in high-stakes situations. The decision to rely on technology should always include safeguards that allow for human intervention when necessary, especially in cases where the ethical stakes are high, such as healthcare, criminal justice, or autonomous vehicles.

12.5.2. *Fostering Inclusivity and Equity in Technological Innovation*

Inclusivity and equity must be central to any conversation about technology and society. Emerging technologies hold the promise of solving pressing global challenges, from improving healthcare and education to mitigating climate change and enhancing governance. However, if not carefully managed, these technologies can exacerbate social inequalities, leaving marginalized and vulnerable populations behind. This has been one of the main criticisms of the technology industry — while new technologies often promise improvements for all, the benefits are frequently unevenly distributed.

Decision-makers must ensure that technological advancements are inclusive by design, and that the opportunities created by technology are available to all people, regardless of their background, income, or location. One way to achieve this is through the active inclusion of underrepresented groups in the development and deployment of emerging technologies. Diversity in design teams, for instance, can help ensure that the needs of various communities are taken into account when creating new technologies. Additionally, prioritizing investments in technologies that address the needs of underserved populations can help ensure that technological innovations benefit all members of society.

The digital divide remains one of the most significant barriers to technological inclusivity. While many parts of the world are experiencing rapid advancements in digital technologies, a large portion of the global population still lacks access to the internet or the necessary infrastructure to participate in the digital economy. Closing the digital divide is essential if we are to ensure that emerging technologies do not deepen existing global inequalities. Governments, organizations, and global institutions must work together to provide equitable access to technology, ensuring that all individuals have the tools, knowledge, and opportunities to benefit from technological progress.

Equity also extends to the development of AI and ML systems. If AI models are trained on biased data or are designed without consideration for social and cultural diversity, they may perpetuate or even amplify existing inequalities. For example, facial recognition systems have been shown to have higher error rates for people of color, which raises serious concerns about fairness and discrimination. Decision-makers must be aware of such issues and ensure that AI systems are designed to be fair and inclusive, reflecting the diverse realities of the populations they serve.

12.5.3. *The Role of Education and Public Awareness*

As technology continues to evolve, the general public must also be educated about the potential risks and benefits of these advancements. Public awareness campaigns, educational initiatives, and transparent dialogue about the ethical implications of technology can help build a more informed society. A well-educated public is better able to make informed choices about technology, demand accountability from technology developers, and engage in debates about the ethical and societal implications of these innovations.

Educational systems must also evolve to equip future generations with the skills needed to navigate a technology-driven world. This includes not only technical skills related to AI, data science, and engineering, but also an understanding of the ethical, social, and cultural implications of technology. By integrating ethics and technology into educational curricula, we can help foster a generation of decision-makers, developers, and leaders who are mindful of the societal consequences of their actions and decisions.

12.5.4. *Moving Towards Responsible Innovation*

While the potential for emerging technologies to drive societal progress is vast, it is important to recognize that technology is neither inherently good nor bad; its value depends on how it is developed, implemented, and governed. Responsible innovation is the key to ensuring that technology serves the common good and contributes positively to society. This requires a comprehensive approach, one that balances technological advancement with ethical considerations, societal needs, and the principles of justice and fairness.

To achieve responsible innovation, decision-makers must prioritize ethics in all stages of technology development, from conception and design to implementation and post-deployment monitoring. This includes engaging with ethicists, policymakers, and affected communities early in the development process to anticipate potential risks and challenges. It also requires the establishment of robust governance frameworks that promote accountability, transparency, and inclusivity, ensuring that technology is used in ways that enhance human well-being and societal progress.

Ultimately, as we continue to witness the rapid advancement of emerging technologies, the role of decision-makers will become even more critical. By embracing ethical governance, prioritizing inclusivity and equity, and fostering responsible innovation, we can harness the potential of these technologies to create a more just, equitable, and sustainable world. In this rapidly evolving landscape, decision-makers must remain proactive, thoughtful, and committed to ensuring that technology is used to serve the common good, safeguard individual rights, and promote a brighter future for all.

References

Bolukbasi, T., Chang, K. W., Zou, J. Y., Saligrama, V., & Kalai, A. T. (2016). Man is to computer programmer as woman is to homemaker? Debiasing word embeddings. *Advances in Neural Information Processing Systems*, 29, 4349–4357.

Brynjolfsson, E., & McAfee, A. (2017). *The Second Machine Age*. W.W. Norton & Company.

Buolamwini, J., & Gebru, T. (2018). Gender shades: Intersectional accuracy disparities in commercial gender classification. *Proceedings of the Conference on Fairness, Accountability, and Transparency*, 81–91.

Floridi, L., & Cowls, J. (2019). "A unified framework of five principles for AI in society." *Harvard Data Science Review*.

Hoffman, B., Kline, R., & Crocker, J. (2020). AI and Ethics: Balancing Technological Innovation and Ethical Considerations. *Journal of Technology and Ethics*, 15(2), 45–62.

Hoffman, S., Novak, T., & Peralta, M. (2020). Addressing digital inequalities: Strategies and implications. *Journal of Digital Policy and Governance*, 2(1), 14–28.

Intel Corporation. (2021). She Will Connect: Transforming lives through digital literacy. Intel Reports. Retrieved from Intel.com.

International Telecommunication Union (ITU). (2022). Bridging the gender digital divide: A report on gender inclusion in technology. Retrieved from ITU.org.

Kattel, R., & Mergel, I. (2020). Estonia's digital transformation: Lessons for policy makers. *Public Management Review*, 22(6), 961–979.

Mittelstadt, B. D., Allo, P., Taddeo, M., Wachter, S., & Floridi, L. (2016). The ethics of algorithms: Mapping the debate. *Big Data & Society*, 3(2), 1–21.

Partnership on AI. (2020). "Annual Report." *Partnership on AI*.

Qudrat-Ullah, H. (2014). *Better Decision Making in Complex, Dynamic Tasks*. New York, USA: Springer.

Qudrat-Ullah, H. (2020). Exploring the dynamics of renewable energy and sustainable development in Africa. Springer Nature.

Qudrat-Ullah, H. (2020). Improving human performance in dynamic tasks with debriefing-based interactive learning environments: An empirical investigation. *International Journal of Information Technology and Decision Making*, 19(4), 1065–1089.

Qudrat-Ullah, H., Spector, M., & Davidson, I. P. (Eds.). (2008). *Complex Decision Making: Theory and Practice*. New York, USA: Springer.

Raman, S., Ghosh, R., & Banerjee, A. (2020). Bridging the cultural gap in digital payments adoption. *Journal of Technology Adoption Research*, 15(2), 67–84.

Smith, J. A., Johnson, B. C., & Davis, E. F. (2022). *Climate Resilience: Dynamics, Technology, and Governance*. New York, USA: Palgrave Macmillan.

UNESCO. (2021). "Recommendation on the Ethics of Artificial Intelligence."

World Bank. (2023). Bridging the digital divide: Internet accessibility initiatives in developing nations. World Development Reports. Retrieved from WorldBank.org.

Zetzsche, D. A., Buckley, R. P., Arner, D. W., & Barberis, J. N. (2018). Regulating a revolution: From regulatory sandboxes to smart regulation. *Fordham Journal of Corporate & Financial Law*, 23(1), 31–103.

Chapter 13

Strategic Foresight and Scenario Planning

Abstract

Chapter 13 delves into the significance of strategic foresight and scenario planning for dynamic decision-making amid emerging technologies. It emphasizes how these methodologies enhance organizational resilience by allowing decision-makers to anticipate and prepare for diverse future scenarios. The chapter explores the role of foresight in identifying potential risks and opportunities, while scenario planning helps in crafting adaptable strategies. It further discusses the dynamic nature of resilience and the importance of continuous learning and adaptation in response to rapid technological changes. The chapter concludes by highlighting the value of these practices in navigating uncertainty and achieving long-term success.

Keywords: Resilience; Scenario Planning; Strategic Foresight' Adaptation; Transformation; Agility; Uncertainty; Disruptions; Dynamic Framework; Technological Innovations; External Factors; Continuous Learning; Risk Management; Organizational Culture

13.0. Introduction

In an era where the pace of technological change, global interconnectedness, and environmental shifts are evolving at unprecedented rates, organizations face increasingly complex challenges that require decision-makers to adopt innovative, flexible, and adaptive strategies. The future, more than ever, is marked by unpredictability, making the need for foresight and strategic planning crucial. The rapid development of disruptive technologies — such as artificial intelligence (AI), machine learning (ML), blockchain, and Internet of Things (IoT) — has created both immense opportunities and significant risks. In this environment, organizations can no longer rely solely on traditional strategic planning processes that are linear or based on historical data alone. The complexity of modern-day challenges demands a more dynamic, proactive approach to decision-making.

Strategic foresight and scenario planning emerge as essential tools for organizations seeking to anticipate and navigate these uncertainties. Foresight, which involves systematically looking ahead to understand potential future developments, equips decision-makers with the insights necessary to identify risks, opportunities, and emerging trends. Scenario planning, a key component of foresight, helps organizations envision multiple possible futures, enabling them to prepare for different eventualities and to develop strategies that are robust and adaptable. By integrating these tools into their strategic frameworks, organizations can build resilience — giving them the ability to withstand shocks, adapt to change, and emerge stronger in the face of adversity (Hodgkinson & Healey, 2011).

The increasing prevalence of AI, ML, and other emerging technologies not only alters the competitive landscape but also raises new ethical, economic, and social considerations. As industries are transformed by automation, digitalization, and connectivity, organizations must be able to respond swiftly and effectively to the challenges that arise from these technological shifts. With foresight and scenario planning, organizations can better understand the implications of these technologies on their operations, workforce, and overall business models. This enables them to craft strategies that are not only forward-thinking but also resilient, ensuring their long-term success in a rapidly changing environment (Schoemaker, 1995).

In this chapter, we explore the critical role of strategic foresight in decision-making, emphasizing its ability to enhance organizational resilience. We will discuss how foresight and scenario planning can be leveraged to build robust strategies, identify emerging risks, and seize new opportunities. The following sections will examine the dynamic nature of resilience, highlighting how continuous learning and adaptation are key to responding effectively to technological change. We will also explore how these methodologies enable organizations to develop adaptable strategies that ensure long-term success, regardless of the challenges posed by the future.

13.0.1. *The Complexity of Today's Environment*

The pace of technological advancements and the growing interconnectedness of the global economy have created an environment characterized by volatility, uncertainty, complexity, and ambiguity — often referred to as a VUCA environment. In such an environment, traditional decision-making processes that rely on static assumptions and linear projections are insufficient. Organizations must be prepared for a range of possible futures, as the rate of change and the emergence of new risks and opportunities make it difficult to predict which direction the world will take.

The complexity of today's environment is compounded by multiple factors, including geopolitical tensions, environmental concerns, social movements, and the rise of new technologies. For instance, technological advancements such as AI and automation have the potential to disrupt entire industries, change the nature of work, and shift societal expectations. Meanwhile, climate change and environmental degradation present long-term risks that may alter supply chains, regulatory landscapes, and public sentiment. To navigate this uncertainty, organizations must develop the capacity for long-term thinking and strategic foresight.

Strategic foresight involves understanding the broader forces shaping the future and developing strategies that are flexible and adaptive to these changing conditions. By considering various potential futures and understanding the drivers of change, organizations can make informed decisions and proactively position themselves to succeed in a range of possible scenarios. This foresight also enables organizations to identify opportunities for innovation and growth, allowing them to stay ahead of the curve and respond effectively to disruptions (Schoemaker, 1995).

13.0.2. *The Growing Importance of Foresight in the Age of Disruption*

In today's rapidly evolving technological landscape, organizations that fail to adopt foresight as a core component of their strategy risk being left behind. The rapid development and deployment of disruptive technologies — such as AI, ML, and blockchain — are transforming industries, creating new competitive dynamics, and introducing new business models. For example, AI is enabling companies to streamline operations, enhance decision-making, and develop innovative products and services. At the same time, it also raises ethical and social concerns related to data privacy, job displacement, and algorithmic bias. Similarly, blockchain technology is revolutionizing industries like finance and supply chain management by providing secure, decentralized systems for transactions and data storage.

As these technologies continue to evolve, organizations must be able to anticipate their potential impact on their operations, workforce, and broader industry landscape. Foresight allows decision-makers to understand the implications of these technologies on their business models and develop strategies that mitigate risks while capitalizing on new opportunities. Scenario planning further complements foresight by enabling organizations to envision different future scenarios based on varying assumptions about technological advancements, market trends, and external disruptions (Ringland, 2010).

For example, in the automotive industry, the development of electric vehicles (EVs) and autonomous driving technologies is reshaping the market. By using scenario planning, companies can assess a range of possible futures, such as the widespread adoption of EVs or the development of hybrid technologies, and prepare strategies for each scenario. This ensures that organizations are not only prepared for potential disruptions but are also in a position to drive innovation and lead in their industry.

13.0.3. *Foresight and Scenario Planning for Building Organizational Resilience*

Organizational resilience refers to the ability of an organization to withstand and recover from external shocks and disruptions. In today's rapidly changing environment, resilience is no longer about simply bouncing back from adversity; it is about the ability to adapt, innovate, and evolve in response to emerging challenges. Foresight and scenario planning are critical tools in building this resilience.

Through foresight, organizations can identify potential risks and disruptions before they occur, allowing them to take proactive measures to mitigate the impact of these events. By incorporating scenario planning into their strategic frameworks, organizations can explore different potential futures and develop adaptable strategies that are not only robust but also flexible enough to respond to unforeseen challenges.

For example, in the context of the COVID-19 pandemic, organizations that had integrated foresight and scenario planning into their strategic decision-making processes were better able to navigate the disruptions caused by the crisis. These organizations had already considered scenarios related to global health crises, allowing them to implement contingency plans quickly and effectively. In contrast, organizations that had not engaged in foresight were often caught off guard and struggled to adapt to the rapidly changing environment.

Resilience is also about continuous learning and adaptation. As new technologies emerge and market dynamics shift, organizations must be able to adjust their strategies in real-time to remain competitive. Foresight and scenario planning provide the framework for this ongoing learning process, ensuring that organizations are constantly revisiting and updating their assumptions and strategies based on new information and insights (Hodgkinson & Healey, 2011).

13.0.4. *The Role of Continuous Learning and Adaptation*

In an environment defined by constant change and uncertainty, organizations must cultivate a culture of continuous learning and adaptation. This requires decision-makers to be open to new ideas, willing to challenge existing assumptions, and prepared to pivot their strategies when necessary. Foresight and scenario planning contribute to this culture by encouraging organizations to think beyond the status quo and consider a wide range of possibilities.

Continuous learning involves not only staying informed about emerging trends and technologies but also being receptive to feedback, experimentation, and failure. Organizations that view failure as an opportunity to learn and improve are more likely to adapt quickly to new challenges and remain resilient in the face of disruption.

Furthermore, continuous adaptation requires flexibility at all levels of the organization, from leadership to operational teams. Organizations must create systems and structures that allow for rapid decision-making, experimentation, and course correction. By integrating foresight and scenario planning into their organizational processes, companies can ensure that they are prepared to navigate uncertainty and capitalize on new opportunities as they arise (Schoemaker, 1995).

13.0.5. *Conclusion: A Proactive Approach to Uncertainty*

As organizations face an increasingly uncertain future, the need for strategic foresight and scenario planning has never been more critical. These methodologies enable decision-makers to anticipate and prepare for the challenges and opportunities that lie ahead. By incorporating foresight into their strategic decision-making processes, organizations can build resilience, adapt to technological change, and position themselves for long-term success.

The dynamic nature of today's business environment requires organizations to adopt a proactive approach to decision-making — one that emphasizes flexibility, innovation, and continuous learning. Through foresight and scenario planning, organizations can develop strategies that are not only robust but also adaptable to the evolving needs of the future. As we move further into the twenty-first century, those organizations that embrace these tools will be better equipped to thrive in an increasingly complex and interconnected world.

13.1. The Importance of Foresight in Dynamic Decision Making

Strategic foresight is a systematic process of exploring possible future developments and preparing for them in advance. In a world characterized by rapid technological advancements, evolving market dynamics, and unpredictable societal shifts, foresight has become an essential tool for decision-makers. It involves scanning the horizon for emerging trends, understanding potential disruptions, and identifying both opportunities and threats before they materialize (Van der Heijden, 2005). Foresight allows organizations to take a proactive rather than reactive approach in shaping the future, which is crucial in environments where decision-making speed and agility are critical. This section explores the importance of foresight in dynamic decision-making, focusing on its role in anticipating changes in technology, market trends, and societal needs, as well as its ability to help organizations craft adaptive and forward-looking strategies.

13.1.1. *Proactive Decision-Making through Foresight*

The key characteristic of strategic foresight is its proactive nature. It enables decision-makers to anticipate potential future developments, rather than waiting for these events to unfold. By integrating foresight into decision-making, organizations can spot emerging trends and disruptions before they occur, allowing them to take strategic actions early. This proactive approach is especially important in industries where technological changes happen rapidly, such as information technology, healthcare, and energy.

For example, in the energy sector, companies that leverage foresight methodologies can anticipate future regulatory shifts regarding renewable energy sources and adapt their strategies to align with these changes (Berdica *et al.*, 2019). Similarly, in the field of AI, companies using foresight techniques can predict advancements in ML algorithms and adjust their product development strategies to incorporate these innovations, maintaining a competitive edge in a highly dynamic environment (Schoemaker, 1995). Without foresight, companies risk being caught off-guard by disruptions, which can result in significant strategic missteps.

13.1.2. *Identifying Emerging Risks and Opportunities*

One of the most valuable aspects of foresight is its ability to identify emerging risks and opportunities before they become apparent to the broader market. This early identification allows organizations to allocate resources effectively, mitigate potential risks, and seize opportunities that others might overlook. Foresight involves not only scanning for trends in technology and market behavior but also understanding broader social, political, and environmental forces that could shape future scenarios.

For instance, the rise of e-commerce platforms has dramatically altered the retail landscape. Traditional brick-and-mortar retailers that failed to anticipate the shift toward online shopping were left behind, while those who used foresight to invest in digital platforms early were able to capitalize on the growing trend (Christensen, 1997). In a similar vein, the COVID-19 pandemic was an unforeseen disruption that required businesses to rapidly adapt their operations. Organizations that had already invested in digital transformation, due to foresight about the increasing importance of remote work and digital services, were better positioned to navigate the crisis (Westerman *et al.*, 2011).

Furthermore, foresight helps in identifying opportunities for innovation. For example, companies that anticipate the growing demand for sustainable products can innovate in the development of environmentally friendly technologies or green supply chain practices, positioning themselves as leaders in the emerging market for sustainability (Ringland, 2010). This enhances their competitive advantage and helps to meet evolving consumer preferences for eco-conscious products and services.

13.1.3. *Foresight as a Tool for Technological Adaptation*

In today's rapidly changing technological landscape, foresight plays a pivotal role in enabling organizations to adapt to and capitalize on new technologies. Technological advancements such as automation, AI, and blockchain are transforming industries, creating new business models, and challenging traditional ways of doing business. The ability to foresee these changes and adjust strategies accordingly can make the difference between success and failure.

For example, in the automotive industry, foresight techniques have allowed companies to predict the rise of EVs and autonomous driving technologies. By recognizing the shifts in consumer preferences and government regulations around environmental sustainability earlier than their competitors, automakers like Tesla and General Motors have made significant investments in electric vehicles, positioning themselves at the forefront of the EV revolution (Ghoshal, 2005). Those who failed to recognize these shifts have found themselves struggling to catch up as demand for traditional gasoline-powered vehicles wanes.

Moreover, in the healthcare industry, foresight enables organizations to identify emerging technologies such as personalized medicine, biotechnology advancements, and digital health platforms. By anticipating these trends, healthcare providers and pharmaceutical companies can adapt their operations, invest in research and development (R&D), and craft strategies that align with future needs. As technological innovations continue to reshape healthcare delivery, organizations that leverage foresight will be better equipped to meet the demands of a rapidly evolving industry.

13.1.4. *Understanding the Broader System: Interdependencies and Cascading Effects*

A key aspect of strategic foresight is its emphasis on understanding the broader system in which an organization operates. Foresight involves recognizing the interdependencies between various factors — technological, economic, social, and environmental — that collectively shape the future. It also considers the potential cascading effects of changes in one part of the system on others, which is essential for making informed and resilient decisions in complex, dynamic environments (Berdica *et al.*, 2019).

For example, the rise of renewable energy technologies has had profound impacts not only on the energy sector but also on industries such as manufacturing, transportation, and real estate. As companies in the energy sector invest in solar and wind power, they are influencing supply chains, technological infrastructure, and even urban planning (Ringland, 2010). Organizations that incorporate this systems perspective into their foresight processes can better anticipate the ripple effects of technological advancements and prepare for the broader changes that may occur in their industry and beyond.

Foresight also helps organizations understand the potential geopolitical, regulatory, and societal changes that could disrupt their business models. For instance, the implementation of carbon taxes or stricter environmental regulations can create new challenges for companies in traditional energy sectors. Those who fail to anticipate these changes may find themselves exposed to regulatory risks and penalties, while those who prepare in advance can develop strategies to mitigate these risks and take advantage of the incentives for clean technologies (Westerman *et al.*, 2011).

13.1.5. *Enhancing Long-Term Strategic Planning*

Foresight plays a crucial role in enhancing long-term strategic planning by providing organizations with a framework for evaluating potential scenarios and their implications. Strategic foresight allows organizations to move beyond short-term operational concerns and think critically about their long-term objectives. It enables organizations to set clear goals, define strategic priorities, and allocate resources in ways that align with anticipated future developments.

By providing decision-makers with insights into future trends, foresight helps organizations develop more informed and resilient strategic plans. For example, companies in the financial sector can use foresight to anticipate changes in global financial regulations, shifts in consumer behavior, and advancements in fintech. This enables them to craft strategies that address these future developments while positioning themselves to capitalize on emerging opportunities (Schoemaker, 1995). As such, foresight helps organizations to ensure their strategic plans are adaptable and aligned with evolving circumstances.

In addition, foresight supports the alignment of organizational goals with external trends and market dynamics, enabling companies to position themselves as leaders in their industries. By understanding potential future developments, organizations can prioritize investment in innovation and capability-building that will enhance their long-term competitiveness. This allows organizations to achieve sustainable growth even in an environment of uncertainty and change (Van der Heijden, 2005).

13.1.6. *Mitigating the Risk of Disruption*

One of the greatest advantages of foresight is its ability to help organizations mitigate the risk of disruption. As technological innovations and market shifts continue to accelerate, industries are facing constant disruption from new entrants, business models, and technologies. Organizations that fail to anticipate these changes risk being left behind, while those that embrace foresight can build strategies that help them adapt to these disruptions before they cause significant harm.

For example, in the media and entertainment industry, the rise of streaming services like Netflix, Spotify, and YouTube has disrupted traditional television and radio models. Companies that used foresight to recognize the growing importance of digital content delivery were able to pivot their business models and thrive in the new digital landscape. Meanwhile, traditional media companies that failed to anticipate this shift have struggled to maintain their market share (Christensen, 1997).

Foresight helps organizations identify the early warning signals of disruption and take action to mitigate potential risks. This can include investing in new technologies, diversifying revenue streams, or developing strategic partnerships with innovative startups. By staying ahead of the curve, organizations can protect themselves from the negative effects of disruption and capitalize on the opportunities that new technologies and business models present.

In conclusion, the importance of foresight in dynamic decision-making cannot be overstated. Strategic foresight empowers organizations to anticipate changes in technology, market trends, and societal needs, allowing them to take proactive measures that ensure long-term success. By providing valuable insights into emerging risks and opportunities, foresight helps organizations craft adaptive strategies, improve their resilience, and navigate uncertainty with confidence. In an era of rapid technological change, foresight is an essential tool for decision-makers who seek to maintain their competitive advantage and ensure sustainable growth in a complex and unpredictable world. Table 13.1 highlights how foresight allows organizations to anticipate changes, spot emerging trends, mitigate risks, and build adaptive strategies, ensuring long-term success in rapidly changing environments.

Table 13.1. Key Features of The Importance of Foresight in Dynamic Decision-Making

Key Feature	Insight/Key Lesson
Proactive Decision-Making	Foresight enables organizations to anticipate future developments and act early, ensuring proactive, rather than reactive, decision-making. This is essential in industries with rapid technological changes, such as IT, healthcare, and energy (Schoemaker, 1995; Berdica *et al.*, 2019).
Scanning for Emerging Trends	Foresight helps organizations identify emerging trends, market shifts, and technological advancements that could disrupt business models. This early identification allows for adaptive planning.
Anticipating Technological Disruptions	By anticipating technological advancements, such as AI and ML, organizations can adapt strategies to maintain a competitive edge and stay relevant in dynamic industries (Schoemaker, 1995).
Adapting to Market and Societal Changes	Foresight helps organizations respond to shifts in societal needs, regulations, and consumer behavior, particularly in industries like energy, healthcare, and consumer goods. This adaptability is key to long-term success.
Shaping Adaptive Strategies	Organizations using foresight can develop flexible, forward-looking strategies that can be adjusted as new information and circumstances arise, allowing for sustainable growth in uncertain environments.
Mitigating Risks	Foresight allows decision-makers to foresee potential risks and disruptions, enabling them to take proactive steps to mitigate adverse impacts. Early risk identification supports strategic resilience (Van der Heijden, 2005).
Enhancing Organizational Agility	By using foresight, organizations can build agility into their operations, ensuring they can pivot quickly in response to unforeseen changes. This is especially crucial in volatile, high-tech sectors.
Gaining Competitive Advantage	Foresight provides a competitive edge by allowing organizations to act on future opportunities and challenges before competitors, maintaining leadership in fast-evolving markets.

13.2. Scenario Planning for Uncertain Futures

While strategic foresight helps organizations identify emerging trends and potential futures, scenario planning provides a more structured approach for exploring multiple plausible outcomes and developing responsive strategies. Scenario planning goes beyond predicting a single future and instead focuses on preparing for a range of possibilities that could emerge based on current trends, uncertainties, and external factors. It allows organizations to test the robustness of their strategies under different conditions, enabling them to make informed decisions and navigate uncertainty more effectively.

The core principle behind scenario planning is that the future is inherently uncertain and shaped by multiple factors. As such, scenario planning is about exploring the future through multiple lenses, considering different variables, and assessing how different scenarios might impact the organization. This section will delve into the various aspects of scenario planning, its significance in dynamic decision-making, and its application in industries facing high levels of uncertainty, such as energy, technology, and geopolitics.

13.2.1. *Understanding the Role of Scenario Planning*

Scenario planning is a strategic tool that organizations use to anticipate a range of possible futures rather than relying on a single forecast. Unlike forecasting, which focuses on predicting a single outcome based on historical data and trends, scenario planning acknowledges that the future is shaped by unpredictable events and complex interactions that cannot always be captured through conventional models. The goal is not to predict specific outcomes but to prepare for a variety of potential situations that may emerge in the future (Schoemaker, 1995).

By developing different scenarios, decision-makers can better understand the key drivers of change in their environments and the possible implications of those drivers. Scenario planning forces organizations to consider a broad range of variables — including technological advancements, regulatory changes, economic shifts, and social trends — thus broadening the scope of decision-making. The exercise allows for the identification of weak signals that might otherwise be overlooked and highlights the uncertainties that may shape future outcomes.

For example, in the context of the global food supply chain, scenario planning has been used to explore the potential impacts of climate change, geopolitical instability, and technological innovations such as genetically modified crops. By analyzing the outcomes of different scenarios, companies can make more resilient decisions regarding supply chain management, production strategies, and investment priorities (Chermack, 2011).

13.2.2. *The Scenario Planning Process: Steps and Methodology*

The process of scenario planning typically involves several key steps, each of which contributes to a more comprehensive understanding of possible future scenarios. These steps allow organizations to move beyond conventional forecasting and develop flexible strategies for navigating uncertainty. The key steps in scenario planning include:

1. **Identifying the Focus Area and Key Drivers of Change**: The first step in scenario planning is to identify the specific focus area, which could be a business decision, a market trend, or an industry challenge. This is followed by a thorough analysis of the key drivers of change that are most likely to influence future outcomes. These drivers can be internal factors, such as technological advancements or organizational culture, or external factors, such as political shifts, economic trends, or environmental changes (Van der Heijden, 2005).
2. **Developing Assumptions and Uncertainties**: Once the key drivers have been identified, decision-makers must develop assumptions about how these drivers will evolve in the future. These assumptions are based on existing data, expert opinions, and ongoing trends. However, because uncertainty is inherent in scenario planning, it is important to also consider the potential risks and unknowns that may affect the key drivers (Schoemaker, 1995). These uncertainties are captured in the development of different scenarios that reflect varying degrees of change and potential outcomes.

3. **Constructing Scenarios**: In this phase, decision-makers create multiple scenarios that reflect different combinations of assumptions and uncertainties. These scenarios should be plausible, challenging, and divergent, meaning that they explore different, potentially conflicting outcomes. By constructing contrasting scenarios, organizations can explore a wider range of possibilities and test the robustness of their strategies under different conditions (Chermack, 2011).
4. **Analyzing the Scenarios and Implications**: Once the scenarios are developed, it is essential to assess the potential implications of each scenario for the organization. This involves evaluating the strategic opportunities, risks, and challenges associated with each scenario and identifying potential action plans for responding to them. The analysis also includes considering the potential interactions between different scenarios and how they might affect the organization's broader strategic objectives (Berdica *et al.*, 2019).
5. **Developing Action Plans and Contingency Strategies**: The final step in scenario planning is to develop action plans and contingency strategies for each scenario. These strategies should focus on enhancing the organization's flexibility and adaptability, ensuring that it is prepared for a range of possible futures. By considering various outcomes, scenario planning helps organizations identify strategic priorities, resource allocation needs, and risk management tactics that are robust and adaptable (Van der Heijden, 2005).

In conclusion, the scenario planning process provides organizations with a structured approach to navigate uncertainty by examining multiple potential futures. Through a series of steps — identifying key drivers, developing assumptions, constructing diverse scenarios, analyzing their implications, and creating adaptable action plans — scenario planning helps decision-makers understand the broad range of factors that could shape future outcomes. By preparing for various possibilities, organizations can enhance their resilience, ensure strategic flexibility, and make informed decisions that align with long-term objectives, thus improving their ability to respond to dynamic and unpredictable environments.

13.2.3. *Scenario Planning for Technological Disruption*

In industries where technological disruption is a significant driver of change, scenario planning plays an especially critical role. The rapid pace of technological innovation creates uncertainty regarding future market demands, business models, and regulatory landscapes. Organizations that rely solely on traditional forecasting methods may fail to account for the transformative impact of emerging technologies. Scenario planning helps bridge this gap by considering a wider range of technological possibilities and their potential effects on the business environment.

For instance, in the energy sector, companies have used scenario planning to explore the impact of renewable energy technologies, changes in government policies related to carbon emissions, and advancements in energy storage systems. By analyzing different scenarios, energy companies can assess the potential risks of relying on traditional fossil fuels versus embracing renewable energy sources, and adjust their investment strategies accordingly (Chermack, 2011).

In the technology sector, scenario planning helps organizations anticipate the impact of disruptive innovations such as AI, blockchain, and quantum computing. By constructing scenarios that consider the accelerated adoption of these technologies, companies can identify potential business opportunities and threats. For example, in the case of AI, companies can explore scenarios where AI adoption leads to increased automation in industries like manufacturing, healthcare, and logistics, and plan their strategies to capitalize on these developments (Westerman *et al.*, 2011).

13.2.4. *Managing Geopolitical and Economic Uncertainty through Scenario Planning*

Another domain where scenario planning proves invaluable is in managing geopolitical and economic uncertainty. Global events such as trade wars, regulatory changes, and political shifts can create significant disruptions in international markets. By using scenario planning, organizations can assess the potential effects of such events and create flexible strategies that minimize risks and maximize opportunities.

For example, companies operating in the oil and gas industry must constantly navigate geopolitical tensions, fluctuating commodity prices, and evolving environmental regulations. Scenario planning allows them to model different geopolitical scenarios, such as changes in oil supply due to conflicts in the Middle East or the impact of new climate policies on their operations. By understanding how these events could affect their supply chains, profitability, and market positioning, companies can devise contingency plans that protect their long-term interests (Van der Heijden, 2005).

Scenario planning is also crucial for businesses that rely on global supply chains. The COVID-19 pandemic, for instance, exposed the vulnerabilities of many organizations' supply chains, leading to delays, shortages, and increased costs. Scenario planning would have helped organizations anticipate the potential disruptions of a global health crisis and develop contingency strategies to mitigate these risks, such as diversifying supply sources or investing in digital supply chain technologies (Schoemaker, 1995).

13.2.5. *Enhancing Organizational Agility and Resilience*

One of the most significant benefits of scenario planning is its ability to enhance organizational agility and resilience. In a world characterized by volatility and uncertainty, organizations must be able to adapt quickly to changing circumstances. Scenario planning equips decision-makers with the tools to assess potential risks and uncertainties in advance, enabling them to make decisions that enhance their ability to respond to unexpected events.

By developing and analyzing multiple scenarios, organizations can build a portfolio of strategic options that they can deploy when needed. This allows organizations to maintain flexibility in their decision-making and avoid being locked into a single course of action. For instance, in the face of an economic downturn, organizations that have used scenario planning may have already developed cost-cutting strategies, diversification plans, or partnerships that they can implement quickly to maintain stability (Chermack, 2011).

Moreover, scenario planning encourages long-term thinking, which is essential for building organizational resilience. By focusing on possible future challenges and disruptions, scenario planning helps organizations develop a deeper understanding of the external forces that shape their success. This understanding enables organizations to create more adaptive business models, improve their risk management practices, and strengthen their capacity to thrive in uncertain environments (Westerman *et al.*, 2011).

13.2.6. *Conclusion: The Power of Scenario Planning in Dynamic Decision Making*

In conclusion, scenario planning is a powerful tool for managing uncertainty and developing strategies that are resilient in the face of change. By considering multiple plausible futures, organizations can prepare for a wide range of potential outcomes and make more informed decisions that enhance their long-term success. In industries that face technological disruption, geopolitical risks, and economic uncertainty, scenario planning provides a systematic approach for analyzing potential risks, identifying opportunities, and improving strategic flexibility. In an increasingly complex and unpredictable world, scenario planning is an indispensable part of dynamic decision-making that enables organizations to navigate uncertainty with confidence.

Table 13.2 provides a summary of the key features and insights of scenario planning for uncertain futures. This table highlights the importance of exploring multiple potential futures, understanding key drivers of change, managing technological disruptions, and enhancing organizational agility and resilience through flexible and well-prepared strategies.

Table 13.2. Key Features of Scenario Planning for Uncertain Futures

Key Feature	Insight/Key Lesson
Understanding Multiple Futures	Scenario planning helps organizations explore a range of plausible futures, rather than relying on a single prediction, enabling them to prepare for various outcomes (Schoemaker, 1995).
Key Drivers of Change	Identifying and analyzing key drivers, both internal and external, allows organizations to assess the factors that could shape their future and prepare adaptable strategies (Van der Heijden, 2005).
Incorporating Assumptions and Uncertainties	The process includes developing assumptions about future changes while acknowledging the inherent uncertainties, ensuring strategies remain flexible and responsive to various possibilities (Schoemaker, 1995).
Constructing Divergent Scenarios	Creating contrasting scenarios enables decision-makers to test strategies against a range of divergent outcomes, ensuring robustness under different conditions (Chermack, 2011).
Analyzing Implications and Interactions	Analyzing the outcomes of different scenarios helps decision-makers identify potential risks and opportunities, and understand the implications for strategic goals (Berdica *et al.*, 2019).
Developing Contingency Plans	Scenario planning facilitates the creation of contingency strategies that enhance organizational resilience, enabling businesses to pivot quickly when unexpected events occur (Van der Heijden, 2005).
Technological Disruption Management	In sectors like energy and technology, scenario planning helps anticipate the impact of emerging technologies, such as AI and renewable energy, allowing organizations to adjust investment and development strategies (Chermack, 2011; Westerman *et al.*, 2011).
Managing Geopolitical and Economic Uncertainty	Scenario planning enables organizations to explore the impact of geopolitical tensions, trade wars, and economic shifts, helping them craft strategies to minimize risk and seize opportunities (Van der Heijden, 2005).

(*Continued*)

Table 13.2. (*Continued*)

Key Feature	Insight/Key Lesson
Enhancing Agility and Resilience	By analyzing different scenarios, organizations can develop a portfolio of strategies to deploy quickly in response to crises, enhancing their adaptability and long-term resilience (Chermack, 2011).
Long-term Strategic Thinking	Scenario planning encourages decision-makers to think long-term, helping organizations develop strategies that are robust, adaptable, and capable of withstanding future disruptions (Westerman *et al.*, 2011).

13.3. Building Resilience through Strategic Planning

Building organizational resilience is crucial for ensuring long-term sustainability and success, particularly in an increasingly volatile, uncertain, complex, and ambiguous world. Resilience refers to an organization's capacity to anticipate, withstand, adapt to, and recover from external shocks or disruptions. For modern organizations, especially those in industries facing technological, economic, or geopolitical turbulence, resilience is not just about surviving disruptions but thriving in them. This section explores how strategic planning, particularly through the lenses of strategic foresight and scenario planning, contributes to resilience by helping organizations prepare for the unexpected, manage risks effectively, and adapt to changes.

Strategic foresight and scenario planning are integral in developing resilience by enabling organizations to identify potential vulnerabilities, anticipate emerging risks and opportunities, and create flexible strategies that allow them to respond to disruptive changes effectively. Given the accelerated pace of technological advancements such as AI, automation, and digitalization, organizations must rethink their strategies to build resilience in a way that empowers them to adapt swiftly to the evolving landscape (Hamel & Välikangas, 2003). This section delves deeper into how strategic foresight and scenario planning facilitate resilience-building, covering the foundational principles, key strategies, and practical applications.

13.3.1. *Defining Resilience in Organizational Contexts*

Resilience, in an organizational context, is the ability to absorb disturbances and adapt to long-term changes, maintaining core functions while also capitalizing on opportunities for growth (Berdica *et al.*, 2019). Organizations that exhibit resilience are not only able to bounce back from crises but also proactively manage risk and use disruptions as opportunities to evolve and innovate. This concept of resilience has evolved from merely "surviving" disruptions to a more proactive approach of "thriving in disruption," which is where strategic foresight and scenario planning become crucial tools.

Resilience goes beyond simply preparing for the worst-case scenario. It is about creating an adaptive culture that anticipates a wide range of potential future states. This includes understanding the internal and external forces that could impact the organization — such as market shifts, regulatory changes, supply chain disruptions, and technological innovations — as well as developing strategies that allow the organization to remain flexible and responsive. Resilience thus becomes a fundamental characteristic that is embedded in the organization's culture, leadership, processes, and systems.

In conclusion, resilience in an organizational context is not just about surviving disruptions but thriving in the face of them. By fostering an adaptive culture that anticipates a variety of potential challenges, organizations can turn disruptions into opportunities for growth and innovation. Strategic foresight and scenario planning are essential tools in this proactive approach, enabling organizations to navigate internal and external changes while remaining flexible and responsive. Resilience, therefore, must be embedded in the organizational culture, leadership, and processes to ensure long-term sustainability and success.

13.3.2. *The Role of Strategic Foresight in Enhancing Resilience*

Strategic foresight is a critical component in resilience-building, as it involves looking beyond the immediate future and considering long-term trends and emerging issues. Foresight allows organizations to explore future possibilities and envision a range of potential scenarios based on current and anticipated developments. By assessing these possibilities, organizations can better understand the external forces shaping their environments and align their strategies accordingly.

For example, in the case of emerging technologies such as AI and automation, strategic foresight allows organizations to assess how these technologies might disrupt their current business models, workforce dynamics, and operational processes. Foresight can help identify early signals of change, such as the automation of routine tasks or the rise of new competitors, allowing organizations to adjust their strategies before these disruptions fully materialize.

Moreover, strategic foresight contributes to resilience by enabling organizations to assess the potential impacts of different technological advancements and market shifts on various areas of their operations. This may involve anticipating changes in customer preferences, shifts in the competitive landscape, or regulatory changes in areas like data privacy and cybersecurity. By integrating foresight into their strategic planning processes, organizations can better manage uncertainty, mitigate risks, and identify new opportunities (Westerman *et al.*, 2011).

In conclusion, strategic foresight plays a vital role in enhancing organizational resilience by enabling businesses to anticipate and prepare for long-term trends and potential disruptions. By considering emerging technologies, shifts in customer preferences, and regulatory changes, organizations can proactively adjust their strategies to remain competitive and adaptive. Foresight helps identify early warning signs, allowing companies to respond to changes before they become critical, thus strengthening their ability to manage uncertainty and seize new opportunities. Integrating foresight into strategic planning ensures that organizations are better equipped to navigate an ever-evolving business landscape.

13.3.3. *The Role of Scenario Planning in Developing Adaptive Strategies*

Scenario planning complements strategic foresight by providing organizations with a structured approach to think through various future scenarios and the potential implications for their strategies. Unlike traditional forecasting, which relies on the assumption that the future will unfold in a predictable way based on current trends, scenario planning embraces the inherent uncertainty of the future and explores a range of divergent possibilities.

Scenario planning is particularly effective in helping organizations prepare for a variety of disruptions, including technological innovations, economic downturns, geopolitical instability, or natural disasters. By developing different scenarios based on varying assumptions about the future, organizations can test the robustness of their strategies and assess how they might fare under different conditions.

For instance, a company operating in the global supply chain may use scenario planning to evaluate how disruptions in one region, such as a trade war or a natural disaster, could affect its operations. Through the creation of different scenarios — such as "business-as-usual," "trade barriers rise," or "supply chain collapse" — the organization can develop contingency strategies that allow it to mitigate risks and respond effectively when a disruption occurs.

Furthermore, scenario planning helps organizations understand the interdependencies between various factors and how they could cascade through different parts of the business. For example, a change in global trade policies could lead to price fluctuations, which might affect supply chains, labor costs, and customer demand. Scenario planning helps organizations account for these complex interdependencies, ensuring that their strategies are resilient and adaptable to changing circumstances (Van der Heijden, 2005).

13.3.4. *Building a Culture of Resilience and Innovation*

Building organizational resilience is not just about having a crisis management plan or a set of contingency strategies in place. It also requires fostering a culture of innovation, adaptability, and continuous learning. Resilient organizations are those that are open to change, able to pivot when necessary, and continuously challenge their assumptions to remain relevant in an evolving environment.

Strategic foresight and scenario planning play a key role in creating this culture. By regularly engaging in foresight and scenario planning exercises, organizations can instill a mindset of proactive adaptation and innovation throughout the organization. This means encouraging leaders and employees alike to think beyond the immediate future and consider the long-term implications of their decisions. In addition, foresight and scenario planning help organizations foster an awareness of emerging trends and disruptions, ensuring that they are not caught off guard by unexpected changes.

Moreover, building resilience involves not only being prepared for external disruptions but also investing in the organization's internal capabilities. This includes upskilling employees, fostering cross-functional collaboration, and developing agile processes that allow the organization to quickly adjust to new information or changing conditions. For example, organizations in industries affected by automation may use foresight to predict the potential job displacements and proactively invest in retraining programs that equip their workforce with the necessary skills for new roles (Berdica *et al.*, 2019).

In conclusion, building a culture of resilience and innovation requires organizations to go beyond crisis management, focusing on adaptability and continuous learning. Strategic foresight and scenario planning are essential tools in this process, helping organizations anticipate future challenges and opportunities. By fostering a culture that embraces change, challenges assumptions, and prioritizes innovation, organizations can remain flexible in the face of disruptions. Additionally, investing in internal capabilities, such as employee upskilling and cross-functional collaboration, strengthens resilience and ensures that organizations are well-prepared for both external and internal changes. This proactive approach to resilience enables organizations to thrive in an ever-changing environment.

13.3.5. *Leveraging Strategic Foresight and Scenario Planning for Long-Term Success*

Organizations that effectively leverage strategic foresight and scenario planning can build a competitive advantage by continuously adapting to changes in the external environment. By integrating foresight into their strategic planning processes, organizations can ensure that they are not only resilient in the face of disruption but also positioned to capitalize on new opportunities as they arise.

For example, companies in the renewable energy sector have used scenario planning to model the future of energy production and consumption, considering factors such as technological advancements in energy storage, shifts in government policies, and changing consumer preferences. By developing and analyzing multiple scenarios, these companies can anticipate the potential impact of these changes and develop strategies that allow them to remain competitive and resilient in a rapidly evolving market.

Similarly, organizations can use scenario planning to explore different future scenarios in their industry or sector, considering the likely outcomes of current trends, such as technological disruption or shifts in consumer behavior. By considering a variety of possible futures, organizations can ensure that they are prepared for any eventuality and have the agility to pivot quickly as the market evolves (Chermack, 2011).

In conclusion, leveraging strategic foresight and scenario planning enables organizations to gain a competitive edge by staying proactive in the face of change. By continuously adapting their strategies to emerging opportunities and risks, organizations can navigate disruptions effectively and position themselves for long-term success. The ability to explore multiple future scenarios allows organizations to be agile and responsive, ensuring they remain resilient and well-prepared for an ever-evolving business landscape. Integrating foresight into strategic planning not only strengthens an organization's resilience but also enhances its capacity to capitalize on future opportunities.

13.3.6. *Continuous Adaptation: The Key to Resilience in a Changing World*

Building organizational resilience is not a one-time effort but a continuous process of learning, adapting, and evolving. As new technologies emerge, markets shift, and societal expectations change, organizations must continuously update their strategic foresight and scenario planning processes to stay ahead of potential disruptions.

This requires fostering a mindset of continuous adaptation, where organizations regularly reassess their strategies, identify emerging risks, and update their forecasts based on the latest information. In this way, strategic foresight and scenario planning become ongoing practices that evolve along with the organization's journey. By making these processes a core part of the organization's strategic planning and decision-making, leaders can ensure that their organizations remain resilient and capable of navigating an increasingly unpredictable future (Hamel & Välikangas, 2003).

In conclusion, continuous adaptation is essential for sustaining organizational resilience in an ever-changing world. By integrating strategic foresight and scenario planning into regular decision-making processes, organizations can stay agile and prepared for emerging risks and disruptions. This ongoing practice enables organizations to evolve alongside external changes, ensuring they remain resilient, innovative, and capable of thriving in an increasingly unpredictable future. Leaders must cultivate a culture of continuous learning and adaptation to successfully navigate the complexities of a rapidly changing environment.

13.3.7. *Conclusion: The Importance of Resilience in an Uncertain Future*

In conclusion, building organizational resilience through strategic planning is essential for thriving in today's dynamic, uncertain, and rapidly changing world. Strategic foresight and scenario planning provide the tools and frameworks necessary for organizations to anticipate risks, adapt to emerging changes, and build the flexibility needed to respond to disruptions effectively. By fostering a culture of resilience, continuous learning, and adaptability, organizations can ensure their long-term success and competitiveness, regardless of how the future unfolds. Resilience is not merely about surviving but about turning disruptions into opportunities for innovation and growth. Table 13.3 summarizes the essential aspects of building resilience through strategic planning and offers actionable insights for decision-makers to create adaptive, forward-thinking strategies.

Table 13.3. Building Resilience through Strategic Planning — Key Features and Practical Insights

Key Feature	**Practical Insights and Key Lessons for Decision Makers**
Defining Organizational Resilience	Resilience is about thriving, not just surviving. Foster a culture that embraces adaptability and innovation to navigate disruptions.
Strategic Foresight for Resilience	Use foresight to anticipate long-term trends and emerging risks. Evaluate the impact of technological advancements and market shifts.
Scenario Planning for Adaptive Strategies	Create diverse scenarios to prepare for a range of disruptions. Develop contingency plans that are adaptable to different future conditions.
Building a Culture of Resilience & Innovation	Encourage continuous learning and proactive adaptation. Invest in employee upskilling and foster cross-functional collaboration.
Leveraging Foresight for Long-Term Success	Integrate foresight into strategic planning to capitalize on opportunities. Stay ahead of potential disruptions to maintain a competitive advantage.
Continuous Adaptation	Resilience is a continuous process. Regularly reassess strategies and update forecasts to keep pace with evolving trends and risks.

13.4. Dynamic View of Resilience and Scenario Planning for Uncertain Futures

The concept of resilience has evolved significantly in recent years. Traditionally, resilience was viewed as the ability of an organization to "bounce back" from a single disruption or crisis. However, in the face of the accelerating pace of technological advancements, global interdependencies, and shifting market conditions, this view of resilience is no longer sufficient. Instead, resilience today is seen as a dynamic and continuous process of learning, adaptation, and transformation (Hamel & Välikangas, 2003). Organizations must now not only prepare for potential disruptions but also anticipate, adapt, and transform in response to an ongoing stream of challenges and opportunities. Scenario planning plays a pivotal role in enabling organizations to build such resilience, providing them with the tools to think systematically about the future and prepare for multiple, evolving outcomes.

As emerging technologies such as AI, blockchain, and IoT continue to reshape industries, decision-makers face new and unprecedented challenges. In an era marked by rapid technological advancements and volatile global conditions, organizations must build resilience through strategies that are flexible, adaptable, and capable of responding to both known and unforeseen disruptions. Scenario planning allows organizations to embrace uncertainty by developing strategies that are not fixed but instead evolve in response to new information and changing circumstances. This section delves into the dynamic nature of resilience and explores how scenario planning serves as a critical tool in preparing organizations for uncertain futures.

13.4.1. *Shifting Paradigms: From Recovery to Transformation*

In the past, resilience was defined as the ability to recover from shocks or disruptions. This was particularly true in industries where disruption was perceived as a temporary event, and organizations could return to a status quo after the immediate effects subsided. However, as disruptions become more frequent and complex, it has become clear that simply bouncing back is no longer sufficient for long-term success. The future is uncertain, and organizations must be prepared not only to recover but to continuously adapt, evolve, and transform their operations, business models, and strategies.

This shift from recovery to transformation is reflected in the changing dynamics of industries, driven largely by technological advancements. For instance, the rise of automation and AI is fundamentally changing the way businesses operate, often rendering traditional models obsolete. Organizations that once thrived on a predictable, stable environment now must navigate constant changes in technology, customer preferences, and competitive pressures. The ability to "bounce forward" instead of "bouncing back" is what differentiates resilient organizations from those that may fail to adapt.

Resilience in this context means that organizations must be proactive, continuously scanning the horizon for emerging trends and potential disruptions, and adapting their strategies accordingly. This dynamic view of resilience aligns with the concept of "anticipatory resilience" (Meyer *et al.*, 2017), which emphasizes the ability to anticipate potential disruptions, integrate foresight into strategic planning, and develop proactive responses to minimize risks while capitalizing on new opportunities.

13.4.2. *The Role of Scenario Planning in a Dynamic Resilience Framework*

Scenario planning is one of the most effective tools organizations can use to build dynamic resilience in the face of uncertainty. Unlike traditional forecasting, which attempts to predict the future based on past data and trends, scenario planning recognizes that the future is inherently uncertain and explores a range of possible outcomes. Scenario planning provides organizations with a framework for identifying multiple potential futures, each with its own risks, opportunities, and challenges, thus allowing decision-makers to develop strategies that are flexible and adaptive to change.

One of the key strengths of scenario planning is its ability to incorporate a variety of external factors — such as technological innovations, regulatory changes, shifts in consumer behavior, and geopolitical risks — into its analysis. For example, organizations in the financial services sector can use scenario planning to assess how emerging technologies like blockchain could disrupt traditional banking systems. By developing different scenarios around the rise of decentralized finance or the introduction of new financial regulations, these organizations can anticipate potential disruptions and create strategies that allow them to adapt to whatever the future holds.

Moreover, scenario planning is not a one-time exercise but an ongoing process that requires continuous updates and revisions. As new information becomes available and the external environment evolves, organizations must revisit their scenarios and adjust their strategies accordingly. This iterative process is essential in a rapidly changing world where the pace of technological innovation and market disruption continues to accelerate. Regularly revisiting scenarios ensures that organizations remain agile and can adjust their strategies in response to new risks or opportunities, maintaining their resilience in an uncertain future (Ringland, 2010).

In conclusion, scenario planning is a crucial tool for organizations seeking to build dynamic resilience in an uncertain world. By considering multiple potential futures and incorporating various external factors, organizations can develop flexible strategies that adapt to shifting conditions. Rather than relying on static forecasts, scenario planning encourages continuous evaluation and revision, ensuring that organizations stay agile and prepared for emerging risks and opportunities. This ongoing process fosters long-term resilience, enabling organizations to navigate uncertainty with confidence and adaptability.

13.4.3. *Building Agility: Adapting Strategies to Changing Circumstances*

One of the hallmarks of a resilient organization is its ability to remain agile and adaptable in the face of change. This requires not only having a set of predefined contingency plans but also fostering a culture that encourages flexibility, creativity, and quick decision-making. Scenario planning plays a crucial role in helping organizations build this agility by providing a structured approach to thinking about the future and preparing for various possible outcomes.

Agility in scenario planning means that organizations are not locked into a single vision of the future. Instead, they remain open to a wide range of possibilities and are ready to pivot when new information arises. For instance, a company may develop a scenario where a new regulatory policy significantly impacts its operations. If such a scenario materializes, the company must be prepared to quickly shift its strategy to comply with the new policy while minimizing negative impacts on its business. Similarly, if a disruptive technology emerges, organizations that have used scenario planning can pivot more rapidly, reconfiguring their business models to take advantage of new technologies or mitigate associated risks.

Additionally, scenario planning fosters a mindset of resilience by encouraging organizations to think about long-term implications rather than focusing solely on short-term risks. By considering different scenarios over extended time horizons, organizations can develop strategies that not only address immediate challenges but also position them for success in the future. This long-term perspective is essential for building resilience, as it allows organizations to anticipate changes before they occur, rather than reacting to them after the fact.

13.4.4. *Collaboration and Knowledge Sharing: A Key Component of Resilience*

In an increasingly complex and interconnected world, resilience is not only about internal capabilities but also about how organizations collaborate and share knowledge with others. The challenges facing organizations today — whether in the form of cybersecurity threats, climate change, or global pandemics — are often too large and complex for any single organization to address alone. As a result, collaboration across industries, sectors, and borders is becoming essential for building collective resilience.

Scenario planning can facilitate collaboration by bringing together diverse stakeholders — such as industry leaders, policymakers, academics, and civil society organizations — to explore a wide range of potential outcomes and develop shared strategies for navigating uncertainty. For example, in addressing global risks such as climate change or cybersecurity, scenario planning can help organizations identify common vulnerabilities and opportunities for joint action. By working together to develop and test different scenarios, stakeholders can better understand the interdependencies and trade-offs involved in managing these complex challenges.

Moreover, scenario planning provides a platform for knowledge sharing, allowing organizations to pool their insights and expertise to develop more robust, well-informed strategies. In the case of a global pandemic, for instance, scenario planning allows public health organizations, governments, and businesses to collaborate in crafting strategies that promote resilience across society. By sharing information about emerging risks and best practices, these stakeholders can work together to mitigate the impact of the crisis and ensure a more resilient response.

13.4.5. *The Importance of Continuous Learning in Building Resilience*

A dynamic view of resilience also emphasizes the importance of continuous learning and adaptation. Resilient organizations are those that are committed to learning from both successes and failures and are able to adapt their strategies based on new insights and experiences. This culture of learning is essential in a world where the pace of technological and market changes is rapid, and new challenges and opportunities are constantly emerging.

Scenario planning supports this learning process by encouraging organizations to engage in regular "what-if" exercises, where different scenarios are explored and tested to uncover new insights. These exercises can help organizations identify potential blind spots, question their assumptions, and consider alternative strategies that may be more effective in responding to emerging challenges. Furthermore, scenario planning encourages organizations to monitor the evolution of key trends and revisit scenarios periodically to ensure that they are still relevant in the context of the changing environment.

By fostering a mindset of continuous learning and scenario testing, organizations can build resilience not only through proactive strategy development but also by ensuring they remain agile and ready to respond to future disruptions with greater knowledge and confidence.

13.4.6. *Conclusion: Preparing for an Uncertain Future through Dynamic Resilience*

The dynamic nature of resilience is central to navigating the challenges of an uncertain future. As organizations face increasingly complex and unpredictable disruptions driven by technological, environmental, and social forces, they must embrace a continuous process of learning, adaptation, and transformation. Scenario planning is a key tool in this process, helping organizations anticipate a wide range of possible futures, develop flexible strategies, and remain agile in the face of change. By fostering collaboration, knowledge sharing, and continuous learning, organizations can build collective resilience and ensure their long-term success, regardless of the disruptions that lie ahead.

Table 13.4 provides a summary of the dynamic view of resilience, emphasizing that organizations must not only prepare for disruption

Table 13.4. Dynamic View of Resilience and Scenario Planning for Uncertain Futures

Key Feature	Practical Insights	Key Lessons for Decision Makers
Shifting Paradigms: From Recovery to Transformation	Resilience now requires continuous adaptation and transformation, not just recovery from crises.	Organizations must evolve their business models and strategies to not just bounce back but to "bounce forward," anticipating and adapting to future disruptions.
The Role of Scenario Planning	Scenario planning helps organizations explore multiple potential futures and prepare for uncertainty.	Decision-makers should integrate scenario planning as a continuous practice to understand risks, opportunities, and evolving outcomes, ensuring strategies remain adaptive.
Building Agility	Flexibility and creativity in decision-making allow organizations to quickly pivot in response to changes.	Organizations should foster a culture of agility by embracing diverse future possibilities and adapting strategies to new information or disruptions swiftly.
Collaboration and Knowledge Sharing	Resilience is enhanced through cross-sector collaboration and shared insights on complex challenges.	Decision-makers must engage in partnerships, utilizing collective knowledge to address global risks and build resilience in an interconnected world.
Continuous Learning and Adaptation	Ongoing learning and revisiting of scenarios allow organizations to refine strategies based on new insights.	Organizations should implement continuous learning mechanisms, testing scenarios and adjusting strategies to remain relevant in the face of technological and market changes.

but also embrace transformation through continuous learning, scenario planning, and adaptability. These strategies help build long-term resilience and ensure organizations are capable of responding to both known and unforeseen future challenges.

13.5. Conclusion

In an era marked by rapid technological advancements, global interconnectivity, and increasing complexity, organizations are faced with the challenge of navigating an uncertain future. Traditional approaches to strategic planning, which often rely on historical data and predictable trends, are no longer sufficient. As new technologies emerge and disrupt existing systems, organizations must be equipped with the tools and frameworks to anticipate change, adapt to uncertainty, and remain resilient in the face of disruptions. This is where strategic foresight and scenario planning come into play.

Strategic foresight and scenario planning are indispensable tools for organizations seeking to understand the potential impacts of emerging technologies, global risks, and market shifts. These methodologies enable decision-makers to think beyond conventional projections and prepare for multiple possible futures, each with its own set of risks, opportunities, and challenges. By integrating foresight and scenario planning into their decision-making processes, organizations can proactively shape their future, rather than merely reacting to change. This proactive approach is essential in building resilience, fostering innovation, and ensuring long-term success in an increasingly uncertain and dynamic world.

This section provides a synthesis of the key insights discussed throughout the chapter, emphasizing the critical role of foresight and scenario planning in navigating uncertainty, building adaptive strategies, and preparing for the future. It also highlights the importance of resilience in today's rapidly changing technological environment and underscores how organizations can leverage these methodologies to drive innovation and transformation.

13.5.1. *The Role of Strategic Foresight in Anticipating the Future*

Strategic foresight is a discipline that enables organizations to look beyond the immediate present and anticipate the future by exploring different possible scenarios. It is not about predicting the future with certainty, but rather about preparing for a range of potential outcomes by considering various factors that could influence the future landscape. By adopting strategic foresight, organizations can identify emerging trends, assess the potential impacts of new technologies, and understand the broader implications of societal, environmental, and economic changes. This enables decision-makers to craft strategies that are flexible and resilient, capable of adapting to both anticipated and unforeseen changes.

For example, in industries such as healthcare, where technological advancements like AI, telemedicine, and genomics are rapidly transforming the way care is delivered, strategic foresight allows organizations to identify the most likely technological trajectories and plan accordingly. By understanding these trends early, organizations can take proactive steps to integrate new technologies into their operations, streamline processes, and improve patient outcomes. Similarly, in industries impacted by climate change, foresight can help organizations assess the long-term environmental risks and prepare for potential disruptions, such as resource scarcity, changing regulations, and shifts in consumer behavior.

Foresight, therefore, serves as a critical tool in helping organizations anticipate and plan for change, ensuring they remain competitive and resilient in the face of emerging risks and opportunities. Through foresight, organizations can reduce uncertainty, improve decision-making, and develop strategies that are not only reactive but also forward-thinking and proactive.

13.5.2. *Scenario Planning: Crafting Adaptive Strategies for Uncertainty*

While strategic foresight provides organizations with insights into potential future trends and developments, scenario planning is the tool that allows organizations to build and test adaptable strategies based on those insights. Scenario planning involves creating a set of diverse, plausible future scenarios — each reflecting a different combination of trends, risks, and uncertainties — and then developing strategies that can respond to each of these scenarios.

The key value of scenario planning lies in its ability to help organizations prepare for the unpredictable. In a world where technological advancements are occurring at an unprecedented rate, and where global challenges such as geopolitical instability, pandemics, and climate change are becoming more frequent, organizations can no longer rely on a single, linear forecast of the future. Scenario planning encourages organizations to think more expansively about the range of possible futures and develop multiple pathways for action.

For example, in the context of emerging technologies like AI and automation, scenario planning can help organizations explore different possible outcomes of these technologies, ranging from highly optimistic scenarios where AI enhances productivity and creates new industries, to more pessimistic scenarios where automation leads to significant job displacement and economic inequality. By developing strategies for both optimistic and pessimistic scenarios, organizations can ensure they are prepared for a variety of potential outcomes, allowing them to respond quickly and effectively to whatever the future holds.

Moreover, scenario planning is a continuous, iterative process. As new information becomes available and the external environment evolves, organizations must regularly revisit and revise their scenarios. This ensures that strategies remain relevant and adaptable to changing circumstances, allowing organizations to stay ahead of potential disruptions and continuously optimize their responses.

13.5.3. *Building Resilience through Adaptability and Innovation*

Resilience is not a static characteristic, but rather a dynamic process that requires continuous learning, adaptation, and innovation. In today's technological landscape, organizations must embrace resilience as a core capability, enabling them to respond effectively to uncertainty, complexity, and disruption. Resilience involves not only the ability to withstand shocks but also the capacity to adapt and transform in response to new challenges and opportunities.

Strategic foresight and scenario planning contribute to resilience by helping organizations anticipate risks and opportunities, identify vulnerabilities, and develop strategies that allow them to adjust and evolve. Through foresight, organizations can prepare for potential technological disruptions, such as the rise of AI, blockchain, or quantum computing, and design strategies that mitigate potential risks while maximizing the benefits of these innovations. Scenario planning, on the other hand, enables organizations to test the robustness of their strategies in different future scenarios, ensuring that they are equipped to handle unforeseen challenges.

However, resilience is not just about avoiding or surviving disruptions — it is also about innovation. Resilient organizations view uncertainty and disruption as opportunities for growth and transformation. By embracing a culture of innovation, organizations can turn potential threats into opportunities, reimagining their business models, operations, and value propositions to better align with changing market conditions and technological advancements.

For example, in industries like energy and transportation, where technological innovations are rapidly transforming the market, organizations that embrace resilience and innovation are better positioned to capitalize on new developments. Companies in these sectors are increasingly exploring sustainable energy solutions, electric vehicles, and digital platforms, leveraging innovation to not only adapt to changing market conditions but also to shape the future of their industries.

13.5.4. *The Importance of Continuous Learning and Flexibility*

Building resilience through strategic foresight and scenario planning requires organizations to cultivate a culture of continuous learning and flexibility. The fast pace of technological change means that organizations must be prepared to learn quickly and adapt their strategies as new information becomes available. This requires leaders and decision-makers to foster an environment where experimentation, innovation, and learning are encouraged, and where organizational structures are flexible enough to respond to change.

A key aspect of continuous learning is the willingness to challenge assumptions, test new ideas, and embrace failure as an opportunity for growth. Resilient organizations are those that view learning as an ongoing process rather than a one-time activity. By continuously refining their strategies based on new insights and lessons learned, organizations can remain agile and responsive to emerging trends, disruptions, and opportunities.

Moreover, organizations must be able to quickly adapt their business models and operations in response to changes in the technological landscape. This requires a high degree of flexibility, both in terms of organizational structure and decision-making processes. Organizations that are rigid in their approach may struggle to adapt to new realities, while those that are flexible and open to changes are better positioned to thrive in an uncertain future.

13.5.5. *Conclusion: Proactive Resilience for Long-Term Success*

In conclusion, the future is increasingly uncertain, and organizations must be prepared to navigate this uncertainty by integrating strategic foresight and scenario planning into their decision-making processes. These methodologies offer organizations the tools to anticipate emerging trends, identify potential risks and opportunities, and develop flexible strategies that can adapt to a wide range of future scenarios. By embracing these tools, organizations can build resilience — allowing them to not only survive disruptions but also thrive in the face of uncertainty.

Strategic foresight and scenario planning enable organizations to shift from a reactive mindset to a proactive one, where they can actively shape their future rather than simply responding to change. Through continuous learning, adaptability, and innovation, organizations can build the resilience needed to withstand and capitalize on technological advancements, market shifts, and global risks. As the world continues to change rapidly, organizations that embrace foresight and scenario planning will be better positioned to lead, innovate, and achieve long-term success in an uncertain and complex future.

References

Berdica, K., Kostić, A., & Djuric, N. (2019). Scenario planning as a tool for managing uncertainty and risk in business strategy. *Journal of Business Research*, 97, 340–350.

Chermack, T. J. (2011). *Scenario Planning in Organizations: A User's Guide*. John Wiley & Sons.

Christensen, C. M. (1997). *The Innovator's Dilemma: When New Technologies Cause Great Firms to Fail*. Harvard Business Press.

Ghoshal, S. (2005). The value of foresight in decision making. *Strategic Management Journal*, 26(9), 933–949.

Hamel, G., & Välikangas, L. (2003). *The Quest for Resilience.* Harvard Business Review, 81(9), 52–63.

Hodgkinson, G. P., & Healey, M. P. (2011). Psychological foundations of dynamic decision making. *Journal of Business Research*, 64(5), 423–430.

Meyer, C. B., Winter, S. G., & Löffler, K. (2017). Anticipatory resilience: Organizational preparedness in an uncertain world. *Journal of Business Continuity and Emergency Planning*, 11(2), 168–184.

Ringland, G. (2010). *Scenario Planning: A Field Guide to the Future.* John Wiley & Sons.

Schoemaker, P. J. (1995). Scenario planning: A tool for strategic thinking. *Sloan Management Review*, 36(2), 25–40.

Van der Heijden, K. (2005). *Scenarios: The Art of Strategic Conversation.* John Wiley & Sons.

Westerman, G., Calméjane, C., Ferraris, P., & Bonnet, D. (2011). Digital transformation: A roadmap for billion-dollar organizations. *MIT Sloan Management Review*, 53(2), 2–8.

Chapter 14

Synthesis and Final Thoughts

Abstract

Chapter 14 synthesizes the book's key insights into emerging technologies and dynamic decision-making. It recaps the transformative impact of technologies such as artificial intelligence (AI), big data, and blockchain on decision processes, emphasizing the need for adaptive frameworks and strategic foresight. The chapter outlines future directions for research, focusing on ethical considerations, technology integration, and sector-specific impacts. It concludes with reflections on the ongoing evolution of decision-making practices and personal insights on navigating these changes. This final chapter serves as a comprehensive summary and a guide for future exploration in the intersection of technology and decision-making.

Keywords: Emerging Technologies; Dynamic Decision-Making; Artificial Intelligence (AI) and Machine Learning (ML); Big Data; Blockchain; Strategic Foresight; Adaptive Frameworks; Ethical Considerations; Technology Integration; Sector-Specific Impacts; Future Research Directions; Technology and Decision Processes; Personal Reflections; Concluding Insights

14.0. Introduction

This chapter serves as a synthesis of the key themes explored throughout the book, offering a comprehensive reflection on the ways in which emerging technologies are influencing dynamic decision-making processes. As we move further into the twenty-first century, the impact of technology on decision-making is becoming increasingly profound, with advances in AI, blockchain, digital platforms, and other technological innovations transforming the landscape of how individuals, organizations, and governments make decisions. From the automation of routine tasks to the introduction of complex, data-driven decision-making frameworks, these technologies are reshaping every aspect of decision-making, from the micro level to the macro level.

The central aim of this chapter is to consolidate the insights derived from previous chapters, weaving together a cohesive narrative that explores the multidimensional roles these technologies play in decision-making contexts. Throughout the book, we have examined the ethical, social, and governance challenges that arise with the adoption of new technologies, as well as the strategies that decision-makers can employ to mitigate risks and maximize benefits. By drawing from real-world case studies, theoretical frameworks, and empirical research, we will highlight the multi-faceted ways in which technologies influence decisions at various levels.

One of the key themes explored in the book is the tension between innovation and responsibility. Emerging technologies offer unprecedented opportunities for improving efficiency, accessibility, and transparency in decision-making. However, they also present new risks, particularly related to privacy, bias, equity, and accountability. In this chapter, we will revisit these challenges and offer insights into how decision-makers can navigate the ethical dilemmas posed by technological advances. We will also emphasize the need for responsible governance frameworks that ensure emerging technologies are deployed in ways that benefit all segments of society, particularly the most marginalized.

Another important focus of the chapter will be the role of inclusivity in technology adoption. While technological advancements hold the promise of creating more efficient, effective, and data-driven decision-making systems, it is critical that these technologies are designed and implemented with an awareness of their potential to either exacerbate or alleviate existing inequalities. The adoption of technologies in diverse and global contexts requires a deep understanding of local needs, values, as well as cultures, and decision-makers must strive to ensure that technology is accessible, inclusive, and equitable. Throughout this chapter, we will offer practical guidance on how to foster inclusivity in technology development, ensuring that technological solutions address the needs of all stakeholders, especially those who are traditionally underrepresented.

The chapter will also explore the intersection of technology and sustainability. Emerging technologies, when deployed thoughtfully, have the potential to drive significant advances in environmental sustainability, social equity, and economic development. However, to realize these benefits, decision-makers must consider the long-term impacts of technology on the environment, society, and future generations. We will reflect on how decision-making processes can be aligned with the United Nations' Sustainable Development Goals (SDGs) to create a more sustainable future. By integrating sustainability principles into technology adoption strategies, decision-makers can not only enhance the effectiveness of technological solutions but also ensure that the benefits of innovation are widely distributed.

Furthermore, this chapter will revisit the importance of transparency and accountability in the implementation of emerging technologies. As technologies become more autonomous and capable of making decisions without human intervention, there is an increasing need for mechanisms that ensure these technologies are operating as intended and in alignment with ethical standards. We will discuss the importance of transparency in algorithmic decision-making, the need for explainable AI (XAI) systems, and the role of human oversight in ensuring accountability. Decision-makers must be equipped with the knowledge and tools to monitor and assess the impact of technological solutions continuously, making necessary adjustments to maintain trust and ethical integrity.

Finally, the chapter will outline practical insights and actionable strategies for decision-makers who are navigating the complexities of technological integration. Drawing from the lessons learned throughout the book, we will present a set of recommendations designed to help decision-makers implement responsible and effective technology adoption strategies. Whether through ethical impact assessments, fostering diverse stakeholder involvement, or aligning decisions with global sustainability goals, these strategies will enable decision-makers to balance the promise of emerging technologies with the need for social responsibility.

In conclusion, this chapter aims to provide a holistic framework for understanding the dynamic relationship between emerging technologies and decision-making. By synthesizing the various insights and principles discussed in previous chapters, it will offer decision-makers a comprehensive toolkit for making informed, balanced, and responsible decisions in an increasingly technological world. As we continue to advance in the era of digital transformation, it is essential that we remain mindful of the ethical, social, and governance implications of these technologies, ensuring they are harnessed in ways that contribute to the common good and the long-term prosperity of society.

14.1. Recap of Key Insights

Throughout this book, we have delved deeply into the transformative power of emerging technologies, including AI, blockchain, big data, and intelligent systems, and their far-reaching effects on decision-making processes across various domains. These technologies are not only reshaping how decisions are made but are also redefining the nature of decision-making itself. One of the core insights from our exploration is the profound shift towards data-driven decision-making. By leveraging vast amounts of real-time data, organizations and individuals can make more informed, accurate, and timely decisions. Big data analytics, coupled with advanced machine learning (ML) algorithms, allows decision-makers to uncover patterns, predict outcomes, and optimize strategies in ways that were once impossible.

Another crucial insight is the increasing importance of adaptive and agile decision-making processes. In a rapidly changing world, where technology evolves at an unprecedented pace, traditional decision-making models that rely on fixed, long-term plans are becoming less effective. The ability to swiftly adapt to new information and to make decisions in dynamic, uncertain environments is now essential. Technologies such as AI and blockchain provide decision-makers with the tools to adjust strategies in real-time, improving responsiveness to emerging challenges and opportunities. This adaptability is particularly important in sectors like healthcare, finance, and logistics, where the stakes are high, and the ability to pivot can make the difference between success and failure.

Moreover, this book has highlighted the critical role of strategic foresight in navigating the uncertainty inherent in technological advancements. The rapid pace of technological innovation introduces new uncertainties that decision-makers must address proactively. Strategic foresight — the ability to anticipate future trends, scenarios, and disruptions — is becoming an indispensable skill for leaders in both the public and private sectors. By using predictive analytics and simulation tools, decision-makers can develop more robust strategies that take into account not only the immediate effects of technology but also its long-term implications. This foresight enables organizations to prepare for potential risks, capitalize on emerging opportunities, and align their strategies with broader societal goals.

The integration of these insights has led to the recognition of the need for dynamic frameworks that are capable of evolving alongside technological advancements. As the technological landscape continues to evolve, so too must the frameworks that guide decision-making. The book has underscored the necessity for decision-makers to adopt flexible, iterative approaches that allow them to continuously assess and refine their strategies. These frameworks must consider the ethical, social, and environmental impacts of technology, ensuring that decisions not only maximize value but also contribute to broader goals such as sustainability and equity.

Furthermore, our discussion has emphasized the interconnectedness of technology and human decision-making. While automation and AI can enhance decision-making processes, human oversight remains crucial to ensuring that decisions align with ethical principles and societal values. The role of humans in the loop — whether through validating AI-driven insights, providing contextual knowledge, or making final judgments — remains central to maintaining accountability and trust in technology.

Lastly, the book has also stressed the importance of inclusivity and equity in technology adoption. Emerging technologies hold the potential to either bridge or widen existing social gaps, depending on how they are designed, implemented, and distributed. Therefore, decision-makers must ensure that these technologies are accessible to all, particularly marginalized and underserved communities. By prioritizing diversity in tech development teams, promoting digital literacy, and ensuring equal access to technological tools, decision-makers can help ensure that technology serves as a force for good in society, benefiting everyone and not just a privileged few.

In conclusion, the key insights presented throughout the book underscore the need for decision-makers to embrace a multifaceted approach to technology adoption. This approach involves integrating data-driven strategies, fostering agility in decision-making, leveraging strategic foresight, and ensuring that decisions are guided by ethical, social, and sustainability considerations. As the influence of emerging technologies continues to expand, decision-makers must adapt to the changing landscape, equipping themselves with the tools and frameworks necessary to navigate an increasingly complex and interconnected world.

14.1.1. *The Dynamic Model of the Integration of Technological Advancements*

Our dynamic model draws on the insights from this book and integrates the technological advancements and their implications. The main elements of our dynamic model are derived from the exploration of emerging technologies, data-driven decision-making, adaptive processes, and strategic foresight, as is shown in Figure 14.1.

- **Key Elements of the Dynamic Framework:**
  1. **Data-Driven Decision-Making (Arrow →)**:
     - This element emphasizes the use of big data, AI, and ML algorithms to inform and guide decisions.
     - It is central to modern decision-making, providing real-time, actionable insights.
     - **Connects to:** Adaptive Decision-Making, Strategic Foresight, and Continuous Improvement.
  2. **Adaptive and Agile Decision-Making (Arrow →)**:
     - This involves the ability to quickly adjust and reconfigure decisions in response to changing conditions and emerging trends.
     - **Connects to:** Data-Driven Decision-Making (enabling informed, real-time decisions) and Strategic Foresight (anticipating future changes).
  3. **Strategic Foresight (Arrow →)**:
     - Focuses on anticipating future developments, trends, and uncertainties.
     - It integrates long-term planning and short-term adaptability, allowing organizations to prepare for future technological disruptions.

- ◦ **Connects to:** Adaptive Decision-Making (ensuring alignment of current actions with future goals) and Data-Driven Decision-Making (using data to forecast trends).

4. **Continuous Learning and Innovation (Arrow →):**
   - ◦ Emphasizes ongoing learning, feedback loops, and a culture of innovation that drives improvement and responsiveness.
   - ◦ It involves embracing experimentation and iteration as part of the organizational culture.
   - ◦ **Connects to:** Adaptive and Agile Decision-Making (which relies on iterative processes) and Data-Driven Decision-Making (which feeds insights into new strategies and learning).
5. **Technology Integration (Arrow →):**
   - ◦ Encompasses the technological systems (e.g., blockchain, AI, intelligent systems) that support decision-making and business operations.
   - ◦ The framework should integrate these technologies into the organizational infrastructure, ensuring they are accessible and usable by decision-makers.
   - ◦ **Connects to:** Data-Driven Decision-Making (as these technologies help collect and analyze the data) as well as Continuous Learning and Innovation (enabling new solutions and strategies).

- **Explanation of Connections:**
  1. **Data-Driven Decision-Making** is the central pillar of the framework, feeding into **Adaptive and Agile Decision-Making**, allowing organizations to respond in real-time.
  2. **Strategic Foresight** ensures that the agility of decisions is aligned with long-term objectives, guiding organizations in anticipating future trends and disruptions.
  3. **Continuous Learning and Innovation** promotes ongoing improvement, feeding back into decision-making processes through feedback loops and iteration, ensuring that organizations stay ahead of the curve.
  4. **Technology Integration** enables the entire framework, providing the tools and platforms for collecting and analyzing data, supporting decision-making, and fostering innovation.

- **The Bi-Directional Relationships in the Dynamic Model**

The symbol "$\leftarrow\ \rightarrow$" represents a **bi-directional** or **two-way relationship** between two elements or concepts. It implies that both elements influence each other, create a feedback loop, or are mutually dependent on each other.

In the context of the dynamic framework, we discussed earlier, "$\leftarrow\ \rightarrow$" indicates that two concepts or processes not only influence each other but are also in constant interaction. This means there is a continuous exchange of information, feedback, or effects in both directions.

- **Examples of Bi-Directional Relationships ($\leftarrow\ \rightarrow$):**
  1. **Technology Integration $\leftarrow\ \rightarrow$ Data-Driven Decision-Making**:
     - **Explanation**: Technology Integration (e.g., AI, big data tools) supports and enables data-driven decision-making by providing the systems and infrastructure to collect, analyze, and visualize data. On the other hand, **data-driven decision-making** influences the direction in which technology is adopted and used. For example, if a company decides to focus on customer personalization, it will drive the development or use of AI algorithms to process data in real-time.
     - **Real-World Example**: In retail, customer behavior data drives the development of ML algorithms for personalized recommendations. These algorithms, in turn, generate new data that can be used to refine decision-making processes further, creating a loop of continuous improvement.
  2. **Strategic Foresight $\leftarrow\ \rightarrow$ Adaptive & Agile Decision-Making**:
     - **Explanation**: Strategic foresight involves predicting future trends and disruptions, which informs the decisions made in adaptive and agile frameworks. At the same time, **adaptive decision-making** based on real-time information or market shifts can help inform and refine long-term strategies. For example, if market conditions change rapidly, agile decision-making might lead to adjustments that influence long-term strategies or force a re-evaluation of forecasts.

- ◦ **Real-World Example**: A company may foresee a disruption in the market (strategic foresight) and respond by pivoting its business model or products (adaptive decision-making). As the company implements new strategies, it may gain additional insights that further inform their long-term outlook.

3. **Continuous Learning & Innovation ← → Data-Driven Decision-Making**:
   - ◦ **Explanation**: Continuous learning within an organization often results from analyzing data, experimenting, and iterating on solutions, which refines decision-making. On the flip side, data-driven decision-making can lead to new insights and better understanding, which fuels further learning and innovation.
   - ◦ **Real-World Example**: A tech company might continuously collect user data on how people interact with its app (data-driven decision-making). This data could lead to new ideas for improving the app (continuous learning), and the improved app then provides more data that continues to feed the learning process.

- **Bi-Directional Relationships in a Feedback Loop:**

In many systems, the exchange isn't just one-time; it happens repeatedly, creating a **feedback loop**. For example:

- **Feedback Loop in Data-Driven Decision-Making**: When a company analyzes customer feedback (data-driven decision-making), it may innovate or change its products. These changes are then tested by the customers, generating new feedback, which starts the cycle again.

In essence, "← →" symbolizes a **mutual relationship**, where both elements are interacting, influencing each other, and continuously evolving together.

'By integrating these elements, organizations can develop a dynamic, flexible decision-making model that not only responds effectively to immediate changes but also anticipates and prepares for the future. This interconnected system creates a robust, resilient approach to managing uncertainty and driving innovation in an increasingly technological world.

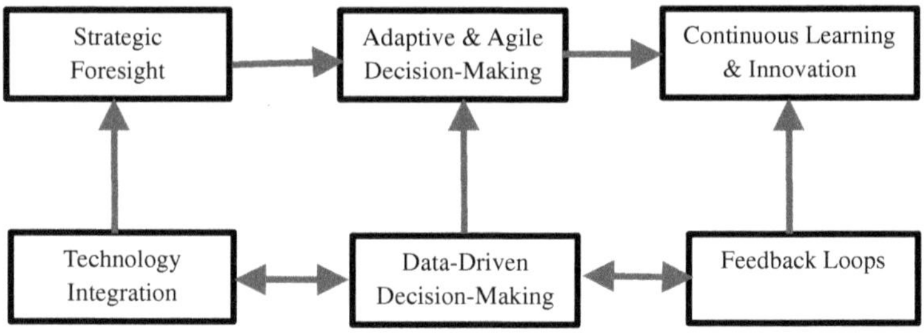

Figure 14.1. The Dynamic Model of Integration of Technological Advancements in Decisions

14.2. The Road Ahead for Emerging Technologies and Dynamic Decision Making

As we look to the future, the ongoing evolution of technologies such as quantum computing, advanced AI, and Internet of Things (IoT) will continue to reshape the decision-making landscape in profound ways. These technologies promise to unlock unprecedented capabilities, enabling decision-makers to process complex data sets, simulate scenarios in real-time, and make highly accurate predictions across various sectors. Quantum computing, for instance, has the potential to revolutionize fields like optimization, cryptography, and ML, allowing decision-makers to tackle problems that are currently beyond the reach of classical computing (Marr, 2020). With the processing power to solve highly complex calculations in a fraction of the time it currently takes, quantum computing could greatly enhance decision-making capabilities, particularly in areas such as supply chain management, financial modeling, and drug discovery.

Advanced AI, including techniques such as deep learning and reinforcement learning, will further empower organizations to automate decision-making processes while also enhancing their ability to recognize patterns and anticipate future trends. In addition to improving efficiency and accuracy, AI systems will be able to support decision-makers in more nuanced, complex environments where human cognitive limitations may hinder the effectiveness of traditional decision-making models. These systems will not only enhance operational performance but also enable strategic decision-making that aligns more closely with broader organizational and societal goals, from optimizing resource allocation to mitigating environmental impacts.

IoT will also play a crucial role in the future of decision-making. With billions of connected devices generating real-time data, IoT-enabled decision-making will allow for unprecedented visibility into operations and systems across industries such as healthcare, transportation, agriculture, and urban planning. This data-driven insight will facilitate smarter, more responsive decision-making, enabling organizations to optimize everything from energy usage to inventory management and patient care.

However, as these technologies continue to evolve, they will also introduce new challenges. The increasing complexity of decision-making processes necessitates a greater focus on resilience and adaptability. As decision-makers integrate these technologies into their workflows, they will need to develop systems that are not only efficient but also robust in the face of uncertainty. This means adopting flexible, adaptive decision-making frameworks that can respond to both expected and unforeseen changes. Technologies such as AI and IoT will play a pivotal role in enhancing these capabilities, providing decision-makers with the tools needed to navigate the complexities of an ever-changing landscape (Daugherty & Wilson, 2018).

Ethical considerations and societal impacts will also continue to be at the forefront of technological development and adoption. As emerging technologies become more deeply embedded in decision-making processes, the need for strong ethical guidelines and governance frameworks becomes increasingly urgent. AI, for example, raises significant concerns about data privacy, bias, and accountability, which must be addressed to ensure that technology benefits all members of society equitably. Moreover, technologies like quantum computing, which could potentially disrupt industries ranging from finance to cybersecurity, will require robust regulatory frameworks to mitigate risks associated with misuse or unintended consequences. As these technologies become more powerful and pervasive, governance structures will need to evolve in tandem, ensuring that innovation is balanced with societal well-being (Floridi, 2020).

Moreover, the road ahead will also necessitate greater collaboration between governments, businesses, and civil society to establish regulations that promote responsible innovation while safeguarding fundamental rights. As technology continues to disrupt traditional industries, decision-makers must embrace a forward-thinking approach to governance that fosters inclusivity, accountability, and transparency. This will involve not only adopting technological innovations but also ensuring that they are implemented in ways that reflect shared ethical principles and respect for human dignity.

In conclusion, the future of emerging technologies in decision-making holds enormous promise but also significant challenges. The continued integration of quantum computing, AI, and IoT will lead to more efficient, accurate, and responsive decision-making across industries. However, to realize the full potential of these technologies, decision-makers must also prioritize resilience, adaptability, and ethical governance. The road ahead will require thoughtful, collaborative efforts to ensure that these advancements are used responsibly and equitably, contributing to a sustainable and just future for all.

14.3. Final Reflections and Future Research Directions

As we reflect on the discussions presented in this book, several key themes emerge that highlight the dynamic relationship between emerging technologies and decision-making. These areas not only illustrate the profound impact of technological advancements on decision-making but also emphasize the complexity and challenges that decision-makers will face as they continue to integrate these technologies into their processes. To navigate this evolving landscape effectively, further research is required to address both theoretical and practical gaps that have surfaced throughout this exploration.

One of the most critical areas for future research lies in exploring the ethical dimensions of technology adoption. As decision-making processes become increasingly influenced by AI, blockchain, big data, and other advanced technologies, questions surrounding ethics, fairness, accountability, and transparency will become ever more pertinent. Research should focus on developing frameworks and guidelines that ensure ethical considerations are embedded in the development, deployment, and use of these technologies. This includes addressing issues such as bias in AI algorithms, the potential for surveillance and privacy violations, and the responsible use of big data in decision-making. Studies that focus on the ethical implications of emerging technologies will be essential in guiding organizations, governments, and policymakers to make decisions that prioritize the well-being of individuals and communities.

Another vital research direction involves developing more sophisticated models for integrating big data into decision-making. As the availability and volume of data continue to expand, decision-makers need more advanced tools and frameworks to analyze and interpret this data effectively. Research should focus on developing models that not only enhance data-driven decision-making but also consider the complexities of data management, including issues of data privacy, security, and the integration of disparate data sources. Additionally, research could explore the development of hybrid models that combine big data analytics with human judgment to create more robust and contextually relevant decision-making systems.

The impact of emerging technologies on various sectors also warrants significant attention. While much has been written about the general applications of technologies like AI and blockchain, there is a need for more sector-specific research that delves into how these technologies affect industries such as healthcare, finance, education, and manufacturing. Investigating the challenges and opportunities that these technologies present in different contexts will help decision-makers understand how to tailor their approaches to maximize benefits and mitigate risks. For example, in healthcare, AI and ML hold great promise for enhancing diagnostic accuracy and patient outcomes, but research is needed to explore how these technologies can be integrated seamlessly into existing healthcare systems without compromising care quality or equity.

Moreover, the dynamic interplay between technological innovations and decision-making processes requires further investigation. Emerging technologies are not static — they evolve rapidly, often in unpredictable ways. Understanding how decision-makers can effectively manage and leverage these technologies will be crucial for maintaining a competitive edge and ensuring long-term sustainability. Future research could examine the role of agility in decision-making, exploring how organizations can remain adaptive and responsive to technological changes while minimizing disruption. Additionally, studies could focus on the organizational processes that support technology adoption, such as change management strategies, leadership styles, and the development of a culture of continuous learning and innovation.

Finally, future research should focus on the relationship between technology and the broader societal impact. While the integration of emerging technologies into decision-making processes offers significant benefits, it also raises important questions about their societal implications. Research should explore how technology adoption affects inequality, power dynamics, and social justice. It will be important to study how emerging technologies can be harnessed to address pressing global challenges, such as climate change, poverty, and access to education, while also ensuring that the risks of exacerbating societal divides are minimized.

In conclusion, as technological advancements continue to shape decision-making across industries and sectors, it is crucial that research keeps pace with these developments. The future of decision-making will undoubtedly be shaped by emerging technologies, but it is through rigorous, interdisciplinary research that we will ensure these technologies are used in ways that are ethical, inclusive, and beneficial to society as a whole. By addressing the ethical, practical, and societal challenges of technology adoption, future research can guide decision-makers toward a more sustainable and equitable technological future.

14.4. Concluding Remarks

In conclusion, this book has provided a comprehensive analysis of the role of emerging technologies in dynamic decision-making. By examining various technologies, decision-making frameworks, and practical applications, it offers valuable insights into how to navigate the complexities and uncertainties of modern decision environments. The integration of technological advancements into decision-making processes represents both a challenge and an opportunity for organizations and individuals alike.

As we have discussed throughout the book, the rapid evolution of technologies such as AI, blockchain, big data, and IoT is transforming the landscape of decision-making across multiple sectors. These innovations have the potential to drive greater efficiency, innovation, and productivity. However, they also introduce new risks, ethical dilemmas, and challenges that decision-makers must address. This dual nature of emerging technologies — offering both promise and peril — requires careful consideration and strategic foresight to ensure that their benefits are maximized while minimizing potential harm.

A central theme of this book has been the need for dynamic, adaptive decision-making frameworks that can accommodate the complexities and uncertainties introduced by emerging technologies. Traditional decision-making models are often ill-equipped to handle the rapid pace of technological change, and decision-makers must be prepared to continuously adjust their strategies in response to evolving technological landscapes. The book has underscored the importance of building resilience and flexibility into decision-making processes, enabling organizations and individuals to not only adapt to change but to anticipate and shape it.

Furthermore, the integration of emerging technologies into decision-making highlights the critical role of ethics, transparency, and inclusivity. As technologies such as AI become more embedded in decision-making processes, ensuring that these systems are fair, transparent, and accountable is of utmost importance. The book has emphasized the need for responsible governance, robust oversight, and ongoing efforts to address biases and ensure that technology benefits all members of society, particularly the most vulnerable.

Looking ahead, the future of decision-making will undoubtedly be shaped by these technologies. However, it is not enough to simply adopt new tools; decision-makers must also embrace a mindset of continuous learning and adaptability. As we have explored, the intersection of technology and decision-making will require collaboration across disciplines, industries, and stakeholders. This book serves as a call to action for researchers, practitioners, and policymakers to continue advancing the knowledge and frameworks that will guide the responsible integration of emerging technologies into decision-making processes.

In conclusion, the journey toward more informed, adaptive, and ethical decision-making in the age of emerging technologies is just beginning. The insights provided in this book offer a foundation for navigating the evolving landscape of technological advancements. As we continue to explore and harness the potential of these technologies, the ultimate goal must be to use them in ways that enhance human decision-making, contribute to societal well-being, and promote a sustainable future.

14.5. My Personal Words

Reflecting on this journey through the book, I am reminded of the vast potential — and challenges — emerging technologies present. From AI to blockchain, big data to quantum computing, these innovations are reshaping not just how we make decisions but the very fabric of human progress.

What stands out is that success in navigating this evolving landscape depends on adaptability and openness. While these technologies offer transformative possibilities, we must approach them with vigilance, constantly evaluating their impact and ensuring they are used ethically and inclusively. The goal is not just to adopt new technologies, but to do so responsibly, with a focus on benefiting all.

I hope this book serves as both a guide and an inspiration, providing insights into the role of emerging technologies in decision-making while encouraging continuous learning and thoughtful engagement. The decisions we make today will shape tomorrow, and we must ensure these technologies are harnessed for the greater good, fostering a future that is sustainable, equitable, and just.

As we look ahead, I encourage you to embrace the promise of these technologies with both curiosity and caution. Let us think critically, act wisely, and engage in the ongoing dialogue to shape a future that benefits everyone.

References

Brynjolfsson, E., & McElheran, K. (2016). The role of data-driven decision making in the evolution of businesses. *Management Science*, 62(8), 2266–2282.

Chen, H., Chiang, R. H. L., & Storey, V. C. (2021). Business intelligence and analytics: From big data to big impact. *MIS Quarterly*, 45(4), 1053–1077.

Daugherty, P. R., & Wilson, H. J. (2018). Human and machine: How AI is transforming the future of work. *Harvard Business Review*, 96(1), 62–71.

Floridi, L. (2020). The ethics of artificial intelligence. *Oxford Handbook of Ethics of AI.*

Marr, B. (2020). The key trends in data science and artificial intelligence in 2020. *Forbes.*

Smith, A., & Houghton, R. (2021). The future of decision-making: Trends and challenges. *Journal of Strategic Decision-Making*, 35(2), 45–59.

Zhang, X., Xu, Y., & Wang, C. (2019). Data-driven decision-making and the role of advanced analytics. *Journal of Business Analytics*, 6(3), 192–206.

Index

5G networks, 166, 272, 482

accessible data, 322
accurate decision-making, 263
actionable insights, 270, 590
actionable strategies, 278, 420
adaptable action plans, 579
adaptable strategies, 599
adaptive business models, 582
Adaptive Decision-Making, 611, 612
adaptive frameworks, 430, 539
adaptive IDSS, 347
adaptive learning platforms, 351
Adaptive Management, 214, 218
adaptive principles, 239
adaptive regulation, 117
adaptive solutions, 236
adaptive strategies, 198, 245, 247, 565
adequate training, 174
adoption decisions, 156
adoption rates, 179
advanced analytics, 308, 345, 393
advanced data analytics, 251
advanced technologies, 265
advancements in fintech, 574
affordable access policies, 545
Agile Decision-Making, 610
agile decision-making processes, 608
agile frameworks, 454
agile methodologies, 443
agriculture, 615
AI, 17, 54, 79, 511, 605
AI algorithms, 5, 28, 54, 59, 127
AI models, 49, 54, 312
AI solutions, 288
AI systems, 22, 356, 515, 521, 614
AI tools, 203
AI-based platforms, 40
AI-based systems, 295
AI-driven analytics, 222, 240
AI-driven automation, 35
AI-driven chatbots, 307
AI-driven decision-making, 98
AI-driven systems, 40
AI-driven technologies, 124
algorithmic bias, 11, 273, 298, 300, 335, 518
algorithmic decision-making, 607
algorithmic decisions, 520
algorithmic fairness audits, 356
algorithmic trading, 301
algorithmic trading strategies, 300
algorithms, 512, 612
alternative strategies, 596
Amazon, 333, 442, 456
AML, 104
Amsterdam, 235
analytical capabilities, 339
analytical techniques, 255, 394
analytical tools, 337
analytics tools, 259
anticipatory frameworks, 537
anticipatory resilience, 593
Apple, 440

array of viewpoints, 502
authoritarian regimes, 29
automated systems, 536
automation, 154, 511, 606
automotive industry, 572
automotive manufacturing plants, 272
autonomous machines, 490
autonomous systems, 105, 107, 258
autonomous vehicle, 49, 66, 148, 269, 272, 278, 554
autonomous weapons systems, 29
awareness, 606

balanced grids, 345
balancing feedback loops, 68
banking systems, 103
best practices, 595
better-informed decisions, 298
bi-directional, 612
Big Data, 247, 256, 287, 399, 405, 413, 414, 419, 421, 423, 425, 426, 608, 617
Big Data analytics, 281, 404, 424, 608
Big Data management, 395
biodiversity, 217
biodiversity preservation, 239
bioengineered bacteria, 480
biotechnology, 123, 479
Bitcoin, 65
black box, 106
blockchain, 2, 19, 42, 101, 511, 605
blockchain technology, 103, 568
brick-and-mortar retailers, 572
broadband expansion, 92
building resilience, 619
business environment, 447
business opportunities, 580
business strategy, 6, 244, 270
business-as-usual, 587

capability-building, 574
capacity-building efforts, 539
carbon capture technologies, 235
carbon footprint, 44
carbon taxes, 573
cascading effects, 221, 573
case studies, 322
causal loop diagrams, 223
CCPA, 273, 523
CDAP, 182
central banks, 222
centralized system, 152
change agents, 166
change management, 185
changing conditions, 5, 246
changing environment, 140, 222, 575, 596
changing landscape, 610
changing technological landscape, 285
Chatbots, 307
China, 31, 103
civil society, 67, 514
CLDs, 226
clean technologies, 574
climate change, 71, 324, 560, 567
climate modeling, 56
clinical guidelines, 40
cloud-based platforms, 143, 286
cloud-based quantum computing, 50
cloud-based solutions, 273
CO2 emissions, 218
Cobots, 359
cognitive load, 487
collaborative approach, 551
collaborative efforts, 52
collaborative framework, 493
common goals, 244
common good, 513
common standards, 159
community forums, 122
community representatives, 532
community workshops, 90
comparative analysis, 54
COMPAS, 519, 553
competitive advantage, 253, 475
Competitive dynamics, 166, 212, 568
competitive edge, 283, 380, 408, 484, 617
competitive pressures, 6, 228
complex calculations, 614
complex decision environments, 378
complex dilemmas, 526

complex environment, 319
complex global challenges, 363
complex landscape, 11, 133
complex problems, 354
complex societal issues, 28
complex systems, 212, 224, 226
complex technological environments, 189
comprehensive analysis, 78
computational power, 18, 102
computational speeds, 100
computer self-efficacy, 174
computing frameworks, 396
consumer preferences, 572
consumer trust, 262, 389
contingency plans, 278, 569
continuous adaptation, 590
continuous evaluation, 594
continuous improvement, 520
continuous learning, 150, 155, 156, 225, 318, 322, 373, 456, 497, 499, 500, 570, 588, 620
continuous monitoring, 297
continuous support, 149
continuously challenge, 587
corporate environment, 177
correction mechanisms, 546
COVID-19, 83, 217, 222, 229, 322, 569
creative thinking, 501
credit risks, 397
creditworthiness, 301
crisis management, 221
CRISPR, 474
crop yield, 59, 373
cross-border payments, 23
cross-chain solutions, 44
Cross-functional teams, 282
cross-sector collaborations, 22
cross-sector partnerships, 139
cross-sectoral collaboration, 199
cross-sectors collaboration, 485
cryptocurrency, 66
cryptographic algorithms, 48
cryptography, 56, 100, 614
cultural change, 443
cultural differences, 547
cultural factors, 223
cultural foundations, 164
cultural implications, 547
cultural transformation, 391, 466
customer engagement, 277, 307
customer experience, 3, 152, 313
customer needs, 258
customer satisfaction, 146, 252, 258, 369
customer service platform, 152
cutting-edge technologies, 183
cybersecurity, 586, 615
cybersecurity measures, 190
cybersecurity protocols, 322
cybersecurity risks, 38
cycles of poverty, 32

daily operations, 151
data accessibility, 286
data accountability, 537
data accuracy, 151
data analysis, 27
data analytics, 270, 293, 295, 386, 415
data cleansing, 254
data collection, 522
data curation, 356
data demands, 406
data diversity, 254
data governance, 254, 279
data handling systems, 523
data infrastructure, 420
data insights, 459
data integrity, 316, 370
data literacy, 400
data management, 617
data privacy, 11, 274, 308, 335, 477, 513, 586, 617
data processing capabilities, 332
data quality, 314, 316
data repositories, 381, 521
data scientists, 282
data security, 191
data security measures, 306
data usage practices, 191
data utilization, 322

data validation, 370
data-driven, 606
data-driven approaches, 333
data-driven culture, 257, 289
Data-Driven Decision-Making, 79, 267, 324, 608, 610
data-driven decisions, 59, 336
data-driven insights, 10, 285, 318, 334, 379
data-driven products, 259
data-driven results, 172
data-driven scheduling, 348
data-driven world, 282
day-to-day basis, 149
DDDM, 389
DDM, 6
DDoS, 99
decentralized cultures, 155
decentralized ledgers, 21
decision cycles, 443
decision outcomes, 252
decision paths, 215
decision support systems, 10
decision-makers, 7, 338, 575, 607
decision-making, 2, 12, 38, 570, 606
decision-making frameworks, 436, 615, 619
decision-making landscape, 6
decision-making models, 2, 5, 608
decision-making outcomes, 9
decision-making process, 3, 8, 72, 108, 161, 343, 482, 514, 605, 607, 609
decision-making skills, 8
decision-making speed, 272
decision-making strategies, 7, 335
decisions, 8, 606, 612
deepfake technology, 514
deforestation, 217
delivery routes, 414
Delivery Trucks, 414
demand, 268
demand fluctuations, 308
demand patterns, 73
demographic groups, 353, 513, 525
deterministic models, 213
developed nations, 233
development process, 529
diagnostic procedures, 106
diffusion models, 169
diffusion phase, 63
digital divide, 555
digital economy, 105
digital infrastructure, 79
digital literacy, 494, 609
digital literacy programs, 545
digital platforms, 129, 605
digital transformation, 184, 344, 572
digitalization, 566
disadvantaged groups, 91
discriminatory outcomes, 390
discriminatory patterns, 519
disease progression, 299
disparate data sources, 341
disruptive technology, 18, 594
distributed energy resources, 345
diverse datasets, 69, 225
diverse environments, 216
diverse groups, 533
diverse needs, 199, 549
diverse perspectives, 225, 498, 507
diverse stakeholders, 527
diversification plans, 582
DPoS, 103
drainage systems, 218
drug discovery, 21, 478, 614
DSS, 331, 340
dynamic adaptations, 269
dynamic approach, 219, 315, 422
dynamic business landscape, 459
dynamic capabilities, 454, 464
dynamic changes, 236
dynamic decision-making, 3, 7, 8, 73, 212, 294, 315, 319
dynamic DSS, 351, 366
dynamic environments, 232, 255, 274, 457
dynamic frameworks, 609
dynamic IDSS, 368
dynamic labor market, 85
dynamic model, 219, 610
dynamic perspective, 58, 62
dynamic pricing systems, 334

dynamic resilience, 594
dynamic systems, 224, 263, 367, 369–371
dynamic technological landscapes, 233

e-learning, 174
ECC, 100
eco-conscious products, 572
ecological assessments, 238
ecological preservation, 239
ecological shifts, 238
Economic conditions, 158
economic downturns, 587
economic growth, 89, 158, 481
economic impact, 82
Economic incentives, 197, 202
economic instability, 30
economic structures, 78
economic uncertainty, 580
ecosystem degradation, 239
edge analytics, 265
educational curricula, 118, 562
educational inequalities, 32
effective decisions, 9
efficiency gains, 148
Effort Expectancy, 176
electric vehicles, 481
emergency management, 302
emergency response, 215, 302
emerging analytics trends, 269
emerging challenges, 568
emerging market, 572
emerging technologies, 2, 10, 19, 26, 64, 73, 129, 182, 240, 341, 541, 566, 605, 607
empirical research, 606
employee productivity, 147
employee training, 165
employment landscape, 84
employment opportunities, 90
employment patterns, 23
empowering individuals, 51
encrypted communications, 49
encryption technologies, 280
energy distribution, 309
energy production, 589
energy sector, 573
energy sources, 233
energy systems, 68
energy-efficient blockchains, 44
energy-efficient buildings, 309
enforcement agencies, 29
entertainment industry, 355
environmental changes, 241
environmental conservation, 242
environmental data, 265
environmental degradation, 567
environmental footprint, 112
environmental forces, 571
environmental impact, 102, 324, 615
environmental noise, 50
environmental patterns, 266
environmental policy, 226
environmental regulations, 573
environmental risks, 599
Environmental science, 25
environmental shifts, 565
environmental sustainability, 222
equitable access, 50
equitable opportunities, 558
equitable outcomes, 553
equitable solutions, 503
ERP, 143
ERP system, 229
error correction, 56
Ethereum, 65
Ethical AI frameworks, 108
Ethical AI systems, 532
Ethical challenges, 105, 124
ethical concerns, 103, 113, 266, 303, 528
ethical considerations, 11, 78, 95, 98, 319, 493, 515, 616
ethical decision-making, 512
ethical design, 69
ethical dilemmas, 38, 489, 505, 532–534, 606
ethical dimensions of technology, 616
ethical discussions, 30
ethical frameworks, 65, 381, 527, 530
ethical governance, 562, 616

ethical guidelines, 615
ethical impact assessments, 607
ethical implications, 481, 525
ethical integrity, 607
Ethical interventions, 69
ethical issues, 120
ethical judgment, 348
ethical perspectives, 26
ethical pitfalls, 530
ethical practices, 45
ethical principles, 30, 113, 118, 538
ethical reasoning, 498
ethical safeguards, 379
ethical standards, 527
Ethical stewardship, 529
ethically aware, 526
ethics review board, 527
European Union, 31
EV ecosystem, 228
EV revolution, 572
ever-changing environment, 430
ever-changing landscape, 461
evidence-based treatments, 332, 374
evolving landscape, 584
EVs, 568
expert judgment, 294
expert systems, 338
external changes, 236
external disruptions, 568
external environment, 588
external factors, 177, 593
external forces, 160
external pressures, 321

Facebook-Cambridge Analytica, 521
facial recognition technology, 29
failure diagnostics, 256
fast-paced business environments, 255
faster decision-making, 153
faster decisions, 253
FCA, 540, 541
feedback loop, 46, 73, 152, 246, 318, 433, 611, 613
financial burden, 183
financial challenges, 183
financial decisions, 296
financial instability, 539
financial markets, 254
financial modeling, 269, 614
financial penalties, 556
financial regulations, 540, 574
financial repercussions, 404
financial risk, 162
financial sector, 158
financial stability, 66
financial transactions, 513
FinTech, 65
flawed decisions, 313
flexible strategies, 204, 448
flood prevention, 218
focus groups, 442
food safety, 44, 55
food supply chain, 578
forecasting accuracy, 306, 321
forecasting methods, 213
foresight, 574
forward-looking approach, 507
forward-looking strategies, 483
forward-thinking, 532, 542
forward-thinking decision-making, 230
forward-thinking integration, 449
forward-thinking strategies, 590
frameworks, 516, 518
fraud detection systems, 388
FTX, 540

GDP, 81
GDPR, 41, 72, 157, 273, 286, 314, 371, 513, 523, 538, 556
GE, 37, 419
gender, 512, 515
gender disparities, 525
gender imbalances, 525
General Motors, 572
geopolitical instability, 587, 600
Germany, 218
gig economy, 85
gig work, 23
gig workers, 80
gig-based employment, 85
global action, 112

global challenges, 22, 32, 61, 73, 120, 324
global competition, 446
global cooperation, 112
global efforts, 91
global framework, 66
global health crises, 71
global inequalities, 561
global interconnectedness, 565
global markets, 82
global pandemics, 595
global progress, 476, 508
global reach, 111
global risks, 595, 598
global supply chains, 224
GMOs, 202
goal-aligned decision-making, 379
Google, 27, 50, 241, 425, 440, 451, 452
governance challenges, 606
governance frameworks, 559, 615
governance models, 549
government agencies, 66
GPAI, 32
greater good, 620
green technologies, 163
greenhouse gas emissions, 68

habitat degradation, 238
healthcare, 41, 81
healthcare diagnoses, 317
healthcare industry, 573
healthcare providers, 300
healthier environment, 47
high-altitude balloons, 545
high-demand periods, 257
high-frequency trades, 272
high-quality data, 316
high-stakes environments, 303
high-stakes scenarios, 520
high-stakes sectors, 299
HIPAA, 144
hiring algorithms, 273
hiring practices, 266, 525
hiring process, 518
historical biases, 520
historical data, 374, 450, 512
holistic approach, 323
holistic problem-solving, 323
holistic view, 295
hospital capacity, 221
human agency, 106, 350
human agents, 353
human analysts, 311, 359
human capabilities, 350
human creativity, 360
human decision-makers, 253, 526
human decision-making, 334, 524, 554
human expectations, 485
human expertise, 460
human experts, 554
human intervention, 607
human judgment, 560, 617
human oversight, 353, 506
human resources, 346
human rights, 65
human strengths, 507
human values, 357
human welfare, 506, 508
human well-being, 516
human workers, 359, 491, 536
human-centered design, 360
human-machine collaboration, 333, 352, 356, 358, 363
human-machine interactions, 362

IBM, 27, 35, 50, 228, 258, 452, 477, 516
IDS, 190
IDSS, 331, 344
IEEE, 98
illegal activities, 102
inaccurate analyses, 402
inclusive future, 99
inclusive policies, 47
inclusivity, 606, 616
individual rights, 403, 563
industries, 619
industry leaders, 595
industry trends, 165
informed decisions, 253, 287, 418
infrastructure readiness, 24
innovation strategies, 228

instantaneous decisions, 269
intelligent systems, 608
interactive graphs, 340
interconnected innovations, 71
interconnected system, 613
interconnected world, 204, 595
interdisciplinary collaboration, 346, 534
interdisciplinary research, 618
international collaboration, 113
international cooperation, 124
international standards, 37
International Telecommunication Union, 93
internet connectivity, 86
interpersonal interaction, 80
inventory levels, 274
inventory management, 305, 412
investment portfolios, 413
investment priorities, 578
investment solutions, 345
investment strategies, 580
IoT, 19, 36, 45, 55, 77, 101, 131, 137, 159, 424, 475, 496, 615
IoT devices, 38, 109, 125, 259
IoT solutions, 36
IoT-enabled vehicles, 268
irrigation systems, 46
IT, 179, 192
IT infrastructure, 150
IT professionals, 319
iterative approach, 441, 609

job displacement, 93, 588
just world, 33

Kenya, 550
Khan Academy, 359
knowledge exchange, 27

labor market, 80
lack of transparency, 522
last-mile logistics, 262
learning approach, 318
learning curve, 173
learning environments, 7
learning loop, 465
learning preferences, 347
learning support, 360
Legacy systems, 142, 401
legal repercussions, 522
lessons learned, 607
level of complexity, 293
linear decision-making, 439
linear perspective, 212
local communities, 87
logistical challenges, 269
long-term competitiveness, 574
long-term growth, 148
long-term strategies, 466
long-term success, 164, 248, 602
long-term sustainability, 466, 585
low-income, 515
low-income communities, 26
low-income households, 92
low-risk environment, 175

machine learning (ML), 520, 608
machine learning algorithms, 8, 127
management practices, 218, 223
manufacturing, 573
manufacturing firms, 143
manufacturing process, 306
marginalized groups, 549
marginalized individuals, 519
market bubbles, 223
market conditions, 198, 287
market demands, 455
market dynamics, 157, 166, 226, 570
market fluctuations, 218
market leadership, 234
market share, 63
market trends, 568, 575
market volatility, 65
marketing campaigns, 307
marketing platforms, 151
marketing strategies, 217
materials science, 21
measurable benefits, 148
medical records, 352
MFA, 190
MiCA, 66, 72

Microsoft, 50
military operations, 106
minimal-impact applications, 171
minority communities, 95
minority groups, 519
MIS, 337
mitigation strategies, 322
ML, 511
ML algorithms, 252, 612
modular architectures, 335
multi-disciplinary approach, 30
multi-disciplinary teams, 340
multi-faceted barriers, 194
multi-faceted ways, 125
multi-modal transit, 240
multidimensional challenges, 130
multidisciplinary approach, 9, 25
multilingual interfaces, 491
multiple sectors, 52
mutual relationship, 613

national security, 31
natural disasters, 301
natural language processing, 343
navigating uncertainty, 598
Negative feedback loops, 68
network effects, 195
Neural Networks, 275
new technologies, 169, 594
NGOs, 88
NIST, 48, 100, 541
NLP, 366, 474
nonlinear interactions, 2
NQI, 52

OECD, 113, 124
older systems, 171
online resources, 150
OPEC, 233
operational continuity, 365, 375
operational costs, 43
operational efficiency, 252, 258, 265
operational management, 40
operational performance, 614
operational processes, 586
operational teams, 569
opinion leaders, 169
optimal solutions, 216
optimization, 614
optimization methods, 211
organizational actions, 270
organizational contexts, 431
organizational culture, 27, 321, 458, 508, 578
organizational goals, 145, 381, 398
organizational implications, 8
organizational performance, 401
organizational processes, 570
organizational resilience, 323, 500, 566
organizational shifts, 27
organizational strategy, 387, 422
organizational structures, 601
organizational success, 426
ORION, 262
outdated systems, 142
outdated technology, 142

pandemics, 245
paradigm shift, 85
participatory assessments, 114
participatory governance, 110
path dependence, 196
patient data, 275, 344
patient harm, 106
patient history, 368
pay-as-you-go basis, 183
people of color, 561
Perceived Ease of Use, 173
Perceived Usefulness, 173
personal data, 307
personal hardship, 83
personal information, 191, 513
personalized experience, 488
personalized medicine, 411
personalized services, 521
pharmaceuticals, 20
policy design, 223, 549
policy frameworks, 88
policy shifts, 235
policymakers, 3, 529
policymaking, 129

portfolio management, 53
PoS, 103
positive attitudes, 149
post-crisis recovery, 221
post-incident analysis, 108
Post-it Notes, 434
potential vulnerabilities, 584
power dynamics, 618
practical applications, 170
practical insights, 274, 461, 607
practical takeaways, 343
practitioners, 517
predictable conditions, 216
predictive analytics, 3, 256, 259, 268, 269, 272, 276, 285, 302, 449, 467, 609
predictive analytics models, 263
predictive capabilities, 344
predictive insights, 247
predictive maintenance, 37, 305
predictive models, 258, 276
predictive text models, 267
prescriptive analytics, 397, 416
prevention systems, 68
principles of fairness, 267
principles of quantum mechanics, 62
privacy concerns, 190
privacy issues, 507
privacy policies, 523
privacy violations, 121, 194
proactive approach, 155, 447, 585
proactive decisions, 279
proactive measures, 526
proactive regulatory environment, 202
proactive strategies, 123
problem-solving, 17, 145, 189, 515
professional development, 188
professional growth, 10
professional networks, 171
programming language, 51
proof-of-stake, 55
proof-of-work mechanisms, 55
protein folding, 48
public awareness, 99
public buildings, 46
public concerns, 122
public confidence, 530
public health systems, 60
public interest, 72, 105
public opinion, 67
Public perception, 22
public transportation, 229
public trust, 47, 484, 526, 547

qualified professionals, 407
quantum computing, 19, 21, 48, 53, 112, 123, 473, 483, 614
quantum ecosystem, 51
quantum principles, 49
quantum research, 52
quantum solutions, 51
quantum supremacy, 37
quantum systems, 51
quantum technologies, 52
quantum-enabled decryption, 100
quantum-resistant algorithms, 37
quantum-resistant technologies, 101
quantum-safe encryption, 50
qubit stability, 56

R&D, 62, 82, 483, 573
R&D Planning, 228
racial minorities, 555
racial profiling, 114
rational choice theory, 211
real-time adjustments, 248
real-time analytics, 283, 415
real-time data, 36, 46, 142, 224, 245, 315, 316, 394, 435
real-time data integration, 338
real-time data processing, 64, 261
real-time decision-making, 273, 339
real-time decision support, 263
real-time insights, 297
real-time responsiveness, 2
real-world case studies, 606
real-world data, 240
real-world decision-making, 224
real-world examples, 259, 431
real-world scenarios, 259
regulatory bodies, 192, 490, 557
regulatory challenges, 11

regulatory changes, 226
regulatory environment, 197, 513
regulatory frameworks, 41, 120, 122, 157, 317, 513, 615
regulatory landscape, 192
regulatory measures, 115, 130
regulatory mechanisms, 128
regulatory oversight, 102, 104
regulatory priorities, 539
regulatory risks, 573
Regulatory sandboxes, 116
regulatory shifts, 571
regulatory standards, 559
reinforcing cycle, 67
renewable energy, 59, 571
renewable energy production, 268
renewable energy targets, 195
renewable resources, 68
renewable sources, 309
representative data, 546
Resilience, 600
resilience of systems, 219
resilience-building, 585
resilient decisions, 573, 578
resilient outcomes, 239
resource expenditure, 145
resource scarcity, 60, 457
resource utilization, 47
response times, 147
responsive solutions, 277
responsive strategies, 276
rise of automation, 592
risk assessment models, 217
risk management, 125
risk of disruption, 574
risk of overregulation, 536
risk-tolerance, 502
risks, 606
robotics, 154
RSA, 100
rule-based systems, 277

safety standards, 45, 72
satisfying experiences, 489
scalability, 62
scalable solutions, 43
scalable technology solutions, 322
scarce resources, 299
scenario planning, 214, 225, 242, 566, 569, 577, 581, 582, 588
scenarios, 579
SD, 214, 226, 228, 242, 244
SD models, 229
SDG 4, 558
SDGs, 607
seasonal patterns, 256
security measures, 522
self-optimizing systems, 266, 278
sensitive personal data, 317
sensitivity analysis, 244
sensor data, 339
sentiment analysis, 262
service industries, 81
shared standards, 514
Siemens, 37, 283
Simulation models, 215
simulation tools, 609
skill development, 287
skilled professionals, 323
skilled workers, 187
smart cities, 4, 378
smart grids, 308
SMEs, 161, 181
social consequences, 547
social considerations, 357
social dimensions, 524
social inequalities, 131
social influence, 167, 176
social justice, 618
social media feeds, 354
social networks, 222
social responsibility, 607
Societal acceptance, 197
societal changes, 573
societal considerations, 235
societal development, 558
societal goals, 557
societal harm, 519, 528
societal impact, 618
societal imperative, 520
societal implications, 28, 111
societal inequalities, 517

societal needs, 73, 556
societal progress, 516, 550, 562
societal safeguards, 540
societal trust, 115
societal values, 530, 531
societal well-being, 553, 619
socioeconomic biases, 512
socioeconomic groups, 31
socioeconomic impacts, 129
socioeconomic implications, 130
software development, 198
split-second decisions, 272
stakeholder engagement, 492
stakeholder participation, 117
stakeholder trust, 283
stakeholders, 606
static analyses, 432
STEM, 548
stockouts, 258
strategic advantage, 226
strategic agility, 234
strategic approach, 57, 257
strategic decisions, 81
strategic decision-making, 272
strategic focus, 460, 468
strategic foresight, 566, 589, 608, 610
strategic framework, 461
Strategic investments, 83
strategic options, 581
strategic planning, 160, 203, 217, 589
strategic priorities, 579
strategic vision, 269
structured datasets, 339
sub-Saharan Africa, 86
subjective judgment, 387
success stories, 166
successful businesses, 146
supply chain, 42, 213, 306, 573, 581
supply chain collapse, 587
supply chain management, 4, 42, 146, 215, 310, 312, 314, 361, 578, 614
supply chain operations, 375
supply chain performance, 432
supply chain transactions, 147
supportive culture, 186
surveillance overreach, 114
sustainability goals, 378, 607
sustainability objectives, 94
sustainable development, 32
sustainable economic benefits, 239
sustainable energy solutions, 601
sustainable fisheries, 239
sustainable future, 94
sustainable growth, 324
sustainable progress, 92
sustainable resource use, 229
sustainable solutions, 230
sustainable world, 110
sustained investment, 546
symptoms of problems, 434
synthesis, 605
System Dynamics, 214
system integration, 141
systemic barriers, 199
systemic biases, 95
systems making, 296
systems thinking, 218, 224

TAM, 138, 144, 172
tech-savvy populations, 93
technical barriers, 53
technical capabilities, 121
technical infrastructure, 179
technical innovation, 99
technical support, 181
technological adoption, 323, 545
technological advancements, 20, 64, 67, 516, 591, 602
technological advances, 606
technological breakthroughs, 195
technological challenges, 42, 138
technological change, 79, 255
technological convergence, 78, 127, 128
technological disruption, 288, 429
technological environment, 598
technological infrastructure, 86, 549, 573
technological innovation, 242, 514, 587
technological integration, 607

technological landscape, 265, 531, 559, 567
technological literacy, 91
technological progress, 67, 72, 116, 550
technological shifts, 156
technological solutions, 606
technological systems, 611
technological trajectories, 599
technological trends, 451
technological uncertainty, 452
technological world, 613
technology adoption, 140, 154, 159, 289, 609
technology adoption decisions, 153
technology adoption process, 156
technology governance, 539
technology-driven decision-making, 310, 314, 315
technology-driven world, 32, 164
technology-intensive fields, 88
Tesla, 241, 455, 572
the United Nations' Sustainable Development Goals (SDGs), 607
themes, 605
theoretical frameworks, 606
threshold effects, 196
thriving in disruption, 585
time decision support, 264
time-efficient manner, 188
tipping points, 196
trade barriers rise, 587
traffic conditions, 277
training programs, 82, 88, 90
transaction patterns, 358
transformative power, 139
transformative progress, 42
transformative technology, 232
transformative tools, 367
transnational challenges, 538
transparency, 607
transparency audits, 288
transparency of decisions, 313
transparent data management, 257
transportation, 573
transportation systems, 269
treatment personalization, 40
trust, 607
two-way relationship, 612

U.S., 29, 519
UK, 29
unalterable chain of data, 42
unauthorized access, 4
uncertain future, 570
UNESCO, 538
unethical practices, 540
unintended consequences, 133, 218, 224, 479, 480
United Nations, 93
United States, 31, 103, 144
unpredictable environments, 579
unpredictable future, 590
unpredictable outcomes, 127
unstructured data, 253, 339, 423
urban centers, 88
urban ecosystems, 223
urban planning, 386, 615
urgency of adoption, 157
user engagement, 69
user-friendly interfaces, 338
UTAUT, 178

vaccination campaigns, 230
value of the technology, 155
verification processes, 403
virtual tutoring, 87
voice-activated commands, 372
volatile business environment, 461
VR experiences, 268
VUCA environment, 567
vulnerable populations, 531

wage regulation, 84
Watson for Oncology, 516
Wearable devices, 60
WEF, 111
widespread adoption, 63, 152, 172, 178
worker movements, 85

workflows, 149, 175
workforce adaptation, 24
workforce displacement, 35
workforce implications, 494
workplace setting, 173
World Bank, 93
World Economic Forum, 497
WRI, 235

XAI, 273, 288, 351, 371, 517, 560, 607

Other Titles by the Author

Riding the Wave: Exploring the Realms of Autonomous Vehicles
ISBN: 978-981-12-9482-2

www.ingramcontent.com/pod-product-compliance
Ingram Content Group UK Ltd.
Pitfield, Milton Keynes, MK11 3LW, UK
UKHW020405150926
8624IPUK00004B/357

9 789819 811892